The Hoover Library on War, Revolution, and Peace
Publication No. 14

Features and Figures of the Past

PUBLISHED UNDER AUTHORITY OF THE
DIRECTORS OF THE HOOVER LIBRARY
ON WAR, REVOLUTION, AND PEACE

VLADIMIR IOSIFOVICH GURKO

The Hoover Library on War, Revolution, and Peace
Publication No. 14

FEATURES AND FIGURES OF THE PAST

GOVERNMENT AND OPINION IN THE REIGN OF NICHOLAS II

By

(Vladimir Iosifovich)

V. I. GURKO

*Late Assistant Minister of the Interior
and Member of the Russian State Council*

Edited by

J. E. WALLACE STERLING
XENIA JOUKOFF EUDIN
H. H. FISHER

Translated by

LAURA MATVEEV

1939
STANFORD UNIVERSITY PRESS
STANFORD UNIVERSITY, CALIFORNIA
LONDON: HUMPHREY MILFORD
OXFORD UNIVERSITY PRESS

STANFORD UNIVERSITY PRESS
STANFORD UNIVERSITY, CALIFORNIA

LONDON: HUMPHREY MILFORD
OXFORD UNIVERSITY PRESS

THE BAKER AND TAYLOR COMPANY
55 FIFTH AVENUE, NEW YORK

THE MARUZEN COMPANY
TOKYO, OSAKA, KYOTO, SENDAI

EDITOR'S PREFACE

VLADIMIR IOSIFOVICH GURKO came of a family which gave distinguished service to the Russian Empire. His grandfather, V. I. Gurko, was an officer in the Napoleonic wars. His father, Field Marshal I. V. Gurko (1828–1901), was one of the principal Russian commanders in the Russo-Turkish War of 1877–78 and was later Governor-General and Commander of the Troops in Poland. The author's maternal grandmother, Countess Sailhas de Tournemire (Elizaveta Vasilievna Sukhevo-Kobylina), contributed under the name Evgenia Tur to *Sovremennik, Russkii Vestnik,* and *Russkaia Rech,* and wrote a number of novels. She was the friend of Granovsky, Turgenev, Afanasiev, and other literary figures of the mid-century. His brother, General Vasilii Iosifovich Gurko, held many important posts during the World War, including those of Acting Chief of the Imperial General Staff and Commander of the Western Group of Armies.

In 1885, at the age of twenty-three, V. I. Gurko graduated from Moscow University, and immediately entered public service in Poland, first as commissioner for rural affairs and later as an assistant to his father, the Governor-General in Warsaw. In these first years of his career Gurko showed the direction of his interest and the bent of his mind. With characteristic energy he turned to the study of agrarian problems, publishing in 1887 *Dvorianskoe zemlevladenie v sviazi s mestnoi reformoi ("Nobility Landownership in Connection with Local Reform"),* and ten years later *Ocherki Privisliania ("Sketches of the Vistula Region").*

Early in the reign of Nicholas II, Gurko was appointed to the Imperial Chancellery, an institution which had been the training school of many Russian statesmen and in which he had the opportunity to observe the working and membership of the State Council, which he here so effectively describes. Gurko's ability was recognized by the head of the Chancellery, the then Imperial Secretary, V. K. Plehve, but his developing bureaucratic career did not turn Gurko from his interest in peasant and agrarian affairs. On the large estates owned by his wife in Voronezh Gubernia he carried on a model farm, studied at first hand the conditions of life and the problems of the peasants, and in 1902 published *Ustoi narodnago khoziaistva Rossii ("Principles of People's Economy of Russia")*.

When Plehve became Minister of the Interior in 1902 he appointed Gurko Manager of the Peasant Section. This appointment was significant, for at the time the government was devoting particular attention to the problems of agriculture and the condition of the peasants. In this office, and later as Assistant Minister of the Interior, Gurko took a prominent part in discussions, interministerial conferences, and the formulation of projects relating to rural administration and agrarian reforms. But his opportunities to observe the involved process of Imperial Government were not, of course, confined to this important question. From such an advantageous post of observation in the ministry most influential in the direction of government policy, Gurko saw the rise and fall of the political fortunes of Witte, Plehve, Sviatopolk-Mirsky, Durnovo, and Goremykin, and he noted the personal traits and contributions of many less-known figures. He saw the blundering progress of Russia's costly adventure in the Far East and the fumbling measures to meet the rising tide of unrest among peasants, workers, and liberals. With his keen mind, his talent for character portrayal, and, it may be added, an eye for the frailties of human nature, Gurko brings to life the scene of the historic years 1902–1906— the clash of personalities and opinions, and the struggle to control and guide the tremendous forces in the social and economic life of the country.

One of the high points of Gurko's public career at this time was his appearance in the First Duma as government spokesman on the agrarian question. Writing of this occasion, Senator G. V. Glinka recalls: "The unsuccessful speeches of the government representatives before the noisy assembly, the feeling of bewilderment, the crushing confusion—and then V. I. Gurko's speech. I remember his slight stature, his loud, harsh voice. Every sentence was charged with feeling, with a biting sarcasm. . . . . The sweeping fire of his eloquence revealed him to be a capable parliamentary fighter. This speech proved his outstanding political genius, but at the same time it aroused great jealousy among those who sided with him and was never forgotten by his political foes."

In 1906 Gurko published his fourth book, *Otryvochnyia mysli po agrarnomu voprosu ("Random Thoughts on the Agrarian Question")*. In the same year his bureaucratic career ended when he was charged with having exceeded his authority in making with a certain Lidval, who failed to carry out his agreement, a contract to supply grain to regions experiencing an acute food shortage. Gurko's political adversaries and the opposition parties in general naturally made the most of this affair; but there were many, including some of other political camps, who believed that injustice had been done. Referring to this affair, P. B. Struve later wrote: "Although I did not know Gurko personally, my conscience has long prompted me to see the injustice of this accusation. Gurko's path, it seems, somehow crossed that of P. A. Stolypin. In reality they were pursuing the same aim and were permeated with the same spirit. But their personal ways crossed and the historical flow of events carried Stolypin forward and pushed Gurko back. . . . . But fate was not just to Gurko, and the fact should be remembered that 'Stolypin's work,' aiming at a Russian peasantry strongly settled on the land, was helped by the gifted and brilliant Gurko. The historian who studies the documents will recognize the role and significance of Stolypin's land reform and of Stolypin himself and of Gurko, and lastly, of the partial realization of their program by A. V. Krivoshein. It remains to state, ... that from a purely historical point of view these three names should be recorded together."

Gurko's forced retirement from the government service did not end his public life. In 1909 he published *Nashe gosudarsvennoe i narodnoe khoziaistvo ("Our State and People's Economy")*. During this year also he returned to live on his family estate in Tver Gubernia, to begin what was in fact a new career as a member of the zemstvo. In this he faced a difficult situation. Not only was he a former bureaucrat—and all bureaucrats were regarded with suspicion by the zemstvo men—but he had been one of the most forthright critics of the policies of the Cadet party, and this party was very strong throughout the Tver zemstvo organizations. Gurko threw himself into provincial work with energy and intelligence, and so successfully overcame local and party prejudice that in 1912 his election to the Fourth State Duma was prevented only by pressure from St. Petersburg. Under this pressure he withdrew his candidacy for the Duma but was elected to the State Council. In this body Gurko, as he explains, did not join any definite party group, but with some twelve or fourteen others, chiefly former ministers of liberal or progressive views, formed a non-party group.

As representative of this group he took part in drafting the program of the progressive bloc in 1915. In the later chapters of this book Gurko discusses the personalities and policies of Stolypin, Kokovtsov, Krivoshein, and their associates and describes events of the years 1914–15 and their effect on public opinion and the prestige of the government as he observed them.

The book ends some months before the February Revolution. Soon after that event the State Council disappeared from the scene and Gurko's political life was over. After the October Revolution he remained in Moscow, actively supporting various groups which were attempting to organize the struggle against the Bolsheviks. In September 1918, being obliged to leave Moscow, he went to the Ukraine, where he continued his opposition both to the Bolsheviks and to Ukrainian separatism. He attempted to negotiate a union between the Volunteer Army, the Don Cossacks, and the Ukraine; but this failed because the Volunteer Army had an Entente orientation and the Ataman of the Don Cossacks and the Ukrainian government looked to Germany for aid. Later Gurko attended a conference of representatives of Russian anti-Bolshevik groups and diplomatic representatives of the Entente at Jassy. This conference had very small results, and Gurko became a member of a delegation sent to France and England to present the case of the Whites to the Allied governments. This mission was equally unproductive, and Gurko returned to Odessa. His account of these events was published in Volume XV of *Arkhiv Russkoi Revoliutsii* under the title "Iz Petrograda cherez Moskvu, Parizh, London v Odessu" ("From Petrograd through Moscow, Paris, London to Odessa"). Gurko left Russia when the French troops evacuated Odessa in 1919, but returned for a brief period to take part, on the invitation of General Wrangel, in conferences in Sebastopol on political and economic matters. During his last years under the difficult conditions of emigrant life Gurko continued his active support of the White cause. He died in Paris on February 18, 1927.

Gurko's contemporaries speak particularly of his intellectual capacity and energy. Struve places him with "that brilliant type of clever, energetic, and extraordinarily hard-working bureaucrat produced by Imperial Russia in such men as M. M. Speransky, F. F. Konkrin, M. A. Korff, D. A. and N. A. Miliutin, and many other notable personalities." In some respects he resembled A. V. Krivoshein, but Struve notes this difference: "Krivoshein possessed a sense of proportion and the will to power which were lacking in Gurko, who was, however, more gifted and more brilliant." Glinka, speaking of Gurko's eloquence, adds that "this gift was enhanced by his extraordinary quickness in grasping the substance of every question, his ability to find his way out of any situation with lightning rapidity; also by the vividness of his imagination which enabled him to build plans on the widest scale. However . . . . Mr. Gurko was immune from a tendency common to many Russians: they are apt, after an impetuous impulse, to cool down very quickly and yield to the inclination to rest after every strenuous effort. Fatigue and overstrain seemed to be unknown to him. His store of energy was inexhaustible. He was as incapable of living without intellectual activity as a fish without water."

The reader of this book can scarcely fail to gain a very clear impression of the author's personality. His judgments of men and events, which are often severe, reflect that personality; they reveal prejudices and predilections, but they are the judgments of a keen and vigorous mind.

In respect to certain matters discussed by Mr. Gurko we have thought it might be useful to include excerpts from the memoirs of some of his contemporaries who were themselves concerned with these events. These excerpts from the writings of D. N. Shipov and A. I. Guchkov, as translated by Mrs. Joukoff, are given in the Appendix. The extract from Mr. Guchkov's memoirs is published with the kind permission of his executors, Messrs. Boris Elkin and V. A. Maklakov. In the Appendix and in Gurko's text, the respective authors' interpolations are enclosed in parentheses, while square brackets indicate in every case interpolations by the present editors.

Mrs. Joukoff, Mr. Sterling, and I are under deep obligation to Madame Gurko for the invaluable help she has so courteously and patiently given us in the preparation of this book. We wish to acknowledge our obligation also to Mrs. Gay Dimick Taylor, who has prepared the manuscript for the press and aided us in many other ways. The index has been prepared by Mrs. Taylor and Mr. Paul L. Hanna.

H. H. FISHER

STANFORD UNIVERSITY, CALIFORNIA
November 5, 1937

TABLE OF CONTENTS

Eastern affairs—Witte's interest in Russian enterprises in Manchuria—Vonliarliarsky and Bezobrazov; the timber concessions and
railway building in northern Korea—The purchase of the Yalu concession with His Majesty's private funds—Strained relations with
Japan—Ito's proposal regarding north Korea endorsed by Baron
Rosen and Colonel Vogak—Their recall and the appointment of A. P.
Izvolsky and Vannovsky—Ito's visits to St. Petersburg and London—
Russia's agreement with China to withdraw from Manchuria—Bezobrazov's continued activities; the opposition of the ministers and
Alekseev's support—The Yalu enterprise as a private stockholders'
company (1903)—The decisions to withdraw troops from Manchuria,
to set up a vice-royalty in the Far East and a Special Committee for
Far Eastern Affairs—Kuropatkin's visit to the Far East and his
views on the situation—Increasing tension and Japan's war preparations—The break in diplomatic relations—The responsibility for the
war—The roles of Witte, Alekseev, Bezobrazov, Kuropatkin—The
innocence of Plehve and Rosen

    Candidates to succeed Plehve—Influence of the Dowager Empress
in the appointment of Sviatopolk-Mirsky—His character, education,
early career, and liberal intentions—The dismissal of Plehve's assistants and the restoration of rights to zemstvos and to individual political offenders—Popular approval of his theory of "sincere trust" in the
public—Mirsky's failure to uphold his proposals for a "regime of
equity" and an enlargement of the State Council with elected members—The congress of zemstvo workers—The Union of Liberation
and the zemstvos—Revolutionary elements in the zemstvos—Revolutionary character of the banquets celebrating the fortieth anniversary of the judicial reforms—Activities of the Union of Liberation,
of the Social Democrats—The Ukase of December 12, 1904—Witte's
attempt to put through the reforms set forth in the Ukase of December 12—The growing revolutionary unrest

    Mirsky's appointment of Kutler as Assistant Minister of the In-
terior—E. A. Vatatsi's influence and work as Director of Department for General Affairs—Composition and importance of Witte's
Special Conference on the Needs of Agricultural Industry—The attitude of the Ministry of the Interior—Mirsky's open letter to the
governors on the work of the Special Conference—Debates of the
Special Conference on the land commune—Goremykin's success in
discrediting Witte and bringing about the closing of the Special Conference—Goremykin appointed chairman of a new conference on
peasant land tenure—The incident on Epiphany Day, January 6, 1905
—Gapon's work in Zubatov's society of factory workers in St. Petersburg—His relations with the Petersburg Governor, Fullon—Gapon's
responsibility for the strike of January 1905—The petition to the
Tsar—Mirsky's conference of January 8 regarding the impending

—The question of proroguing the Duma and reorganizing the Council of Ministers—Failure of the liberal ministers and the Progressive Bloc to persuade Goremykin to resign—The dismissal of the liberal ministers—The widening breach between government and public— The significance of the Tsar's refusal in 1915 to meet the moderate suggestions of the public and his liberal ministers

EDITORS' NOTES

APPENDICES

INDEX

FEATURES AND FIGURES OF THE PAST

AUTHOR'S PREFACE

"Not a fighter, but a mere chance visitor in both camps, bought by neither—no matter under whose banners I was fighting, I would not bear my friends' prejudiced zeal but would defend the honor of my enemy."— COUNT A. TOLSTOI

Old Russia has disappeared into the past. What new Russia will be we do not know. But one thing is beyond dispute: the sweep of events has created a vast abyss between the old and the new. The recent Russian past is still near to us in time, but it is so far removed in other respects that we may study it almost objectively. Yet the living witnesses of this recent past, who had an opportunity to observe the state machine at work and to take part in Russian political life, are steadily decreasing in number. This fact, together with the extraordinary events they experienced during the Revolution and the conditions of their new existence, tend more and more to obscure the happenings of yesterday. The internal organization of old Russia, her political and social institutions, and those details of her life which are not reflected in literature and yet are of a certain value to future historians are being forgotten.

We are beginning to forget, too, the personal traits of her statesmen and her public men. As time goes on, it will be even more difficult to reconstruct their personalities from the written documents of the period of their activities, especially since many of the state archives have been destroyed, and private ones, particularly rich in information concerning certain men, have for the most part disappeared. Yet when an attempt is made to reconstruct the history of the period of Nicholas II, these details also will be significant.

The purpose of this work is to present in written form salient points in the political past of Russia, to point out the principal trends of public and bureaucratic thought in pre-revolutionary Russia, and to draw a few character sketches of her prominent leaders. The author fully realizes the many defects of this work, especially the disproportionateness between its several parts. But this is an inevitable characteristic of any account of historical events by a contemporary, because to him certain events are better known than others and thus claim his attention more completely. It is but natural, therefore, that in recording even the most important events of an epoch he would emphasize some facts more than others and would relate at considerable length those happenings in which he took part. It has been especially difficult for the author of this work to avoid these natural faults because in his present exile he has had access to only a limited number of sources. He has been obliged to depend chiefly on his memory for the facts here set forth, but he has always striven to verify the accuracy of these facts by conversations with persons who were closely connected with the events and circumstances described. But despite this verification grave errors may still remain. Even so, there is a distinct advantage in publishing one's personal impressions while other contemporaries of the events described are yet alive, for errors may be recognized and corrected by them.

The author will undoubtedly be reproached repeatedly for expressing his sincere and unadulterated opinions of the activities and personal characteristics of certain persons who are still alive and with whom he comes in personal contact. Yet be it said in justification of the author's effort that, in attempting to characterize those two forces, the government and the public, he has not only endeavored to be as impartial as is humanly possible but has had no difficulty in maintaining such an attitude. For more than twenty years the author worked in the ranks of the government and then he took his place in the ranks of the public, for which he has labored to the best of his abilities ever since. During this time he was able to familiarize himself with both government and public groups and to observe and realize that both camps had undeniable weaknesses as well as incontestible merits.

The author wishes to conclude this preface by saying that he has always followed the principle: *"Amicus Plato, sed magis amica Veritas."*

V. I. G.

PARIS, FRANCE

INTRODUCTION

The reign of Emperor Nicholas II[1]* can be divided into two parts, namely: the period of autocratic government (1894–1906), and the period following the establishment of constitutional government (1906–1917). But it is also possible to divide his reign into four separate periods which either may be named after statesmen of great authority, influence, and activity or are characterized by distinct social forces and tendencies.

During the first of these four periods, which extended from his accession to the throne (1894) until the spring of 1902, the young sovereign, realizing his inexperience in state affairs, relegated nearly all authority to his ministers, the majority of whom had held their posts during the reign of Alexander III.[2] Among those ministers the first place was occupied almost from the outset by the restless, fiery, and progressive Minister of Finance, S. Y. Witte,[3] who at that time enjoyed the complete confidence of Nicholas II. The Emperor supported Witte in all his financial and economic ventures, and as a result economic problems dominated state policies. Industrial development went ahead by leaps and bounds; both domestic and foreign trade were revived; state finances were strengthened. The state budgets showed a marked increase of revenues over expenses from year to year. Private fortunes were accumulated. A strong and influential industrial and merchant class appeared and, as it expanded, became ambitious for increased honors and power. A proletarian class also appeared. But the masses of the peasantry did not benefit from this new wave of prosperity. In some localities, indeed, they experienced a change for the worse. This was due to the general neglect of agriculture and other branches of rural economy. The poor organization of the grain trade, the poverty of the producer who was forced by his own condition to sell his produce at any price, and world conditions resulted in a steady decline of grain prices. This decline was harmful no less to the peasants than to the landowners.

During the last years of this period—a time of comparative quiet undisturbed by any serious domestic troubles—political passions

* [See Editors' Notes on page 589, at end of text.]

began to awaken among the public. This awakening found expression mainly in student disorders, which toward the end of the nineteenth century became an almost chronic phenomenon. The period terminated in a series of terroristic acts directed against representatives of the government: the Minister of Education, Bogolepov,[4] was murdered, and soon afterwards the same fate befell the Minister of the Interior, Sipiagin.[5] Nor were these murders greeted with indignation by the masses of the people; on the contrary, they were accepted with silent approbation. The opposition press strove, as much as conditions of censorship permitted, to prove that these acts were a natural and even an inevitable product of the existing regime.

The murder of Sipiagin and V. K. Plehve's[6] appointment as Minister of the Interior, in April 1902, mark the end of the first and relatively peaceful period of the reign of Nicholas II.

The second period, lasting until 1907, was very turbulent. It may be divided into two parts, which, though really very similar, seemed to be very different from each other in their external manifestations. The first part was occupied with the struggle between the government and the awakened public. Plehve sincerely desired to do the country good; he endeavored to inaugurate certain reforms designed to improve the state machinery and to relieve the peasantry, but in practice he limited himself to conducting a peculiar struggle against the public. This struggle was characterized by the fact that no distinction was made between the different elements of the opposition. Those who professed moderate constitutional aspirations were persecuted just as severely as were the truly revolutionary leaders. Plehve manifested a faultfinding, hypercritical attitude toward everything and everybody but instituted no decisive general measure. This caused universal dissatisfaction among the most widely different strata of society, which became antagonistic without having been weakened. In a word, if the first period of the reign passed under the "sign of Witte," the first half of the second period passed under the "sign of Plehve" and ended with his assassination.

During the second part of this second period the struggle between government and public continued but with the former making some concession. Plehve was succeeded by Prince Sviatopolk-Mirsky,[7] who strove to appease the more moderate elements of public opposition and to sever their connection with the revolutionary groups. He proclaimed an era of confidence in the public, but the public was not to be so easily pacified and continued to express its restless dissatisfaction. The unfortunate Japanese War only made matters worse, with the spirit of unrest spreading in ever widening circles and expressing itself more and more clearly and strongly.

The public turned from the defensive position it had maintained under Plehve to take the offensive, and besieged the government with increased energy and arrogance. It was spiritually and at times actually allied with revolutionary elements. The controversy began to include lower masses of the population, especially the industrial workers, who were under the guidance of the Socialist-Revolutionists.[8] The government contented itself with a policy of self-defense which it expressed with varying degrees of forcefulness. Different men followed one another at the helm of state, but not one of them charted a definite course for state policy. The most pronounced, although more or less passive, resistance to the insistent demands of the public was made by the Tsar himself. Nevertheless, the public, aided by the uprisings and the general railway strike of 1905, gained a partial victory. The Manifesto of October 17, 1905,[9] proclaimed the establishment of representative government and stipulated that no law could be promulgated without the consent of the people's representatives; but it failed to bring order to the country. Witte, as head of the new government, vainly attempted to come to an understanding with the different elements of the opposition. Revolution walked the streets. There was an armed uprising in Moscow. Serious troubles broke out in many parts of the vast empire. There were mutinies among the troops. The regime tottered on the brink of an abyss. It was saved by a member of the Witte cabinet, the Minister of the Interior, P. N. Durnovo,[10] who adopted an almost independent policy and by merciless persecution of the revolutionary elements re-established a certain degree of order in the country. The act of October 17 marks the legal division between the old, definitely autocratic regime and the new order, which was a peculiar mixture of constitutionalism and absolutism.

The first efforts of the people's representatives served as a beginning for collaboration between government and public. But this did not bring government and public together. On the contrary, and especially in the new legislative body, differences were more acute and public unrest was stimulated to a considerable degree. The First Duma, although led by bourgeois elements, showed definite revolutionary tendencies. I. L. Goremykin,[11] Witte's successor as Chairman of the Council of Ministers,[12] was at first content with a passive resistance to the opposition, but he ended his short term of office with a decisive act: the dissolution of the Duma.

P. A. Stolypin[13] succeeded Goremykin as head of the government. His first concern was to quiet public opinion. He wished to do it by carrying out on the Tsar's authority by means of Imperial ukases the liberal measures which had been so insistently demanded by the progressive elements of the country. Accordingly, when the Duma was not in session, all crown and state tillable land was transferred to the Peasant Land Bank[14] to be sold. At the same time regulations were issued concerning the procedure by which individual peasants might be permitted to leave the land communes (*pozemelnaia obshchina*).[15] By these measures it was hoped to develop among the peasants a sense of individual proprietorship and to create a stratum of strong and well-to-do peasantry.

The Second Duma, which met in November 1906, did not seem satisfied with the measures that had been adopted since the dissolution of the First Duma. In fact its opposition was more vigorous than that of the First Duma. In addition, it manifested a tendency toward a social rather than a political upheaval. But the people, weary from the troubles of previous years, reacted but feebly to the fiery revolutionary speeches in the Duma.

Realizing that the government could not work with the people's representatives elected according to the law of December 11, 1905,[16] Stolypin decided to break the basic law. By a ukase of June 3, 1907, the Duma was declared dissolved and at the same time a new law concerning elections to the Duma was promulgated on the authority of the Monarch;[17] this sought to guarantee that a majority of the Duma members would be supporters of the government. This act terminated the period of sharp struggle between public and government and inaugurated a period of collaboration between the two. This third period was characterized by the administration of strong-willed men, distinguished for their initiative and energy. Stolypin undertook to increase the prestige of the government and at the same time to win for it the support of the moderate elements of the zemstvo and of the well-to-do peasantry, an undertaking in which he met with considerable success. The Minister of Agriculture, A. V. Krivoshein,[18] was no less energetic. He achieved brilliant results in improving the conditions of rural economy and the methods of peasant agriculture, and after the assassination of Stolypin, September 1911, while V. N. Kokovtsov[19] was Chairman of the Council of Ministers, he exerted considerable influence upon the entire scope of state policy.

During this period the Third Duma, which had been elected in accordance with the new electoral law, played an important part in public life. In working with it, Stolypin realized his dream of transforming the Duma from an institution fundamentally hostile to the government to an active and powerful collaborator. On its initiative many legislative measures for improving general standards of living and education were adopted. As a result, the prosperity of the people and the entire country increased by leaps and bounds. The pace of economic life was quickened with every passing year. Both state and local budgets, such as those of zemstvos and towns, increased steadily and revenue markedly surpassed expenditure.

Little by little, the relations between the government and the broad masses of the people became more harmonious. The revolutionary elements began to lose ground and became appreciably weaker. The opposition continued to defy the government but did not rise openly against it. In a word, internal peace was established.

This internal peace lasted until the middle of 1914—up to the very beginning of the World War, when Russia entered the fourth and final period of the reign. At first the war seemed to draw the public and the government more closely together; but the serious defects in our military supplies became apparent toward the beginning of 1915 and stimulated public discontent. Then Rasputin[20] rose to fame. Rasputin was an ignorant peasant who wormed his way into the Imperial palace—a fatal personality endowed, unfortunately, with certain hypnotic powers. Actual control gradually passed from the Tsar to the Tsarina, Alexandra Fedorovna,[21] and was finally concentrated in her hands. She became the real ruler, experiencing only more or less passive resistance from the Tsar. Krivoshein's influence began to wane and soon disappeared entirely, and he was removed from his ministerial post. Then began a continuous shifting of those in power. Goremykin, again appointed Chairman of the Council of Ministers in January 1914, was now weighed down by years; not only had he lost all his energy, but also he was imbued with antiquated political ideas. Early in 1916 he was replaced by Stürmer,[22] who was entirely engrossed in his own private interests and criminally indifferent to the well-being of the state. During the autumn of 1916 tremendous influence was exerted by the unbalanced Protopopov,[23] who had been appointed Minister of the Interior at the instigation of various dubious forces. At this time the strongly prevailing opinion that Rasputin was the actual ruler of the country was of great psychological importance. The word "treason" was heard, and public opinion did not exclude from the ranks of traitors many persons of authority —even the Tsarina herself. The public was tremendously excited. It insisted that positions of responsibility should be filled with persons enjoying public confidence, but its insistence met with neither approval nor serious resistance. Revolutionary elements were quick to use the situation for their own ends. Supported in part with German money, they carried on an intense propaganda among the workingmen and among the army units behind the front. Public opinion was left to follow whatever course it would; the government made no effort to win its support. The country was filled with vast amounts of combustible human material. The situation was ripening for a complete upheaval and destruction of the existing state order. The Tsarina realized this fully but had neither the skill nor the political tact necessary to restore a normal social atmosphere. Nor was she able to find anyone capable of taking over the helm of state.

In summary, therefore, we may say that two periods of the reign of Nicholas II were creative: the Witte period from the accession of Nicholas II until 1902, and the seven-year period (1907–1914) of Stolypin and Krivoshein, when these two talented statesmen worked in co-operation with the majority of the Duma. Between these two periods lay the unfortunate war with Japan and, as a result of that war, the open struggle between the public forces and the government. But the troubles born of this struggle gradually subsided. The state entered upon a new road full of promise for the development of the country's economic and cultural forces.

The fourth and final period covered less than three years. Aside from the World War, which, of course, was the source of all subsequent evils, this period is characterized by the Tsar's gradual renunciation of his authority. In the beginning Nicholas relegated his authority almost entirely to the Tsarina, who unwittingly acted under the influence of dark forces; in the end he abdicated. His abdication left the country with no ultimate authority.

PART ONE

The First Years of the Reign of Nicholas II

CHAPTER I

THE DEATH OF ALEXANDER III AND THE ACCESSION OF NICHOLAS II

October 20, 1894. A clear sunny day in St. Petersburg. The streets are filled with people, but the spirit of the crowd is far from festive. On the Nevsky, people are standing at each street corner, reading with worried care announcements pasted on the walls: the health bulletins of the ailing Emperor Alexander III, now at Livadia on the southern coast of the Crimea. On Kazan Cathedral Square there is unwonted agitation. In the cathedral a crowd of worshippers listens to a *Te Deum* being sung for the recovery of the sick monarch. The crowds are worried and depressed.

The Emperor's illness, which had taken a sudden turn for the worse, involved the possibility of a change of sovereigns. It had been entirely unexpected. Alexander's giant stature, his age (he was in his prime), his appearance, which showed no traces of ill health—all had seemed to assure the country a long, uninterrupted rule. The news of his illness was all the more unexpected since it had become known only after his condition had become very serious. Before the country had had time to inform itself of its sovereign's illness it learned that his illness would be fatal.

The population of the capital realized all this not so much by reasoning, perhaps, as by intuition. The St. Petersburg bureaucracy and its prominent members were fully aware of the situation. Their eyes turned instinctively toward the future, trying to foresee how it would be affected by the character and personal traits of the heir to the throne. But the Tsarevich was little known and his personality was described in many different ways. The personality of the future Nicholas II was at that time not yet known, largely because he had taken no part in state affairs. He was, it is true, Chairman of the Committee to Supervise the Construction of the Siberian Railway,[1] but his chairmanship was purely honorary, and it was common knowledge that he exercised no influence upon the decisions of this committee. There were many different opinions on

13

this matter, it is true; but on one point all seemed to agree: the future ruler of Russia had had no experience in statesmanship.

It is not strange, therefore, that under these conditions the future seemed both insecure and uncertain. I had an occasion to witness the apprehensions commonly shared at that time by the administrators. On the morning of October 19, 1894, I had a talk with the Minister of the Navy, N. M. Chikhachev.[2] I had arrived that day from Warsaw and when I handed him a letter from my father I asked what news there was from Livadia. "As bad as possible," answered Chikhachev. "There is no hope of recovery; in fact, I am sure the Emperor has already passed away. Tell your father," he added, "that to us the future seems veiled in mist. The heir is a mere child, without experience, training, or even an inclination to study great problems of state. His interests are still those of a child, and it is impossible to predict what changes may be effected. At present military service is the only subject that interests him. The helm of state is about to fall from the hands of an experienced mariner, and I fear that no hand like his is to grasp it for many years to come. What will be the course of the ship of state under these conditions the Lord only knows."

Chikhachev's guess, that the Emperor was already dead, was an accurate one. That same day about 9:00 P.M. extra editions of the papers announced the death of Alexander III. They appeared just as the express train was about to pull out of St. Petersburg's Nicholas station for Moscow. The news caused so much consternation that the passengers in my carriage (I was leaving too), friends and strangers alike, engaged in general conversation, exchanging their views on this significant event. The question on everyone's lips was: "What will come of it all?"

When I reached Moscow the following day, I was greatly surprised at the appearance of the old capital. The calm there was in striking contrast to the excitement in St. Petersburg; Moscow seemed indifferent to the change in sovereigns. Of course requiems were sung in all churches for the soul of the late Emperor and church bells tolled mournfully, but no large crowds gathered at the church doors and the people in the streets showed no agitation such as prevailed in St. Petersburg. On the contrary, the people in the streets were the ordinary everyday business crowd with everyone hurrying about his own affairs, showing no concern for the future. Nor did I find among the local Moscow nobility, whose ranks were even at that time very much thinned out, but whose members were the leaders of Moscow cultural circles, any particular anxiety over the change in reign. I was involuntarily reminded of the events that had occurred thirteen years before, on March 2, 1881, when Moscow learned of the assassination of the Emperor Alexander II.[3] Then Moscow had been as troubled as an overturned beehive; commonplace worries were forgotten; the attentions of the masses and of the upper social circles alike were absorbed by questions of national significance. But now the sharp difference between the mental attitudes of St. Petersburg and Moscow would have impressed any person who was at all observant. Perhaps because so many of its citizens would be directly affected by any change in administrative circles, bureaucratic St. Petersburg was far more alive to political possibilities than was Moscow, which was becoming more and more an industrial center. Moscow, deep in the pursuit of its own private interests, seemed to be in danger of losing the political instincts so essential to a healthy national organism; nor did it seem to realize the close relation between private interests and the general state of national affairs.

But the industrial circles were not the only ones indifferent to questions of state. Those circles of the intelligentsia that were in the habit of striking the tone for the prevailing public moods appeared now to be engrossed in their own special ideas and plans. The students who in the 'seventies had been accustomed to express their feelings so passionately had quieted down surprisingly, had abandoned to a great extent their idealistic aspirations, and had become absorbed in petty philistine interests. The middle classes had produced only those dull, homely types so effectively portrayed by Chekhov.[4] In a word, that passionate development of public thought, so noticeable in the 'seventies, had come to an end. This may have been due to the fact that the local nobility and gentry, shaken by the reform of February 19, 1861,[5] had already lost from their ranks their more easily excitable and active elements, which had gone to swell the ranks of the revolutionary movement of the 'seventies, while the strata of the population known as *raznochintsy*,[6] although very much increased in number, had had no time to develop definite political opinions and contented themselves with endeavoring to satisfy their modest material needs.

It is easy to understand that St. Petersburg, the city of the bureaucrats and the center of the country's cultural life, was more likely to react to state problems than was Moscow, the city of the people. There was a widespread opinion in Moscow that St. Petersburg had lost its contact with the mother country and had lost all national feeling. Yet St. Petersburg, perhaps because of its higher cultural level, appraised the significance of the change of sovereign much more accurately than did Moscow, absorbed in selfish material interests and with the upper classes greedy for profits and wealth. St. Petersburg, the center of administration, reflected the current tendencies of public thought.

In the October days of 1894 these two cities impressed me as typifying two forces which, if not openly hostile, were certainly alien to each other and reacted to events in different ways. What reason could there be for this estrangement, which in one way and another had been evident for a considerable time? Formerly, Moscow had been far more sensitive to deep-rooted national interests, and St. Petersburg had held itself rather aloof. One would have thought that the thirteen peaceful years of Alexander III's reign would have tended to establish some understanding between the bureaucratic and the public points of view; yet the very antithesis of understanding seemed to exist. What, then, could be the reason? The importance of the achievements of Alexander III's reign in developing Russia's national strength and international prestige cannot be denied. The briefest comparison of conditions at the beginning of the reign with those at its end would prove this point incontestably. When Alexander III ascended the throne, red with the blood of the Tsar Liberator, he inherited an enormous empire virtually in a state of chaos. In fact, during the last years of the reign of Alexander II there had been neither continuity nor stability in Russia's national policy. A continual shifting of the political course, now toward liberalism, now toward reaction, now toward directing all efforts of the government against so-called treason (*kramola*),[7] now in an endeavor to appease public opinion by a series of measures intended to introduce a regime of equity in Russia—all this had deprived the government of much prestige. The condition of both the state and the people's economy was very unsatisfactory. State budgets showed yearly increasing deficits. At the same time our economic dependence upon the states of Western Europe was reflected in the depreciation of our paper currency. Arrears in tax payments, and particularly in redemption dues,[8] increased from year to year, showing clearly that the standard of living among the people in general and the peasants in particular was sinking lower and lower. The Russo-Turkish War, although marked by brilliant military successes culminating in the Treaty of Berlin,[9] which wounded national pride deeply, revealed our weakness before the threats of a united England and Germany and was utterly without profit to us.

During the thirteen years of Alexander III's reign these conditions were radically changed. This reign exemplifies in a striking manner the great value of a clearly defined and constant course of political conduct. Because Alexander III followed such a course, even though it ran counter to the hopes of society's progressive circles, his reign experienced neither sharp protestations nor open uprisings. The external appearance of strength which was expressed so well in the tremendous physique of Alexander III was in complete harmony with the force and stability of his spirit and will. The progressive circles felt instinctively that to engage in an open struggle with this will would have been both useless and dangerous. Under the leadership of this powerful directing will, all those persons who were placed at the head of different branches of government shared similar qualities of stability and constancy, assuring the state of an even and consistent progress in all its aspects. This program was helped by the fact that the change of men responsible for the country's policies, both foreign and domestic, occurred but on rare occasions. N. K. Giers[10] was Minister of Foreign Affairs throughout the entire reign. After the discharge of Count N. P. Ignatev,[11] who had been inherited from the previous reign, D. A. Tolstoi[12] was Minister of the Interior until his death, when he was succeeded by I. N. Durnovo.[13] Changes in other departments were just as infrequent. Thus P. S. Vannovsky[14] was Minister of War during the entire reign. As a result Russia enjoyed civil peace and gradually recovered her strength and prosperity.

The foreign policy of Alexander III achieved equally brilliant results. It was sincerely pacific in character, devoid of all wild and fantastic schemes, full of dignity, and always on guard to protect the interests of the state. Toward the end of the reign the prestige of both Russia and her sovereign attained unprecedented heights. It may be said without exaggeration that in the beginning of the 'nineties Alexander III was the recognized chief arbiter for all Europe. All states of the world listened to his rarely expressed but weighty opinions. This was mainly due to the fact that Russia had no alliance with any country at that time. Alexander's memorable toast: "To the health of my only friend, the Prince of Montenegro," the territory of whose domain was no larger than one Russian uezd, served to show that the might of Russia needed no outside assistance and that Russia would enjoy complete freedom of action in the event of any conflict among the states of Western Europe. Uncertainty as to Russia's action restrained the states of Western Europe in their mutual feuds and so promoted international peace. The foreign policy of Alexander III gave to Russia the luxury of that "splendid isolation" which up to that moment only England, by virtue of her insular position, had been able to maintain.[15]

Yes, it was all of this. At home and abroad Russia's position was indeed strong. Yet those were also right who likened Russia's internal peace and quiet to the Roman peace of which Tacitus said: *"Solitudinem faciunt et pacem appellant."*

Public thought was undoubtedly restrained by the political and the censorial vise. As a result, the instinct of statesmanship became atrophied even among the intellectuals, and their efforts were directed exclusively toward the attainment of personal well-being. This created indifference toward questions of state such as was demonstrated so clearly in Moscow at the time of the death of Alexander III. The intelligentsia were denied participation in the building of the state and consequently they, as well as the masses, naturally lost all interest in any question which did not touch immediately upon their own private interests.

This of course was not the attitude of those persons who, because of their individual characteristics and the breadth of their intellectual horizons, were interested and engrossed in great political and social problems. They had long been discontented with the existing political regime and were waiting only for an opportunity to throw off the yoke that weighed heavily upon the educated elements of the population, to place themselves at the head of the intellectual masses, and to proclaim the people's right to a direct participation in the building of the state. Both as heir to the throne and later as sovereign, Alexander III had had opportunities to develop definite political opinions. The fact that his successor was a youth inexperienced in state policy was full of import for these farsighted persons.

The remains of Alexander III had not yet been interred when a certain portion of the press hastened to expose the negative aspects of his policy. Such important monthlies as *Vestnik Evropy*[16] and even the moderate *Istoricheskii Vestnik*[17] took the lead in this activity. These publications clearly pointed out the necessity of shifting the political course in a more liberal direction. The same stand was taken by several public institutions, among which the zemstvo assembly[18] of Tver Gubernia was particularly conspicuous. Supported by I. I. Petrunkevich,[19] F. I. Rodichev,[20] and I. A. Korsakov[21]—the godfathers of the future Cadet party[22]—this assembly openly suggested to the young sovereign in a most humble address[23] the necessity of introducing a constitutional regime in Russia.

What answer could the young Tsar make to all this?

Completely bewildered by state problems, which were especially obscure to him, since he had no natural inclination in that direction, and completely under the influence of his mother, the Dowager Empress,[24] who naturally admired the policy of her late husband, Nicholas II could have no other desire than to follow meekly in the footsteps of his father. This he expressed in his first manifesto. But the policy of Alexander III was the natural outcome of his personality, with which it was in harmony. To continue such a policy without possessing those qualities upon which it had rested was to undertake the impossible; it would have meant attempting to accomplish the task without the proper tools. It was not long before everyone realized this. In truth, perhaps the main reason for all the internal troubles which disturbed the reign of Nicholas II and which finally led to the downfall of the Empire was Nicholas' attempt to preserve a policy which he was quite unfitted to follow, and to be an autocrat without possessing the qualities which such a role demanded.

This became apparent during the very first months of his reign and was first evidenced in his address to the many town, zemstvo, and class organizations which presented themselves to him on the occasion of his accession. This address contained the expression "senseless dreams" in referring to the address of the Tver Zemstvo Assembly. This was a very ill-chosen phrase. It was given immediate and wide publicity and became a target for hostile and mocking criticisms. In fact, it clearly showed the young ruler's immature political outlook and his lack of political tact. A less harsh response based on a definite point of view or even a reprimand would undoubtedly have made a far better impression. But his attitude, so childishly expressed, toward the proposed state organization, such as had already been accepted by all civilized countries, not only revealed the immaturity of the new sovereign but also provided ammunition for the opposition.

From the beginning, therefore, an imminent conflict between the two forces, government and public, cast its shadow over the reign of Nicholas II. But the struggle did not begin immediately. Just as the calm sea does not at once become turbulent before the rising storm, so the inert masses of the people could not throw off their apathy and rise at a moment's notice. For this very reason, the first years of the new reign did not differ much from the previous period as far as internal administration and public opinion were concerned. To all appearances the political machinery of the country experienced no alteration; the first sign of the impending sharp change was manifested in the younger generation, among the students in the country's higher institutions of learning who had not felt the spiritual force of Alexander III. But it was soon evident that despite his fond desire to follow in the footsteps of his father, Nicholas II had failed to do so in so far as the state policy of the first few years of his reign was concerned.

The domestic policy of Alexander III had been centered on strengthening the existing order by stabilizing the position of the local gentry, by lending economic support to the peasants, by exalting the church. In accordance with this policy there had been founded the Bank of the Nobility,[25] the Peasant Bank, and the institution of the *zemskie nachalniki*,[26] based to a certain extent upon principles of patrimonial authority. The statutes on town and rural self-government had been revised in order to increase the number of taxpayers; a great number of parish schools had been organized; and church building had been encouraged. In so far as the non-Russian population of the country's far-flung borders was concerned, Alexander's policy was to permeate them steadily with Russian state principles.

In all these fields the policy of Nicholas II brought considerable changes and, above all, showed a total lack of system and stability. As regards the border regions this change was evidenced by the dismissal, at the insistence of the Dowager Empress Marie Fedorovna, of the Governor-General of Warsaw and Commander in

Chief of Troops of the Warsaw Military District, I. V. Gurko,[27] an ardent champion of Alexander III's aims. As regards domestic policy, it was manifest in the encouragement of trade and industry and in the discontinuation of those measures intended for the support of civil-service employees. Nicholas' personal relations to this class seemed to remain unaltered, but the state policy regarding it changed radically. There was also a change in international policy. Outwardly it remained the same, but essentially it assumed quite a different character.

During the reign of Alexander III the friendly relations with France were but a diversion and a retaliation for the Treaty of Berlin, which had been forced upon Russia, and not in any way a manifestation of Russian enmity toward Germany.[28] Nicholas' visit to Paris in October 1896 was an open declaration of that friendship in the face of Germany. The evolution of our friendship with France into a definite alliance not only imposed tremendous obligations upon us but also broke the centuries-old traditional friendship between the Romanovs and the Hohenzollerns. Both steps deprived us of that freedom of action which Alexander III had justly considered to be of such great importance.

Thus, there really was no "following in the footsteps," and the footprints themselves were gradually obliterated.

But why should this have been so? To this there can be but one answer. In the hands of Nicholas II, autocracy, conceived as a personal and independent direction of state problems, had ceased to exist. It was actually supplanted by an oligarchy of a dominant group composed of several chief administrators, who were united by no common political opinion and therefore were in continual opposition to one another. Among these men, who bore the title of ministers, now one and now another assumed a temporary leadership which was really confined to the limits of his own department.

The nucleus of political life, at least outwardly, was concentrated in the State Council.[29] This institution very clearly indicates current political forces. It also affords the best background for a picture of the personalities and individual idiosyncracies of the statesmen. For this reason, it is fitting briefly to survey domestic policy during the first period of Nicholas' reign as portrayed by the activities of the State Council, and to draw a few sketches of the persons in authority at that time.

CHAPTER II

THE STATE COUNCIL BEFORE THE REFORM

The State Council was the supreme institution of an empire of more than one hundred and fifty million people. It deliberated upon and edited laws governing the destinies of the people of one-sixth of the inhabited globe. At the beginning of the reign of Nicholas II it consisted of less than one hundred men, for many of whom some of the fields and aspects of administration were literally *terra incognita.* Of these hundred members less than forty took an active part in the debates on proposed statutes. Before projects of laws were submitted to the State Council proper, they were usually discussed in its departments with the participation of those members who had been appointed especially for work in these departments.

There were at first three departments: Legislative, State Economy, and Civil and Ecclesiastical Affairs. In 1899 a fourth was added: the Department of Industry, Science, and Commerce. This name, in which science was linked with trade and industry, was characteristic of the general trend of the time. Under the irresistible drive of S. Y. Witte the development of Russian industry was considered the most important and pressing task of the state, while science, that is, public education, was relegated to second place.

Those members of the Council who were not appointed to specific departments took part only in the general sessions of the Council. They did not ordinarily debate proposed laws but passed upon only those matters which had not been settled in the departments. They were not called upon to make such decisions frequently, but when they were, the matter usually concerned some general principle, and the arguments that ensued were for the most part not between members of the Council, but between the heads of the different ministries who had a right to attend the sessions ex officio. The votes of the members of the Council were divided in support of the different ministerial advocates.

But even of those members of the Council who were appointed to different departments, not all took an active part in the debates. This is not surprising when we consider the method by which men became members of the Council. They were, as a rule, old men—former ministers, governor-generals, and ambassadors—who were little fitted for further work. Several of the abler senators were appointed to perform the actual work in the Council, but even these were not particularly youthful, and, since appointment to the Council was for life, they automatically became members of the general sessions, thus augmenting the useless load that weighed upon that institution.

During former reigns the addition of new members to the State Council had been given close attention and consideration. It had been absolutely impossible to become a member through the good offices of friends and patrons and therefore no attempts had been made to attain such an end. But after the accession of Nicholas II, persons possessing the friendship of influential officials and members of the Court found their way into the country's highest institution and took their place among those who, by virtue of their personal qualities or their past performances, had an indisputable right to membership.

The sessions of the Council were conducted with strict formality, even with solemnity. This was particularly true of the general sessions, which were held in the superbly decorated Mariinsky Palace,[1] in the famous round hall depicted in Repin's[2] well-known painting. This hall had overhead lighting; pillars supported the balcony. It was carpeted with a dark crimson rug and furnished with comfortable armchairs and two round concentric tables covered with velvet cloth of the same color as the rug. Portraits of the Emperors who had reigned since the formation of the Council hung between the pillars. The whole setting gave the hall, particularly in the evening, an air of solemnity and even of mystery. It seemed a fit meeting-place for the sessions of a Masonic order or a council of the Doges which had to be concealed from the eyes of the uninitiated. Nor was this impression dispelled by the appearance of the members: venerable old men, white-haired or entirely bald, with wrinkled skin and often quite bent with age, wearing uniforms and adorned with all their decorations—they produced the impression of a living historical tableau.

The inauguration of a new member was conducted with theatrical effect, and this accepted order of inauguration was retained even after the inclusion of elected members in the Council. When a new member appeared for the first time at a session of the Council he was welcomed by the chairman; he then rose and bowed to the chairman and to all the members; whereupon all the members rose and bowed to the new member. In addition, each new member had to sign a special pledge, the text of which had not changed since the day the Council was organized, and to record his name in a book bound in green suede leather. This book was something indeed unique, for it contained the signatures of all members of the Council since its first meeting, among which were those of the Emperors Alexander II, Alexander III, and Nicholas II, who had been members of the Council before they ascended the throne. I wonder what has become of this historical relic!

The sessions were conducted under the chairmanship of the Grand Duke Mikhail Nikolaevich,[3] or, in his absence, under that of the senior chairman of the departments, at that time D. M. Solsky.[4] They usually began with the Imperial Secretary (Plehve at the period described) reading aloud those Imperial ukases that concerned the Council and reporting on those legislative projects accepted by the Council which had been accorded Imperial confirmation. If there had been disagreements in the Council he reported which opinion had been approved by the Emperor. Then one of the officials of the Imperial Chancellery read aloud those legislative projects that had been adopted by the different departments of the Council. This duty generally fell to the Assistant State Secretary, N. F. Deriuzhinsky,[5] (who became Assistant Imperial Secretary in the reformed State Council) because of his fine and pleasant voice, his clear and rapid reading. As I have already said, there were no debates. If a member desired to express an opinion on some project that had been unanimously adopted by the department concerned, he was obliged to announce this intention to the chairman beforehand. This happened very rarely; when it did, the project was usually returned to its department for further consideration of the disputed point with the participation of the objecting member. There was never a case in which the general session revised a project after it had been adopted by a department.

The discussion of questions that had caused some disagreement in the departments usually took the form of speeches delivered by the representative of the ministry presenting the project, by those who were opposed to it, as well as by the representatives of two crystallized opinions among the members of the Council. The spokesmen representing the different opinions, usually the same on each occasion, sought to dumfound the audience with their eloquence. Their speeches were later discussed with some animation by the members of the State Council and the orators were complimented upon their efforts. After the speeches the votes were taken by the officers of the Imperial Chancellery, who made the rounds of the members. The question was generally put in this form: "Is your Excellency with or against Minister So-and-so?" This made voting very easy, for many of the members had no opinion whatever on the matter under consideration and had not read the project, and even had they done so they could hardly have been expected to understand it because of their senility. Among this group were some men who had formerly been outstanding government leaders, but who by that time had lost their mental vigor and their capacity for work; such were the former Minister of Justice, Nabokov,[6] and the hero of Plevna, General Ganetsky.[7] At times there were curious situations. For example one member, General Stürler, who was making his career by holding various offices at court, announced on one occasion that he was with the majority, and when the officer who was taking the votes respectfully reminded him that there was no majority as yet, as it could be determined only after the voting, he answered with some displeasure: "I still insist that I am with the majority" and refused to be moved from this stand.

General sessions took place once a week and usually lasted about an hour. But the month of May, that is, the last month of the Council sessions before the summer vacation, was an exception, as in this month all departments presented to the general session their long and complicated projects, prepared by them throughout the winter term. The number of the projects included in the order of the day for the last general session sometimes reached a hundred, while in the winter months it did not exceed twelve to fifteen.

The meetings of the departments of the Council were characterized by a higher level of efficiency and vivacity than the general sessions. They were held four times a week and, with a half-hour recess, lasted from 1:00 P.M. to 6:00 P.M., which was accepted as the end of the business day. Formalities were observed to a nicety: all those present wore uniforms; smoking was not allowed; there were no sharp retorts or personal bickering; and fiery debates were very rare. Observation of rank was carried to an extreme: non-members of the Council, with the exception of assistant ministers representing the ministers and in that capacity having a right to vote, sat at a separate table; even the Imperial Secretary and the State Secretary (who was the head of the department which was sponsoring the project under debate) sat at a small table near the large table occupied by those who were members of the Council. Persons "invited to present explanations" were seated at a separate table next to the official whose duty it was to take minutes of the discussion. Persons so invited were generally the directors of the departments of that ministry which had submitted the project. The only exception that I ever witnessed was the case of the Governor of the City of St. Petersburg, who was usually invited when there was any discussion of the city's affairs or, more strictly speaking, of its police department. Twice General Kleigels[8] was invited to the meetings and on each occasion he was seated at the large table with the Council members and was shown much consideration. On the other hand, the Director of the Board of Weights and Measures,[9] Professor D. I. Mendeleev[10]— a world celebrity—not only was seated at the *Katzentisch,* but was even sternly reprimanded by one of the members because, without being invited to do so by the chairman, he attempted to give some explanation concerning one of the paragraphs of his draft of the new Regulations on Weights and Measures. According to custom those "invited to present explanations" could do so only after some member of the Council had asked for their opinions. This made their presence usually quite unnecessary, as they were seldom asked anything. All such inquiries were addressed either to the minister who had submitted the project or to his assistant acting in his stead, and these believed that to show the slightest hesitation on a subject the details of which they could not possibly have known would amount to defeat. At times, therefore, their explanations did not at all fit the reasons for the project, and would cause a better informed person "invited to present explanations" to become restless; sometimes the latter would rise, approach his chief and whisper to him, but usually the chief merely waved him aside.

Public men[11] were never invited to give explanations. The only exception, if I am not mistaken, was in 1900 when the regulation on port duties and taxes was being revised. Then the representatives of the municipal administrations of all large port cities were invited to attend. This invitation caused much discussion and was considered an exceptional phenomenon. Of course these representatives were not to take part in the discussions of the project that touched so closely upon the interests of all ports. According to the project—and this fact was realized later—the port duties and taxes, which formerly had been considered as the revenue of the port cities in which they were levied, were to be appropriated by the Treasury to form a special fund out of which our seaports were to be equipped according to their actual and peculiar needs and without regard to the actual amount of taxes collected in each. The representatives of the municipal administrations were ushered into the assembly hall before the debates began and seated at a table at the more remote end of the hall. Each one was asked to give his opinion. After each had stated his side of the case, the substance of which was that the collection of the sums and their distribution should be left to the cities, the municipal workers were asked to leave the room and the project was not further discussed until all of them had done so. It must be admitted, however, that with few exceptions the explanations of the municipal officials contained no new data and were, on the whole, very unconvincing: the exceptions were those of the representatives of the Baltic ports— Reval, Riga, and Libau—who defended the interests of their cities with animation and courage. Those members of the Council who were of Baltic origin lost no opportunity to comment on this in unofficial conversations; the Assistant Imperial Secretary Baron Uxkull-Gyllenband[12] even saw fit to remark: "In the Baltic you have a product of a superior culture, something different from your Russian Assembly." This Russian Assembly was a newly formed Right-wing and definitely nationalist organization; it was a source of continual irritation to the Baltic population, not because of its leanings toward the Right, but because of its nationalist and Russianizing tendencies.

But the role played by the State Council in the affairs of state was far from insignificant in spite of its lack of life. Yet this role was reduced mainly to a very conscientious examination of the details of legislative projects, and in so far as these projects concerned politics the majority of the Council was invariably in favor of limiting arbitrary administration, of exacting stricter legality, and of protecting the rights of private citizens against willful encroachments by the authorities. This statement must be taken relatively; yet one may say that usually the Council was much more liberal than the representatives of the administration.

Like any assembly of persons which is not immediately connected with government, exercises no direct authority, and bears no responsibility for its decision—which, from a legal point of view, was no more than advice—the State Council was willing to make more concessions to public opinion than were those who were directly connected with government. Of course some members of the Council were reactionaries, but these were in a minority. A much larger number of them were indifferent, adjusted their own opinions to the moods of those at the top, and feared most of all to subscribe to an opinion which was contrary to that of the Supreme Power. Yet the State Council sometimes acted as a check, especially upon a minister who wished to introduce a distinct and bold innovation. This was because the members of the Council, mostly former ministers, invariably opposed the ventures of their successors and also because their advanced ages naturally led them to give hesitating and careful consideration to all questions.

The effect of age showed itself in still another way. Some of the members of the Council's departments—particularly the chairmen of departments who determined when a given project should be heard— liked to avoid difficult and complicated matters, the examination of which necessitated hard work. Sometimes, therefore, projects on such matters were returned under some mere pretext to the office from which they had originated. Such was the fate of the complicated project of Russian naturalization and expatriation—a matter that had demanded years of hard study. It was returned to the Ministry of the Interior merely because the Chairman of the Legislative Department of the State Council (1898), Ostrovsky,[13] was very ill and unable to deal with it. He used a projected change in the revision of laws concerning Finland as a pretext for its return.

The importance of the Council was further weakened by the fact that it enjoyed no legislative initiative, that is, it was not a legislative body. The importance of such a privilege cannot be too strongly emphasized, as it obliges the government of a state to carry out the instructions of its legislative body. The State Council was empowered to give such instructions, and it used this privilege extensively, but, since it had no way to enforce its wishes, the privilege amounted to nothing in practice. The various government offices paid little or no attention to the instructions of the Council, and I cannot recall even one project submitted to the Council in execution of an instruction that it had given.

Of course these instructions pertained only to matters of secondary importance—properly speaking, to the technique of administration. In its instructions to the government offices, the Council did not broach any extensive political problems and actually could not have done so, for it is certain that any such attempt would have been nipped in the bud. I recall one such instance. During the examination of some proposed statute it was discovered that the Buriats were exempt from corporal punishment, whereas the Russian population living in the same regions were subject to such punishment upon the decision of the volost courts.[14] Considering this a patent injustice, the State Council recommended universal abolition of corporal punishment. This recommendation was entered in the minutes of the departments as a resolution, but was later changed to a mere statement of opinion expressed at a general session of the Council. This change was made at the instance of experienced members of the Council, who unofficially expressed the fear that such a display of initiative by members of the Council might provoke the Tsar's displeasure, since it seemed that he wished to abolish this type of punishment by a special manifesto to celebrate the birth of an heir to the throne. These members proved to be perfectly right. The Council's recommendation, mild though it was, evoked a sharp retort from Nicholas II: "This shall be done when I so desire." It goes without saying that this rebuke called forth many different opinions among the members of the Council. The timid members were terrified, and the brave ones expressed open indignation. The Minister of the Interior, D. S. Sipiagin, whose avowed reactionary policy had been continually opposed by the majority of the Council, immediately took advantage of this opportunity to characterize the Council to the Emperor as an almost seditious institution, as one that was certainly attempting to enforce its own desires without bothering to co-ordinate them with the wishes of the Tsar. This insinuation was grossly false, but it aroused in Nicholas II unfriendly feelings toward the institution, the members of which he himself had appointed.

There was one field, however, in which the Council enjoyed considerable importance—in rendering conciliatory decisions on subjects on which individual offices had been unable to reach an agreement. In effect the Council was really nothing but a court of conciliation for quarreling ministers and government offices in general. The Council's stand was decisive, particularly in the examination of projects for state revenues and expenditures. All departments and government offices naturally tried to increase the sums annually allotted to them. The Ministry of Finance, although it allotted considerable sums to itself and acted almost independently in so doing, invariably opposed any increase in the expenditures of other departments even if these expenditures were designed to meet urgent state needs. The State Control[15] was the faithful ally of the Ministry of Finance in such protestations. But the State Council had the last word in deciding these disagreements, for the Ministry of Finance did not dare to defy the decision of its majority.

Not only did the members of the Council try to avoid differences of opinion in the Council, but even more so the ministers, at least in matters of secondary importance. They did not wish to bring these matters to the attention and decision of the Supreme Power, especially since the Tsar invariably agreed with the decision of the majority of the Council. But on such occasions the personality of a minister played a very important role, as did the degree of his influence, his hold upon his position, and, alas, the amount of worldly goods at his disposal. As a matter of fact the ministers of the end of the last century, and probably long before that, could be divided into two categories: those who wanted to impress the Council by their importance and treated it in a half-condescending manner; and those who were obsequious toward it in attempting to assure themselves of its favor in their struggles with other ministries.

Speaking generally, the State Council reflected clearly and distinctly all peculiarities of our state structure. This structure was mistakenly called an autocracy. Some thought that the continual conflict among the ministers, which seldom had a foundation in personal aspirations and interests, but was most often based upon different conceptions of immediate state problems, indicated a certain weakening of the principle of sovereign authority. It was often remarked: "Therein lies the essence of our Russian constitution." But this was not true, at least in the later period. There was really a continually changing group of oligarchs at the head of the different branches of administration and a total absence of a single state authority directing their activities toward a clearly defined and recognized goal. These oligarchs, in the fullest sense of the word, undermined the state authority and brought it to naught, since they were not able to vest themselves with a single portion of this authority even within the limits of their subordinate offices.

State authority as such ceased to function. An arbitrary and often unexpected change was going on in the ministerial body. There was an arbitrary control over individuals; there was a complicated system of checks and hindrances to free exercise of initiative and energy in every branch of endeavor; but there was no constructive force directing the life of the people and working for the well-being of the country as a whole. Essentially, the state apparatus had no influence at all upon the lives of the people. Life went on of its own momentum, breaking little by little those fetters which encumbered it, and so developed, in spite of the state authority which either had no influence or exercised its influence in a negative way, a hindrance and an encumbrance which exasperated all healthy creative forces in the country.

This was the general situation. Sometimes it seemed to change, to stop in its course, such as when there rose to prominence some minister who had definite creative plans and enough strength of character and influence to silence his adversaries. Such a minister was Witte, who left his imprint upon a whole period of the reign of Nicholas II; such also was V. K. Plehve, who left no mark because of the shortness of his term as Minister of the Interior and because his personality was less decisive. Yet the influence even of such men obviously could not affect all branches of public life. This caused a deformed, one-sided development of certain phases of public life and the stagnation and suppression of others.

Stagnation was not the only aspect of the situation. There developed also a stratification of state policy. While the weak colleagues of a powerful statesman were not able to pass real reforms and to accomplish their aspirations and desires, the satrap of the moment was equally powerless to force his companions to co-ordinate their current policies with his undertakings and plans. As a result the well-meaning and forceful ventures of a person who used his authority were often weakened in their actual effect for want of favorable conditions.

I shall illustrate my point by citing one of the most patent examples of lack of co-operation and system in one and the same field of state undertaking, namely, in the question of the interrelation of capital and labor in our industry. The Ministry of Finance controlled the Department of Factory Inspection.[16] This ministry endeavored, through the medium of that institution, not only to protect the workingmen from undue exploitation by their employers but also to promote a more friendly feeling between labor and capital. But besides the Department of Factory Inspection there existed an institution of an administrative-police nature for the supervision of the workers. This institution not only often hindered the attempts at conciliation, but was usually not averse to taking drastic action against the workers during labor strikes. It often did so without waiting for any request from the employers and even against their clearly expressed wishes to come to some peaceful understanding with their employees by direct negotiations. Such was the state of affairs up to the well-known time of Zubatov;[17] and although the situation did not change even then, it acquired different aspects.

Then one has only to consider our censorship, which extended more or less over all the ministries—it often happened that one ministry published at the state's expense something which another minister, the Ministry of the Interior and its Chief Administration for the Affairs of the Press,[18] prohibited.

The powerlessness of individual ministers to deal with those problems which touched even slightly upon the sphere of another ministry brought about a peculiar phenomenon, namely, a desire of a minister, who was most influential at the moment, to include in the jurisdiction of his ministry all subjects that even slightly concerned it. Thus Witte so enlarged the sphere of the Ministry of Finance as to render the authority of the Ministries of Ways and Communications and of Agriculture practically nil. This was unquestionably the ambition of Sipiagin also, who aimed even higher; he endeavored to make his successive offices—first His Majesty's Private Chancellery to Receive Petitions[19] and later the Ministry of the Interior—supreme over all other offices. This was obviously the aspiration of Plehve also, although he sought to carry it out in a different and more modest way. He dreamed of including within the competence of the Ministry of the Interior the Land Banks— namely, the Bank of the Nobility and the Peasant Bank—on the one hand, and the Department of Factory Inspection on the other, and to this end he planned to institute chief administrations for both rural affairs and labor and to attach these administrations to his ministry.

Moreover, within the ministries themselves the various departments did not always act in co-ordination. For instance, in the early 'eighties a police search discovered a manuscript which caused the deportation of its author, Borodin, to Siberia. The manuscript dealt with economic conditions in Viatka Gubernia, and after Borodin's departure was published in the magazine, *Otechestvennyia Zapiski*[20] over Borodin's name, but the editor of the magazine was not censored or punished.

Finally, the action of the administration and the courts was not co-ordinated. I recall a case in 1897 when the Tver Gubernia Special Board[21] reprimanded two zemskie nachalniki and the chairman of the uezd court for refusing to try a certain case, whereas the Tver District Court supported them in their refusal. Thus were government officials reprimanded on the one hand, and were supported on the other by government bodies to which they were subordinated.

At the beginning of the twentieth century there was a series of jubilees for most of our government institutions. For the State Council and many ministries it was the celebration of their hundredth anniversaries. Strange as it may seem, these celebrations were somewhat sad, as if the celebrators were burying their past and had no hope for the future. The jubilee of the State Council in 1901, in spite of its outward splendor, was particularly depressing. To begin with, the Emperor made two serious changes in the draft of the Imperial Ukase to be issued to the State Council on this occasion. The draft read in part, that the Council was an institution that had been established in 1801 and was formed of persons "honored with the confidence of the Monarch and the people." The Tsar crossed out the words "and the people." He also struck out part of the following sentence: "the opinions of the Council have been heeded with consideration by our crowned forefathers, our lamented grandfather, and our unforgettable father . . . ," namely, the words "with consideration." The significance of these corrections, or rather exclusions, was perfectly clear to the members of the Council. They revealed that the State Council, composed entirely of persons appointed by the crown and for the most part of persons who were tried workers for the throne, did not enjoy the favor of the Tsar. An absolutely loyal association of persons, the majority of whom, in spite of their great age, were devoting their entire strength to the service of the country and the throne, was under suspicion.

This was made particularly evident on the very day of the jubilee, commemorated by the artist Repin in his famous painting of the solemn session of the Council. The Emperor, arriving at the session, was met by all the members in the vestibule of the Mariinsky Palace; he passed immediately to the assembly hall and opened the session. Since the whole program consisted of the reading of the Imperial Ukase and the distribution of anniversary medals to the members of the Council by the officials of the Imperial Chancellery, the session lasted only a short time. There were no speeches, no congratulations of any sort; a depressed silence reigned in the hall, an embarrassing stiffness that was felt by everyone present. Instead of a festive or even slightly cheerful mood there was an all-pervading air of dejection and constraint. An invisible but dense veil hung between the bearer of supreme power and his councillors.

His Majesty departed without entering the adjoining hall, where a buffet lunch with champagne had been prepared and where, it had been expected, the Chairman of the Council would offer a toast to the Emperor, after which the Emperor would drink the health of the members of the Council. This demonstratively cold treatment at the hand of the Tsar, who had not deemed them worthy even of a few words, deeply offended the venerable men who had given all their lives to the service of Russian monarchs.

The State Council was at that time on the brink of its grave, but the reason it had not served the country to better advantage lay not in itself, nor even in its composition, nor in the advanced age of some of its members. Upper legislative chambers of Western Europe also include a number of men who have lost their former power and great energy. There are members of the British House of Lords who have reached a great age, yet until the last few years this institution was one of the creative forces of the country. Neither had the work of the Council been hampered by the solemn ceremoniousness of its sessions. The British House of Commons, even though it is inherently much more democratic, is distinguished by a far more elaborate ritual, unchanged for many centuries. The activities of the State Council were handicapped, in the first place, by the fact that its sessions were not made public, and chiefly because of its usual role of conciliatory agent. Had we had a uniform government on one side and on the other a free and public expression of its opinions by a body of former administrative workers enriched by experience, the activities of the State Council would have produced different and much more effective results.

CHAPTER III

THE IMPERIAL CHANCELLERY

In the organization of the old State Council, the Imperial Chancellery occupied a place of considerable importance. It was not, strictly speaking, a public institution, since it had no direct contact with the public, no concern with private civil affairs, and observed no regular office hours. The officials, with the exception of some young members of the staff, worked at home and as a rule appeared at the Mariinsky Palace only for the sessions of the Council or its departments. On other occasions they regarded the Chancellery as a sort of club, where they could sit about with a cup of tea or coffee served by footmen in court liveries and exchange city news and current political opinions—an exchange which often led to fiery arguments.

The meeting place of the Chancellery staff was the reading room of the State Council, which, as the members of the Council seldom visited it, had been virtually appropriated by the Imperial Chancellery. Later, in 1906, when the Mariinsky Palace was reconstructed, this room was rebuilt to serve as an extension of the Council's session hall. To be sure, different sections of the Chancellery, each associated with the corresponding department of the Council, had their own quarters, but these were reserved for various clerks and for the reading back, usually by the young men attached to the Chancellery, of the corrected minutes of the Council's sessions, as well as for the compiling of references required for projects that were to be discussed by the Council. These references were compiled quite mechanically—by the employment of scissors and a pot of glue. They consisted for the most part of separate articles of existing laws bearing on the project in question. The separate articles required for a particular project were cut out of editions of the Code and the Collection of Regulations, pasted on sheets of paper, and sent to the State Printing Office, where enough copies were made to supply all members to whom the project was sent for consideration. Such cutting and pasting required that there be many copies of the Code and of the Collection of Regulations, but it facilitated matters for the members of the Council. Yet hardly any member of the Council, with the possible exception of Golubev,[1] ever used these references, and Golubev with his inbred skepticism, his precision, and his conscientiousness would more likely have been driven to the volumes themselves.

Positions on the Chancellery staff were highly prized. The Chancellery granted a four months' vacation during the Council's summer recess; it permitted its staff members to use their time almost as they saw fit; it assured proximity to the center of administration, information on all important political issues, constant contact with ministers, and, therefore, a possibility of making a career if one was willing to work; finally, it provided a congenial company of co-workers. Such exclusive advantages attracted many, so that those in charge were generally able to select talented and honest workers. Some members of the staff, of course, were not of this brand; in fact, the members could be divided into two groups, whom Plehve characterized, respectively, as "distinguished foreigners" and "white slaves." With few exceptions, however, the "distinguished foreigners" did not make much headway toward a career, but usually occupied supernumerary positions with little or no pay. In advancement to responsible positions, there was little favoritism shown. It was really impossible to do so since the work of the Chancellery demanded men with well-trained minds, experience, and industry. If the staff members were more or less free to order their own days, their nights were as often as not spent at their desks, even though these were in their own homes.

An idea of the significance of the Imperial Chancellery can be gained from the fact that separate articles of a law were never in their final form when adopted by the departments of the Council, still less by the general session of the Council. The Council accepted the principle of a law, but its final wording was generally left to the Chancellery. In these cases the Chancellery had great freedom of action. Frequently it introduced fundamental changes of form and presentation despite the fact that the changes it made were supposed to be purely editorial. Of course these changes were limited to details, and left severely alone all of the essential, especially the political, aspects of the projected law. But considering that the majority of laws* passed at that time were of a technical

* For example, the Statute on Weights and Measures, passed in 1901, and the Statutes on Mutual Insurance for the zemstvos and on Liquor Production were en-

nature, it must be admitted that the Imperial Chancellery was a significant factor in Russian legislation.

The fundamental work of the Chancellery—that of editing and compiling the minutes of sessions of the Council's departments and of adjusting the text of legislative projects to fit accepted decisions —made for logical thinking and clear expression. The minutes were given careful, perhaps too careful, consideration, and, as regards those of the Legislative Department, their composition was faultless. A future historian of Russian legislation and a student of our state structure in the nineteenth century will find in them much valuable material. They constituted a detailed and exact account of the essence of the project under discussion as well as of the circumstances and reasons which had caused it to be drawn up; then followed an enumeration of all opinions concerning the basic provisions of the project as expressed by the departments; and in conclusion there was a statement of the decisions and of observations concerning separate articles. The project itself, in its final revised form, was appended to the minutes. The fact that the minutes, though detailed and exact, had to be brief, made the work on them much more difficult. Even Voltaire sought to excuse the lengthiness of his writings by saying that he had too little time to be brief.

Ludicrous formalities sometimes attended the writing of these minutes. Thus in describing an argument one was obliged to give each debater an exactly equal number of pages, even lines. It seems that the weight of an opinion was to be measured, not by specific gravity, but by the yard. But in recording a unanimous decision, the editor had free rein. He was not hampered by what was said in the department meetings and was allowed to suppress or develop some detail or even add a series of his own opinions which served to support the decision taken. Such editing was possible because individual opinions were recorded impersonally, as if they were those of an entire department. Consequently, a member of the Council was at liberty either to accept responsibility for an expressed opinion or to ascribe it to a colleague. In reporting arguments the editors kept more closely to facts; but since even here arguments

tirely rewritten by the Imperial Chancellery. And by way of comment on this phase of the Chancellery's work, may I say that D. I. Mendeleev, the author of the Statute on Weights and Measures, who had formerly been horrified at the changes made, was completely reconciled to the final edition and even expressed his gratitude to the members of the Chancellery staff for their conscientious and minute elaboration of the details.

represented opinions of groups of members, it was often necessary to expand the argument of one group to make it equal in length to that of another. To a well-informed editor with a mind of his own, it was a difficult and disagreeable task to state in a convincing way two diametrically opposite opinions, and it could not fail to exert a pernicious influence upon him. While it gave training in dialectics and, to a degree, in impartiality, it also developed a skeptical, indifferent attitude and an inclination to compromise—characteristics of our governing class even at its best. The diversity of problems and business that passed through the hands of the editors tended to make them feel that they knew everything and could do anything, and this was reflected in their subsequent activities.

The fact that the activities of the Imperial Chancellery were all-embracing and on an all-Russian scale made it a real training ground of future high officials. Many of our last ministers—Kaufmann,[2] Kharitonov,[3] Rukhlov,[4] Filosofov,[5] Kokovtsov, Trepov,[6]—started there. All of them were remarkable men, but hardly all of them were well-fitted to their positions. Still, I doubt that many constitutional ministers of the West—journalists, physicians, lawyers, who have served in parliamentary institutions—have had better training and more actual experience than these men.

Still greater influence was enjoyed by the state secretaries, who, though heads of the sections of the Imperial Chancellery, also took charge of the business of the corresponding departments of the Council and each had an assistant state secretary. Their influence was based on the fact that not only the final editing of a law rested with them but also each of them reported to the chairman of the corresponding department of the Council on projects coming up for discussion. These chairmen were usually experienced and efficient, but rather old-fashioned. It was difficult for them to study all the details of complicated statutes which necessitated minute comparison of separate articles. It devolved therefore upon the state secretary to interpret the project in question or at least to draw the chairman's attention to some particular part of it.

During the period 1897–1902 these state secretaries were usually men of wide experience and therefore able to familiarize themselves with many complicated questions with which they had formerly been unfamiliar. Their knowledge of a question was, of course, theoretical. They knew little of the life of the people and even less of their current problems. Official administration of a problem never brought them into actual contact with the problem itself, so they were shut off from studying at first hand the needs of the people and of the state. Their outlook was quite broad, for they were not limited in their actions by time or space; the legislative projects which they drafted bore evidence of a desire to render uniform everything and everybody throughout the whole extent of the Empire, to make everything conform to some common standard. This was particularly evident in those statutes which pertained either wholly or in part to Russia's border regions.

Some of the state secretaries of this period might be mentioned. In the legislative section, Baron Uxkull-Gyllenband was state secretary. He was a true Balt at heart and applied himself wholeheartedly to the protection of the baronial interests, although he tried very carefully to conceal his partisanship and to appear to be considering the interests of all Russia. He was, it appeared, a sincere admirer of German culture and denied that the Russian people were of any cultural significance. He was well suited to edit the projected laws, having a perfect knowledge of legislative technique. Projects submitted during his term as state secretary were subjected to a most minute study in which all officials of his section took an active part. That is, section conferences were held which were conducted as follows: first, the person responsible for the project presented the substance of its parts and offered his criticism of it. Then all the rest of the officials, including the most inexperienced, joined in discussing it. This procedure made it easier for the state secretary to familiarize himself with the project and consequently to help the chairman of the department to become acquainted with it and at the same time provided a fine schooling for the officials. It not only served to interest them in the work under consideration and to excite useful competition, since each strove to display his familiarity with the subject and his general knowledge, but it was also of educational importance: it enlarged their horizons, introducing them to problems of state and to the intricacies of administration.

But not all state secretaries possessed those attributes which distinguished Baron Uxkull. His successor, G. I. Shamshin (brother of the member of the State Council, I. I. Shamshin[7]), was of an altogether different type. Shamshin was a bureaucrat and little concerned with the substance of his work; he was mainly concerned about the "presentability" of the minutes. In his opinion the minutes must contain nothing of a sharp or even of a very clearly defined character. "You know," he used to say, "just as a swallow, while flying over water barely touches the surface with its wings—so must we in our minutes barely touch upon the substance of the matter—just barely touch upon it, so as not to hamper the Council in its further decisions on analogous cases."

Yet Shamshin was extremely industrious. He had such fiendish patience that he would rewrite all first drafts of the minutes presented to him. He could write an absolutely new text in the finest and tiniest script upon the margins of the corrected text, and so phrase it that it contained only smooth-sounding words with little meaning; this was his particular talent. On the other hand, he paid but scant attention to the task of editing projects of laws and generally left them in the form in which they were presented to him.

D. A. Filosofov, State Secretary of the Section of Industry, Science, and Commerce, 1900–1901, when he was appointed Assistant State Comptroller, displayed an altogether different attitude to his work. He was a very intelligent, even talented man, noted for his amiable effrontery and good-natured impudence. He was very ambitious for power, but at the same time extremely lazy; yet he possessed the capacity of many intelligent but indolent men, that of selecting subordinates whose work he could unhesitatingly attribute to himself. Still, when it was absolutely imperative, he could do any work unaided; he wrote with distinction and not in the usual official style. He owed his appointment as state secretary to his own work, specifically, to his presentation to the State Council during its session in 1897–1898 of a project on *promyslovyi nalog,* the taxation of business concerns.

Filosofov paid little attention to opinions expressed in departments, and his editing of minutes reflected only approximately what had actually been said there. But he was really interested in his work, and his influence on the decisions of the Council exerted through the Chairman of the Department of Industry, Science, and Commerce, Chikhachev, was continuously felt.

Filosofov was an economist. He had no firm political convictions, and those he had he rarely expressed, avoiding identification with any political group. He desired above all else to make a career, and, realizing that times and conditions can change, he knew how to keep on friendly terms with all camps, including the zemstvos, attending religiously the sessions of the zemstvo assembly of

Pskov Gubernia of which he was a member. There he was considered a moderate progressive, although he took part only in the discussion of economic problems. Later, in 1905, he seemed to move to the Left. As State Comptroller in Witte's Cabinet, he attended the discussion of the regulations on elections to the Duma and did not hesitate to express himself definitely in favor of the "four-tailed" (*chetyrekhvostka*)[8] formula of election. This, of course, did not prevent him from accepting the post of Minister of Commerce and Industry in Stolypin's Cabinet and as such taking part in the passing of the law of June 3, 1907, which radically altered the original electoral law in favor of an eclectic system of election. But he did not hold this post very long. On December 6, 1907, he died suddenly in the Mariinsky Theater in the presence of the Emperor during a gala presentation of the opera, *A Life for the Tsar*.

P. A. Kharitonov, State Secretary for the Section of Civil and Ecclesiastical Affairs, was less ambitious than Filosofov and made his career by dint of hard work. He persistently subscribed to the opinions of his superiors and never hesitated to alter his own to correspond to a changed attitude of his chiefs or to altered circumstances. During the period being discussed he was the closest co-worker of Plehve in drafting different measures concerning Finland, and strongly supported the opinion that that country should be deprived of all traces of independence. Because of the participation of Plehve (at the time, Imperial Secretary) in our Finnish policies, this issue was often the subject of argument and discussion among the officials of the Imperial Chancellery. Kharitonov often took part in these arguments, which usually took place in the reading room, and never hesitated to express most reactionary opinions. I remember one occasion when the conversation turned away from Finland and touched upon the question of local self-government and the zemstvo organizations. The majority of those present expressed themselves in favor of the zemstvos—of greater zemstvo independence and emancipation from administrative censorship. Kharitonov objected, and finally declared that he saw no difference between the zemstvo organizations and those of the central administration: both were supposed to concern themselves with administrative questions and therefore should be equally subordinated to government administrative agents. Obviously nettled by such a point of view, one of those present replied: "Nevertheless, there is a good deal of difference. It can be expressed thus: If you were to say something to me here, in this institution, I should be obliged to answer, 'As you wish it, Your Excellency.' But if you and I were members of the zemstvo, I should answer, 'Nonsense, Petr Alekseevich.' " Here the argument ended abruptly in an awkward silence.

Then came turbulent 1905. Plehve was in his grave and Kharitonov had become a fervent defender of the parliamentary system based upon a most democratic election of popular representatives. During an argument in the First Duma over the zemstvos, Kharitonov thundered against his interlocutor mentioned above for voting against the project submitted by thirty-three members of the Duma on the compulsory expropriation of privately owned lands. How sincere Kharitonov's change was, I cannot judge, but no one can deny the audacity of the volte-face. In his activities in the Imperial Chancellery Kharitonov displayed exceptional industry, especially during the passing of the new criminal code. Later, when appointed State Comptroller, he failed to display sufficient courage to expose those serious misdeeds which came to light from time to time in the ministries. While he occupied this position, the State Control worked very diligently, as it had done under his predecessor; but its work consisted of tracing misspent rubles and kopecks, while millions were squandered unnoticed. At most, these millions were mentioned in private and absolutely secret "most humble reports" made yearly by the State Comptroller to the Emperor.

Another state secretary who later became a minister was S. V. Rukhlov. He was an authority on budget regulations and, being in charge of the Section of State Economy, had to compute the yearly government table of revenues and expenditures in accordance with changes introduced by the department in the original draft of the project. This work was particularly difficult because it was always urgent. The department started to consider this table after the first of October—i.e., after the State Council had resumed its sessions—and by January 1 the table of revenues and expenditures had received all necessary confirmation and was published for general information. The Department of State Economy and all persons concerned with the work, including Rukhlov, must be given their due, for the original draft of the table was usually studied very carefully and underwent changes which were always for the better.

Rukhlov was an opponent of Witte's policy. He insisted, among other things, that our entire metallurgical industry had been created artificially, and that it was maintained only by government orders and mostly for the needs of our railways, these orders being filled at a very high price. Later, as Minister of Ways and Communications, 1909–1915, he set himself the task of increasing the revenues of our railways. He achieved success in this, it is true, but only by reducing the capital value of the railways by limiting almost to the vanishing point the supply of new rolling stock and by leaving the tracks in disrepair. He also discontinued the building of new railways, although this latter can hardly be ascribed to him alone. But throughout he retained his former opinion of our metallurgical industry, although it must be said that at least during his ministry the metallurgical industry was not maintained by government orders. Yet the state did not profit, and when the war started it was necessary hastily to increase our rolling stock. But our factories were not equipped for this purpose because they had lacked large orders in previous years; so Russia was obliged to place extensive orders abroad, mainly in America. Our factories, too, had to be paid for their war orders at the new and much higher rates.

Lively and agile, though somewhat shifty, Rukhlov was undoubtedly an honest man and a conscientious worker. But he was not a statesman. His shortcomings in this respect were not so much a matter of brains as of vision and driving force. He fitted perfectly the French proverb: *"Tel brille au second qui s'éclipse au premier."* As a state secretary he was outstanding, but when advanced to first rank he did not justify the hopes placed in him by many and at best remained a mediocrity.

A few words must be said about the section of the Imperial Chancellery known as the Section for the Affairs of the Imperial Secretary. This section was actually divided into two offices, one of which was occupied exclusively with the compilation of the so-called memoranda. These included, in very brief form, the substance of a project, the debates it had occasioned, and the changes introduced in it by the Council; where there had been disagreements it gave the essence of the diverging opinions and listed the members and ministers who shared each of them. These memoranda were then presented to the Emperor. The pages destined to bear the Imperial decision were marked by special slips which contained the wording of such decisions as were needed to make the project law. The conflicting opinions were reconciled and resolved by the fact that under the opinion shared by the Tsar he would inscribe with his own hand: "This is also my opinion." Since it sometimes happened, although infrequently, that the Tsar confirmed the opinion of the minority, the return of these memoranda was always awaited with much impatience, especially where acute and burning questions were involved. As for unanimous decisions, the Tsar invariably confirmed them.

No matter how briefly the memoranda were compiled, during spring months they grew to alarming proportions, the larger part of them being devoted to the projects themselves. These memoranda were official documents and were sent to the Senate for publication as adopted laws. But for convenience' sake, briefs were made of them explaining the meaning of the projects represented and the opinions of the debaters. When Polovtsev[9] was Imperial Secretary, he himself drafted, if he did not write, these briefs. Under Plehve's predecessor, Muravev,[10] this method was abandoned. The briefs were typed on ordinary paper without letterheads and attached to the memoranda.

The other office of the Section for the Affairs of the Imperial Secretary was concerned with all matters pertaining to the personnel of the State Council and the Imperial Chancellery. This office dealt with all appointments, money gifts, and increases in salaries. There was no definite scale of salary provided by law for members of the Council, and salaries were fixed for each newly appointed member. These salaries could not be considered excessive. Usually they were fixed at 10,000 rubles a year; later they were raised to 12,000 rubles; sometimes they even reached 14,000 rubles. Persons who for a long period of time had occupied ministerial posts received about 15,000 rubles; only a few of them received as much as 18,000. Of course, for many of the members these salaries were nothing but pensions, since they did no actual work in the Council and were not even obliged to attend sessions. But, even considered as such, these salaries were not too large for persons who had devoted all their lives to the service of their country and had occupied some of the highest posts.

Personnel matters were considered highly confidential, so that even the state secretary in charge of this particular office of the Section for the Affairs of the Imperial Secretary was not always initiated into them. They were the immediate concern of the Imperial Secretary and were taken care of by the filing clerk of this office, I. T. Tatochka,* who was well known and held in much esteem by the entire Council.

I should like to mention just one more section of the Imperial Chancellery, the Codification Section. Originally the functions of this section had been performed by the Second Section of His Majesty's Private Chancellery.[13] Then these functions were taken over by a Section of Codification proper, which was abolished in 1893 when its functions were transferred to a section of the same name attached to the Imperial Chancellery. These functions consisted of correlating the newly passed statutes with those already included in our Code. This work of correlating necessitated a con-

---

* Tatochka[11] had been promoted from an ordinary clerkship. He had had no formal education but knew office routine to a nicety, and as regards confidential matters could be as silent as Pharaoh's tomb. He was tall, a bit stout, and had small squinting eyes full of Ukrainian slyness set in a round plump face. He was Plehve's closest confidant, and when the latter became Minister of the Interior in 1902, he wished to retain Tatochka as his private secretary, but Tatochka declined the offer in spite of its obvious advantages. He profusely thanked Plehve but flatly refused to accept, and after much hedging he explained his decision in this way: "They will probably assassinate Your Excellency quite soon, and then where should I be? The new minister would appoint his own man in my place, and I should lose my position, and whatever pension they pay me will be much smaller than the one I may count upon here." What could Plehve say? Yet they found a way out. Plehve obtained an Imperial order fixing Tatochka's pension in advance at a rather respectable sum—three thousand rubles a year, if I am not mistaken. Tatochka's foresight turned out to be justified; he used the Imperial order in due time, but did not seem to enjoy the pension. After leaving service he became low-spirited and grew thin.

Another familiar figure associated with the State Council but having no share in its official tasks was Colonel (later General) Shevelev, superintendent of the Mariinsky Palace building. He had served as an officer in the Infantry Guards during the Russo-Turkish War of 1877–78 and still retained his military bearing and old-fashioned army mannerisms, wearing a tightly buttoned uniform of the period of Alexander II. Under his all-seeing eye the servants of the palace staff were models of discipline and courtesy; Shevelev was indeed an excellent manager.

It used to be said of Prince Volkonsky,[12] Court Minister of Nicholas I, that he had won his Field Marshal's baton *"au feu des batteries de cuisine"*; it could be said of Shevelev with equal justification and not a little exactness that he had won his generalship behind a coffee pot. He was an expert blender of coffee; nothing gave him greater pleasure than praise of his really fine beverages.

Shevelev retained his position through the February Revolution, even concealing in his apartment several ministers marooned in the palace by the sudden uprising, and through the period of the Provisional Government. If it was his lot to see the palace, which he had kept for so long in such exemplary order, looted in the October Revolution by the sailors of Kronstadt, "the pride and beauty of the Revolution," what a sad lot it must have been! What pain he must have felt at witnessing such barbarity.

tinual publication of new volumes of the Code, and therefore demanded much work, unremitting attention, and painstaking study of all sixteen volumes of the Code. This was because actually only a few statutes were published which entirely supplanted the old ones; the majority were passed "to alter, complete, or abolish" those already in force.* The system of codification adopted in Russia, by reason of its extreme complexity, exists nowhere else in the world, if I am correctly informed, although it presents many facilities for those working with the legislation of a country. It is little to be wondered, then, that its realization in our purely bureaucratic institutions had left much to be desired and, therefore, it had been decided when the business of codification was transferred to the Imperial Chancellery to attract our scientific workers to it. The new section was headed by the celebrated Russian criminologist, Professor N. D. Sergeevsky,[14] and among his colleagues were to be found such men as the well-known authority on constitutional law, Professor N. M. Korkunov,[15] and Professor of Constitutional Law, Malyshev.[16]

Sergeevsky belonged to that smaller group of our scholars who professed conservative views. Thus, he was an advocate of corporal punishment, which caused him to be nicknamed "Knoutophile." While defending his Doctor's thesis dealing with criminal punishment in the Middle Ages, he was imprudent enough to say that one of the reasons for a remarkable frequency of capital punishment in those times was the cheapness of this measure, since it freed the government of the expense of supporting the criminal elements of the population. This statement excited among the official opponents of Sergeevsky a veritable storm of indignation, although it would be difficult indeed to understand the reason for this. In fact, Sergeevsky only tried to explain the reasons for the frequency of capital punishment in the Middle Ages, and did not in the least suggest that modern governments should follow this example. As to his personality, one may say that although his manner of speaking and his looks were somewhat uncouth, he was a very fine man by nature; his outstanding trait was ardent patriotism with a slight trace of chauvinism. This trait was used by Plehve, who employed him in the working out of different problems

* The case of the Regulations and Instructions on Penalties imposed by Justices of the Peace was an exceptional one. New articles were added to them directly and numbered as continuing articles.

dealing with Finland, and appointed him chairman of a special commission for the codification of the laws of the Grand Duchy of Finland. This commission was attached to the Codification Section of the Imperial Chancellery, and with its establishment the Codification Section and its chief, the Imperial Secretary, acquired great political significance; it changed from a purely bureaucratic institution and office to one included in the number of institutions and persons concerned with state policies.

In concluding this chapter I should like to say something of V. K. Plehve, as he was Imperial Secretary and as such head of the Imperial Chancellery for almost ten years. Plehve did not concern himself with the daily business of the Chancellery, leaving this to the state secretaries in charge of the business of the various departments of the Council; but he did make all appointments to the Chancellery staff and, indeed, succeeded in assembling and training a group of excellent workers. And although he had little personal contact with any of his staff, he was fully aware of the traits and abilities of all its members. Plehve's attitude to his subordinates was not merely one of superiority but was even majestic. A summons to appear before him brought the summoned person to Plehve's office muttering prayers for the meekness of King David. Plehve was known to have a sharp and even malicious tongue; often his biting sarcasm threw a timid subordinate into great confusion. Even subordinates, in whom he showed special confidence by entrusting to them particularly responsible work which interested Plehve himself at that time, did not escape his caustic comment.

No one can deny the importance of the role played by Plehve when he was Imperial Secretary. But this importance bore little relation to his position as head of the Imperial Chancellery. Rather was it based on the fact that he took part in almost all special commissions of the Council that dealt with pressing political problems and, what is most important, that he had a share in appointing the members of these commissions as well as in appointing new members to the State Council from among the Senators, to which end he worked through Grand Duke Mikhail Nikolaevich, the Chairman of the Council. This gave Plehve great influence, but not enough to satisfy him. Plehve had formerly been Director of the Police Department of the Minister of the Interior, and, later, Assistant Minister of the Interior under the Ministers Count D. A.

Tolstoi and I. N. Durnovo. In these positions he had wide influence in matters of government and administration, a field of endeavor that appealed to him more strongly than did his duties as head of the Imperial Chancellery. He longed to return to the administrative arena and to obtain a ministerial post. Men of less experience and influence attained such posts—Sipiagin for instance. Why could he not do the same? To attain this end Plehve became convinced that he must put himself in a position in which he came into more frequent contact with the Emperor. As Imperial Secretary he did not make regular reports to the Emperor; he had to solicit audiences with His Majesty for each and every separate need; and these audiences were not frequent, coming usually only when there was to be an appointment to the Imperial Chancellery. The first step therefore seemed to be to find some matter which would give occasion for frequent audiences with the Emperor. The opportunity to reach this goal was presented by the Finnish problem; and although this matter was initiated by the Ministry of War and not by Plehve, the latter speedily appropriated it for the achievement of his own purpose.

The Ministry of War planned to reorganize Finnish troop-units that were composed exclusively of Finns and to incorporate the Finns into Russian troop-units. But there were obstacles in the way of realizing this plan. All statutes concerning Finland had to be passed by the Finnish Diet, a body which could not be expected to pass a statute in accordance with the War Ministry's proposition. It was imperative, therefore, that the system of Finnish legislation be altered. To this end a special commission of the State Council was formed under the chairmanship of the Grand Duke Mikhail Nikolaevich; its driving force was State Secretary Kharitonov, who was charged with secretarial duties. This commission worked out the basic principles of the regulation on Finnish legislation which also affected the interests of the Russian Empire. The regulation, confirmed on February 3, 1899, excited much indignation among the Finns. As is well known, Finnish politicians stated that this regulation violated the Finnish constitution confirmed by Alexander I when Finland was joined to Russia; the Russian investigators, on the other hand, insisted that Alexander I had meant to preserve the constitutions (that is, the fundamental laws) of Finland and did not at all refer to a Finnish constitution. At any rate, on the basis of the new regulation of February 3, 1899, the laws of Finland which the new regulation affected were to be examined by the Russian State Council and were to be considered as passed only after they had been confirmed by the Russian Emperor.[17]

This circumstance was seized upon by Plehve in order to approach the Finnish question. He pointed out that since the Council was to consider some of the laws of Finland, it must familiarize itself with the legislation of this country and to this end Finnish laws must be compiled and systematized. For this work, and a very minute and difficult one it was, a special commission of the Codification Section was formed under the chairmanship of Professor Sergeevsky, as I have already mentioned. As its members certain Russian authorities on Finnish legislation were also engaged, such as Professor Berendts,[18] appointed for this reason Assistant State Secretary of the State Council, and General Borodkin,[19] appointed to represent the War Ministry. As soon as the Commission began to function, a number of arguments and undecided questions arose which permitted Plehve, as Imperial Secretary under whose direction the commission was working, to go to the very bottom of Russo-Finnish relations and make frequent reports to the Tsar on this subject. So he attained his end.

There can be little doubt that on many points Russian investigators of the Finnish problem, such as Ordin,[20] Elenev,[21] and Plehve's colleagues, were in the right. It was but natural that the Finns should wish to protect the independence of their country, but they used utterly unfair means and even forgeries to this end. They intentionally made mistakes and errors in translating, from Swedish to Russian, laws passed during Swedish supremacy in Finland, and they introduced into their translations into the local languages, Finnish and Swedish, just as many errors of Russian texts of statutes concerning Finland. There were some strange incidents in this connection. For instance, Professor Tagantsev[22] discovered that some statutes of the criminal code in force in Finland were complemented by articles published in Sweden after Finland had been separated from Sweden. Nevertheless, the Russian treatment of the Finnish problem was basically unsound. It accomplished nothing in the sense of assuring Russian influence and protecting Russian interests in Finland; it tended to irritate the Finns and destroy all their fear of and respect for Russian authority. This happened because all measures pertaining to Finland were essentially only half-measures and were actually not enforced at all. This was due to two causes. First, the Russian government was utterly impotent to carry out any daring and decisive policy, since this government was shared by a dozen or so ministers who were always in each other's way and who differed in their political outlook. Second, the Russian government itself realized dimly that not all its projected measures were necessitated by state needs. The question was not whether the Finns had made faulty translations of Russian and Swedish legal texts but whether these errors of translations did Russia any harm. It was generally realized that they did not. Russia's only interest in Finland was in being absolute master of the Finnish Gulf and the Finnish coast and in having an absolutely secure frontier line between Russia and Finland in view of its proximity to St. Petersburg. This could have been accomplished by other measures than the ones adopted for Finland; the measures adopted were not enforced.*

Even if Plehve developed the Finnish question for personal reasons, he soon undoubtedly became sincerely interested in it and in giving it a more logical solution. He must certainly have realized that the method adopted by the War Ministry was absolutely unsuitable to the work at hand. Therefore, he approached it very cautiously, and when, in the spring of 1899, he was appointed State Secretary for Finnish Affairs (while remaining Imperial Secretary) he endeavored first of all to establish friendly relations with those Finnish statesmen who were most favorably inclined toward Russia, and to find a golden mean whereby he could assure Russia's interests and dignity as a sovereign state and at the same time not alienate the Finns. But his attempts in this direction proved fruitless, and his efforts were mainly confined to relations with a prominent Finnish statesman, Count Armfelt.[24] Then Plehve had another idea, and a very good one, too. He proposed to exclude from the Grand Duchy of Finland so-called Old Finland—that is, that

---

* The law incorporating Finnish soldiers into Russian army units[23]—the very question that precipitated the regulation of February 3, 1899—is a flagrant example. Of the 26,000 Finns liable for military service only 280 were drafted in 1902 and only 190 in 1903. This small increase in the Russian army was purchased at the cost of infuriating the Finns beyond reconciliation. All the 26,000 were called up annually for military medical examination and held in suspense as to whether they should have to serve. As if in admission of its utter stupidity, this law, passed by the State Council over strong opposition headed by no less a person than Witte, and then published, was never put into force.

part of it which had been annexed by Peter the Great and constituted Viborg Gubernia[25]—and to leave the rest of Finland more
or less independent. This course was the more feasible since Finland's economic dependence upon Russia enabled us to force her
not only to be perfectly obedient but even voluntarily to demand
closer contact with Russia, the chief market for Finnish products.
Tariffs against Finnish goods would have brought Finland into line.
A special commission headed by Filosofov was actually established
to work out tariff norms for Finnish products, but nothing came
of it. The Russian government of the beginning of the twentieth
century could not have adopted such a definite course of action. As
Professor Sergeevsky justly remarked, measures adopted at that
time were strong as oak, but the wills of those who were called upon
to enforce them were like trembling aspen. Besides, Plehve had
attained his desired end—he was appointed Minister of the Interior
in 1902—and had neither time nor inclination to occupy himself
with Finnish affairs, although he did remain State Secretary for
Finnish Affairs.

Thus the Finnish problem died down somewhat. It left behind,
however, one serious effect which in no way concerned Russo-
Finnish relations, namely, a marked aggravation of the relations
between Witte and Plehve. This was first revealed during the discussion of Finnish legislative projects in the Council. Two bears
are always somewhat crowded in one den. Conflict between these
two strong and commanding personalities was bound to develop;
the Finnish question furnished a good pretext for debates which
found Witte and Plehve on opposite sides and left them bitter
enemies. The winter of 1902–3 witnessed their final struggle.*

* Although Witte had little concern for the Finnish problem, he was particularly energetic in leading the opposition in the State Council to Kuropatkin's[26] plan
for drafting Finnish recruits into the Russian army. In fact, he succeeded in uniting the entire liberal part of the Council in opposition to the project. Witte's stand
was really a reply to the insistent demands of the Ministry of War for appropriations wherewith to increase our military strength in the Far East, especially at Port
Arthur.[27]

CHAPTER IV

SERGEI YULIEVICH WITTE AS MINISTER OF FINANCE

In its influence upon state policy, the State Council was, as I have said, above all a chamber of conciliation for arguing, and at times quarreling, ministers. It is easy to understand that under these conditions both the general trend of policy and the personal traits of individual ministers appeared in it in a particularly strong light in so far as they had anything to do with general state policies. Of the ministers the most important was S. Y. Witte.

Witte's outstanding importance was due mostly to his influence and authority, and to some extent to his personality, for even when his position was more or less unstable his influence upon the decisions of the State Council remained unshaken. He was a discordant note in the orderly routine of the State Council. His huge, rather burly figure; his enormous arms too long for his body; his rather expressionless, ordinary, homely face; his plain, unadorned, somewhat rough and uncultivated speech, with its pronounced Odessa accent; his utter disregard of the traditions of the "great assembly"—all these combined to produce an odd and not particularly favorable impression. He could not be termed an orator; his language was not adorned with the flowers of eloquence, nor was it always coherent and logical; yet when he spoke he managed to create a strong impression. Witte was obviously a master of psychology and, despite his apparent simplicity and artlessness of speech, he understood the men with whom he was dealing and put his arguments accordingly. He used flattery, at times quite openly; or, if the occasion called for it, he attacked his adversary with insinuations. If actual facts were not sufficient he sometimes resorted to fabrication.

By and large, Witte's attitude toward people was based on a deeply rooted contempt for all humanity. Yet he was kind and considerate by nature. He showed this clearly in his relations with his assistants and subordinates, whom he tried to assist and whose future he tried to arrange, even though sometimes such consideration was not deserved. A case in point is Maksimov, head of the Department of Railways, whose official career culminated in scandal.

Witte brought all these abilities and tactics into play in his relations with the State Council. He directed all his attention to the most important and influential members of a group and to assure himself of their assistance and particularly of freedom from their opposition, he used all sorts of methods which may be described by the blanket term—bribery. If flattery failed, he used—and this, alas, was usually the case—more material bribes. Witte had it in his power to confer material advantages. As Minister of Finance he controlled the disposal of a great number of remunerative positions; he also controlled state credit. He was in charge of the State Bank[1] which made trade and industrial loans, of the Bank of the Nobility and of the Peasant Bank, which could purchase lands at almost any price.

Now and then, of course, Witte met with a sharp rebuff from those he was trying to win to his side. When he suggested to the newly appointed Minister of Foreign Affairs, Prince Lobanov-Rostovsky,[2] that his salary might be raised to correspond to that of an ambassador (the difference being some 30,000 rubles yearly), the Prince answered: "Has anyone told you that I have applied for such an increase? If so, you have been misinformed."

But such sharp answers did not change Witte's customary policy. He nearly always succeeded in disarming a great number of influential adversaries; those whom he could not disarm he attacked directly; and sometimes he even terrorized them. Witte demonstrated the latter method in the State Council over the question of an additional assignment of some two million rubles for the founding of the St. Petersburg Polytechnical Institute. The preliminary scheme of erection and equipment called for about five million rubles, if I am not mistaken; and, later, two more appropriations of large sums were needed. With the last appropriation of two million, the cost of the Institute's organization would have reached almost ten million rubles. The State Comptroller, P. L. Lobko,[3] considered this sum entirely too large and persisted in trying to have it reduced. In a meeting of one of the Council's departments Lobko sharply criticized the Ministry of Finance in connection with the establishment of the Institute. Witte's retort was no less sharp and Lobko, offended by some of Witte's statements, could not constrain himself. He charged that the conduct of the Ministry of Finance in this affair could be judged by the fact that the land on which the Institute buildings at the Lesnoi were to be erected had been purchased by the Ministry for 200,000 rubles from a Mr. Segal, who had paid 30,000 rubles for it a few months before. The chairman sought to hush up the incident by saying that it was not the strict concern of the State Council, and as it was late (almost 6:00 P.M., the customary time of adjournment) he suggested that they vote on the matter. But he had not reckoned with Witte, who was not the man to allow such a challenge to pass unheeded. "We shall remain here until midnight," he announced, ignoring the rights of the chairman, "for, since one of you has chosen to engage in insinuations, I shall not remain silent." In a very brilliant improvisation Witte successfully opposed Lobko's ill-timed attack, and the appropriation was unanimously accepted — even Lobko himself voted for it.[4]

Another incident is very typical of Witte. The State Council was debating the taxation on diocesan candle works. K. P. Pobedonostsev,[5] Ober-Prokuror of the Holy Synod,[6] was opposed to the measure, and his arguments were, as always, accorded great attention; for although he spoke infrequently he spoke well, and although he was not a creative thinker he had a keen analytical mind and was at his best as critic. To see Pobedonostsev was to remember him. He was extremely emaciated; his skin was like parchment; his face was that of an ascetic and was made more striking by a pair of large horn-rimmed glasses; he gave the appearance of a clerk or barrister of the ante-reform courts who was versed in all the niceties of legal casuistry, as indeed he was. On those occasions when in his excitement he raised both arms and pictured the horrors awaiting the Empire if the measure he happened to be opposing should be adopted, he was something worth seeing. And now in opposition to the proposed tax, he held that there existed a sovereign ordinance exempting diocesan candle works from taxation. This roused Witte. "I cannot exhume all sovereign ordinances," he said. "I have no time to do so. And anyway, what do they matter?" Never had such a statement been heard by the State Council; yet coming from Witte it aroused no comment, so accustomed was his audience to his sallies.

By the time of the accession of Nicholas II, Witte had had time to demonstrate his particular qualities: courage, determination, and a great deal of creative energy. He had established the government liquor monopoly, and he had gone through a customs war with Germany as a result of the tariff he had established on German industrial products. According to the commercial treaty of 1894[7] a tariff was retained; but it was a lower one, and Germany modified her tariff on Russian agricultural products. However, the most important accomplishment of Witte in the new reign was the establishment of a gold standard for Russia (1897).

When Witte was appointed Minister of Finance[8] in 1892 he had only a vague understanding of finances and their practical management. By education he was a mathematician, and by profession a railway man; yet with characteristic self-assurance he undertook a series of most decisive reforms which broke all the established precedents of the Ministry of Finance. At the outset he did not contemplate the establishment of the gold standard; on the contrary, he planned, as a means of speeding up national economic progress, a "satiating of the shallowest channels of monetary exchange." This was to be accomplished by increasing the issue of new bank notes, a plan supported by Katkov,[9] who had helped Witte to secure the appointment of Minister of Finance. This plan, together with Witte's scheme to support the building of the entire Trans-Siberian Railway with paper currency, had served to win him the appointment.

During the first years of his activities as Minister of Finance Witte subscribed so fully to this plan that he prevented the realization of certain measures for stabilizing our monetary unit, measures which had been projected and partially realized by his predecessors, Bunge[10] and Vyshnegradsky.[11]

Witte's first financial adviser was a former professor of Kiev University, Antonovich,[12] whom Witte appointed as his assistant. Antonovich was strongly in favor of expanding trade and industry in Russia by increasing the amount of money in circulation within the country, and to this end revised the statutes concerning the State Bank. According to the new statutes, the Bank was expected to increase considerably its loans to industry. But the new statutes had hardly been put into effect when Witte completely changed his attitude both toward the question of an increased issue of banknotes and toward Professor Antonovich. Once he had succeeded in orienting himself in this unfamiliar field of finance he felt no hesitation in altering radically his course of action and in parting

with Antonovich, who was supplanted as adviser on financial problems by Rothstein, a newcomer from Berlin and a director of the
International Bank. With the close assistance of this banker Witte
succeeded in passing a monetary reform and in stabilizing our
monetary unit, although the State Council's opposition to this reform obliged him to carry his project through the Finance Committee[13] and to have it confirmed by an Imperial Ukase. Witte's
prestige was then (1897) at its height. His use of the unlimited authority of the Tsar to gain his end was not entirely without danger, for it not only made him solely responsible for his actions but
also roused many influential persons and groups against him. But
Witte was willing to run this risk. At that time he considered
authority not as a goal in itself but as a means of carrying out his
creative ideas, as a field in which to apply his remarkable talents.

The part Witte played in the development of Russian industry
is well known. His influence in this direction was all the more
remarkable since his measures were directed to the single end of
creating a situation favorable to the development of Russian industry. Yet this situation had its dark side, and a rather important
one. Some of the measures were artificial and consequently temporary; and when their practice was discontinued, some branches
of industry began to weaken. This was especially true of the metallurgical industry, which had been developed mainly by large governmental orders designed to meet the needs of state railways. With
the termination of railway construction, the factories engaged in
supplying railway materials were left without a ready market for
their products.

But with all his talent in matters of finance, Witte was not a
statesman. Entire spheres of state organization remained a closed
book to him to the end of his days. He had but a hazy understanding of Russia and of the Russian people, a fact which became particularly evident in 1905 when he became head of the
government. Although his business acumen guided him in the
solution of those varied problems of the day with which he was
faced, it did not give him that vision of the future which is the
indispensable attribute of all true creators of public welfare and
state power. Thus, Witte's economic policy was but a program to
meet the current need and showed that simplicity of conception
which was his distinctive trait. This policy was, in brief, the
accumulation of funds in the state treasury and the accumulation of

private capital in the country. Realizing that the best method of increasing state resources was to develop the country's economic life, he encouraged such development; but he considered that the only means to attain this end was to develop industry, heavy industry especially, since it was the source of all great private fortunes.

Witte's views on agriculture reflected those of Friedrich List,[14] on whose doctrine he had compiled a little treatise. Witte held that agriculture is but a limited field for the application of human labor, while industry, unconfined by material limitations, may develop indefinitely and thereby use an indefinite amount of labor. Agriculture to him was a necessary but purely subordinate branch of public economy; agriculture was necessary to feed the population, but could not serve as the sole source of its well-being. This explains his negative attitude toward all measures designed to improve the agricultural situation.

At first glance it is difficult to understand Witte's indifference toward the great fall in prices of agricultural products during the 'nineties throughout Russia. These low prices, particularly for cereals, caused a severe agricultural crisis. Witte denied the existence of such a crisis when he exclaimed with mingled pathos and irony in his most humble report: "How strange that there should be such a crisis when the price of land is steadily increasing."*

In making this statement, Witte did not take the trouble to find out whether or not the productivity of the land corresponded to its market value. To deny that there was an agricultural crisis in the 'nineties (that is, during the very time of Witte's activity as Minister of Finance) would indeed be odd. Yet, when the price of rye in the Volga region and other central gubernias fell to twelve kopecks a pud, and when even in Moscow, the center of the grain trade in Russia where the average price for grain was established for the whole country, the price was not over twenty kopecks, Witte was content to engage a group of economists, headed by A. I. Chuprov,[15] to compile a series of articles under the title:

---

* This statement that the price of land was increasing was also untrue. The price of land had reached approximately one hundred rubles a desiatin in the black-earth belt in the 'seventies, and remained at this level for a number of years. Not until the 'nineties—that is, at the time of Witte's report—did the price begin to rise again, and this after the crisis, which had reached its peak in 1893–94, had begun to recede. This rise in land prices was also influenced by the devaluation of our monetary unit which, with the introduction of the gold standard, had become stabilized at two-thirds its former purchasing power.

*Vliianie urozhaev i khlebnykh tsen na nekotoryia storony russkago
narodnago khoziaistva* ("*The Effects of Crops and Grain Prices on
Various Aspects of Russian People's Economy*"). These articles
may be considered a code to Witte's policy. Their purpose was to
silence press comment on the deplorable effects of low grain prices
upon the lives of the agricultural elements of Russia, elements which
made up eighty per cent of the entire population. To the extent of
several hundreds of pages and with tables of complicated statistics,
these gentlemen expounded the theory that the Russian peasant was
not really the producer but the consumer of the grain—at least of
that part of it which finds its way to the market—and, therefore, a
low price for this commodity could only be to his advantage.

This conclusion was reached from two simple facts: on one
hand, a recorded increase of consumption of breadstuffs by the
peasants; and, on the other, a shrinkage of the area of tillable land
under cultivation. Those lands which were rented or used on a
half-and-half basis by the agricultural population were not considered. Of course, the conclusion arrived at was an easy mark for
the critics; but since the learned scholars had decided that high grain
prices were profitable only for those landowners possessing income-
yielding estates, our radical press did not attack but praised the
articles.

"It is harmful for the buffaloes [i.e., the conservatives], therefore fine for the country." This was the amazing, plain, and
straightforward conclusion of the radical elements. And yet, the
fact that over one billion puds of all grain produced in the country
found its way to the market, and that this billion puds was the
result of peasant labor, clearly revealed that it was not the landowners alone but also the entire peasant population who suffered
from low prices. Indeed, even supposing that this entire amount of
grain was produced on the estates of the landowners (which, of
course, is not true), still a great portion of the market value of the
grain (in fact its entire value at that time) was expressed in payment for the labor applied by the same rural population to the
cultivation of the land and to the harvesting of the crops. It was
self-evident, therefore, that the lower the price of grain, the lower
the price of labor necessary to produce this grain. Later, when
grain prices showed a marked rise, this argument was confirmed by
actual fact; for the price of agricultural labor rose also.

How could Witte, with his intelligence and practical perception, fail to understand this simple and obvious fact? Perhaps he did understand it. But if so, why was he indifferent to the fall in grain prices? Perhaps because he was unable to raise them. Yet, this is not so. It was, of course, beyond his power to influence world prices. All our export trade prices depended upon prices in Germany; export prices naturally influence domestic prices, and Witte was powerless to force Germany to lower the tariff on Russian grain. To accomplish this we should have had to make concessions in our protective tariff on German industrial products, which would have rendered our own industry utterly unable to compete with German industry even in our own domestic markets and would have wiped out many branches of Russian industry. Yet there was a method that might have been used to secure higher prices for Russian grain in foreign markets. Western Europe could not have done without Russian grain at that time. It would have been quite feasible to establish a network of grain elevators, to introduce a warrant system for the grain kept in them, to enlarge credit operations on grain, to guarantee the quality of exported grain, and so on. The low price of Russian grain was caused to a great extent by the fact that the producer lacked floating or any other kind of capital and was forced to dispose of all his crops immediately after the harvest at the existing price. This situation was exploited by grain traders and by exporters. Each year toward threshing time, when there was a reasonably good crop, domestic prices for grain declined sharply, then rose again in the spring. The measures mentioned above would have gone far to check such practices, and Witte was perfectly capable of conceiving them, the more so since he had been advised by a number of people to resort to such measures. Yet, if he put these measures into effect at all, it was on such a small scale that they were without significance and served only to enable him to say that he was making efforts in that direction but could not extend his undertakings because of the great expenditures entailed and because actual experience showed that they were not successful anyway.

What, then, was the real reason for his inexplicable attitude? Undoubtedly there was one: Witte, eager to develop Russian industry at any cost, saw the need of providing cheap labor for this industry. Lacking a rich and elastic domestic market, Russian industry could hope to compete with western Europe only if it had a ready supply of cheap labor. With inferior technical equipment and poorly trained workers, who had but recently been attracted to industrial occupations,

Russian industry could not develop without such labor. At Russia's then economic level the cost of labor was almost directly dependent upon the cost of foodstuffs. Again, low profits in agriculture would have assured a continual influx of workers into factories. Witte's stand on these matters was influenced by D. I. Mendeleev, whose opinions he valued highly and whose ideas as to the influence of cheap foodstuffs on the development of industry were later expounded in his well-known book: *K poznaniiu Rossii* (*"Toward the Understanding of Russia"*). The keeping of grain prices at a low level corresponded in every way to the grandiose plans of Witte, who repeatedly affirmed that in a few more years Russia would be the first industrial country of the world.

Here, in my opinion, lies the answer to the riddle of Witte's attitude toward agriculture, particularly as regards profit-yielding landownership. Admitting that fortunes in the form of ready capital could not be made from agriculture under any conditions, he considered that great agricultural development and extensive employment of high-priced labor would be a serious handicap to the development of our industry. Witte was but a son of his time; a fervent admirer of the capitalistic structure of society and of capitalism in general. But in his mind this capitalism was connected with trade and industry and not with agriculture. Nor must it be forgotten that Witte's paramount aim was not so much to bring happiness and prosperity to individual citizens of the country as to assure the greatness and might of the empire as a whole. To him different classes of society were so much building material with which to erect the edifice of a great state.

Witte's unconcern with agriculture, a result of his policy of industrialization, was greatly increased by the opposition he experienced from the agricultural element, an opposition which was not wholly disinterested. The criticisms directed at Witte because of his establishment of the gold standard and because of his tariff policy for the protection of our industry were mostly unfounded. Even so, it was natural that he should be disturbed by this critical attitude which threatened to undermine his position and frustrate his plans. Very soon, therefore, his indifference toward landowners changed to open animosity, and invariably he included in this class all landed gentry, whom he accused of furthering solely their own class interests.

Be it noted, however, that Witte's hatred was directed not at the landed magnates but at the small and average landowners whom he described as a ruined class living from hand to mouth. He treated the landed aristocracy altogether differently and endeavored to separate it from the mass of landed gentry and to interest it in industrial undertakings in order to break up its economic solidarity with the smaller landowners. Witte needed the support of this class of great landowners in order to strengthen his position with the throne—since the members of this class had access to the court—and in order to gratify his petty vanity. So that he might enter St. Petersburg's high society he ingratiated himself with their representatives and tried hard to gain their friendship. He arranged to sell state lands to some of them at moderate rates; to others he advanced considerable industrial loans and subsidies; from others he purchased land for the Peasant Bank at a nice price. Yet, after spending so much energy in tempting them, in his *Memoirs* Witte accuses them of currying favors and of boundless cupidity and avarice.

Witte's malice toward the lesser landed gentry is reflected in his reminiscences of the Special Conference for the Affairs of the Nobility,[16] which functioned from 1897 to 1902. Not without significance is his statement that this conference was organized primarily to find means to assist the small landed gentry, for neither the name nor the documents of this institution specify its purpose as such. It is true that the small and moderately well-to-do landed gentry were in severe economic straits, and any objection to supporting them as a class could have been only theoretical. In fact, this class included nearly all of the landowners who were fighting poverty. The agricultural crisis had dealt just as hard a blow to these owners as to the peasant population. They loved the land with a love developed through generations, yet they were often forced to abandon their traditional occupation and seek some other means of livelihood. They did not seek exceptional profits, but merely a chance to make both ends meet, to support their families, and to educate their children. These were the men whom Witte denounced for their cupidity, their class aspirations, and their desire to improve their own welfare at the expense of the rest of the population. As a matter of fact he was opposed to and even contemptuous of these people because of their poverty and their inability (due to circumstances quite beyond their control) to accumulate fortunes. Prominent financiers making millions, industrial magnates who had doubled their fortunes within a few years—these were the persons he respected and whose wishes he treated with utmost consideration.

Witte refers to the Conference for the Affairs of the Nobility as an association of individuals who were enemies of the people; he saw to it, therefore, that this conference should do nothing of importance. Of this there can be no doubt. But Witte does not mention which side of the conference's activities met with his open opposition. This opposition became particularly manifest when the conference turned from a discussion of purely class problems (admission to the ranks of the nobility, the sphere of activity of the assemblies of the nobility, etc.) and began to consider questions of public importance. For this latter purpose the conference was divided into commissions, the economic commission being headed by Minister of Agriculture Ermolov.[17] From the first this commission adopted the stand that the economic interests of the nobility were indissolubly connected with those of the entire agricultural class, and that of all measures intended to assist the landed gentry only those could be effective which would raise the level of Russia's entire rural economy. Witte's representatives on the commission informed him of the stand it had taken, whereupon Witte immediately announced in a very sharp letter to its chairman that the commission had overstepped the limits of the problems it had been called upon to discuss, and that he, Witte, was decidedly opposed to its further activities in that direction. Ermolov's attempts to defend the commission's freedom of action proved fruitless, as did all his attempts to oppose Witte. Nor was this to be wondered at. Witte was then at the summit of his power and his nearness to the court was so marked that he was charged with giving some lectures on political economy to the Heir Apparent, Grand Duke Mikhail Aleksandrovich.[18] Witte's account of this incident passes over the obvious contradiction in his own opinions, but this contradiction is set forth clearly in that part of his *Memoirs* which deals with the Special Conference on the Needs of Agricultural Industry and with the organization of the agricultural committees.[19] Here he asserts that these committees had expressed themselves as being primarily in favor of providing for the needs of the peasants, of abolishing their class distinction, and of satisfying the wants of the population in general. But the heads of these committees were none other than uezd marshals of nobility and their members were for the most part members of the landed gentry, some of whom were zemskie nachalniki. *Horribile dictu!* Witte seemed to hold on the one hand that the nobility was an enemy of the people, and on the other that it was the first to show sincere concern for popular needs.

Witte's hostile attitude toward the agricultural elements and the representatives of the landed gentry was carried over from them to the zemstvo, which rested exclusively on these elements. In 1899 he made a report concerning the project to establish zemstvo institutions in the western gubernias,[20] and in this report he tried to establish the idea that under an autocracy the zemstvo was an ineffective and dangerous administrative organization, and pronounced himself definitely for the curtailment of its activities. Witte further developed this latter idea in another report of the same period dealing with public education. In this he argued in favor of exempting all schools from the authority of the zemstvos and of transferring them to the authority of the Synod. Of the cultural role of the zemstvos, the importance of which no one has ever denied, Witte said not a word; on the contrary he insisted that the zemstvos were "overtaxing the peasantry."

But Witte's animosity to the zemstvos was caused by something more than his hostility to the landed gentry. The zemstvos enjoyed the privilege of levying their own taxes. As this did not accord with Witte's policy of directing the greatest possible amount of the public wealth into the state treasury, he endeavored to curtail this zemstvo privilege. It was to this end that he tried to deprive the zemstvos of their administration of public education. He affirmed in the report mentioned above that the zemstvos spent for educational purposes seven million rubles a year, a sum which the state could administer to far better advantage. But he went even farther in his attack on zemstvo privileges. In 1900 he, together with Minister of the Interior Sipiagin, submitted to the State Council a project which sought to limit the zemstvos' right of taxation. There was much discussion and some objection, and when the project was finally adopted it was in a much-moderated form. The limits set to the zemstvos' right of taxation were specified in the law itself and were not left to the discretion of the administration, as the original draft had stipulated.* In practice this law had essentially no effect, yet

* Theoretically this law limited the taxing power only of those zemstvos, gubernias, or uezds whose taxation had been smallest. Zemstvos were to be allowed a yearly increase in real estate taxes of not more than three per cent of the previous year's taxation. That is, taxation of 300,000 rubles could be increased only by 9,000, whereas taxation of 3,000,000 could be increased by 90,000. The percentage of increase was the same in both cases, but the absolute increase was vastly different, permitting the greater taxation to increase rapidly and freely while the lower was prevented from expanding according to its needs. Under this law, for instance, the

it produced a most unfavorable impression. It was, in short, one of those pinpricks which undermined the prestige of the government and aroused the dissatisfaction of the public.[21]

One of Witte's glaring inconsistencies is to be seen in a comparison of his attitude to the zemstvos on the one hand and to the municipal administrations on the other. The latter as well as the former had the right to levy taxes; and actually both organizations were anomalous in an autocratic regime. But Witte never opposed the municipal administration because he never opposed the industrial classes. Not only did he refrain from handicapping any sort of social organization allied to industry but often he endeavored to increase its strength. In 1899, for instance, it was decided on Witte's initiative to allow periodical conventions of representatives of the metallurgical and other industries and of the railway-construction shops and machine factories of the Northern and Baltic regions. Many of these conventions were later transformed into permanent organizations to further the interests of the industry they represented, and acquired much power and influence. Witte feared the privilege of the zemstvos indefinitely to raise the tax rate on real estate as one that might harm the interests of the industrial class whose property consisted of factories, was generally situated outside the city limits, and was subject to zemstvo taxation, although the representatives of the industrial class were always in the minority in the assemblies of the zemstvos.

Witte's opposition to local self-administration, evident in his report on the zemstvos, at first seems strange and even inexplicable. Witte, the author of the Manifesto of October 17, 1905, was the first to recognize the significance of public opinion and missed no opportunity to gain its support, as he often succeeded in doing. His ability in this respect was clearly shown in America during the peace negotiations with Japan that led to the Treaty of Portsmouth. In a few days he succeeded in winning the sympathy of the American public, a factor of the greatest importance in establishing the conditions of the treaty. But the fact remains that with Witte public opinion was one thing and public activities were another. By nature Witte was a very masterful man and, perhaps unwittingly, a rational

zemstvo of Izium Uezd increased the tax on one desiatin of land to six rubles—an enormous sum considering the productivity of that area. But actually zemstvos with really low tax rates were permitted to exceed the three per cent increase with the permission of the government, a permission which was seldom withheld.

absolutist. He was an ardent champion of public education; he strove impatiently and passionately to carry through reforms that would develop the country's general economic strength; but at the same time he was firmly persuaded that this end could be attained far more quickly by an autocratic power, unlimited and free from all inter- ference, than by elected institutions, obliged to consider the shifting opinions of a democracy. Accordingly, public opinion was important to Witte not in itself, but as an indication of what course of action to follow, not as a factor of public life, but as a means of accomplish- ing his own definite ends. His sceptical attitude toward all humanity convinced him that the people ought to have no active part in govern- ment, and that the rulers, merely in order to strengthen their position and their power, should so present their measures as to gain public approval. His formula of absolutism was: *"und der König absolut wenn er unsern Willen thut."* But do not the defenders of democracy adopt another formula which is essentially the same: *"et le peuple souverain, si son désir est le mien?"* And is not the entire problem often reduced to a consideration of the means by which this end can be gained? In Witte's position as Minister of Finance it was undoubt- edly easier for him to act through an absolute authority; it is natural then that he should become its advocate and that public opinion should be for him an important but decidedly secondary factor in strengthen- ing his position.

Witte was alive to the tremendous influence of the press on public opinion, and endeavored to be on the best of terms with press lumi- naries and representatives, using all manner of tactics to this end. He knew how to enlist the services of specialists in order to secure the best possible advice on different problems and to gain proof of the justice and wisdom of his policy. Certain economists, for instance, who were devoted to him and to their own interests, wrote in defense of his financial measures, and the pages of *Novoe Vremia*[22] were used to make these writings public. On the other hand, he never hesitated to muzzle the press if its opinions did not fit in with his plans. *Russ- koe Delo*,[23] the weekly publication of S. F. Sharapov,[24] the lifelong opponent of Witte's economic policy, was suppressed because of its opposition. But Witte used such tactics infrequently, realizing, no doubt, their futility and even adverse effects. Sometimes, indeed, he played to the public, as when he removed the censor's prohibition on a booklet by one Tsion[25] which had been published abroad and contained criticisms of Witte's financial policy. Nor did Witte forget to inform the public that it was he who had had the restriction removed. But an occasional booklet of purely malicious character was one thing; the continual biting and witty criticisms of an established organ such as Sharapov's *Russkoe Delo* was another. Witte, however, was equal to the occasion. First, it was noticed that Sharapov discontinued the publication of his weekly and issued a series of booklets, although the substance of the printed matter and the writers remained essentially the same. But soon, when Sharapov's publications ceased altogether, he was advanced a subsidy with which to develop his shop for the manufacture of lightweight peasant plows.

But if Witte is to be criticized for his methods, it should also be said that in the pursuit of his plans he was confronted with great difficulties which were all the more disheartening and aggravating because they usually consisted of innumerable petty and hidden checks. In his efforts to overcome these obstacles Witte sought support wherever he could find it. Prince Meshchersky,[26] famous editor of *Grazhdanin*,[27] General Bogdanovich,[28] who bartered his own patriotism and monarchism to suit his own ends, and even such an adventurer as Andronnikov were among the unprincipled persons to whom he turned for aid and for whom he felt nothing but contempt. Under different circumstances Witte would undoubtedly have been more discriminating, but those with whom he had to contend were not famous for the scrupulousness of their methods; and Witte invariably acted on the motto that "To live with wolves one must howl like one of them." If his adaptability, powers of discernment, and innate lack of principle enabled him to become a veritable virtuoso in intrigue, that does not at all mean that his contemporaries and associates were without guilt in this regard. His *Memoirs* sometimes show partiality, but they also reveal that he hated his enemies with a bitter hatred and cherished no illusions about his friends. Witte had conceived of or initiated his most notable reforms under Alexander III, to whose memory he was unswervingly loyal and whose support had been all that was necessary to carry through a measure. When the death of Alexander III removed that support, Witte saw conditions change and was obliged to call upon all his resources and energy to carry out his plans. Afterward Witte used to say that if some of his measures were insufficiently worked out it was because he had had to hurry them through, as he was never quite sure what the situation would be on the morrow. As to selection of method, Witte was, as has been pointed out, an opportunist; he was facile also in shifting his opinion when he considered such shifts advisable. But his aim of promoting the economic development of Russia as a basis for political strength was steady and unswerving.

In summary, Witte's accomplishments as Minister of Finance reveal his great merit as an organizer of our state economy. He brought order into the state budget, avoided deficits, and achieved even a pronounced increase of revenues; he strengthened Russian finances as much by the introduction of the gold standard as by his successful conversion of state loans to a lower rate of interest, to four instead of six per cent. He extended the network of our railways; he introduced and developed university and secondary technical education; he assembled a fine group of assistants and other officers in the Ministry of Finance; he organized the department of tax supervision; he most successfully introduced and organized the large-scale liquor monopoly. All these were the fruits of Witte's strenuous labor. Thanks to him our industry began to develop at an almost incredible speed and attracted a part of the population away from agricultural pursuits which could not absorb all the peasant labor as the population increased.

Had Witte used his outstanding abilities and capacity for work to further the development of agriculture, his activities would have been of even greater historical significance. If, in good time, he had directed his attention to the question of rural economy, he would have realized that the center of gravity lay in the formation of large peasant holdings which could supply the markets with produce; at the same time he would have preserved the gentry who owned profit-yielding farms and who were responsible for the development of Russian agriculture. Had Witte studied the peasant problem, he could have hastened the abolition of the communes and the law on the inalienation of periodically repartitioned communal land. This last step would have tended to give free play to the country's economic forces, and would have furthered the transference of the land into the hands best fitted to make use of its productive forces. Such a policy would have strengthened industry by improving the domestic market; it would have raised the level of our rural economy; and, most important, it would have prevented Russia from slipping into that abyss into which she was pushed by the fanatics that are still oppressing our country. They would have been opposed by an enriched and consequently better-educated peasantry, able to see that the well-being of the Russian tiller of the soil would be assured not simply by additions to his lot of tillable land but also by improvements in the methods of its cultivation.

But, alas, Witte could work with spirit only for that which depended upon him directly, that which was under his personal and unrestricted authority. Agriculture and rural economy were not in his sphere of activity, and he treated them at first with indifference and, later, when their representatives opposed his policies, with open hostility. Still later, as Chairman of the Committee of Ministers and then of the Council of Ministers, he seemed to take some interest in the peasant and land problems. But really, to him the peasantry meant merely cheap labor for industry and the landowning peasant was to him not so much a source of national wealth as a taxpayer who paid his taxes mostly through his consumption of liquor.

For this onesided policy, which his successors, Stolypin and Krivoshein, tried in vain—unfortunately too late—to straighten out in order to avert the threatening catastrophe, Russia is now paying with her whole being. And the cataclysm has effaced all traces of Witte's great work.

It is to be hoped that this cruel lesson has not been in vain; that future rebuilders of the Russian state will realize that the foundation of the well-being of the Russian people consists in an organized and technically improved agriculture which uses the people's labor to the best advantage; that they will see that all this labor cannot be utilized for agriculture alone and that a part—a great part—must be attracted to a non-agricultural field of endeavor because the development of industry is just as important for Russia as the intensification of her agriculture.

CHAPTER V

ALEKSEI SERGEEVICH ERMOLOV AS MINISTER OF AGRICULTURE

A. S. Ermolov, Minister of Agriculture and State Domains,[1] was very different from Witte, although both were unaffected in manner and unfamiliar with bureaucratic formality. His thickset, commonplace figure did not give him the appearance of an important public official; and this impression was emphasized by his habit of half turning away from persons with whom he was conversing as if at any moment he might leave them in the middle of a sentence. Yet he was very well educated, well-read, conscientious, and completely devoted to his work. He was the author of many works on agriculture, some of which possessed undoubted merit, but he was without organizing ability and was therefore unable to put his theories and plans into practice. In his writings, which were the reason for his appointment as Minister of Agriculture during the reign of Alexander III, he had outlined in an extensive program those measures which he deemed necessary for the development of Russian agriculture. One of these was a project for raising the level of the Caspian Sea and another for establishing ostrich farms in Russia. In practice, however, Ermolov did not succeed in raising any sea levels; in fact during his long term as Minister of Agriculture he carried through no important measures.

Ermolov's unpretentiousness and lack of organizing ability were immediately apparent to anyone who entered the beautiful ministry house he occupied, a house built by Count Kiselev[2] in the expansive style of the period of Nicholas I. The enormous and splendid waiting room gave the impression of an abandoned country house that had fallen into complete disrepair. Shabby walls covered with cobwebs, antique mahogany furniture with worn and threadbare upholstery, superb but faded window drapes, dirty panes, double window frames which gave evidence of not having been touched by human hands for years—all this was eloquent testimony to the fact that the master of the house was completely indifferent to any display of elegance, but it also proved that he could not discipline even his servants. His numerous subordinates treated him as an equal, and carried out his orders as they pleased. He did not know how to allocate work between himself and his subordinates; for example, he himself read copy for the agricultural newspaper published by his ministry. He inspired no enthusiasm in his subordinates, some of whom were energetic and well informed, and any native enthusiasm for their work was dampened by the realization that their initiative would not prevail against their chief's lack of directing skill. In the "Green Ministry," as this ministry was called because of the color of the piping on its uniforms, overpowering dreariness and mental listlessness reigned supreme. On a door in the ministry offices was a sign: "Office of Sand Dunes and Gullies," which might well have been applied to the whole ministry. Ermolov's term as minister left Russian agriculture, about which he had so much information and which was so dear to him, in the same undeveloped condition in which he had found it.

Lack of organizing ability was not Ermolov's only handicap. He was further prevented from improving Russian rural economy and from exploiting the state domains by the systematic refusal of the Ministry of Finance to advance sums adequate for his purposes. And here also Ermolov's peculiar personality was mainly responsible. He had a weak will and failed to insist upon his demands. Nor would he resort to underhand methods to gain his ends, for his honest, straightforward nature made him incapable of intrigue under any circumstances. Consequently, in St. Petersburg bureaucratic circles, where subtlety was a prerequisite of success, he accomplished nothing. His inability to use his position in a bureaucratic world to create such relations as were necessary for the realization of his plans can be shown by one fact. Under his predecessors it had been customary to pay all money loans made for a period of from three to twelve years to persons well established in the Civil Service out of the revenues from state domains; these had been apportioned on the recommendations of the Minister of Agriculture and State Domains to the Emperor. But Ermolov was so unaccustomed to such methods that this opportunity entirely escaped him, only to be grasped by his colleagues and even by his adversaries. Without Ermolov's knowledge they solicited loans for persons useful to them, and Ermolov was simply ordered by the Emperor to pay the sums that had been requested. It went so far that Witte attempted to bring the disposal of these sums under his own authority by suggesting that in the future all such recommendations should be made by the Ministry of Finance. On this occasion, however, Ermolov displayed unexpected energy and firmness, and Witte was defeated.

Current gossip had it that Witte's refusal to grant Ermolov the sums he needed to carry out his plans was to be explained by a personal feud between the two men resulting from the fact that the wife of one had not made a social call on the wife of the other. But this was not the reason. The real reason lay in Witte's anxiety to avoid disbursements that would decrease the amount of cash in the State Treasury and in his general attitude toward agricultural development as set forth in the previous chapter. In addition, Witte completely distrusted Ermolov's ability as an administrator and believed that sums placed under his control would not be employed to any useful end. "Give me another Minister of Agriculture," he would say, "a man of decision and business ability, and I shall flood him with money." The sincerity of this remark is open to question; Ermolov's shortcomings unquestionably provided Witte with a convenient pretext for withholding funds.

A successful struggle with Witte was entirely beyond Ermolov's capacities, especially since he had not enough courage to state the issue clearly: "Either provide me with means, or free me from my responsibilities." All he could do was to take the first steps of his different undertakings and hope that, should conditions change, these beginnings could be expanded to meet the actual needs of the country. There was no phase of the activities of his ministry on which Ermolov did not present a project for consideration by the State Council. But nearly all these projects represented abstract considerations and regulations, either with no estimate of the sums required for their fulfillment (in this case it was expected that these sums would simply be granted by the Ministry of Finance in accordance with the estimated yearly expenditures of the Ministry of Agriculture) or with an estimate which was exceedingly small but which, nevertheless, always met with objections from the Ministry of Finance. These objections are easily understood. It was to be expected that Witte, in spite of his unfriendliness to agriculture, would be more favorably disposed toward large and adequate appropriations than to small grants which were rendered ineffective by their very smallness. This was true in the case of the project to establish inspectors of rural economy. The project called for one for each gubernia, to be appointed gradually, in turn. At first twelve were to be appointed, if

I remember correctly. The same fate awaited the project to secure loans for improving the land and for equipping peasants with agricultural machinery and implements and for organizing enterprises to supply agricultural needs. Ermolov's project for improving the land involved the securing of loans without interest for work that was not financially profitable but was nevertheless important for the state, namely, measures to check the shifting of sand dunes and gullies. This project was defeated by Witte in the State Council. The project for establishing experimental farms and stations, etc., met the same fate and was reduced finally to one for the establishment and classification of different types of such organizations. While this project was being considered by the State Council it became evident that although the sums at the disposal of the Ministry of Agriculture, which were intended to subsidize zemstvos and other social organizations to maintain experimental stations, workshops, etc., were quite considerable, yet they were entirely inadequate; moreover, they had been spent very unwisely. The organizations to which loans had been made were numerous and the amounts advanced them were at times ludicrously small— in some cases a mere twenty-five and even ten rubles a year. Ermolov's gentle disposition led him to grant any petition for a subsidy, no matter how small.

This characteristic of Ermolov and his own awareness of it were revealed in the State Council's debates on the project for establishing inspectors of rural economy. One clause of this project provided that special agronomic training should be required for appointment to these positions. It was argued in the Council that this requirement would make it impossible to find enough men and that, therefore, men with general university training should be used to make up the necessary number. But Ermolov stood firm. Later, in private conversation, he admitted that he had to have this provision else he would have been overwhelmed by candidates for the position. Even so, in the end some of his first appointees had no special agronomic training and in some cases very little knowledge of agricultural problems.

But even more numerous than the projects Ermolov submitted during his term as Minister of Agriculture were the commissions under his chairmanship, both those of his own ministry and those formed jointly with other ministries. Nothing concrete ever came of these commissions, owing partly to Ermolov's personality, partly to the atmosphere in which he was obliged to work, and partly to his deficiencies as chairman. He began the work of every commission by making a lengthy speech, in which he displayed his acquaintance with the problems to be discussed, and outlined in general terms broad and vigorous measures for their solution. Here his participation ceased. Thenceforth the commission went its way without interference or direction from him. The members of the commissions were nearly always the same men; they realized what they had to contend with and consequently had no interest or energy for the work. The representatives of the Ministry of Finance in these commissions were apparently instructed to object to everything that was discussed, and they succeeded in doing this without much effort. To send a problem to one of Ermolov's commissions was at that time tantamount to sending it to the archives.

But through it all Ermolov himself never lost his peculiar form of energy. Accomplishing nothing, or practically nothing, he was continually striving to achieve something, and there was no problem close to his heart that he did not attempt to solve in one way or another. As minister he sought, as far as conditions would permit, the co-operation and support of public men. In the project for organizing the local branches of the Ministry of Agriculture he desired to link up their activities with those of the zemstvo organizations. With his support there met at Poltava a regional congress of homecraft industries, and at St. Petersburg in 1902 there was an All-Russian Homecraft Workers' Congress under the chairmanship of Count P. A. Heyden,[3] who later became famous for his activities in the First Duma. This latter congress was not limited in its activity by any program and was an outstanding public event of the time. But the resolutions of the convention, many of which had only a remote relation to homecraft industries—as for example, the abolition of corporal punishment—were only paper resolutions and had no concrete results.

Ermolov's other attempt to attract public co-operation for the work of his ministry—namely, the organization of a Council on Rural Economy attached to the Ministry of Agriculture — was equally fruitless. Ermolov invited public men and well-known landowners to take part in the sessions of this Council, which met once a year for about two weeks but which did nothing for Ermolov or his work and, like all his undertakings, gradually sank into oblivion.

If Witte was a minister who bullied the members of the State

Council, Ermolov was one who looked to the Council for help and support. Those members of the Council who had not enough courage to check Witte's sharp sallies treated Ermolov condescendingly and never failed to reproach him for the lack of detail and faulty wording of his projects. Finally, in 1898 Ermolov asked the State Secretary of the Legislative Section of the State Council, Baron Uxkull-Gyllenband, to be his assistant, since Uxkull was an experienced editor familiar with the legislative technique of the Council. This was a peculiar appointment. Uxkull knew nothing of agricultural problems; he said that he had never seen a potato except on his plate. Subsequently the text of Ermolov's projects improved, but their net result remained the same.

Politically, Ermolov belonged among the liberals. In the turbulent days of 1905 he gained so much courage that at a large banquet he demonstratively drank a toast to a democratic constitution in Russia; the toast had been proposed by the famous actress of the Imperial Theater, M. G. Savina.[4] At that time Ermolov was no longer a minister but merely an ordinary member of the State Council.

In conclusion I cannot refrain from relating an anecdote which Ermolov would tell about himself and which was very typical of him. It appears that one Passion Week he went to St. Isaac's Cathedral[5] to confession and, being very modest, took his place in the long line of worshipers. When his turn came to confess, the priest, curious as most of them are, asked him his occupation and, upon hearing that he worked in the Ministry of Agriculture, wished to know his official position. Ermolov told him the truth. "You should be ashamed of yourself," thundered the priest. "You have come to confess and yet you lie most impudently. As if anyone would believe that you are a minister."

CHAPTER VI

IVAN LOGGINOVICH GOREMYKIN AS MINISTER OF THE INTERIOR

In 1895 Goremykin succeeded I. N. Durnovo as Minister of the Interior and held this office until 1899. Later, after 1905, he was twice appointed Chairman of the Council of Ministers, but at that time he was an entirely different personality and professed different political opinions. Goremykin was a clever man and something of a philosopher. Long service in the Second, the so-called Peasant, Department of the Senate[1] had led him to respect law and to dislike arbitrariness in administration. When he was appointed Minister of the Interior he was considered not only a liberal—for his friendships were in that circle of the Senate—but even a disciple, platonic of course, of Tolstoi's gospel. But his outstanding characteristic, which became more pronounced as the years went by, was an imperturbable calm which approached indifference. It was perhaps this very trait which led him to sympathize with Tolstoi's theory of non-resistance to evil. *"Laissez faire, laissez passer!"* was essentially his motto. *"Quieta non movere!"* Let it alone!—his fundamental principle. His favorite and most common expression was, "It is a trifle," which meant: "Don't get excited; don't worry; wait calmly until events and time dull the sharp edges of the question. Then everything will arrange itself, and the ripe fruit will either fall into your hands or will rot away and disappear."

Goremykin's course of action was also influenced by the fact that he was incurably lazy. By this I do not mean a laziness of mind—for his mind was always busy and quite able to comprehend any situation that might arise—but an aversion to all forms of physical effort, a fear of anything that might disturb his serenity. Goremykin was a profound egotist and sybarite; he put a great value upon all forms of comfort and avoided anything that might trouble the placid, measured, carefully planned and settled course of his existence. He managed his personal affairs to perfection. He was scrupulously honest, but he amassed a considerable fortune by dint of economy and good management and by an ability to use his wide relationships and many friends.* Indeed, Goremykin had a talent for using people, for selecting useful co-workers and for exploiting to the fullest extent the knowledge and abilities of each. As the proverb says: "Others poked his fire." He did not possess great breadth of vision. He was not distinguished for his generosity and could not even be relied upon to feel gratitude for services rendered. He was fond of no one except his immediate relatives. His policy was based upon personal rather than state interest, and when these two interests clashed he gave allegiance to the former.

Goremykin treated humanity with contempt. Witte, too, held people in contempt; but his contempt was for individuals with whom he came in contact and upon whose worst traits he played. Goremykin's contempt, however, assumed another form and found expression in his consummate indifference. To Witte power was not an end in itself or even a means of satisfying his personal ambition and of assuring his material well-being.† He sought power so that he might use his great constructive ability. To Goremykin power was of no value in this sense. Its importance to him lay in the prestige, material wealth, and comfort that it brought. Such a trifle as the use of living quarters provided by the state was of tremendous importance to Goremykin. Witte stopped at practically nothing in holding to his power; but he could not have renounced his active mode of life, the realization of his plans and ideas. Goremykin, too, strove to hold his power and after he had lost it strove to regain it; but he did not resort to the methods employed by Witte. It was alien to his nature to work with the various shady figures whose aid Witte never rejected. The use of bribery, as a means of getting supporters, was equally foreign to Goremykin's nature.

Once Goremykin had reached a position of authority, he tended to become inactive, or at best, slow and cautious. He saw trouble for himself in each new problem and approached it with the utmost

* When he was Ober-Prokuror of the Senate Goremykin laid the foundation of his fortune by compiling decisions in cassation made by the Senate's Second Department. This compilation was essential to all peasant institutions of the empire and passed through several editions; and, as the later ones included new decisions, all who were concerned with the peasant affairs were obliged to buy the new editions.

† In his private life Witte was just as venturesome as in his state policy and spent great sums of money; but he was never a sybarite and money to him was a tool rather than a goal—an indispensable tool, for he did not stint himself in anything.

caution. If he could ignore it or wave it aside, he did so; otherwise he undertook to carry it through as slowly as possible, hoping to kill it by delay and to exhaust its urgency, taking care beforehand to secure support for his proposed solution, especially from those in the highest positions.

Sitting complacently in his armchair in the seclusion of his private office, Goremykin planned his moves. He outlined in some detail the results which he desired to secure and also the reasons why such results should be attained. Then he summoned experts to prepare notes for him on the basis of these outlines. When the notes together with the original outlines were returned, he always revised the notes in meticulous detail, making changes here and there. The real authors of the notes never knew how much of their work would survive this revision. By such petty methods as these Goremykin built his career, and because they had served his personal interests so well he was sure they would function equally well in building up the state.

As long as he was Minister of the Interior, Goremykin never concerned himself with public opinion to any great extent; but he assiduously avoided any act that would annoy it, since he was always unwilling to disturb the peace of his private existence as well as that of the public. He endeavored to preserve not only peaceful but even friendly relations with the zemstvo organizations, especially since he, as a former member of the zemstvo assembly of Borovichi Uezd, was in a way connected with them.

His dismissal of N. D. Akhlestyshev as Governor of Tver Gubernia was a move to win the favor of Tver Zemstvo; nor was Goremykin deterred in this move by fear of Akhlestyshev's powerful friends in the Right group. Akhlestyshev's activities as governor had been so unpopular with the zemstvos that the government had considered it the better part of wisdom during his governorship to appoint the members of the Tver Gubernia Zemstvo Board,[2] instead of having them elected as was customary. Goremykin understood perfectly well that to continue the practice of appointing the zemstvo members would be to breed resentment against the government. Consequently he had the practice of election restored. Nevertheless, by negotiating with the representatives of the majority of the Tver Gubernia Zemstvo Assembly he succeeded in securing the election to the Zemstvo Board of members more to his liking without giving the appearance of capitulating to the zemstvo.

But Goremykin did not limit himself to such palliatives. He also suspended the enforcement of a new medical regulation which deprived the zemstvos of control over those hospitals and ambulatory clinics which were maintained by their money. He also stopped the development of other projects under way in the Ministry of the Interior for limiting the authority of the zemstvos; he even asked for the recall of a project which had been submitted to the State Council by his predecessor and which sought to deprive the zemstvos of authority over the business of provisioning.

Still more decided was his stand in connection with a project he submitted to the State Council in 1898 concerning the establishment of zemstvos in our eastern gubernias—Astrakhan, Orenburg, and Stavropol. In opposing this project Witte characterized the zemstvo as "an inadequate method of government," and in reply Goremykin wrote with feeling: "The basis of a state's true might, no matter what its form of government, is in human personality, educated and inured to self-reliance; only the habit of self-government can develop a people's capacity for organization and self-assertion; an emphasis on bureaucracy and governmental guardianship can create nothing but depersonalized and disunited masses of people, mere human dust." But it was this project which Witte used to undermine Goremykin's position with the Tsar by harping upon Goremykin's desire to exploit public forces in order to satisfy local needs, upon his insistence on the necessity of developing local self-reliance and preparing the educated classes of society for participating in the work of the state. These ideas Witte interpreted to Nicholas II as evidence that Goremykin was striving to limit the authority of the Monarch and to introduce a constitution in Russia. This was essentially untrue. Goremykin considered that the existing regime was founded upon an immovable rock; and the strength of his conviction can be judged by his comment on a remark of King George of Greece,[3] whom he met on a trip to the Mediterranean on the yacht of the well-known millionaire Zaharoff.[4] The King told Goremykin that it would be to the best interests of Russia and the Imperial family for the Tsar to preserve the constitution, and quoted his own example: "As long as I keep close to the constitution, I am perfectly sure of my future." Goremykin used to quote these words as an example of a foreigner's ignorance of Russian conditions: "Does he imagine there is any similarity between the Russian Tsar and the king of a people who trade in sponges and currants? The more apparent the authority of the Tsar, the greater it is." So Goremykin was accustomed to end his story.

Although Goremykin was lacking in energy, he possessed both force of character and perseverance. He was well versed in administrative technique and was an able director of his staff. He always knew exactly what he wanted and went after it slowly and carefully but with assurance. He undertook any new task without enthusiasm; he always made a long and careful study of the problem involved, but once he reached a decision he knew no hesitation in carrying it out. In this respect he was very different from Witte, who, for all his activity and energy, was not distinguished for either stability of character or will power. Difficult situations disturbed him and he was apt to lose his presence of mind. The difference between these two men was particularly evident in 1905 and 1906.

Goremykin being what he was, it is easy to understand why his four-year term as Minister of the Interior had no particular effect upon the country as a whole or even upon his ministry. One reason for his appointment had been that he might take action on the matter of peasant legislation, in which field he was a recognized authority. He had been made Assistant Minister of the Interior in 1894 and, if I am not mistaken, it was under his direction that the problems of peasant administration were drawn up for the use of the gubernatorial conferences which were established in 1894. These conferences, under the chairmanship of governors and with local public men (selected on the recommendations of the administration), were to terminate their activities in 1896. But when Goremykin was appointed minister he made no use of the work of these conferences and during his entire term assembled his colleagues only once for consultation upon the peasant problem; even then he gave them no instructions or directions, and a two-hour speech concluded his activities in this field.

This attitude toward peasant legislation was deliberate. He fully realized the tremendous difficulties connected with any reform of peasant affairs and the many-sided opposition and hostility which might arise from a suggested revision of the statutes of February 19, 1861.* To face this opposition and hostility meant to jeopardize

* This hostility was to be expected either from the partisans of the commune or from the defenders of individual ownership and, on another issue, either from the partisans of special peasant administration and courts or from those who favored a non-class organization of administration and justice.

his peace of mind and his official position. Neither prospect attracted Goremykin. Besides, he had retained a certain inclination toward the ideals of the 'sixties and had been known to boast of his participation in the reform of 1864 in the Kingdom of Poland,[5] where he was at that time acting as vice-governor. He was also author of several essays on the Polish peasants in which he expressed himself as being in favor of the state control of peasants. As one of the official members of the Senate commission that made a survey of conditions in Saratov and Samara gubernias he had also done research (1880) on the economic conditions and the legal status of the local peasantry. His report had great merit as a record of facts, but contained no definite suggestions for improving peasant conditions.

Even though his report expressed sympathy with the ideas of the *Narodniki*[6] a sympathy which echoed, though faintly, in his speeches even as late as 1905, the fact remains that during his term as Minister of the Interior Goremykin apparently saw no need for a revision of the statutes of February 19, 1861. He must have realized that they were obsolete, but he probably hoped that in the future they would either fall into oblivion or be partly changed by the Senate's decisions in cassation—or, more exactly, by those of the department in which he had recently worked as Ober-Prokuror.

Goremykin's attitude toward the peasant problem throws additional light on his character; his passion for peace and quiet; his policy of lulling public opinion to sleep with large doses of soothing potions, of avoiding questions that would excite public opinion, of refraining from actions likely to attract criticism, and of endeavoring to be on good terms with everyone. Only in case of need was he ready to take decisive and irrevocable measures. Even so, his policy was preferable to one very frequently used in Russia: noise, threats, continuous irritation of public opinion, and the antagonizing of the population of the frontier regions, together with a total absence of system and stability.

Goremykin's policy, naturally, was not one to put forward any important or complicated legislative project. Consequently Goremykin appeared but seldom in the State Council. He took no part in the give and take of vehement argument; nor did he intrude in affairs which did not concern his ministry. Consequently it was difficult to determine his politics in the State Council. Of all its sessions in 1897, 1898, and 1899, I recollect seeing him in attendance only once, on the occasion of the discussion concerning the project for the additional lists of the St. Petersburg mounted police. And how artfully he handled the project! Never once did he touch upon the essence of the matter; he related what had taken place on the streets of St. Petersburg during a recent visit (1897) of the President of the French Republic,[7] and persuaded his audience that the measures he had taken to preserve order were really liberal and had permitted the population to participate freely in greeting the highest representative of a democratic republic. He then referred to our domestic policy and did so in such a way that it appeared he was giving the members of the Council a glimpse behind the scenes of politics, as if in informal conversation. Stroking and fluffing up his luxurious whiskers—a favorite gesture—as amiable as could be, and with eyes twinkling with suppressed mirth, he seemed to be making confidants and colleagues of all his listeners, who were genuinely pleased and flattered. They felt themselves practically helpless to criticize the measures the speaker proposed for the police protection of the Imperial residence. Goremykin made several concessions with entirely good grace, victoriously carried his project, and left the room amid a chorus of cheers.

But in spite of his diplomacy, during an absence in the autumn of 1899 Goremykin was supplanted by D. S. Sipiagin. Evidently Goremykin had overlooked one rule, namely, that the absent man is always in the wrong. His unexpected dismissal, of which he first learned upon his return from Paris, was a terrible blow.

I cannot say definitely what was the reason for his dismissal. All I can do is to state the reason that seemed most plausible at that time but which to my way of thinking is of little value: the struggle between Goremykin and Witte over Goremykin's defense of the rights of the zemstvos. It was at this very time that Witte wrote his report on the incompatibility of zemstvo self-government with an autocratic regime, and it seems to me that Witte selected this question as the one which promised the best chances of success in effecting Goremykin's dismissal.[8]

These two men, with their extremely different personalities, temperaments, and methods, could not work together; the more aggressive adversary, championing the preservation of the Sovereign's privileges, emerged victorious over the sagacious cunctator, who was inherently more devoted to autocracy.

CHAPTER VII

DMITRII SERGEEVICH SIPIAGIN AS MINISTER OF THE INTERIOR

Goremykin's successor, D. S. Sipiagin, was a typical scion of old-time Russian gentry and his ideas of state administration were those of his class. In his eyes Russia was a domain to be governed paternally by the Tsar. He was a university graduate but could not be considered well-educated, and was endowed with but limited intellectual capacity. He was unaware of the complex and pressing problems concerning Russia's future. True, he saw, as did every one else, that the Russian ship of state was not sailing any definite course but was being helplessly tossed about; yet he failed to comprehend the underlying causes of this menacing situation. In Sipiagin's eyes the root of all Russia's political evils lay in the fact that individual ministers were not making enough effort to preserve the prestige of the Imperial authority and that at the same time they often made use of this authority to carry out measures tending to undermine the principle of autocracy and to lower the prestige of its representatives.

The essence of his point of view had become apparent even before he was appointed minister. When he was Head of His Majesty's Private Chancellery to Receive Petitions, he made a report in which he proposed a general obligatory rule that all projects of general measures or legislative suggestions of state significance should be submitted to His Majesty's Private Chancellery before being presented to the Tsar for his approval. In this way the Head of the Private Chancellery (Sipiagin) would be enabled to present them to His Majesty. This disingenuous measure, he thought, would put an end to all dissension on state policies and serve to detect malicious attempts to undermine the patriarchal, autocratic, and class-differentiated administrative structure. This unbelievably odd suggestion, which proposed virtually either a resurrection of the *Oprichnina*[1] or the establishment in His Majesty's Private Chancellery of a sort of *Eminence-grise,* seemed to Sipiagin a sure method of co-ordinating the activities of individual ministers and of permitting the Emperor to take a more direct part in governing the Empire. Evidently Sipiagin did not realize that his project would merely create one more hindrance to the development of the state, and that it would be powerless to co-ordinate the policies of the separate branches of the administration, since these policies were reflected in the general trend of administration and not so much by separate measures or reforms as by the fact that a great many individual and unco-ordinated decisions and orders were made and given every day. Yet there was the germ of a good idea in Sipiagin's project: given an autocratic regime, unity of policy among the heads of administration could be attained only by the formation of a uniform cabinet under the leadership of one person, who should be not only responsible to the throne but also vested with authority over the other members of the cabinet and empowered to appoint them from members of his political group. Sipiagin was perfectly well aware that the realization of such an idea would be possible only if the idea were camouflaged; so he sought to advance his scheme under deceptive colors. At first he may have planned merely to put himself in a position to control the political activities of the ministers, hoping that later he might become their directing genius and finally their official head.

All the ministers were horrified at Sipiagin's project. Personal considerations made them opposed to the idea of passing all their projects through Sipiagin's sieve, and they also realized the absurdity of his invention. Meanwhile Sipiagin used his extensive backing at the Court to obtain a preliminary approval of his project. It became imperative, therefore, that all weapons should be used and all strings pulled to defeat it. This was done by an old, proved method for defeating undesirable measures—a special commission, composed of persons of some authority and prestige by reason of their former position, was appointed to consider Sipiagin's project. After much time and effort the commission reached a decision and succeeded in persuading Sipiagin to withdraw his project, and thus put an end to the whole problem. But when Sipiagin was appointed Minister of the Interior, he made another attempt to realize his primary ambition—the unification of the ministerial college under his leadership. This time, however, he employed different methods. Immediately after his appointment he hastened to withdraw from the State Council his predecessor's project for extending zemstvo self-administration to the western and some of the eastern gubernias, and to develop his own policy for strengthening the nobility as a civil service class. To this end he sought to organize within his ministry a special department for the affairs of the nobility. He submitted a corresponding project to the State Council, and had even selected a candidate to be director of the new department—the Ekaterinoslav marshal of the nobility, A. P. Strukov,[2] who was noted for his conservatism and particularly for his devotion to the plan of assuring to the nobility the role and importance of a basic civil service class. But fate intervened. Before the State Council had an opportunity to consider the project, Sipiagin was assassinated. His successor, Plehve, withdrew it.

Sipiagin also nursed a desire to glorify the office of governor and to give it an important place in the administrative machinery. He had served for some time in that capacity and felt that governors should be not mere administrators but representatives of the Imperial Power, representatives of the person of the Monarch,* as were ambassadors at foreign courts. But the method he employed to carry through his scheme was just as childish as the one he had used for the advancement of the nobility: he persuaded the Emperor to give separate audiences to governors who came to St. Petersburg and to hear their reports on the conditions and needs of their respective gubernias. After a time Sipiagin himself seemed to realize that the discord which was bound to result from this measure would only increase the general chaos; at any rate, the practice was discontinued and Sipiagin made no effort to re-establish it.

As regards the administration of his ministry, Sipiagin considered the Minister of the Interior to be a governor on an all-Russian scale. He overlooked nationally important questions and devoted himself to administrative details. He seemed to think that from his office on the Fontanka he could take an active part in solving all local problems. Accordingly, he spent nearly all his time conversing with representatives of the local administration on their visits to St. Petersburg. He established a curious routine for these

---

* This scheme of Sipiagin had some foundation in law. Bibikov,[3] Minister of the Interior under Nicholas I,[4] had written an instruction determining the character of a governor's activity and this instruction had been later incorporated into the statute on provincial administration. There was no legal provision, however, determining the extent of a governor's activity.

conversations: each governor, upon arrival in the capital and prior
to his conference with Sipiagin, had to submit a list of the questions to be discussed with the minister. These questions were then
distributed among the proper departments of the ministry, in order
that exhaustive information on them might be collected and presented to the minister. After studying this information Sipiagin
would meet with the governor and spend hours discussing a bridge
which the governor felt was needed by some region of his gubernia,
or a decision of a Gubernia Special Board for Zemstvo and Municipal Affairs,[5] which had been appealed to the Senate. These conversations were generally useless, as was to be expected; but this
fact seemed to have no influence upon Sipiagin, and he continued
the system during his whole term as minister, continually adding to
the amount of information he needed for these interviews. It finally
reached a point where the entire work of the departments was reduced to the compilation of these notes. It was a standing joke among
the employees of certain departments to dub this ministry "Kapany-
gin's office," after a well-known St. Petersburg establishment for
renting and leasing houses.

With Sipiagin so engaged it is not surprising that during his
term of office the ministry neither studied nor carried through any
measures of general importance. Even the routine work was delegated to assistants. Sipiagin created the office of Third Assistant,
to which he appointed A. S. Stishinsky.[6] He selected, as successor
to Assistant Minister Baron Uxkull-Gyllenband, P. N. Durnovo,
who had been Director of the Police Department[7] and later a member of the First (administrative) Department of the Senate under
Alexander III. Gradually the most important part of the minister's
activities came to be handled by Durnovo, but the work that should
have concerned Stishinsky, namely, that dealing with peasant institutions, was left to shift for itself. Stishinsky was a very fine and
honest man, a stranger to intrigue, devoted to his work and distinguished for his conscientious industry, but he was completely lacking
in administrative ability.

Although Sipiagin's intellectual equipment was limited, he was
endowed with a certain intuition, a quality which was sorely lacking
in Witte. Thus upon his return from a trip through Russia in 1900,
during which he saw only the impressive side of things and met only
representatives of the administration and of that part of Russian
society which at that time had no revolutionary aspirations, he

dumfounded the officials who had accompanied him by stating that there was something radically wrong with Russia and that she was on the verge of revolution. Witte was fully aware of Sipiagin's mental limitations yet conceded him a sort of "feminine intuition." But intuition, even though it be feminine, was not enough with which to govern Russia. The realization that there was "something rotten in the State of Denmark" was no substitute for finding a sane and solid corrective for the decay.

Sipiagin appeared but seldom in the State Council—usually he sent his assistants instead—and on occasions when he did appear he made a sorry impression. Possessing neither eloquence, clear thinking, nor knowledge of his business, he became helplessly entangled in his own explanations. Yet his projects, having provoked conflicting arguments and having been considerably cut down, passed the Council, though many of them did not please its members. For instance, Sipiagin extended the statute on zemskie nachalniki to the three northwestern and three western gubernias, and succeeded in transferring from the zemstvos to peasant organizations all business concerning food supply. Sipiagin enjoyed too much influence for the majority of the Council to oppose his plans. Besides, he often had a powerful ally in Witte. The transfer of the business of food supply to the zemskie nachalniki and uezd congresses (*uezdnye sezdy*)[8] was actually the work of Witte who probably hoped that with this transfer the yearly assignments of the Treasury to gubernias with crop shortages would be reduced. It must be admitted that the various zemstvo institutions managed this business very poorly, especially the business of having peasant communities replenish rural food supplies. The zemstvos had no power of enforcement; they were unable to force peasant communities to lay aside a reserve stock of these supplies.

Witte had well estimated Sipiagin's possibilities and how to use him for his own ends. It was interesting to see Witte take Sipiagin's arm and walk with him along the halls of the Mariinsky Palace during recesses. It would be difficult to find two men more different in appearance: the handsome but dull-eyed nobleman, Sipiagin, with his carefully brushed beard and his well-fitting clothes, seemed to have nothing in common with the carelessly dressed but indisputably intelligent plebeian Witte. It did not take much perspicacity to realize that Witte used all his free moments to mold Sipiagin's view to fit his own. He frequently won Sipiagin's support with the

Tsar and, in addition, often succeeded in influencing Sipiagin to issue certain general orders which enabled him to carry out schemes in his own ministry. It was with Sipiagin's help, for instance, that Witte succeeded in establishing a different treatment of tax-supervisors by representatives of local gubernia and uezd administrations. By Sipiagin's ordinance tax-supervisors were even included as full-fledged members in executive boards of uezd congresses on peasant affairs, and Witte saw to it that these tax-supervisors were carefully selected and entirely satisfactory. Factory inspectors, who were not great favorites with the gubernia administration, were to some extent protected by Witte through Sipiagin from the interference of the local police.

Although Sipiagin's two years as Minister of the Interior left no mark upon the country, he succeeded in erecting a monument to himself in the form of the ministry building, the Fontanka Palace.[9] Witte willingly appropriated considerable funds for this purpose, and Sipiagin gave the enterprise personal supervision. It was according to the latter's instructions that the dining hall was given a vaulted ceiling and its walls were decorated in old Russian style. Sipiagin was a great and amiable host; he loved good food and was fond of entertaining his friends at a fine dinner; he was a connoisseur of culinary art and a lover of Russian antiquity in all its forms; and he spared no state money in perfecting this, his favorite dwelling place. Artistic murals decorated the walls of this dining hall; one of these represented the calling of the Tsar Michael Fedorovich Romanov[10] to the Russian throne. And, curiously enough, the leather upholstery of the chairs bore Sipiagin's own monogram. It was Sipiagin's ambition and purpose to invite the Tsar there. In fact, this had been the primary reason for the whole undertaking. But cruel fate intervened. Sipiagin was assassinated the day before he was to give his dinner for the Tsar. He had lived only a few short months in his beautiful mansion.

Popular superstition had it that in this very room he had had a sign of the coming tragedy. On the day he arrived at the Palace, the heavy bronze chandelier of old Russian design fell from the ceiling and broke into splinters the table which was already set for a meal. It was said that this occurrence greatly depressed Sipiagin. Later, after the assassination of Plehve, who also occupied the house, it was popularly believed that the house brought ill luck to all its occupants.

Outside of Sipiagin's immediate family circle, probably no one, with the sole exception of Witte, lamented his death. Witte not only was deprived of a valuable aid and partisan before the Tsar, but also acquired in the person of Plehve, Sipiagin's successor, a serious and dangerous adversary, who finally succeeded in overthrowing him.

CHAPTER VIII

NIKOLAI VALERIANOVICH MURAVEV AS MINISTER OF JUSTICE

The ministers of this period, with the exception of those whose personalities I have been trying to sketch, seldom troubled the State Council with serious legislative proposals; neither did they take an active part in the consideration of projects submitted by other ministers. Their political characters, therefore, were seen only indistinctly and occasionally. Legislation concerning the army and navy did not fall within the competence of the Council. The State Council was not called upon to act as a conciliatory agent—its most important role—between the ministries of War and the Navy and some other ministry. Except for some accidental and unimportant sums the expenditures of the ministries of War and the Navy were settled in special commissions and presented to the State Council only after an agreement had been reached with the Ministry of Finance. To object to such an agreement would have been to object to administrative decisions which were outside the field of legislation. The State Council did not dream of doing such a thing.

All our foreign and commercial policy was determined outside the State Council also, and although the Council passed upon custom treaties, this was mere formality. The Minister of Foreign Affairs was completely independent of the Council, and therefore had no influence there. Neither was there any interference from the State Control, which limited itself to purely formal discussions, on matters such as the question of classifying some newly created office with regard to state pensions. Two Ministers of Education during the period described, Bogolepov and Vannovsky, acted almost entirely within the limits of their office; they never took the floor in the State Council; neither was outstanding. The Minister of Ways and Communications, Prince Khilkov,[1] a self-made man (he started his career as a machinist in America), was a technician par excellence. He never showed his clearly democratic opinions in the State Council except that he always voted with the most liberal group.

N. V. Muravev, Minister of Justice, was outstanding in all respects. He was an experienced lawyer (although he was only public prosecutor [*prokuror*]), scholarly, well educated, and a splendid orator. He was consumed with unbounded ambition, paid close attention to the opinions of the highest administrative circles, and plotted his course accordingly. Thus, in 1895, when he was opening new legal institutions at Reval, he made a brilliant speech which was in harmony with the ideas and aspirations of the time and which attracted great attention. The speech was an attempt to show that the mighty wings of the Russian eagle could give shelter to all nationalities. "Within the Russian Empire," he said, "there is neither Greek nor Jew." In the same year, 1895, in opening the sessions of the commission for the revision of our legal statutes, he once more expressed the idea that justice must be impartial and free from all outside pressure. As the years went on, his attitude toward this principle experienced a great change, which, in my opinion, was due partly to the changed attitude of the Government, and partly to his passionate desire to become Minister of the Interior, an office which called for a profession of real conservatism. Muravev was naturally inclined in that direction. As Minister of Justice he realized that he had to uphold law and justice, and at the same time to support the independence of the courts. The prudent Muravev tried to find a way out of this dilemma by avoiding all important official appearances and by concentrating his energies upon the completion of a new criminal code which had been begun in 1881, and upon the reorganization of our legal institutions which the new code made necessary. He succeeded in passing the new code through all the numerous commissions which were appointed to consider it—the State Council considered it in 1903—but he did not succeed in changing the legal authority of the zemskie nachal-niki. Nor could he have done so, since this would have necessitated an agreement with the Minister of the Interior and entailed a profession of a definitely conservative or liberal point of view, a profession which he did not intend to make. The result was that the new criminal code confirmed in 1903 was never put in force in its entirety. It was possible actually to apply it only as it dealt with state crimes. Another measure which Muravev carried through with much ado was the substitution of imprisonment for exile at the discretion of the courts. The measure also provided for the abolition of exile, at the decision of peasant communities, in cases

of peasants convicted of criminal offenses, and the introduction of
police supervision in its place. This measure passed the State Council
in 1900 and was the occasion of a brilliant speech by Muravev at a
general session. He said in part: "The Minister of Justice of Emperor Nicholas II declares: 'There is no more exile.'" But his proud
announcement remained nothing but an announcement; the custom
of exiling to Siberia continued.

CHAPTER IX

THE CHAIRMEN OF DEPARTMENTS AND OTHER MEMBERS OF THE STATE COUNCIL

Of the members of the State Council only the chairmen of departments had any definite, although limited, influence upon the fundamentals of our state policy in so far as it was reflected in legislation; and the influence they exerted depended to a great extent upon the fact that they were at the same time members of the Committee of Ministers. The ministers valued the chairmen's support very highly, as their voices were often the deciding factor in cases where differences of opinion arose. Yet the influence of the chairmen of departments was not so much evident at the department meetings as behind the scenes. Before submitting a legislative project of any importance to the State Council, especially when it was a project of political importance likely to arouse argument, a minister usually came to some understanding with the chairman of the department which was to be concerned with the project.

During the period described the following persons were chairmen of the departments of the State Council: the Legislative Department, M. N. Ostrovsky, and—after the autumn of 1899— E. V. Frisch;[1] the Department of Economy, D. M. Solsky; the Department of Civil and Ecclesiastical Affairs, the same Frisch and —after 1899—I. Y. Golubev; the Department of Industry, Science, and Commerce after its organization in 1899, N. M. Chikhachev.

Of these persons Solsky was the most influential, partly because of the fact that he was also Chairman of the Finance Committee, an organization not provided for in the Code of Laws but possessing a great deal of importance, since it debated all the principal problems of financial policy. Solsky was a bureaucrat of the old school, having been State Comptroller under both Alexander II and Alexander III. He was an undisputed authority on financial problems, had had great experience in all matters of budgeting, and each year carried a tremendous load of work when his department was busy with the state budget; and when the individual articles of this budget were discussed he was always in a position to see that they were carried out in the way desired by himself. The Ministry of Finance never dared to oppose any of his opinions. As regards the more basic and important questions, Witte always tried to come to some arrangement with Solsky before they were discussed, and usually succeeded in doing so.

Ostrovsky also was a member of the old school. He had been Minister of State Domains during nearly the entire reign of Alexander III. He was a half-brother of A. N. Ostrovsky,[2] the author, and himself a man of great erudition. He was conscientious and honest but he was not endowed with the farseeing mind of a statesman and possessed organizing talents in even a lesser degree. He had had some hard experiences in his youth and had advanced himself by dint of perseverance in a time when a superior was held to be infallible. To the end of his days he greatly valued the position he had attained and preserved a reverence for the opinions of those in authority. This tended to make him cautious and alert to avoid conflicts with persons in a position to do him harm. He was especially careful in his relations with Witte—doubly so since he was aware of his difficulties in understanding economic and financial questions.* Of course Ostrovsky's position was not unique. A lack of knowledge of economic problems was typical of many nineteenth-century Russian statesmen of considerable education and of important official position. In fact, until the appearance of Witte (one seems to be forced to return to him continually) there had been no Russian economic policy to speak of, and all

---

* I recall his plight in the winter of 1898 when he served on the special commission under the Tsar's chairmanship to consider Witte's project for attracting foreign capital into Russia. When he had seen Witte's report, Ostrovsky turned to some persons whose knowledge of economic questions he thought trustworthy. But these persons happened to belong to the group which was opposed to the influx of foreign capital. They persuaded Ostrovsky that their opinions were sound and contended that he should support them against those advanced by Witte. Ostrovsky looked with misgivings and some trepidation upon the possibility of a clash with Witte and was hesitant to commit himself. It was V. I. Kovalevsky,[3] director of a department in the Ministry of Finance, who, at Witte's direction, finally brought Ostrovsky to a decision. When Ostrovsky freely expounded to Kovalevsky the reasons which made him hesitate to join Witte's party, Kovalevsky not only said that he shared Ostrovsky's point of view but also expressed amazement at his detailed information on the subject. This unexpected support from a member of Witte's own ministry decided Ostrovsky to oppose Witte. In the end Witte's project was quashed and the Committee of Ministers was given the right to decide on all matters concerning the attraction of foreign capital into Russia.

financial problems had been reduced to one: how to avoid a deficit in the state budget. And the only means used to attain this end had been to increase old taxes and impose new ones. No one thought of augmenting the wealth of the population or of increasing the country's private and public resources. Even though Ostrovsky had worked in the State Control for many years, where he had been an active collaborator of Tatarinov,[4] the creator of our system of state control, and then had been for over ten years in charge of the Ministry of State Domains, he was still a stranger to these problems.

In addition to the handicap of a one-sided knowledge, Ostrovsky was, at that time, greatly hampered by ill health. But by summoning all his strength and taking great precautions he was able to keep up attendance at the sessions of the State Council, and by making desperate efforts succeeded in holding his position until his death. The State Council, indeed, had its personalities: Solsky, who was for a long time unable to use his legs and moved about painfully with the aid of two canes; and Ostrovsky, who during sessions was completely surrounded with a tall heavy screen to shield him from draft, in spite of the fact that there were three sets of panes in the windows with interior heating between them.

Frisch, the Chairman of the Department of Civil and Ecclesiastical Affairs, was an authority on law, an industrious worker, and gave the impression of a formalist and bureaucrat who was not superior to the average intelligent and educated man. I did not know him well enough to discuss him further.

Frisch's successor in this office was I. Y. Golubev. The fact that his face was absolutely hairless gave him an unusual appearance. He was an outstanding lawyer, and long before his appointment as chairman of the department he had acquired the reputation of being the most industrious and conscientious man in the State Council. No legislative project was submitted to the Council that he had not studied in detail, and there was no first draft of the minutes of a session that he had not read with utmost care and upon which he had not expressed his opinion in writing. Although a specialist in civil law, he concerned himself with any question that came up and voted on every one. But his opinions on questions that did not pertain to civil law were petty. He was also exasperatingly critical when it came to the wording of a law.

Politically speaking, Golubev was a curious mixture of a typical formalist and bureaucrat and a liberal lawyer. At that time the

old regime appeared unshaken and unshakeable, and Golubev observed all niceties of rank and obediently carried out all orders
from above. He deeply appreciated favors from above and at times
was guilty of petty ambition. But as the old order began to show
signs of decrepitude, and the public appeared to gain power, Golubev took good care to acquire the approval of the latter while still
striving to express his devotion to the throne. For instance, when as
vice-chairman he was presiding over the sessions of the reformed
State Council, he succeeded in persuading its members that no formal
or undefined limitations would be set to the free expression of their
opinions. He accomplished this effect by arranging preliminary
consultations with the leaders of the opposition, whom he usually
told that he would be very glad to permit them to express their
opinions with perfect freedom but that this would result in his
dismissal, which would help them very little and would hardly be
to their advantage. Yet during the last months of the old regime,
in December 1916 and January 1917, Golubev came to display considerable courage. When certain questions were expected to be
discussed, he notified those members of the Council who formed an
opposition to the government that their criticism in the forthcoming
discussion would be quite timely. It is true that he refrained from
interrupting speakers during their orations, but later he revised the
stenographic reports of their speeches, crossing out all remarks to
which exception might be taken, so that he could not be blamed for
leniency. He did so, however, only after he had obtained the consent of the speakers. Consequently Golubev was popular with and
enjoyed the particular esteem of the Council members, especially of
those who were elected. After the February Revolution in 1917 they
formed a special fund, which they named after him, to provide
subsidies for an institution of public education to be decided upon
by Golubev himself. The old man—he died shortly afterwards—
seemed to be particularly touched by this mark of respect. When
the members of the Council appeared at his house to tell him of
the fund, Golubev, in a discussion of recent events, expressed the
opinion that the most imperative step was to preserve the bicameral
legislative system in Russia. With Russia being undermined in-
ternally by a group of fanatics supported by German money, draped
in the mantle of friendship for the proletariat, and surrounded by a
mob of highwaymen, and being attacked externally by a powerful
enemy—amid all this, Golubev was concerned with the state struc-

ture of civilized countries and had come to the conclusion that Russia's salvation lay in the preservation of the bicameral system. Such were the peculiarities of his intellect.

Admiral Chikhachev, Chairman of the Department of Industry, Science, and Commerce, had once been Minister of the Navy, but had attained fame as the organizer of the Russian Navigation and Trade Company, the largest steamship enterprise in Russia. He was Chairman of the Board of Directors of this enterprise, and contributed much to the exploitation of the northern shores of the Black Sea and particularly of the southern shores of the Crimea. He was no economist, but he possessed much practical knowledge of trade and industry. When he was appointed Chairman of the Department of Industry, Science, and Commerce he had lost a great deal of his energy and ability to work and meekly followed the lead of D. A. Filosofov, the state secretary for that department. Chikhachev belonged to the liberal group of the Council and openly professed Semitic sympathies. His abilities as chairman were by no means outstanding.

I wish also to mention some specialists who served in the Council's departments where projects of new laws were studied in detail. These specialists, by conscientious study and effort, sought only to improve the projects submitted to the departments. In the period under discussion, the following were specialists in financial and economic questions: V. V. Verkhovsky, N. V. Shidlovsky[5] and F. G. Terner.[6]

Verkhovsky, for all his talent and eloquence, was less a serious economist than a dilettante who grasped every subject too easily—on the wing, so to speak. He was known in the Council as a resolute opponent of Witte and his financial policy. He was particularly firm in opposing Witte's project for the establishment of the gold standard in Russia, at which time he was but a mere assistant to Protasov-Bakhmetev,[7] the Supervisor of the Institutions of Empress Marie,[8] and was not, strictly speaking, a member of the Council; nevertheless, because he constantly represented his chief in the Council, he succeeded in forming such a large group of opponents of the project that Witte was obliged to withdraw it and carry it out later by means of an Imperial Ukase. Later, Verkhovsky lost a great deal of his brilliance; and, although he continued to oppose all measures suggested by the Minister of Finance, he was no longer able to mobilize the opposition against Witte.

N. V. Shidlovsky was less talented than Verkhovsky and possessed but a superficial knowledge of economics. Yet he was very precise and considered carefully every detail of a project. This trait may be explained by the fact that he had formerly been state secretary in one of the sections of the Imperial Chancellery and had become well trained in legislative technique. He, too, was a fervent opponent of Witte, and proved a constant thorn in the flesh of the Ministry of Finance during sessions of the departments.

Terner was perhaps the most impartial, even the most impassive, participant in arguments on financial problems. He had formerly been a professor in the University of St. Petersburg and was the author of some interesting works on economics. He was inclined to subject to scientific analysis those financial or economic projects which were likely to become a part of public life. He had fallen somewhat behind in the march of science, however, and, generally speaking, was rather old-fashioned; his influence was rather slight.

These three men and others carefully studied budget and taxation problems and any changes they suggested were usually for the better. The project on *promyslovyi nalog* (taxation of business concerns), the first attempt at a progressive income taxation, is a case in point.

Of the older statesmen, those who had served under Alexander II and early in the reign of Alexander III, I wish to mention only a few.

Count Pahlen[9] was a pure-bred Baltic German and spoke with a German accent. He had been Minister of Justice during the reforms of Alexander II and had succeeded in preserving the authority of the courts from all outside pressure and influence, using the utmost caution and discrimination in appointing judges and prosecuting attorneys so as to retain the high moral standard of justice. He was famous for his straightforwardness and honesty and in spite of his advanced age had retained a truly admirable clarity of mind. He spoke infrequently but seriously and persuasively. In spite of his peculiar Russian* he made one feel that the opinion he expressed was sincere and uninfluenced by outside pressure. In 1901 he was appointed chairman of a special commission

* There were many stories told of Pahlen's Russian. Once when he tried to be particularly kind to one of his visitors, who came to plead for something and was terribly depressed, he said sympathetically: "obotrítes dukhámi" [Spray yourself with perfume] when he meant to say: "obódrites dúkhom" [Take courage].

of the State Council to study the new project of the criminal code, and despite his many years he displayed exceptional assiduity and business ability. The work of the commission, in which such authorities in criminal law as Tagantsev, Rosing, and Derviz[10] took part, went along at a surprising pace and by 1903 the project was confirmed without alteration by the Council.

Count N. P. Ignatev was in some respects the direct opposite of Count Pahlen. During the reign of Alexander III he had been Minister of the Interior but had been obliged to resign this post when he failed to carry his suggestion that a national assembly (*zemskii sobor*) be convened, a step which would have meant, if not a constitution, then at least the beginning of one. Count Ignatev was highly intelligent, subtle, and resourceful, and as Russian envoy to Peking after the conclusion of the Treaty of Aigun[11] he proved himself a remarkable and valuable diplomat. Later he was envoy to Constantinople, where he raised the prestige of Russia to an unprecedented height and enjoyed great personal popularity and respect. But during the years being described he had given up public activity and attended the sessions of the Council but seldom. Toward the end of his days he became engrossed in activities which swallowed up his entire fortune.

Another living monument to former times was P. P. Semenov-Tian-Shansky,[12] who continued to take part in the work of the departments of the Council despite his advanced age. He had been personal secretary to Ya. I. Rostovtsev,[13] first chairman of the commission editing the statutes of February 19, 1861; and, since he still considered himself the guardian of the traditions and ideals of the authors of the reform, he was always ready to defend the statutes of February 19 in their entirety. To him the commune with its periodical re-allotments of land was sacred, and only enemies of Russia would dare raise a voice against it.

P. S. Vannovsky was another elder statesman. He had been Minister of War during the entire reign of Alexander III. In 1901 he was dug out of the archives and appointed Minister of Education, in which office he limited his activity to proclaiming the "policy of affection" in matters of public education. This policy was absurd but was justified by the character of the ministry's previous policy. Vannovsky was not cut out for a military man but had proved an able military administrator. He also proved to be a good director of his new ministry but had little in common with pedagogy, although he had at one time worked in the field of military education.

I must mention also E. A. Peretts,[14] a former Imperial Secretary. Peretts was a typical bureaucrat of the time of Alexander II, with a clean-shaven face adorned with side whiskers. He was a brilliant orator; his speech was polished, his ideas were well arranged, invariably including some abstract thought designed to give the impression of erudition, at least of broad political outlook. He, too, appeared in public but seldom.

Although these older men took but small part in the work of the State Council, they exerted an influence on affairs of state that cannot be disregarded, even though this influence was indirect. For instance, when a minister was about to attempt to pass a measure which was likely to meet strong opposition or—and this was more frequently the case—when there was need of defeating some proposed measure, then it was customary to solicit the permission of the Monarch to appoint a special commission to consider the measure in question. To this commission these former authorities were brought as if they were so many ikons and the ministers appealed to their "proved state experience and intelligence."*

In questions of administration and domestic policy in general, as well as in those pertaining to school and education, the most important role was played by A. A. Saburov,[16] a Minister of Education during the reign of Alexander II. He was the most outstand-

---

* Such a commission was appointed to consider Sipiagin's project mentioned above, pp. 82–83.

Another was appointed to consider the project of Civil Engineer Balinsky for a subway in St. Petersburg. This project was drawn upon a magnificent scale and called for no less than 380 million rubles. (Our state loans at that time were never over two hundred millions.) At the same time, foreign capitalists who had agreed to finance the undertaking wished to get a state guaranty for a certain percentage of the capital involved. Witte was against the project, but Balinsky had acquired strong support. He was, for example, supported by his friend, Goremykin, by Minister of the Interior Sipiagin, and by the well-known ballerina Kshesinskaia,[15] who was instrumental in securing the Tsar's preliminary approval of the project. Witte saw that he could not defeat the project single-handed and had recourse to a tried method—the establishment of a special commission under the chairmanship of Solsky. The commission unhesitatingly decided against the project but recommended payment of the engineer's expenses incurred in drawing up the project, some 100,000 rubles, if I remember correctly. Balinsky's project must have had its merits, however, because the foreign capitalists, after the Russian state had refused to give any guaranty, volunteered to build the subway on condition that they be given the right to import necessary materials and parts free of duty. Witte was able to quash this by himself.

ing representative of the liberal group of the Council and concerned himself only slightly with the details of the discussed projects, being content to limit himself mostly to a criticism of their more reactionary points. His influence was manifested mostly behind the scenes, in the lobby of the State Council, a clearinghouse for all sorts of understandings and agreements among the adherents of different opinions, particularly among representatives of different ministries. The liberal opposition had private informal conferences in their homes as well. But since the representatives of this liberal opposition had all been appointed by the government, they could not have developed anything that resembled a political party that could work effectively against the government.

The position of those of the members who strove to uphold the rights of public bodies was especially difficult. All attempts, however innocent, in this direction were at that time deemed little short of revolution. It came to such a pass that on one occasion when a project suggested that the zemstvos be granted some new privilege the reference to the significance of the zemstvos and public initiative contained in the minutes of the session was excluded almost entirely by the state secretary, Filosofov, and this in spite of the fact that Filosofov was himself a zemstvo worker and a supporter of local self-government. In view of the fact that the minutes of the sessions were not made public and never went beyond the general sessions of the Council, whence they were sent to the archives, the incident may serve as eloquent testimony of the fearful attitude adopted by the administrative heads toward this side of public life.

Another prominent member of the liberal group, who also was active in considering all projects pertaining to administration, was Prince D. D. Viazemsky, a former Supervisor of Udels (Crown lands) and previously an Ataman of the Ural Cossacks. The members of the Council remembered Viazemsky as having been involved in a disagreeable incident: He had been rebuked in a Sovereign order to the Ministry of War for interfering with the orders of the government, and at the same time had been forbidden to take part in the sessions of the State Council for a considerable period of time because he had interfered with the activities of the police while they were engaged in dispersing a demonstration (composed mostly of students) before the Kazan cathedral, and had used his military rank to protect several girl students from the whips of the Cossacks.

The other members of the State Council attended sessions of the Council as they saw fit, usually when problems, with which they were familiar from previous experience, were being considered. Some of them had particular hobbies. Thus, for example, I. I. Shamshin, chairman of the special commission for the working out of new civil service regulations, invariably announced, when the organization of some new office was proposed, that the question must be postponed until the regulations his commission had worked out were confirmed, so that the new institution might be put in line with the provisions of these regulations as regards enrolling employees, classifying them, and fixing their pensions. Shamshin usually got nowhere, but this did not prevent him from repeating the performance. And so it went on for many years. But the new regulations, Shamshin's brain child, not only never saw the light of day, but were not even submitted to the State Council. Yet there was great need for some regulation of this sort, since the establishment of a new rate of pensioning, adjusted to changed conditions, was very necessary.

Members of Baltic origin occupied a particular position in the State Council. Our German barons treated with relative indifference all legislative projects not related directly to the Baltic provinces. On the other hand, everything that touched upon the interests of these provinces, and especially upon their nobility, received their close and united attention. Nor was this attention entirely confined to the State Council. They had compatriots in all ministries, especially, at court, and used the most diversified methods to gain their ends.

An example of a clever and efficient method used by the barons to safeguard their interests may be seen in the matter of the right of private ownership on the part of local societies of the nobility of the so-called Baltic estates. These estates had been transferred out of state domains to Baltic societies of the nobility in the eighteenth century upon condition that the revenue from these estates should be used by the local nobility to fulfill certain public duties, such as the maintenance of local police. Later the local nobility was freed from the fulfillment of these conditions—the state assumed these responsibilities—but the societies of nobility retained possession of the estates. In 1890 there arose the question of the organization of these estates and particularly of the establishment of the status of the peasants who were settled upon them and who had remained in virtually feudal relationship to the estate-owners. The Ministry of the Interior was obliged to ascertain where the title to these lands really lay—with the state or with the nobility. Upon the solution of this question depended the status of the peasants living upon the lands in question, since there was one ordinance concerning peasants on private estates and another concerning those on state domains. Had the affair not concerned the Baltic nobility, the ministry would undoubtedly have decided the question itself or would have made some definite representation of the matter before the State Council or the Senate. But since it concerned the Baltic barons there could be no question of solving the argument so simply. So a special commission was appointed under the chairmanship of the member of the Council, Gerard; appointments to the commission were made from the representatives of the four Baltic societies of the nobility. The first step of the Balts was to lodge before the Imperial Secretary a complaint against the official of the Imperial Chancellery in charge of the commission's affairs. They charged that this official had prepared a memorandum which proved that the question of the estates could not be solved according to the provisions of civil law but only on the basis of public law; that is, that it must be considered from the point of view of public benefit. Practically, this meant that the state should preserve the right to control the estates in question. Such a standpoint was unsatisfactory to the Balts. So they applied all their efforts to the task of securing the dismissal of the official in question and replacing him with another more sympathetic to their interests. Working through their compatriot, Assistant State Secretary Baron Uxkull-Gyllenband, they pointed out that the official had overstepped the limits of his office and had permitted himself, in a strictly special memorandum, to indicate what the decision of the commission should be. Strictly speaking, this charge was untrue; for the memorandum did not question the commission's right to decide the question as it saw fit. Essentially, however, the memorandum did prescribe the decision by explaining the true meaning of the law. The barons' attempt to hush up the memorandum proved ineffective since it was distributed among the commission members "at the order" of the chairman. Recourse was then had to another method: the barons succeeded in adding to the commission, as an authority on Baltic civil law (which, by the way, had no bearing whatever on the case), Senator Gasman, of whose favorable attitude they were certain. But even then they did not succeed in proving that the estates in question were the property of the nobility—the contrary was much too evident. But apparently the commission did not dare leave the title to the state. It limited itself to deciding the status of the peasants living upon these lands, to the effect that they should be classified as living upon state lands and not upon private estates. The question of ownership was left open. This decision received Sovereign confirmation, and the estates continued under the management of the societies of the nobility, which also preserved the right to dispose of the interest on the capital paid by the peasants for the land allotted to them. Still the Balts were not satisfied. After a few years—in 1905—they succeeded in obtaining the right not only to dispose of the sums mentioned above but also to mortgage the land left over from the peasant allotments, and freely to use the mortgage moneys. The reason for their petition for these rights was that some of the baronial estates in the Baltic provinces had been looted by the peasants and sums involved were really meant to be compensation for the losses the nobles had sustained. It would not be amiss to note that the mortgaging was done with the Prussian Credit Society and to the full value of the land, thus preventing all attempts of the Russian government to regain the ownership of these lands.

"La charité bien ordonnée commence par soi-même"—this was the principle which the Baltic nobility mastered and applied to the fullest extent. But it should hardly be blamed for the odd fact that the interests of a handful of Baltic Germans were given closer attention than those of the Russian state and those of the majority of the local alien population.

PART TWO

The Period of Plehve's Ascendancy, 1902–1904

CHAPTER X

VIACHESLAV KONSTANTINOVICH PLEHVE AS MINISTER OF THE INTERIOR

Early in April 1902 P. A. Kharitonov entered the private office of the State Secretary of the State Council, Baron R. A. Disterlo.[1] He moved with his usual slow and noiseless gait, and after greeting Disterlo and the others present made himself comfortable in an armchair, then he announced in a tone full of mock veneration and respect: "He has visited Tsarskoe Selo. He has been offered the Ministry of the Interior and he has accepted it." Everyone present understood perfectly who "he" was—the Imperial Secretary, V. K. Plehve.

The appointment of a new Minister of the Interior had been delayed somewhat after Sipiagin's assassination and had become a matter of great interest to the bureaucratic circles of St. Petersburg. They had named three candidates: Plehve; N. V. Muravev, Minister of Justice; and P. N. Durnovo, Assistant Minister of the Interior. The appointment of one of these would decide the fate of many officials of the Ministry of the Interior, the Minister of Justice, and the Imperial Chancellery. Had Muravev been appointed, many officials of the Ministry of the Interior in St. Petersburg would undoubtedly have been supplanted by legal workers; now, however, the appointment of Plehve meant that these officials would be supplanted by men from the Imperial Chancellery, which in turn would lead to a general promotion all along the hierarchical scale of officialdom in this latter institution.

But Plehve's appointment provoked many considerations not dictated by personal interest. Everybody was aware that Plehve and Witte advocated different policies and that there was deep animosity between them. It was common knowledge, too, that Witte's position had been shaken while that of Plehve was becoming increasingly secure, as usually happened in the case of a new minister. It was with some reason, therefore, that the bureaucratic world looked forward to a clash between these two powerful and clever men and to the pleasure of watching the conflict. They even began to speculate on the outcome. Many who secretly wished that it might be so prophesied Witte's retirement. Witte had done much to make enemies for himself. With the passing years he had become more and more arrogant. He had manifested an increasing lack of consideration for the rights and dignity of the State Council by endeavoring to pass his more important measures by direct resort to Imperial ukases. Finally, as Minister of Finance, his control of appropriations made other ministers dependent on his will. Consequently there were many, both in administrative circles and in the State Council, who wished with all their hearts for his downfall, even though they did not dare to oppose him openly.

Yet it could not be said of Plehve that he was especially popular. He had fewer personal friends than Witte, who was known for his sociable disposition, despite the fact that Plehve had been a part of St. Petersburg's bureaucratic world for the longer period. Besides, Plehve made friends much more easily with women than with men.

Plehve had acquired renown as Director of the Police Department, to which post he had been appointed shortly after the murder of Alexander II on March 1, 1881. He had been so successful in organizing the police system that it had had little trouble in almost entirely disrupting the revolutionary party of the *Narodnaia Volia* (Will of the People).[2] The terrorism that had been so prevalent during the last years of Alexander II's reign ceased, and every attempt to revive it had been nipped in the bud. As Assistant Minister of the Interior, at first under Count D. A. Tolstoi and later under his successor, Ivan Nikolaevich Durnovo, Plehve had shown definite administrative talent. He actually directed the whole Ministry, as Durnovo and especially Count Tolstoi took little part in its affairs although they jealously preserved all their privileges as ministers.

But Plehve's personality remained a closed book to his associates. He was considered intelligent and efficient, but hardly anyone knew his real opinions on problems of administration. The consensus was that he was primarily concerned with developing a career and so professed only those opinions which it was most profitable to profess at any given moment. P. V. Orzhevsky,[3] who was noted for his bitter tongue, used to say of Plehve: "Even a dead fish can go with the current."

This remark was popular; but was it apt? A closer knowledge of Plehve reveals that it was not. It is true that he was ambitious for a career and that actually he had tried very hard to secure the appointment of Minister of the Interior. It is also true that he professed those opinions which were viewed favorably at the time. But it is altogether untrue that in doing so he went against his inner convictions, or that he had none against which to go. Plehve was not given to indifferences. He had a deep and sincere affection for Russia; he thought deeply about her destiny, realized the gravity of the crisis through which she was passing, and tried earnestly to find a way out. Being a confirmed believer in the absolute monarchy, Plehve was of the opinion that neither the Russian people in general nor the educated circles in particular were sufficiently well trained to be allowed to govern their country or even to take an extensive part in the government. The Russian people, with their colorless agricultural masses, reminded him of the sphinx, and he was wont to say that Russia's future depended upon how correctly the government solved the peasant enigma. Plehve apparently thought that the most efficient way to insure the future peaceful and systematic development of Russia would be to perfect the state machinery. But he avoided any expression of opinion on this subject, realizing, no doubt, that the life of a people depends upon its inherent characteristics and not upon mere administrative measures mechanically applied to the nation's organism. Be that as it may, in practice he concentrated all his energies on perfecting the governmental apparatus. In so doing he came to realize that the development of Russian administrative machinery could not keep pace with the changing conditions of public life.

Plehve preserved a critical attitude toward the personnel of state institutions. He possessed a capacity for finding out everything about the private life of nearly all prominent bureaucrats, a capacity still more developed by his former work in the Police Department, and he was not averse to telling anecdotes concerning them when occasion presented itself. These anecdotes, moreover, showed that he did not have a particularly exalted opinion of them.*

* Plehve's service in the Police Department had developed in him the deplorable habit of prying into private correspondence. He was particularly interested in the correspondence of his colleagues and friends and the remarks concerning him which this correspondence contained. In general, the reading of correspondence was done officially by a special office of the Police Department and by one of the offices of the Chief Administration of Posts and Telegraphs; and its results, filed in order and compiled annually into reports, provided a cross-section view of the different opinions in vogue among the different classes of society. Not only the correspondence of revolutionaries was read but also that of government officials and even of members of the Imperial family. When this practice is pursued as a part of official duty and allegedly for purposes of state its baseness is apt to be very soon lost

In money matters Plehve was a man of undoubted probity. He came from a family of moderate means—his father was an auditor of a military district court[4]—and the hard experiences of his youth had taught him the value of money. He had no inclination to live on a grand scale as did Witte, who was accustomed to make great expenditures in both public and private life, nor did he have Goremykin's sybaritism; he limited his expenses to the necessities of personal comfort and was indifferent to any outward show. He was careful without being parsimonious; he had neither the inclination nor the ability to speculate and apparently had no desire to accumulate a large fortune. The sum total of his property was represented by a tiny unprofitable estate in Kostroma Gubernia where he spent his summers and made his only contacts with public life. After his death it was learned that during his long term of service in many well-remunerated posts he had saved only some forty thousand rubles.

Plehve's reputation as a stern and even cruel man was ill-deserved. While outwardly severe, grave, and reserved (he had nothing of Witte's adaptability), he could become deeply concerned over the misfortunes of others. True, he kept his subordinates in constant awe of him and finally lost their sympathy because he gave vent to a caustic humor at their expense. Yet he had a noticeable preference for persons who could hold their own ground and preserve their dignity, and toward such persons his manner instantly changed. Conversely, he despised persons who bore his attacks with patient humility. B. V. Stürmer (at that time Director of the Department for General Affairs of the Ministry of the Interior)[5] could be placed in this latter category. He was ready to suffer any ignominy in order to retain his position, which was a great source of comfort to him, and he bore in silence all of Plehve's most insulting remarks even when made in public. Plehve did not use for his personal needs either directly or indirectly the large sums which were at his uncontrolled disposal. But he never refused to help his subordinates if they were in real need of assistance, and it often happened that he would give a larger sum than had been requested. He knew what poverty

---

sight of, but it is dangerously easy for a person thus engaged to slip to the perusal of letters for no other purpose than to satisfy his own curiosity. In Plehve's case, for instance, an examination of all documents in his study after his death revealed that he had kept certain letters which he should have turned over to the proper censorship office. These letters, moreover, were written by persons whose participation in a conspiracy could not have been suspected by even the wildest imagination.

was, and often used to say that the best way to get good work from a horse was to feed it well.

The talent for administration that Plehve had shown in each of his several offices he now applied to the Ministry of the Interior. But fate denied him time to achieve his usual degree of success. He sought to select men for responsible positions who were best able to do the work in question. This does not mean that in making appointments he was impervious to outside interference and considerations. As a product of the St. Petersburg bureaucratic milieu he knew perfectly well that it was impossible to accomplish anything unless one was willing to humor influential persons by granting some of their demands. But if the persons who were appointed from such considerations were of inferior ability, Plehve appointed them to some sinecure, a number of which always exist in every government. In the Ministry of the Interior such positions were represented by membership in the Council of the Minister[6] and in the Council of the Chief Administration for the Affairs of the Press. For young men there were such positions as special duties clerks with the minister.

But with all his talent and his eagerness to comprehend state problems, Plehve was incapable of that conception of things which characterizes a statesman. It could be said of him, as had been said of Speransky,[7] that he was "a superlative clerk." He had been born in the family of a clerk, that is, in that category of the Russian public which had no strongly rooted connections with any organic class of Russian society; he had been educated to be a legal clerk, and his opinions were those of a clerk—a very superior clerk it is true, but a clerk nevertheless. As mentioned above, he thought that Russia's future depended upon a reorganization of the state machinery and his inability to fathom the complex problems of his age precluded for him the possibility of a different point of view.

Plehve was one of those Russian state officials who failed to comprehend the problems of national economy which confronted Russia in the last quarter of the nineteenth century. His policy of meeting Russian problems by perfecting the machinery of government would have served the state well in the period before the Turkish War of 1877–78, which forms a sort of dividing line between the old economic order and the new. But in the early twentieth century such a policy did not take into account the economic changes of the previous few decades. Up to the Turkish War the theory of natural economy had dominated Russian economic practice and private enterprise had developed in its own way, generally unrelated to the economy of the country as a whole. State economic policy was concerned primarily with the balancing of revenues and expenditures in the state budget, and was concerned with national economy only in so far as it served to fill the state treasury. New economic conditions called for a new state policy. No mere administrative reform could solve the economic crisis through which Russia was passing. For such a solution it was imperative to remove all class barriers by bringing all classes under one uniform civil code, thereby introducing order into economic relations and liberating the energies of the people. But this need was not generally recognized, especially by the administrators of the old school, whose training in economic problems was woefully deficient. To them the governmental system remained the backbone of the state and they devoted all their efforts to strengthening it.

Plehve himself did not realize how deeply steeped in bureaucracy he really was. He opposed any increase in the personnel of administrative institutions because his experience had taught him that in every office the work was done by the few, the others resting content merely to be "present." Possibly he regarded this stand as a manifestation that he was not a slave to bureaucratic tendencies; apparently he did not realize that the demands of a growing population and of changing conditions made necessary the creation of new offices.

When Plehve took over the Ministry of the Interior he had three distinct ambitions: first, to organize the activities of the Police Department in such a way as to put an end to the terrorism which had become a chronic menace; second, to reform the central and local administrative apparatus, to adjust its functions to the changed conditions of life, and to place it in direct contact and co-operation with the activities of the public organizations of the municipalities and the zemstvos; and, third, to reform peasant legislation. As is well known, he did not achieve any one of these aims; in fact, his attitude toward the essentials of these projected reforms experienced a marked change as time went on.

Plehve's attitude toward the problem of "exterminating treason" changed during his first month as minister. At the outset he seemed to be of the opinion that the failure of attempts to combat this "treason" was due to the poor organization of police supervision and the secret service. He expressed this opinion when he visited the

Police Department soon after he assumed his new office. He said that it appeared to him that the Police Department had bent its efforts to ruin the organization he had built up when he was director of that department. He criticized the department for its practice of detaining or watching great numbers of persons; in his opinion the safety of the state was to be secured by arresting not large numbers of revolutionary-minded citizens but a limited circle of revolutionary instigators and leaders. As a result of this visit the director of this department, Zvoliansky, resigned.

In May 1902, on his way to Kharkov and Poltava where there had been agrarian disturbances, Plehve expressed to D. F. Trepov,[8] Moscow Chief of Police, his disappointment at the activities of the Moscow secret service. He criticized the activities of Zubatov, head of the secret police there, who was then applying in Moscow with the encouragement of the local authorities the system of police socialism that made him famous.

But Plehve soon came to believe that police supervision was not enough, that police measures alone were inadequate for the suppression of the revolutionary movement or even for the prevention of terroristic acts. Broader measures were needed. Of the reasons for this change of opinion I believe the first was this: It was not until Plehve assumed the responsibilities of the Minister of the Interior that he realized the deep changes which had taken place in the national organism during the ten years that had passed since he had left that ministry. In the 'eighties, when Plehve had succeeded in breaking up the revolutionary organization Narodnaia Volia, there had been no united revolutionary movement in Russia but only attempts of a small group of persons to organize such a movement. In the twentieth century he was faced with a different situation. Industrial development had created in Russia a new proletarian class in which socialist propaganda, mostly Marxist, found fertile soil and which was fully aware of existing social and economic conditions and was striving to improve them with definite ideals in mind.

The condition of the Russian peasantry, too, had changed greatly since the 'seventies, that is, since the "To the People" movement.[9] Increase in agricultural population had reduced the size of individual peasant holdings. This handicap had not been offset by an increase in the productivity of the land or by the introduction of improved methods of agriculture. The result was an acute situation, most acute in some regions of European Russia. Thus, even among the peasant population there was favorable soil for the sowing of revolutionary seed.

Plehve first became fully acquainted with this changed state of affairs while studying the agrarian uprisings in Poltava and Kharkov gubernias mentioned above. These uprisings had been on a rather large scale. They had started March 30, 1902, in Konstantinograd and Poltava uezds, where fifty-four estates were destroyed in the first four days. On the fifth day there was an uprising in Valki Uezd of Kharkov Gubernia, where the rioters looted the landowners' estates, setting fire to two of them. These uprisings were very savage in character; not only landed gentry lost their estates, but also some well-to-do Cossacks. Grain, equipment, and livestock were plundered. Houses were torn beam from beam. When the zemstvo hospital was looted the peasants stole even the mattresses from the patients' beds. From Valki Uezd the uprisings spread to Bogodukhov and the city of Valki. Here, however, the mob, mad for loot, was checked by troops sent there for that purpose. All sorts of people had taken part in the looting. Among those convicted of robbing local sugar refineries was the deacon of a local church. Information at the inquiry showed beyond doubt that these uprisings were not a separate and strictly local occurrence but part of a widely planned and carefully executed revolutionary act. Plehve learned of the widespread activities of the propagandists and the susceptibility of the masses from this inquiry as well as from a detailed report by Zubatov, which dealt with the activities of the revolutionists in Moscow's industrial district.

S. V. Zubatov had begun serving the state by betraying a whole revolutionary group of which he himself had been a member. Nevertheless he was a man of ideals. He had studied all socialist theories and acquainted himself with the works of all the luminaries of socialism, and although he remained a staunch champion of the rights of the proletariat he had become a confirmed monarchist. He considered police supervision, suppression of carefully designed terroristic acts, and arrests of propagandists as of secondary importance in the government's struggle against the revolutionaries. It was his opinion that the main activities of the government should be directed toward paralyzing the spread of revolutionary ideas among the working proletariat, and that this could be achieved in two ways: first, the theories of different socialist groups should be fought with counter theories; second, the government should take definite steps to protect the workingmen from exploitation by the capitalists.

Some measures which Zubatov sought to effect were actually those advocated by socialists, as for example the introduction of the eight-hour working day. Zubatov, however, intended to effect a gradual change in the social order while preserving the old administrative order. The Tsar and the People! Such was the slogan he advanced, a slogan which was in no way new.

Applying his theory to practice, Zubatov arranged for a special instruction to be issued to the factory inspectors as a guide to the regulation of labor conditions in the factories. This instruction was drafted by a certain Trutnev, an official in the office of the Moscow secret service under Zubatov.

The instruction met with much opposition from the Moscow Board for Factory Affairs,[10] since it made demands upon the employers which were not provided for by law. It was complied with by the latter only upon the insistence of the Moscow Governor-General, Grand Duke Sergei Aleksandrovich,[11] who in this instance was influenced by D. F. Trepov, who, in turn, shared and supported Zubatov's views.

To explain Zubatov's point of view it is necessary to recall that as early as 1886 a law had been passed regulating the employment of women and minors in factories. In its day, this early law was undoubtedly far in advance of the western European legislation on the same subject, and proved once more the extent to which an absolute monarchy could go in protecting the weak against the strong. Zubatov intended to follow this example.

That this instruction determining the relations between employers and workingmen was issued by police organs is an adverse comment on Witte's administration. Until 1905 the Department of Factory Inspection was in the Ministry of Finance and Witte should have taken a hand in employer-workman relations. Yet he seems never to have realized that the development of industry would bring in its wake a large working class and the many problems of the proletariat. In short, he was a Russian Colbert[12] set in the atmosphere of the nineteenth and twentieth centuries, with a seventeenth-century attitude toward world affairs and social problems. He considered it important to create favorable conditions in which capital could develop large industrial enterprises. This was his sole concern. The helpless position of the workingmen, their lack of organization, their low level of culture, and, consequently, their utter dependence upon their employers—all this well served the purposes of capital. Why, therefore, should he alter this state of things in order to insure the workingmen even a minimum of rights?

Be that as it may, at that time Russia had no industrial legislation to cope with the demands of a growing industry, and the factory inspection did not work efficiently (which may be explained to a degree by the fact that it had hardly any basis in law upon which to act). Consequently persons responsible for the preservation of order in the country were practically obliged to take steps which were in excess of their authority. Zubatov thought that the police might successfully combat the spread of revolutionary propaganda by persuading the working classes of the fallacies of revolutionary systems and ideas and of the harm that would come to the workers themselves from adopting them. He believed that the only true and steadfast protector of the people's interests was the Sovereign, whose office made him above personal considerations and whose authority was so great that he could force representatives of the capitalist class to fall in line with his plans for furthering the well-being of his people.

Zubatov was encouraged in believing that this scheme might be effective, since groups of workers in Moscow factories had displayed real interest in education and in learning more about the problems and relations of the different classes of society. The workers had even requested some of the Moscow professors to give a series of public lectures on this subject. To educate the workers in a definite direction was exactly what Zubatov planned that the police should do. He attracted to this task men who had at one time taken part in revolutionary activities but had seen the error of their ways and changed their opinions.* He laid his plans to a large scale. He organized in Moscow special courses for officers of the gendarme corps, who were taught the manifold theories of socialism and learned of the socialist parties of western Europe and of Russia. They had to study the works of Marx, Sombart,[14] Hertz,[15] and Kautsky,[16] and of the Russians Prokopovich,[17] Plekhanov,[18] and others. The purpose seemed to be to make these officers capable of carrying out their duties of police control and also to give them such information as might enable them to fight revolutionary socialism by refuting its

---

* One of these was L. A. Tikhomirov,[13] a former prominent member of the Narodnaia Volia party, whose change of allegiance was so sharp that after becoming a partisan of autocracy he became editor of the very reactionary *Moskovskiia Vedomosti*. He was also author of a booklet quite well known in Russia—*Pochemu ia perestal byt revoliutsionerom ("Why I Ceased to Be a Revolutionary")*. Very likely he was godfather of the system which came to be called *Zubatovshchina*.

theories and advancing others instead. This education also helped officers to question and to influence arrested revolutionists. This system was very similar to the method employed by Sudeikin[19] in trying the case of the revolutionary Degaev[20] in the early 'eighties. Sudeikin so persuaded Degaev of the falsity of his former convictions that the latter agreed to serve as informer on his companions while continuing to remain a member of their organizations. Sudeikin paid for this with his life in 1883. But Zubatov wanted to go further. He was not content to secure information by permitting converted members of revolutionary organizations to remain members of these organizations. In addition he intended to convert some able proletarian party workers into opponents of revolutionary theories and let them conduct counter-revolutionary propaganda among the workers. Just as Gorky[21] organized at Capri a school for the study of socialism in order to train revolutionary propagandists, so Zubatov dreamed of organizing a school for the education of counter-propagandists and apostles of autocracy.

Such plans were fantastic and bound to end in disaster. To unite under one roof the activities of the police and an educational system which aimed at altering the ideology of the working proletariat was to ruin both. Educational activity among the workers was combined with police measures and thereby acquired a special character. Thus, at meetings organized in Moscow labor districts by the secret police not only opponents of socialism spoke but also its leaders; frequently, however, the latter would be arrested after the meeting adjourned.

The converting of revolutionary workers arrested by the police amounted to creating a staff of revolutionists who were devoted to the government, but it provided no assurance that such conversions were not due merely to the fact that the government not only exonerated them but also provided them with a means of livelihood. It is hard to determine the sincerity or tenacity of a person's convictions. It is even harder to discover why a person holds the convictions he does. But when the change of a person's convictions inevitably leads to the improvement of his material condition, it is sheer naïveté to trust the sincerity and depth of his new credo. Yet such naïve trust was the basis on which reformed revolutionists were used as collaborators. I doubt if anybody failed to realize that revolutionists admitted as collaborators were nothing more than traitors attracted by pecuniary considerations.

It must be admitted, however, that Zubatov's attempt to alter the ideology of the working masses met with some success, at least outwardly. On February 19, 1902, there was a huge workers' manifestation in Moscow in commemoration of the emancipation of the peasants. A large crowd of more than fifty thousand workers marched through Moscow, assembled before the monument of Alexander II at the Kremlin, heard a requiem mass for him, and placed a wreath on his tomb. All high officials, headed by Moscow's Governor-General, Grand Duke Sergei Aleksandrovich, were present at this ceremony. This manifestation was to demonstrate the solidarity of the Tsar and the working masses.

But a nightingale cannot be fed on fairy tales. The workingmen might have been persuaded that their best friend and their only protector was the government, but they had yet to see any actual evidence that this was true. Then, at the psychological moment, there was an accident! A worker in the Goujon factory lost an arm. For some reason the owners refused to pay him suitable compensation. Zubatov's agents organized a strike at the factory and the government authorities took the matter into their hands and forced the owners to pay the crippled worker a large compensation. This solution of the question may have been entirely just, but it associated the government authorities with lawlessness and introduced into the relations between workers and employers an element of arbitrariness which ultimately had deplorable results. The same procedure was applied to an accident in the Danilov factory, when the police organized an uprising as a result of the owner's refusal to comply with some demand of the workers.

It goes without saying that no administration can go far along this hazardous path. It can never satisfy or even hope to satisfy all the demands of the workers, and each of its failures will only assist revolutionary elements in sowing seeds of discontent among the working masses. Moreover, this discontent will be directed not against employers and capitalists but against the government, which with unfortunate shortsightedness had undertaken to protect the interests of the workers not within the law but at its own discretion. It is quite another matter to create by legislation a set of conditions whereby the workers themselves can protect their own interests.

How can it be explained that Plehve, who must have realized this, not only made no attempt to stop Zubatov in his activities but even transferred him to St. Petersburg, thus tacitly approving his system or at any rate allowing him to apply it on a still wider scale? Several explanations might be suggested. First, and most important, Plehve hoped that Zubatov, working in St. Petersburg under Plehve's more immediate control, would not go to the extremes to which he apparently had gone in Moscow. Of course, Plehve was powerless to stop Zubatov's activity altogether. His conferences with the Grand Duke Sergei Aleksandrovich, who was under the influence of Trepov, had convinced him that he could not alter the Grand Duke's support of Zubatov, and a struggle with the Grand Duke was out of the question. Nevertheless, he hoped to keep Zubatov's activities within limits. Second, Plehve intended to familiarize himself with the results of Zubatov's policy and, using the data furnished by Zubatov as a point of departure, first to bring under his own control the factory inspection and later to undertake a radical reform of industrial legislation. To this end he wished to establish within his ministry a special Chief Administration of Labor, thereby following up an idea which had originated in the ministry in Sipiagin's time. Plehve realized that such a step would involve him in conflict with Witte, but he was preparing for this struggle.

In Plehve's estimation, therefore, Zubatov's work was in one sense a preliminary test and in another a step toward putting the entire labor problem upon an altogether different footing.

Zubatov himself did not regard his work in this light. He planned to extend his anti-socialist propaganda through all large industrial centers, organized and controlled by local sections of secret police.* In pursuit of this plan he came into close contact with the priest, Gapon,[22] whose activity showed its full results in January 1905. Also as a result of his system, the secret police penetrated into revolutionary circles by means of its revolutionary collaborators and, wittingly or unwittingly, converted these collaborators into *agents provocateurs*. In order to secure material for their reports and thereby to justify the receipt of money paid them for their "services," these *agents provocateurs* as members of revolutionary organizations were obliged to adopt the practice of inciting their fellow-revolutionists to revolutionary acts and uprisings. Nor was the secret police averse to creating fictitious terrorist plans on the basis of which they could arrest the most outstanding revolutionary workers. It was indeed a vicious circle. Secret police agents penetrated into revolutionary hid-

* For an account of the results of this program see below, pp. 342–48.

ing-places, and in return the revolutionists penetrated into the sanctum of the secret police. It was almost impossible to determine where secret police agents stopped and revolutionists began.

Plehve made a grave mistake in permitting the Zubatovshchina to continue, and he paid for this mistake with his life. Yet this was not his only nor his gravest mistake. He erred even more seriously in failing to differentiate between those revolutionary elements which strove to undermine the political and, to an even greater degree, the social structure of the state, and those public forces which, although in opposition to the government, were nevertheless opposed to the radical changes advocated by the socialists.

Years have passed. Today we have advanced far beyond the ideas popular in bureaucratic circles at the beginning of the century, and we can hardly believe that intelligent, educated statesmen devoted to the interests of Russia could have considered liberal zemstvo circles and other circles of Russian society in the same light as they considered the purely revolutionary elements. Even less can we justify their use of the same punitive measures against revolutionists and liberals alike.

A year before the manifesto of October 17, 1905, the very word "constitution" was illegal in Russia and had to be camouflaged under the expression "regime of equity." The use of even this modified form brought severe censure. This seems hard to believe, yet it is true, and Plehve considered it necessary to combat the liberal constitutional movement with the same ruthlessness as he fought the Socialist-Revolutionist movement. It appeared that the upper circles of the administration feared the constitutional movement more than the popular revolutionary one, for the revolutionary workers were persecuted only in so far as they were the executors of terrorist acts. The constitutional movement, which would have brought about the next and inevitable change in the form of government and was therefore open to suspicion, seemed to be much more formidable and dangerous.*

* Prince V. P. Meshchersky, talented and cynical publisher of *Grazhdanin,* had assisted Plehve in securing his appointment as Minister of the Interior; but directly after Plehve's assassination Meshchersky turned against the policy Plehve had followed. The Prince has aptly described the activity of the Police Department: "The police knew who subscribed to and read the prohibited foreign publications; they knew who criticized the government and how severe the criticisms were; they knew that there were printing shops which issued proclamations; they knew what was being written about the Minister of the Interior in correspondence between friends—in short, the police knew many things which it was not absolutely

This lumping together of all the elements of opposition had the most deplorable results for the country. It united in the struggle against the existing state order the elements which previously had had nothing in common, either organically or in their aspirations. On the contrary, these diverse elements had been even more hostile to each other than, let us say, the liberal zemstvo or even the municipal public circles had been toward the supporters of autocracy.

Plehve's second ambition was to reform central and local administration in such a way as to adjust its functions to changed conditions and put it in direct touch with the municipality and zemstvo organizations. Actually, however, hostilities between representatives of liberal zemstvo circles and the government grew sharper during Plehve's administration. Sipiagin, in spite of his archaic interpretation of the duties of government and his patently reactionary sympathies, was closer to the liberal zemstvos and understood them better than did Plehve with all his intelligence, his education, and his considerably deeper understanding of state problems. Sipiagin had begun his career as an elected official and had belonged to a Right-wing zemstvo; he spoke the zemstvo language and knew the zemstvos too well to consider them dangerous to the state. With Plehve on the other hand, everything, even his manner—his courteous but cold imperious treatment of the chairmen of zemstvo boards and of city mayors— antagonized them. He never did win the support of the vital forces of the country. Industrial circles could not become reconciled to the Zubatovshchina and in consequence sharply opposed the government. The zemstvos and landed gentry regarded him as a stranger who was powerful and influential only by virtue of the official posi-

necessary for them to know. One thing only the police did not know, and that was the most important. They did not know what was going on in the dark terrorist circles. This state of affairs had come to exist since the days of the Third Section,[23] whose function it had been to direct and control Russian thought. To this function was now added the surveillance of a mass of purely personal affairs; it seemed like probing into the private lives of people in search of gossip. The regular routine work of secret police—that is, the safeguarding against and prevention of unlawful actions—was but a drop in the sea as compared with the tireless and meticulous efforts of the Third Section to ferret out information about people's private lives. As a result, the Third Section proved to be unable to check various recent plans of the terrorists, who carried out their plots unhindered. Inquests showed that invariably the success of a terroristic act was directly due to the unpreparedness of the police. And at this same time numbers of people were being put under arrest for the opinions they held. The Police Department had inherited the logic of the Third Section and now its main concern was to discover what the people were thinking."

tion he held. But at that time high official position was not sufficient to effect the materialization of plans and ambitions. The public, silenced and oppressed, could not accomplish anything either, it
is true; but its power of passive resistance was too great for any
police or administrative measures to overcome.

Plehve can hardly be blamed for his faith in the power of the
government, for who among his colleagues, many of whom later
rushed to the Left, did not at that time believe that the bureaucracy
was capable of realizing any measure and accomplishing any end.
Actually, Plehve was more farsighted than many of his contemporaries, for he had an apprehension that the existing state apparatus
was unable to handle all sides of national life or satisfy all public
wants and his first step as Minister of the Interior was to introduce
into the State Council representatives of the upper strata of public
circles. When he went to Poltava to investigate the agrarian uprisings there, he convoked an assembly of the zemstvo workers and
placed before them a question of great state significance. He spoke
of the troubles which beset the country, pointed out the necessity of
close co-operation between the government and the public, and asked
them to say by what means, in their opinion, such co-operation might
be effected. He virtually told them how to answer: that the public
should be given a more direct participation in the government of the
country. But the zemstvo men, terrified by the looting of private
property, suggested nothing except the need of an ordinance for increased protection in their gubernia. Plehve returned to St. Petersburg and in his first report to the Tsar said: "If twenty years ago,
when I was head of the Police Department, someone had said that
Russia was on the verge of revolution, I should have smiled. Now,
Your Majesty, I am obliged to regard the matter differently."

Plehve then began to study all former projects which suggested
that representatives of the people should have a share in the government. He excavated from the archives the projects of Valuev,[24]
Loris-Melikov,[25] and Count N. P. Ignatev, all of which discussed
the matter of popular representation in government. Cautiously and
gradually he acquainted the Tsar with these projects without initiating even his colleagues into his plans; as a consequence his
plans remained unknown to the public and even to St. Petersburg
bureaucrats. At the same time he tried to establish closer contact
with the leaders of the zemstvos through D. N. Shipov,[26] Chairman
of the Zemstvo Board of Moscow Gubernia. But here he met with

open hostility. Shipov bluntly announced that the progressive zemstvo could not and would not make friends with the present personnel of the administration and with Plehve in particular.[27] Plehve soon abandoned his idea of introducing a constitutional regime into Russia, especially since the idea was not supported by the Tsar.

But Plehve persisted in the opinion that co-operation between government and public was of utmost importance. He resolved to begin at the bottom. Accordingly he projected a gubernia reform which was to affect not only institutions of the central government but also those of the zemstvos and municipalities. He aimed not to narrow down the ranks of the municipal electors and the scope of their activities, but to co-ordinate their activities with the work of the central government. In many instances he provided that the public should have the last word in its co-operation with the government.*

Had Plehve's system been adopted in 1866, when the zemstvos and municipal self-government were established, it would probably have prevented that antagonism which gradually developed between many officials of the central government and institutions of local self-government. Perhaps it would have prevented the hostility which grew up between these two camps which Krivoshein dubbed "we" and "they." But at the beginning of the twentieth century, after the institutions had been in existence nearly forty years, it was hopeless to attempt to unite into one organism working to one common end the institutions of the zemstvos and municipal self-government with the central governmental organs. Even the most conservative, the least progressive, zemstvo workers would have opposed such a union. In fact this division into "we" and "they" was

---

* Plehve had in mind the French system by which the organs of local self-government work in close contact with local representatives of the central government so that the Prefect takes part in the local department meetings of deputies (which correspond to our gubernia zemstvo assemblies) and has also the right to confirm separate articles of local budgets if these articles exceed three hundred francs, since in French law *la commune est mineure*. The commune of Paris is the exception. It has a different organization and its head is appointed by the central government and not elected.

But Plehve failed to take into consideration that the French government was the outcome of public tendencies, and that it worked under the constant and vigilant supervision of an organized and well-developed public opinion. Under these conditions representatives of the central government do not abuse their right of veto and their powers of initiative in local self-government. On the contrary, they are rather unwilling to exercise these powers and are criticized for their unwillingness.

not only manifest in the relations between the representatives of the central government and the most advanced zemstvo elements but was also reflected, only in a more subdued form, in the critical attitude of all zemstvo representatives toward all bureaucrats.

Thus, it was not uncommon even among the more conservative circles of the zemstvo to hear it said of some deputy of the zemstvo who was also in the service of the government, "Oh, he is one of us; he is a zemstvo man." In a word, there was submission to the government, but the governmental personnel was considered something alien, something characterized by bureaucratic formalism. Curiously enough, this attitude was shared even by bureaucratic circles both in the capital and in the provinces. It was a patent example of innate Russian anarchism, a distinctively Russian attitude of half-scornful, half-hostile treatment of any authority; it was possibly a heritage of the ancient Tartar dominion when authority was actually the enemy of the entire people. Undoubtedly the Bolsheviks encouraged this attitude.

Plehve succeeded in carrying out some of his plans concerning the unification and co-operation of government and public. He issued a new regulation concerning the municipal government of St. Petersburg whereby the chairmanship of the Gubernia Special Board for Municipal Affairs[28] was given to a person appointed by the Sovereign and not to the city mayor. This was intended to be a mark of particular consideration for the city Duma. At the same time the privileges of this Board in the regulation of city affairs were increased. It was given the right to protect certain interests of the city population in the event that the city Duma did not do so. To this end the Special Board was apportioned a yearly sum of 25,000 rubles. The liberal press approved the new regulation chiefly because it increased the number of electors of city deputies by including persons who resided in the city and paid no less than 1,080 rubles annual rent for lodging.

Another measure, also intended to effect closer co-operation between the public and the government, produced several different reactions when its separate clauses were studied. It proposed that a special council, which was to include representatives of various ministries and the representatives of zemstvo and municipal institutions, be attached to the Department of Economy in the Ministry of the Interior. This department was renamed in 1904 the Chief Administration and Council for the Affairs of Local Economy. This special council was to meet annually and deliberate on questions of local concern, including those entailing new legislation.

The measure was generally well received, but the progressive circles of the municipalities and zemstvos were very much displeased with the provision whereby representatives of local self-government were included in the council not as deputies elected by zemstvo assemblies and city dumas but as appointees of the Ministry of the Interior. To be sure there were technical difficulties in the way of having the zemstvo assemblies and city dumas elect their own representatives to this council. For instance, the number of zemstvo and municipal representatives that were to participate in the work of the council was smaller than the actual number of gubernias and cities which enjoyed the right to elect representatives; consequently it was impossible to have each gubernia and each municipality represented in this council. Yet there was no special organization at that time which united all zemstvos and all municipalities. The difficulty of having each gubernia and each municipality represented could have been overcome by the introduction of a two-grade system of election to this council, but this was not according to Plehve's plans; for to unite all organs of local self-government into one whole was to give them more significance and power.

Another objection to the measure was raised on the following ground: There is no doubt that the inclusion of the zemstvo men in some central administrative institutions or temporary commissions was a mighty weapon in the hands of the Minister of the Interior; it served to encourage those of the zemstvo men who were more devoted to the government than were their fellows, and it also enabled the administration to obtain the support of moderate zemstvo circles in the solution of some problems. The zemstvo dubbed this measure "a falsification" of public opinion, a characterization which was adopted by all zemstvo workers irrespective of their political inclinations. It was pointed out that the inviting of chairmen and members of the zemstvo boards as representatives of the opinions of the zemstvos was essentially incorrect. The zemstvo assemblies elected their boards merely for the purpose of managing local economies and did not vest them with any authority to express zemstvo opinions regarding questions pertaining to the essence of zemstvo organization. This attitude was characteristic of the representatives of a moderate group of the zemstvo workers. "We elected them," they would say, "to attend to the laundering of the sheets of zemstvo hospitals, and not to represent our opinions and wishes." This same attitude was reflected also in the circles of the landed gentry, even among the most moderate ones. Count Dorrer, marshal of the nobility of Belgorod Uezd in Kursk Gubernia and later the leader of the extreme Right faction in the Third Duma, raised this question before the Kursk assembly of the nobility. He took his stand upon the new regulation of the State Council published on the occasion of its centennial jubilee. This regulation authorized the chairman of the State Council to invite for work in different preparatory commissions, dealing with the examination of complicated and serious legislative projects, persons whose occupations and experience made them of value in performing the work in question. Stressing the element of guesswork which dominated the selection of "informed persons" (*sveduiushchie liudi*)[29] Count Dorrer suggested that the assembly petition that assemblies of the nobility be given the right to elect from their number certain persons whom they considered worthy of representing them in various government conferences and commissions. This procedure, according to Count Dorrer, would assure "fairer representation and prove more efficacious than the one now in use."

Plehve's hope of unifying the public and the government by attracting zemstvo workers to share the work of the central administration went unrealized and failed to win for him the sympathies of the zemstvos; in fact, it never attained any real significance, especially since elective legislative bodies were soon to appear to which expression of public moods and hopes gravitated. Besides, the projected council for the affairs of local economy had not even convened before Plehve's death.

Plehve achieved even less success in his efforts to correct the extreme centralization of government which affected even the remotest regions of the empire. He fully shared Lamennais'[30] opinion: *"La centralisation amène à l'apoplexie du centre et à la paralysie des extremités."*

The central administration was overburdened with questions of secondary importance pertaining to the border regions. This burden became more and more difficult to bear with each passing year. But it was the border regions themselves which suffered most from this centralization both in questions touching upon the interests of private persons and in those of general regional interest. Legislation pertaining to regional needs was perforce lacking in consideration of local peculiarities, since it was drafted usually in St. Petersburg offices by persons unfamiliar with the region. Not that these legislative projects were worked out carelessly; on the contrary, they were usually the result of concentrated effort and hard thinking. But the total amount of work our ministries had to do was tremendous and they were not equal to the task.*

But there was one obstacle in the way of relieving the ministries of their load and transferring the bulk of the work to the regions: local administration could not be relied upon. The more remote a region was from the metropolis, the more did local ways differ from those of the capital and the more insistent was the need of transferring to it the decision of purely local problems; but because of its low cultural level it was the policy of greater danger to make the local government wholly responsible for its own administration. When persons who worked modestly and conscientiously in St. Petersburg were transferred to some border region they fell victims to the general atmosphere prevailing there and became stupid, headstrong autocrats. When even governors of our central gubernias sometimes acquired the habits of satraps, one can easily imagine what often happened to administrators in obscure and remote regions populated by non-Russians. The reason for their satrap-like ways was the extremely low cultural level of the masses. There was no organized and influential public opinion, such as existed in St. Petersburg, which alone could have made these petty autocrats more temperate and more attentive to the wishes of the people. Even in such important gubernias as Kharkov, Kiev, and Odessa, the administrative power was the Alpha and Omega; public opinion was nonexistent. This situation made for a ridiculous parade of authority and was a factor in creating the almost standard type of "lady governor" (*gubernatorsha*). For instance, there were occasions when a play in a theater would be delayed awaiting the arrival of the "chief of the gubernia," or even when all traffic in the streets would be halted in the expectation of his appearance. Even zemstvo workers upon being appointed to administrative posts in the gubernias, which happened quite often, speedily acquired auto-

---

* Take for example the question of the national minorities. How could one small office hope to cope with the extensive and complicated problem of the administration and agrarian organization of the Kirghiz, Bashkirs, Buriats, Kalmyks, and many other small nationalities? This small office was in the Peasant Section (*Zemskii Otdel*)[31] of the Ministry of the Interior, and numbered only three workers!

cratic traits which they had formerly criticized very bitterly. It was far more permissible for a gubernia publication to criticize the activities of the government in general than to disapprove of a specific act of the gubernia or even the uezd administrator. On the one hand this may be explained by the low level of education of the local press employees and of the population at large. A criticism of the central authority and institutions had no practical effect upon their standing, but a criticism of the local authorities would have quite another effect. The local satraps considered that such criticism undermined their authority and lessened their prestige. On the other hand, the prestige of the government's representative was absolutely necessary for the maintenance of order in many regions of Russia, particularly in her eastern parts, where population was sparse. To permit criticism of local administration was to undermine the foundation upon which rested the public order of many localities. The combination of these circumstances presented a dilemma: either to limit the competence of local administration, and thus bring about a slow and ineffective solution of local problems; or to vest local administration with complete power, which might increase its arbitrariness, since there was no guaranty that the local administrators would correctly understand the interests of the state and mete out justice to individual interests. And as the years went by and the economic activity of the population increased without a corresponding rise in its cultural level, the dilemma became more perplexing.

The matter of centralized administration for our possessions in Central Asia and the Far East and the attempt to extend to them the laws and administrative customs in force in Russia proper presented still another aspect of the problem. This aspect was psychological. These possessions were really no more than colonies. Now the term "colony" usually implies a possession separated from the parent state by intervening foreign territory or by water, particularly the latter. But our possessions, though peopled by alien nationalities, were territories contiguous to Russia proper and were regarded by state authorities and public alike as a part of the empire which should have an administrative system corresponding to that of the central government. What should have been done was to establish another ministry for these territories, say, a Ministry of Colonies, and apply to them some colonial system. We should then have avoided such nonsense, for instance, as the granting to half-savage tribes of Kirghiz, Buriats, and Bashkirs the same electoral rights as were given the inhabitants of central Russian areas.

Despite all this Plehve took a step toward the decentralization of administration. At his instance the Tsar convoked under his own chairmanship a special conference of ministers (1903) to consider problems of remote regions. The ministers were requested to make lists of those problems which were then under their competence and which might be transferred to the competence of those regions. All departments of the Ministry of the Interior were ordered to compile such lists and were requested to make them as inclusive as possible. Consequently the list submitted by the Ministry of the Interior was rather large. As far as I can remember, it was confirmed by the Tsar in its entirety and the changes in local government, which could be made without legislation, were effected by the Sovereign order of December 10, 1903; the rest were transferred to a special "Commission on Decentralization" under the chairmanship of State Councilor (*statskii sovetnik*)[32] Platonov. The State Council approved the recommendations of Platonov's commission and these became law when confirmed by the Emperor on April 19, 1904.

But Plehve's decentralization measures had no essential significance. Actually, the ministries had never worked out the matters of which they were now relieved; they had merely made final decisions on measures proposed by local authorities. All that had been accomplished was to decrease useless bureaucratic correspondence and, perhaps, to speed up administrative procedure; provinces remained just as dependent upon the central government as before.

Plehve projected still another reform, also of a bureaucratic nature. He proposed to reorganize most departments of the Ministry of the Interior by merging some of them into several chief administrations. This measure aimed to free the minister of the necessity of studying and elaborating routine matters and technical legislative projects. Plehve proposed that the heads of such chief administrations should communicate directly with the heads of other ministries and even submit projects to the State Council and defend them before this body. This was but a recognition of the established fact that all such projects were decided by the directors of departments anyway and that the minister's signature was affixed as a matter of course. True, some ministers were more scrupulous and considered it their duty to read all documents which they signed; but these were exceptions to the general rule. Plehve used to say that he often found I. N. Durnovo, former Minister of the Interior, stupid with fatigue and with his eyes literally bulging as a result of reading the enormous number of such documents; yet Durnovo never made any changes in the projects his ministry submitted to the State Council. Even had he wished to do so it would have been almost impossible, since he was presented with the documents in their final draft and in printed form. It was equally fitting that the heads of chief administrations and directors of departments should defend the projects in the State Council, since the minister seldom appeared there and generally delegated one of his assistants to perform this task.

The freeing of the minister from direct participation in matters of secondary importance would have enabled him to analyze freely and calmly the fundamental problems of state life. It would have made the minister not a mere cog in the machinery of the state but a statesman in the true sense of the word. All ministers of any prominence realized the necessity of this step, but in practice they got around the difficulty of too much work by transferring the bulk of it to their assistants. Plehve, for particular reasons, did not wish to follow this practice. He had inherited his assistants from Sipiagin. With all of them he had formerly been closely associated, and he could not bring himself to dismiss any of them. On the other hand, he had personally selected many directors of departments whom he trusted to a far greater degree than he did his assistants. It was inevitable, therefore, that the center of gravity in his ministry should shift to the directors of departments. Besides, by making the Minister of the Interior the directing and controlling head of a number of chief administrations, Plehve intended—and of this more will be said later—to make the Minister of the Interior the actual, if not the official, controller of the entire state policy. This ambition did not develop in Plehve's mind until later. At first he strove merely to improve the organization of the ministry so that he might have more leisure to decide upon matters of general importance. The Emperor himself had once told Plehve that he, Nicholas II, was always glad to get away from the capital to Livadia, where there were no daily reports to hear and people to see and where he could forget everyday cares and considerations and engross himself in questions of state significance.

CHAPTER XI

THE PEASANT PROBLEM

Plehve's third project, the reform of peasant legislation, also remained unrealized, but the work he did accomplish in this direction led to the Imperial Ukase of November 9, 1906,[1] which cleared the way for the solution of the land-commune problem.*

The need of a revision of peasant legislation had become evident as early as the reign of Alexander III, but nothing had been done except to make (1895) certain preliminary investigations of local institutions through the medium of special gubernia conferences, and to publish the material gathered in this way. It fell to Sipiagin's lot to go a step farther. In accordance with his suggestion, an Imperial Ukase of January 14, 1902, directed the Minister of the Interior to revise peasant legislation so as to "co-ordinate it with the real needs of the population and the well-being of the Empire." This was vague direction, but no other instruction was given. It reminded one of the famous resolutions passed by the Chinese authorities charging "the proper administration to take appropriate measures." I do not know how Sipiagin intended to go about the work of revision; in fact I have some doubts that he himself knew clearly what he would do. But one thing is certain; he did not intend to introduce any radical changes in peasant conditions; the entire reform would be very conservative. This was guaranteed as much by the personality of Sipiagin as by the fact that the work was to be conducted under the direction of A. S. Stishinsky, Sipiagin's assistant.

When Plehve was appointed Minister of the Interior in May 1902, this preliminary work had gone no farther than an exchange of correspondence with the Ministry of Finance on the subject of money appropriations for this work, and, if my memory serves me right, the rather large sum of some 120,000 rubles a year for five years had been requested. The Ministry of Finance had con-

---

* I was very closely and constantly associated with this part of Plehve's work and for that reason I hope to be excused for treating this part of my memoirs more personally.

sidered this amount excessive and had indulged in lively arguments with the Ministry of the Interior. The only other beginning had been made by the Peasant Section which had compiled a rough project on village communal taxation (*mirskie sbory*).[2]

Hardly anyone was certain what direction this work would take under Plehve. Conflicting political opinions complicated the peasant problems. The group of the extreme Right made a fetish of the land commune just as the revolutionary democratic circles did, though, of course, from another angle. Similarly, a portion of the intelligentsia with socialistic sympathies defended the idea of peasant-class courts and peasant-class self-government with just as much fervor as did the majority of the ultraconservatives.

Like everyone else, I had no idea what policy Plehve would follow. I did know, however, that no matter what policy he adopted he would apply all his strength to carry it through. I had a strong desire to participate closely in this work. I had begun my government service in the government's Board for Peasant Affairs in the gubernias of the Kingdom of Poland.[3] I was familiar, too, both as landowner and as a regular summer visitor in the country since childhood, with the conditions of peasant life in Great Russia. My experience had formed in me a strong conviction that the most formidable barrier to the development of the peasant masses, and therefore of the entire empire, was that anachronism, the land commune. It was therefore my dream to become closely associated with the revision of peasant legislation in order to contribute as much as I could to the immediate dissolution of the commune. In this respect fortune smiled upon me. One of the first persons Plehve dismissed from a responsible position in the Ministry of the Interior was Savich,[4] the Head of the Peasant Section. This section had charge of the entire peasant problem, and was now to carry out the work of the revision. I decided to take advantage of the situation and sent Plehve a letter stating my sincere desire to be appointed to the vacant post.

My procedure was unusual. Persons striving to obtain some position or other usually worked through third persons who had influence or were closely related to the person on whom the appointment depended. But, as far as I know, no one had ever attempted to petition personally for a position, especially in writing. Moreover, Plehve had met me only in the Imperial Chancellery, where I had been an Assistant State Secretary. Our official relations had been limited to the fact that I had composed several letters* in French for him when he was appointed State Secretary for the Grand Duchy of Finland.

I have no doubt that my action surprised Plehve; but it brought results. In a courteous note he invited me to call on him to discuss my letter. When I called he explained frankly that as yet he had no one in mind for the vacant post but that he would have to be very cautious in filling it, since it would require a man who with the help of some assistants could handle the actual revision, an undertaking which both he and the Tsar considered of the utmost importance. "All I can suggest," he said, "is that you should use the four months' vacation, granted by the Imperial Chancellery, to compile a project for a new peasant self-government. Some officials of the Peasant Section will assist you." Before I left, he invited me to a conference which was to be held in a few days under his chairmanship and which was to discuss the Peasant Section's project on the taxation of the peasant community.

During this conversation Plehve did not state the basic considerations upon which the revision was to be worked out; nor did he ask my opinion on this subject; nor did I offer it. But as a matter of fact, during the winter of 1902–3 I had published in *Novoe Vremia* a series of articles entitled "Zemledelie i Zarabotki" ("Agriculture and Earnings"), and in these I had pointed out that the education of the peasant masses, desirable as it was, would be of little use in developing agriculture as long as the land commune existed. The commune, I maintained, held its members to the level of the dullest and least energetic, and nullified the progressive efforts of those who were more intelligent and more energetic. The only sure way to break the fetters that bound Russian peasants and to raise the level of peasant prosperity was to remove the restrictions upon the peasants themselves. Since *Novoe Vremia* was widely read, I had reason to suppose that Plehve was already aware of my opinion on this subject. Later I found I had been mistaken.

At any rate, I accepted Plehve's invitation to the conference and hastened to familiarize myself with the project the Peasant Section had worked out. In my conversations with the officials in that section, I discovered two things: First, that the self-government

* These letters had been addressed to representatives of the Old Finnish party, which was less hostile to Russian rule and with which Plehve tried to establish friendly relations and a common line of conduct.

of the peasant class was to remain unaltered so that there could be no talk of organizing an all-class volost or a small zemstvo unit;[5] second, that the main reason for the proposed revision of peasant legislation was Witte's desire to decrease as much as possible the dues levied by village communities in order that peasant payments might find their way into the central treasury in the form of direct taxation and in payment of redemption dues, the arrears on which continued to grow. This was the same idea that Witte had had when he applied in 1901, with Sipiagin's help, the law of June 12, 1900,[6] limiting zemstvo taxation. He had also persuaded Sipiagin to revise peasant legislation; and now, in accord with this scheme, the first question to be put before the Ministry of the Interior was the revision of the regulation on the taxation of the village community, regardless of the fact that such revision had no direct connection with the general question of reorganizing peasant self-government.

The conference soon met, including among its members A. S. Stishinsky and P. N. Durnovo, assistants to the Minister of the Interior, and Ya. Ya. Litvinov[7] and G. V. Glinka,[8] assistants to the Director of the Department of Peasant Colonization.[9] I opposed the drafted project on the ground that there could be no satisfactory solution to the problem of taxation of the village community until this community, which took charge of certain general matters of economy and administration, was separated from the land commune, which was merely an economic association, or rather an agglomeration of co-owners of a definite land area. This separation, I held, was all the more necessary since the village communities were not coextensive with the land communes in membership and territorial limits; some of the village communities included several separate land communes whereas others included only some members of a certain land commune. Besides, there existed in Russia a great many large so-called "mixed" estate villages—that is, those which before the liberation of the serfs had belonged in part to several landowners and therefore were composed of several separate land communes and just as many separate village assemblies. Consequently, there did not exist in such a village any common organ of local authority to attend to the affairs of this village as a whole.[10]

Litvinov answered my criticism with considerable agitation. I learned later that he was the author of the project and had some hopes of being appointed Head of the Peasant Section. His defense of his project was weak, and was made more so by his unfortunate stuttering, which his excitement aggravated. His arguments brought forth from Plehve only a sardonic smile. My other critic, Stishinsky, concentrated his efforts not so much upon defending the project as upon defending and justifying his colleague Litvinov. Stishinsky was an authority on existing peasant legislation, and was now obliged to admit the correctness of my differentiation between the village community—an administrative unit—and the land commune—a purely economic unit. But he pointed out that this differentiation had no practical significance, that the peasants were accustomed to distinguish the affairs that came under the competence of the village assembly and that they convoked private assemblies composed only of members of the land commune for the discussion of land-commune problems, and held general assemblies for the discussion of affairs of the entire village community. Stishinsky characteristically insisted on the preservation of the existing law while admitting its formal incongruity.

I awaited Plehve's decision with trepidation. My future as well as the direction to be given to the work of revision depended upon his decision. A plan based on my point of view would anticipate the development of a project on peasant self-government which with little additional work could be transformed into a statute establishing the principle of an all-class village community and an all-class volost. For this, two steps were necessary: First, to recognize as an institution of civil law the land commune, which was a distinct class organization made so by a sacred and inviolable regulation on the non-transferability of allotted lands to any class but the peasants; second, when this had been accomplished, to include in the membership of a volost all who owned immovable property within the confines of the volost, thus forming an all-class volost.* I had hopes, moreover, that such a plan would be successful. My hopes were based on the fact that new projects on peasant legislation would be first submitted for discussion to local people in collaboration with local public men. These, I was convinced, would suggest changes in keeping with their long-standing desire to break down the existing wall of legislation which separated the peasants from all other rural classes.

---

*In the spring of 1914 in the State Council I defended the small land unit against the attack of the Right. The project for organizing a small all-class self-governing unit had been adopted by the Duma, but with only indifferent support from the government it was defeated in the upper chamber.

In the course of the discussion it was clearly revealed that Plehve and the others were not too familiar with the peculiarities of peasant life. I happened to mention that the only important difference between communal [i.e., repartitional] and hereditary household land tenure, particularly in those communes which no longer reapportioned the land periodically, was that the members of the commune had no right to sell their allotments while one whose land was held in household tenure had such a right. Yet in localities where both forms of land tenure existed and in communes which had not reapportioned the land for some time it often happened that even commune members sold their allotments, usually to their fellow-villagers.

When Plehve heard this, he asked with great surprise: "Are you sure of that?" and turned for corroboration to Stishinsky, who confined himself to observing that such sales were absolutely illegal and that should such a transaction come to the knowledge of the Senate it would no doubt be voided. I admitted that Stishinsky's observation was perfectly correct but maintained that it did not alter the facts of the case. Under either system of land tenure the owner was unable completely to exploit his allotment. In neither case, for instance, did he have the right to fence off his narrow strips of land scattered in the different fields. These strips, when they were left fallow or after harvest, were turned into common pasture on which the cattle of the entire village population would graze. This prevented the land cultivators, even though their land was their own possession, from utilizing their land as they thought best. As a result both types of peasants had to submit to the rotation system adopted by the land communes—they had to let their lands lie fallow at the same time and sow the same crops which would ripen about the same time so that the entire field might be turned into a pasture at once. I pointed out that a similar situation had once existed in western Europe and still existed in some localities. There was a special German name for it: *Flurzwang*.

My arguments seemed to convince Plehve that my information was correct and to give him a rather exaggerated opinion of my knowledge of peasant customs and life. At any rate, he charged me with the compilation of a project on peasant self-government based upon the views which I had just expounded. At the same time he told Litvinov and Glinka that he wished them to aid me. We three agreed to meet in the evenings to discuss the problem.

I set to work the very next day. At first my collaborators assumed toward me a cool and critical attitude, which became more pronounced after I announced that I hoped to finish the task in two weeks, after which I intended to go to my country estate to write a memorandum to be attached to the project. Their attitude was quite understandable. They had had but little experience in central legislative or administrative matters—Litvinov had been a member of Simbirsk Gubernia Special Board and Glinka of Smolensk Gubernia Special Board. With their provincial outlook, they expected to see in one who had spent five years in the Imperial Chancellery the quintessence of bureaucratic formalism. But as our work progressed and my colleagues became convinced that even less than two weeks would be necessary to complete it, their attitude changed. Very likely also they began to suspect that I would be their permanent chief.

In our work we took from the recently published supplement to Volume IX of our Code the existing regulations on peasant self-government and, with these as a basis, outlined the changes we considered desirable. When we had finished I went to my estate near the city of Tver,* where I worked over what we had done and set about writing the memorandum to be attached to our project. I tried to be as brief as possible and to discuss only the essence of the problem and the solution proposed. An attempt at brevity was a departure from custom, for projects and memoranda usually attained the proportions of large folios.† By the beginning of August

---

* Before leaving St. Petersburg I had asked Plehve's permission to familiarize myself with the activity of the volost boards (*volostnoe pravlenie*)[11] by studying them in several volosts of Tver Gubernia. He had willingly consented. This study took quite a time and aroused the open displeasure of the Governor of Tver, Prince N. D. Golitsyn[12] (later, Golitsyn became the last Chairman of the Council of Ministers). My explanations that my study was in no sense an inspection availed nothing and the governor insisted that he could not permit me to carry on this study except in the presence of a member of the Gubernia's Special Board. Consequently I had to drag after me everywhere an incompetent person who remained idle while I conducted lengthy conversations with volost elders (*starshiny*) and clerks, and familiarized myself with the incredible variety of affairs that came under volost boards. Most of these affairs had no connection whatever with peasant self-government and should obviously have come under the head of general administration.

† Since I was not inclined to fly in the face of current practice I entitled my memorandum: "An Extract from the Memorandum on the Project of the New Statute Concerning Peasant Self-Government." This title later caused some amusing misunderstandings. Persons interested in peasant reform somehow got hold of a copy of my report, the so-called "Extract," which was printed but not signed, and spent much time looking for the full memorandum when such a memorandum did not exist.

I was able to present my work in printed form to Plehve, who called another conference of the same personnel as had made up the previous conference in the beginning of June. This second conference was to examine and discuss the work my collaborators and I had done in the interim.

I was worried as I awaited the conference, since I had included in the project some innovations which I feared would not be acceptable to such a champion of the existing order as Stishinsky. The project made the volost a territorial unit that included the lands of peasants and of all other classes as well. In step with this it provided for a reformed volost assembly of fewer members than were provided for by the existing law. It looked forward to the unification of separate small volosts into larger groups, so that a volost board could be made into a collegiate assembly under the chairmanship of a volost elder; this grouping of small volosts into larger ones would also enable the volosts to be transformed into small zemstvo units. The minimum salary to be paid to the volost elders was stated and the discretion of the zemskie nachalniki was definitely limited; for instance, they were deprived of their right to put volost elders under arrest. All these provisions were mild and palliative, primarily because the existing law of taxation did not permit the levying of volost taxes on non-peasant lands, although situated within the volost. Volost taxes were levied only on persons belonging to the so-called former taxpaying classes.[13] It was absurd to preserve a system which made the peasants bear the whole burden of volost self-government, especially when this self-government acted on behalf of all persons residing in that volost regardless of their class. I had an idea that when my project was examined further, this point would be sure to attract the attention of partisans of an all-class volost, of whom there were a large number in the State Council.

The project also provided that peasants who had received secondary education and had the rank of honorary citizen were not to be excluded from the land commune, as under the existing law, and were not to lose their allotments of land, but were to remain members of their respective communes.

This was a serious innovation, since it made a break in the peasant world which had been impregnable against the penetration of alien elements. Current opinion regarded the peasant class as a uniform mass which was sure to be corrupted by the admixture of elements that had a different outlook on life and education or came from a different class. This point of view was supported both by the extreme conservatives and by the intelligentsia who had socialistic sympathies. Thus, as early as 1905, *Russkoe Bogatstvo,*[14] a magazine of definite Narodnik tendencies, expressed the opinion that "the peasants have common feelings, common movement, and no individual differences." On the other hand the revolutionary Emancipation of Labor Group[15] affirmed in the draft of a program of the Russian Social-Democrats published by it that only the working proletariat could lead the social movement in Russia; "the land commune, binding the peasants by communal interests alone, hinders their political and mental development." The members of the government seemed to have shared this opinion and supposed that the bringing together of the peasants and other classes, if only to consider common economic problems, would disrupt the unity of peasant views and conceptions and would furnish an opportunity for the penetration of pernicious revolutionary propaganda among the peasants. Obviously, this conception was erroneous. By the beginning of the present century the peasantry had given up its primitive ideas and was not a homogeneous mass with common feelings and ideas. During the preceding thirty years most of the peasants had served their terms in the army. Also they had been obliged in ever-increasing numbers to seek work away from home, and consequently many were rapidly becoming intermixed with factory workers. Artificial isolation of the peasants from the other agricultural classes in the field of rural self-government did not prevent the spread and the acceptance of revolutionary propaganda; but it did prevent the association of peasants with representatives of more cultured classes, an association of undoubted value, as was proved by the collaboration of the peasant class with the landed gentry in the uezd zemstvo assemblies. Here the peasants learned that the landed gentry was sincerely working for the best interests of the people, directing their energy to assist the peasants, and paying zemstvo taxes. But the advantages derived from their zemstvo work were small. Public education, medical aid, fire insurance, and agronomic measures—all these were intended to benefit the peasant population; the landed gentry benefited but little. The only thing that might have benefited the landed gentry was the construction of roads and bridges, and in these improvements a mere beginning had been made before the revolution because of shortage of funds.

The authorities feared that the pseudo-intellectuals with their revolutionary ideas would penetrate into the peasant class, which they did in the capacity of rural statisticians doing useless appraisal work. But this attitude of the authorities only resulted in isolating the peasants from the most cultured and essentially conservative elements of the population.

Since the emancipation of the serfs in the early 'sixties, the government had been in a difficult position. During the period of the reforms of Alexander II, it had been sincerely in favor of promoting the education and self-reliance of the masses. But from the very beginning it had had to contend with the revolutionary movement, which endeavored to use every move of the government to attain revolutionary ends. Even the Sunday schools, whose organization the government had wholeheartedly encouraged during the 'sixties, were invaded by anarchists like Kropotkin,[16] who succeeded in turning them into centers for revolutionary propaganda; and although the masses did not comprehend the philosophical aspect of this propaganda they were ready to accept that aspect of it which taught destruction. The government had a perfect right, in fact it was duty bound, to protect the state from the designs of men who were trying to undermine its very foundations. Nor is the guilt of the Russian revolutionary groups limited to the direct and unfathomable harm they did the Russian people by their propaganda of social and proprietary equality. Their most serious crime was that they hindered the government in all its efforts in the field of public education. Their doctrines were unsuited to the cultural level of the Russian people and were interpreted by the masses as advocating the forceful expropriation of another person's property. The motto, "Loot the looters," was not introduced by the Bolsheviks; it was the basis of the teachings of the various revolutionary groups and parties. Conflict with these groups and parties was unavoidable, and the Russian government should not be blamed for waging this conflict; it is to be blamed rather for its failure to win the support of the cultured classes, and for its desire to identify these classes with the open enemies of the state. Plehve never did realize the error of this policy. Nor did the majority of persons in the government until the Revolution of 1917.

No wonder then that I feared that my tentative effort to unify the peasantry with the rest of the agricultural classes would meet with Plehve's violent disapproval. Yet to my great surprise, my fears proved ungrounded. Stishinsky had, as usual, studied my project at length and had drawn attention to one of its provisions whereby all peasants who had attained a certain educational status were not to be automatically excluded from the peasant class. But his representations met with little encouragement from Plehve and he soon ceased to insist upon them. To Stishinsky the opinion of his superiors was something sacred. The project was unanimously approved and was sanctioned by Plehve. Immediately after the conference Plehve told me that he intended to grant my wish and appoint me Head of the Peasant Section and charge me with the complicated work of revising peasant legislation, "if," he hastened to add, "His Majesty deigns to agree." He told me that the Tsar considered the proposed reform very important. Plehve was always careful to point out that he was merely the transmitter and executor of the wishes of the Tsar for whom he always showed deep reverence. Yet he never tried to rest upon the throne for support of his actions and measures which did not meet with public approval.

Very considerately, Plehve postponed my appointment until the autumn so that I might be able to profit by the summer vacation to collect my strength for the coming winter's work. So it was September 1902 when I became Head of the Peasant Section. I began immediately to look for persons capable of editing the new projects of peasant legislation as quickly and as efficiently as possible. From the very first I saw clearly that my immediate collaborators were little fitted for this kind of work. The four assistants to the Head of the Section were well acquainted with legislative technique but had little knowledge of peasant life and were therefore incapable of drawing any general conclusions. Litvinov, who succeeded me as Head of the Section, was a physician by training and, although a small landowner in Simbirsk Gubernia, a zemskii nachalnik, and a permanent member of the Gubernia Special Board, he knew little of peasant conditions except as they were reflected in the work of the peasant institutions. He was in no way outstanding for original ideas or editorial talent; but, conscientious as he was and extremely honest, he could be implicitly trusted to supervise routine work, and of this I put him in charge, knowing that he would not attempt to decide any doubtful issue without consulting me.

G. V. Glinka, Assistant Head of the Chief Administration of Land Organization and Agriculture[16a] under Krivoshein, and director of the department of the same name, was made of quite different stuff. His talents suited him more to the work of administration and organization than to that of study. He was in charge of that office of the Peasant Section which attended to rural food supply. This office occupied his entire time, so that there was no possibility of attracting him to active participation in the work of revising peasant legislation.*

The third assistant was Ilimov, who had been transferred to the Ministry of the Interior from the Ministry of Justice. He was a dull man in charge of peasant judicial institutions, and at the same time was something of a legal adviser to the Peasant Section. It was unthinkable, however, to use him for the work of reorganizing the volost courts. He soon returned to the Ministry of Justice and I gave his place to K. K. Stefanovich (son of the Dean of Kazan Cathedral), who was recommended to me by Senator A. I. Neratov. Stefanovich had been Vice-Governor of Tiflis and later of Lublin, and still later had been appointed Senator. When he was added to the Section the work of revision had been distributed; consequently he had no share in it; anyway, I doubt if he had any aptitude for it. Later he became the inspector of local peasant institutions, an office to which his talents were well suited.

The fourth assistant was N. N. Kupriianov,[20] a serious and clever man. In politics he was a confirmed conservative and nationalist, but by a trick of fate was closely related to the most progressive zemstvo workers of his native Kostroma Gubernia. He was very masterful and exigent in his official relations and, unfortunately, was known for his heavy and even malicious disposition. He represented the old Russian officialdom, for which the glory of the country was of prime importance and which was little concerned

* Since Glinka and I did not get on very well together, my characterization of him may be considered not entirely dispassionate. To me he was a man without stable opinions of his own. For instance, during the Revolution of 1905, he zealously advocated the expropriation of private estates. He was at that time employed in the Ministry of Agriculture and supported Kutler's[17] project for the compulsory alienation of such estates. Later, when the reaction set in, Kutler was dismissed and Krivoshein became Minister of Agriculture. Glinka then changed his credo and advocated the settlement of peasants on separate, individually owned farms (*khutora*). Years later, as General Wrangel's[18] Minister of Agriculture, he drafted an agrarian law by which all privately owned estates were to be turned over to peasants of the particular local volost. In spite of the fact that such a law was obviously a bid for peasant support, Glinka seemed to consider it a means of solving the entire agrarian question. He would not have excepted even Asconia Nova, the famous estate of Falz-Fein,[19] with its unique home of wild animals gradually becoming domesticated, an estate spared even by the Bolsheviks.

with satisfying the needs of the people. He treated with indifference all questions dealing with the conditions of the Russian peasantry, but he did know the peasant conditions in the Kingdom of Poland and staunchly defended the interests of the Polish peasantry against those of the Polish landed gentry, believing that this attitude would further Russian state interests.

Among the other officials of the Section there were many outstanding men, but very few of them could be used in my work. I. M. Strakhovsky was a man of broad culture, well versed in constitutional and particularly administrative law, and a talented writer. His help in drafting the project of peasant self-government would have been valuable, but Plehve intentionally had not included him among my collaborators.*

D. I. Pestrzhetsky was in charge of matters concerning peasants of the mining regions. He was a great source of information on the whole field of peasant legislation and the agrarian problem, but never in my life have I met a man of such knowledge with so little ability to systematize it and arrive at a definite conclusion. The system of land administration pertaining to the peasants of the mining regions was seriously in need of revision. I had no time to undertake this task, but with Pestrzhetsky's help I tried to analyze the situation. He knew by heart all the statutes and regulations of the Senate pertaining to the problem but was utterly incapable of giving a direct answer to a direct question. Instead of a "yes" or a "no," he answered with a hail of citations from the Senate's decisions in cassation. It would have been most unwise to charge such a man with the task of revising this phase of peasant legislation. Pestrzhetsky took his exclusion from this work as a personal offense. He was vain and ambitious, and sought to explain his ex-

* Strakhovsky was not included because he was connected with the liberal periodical *Pravo*,[21] whose editorial staff later formed the nucleus of the Cadet party. In this magazine Strakhovsky advocated that peasants should be placed under the same system of law and justice as other classes and that zemstvo institutions should be independent of the central government. Plehve, who in some mysterious way seemed to know the histories of most workers in the ministry, once characterized him to me, half-jokingly, as "an infamous liberal" whose place was certainly not in the Ministry of the Interior. Yet Plehve chose him to fill the newly created (1903) post of fifth assistant to the Head of the Peasant Section. Strakhovsky's liberalism broke down in practice. Later, as Governor of Viatka, he who had so vigorously defended zemstvo rights engaged in fierce combat with his own zemstvo, and still later as Governor of Tiflis he acquired the reputation of a confirmed reactionary.

pulsion by saying that I was jealous of him and feared he would expose my ignorance. Pestrzhetsky was also the author of several publications which contained much valuable material, mainly of a statistical nature, but no new ideas or clearly expressed conclusions. His book, *Okolo Zemli* (*"Close to the Land"*), published in 1922 contains precious but undigested material on the results of the Bolshevik land reforms. Shortly before the revolution, he was appointed to the Second (Peasant) Department of the Senate, where, undoubtedly, he delivered long and vague speeches as each problem came up for discussion.

And, if I may digress further before resuming the discussion of the work of revising peasant legislation, I should like to mention a few more of my colleagues. It is a source of great pleasure to me, living in exile and mourning for my great and beloved country now so devastated, to recall those with whom I worked to the best of my ability to strengthen and develop Imperial Russia. First of all I must mention G. G. Savich, my predecessor as Head of the Peasant Section. He was lazy but talented. He had an understanding of men and a marked ability to select able and apt workers. With few exceptions each of the sixteen offices of the Peasant Section were headed by men than whom no better could have been chosen. Yet under Savich these men were not permitted to display any initiative; their efforts were confined to routine work and to compiling memoranda for Sipiagin, who, as already mentioned, thought he could direct from St. Petersburg all local affairs. Savich even added to these labors by insisting upon short written reports, a practice which I stopped.

I found that when the office workers of my section were given headway nearly all of them showed a positive interest in their work. At their initiative, for instance, some work was done which had needed doing for a long time: A study was made of all the circular orders of the ministry pertaining to the peasant problem that had been published since the emancipation of the serfs. A great number of them needed to be repealed, and the remaining few needed re-editing in briefer form.

Still more necessary was the publication of an instruction (*nakaz*) to the zemskie nachalniki concerning their administrative activities, in which the limits of their competence to arrest or fine the peasants in their districts were defined. An instruction of this nature should have been published when the office of zemskii nachalnik was established in 1889; but this had never been done, a fact which may explain some of the defects in the work of this institution. The instruction now published was compiled by Strakhovsky and discussed by members of the Peasant Section. Certain steps were taken also to improve the personnel of the zemskie nachalniki. Persons without university training were required to spend a certain period as candidates for the office of zemskii nachalnik in some Gubernia Special Board and to pass an examination before being appointed zemskii nachalnik proper. At the same time special classes were organized in the Peasant Section for persons who wished to apply for such positions, and examinations for those who had completed the course. To facilitate the work of volost self-government, there was published a special manual of regulations selected from the sixteen volumes of the existing code. These were classified according to the different branches of work handled by volost self-governments. This manual soon became the handbook of all organs of volost self-government. On the initiative of V. I. Baftalovsky,[22] who was transferred to the Peasant Section from the Special Board of Saratov Gubernia, a magazine was published in which were set forth, in addition to the new orders and regulations of the government and certain decisions of the Senate pertaining to the activities of the peasant institutions, articles on problems of peasant or agrarian law, extracts from reports of inspections of peasant institutions, and a column of questions and answers concerning the many misunderstandings which arose in applying the provisions of our indefinite peasant law. This column soon became a favorite with local peasant institutions, as was evidenced by the number of questions sent to the magazine. The magazine itself was used by the press, which often quoted it. All workers of the Peasant Section were eager to improve the work of the zemskie nachalniki and to make it strictly legal. Here I must observe that the broad accusations which were showered upon the zemskie nachalniki were greatly exaggerated. In an institution which numbered some six thousand men, there were unquestionably some not entirely suited to their positions; but there were also a great many who were genuinely devoted to their work and were esteemed by the rural population, which readily turned to them with their manifold problems. In the main the institution of zemskie nachalniki had a beneficial influence upon the course of peasant administration. It was founded on a sound idea, but was harmed, unfortunately, by having judicial

functions included in the sphere of its activities. Moreover, with
the decreasing numbers of the landed gentry, especially of those
who preferred to live on their estates, the level of the zemskie
nachalniki personnel fell noticeably, and it was very difficult to
entice into the rural wilderness for a small salary a man who had
a chance of making a livelihood in more or less cultured urban surroundings. Even the housing problem was difficult: landowners at
least had their own estates, but an outsider was put to it to find
living quarters within his district.*

Perhaps the main reason why this institution was not always at a
high level was that the zemskie nachalniki, once appointed, were left
to shift for themselves without any leadership. Stishinsky must
bear the responsibility for this, since he was at the Head of the
Peasant Section when zemskie nachalniki were first established and
still considered himself the spiritual parent of that institution. He
had compiled the statute on the zemskie nachalniki under the supervision of Pazukhin, head of the Chancellery of the former Minister
of the Interior, Count D. A. Tolstoi. He saw in each attempt to
direct or discipline zemskie nachalniki a move to discredit their
value. He considered them not representatives of the government

* I recall an incident which shows the part played on occasion by the personal
connections of candidates for these positions. In 1903 the Governor of Kursk
Gubernia, in agreement with the local marshals of nobility as the law required,
had advanced the candidacy of one Beliaev. By training Beliaev was a surgeon's
assistant (*feldsher*) and at the time was employed at Vladikavkaz in a hospital for
the violently insane. When I investigated the case I learned that Beliaev had eloped
with and married the daughter of Prince Kasatkin-Rostovsky, a highly esteemed
local landowner. The bride's parents, anxious to find for their son-in-law a more
desirable position than that of guarding lunatics, had prevailed upon local authorities to propose Beliaev for the vacant post of zemskii nachalnik of Staryi-Oskol
Uezd. Our ministry refused to confirm his appointment and in consequence was
flooded with petitions in Beliaev's interest. Many people called personally, and
among these was N. V. Raevsky, chairman of Kursk Zemstvo Board, who petitioned so insistently on behalf of Beliaev that I agreed to give the latter an
audience. In less than a week Beliaev—short, thickset, uncouth—put in an appearance. I asked him one question: "What volume of the Code would you use in
performing the duties of zemskii nachalnik?" "Volume One," he replied. Further
conversation was useless; I persisted in my rejection of his candidacy. But petitions
and personal visits continued. Finally, Beliaev's old mother-in-law came to plead
for him. She cried so bitterly and begged so piteously before both Plehve and
myself that our resistance collapsed. Beliaev was appointed. Two years later, in
an agrarian uprising of that revolutionary period, the estate of Prince Kasatkin-
Rostovsky was looted. Among the looters was Beliaev. He had lost his position
a short time previously and his wife had left him after he had given her a terrific
beating.

strictly regulated by existing law, but rather agents of patrimonial authority whose actions and decisions were based upon an understanding of the peculiar circumstances with which they had to deal. This explains why they were left to their own devices from the beginning. Not until 1904, fifteen years after the institution was established, was there an inspection of the zemskie nachalniki; and this first one was to embrace twenty-four uezds in three gubernias. From the outset it was evident that there was a multitude of problems in need of immediate solution. It became apparent that there was virtually no supervision over the activities of the zemskie nachalniki other than that some of their administrative decisions were revised as a result of complaints lodged against them. One reason for this lack of supervision was that the legal supervisors, the uezd marshals of nobility, very seldom carried out their duties and even avoided them lest they offend their subordinate zemskie nachalniki, who played an influential part in electing the marshals of nobility. It also became clear that the chief sin of the zemskie nachalniki was not arbitrariness but laziness and indifference.

To return to the personnel of the Peasant Section. The chief of the office in charge of the special renting of land (*chinshevyia dela*)[23] in the western gubernias was V. I. Yakobson, a clerk typical of the eighteen-fifties—tall, lanky, and clean-shaven, a man who would not dare appear before his superiors except in uniform and wearing the appropriate decorations. Long service at his post had won for him the rank of statskii sovetnik. His outlook was narrow, but he knew the complicated business of land-renting to perfection and treated it with a peculiar tenderness. It was interesting to see him state in minute detail and with evident relish some exceptional and significant case.

I. I. Kraft, the head of the non-Russian population office, and later Governor of Yakutsk, was altogether different. He had had no formal education whatever; he had started his career as a postal clerk in Siberia in localities with non-Russian population. His Asiatic origin (his mother was a Buriat) was revealed in his features and stature; he hardly looked the part of an official in the Ministry of the Interior. He was distinguished for his vivid imagination, his original mind, and his close acquaintance with the life and peculiarities of the varied nationalities inhabiting Asiatic Russia. Buriats, Bashkirs, Kirghiz—he knew them all and spoke their languages fluently. At the same time he fervently defended their rights to their vast and little-worked territories. Everyone coveted these lands. The War Ministry desired to get hold of them in order to transfer them to various Cossack voiskos; the neighboring Russian population made claims on them; the Department of Peasant Colonization was eager to obtain them for Russian settlers. All these designs Kraft considered as little short of criminal and defended the right of the nomadic tribes to preserve their mode of existence, for which extensive land areas were indispensable. He regarded the state authority from an ancient, patriarchal point of view. I used to tell him that his idea of justice seemed to be that of a ruler holding court under some spreading oak and basing his decisions on considerations of abstract right and not well-defined law. By and large, I do not think I have ever met a more fortunate combination of common sense, extensive and varied experience, self-acquired and broad education, and extraordinary assiduity. Kraft compiled a project on the land-organization and administration of non-Russian nationalities, but it was lost sight of in the inter-ministerial shuffle and correspondence which generally preceded the presentation of any legislative project to the State Council.

Baron A. F. Meyendorff[24] was another well-informed and painstaking worker. He was head of the office for the affairs of the Baltic peasants, and at the same time was assistant professor at St. Petersburg University. Later he was a member and Vice-Chairman of the Duma. The degree of his fairmindedness may be judged from the fact that he flatly refused to take part in the work of making certain legislative changes regarding the affairs of Baltic peasants and even left the section saying that as a member of the Baltic nobility, who to a certain extent shared its views, he could not be sure that his treatment of the whole business would be impartial.

Acquaintance with my immediate co-workers in the Peasant Section showed me clearly that I could not hope to find among them collaborators for my proposed work of revising peasant statutes. They were admirably fitted for the work they were doing, but would not do for the special work I had in hand. I had then to look for collaborators among the lesser officials of the Peasant Section, and was fortunate enough to find among them two very capable workers: I. F. Tsyzyrev, assistant professor in Constitutional Law at St. Petersburg University, who worked out a detailed memorandum on the project of peasant self-government with explanations for each article; and P. P. Zubovsky, who was at that time employed as junior assistant to the Secretary of the Peasant Section.

I. F. Tsyzyrev was well educated and possessed some talent as a writer; he was capable of grasping another man's point and therefore made a fine editor; but, as he was not very well trained in legislative technique, I did not use him in the work of compiling the project itself. For some reason unknown to me he was almost the only one of my immediate collaborators who did not advance along the hierarchical scale; and, if I remember correctly, the revolution found him occupying the post of an assistant to the Head of the Peasant Section. P. P. Zubovsky, on the other hand, rose rapidly. A junior assistant to the Secretary of the Peasant Section in 1903, he became in 1907 Director of the Department of Land Organization, and at the time of the 1917 Revolution was Assistant Minister of Agriculture. He had early become a person of importance in the entire business of peasant land management and an advocate of a scheme for settling peasants on separate individually owned farms and separate family holdings. Even so, he remained the assimilator and developer of other people's plans and ideas; for during the period 1907–1915 it was Krivoshein who initiated and directed the work of peasant land management. After the revolution, as Glinka's assistant in the Crimea, Zubovsky continued to display his capacity for complying with the ideas of others and did his best to effect the realization of General Wrangel's absurd agrarian law, a law which differed radically from those principles of land management Zubovsky had championed at an earlier date. Zubovsky's success was due to his great industry and to his ability, but I doubt if he understood the significance of his work; he probably thought but little about its influence upon public life. Yet he was very exact in drafting the text of a law. So eager was he to make the law cover all possible eventualities that under his drafting the law sometimes lost the character of a statute and appeared as a minute and casuistic classification of rules and exceptions. The dear Petr Pavlovich had to be reproved, not for insufficient elaboration of a law, but for a too detailed treatment. He was so conscientious and painstaking that I had to say to him, "Leave something to the Senate whose duty it is to interpret the law as applied to individual cases."

But these two men were not enough for a speedy accomplishment of the projected legislative work, and I had to look outside the Peasant Section for others. There was no lack of willing persons.

Many offered their services. I suppose the main attraction was the pay outside workers would have received whereas department officials received only a bonus. The sum allocated for this work was smaller than had been asked for by the Ministry of the Interior but was nevertheless considerable. From 1902 to 1904 more than 100,000 rubles were apportioned, a large part of which was used to print: (1) several thousand copies of the projects, which, accompanied by detailed explanatory notes, comprised six rather large volumes; (2) a great number of questionnaires distributed among the gubernia conferences which were called to discuss the projects.

Many addressed themselves directly to Plehve, who sent some of them to me; for, after entrusting me with the work, Plehve gave me a free hand in selecting my associates, limiting himself to sending certain persons to me with the observation that they, in his estimation, possessed certain qualities. Since Plehve knew far more officials than I did, all but one of those attracted to the work of legislative revision, excepting persons working in the Peasant Section, were selected by the minister himself. These were A. I. Lykoshin,[25] P. P. Shilovsky, and A. A. Bashmakov.[26]

The most useful of the three was Lykoshin, a former "member of the group of legal advisers attached to the Ministry of Justice" and before that, Assistant to an Ober-Prokuror of the Senate. His creative powers were hardly less developed than those of Zubovsky, and he was very familiar with existing peasant law, the extensive practice of the Senate in this field, and the literature concerning peasant land customs. He had written an essay on the project for regulating peasant land tenure and by using all the information in his possession had given his essay the character of serious scientific research. Yet he had no such devotion to his work as had Zubovsky; he treated the regulations, which he edited and promoted, and their results with a good deal of indifference. He was not exact to the point of pettiness as was Zubovsky. His first consideration was always his career. His outstanding trait was extreme obsequiousness and a flattering attitude toward his superiors. As a personality he was inferior to Zubovsky. Each performed the will of his chief; but where Zubovsky assimilated the idea of his superiors and endeavored to develop and perfect them, during which process he exhibited a good deal of initiative and put forward his "supplementary" ideas, Lykoshin introduced no personal initiative into his work and never opposed his superiors when they made corrections. After he was appointed Assistant Minister of the Interior, he exhibited no independent initiative and took no part whatever even in the work of peasant land management on which he had spent so much effort. It is true that by that time this matter had been transferred to the Chief Administration of Land Organization and Agriculture; yet as Assistant Minister of the Interior Lykoshin was a member of the Committee for Land Affairs[27] and as such might have exercised some influence on it. But at that time Krivoshein's star was in the ascendant, and Lykoshin preferred to agree with everything Krivoshein said or did. After his appointment to the State Council, in 1914 I believe, Lykoshin showed the same blind submission to the will of his chiefs. He became a member of the Right wing of the Council and confined his legislative activity to voting with the government.

A. A. Bashmakov was a quite different and very interesting type. He was a man of enormous erudition and a courageous thinker with a lively imagination. Yet he was utterly powerless to co-ordinate either his ideas or his knowledge. His brilliance as an orator was dulled by a tendency to lengthy digressions, which made it difficult to follow his argument. Bashmakov was entirely unfitted for any specialized work. He had been dismissed from the work of drafting a new civil code because he could not even draw up a clear brief. But he was of value to the work of peasant legislation because of his deep knowledge of the customary peasant law, especially of the part dealing with inheritance. His attempt to express logically the spirit of the customary peasant inheritance law was a dismal failure, and this task had to be transferred to V. G. Petrov, a young man of whom I shall say more later. In many ways Bashmakov strongly reminded one of Turgenev's Rudin.[28] He soared easily into ecstasy and fired others with his own enthusiasm, but he could not bring himself to analyze any subject closely.

Bashmakov had been educated in Switzerland and France and had had an opportunity to become permeated with the spirit and ideals of Western culture, but actually he was a confirmed conservative Narodnik and an admirer of autocracy. He was a Slavophil, a violent enemy of German influence, a member of the Slavic Society, and at the same time a partisan of the commune, a specific peasant organization, and of customary peasant law. It was but natural, therefore, that when he joined the extreme Right party in 1905, he advocated the expropriation of privately owned lands. Later, strange as it may seem, this chaotically minded man, who had so much originality and animation, became editor of *Pravitelstvennyi Vestnik!*[29] But this can be easily explained. Bashmakov was a man of very modest means and the head of a large family. All his life he had looked for a permanent position, but because of his peculiarities he could not stay anywhere for long. The work of editorship demanded only mechanical application; and this suited him nicely, as it gave him time to become engrossed in the most varied problems without bringing them to any concrete conclusions.

The third person appointed on the recommendation of Plehve was P. P. Shilovsky, who was put to the task of compiling for the volost courts a regulation on penalties. Formerly he had served in the Ministry of Justice as an examining magistrate. Shilovsky was very ambitious and not fastidious as to the methods he used in advancing his career. An obsequiousness before his superiors combined with continual plotting and intrigue against them were his outstanding traits. His interest in questions of general importance was that of a dilettante. His very vivid and interesting work, *Sudebnye ocherki Anglii ("Essays on the Legal Customs of England")*, is a patent example of his dilettantism and his total lack of scientific method and impartiality. His failure to develop powers of analysis and criticism deprived his work in the field of law of serious value. His project for regulating penalties imposed by volost courts underwent many discussions and was finally re-edited by the Petrov mentioned above, and then included in the projects on new peasant legislation compiled by the Peasant Section. Later Shilovsky was appointed Governor of Kostroma by the then Minister of the Interior, A. A. Makarov,[30] with whom he was in close personal relation. Later still, in 1912, he engineered an intrigue against Makarov in connection with the Emperor's projected visit to Kostroma in 1913 in celebration of the tri-centennial jubilee of the House of Romanov. The intrigue failed. Its discovery led to Shilovsky's transference to Olonetsk Gubernia, though still as governor. He retired soon afterwards.

I have already referred to V. G. Petrov. This man was the author of the project on the regulation of peasant contracts and also, as I have just said, the final editor of the project on regulation of penalties for peasant offenses and on that of land inheritance. He had just graduated from the university and was serving in some minor position in the Ministry of Agriculture. I had known him personally while he was still a student and had had occasion to note his outstanding intelligence and pedantic exactness in formulating ideas. When he was transferred to the Peasant Section and given the opportunity of working at the projects on volost court organization, he displayed an altogether remarkable capacity for legal thought. He was a born lawyer and, had he chosen an academic career, would probably have made a name for himself. But fate threw him into the Ministry of the Interior, and later into the Chief Adminstration of Land Organization and Agriculture. Here the revolution found him an assistant director of some department. He had done well.

I should like to mention again G. G. Savich, my predecessor as Head of the Peasant Section. He assisted me in the work of revising peasant legislation by compiling a project of volost court organization and practice.

As the collaborators were secured, the work of revision was organized and set in motion. It was carried on in almost the same manner followed by Litvinov, Glinka, and myself in composing the project on peasant self-government. The only difference was that I tried to attract a wide variety of persons to discuss the first draft of the project. Among those invited to participate in drafting the statute on land tenure was A. V. Krivoshein, who at that time was Director of the Department of Peasant Colonization. Yet he tried in every way to avoid participating in the conferences on this matter, either by not appearing at all or, when he did appear, by maintaining an obstinate silence. Rudin,[31] the Assistant Head of the Land Surveying Office of the Ministry of Justice,[32] played a very active part, especially in the question of land allotment. We invited also a number of specialists in different fields to attend the discussions on matters on which they were authorities.

These conferences were under the chairmanship of Stishinsky. Why Plehve appointed him to this position when the entire work was under my direction, I do not know. Perhaps Plehve was eager not to offend Stishinsky by putting him aside. Perhaps it was out of consideration for form and hierarchy. Perhaps also Plehve intended Stishinsky to act as a sort of gendarme-supervisor and guardian of conservative principles. Plehve seemed to have misgivings about my own conservatism, at least as regards the peasant problem; but he had known Stishinsky for a long time, knew his loyalty to the existing regime, and felt that his conservatism was trustworthy. Plehve was also aware, however, of Stishinsky's slowness, indecision, and incapacity to grasp the fundamentals of an issue. He knew that

Stishinsky's extreme thoroughness impelled him to examine personally all documents he signed and to correct not only their contents but
even their style—a commendable conscientiousness but one which led
Stishinsky to hold documents for weeks and months.* He realized
that to put Stishinsky in charge of the revision of peasant legislation
would be to bury the matter. But one characteristic of Stishinsky
Plehve did not know. It is true that Stishinsky was opposed to legislative innovations, but should such an innovation be adopted and
made law Stishinsky would then oppose its alteration with the same
fervor as he had opposed its adoption. Witness how he defended the
institution of zemskii nachalnik, which, as I have said, he regarded as
his favorite child.

I knew, though not too well, all these peculiar traits of Stishinsky,
as I had had some experience with him during our work in the Special
Conference for the Affairs of the Nobility. I had some misgivings,
therefore, as to how our common work would progress and how we

---

* An illustration may give more point to this characteristic of Stishinsky.
Complaints against the decisions of local peasant institutions of the central government were made to the Senate, which turned them over to the Ministry of the
Interior—that is, to its Peasant Section—for study and recommendation. Stishinsky, when he was Head of the Peasant Section, had paid particular attention to
such cases, not only because he was interested in them, but because during the
forty years since the emancipation of the serfs peasant legislation had been based
more upon Senate decisions than upon the provisions of the emancipation law,
which had been inadequately worked out. But in his attention to these cases Stishinsky had delayed returning to the Senate the recommendations of his Section.
He had left his successor, Savich, a large number of these that had been awaiting
final solution for many years. Savich did nothing to improve matters, and when
Plehve became minister in 1902 the number of these unfinished cases had reached
the eight hundred mark, and some of them, especially those concerning the southwestern region, had been awaiting final solution for more than twenty-five years.
In fact this circumstance was one of the reasons for Savich's retirement. Stishinsky was again put in charge of the department temporarily, but Plehve insisted
that all cases should be liquidated within the year. This was done; but it took
tremendous effort on the part of Stishinsky and the Peasant Section. Be it said,
however, that Stishinsky's examination of documents was never colored by consideration of his own personal interests. Where many a person's opinion of a
document was apt to be influenced by the importance or power of the man who had
signed it, Stishinsky's estimate of it was unfailingly impartial and objective. It is
interesting to note in this connection, however, that when there arose a question
of land management involving large interests of peasants and landed gentry, Stishinsky, perhaps unconsciously, ranged himself on the side of the peasants. Some
time in the past Stishinsky, in collaboration with one Matveev, had compiled a
small manual of peasant customs concerning inheritance; and thereafter he considered himself called upon to defend the peasant courts, which were based upon
tradition.

should get on together. Fortunately there was no friction; everything went well. This was due first to the fact that in Stishinsky's eyes the desire of his superiors was sacred and commanded obedience as unquestioningly as did the existing law. To Plehve, who had been his chief for a long time, he was doubly submissive; and, since Plehve had put me in charge of the revision of peasant legislation and had made Stishinsky only chairman of committee meetings involved in this work, Stishinsky accepted this arrangement without demur. It was due, secondly, to the fact that Stishinsky was a thorough gentleman. He was above intrigue and without envy or petty pride. Consequently it was not difficult to come to a working agreement: all current business of the Peasant Section, including the majority of the reports to the Senate, passed directly to Stishinsky, who, working with my collaborators, dealt with them. All matters of general significance, all current business of primary importance, and all personal recommendations and appointments to positions in the government's peasant institutions which Stishinsky passed I reported directly to Plehve. These reports were supposed to be made in Stishinsky's presence, since he was Assistant Minister; but this rule was disregarded. Plehve deliberately set the hours for my reports at a time when Stishinsky had to attend sessions of the Second Department of the Senate. Stishinsky in no way concerned himself with the direction of the Peasant Section; in fact, he was not always advised of its work. Many legislative projects were sent to ministries for confirmation before Stishinsky was aware of their existence. As a rule he learned of them just before they were to be discussed in the State Council; yet he defended them there in minute detail.* Sometimes, however, my colleagues, who disliked Stishinsky's attention to detail, could not reach an understanding with him and requested me to have a talk with him. As a matter of expediency, I usually resorted to another policy: I presented the matter to Plehve, who passed upon it without reading the documents involved. Stishinsky never suspected this procedure, because he quickly forgot each issue as it passed from his immediate attention.

* Further evidence of Stishinsky's conscientiousness and tact is to be seen in the fact that he considered it his duty to ask my opinion on matters of importance that came to him directly. He usually sought my opinion over the telephone, and at night. Sometimes this practice drove me nearly insane, as things which seemed of importance to Stishinsky did not seem so to me; moreover, I loathed long drawn-out explanations over the telephone. But Stishinsky was persistent and would not abandon this practice until he saw he could get nothing out of me in this way.

In an equally satisfactory manner we aranged to hold the discussions on the project of peasant legislation under Stishinsky's chairmanship. In the beginning he attempted to include in the new laws all pertinent Senate decisions—that is, to reduce the work to simple codification of these decisions, as he was particularly fond of this kind of work because it had been his special occupation as Assistant State Secretary. His attempt failed, however, and he did not press the issue. I cannot recollect a single case, however insignificant, when he did not agree with my opinion; and once he had accepted a new idea, even though after stubborn argument, he considered it sacred and welcomed all suggestions for its realization. This was the case with the project to encourage peasants individually to own farms and at the same time to change their allotment lands into family holdings. At first Stishinsky thought this would cause the disintegration of the commune, which he considered should remain inviolable. But when he was won over to the project he became its ardent partisan and we profited greatly from his participation in our discussions, since he was a great authority on Senate activity during the last forty years and could explain Senate decisions which shed so much light upon many sides of peasant life and administration.

In spite of the differences in our political convictions—a difference which became ever more marked with the passing years—Stishinsky and I were friends, and I cannot refrain from stressing once more the nobility of his character and his extreme modesty. I know of no other man who would have accepted the conditions of the situation in which Plehve placed us, no one who would have consented, without a trace of bitterness or hidden hurt, to become the subordinate of a man who was hierarchically his own subordinate. Only a man of genuine nobility of character, devoid of all traces of petty pride, could have treated me, as he did, without the slightest trace of hostility. This was especially true after Plehve's death, when there was no longer any reason for according me his former friendship. Stishinsky may have looked at the world through a tiny crack in the wall, but he was sincerely devoted to his work and to Russia.

The revolution was a severe blow to Stishinsky. His arrest by the Provisional Government without formal accusation and his incarceration for more than a month in a cell in the Peter and Paul Fortress left him broken both physically and mentally. I saw him almost immediately after he was set free and was greatly surprised at the change in him, but even more by the utter lack of bitterness toward the persons who had subjected him to this unexpected and unmerited treatment. He lost his entire fortune and was obliged to work, first in Odessa and later in the Crimea, as an interpreter for the French Mission. He was paid a miserable sum; yet with what simple, uncomplaining dignity this seventy-year-old man, who had been accustomed to comfort all his life, submitted to the reverses of fortune. The last time I met him was in 1920 in the Crimea, when General Wrangel was there with his army. I was amazed to see how easily—that is, how bravely— he had borne the countless trials of fate during the preceding four years. Later he went to Constantinople, where he lived for over a year earning his living by hard work. But his strength had left him; a cold brought him to his grave. May he lie in peace in that foreign land. . . . .

To return to the work of revision. As I have already said, the main purpose which I kept in view was to abolish the land commune by any means possible, and to make the peasants the owners of their allotted land or of those lands they acquired as former members of village communities and land associations. Plehve had no definite opinion on this subject. On the one hand, he seemed to think that the commune was an indispensable aspect of peasant organization; and in this opinion he was supported by representatives of the Right group of the Moscow nobility and Moscow zemstvo, whose opinion he valued highly.* On the other hand, Plehve had to admit that the conception of private property could be inculcated into the Russian peasantry only by transforming the Russian peasants themselves into private owners of the land they used. Moreover, he was rather prejudiced against the commune because socialist and revolutionary circles ardently supported the communal form of land tenure. But Plehve was totally incapable of taking a decisive step in either direction, both because he was insufficiently acquainted with the question and because he was not a reformer by nature. Consequently he issued no definite instructions on this subject. It was implied, however, that there could be no question of abolishing the commune by law; on the other hand, no steps had been taken to facilitate the disruption of the commune by some other means.

* In a special conference called to establish the main principles, which would form the basis of the work of revising peasant legislation, the Muscovites voted unanimously for the complete preservation of the commune. The conference itself did not formulate any conclusions or decisions.

To me it was obvious that there was no possibility of open warfare against the commune as an institution—such methods would bring no results. It would be necessary to progress slowly and as far as possible under camouflage; arguments concerning the question of the commune would have to be transferred to another plane. The commune must never be mentioned. Instead, a rational system of land tenure must be advocated under which a transference to private peasant landownership would become indispensable but would not constitute the declared aim of the reform. If the problem was approached from this angle, the purpose of the revision would appear to be the increase of the productivity of peasant land. With such a purpose there was no quarrel. Accordingly, I used all means at my command to emphasize those parts of the new project which dealt essentially with the organization of peasant property. We worked out detailed regulations concerning the abolition of fractional and stripped land lots situated at a considerable distance from the village homes. This defective system of tenure, common to the central part of the "black-soil belt" and somewhat to the Ukraine, was to be found in both communal [i.e., repartitional] and household land tenure. It could be abolished only by breaking up large villages into small ones. The new project aimed to break up the large villages by granting a certain number of peasants and members of the commune the right to leave their former villages and form another settlement. The new settlement would comprise lands in a more compact area so that tillable lands would be situated nearer the homes. Yet it was not possible to do away entirely with these defects, nor was it feasible to give each individual peasant the right to manage his property as he saw fit, independently of the accepted system of land cultivation practiced by peasants; that is to say, to allow the individual peasant to exploit his land more intensely by improved methods of crop rotation. Such a system of land cultivation was possible only if all the land area in his use constituted one individual land allotment. Accordingly, it was generally supposed that the basic and final purpose of the new organization of peasant land holdings was to distribute peasant lands as separate individual lots and to move houses and out-buildings to these lots, in other words, to form individual farms. But it is evident that such a farm system was feasible only after the right of private ownership of land had been recognized. By its very nature, a commune ceases to be a commune when the land is exploited by any one individual, since individual ownership of land does not permit of

any land reapportionment. Yet the measures we proposed were meant
to allow the individual members of a commune to leave it and aimed
to re-assign as the private property of the peasants the land allotted
them as members of the commune. These measures sought to do
nothing more than to raise the technical level of peasant agriculture,
that is, peasant well-being. Their purpose was essentially economic;
the juridical problem, which involved the disruption of the commune,
was tactfully avoided.

This procedure was slightly paradoxical and later served to make
ambiguous the meaning of the Imperial Ukase of November 9,
1906. The persons who edited the ukase were guided by the provisions of the Peasant Section's project and were evidently ignorant of
the fact that when these provisions were composed no one expected
that they would become law or put into effect without some alterations. The provisions had been worked out in the hope that when
they were examined by outstanding local men the latter would reject
them in favor of a more complete and speedy abolition of the commune and the introduction at least of the household system of land
tenure. I thought it necessary to emphasize, not the political, but
the economic aspects of the problem in order to make clear the necessity of granting the peasants the right to private ownership of their
lands. Besides, it was perfectly clear to me that in many regions of
Russia the peasants were not fitted to pass directly from communally
to individually owned farms. The new project did not provide for
any natural evolution of peasant land tenure. A direct transition
from communal to private ownership which skips the intermediary
period mentioned above of, say, household tenure could not be effected
on any large scale. To me the camouflaging of the measure was only
a tactical device by which it might be possible under the existing
situation to smuggle under the government seal the contraband question of abolishing the commune. For by using this method it was not
necessary to make direct reference to the commune; on the contrary,
it was possible to speak jointly of communal and hereditary household land tenure, since from an economic point of view these two
types had the same defects. As I said before, the idea was to make
the problem one of agricultural and not social or political reform.
But in achieving agricultural reform the transition from communal
to private ownership would also be effected.

At that, the right of individuals to leave the commune and to
receive as their private property an area of land corresponding to

the one allotted them as members of the commune was necessarily limited to individual cases. It was granted to individual peasants when the usual reapportionments of the land were made by the commune; at other times, it was given only to groups of peasants, if my memory serves me right, numbering not fewer that twenty persons, or not less than one-fifth of the members of the commune.*

I want once more to stress the fact that I thought the main, if not the only consideration was to emphasize the chief defects of our peasant organization and at the same time to leave room for local persons, familiar with certain problems and inclined to a certain way of thinking, to portray conditions as they really were.

Concerning the matter of peasant self-government, I tried to introduce the idea of an all-class volost and to build my project of village and volost public organization in such a way that it might be turned, by a few easy editorial changes, into a project for organizing an all-class village or volost society.

Concerning the matter of peasant land-exploitation, my main object was to show the utter impossibility of raising the level of peasant welfare without abolishing the commune, and, at the same time, to outline those extensive measures pertaining to peasant land management which could be realized only after the peasants had been granted the right of private ownership of their lands. Here again I was hoping that the local workers would express themselves in favor of measures far more decisive than the ones I was able to introduce into the projects worked out by the Peasant Section.

I was much less interested in volost judicial reform—namely, volost court organization and practice—and in village regulations on penalties, contracts, and inheritance of allotted lands. I was not a practicing lawyer; I had no legal education and could hardly have had any competent opinion on the subject. But from my layman's point of view it appeared that it was hardly possible to extend the action of our general legal institutions over the entire population of the empire. There were many material reasons why this was so. For instance, there was not a sufficient number of suitably trained persons to fill all legal positions in our rural districts (our volost courts numbered more than 28,000) ; also the State Treasury did not have

---

*It is a curious fact that an almost identical regulation was unanimously projected at the agronomic congress at Moscow in 1922, although the great majority of the congress were Communists or Social Democrats, for persons of other than socialistic parties were deprived of the right freely to express their thoughts.

the sums necessary for their remuneration; finally, it was utterly impracticable to force the volost peasant courts to govern themselves according to the provisions of the tenth volume of the Code. It seemed more advisable, therefore, to improve upon our volost-court organization and practice and give the volost judges some written standards of law rather than to leave them in the primitive state in which they actually were and to allow them to continue to use in their decisions the customary law, which in many localities was nonexistent and which on a great many subjects was vague and indefinite.

It is but natural that under these conditions I was not particularly insistent upon composing projects of peasant legislation which should be perfect in every detail. I realized that before they were finally incorporated into the existing law they would pass through a great number of intermediate stages in the course of which they would undergo such changes as might be necessary to realize the principles upon which they were based. But one thing I insisted upon, and that was speed. Knowing from experience what an insufferable time it took to pass a law of any importance, I considered it most important to take into account the element of time. Unfortunately, Stishinsky was of the opposite opinion. His conscientiousness and his organic incapacity to look ahead and foresee the course of events made him think that each article we drafted would turn into law overnight without the slightest alteration. He considered the idea of sending the project to local people for examination as a mere formality with which he personally would have gladly dispensed. To him the possibility of changes being made in the basic principles of the project was out of the question.

Throughout the entire winter of 1902–3 we met at least three times a week to consider the work in hand; yet after six months' effort we had not completed any one item. We had finished the work on separate parts of several projects, but as yet they were unrelated. The work given Shilovsky and Bashmakov was in a state of chaos. They had not yet completed their explanatory notes, especially those dealing with each separate article. Nor had there been prepared the general note which was to explain all the basic stipulations of the projects and give a résumé of the provisions contained in them.

Both my colleagues and myself were too busy with other work to concentrate entirely upon the revision of peasant legislation. We had worked out a very complicated project whereby we proposed to annul special servitudes (*servitutnyia prava*)[59] of the peasants who were already living on privately owned lands in the nine western gubernias. A large conference of local administrators and local land-owners had met to discuss the project. We were also working under Plehve's chairmanship on another project which was designed to reform the system of food supply and distribution. In this we were assisted by several chairmen of gubernia zemstvo boards. I decided, however, that before the end of the year 1903 all preliminary work of the peasant reform must be not only finished but also tech-nically complete and printed.

The only means of accomplishing this was to free myself and my chief collaborators from all other responsibilities. To do this we should have to separate ourselves from the Peasant Section; so I asked Plehve for six weeks' leave of absence on my estate near Tver and for permission to take with me some of my colleagues. Plehve agreed willingly, and early in June I left St. Petersburg with five co-workers: Zubovsky, Tsyzyrev, Shilovsky, Znosko-Borovsky, and Petrov. Our work in the country went on at a brisk pace. We worked in the daytime and in the evenings discussed such doubts and misunderstandings as had arisen during the day. At the same time, Zubovsky was making a final edition of the regulation on peasant self-government supplemented by that on the taxation of village communities. As for myself, I supervised their work and undertook the composition of the general explanatory note, a part of which—that dealing with peasant self-government—had been drafted by Tsyzyrev.

I wrote this note as if it were the report of a commission which had been set up by the Ministry of the Interior under the chairman-ship of Assistant Minister Stishinsky and which was engaged in revising peasant legislation. I quoted different considerations and opinions which no one had ever really expressed while the work was being done. In view of the fact that our work was not supposed to bear the ministerial stamp, that is, the sanction of the minister, it seemed to me that the ministry was not to be officially involved in the work done and that its opinion was to be expressed only after the project had been examined by persons "honored by public confi-dence," in the words of the Manifesto of February 26, 1903.[34]

I divided the note into three parts. The first part dealt with the defects of the existing peasant self-government and set forth the reasons why it would be premature to unite the peasant class with others in the field of self-government. The second part contained a sharp criticism of the activities of the existing volost courts and their prevailing customs. It also brought out the fact that, owing to the absence of definite legal standards which these courts might have used, "the peasants know nothing either of their own rights and obligations or of those of their neighbors." The third and final part enumerated the many defects in land tenure and land-organization, stressed the idea that the level of peasant welfare depended upon a speedy abolition of these defects, and enumerated the measures by which the defects might be eradicated.

When I returned to St. Petersburg I hastened to present a copy of the printed note to Plehve, who read it with much attention and made several minor corrections. Unfortunately I no longer have in my possession the copy of the note with Plehve's remarks, and I fear that it has disappeared together with all my extensive personal and family archives. But, as far as I can remember, Plehve's corrections were mostly intended to modify the criticism of peasant self-government and volost courts. I must add, also, that Plehve knew no more of the projects than what he read in the note. To be sure, he knew the fundamentals of the projects, but he was not familiar with the details. Still, he was right in not wishing to spend his time reading them; he understood what Stishinsky was unable to grasp, namely, that these projects had to pass through a series of stages before they reached final form. The note interested Plehve because it was intended for the Tsar, and if it should meet with his sovereign approval it was to be published immediately.

Stishinsky, who was nominally responsible for the note, since it was written by a fictitious commission headed by himself, took no part in either its composition or its confirmation and did not express either surprise or displeasure concerning it.

After the Tsar had approved the note it was reprinted in full in *Pravitelstvennyi Vestnik* and created much discussion in the press. The progressive, i.e., the Left liberal section of the press severely criticized the ideas it contained. The liberal papers did not fail to note the discrepancy between accepting the volost as a single territorial unit and limiting the composition of organs of volost self-government to representatives of the former taxable classes. Some sentences of the note* were quoted in nearly the entire liberal press.

* "Those interests and affairs entrusted to the competence of the volost organs of self-government appear to be not limited interests of separate villages but wider interests of public economy and administration pertaining to a definite region of

Vestnik Evropy stated that "from all the indisputable statements of the note, but one logical conclusion can be drawn, namely, that the volost, embracing the entire territory of a given region and approaching in its duties those of the zemstvo institutions, is to be an all-class unit." "Yet," continued the *Vestnik,* "the commission does not mention the reasons which caused it to repudiate its own premises and limit the composition of the organs of volost self-government to members of the former taxable classes."

The press detected the same discrepancy in that part of the work which dealt with the volost courts. Here it quoted statements I had written: "The fact that two different systems of law exist side by side in the country, a written one—that is the general civil code—and an unwritten one—that is, customary law—will always make for conflict between the two systems, and written law will always prevail over custom. The legislator not only must take care to create no obstacles to the task of unifying the peasant class with the other classes of society in the realm of civil law but must further this unification as much as possible. The population of a country can be fused into one powerful and complete social organism only when all its component parts are completely unified in the sphere of civil law." The liberal press considered that these were elementary truths and expressed its astonishment that, in direct opposition to them, the "commission" had proposed to preserve the volost court and arm it with written regulations which did not entirely correspond to the provisions of the tenth volume of the Code and which actually represented a summary of customs which were being repudiated by the commission.

Not all the progressive elements of the country shared these ideas. Count Bennigsen,[35] for instance, who later became a member of the Duma and belonged to the Left wing of the Octobrists, wrote a booklet, *K voprosu o peresmotre krestianskago zakonodatelstva* (*"On the Question of Revising Peasant Legislation"*). In the main, the booklet was liberal in view and was approved by the liberal press. In it Count Bennigsen expressed himself in favor of preserving the volost courts and opposed to extending the application of the general civil code to the peasants. "The consideration of justice,"

___

an uezd. In this sense the volost organization has some characteristics of the zemstvo organization, and therefore eligibility to membership in the volost organs of self-government must be determined mainly by the ownership of real estate within the boundaries of a volost territory."

he wrote, "underlies all decisions of the volost courts and serves as
a code upon which they base their decisions. Our volost courts," he
said elsewhere, "have all the elements for developing into a true expression of popular legal consciousness."

The journalist, Slonimsky,[36] a Narodnik writing in *Vestnik Evropy,* expressed himself just as decisively in favor of preserving the
volost courts: "The peasants create their own law."

There was the same diversity of opinion on the question of the
commune, although one has to admit that the most important part of
the work of the "commission," namely, that concerning the land
tenure of the peasants, was subjected to the least criticism.

It is evident that the press failed to see behind the cloak of economic considerations which covered the political issues of the measure. It did not see that the measure was really a modest but decisive
attack upon the commune. The most perspicacious was the extreme
Left press. *Russkoe Bogatstvo* stated flatly that the entire project
was directed toward "an artificial stratification of peasant society"
and saw in it, not without reason, that policy of "backing the strongest" which Stolypin was later to proclaim. As a proof of the contention that the Russian peasantry had common feelings and shared
in one common movement, the *Russkoe Bogatstvo* advanced the
argument that both the poor and the rich peasants had taken part
in the agrarian uprisings and therefore the uprisings were "not
robbery but an elemental movement."

It goes without saying that the opponents of the commune
thought that the project did not contain measures adequate to put an
end to that institution. In their estimation the evil of the commune
was fundamental. Before the projects were made public, A. P.
Nikolsky[37] had published in the *Novoe Vremia* articles entitled "Krestiane, obshchina i X tom" ("The Peasants, the Commune and
Volume X"). These proclaimed prophetically that "the people are
breeding the dangerous germs of destructive socialism because the
conditions and customs of communal life develop in them only the
idea of communal property and not the idea of private property."
Speaking of those prospects which further segregation of the peasantry might achieve in the future, he exclaimed: "The reason, the
conscience, and the feeling of patriotism have become perturbed by
merely supposing that these sad prospects may become a reality."

The more actively progressive part of society, then, was not
pleased with the projects. This is to be explained by the prevalence

in Russian society of divergent opinions on the subject of the peasant question and by the very character of these projects. Behind the "commission" everybody saw the Ministry of the Interior, or rather Plehve; and by the time the explanatory note appeared in the press the majority of society had already developed a definitely negative attitude toward him.

Here I cannot refrain from pointing out Plehve's inability to use that device so widely used by all governments, so extensively used by Witte—publicity. He was closely associated with such publications as *Moskovskiia Vedomosti*[38] and *Grazhdanin;* these, however, were not only without influence but were even despised in large public circles. The support of these publications only served to harm his public position and the measures he undertook. Plehve failed to use to his own advantage even so loyal a publication as *Novoe Vremia,* which was always ready to support the government.

I must confess, however, that I, too, was very little concerned with this side of the question. At that time the center of gravity was in certain government circles, and I thought that this was where I should look for support, hoping that when local people had become acquainted with my projects they would support and enlarge upon the provisions contained therein. But I also realized that I had to hurry my work. I therefore used every means in my power to speed up its completion. Only the technical work remained—the printing of the necessary number of copies of the "commission's" extensive work. Curiously enough, by the time the task was completed I, too, almost came to believe that the "commission" had really existed.

Finally, in January 1904, everything was finished and a detailed program of the plan of procedure for examining the projects was drafted. An Imperial Ukase of January 8 ordered that the projects should be examined by gubernia conferences organized for this purpose. This plan of procedure was intended to facilitate the complicated work of these conferences and the future work of compiling their decisions, but it was not intended to restrict the freedom of their activity. In fact the plan of procedure stressed the need of obtaining definite answers to questions of a general character associated with the problem of peasant legislation. The appended questionnaires provided a special space for the recording of the opinions of the majority and the minority, and for any diverging opinions pertaining to aspects of the problem which had not been foreseen or provided for by the projects.

It was my hope that not later than the autumn of 1904 the recommendations of the gubernia conferences would be coming into the ministry and that by the beginning of 1905 we could revise the projects in accordance with these recommendations and present them to the State Council. At the same time there was a plan to solicit the Tsar's permission to organize within the State Council a special commission to examine these projects, just as had been done for the new penal code; this would have speeded up the matter considerably so that there was a possibility of having everything finished by the end of 1905.

I was not at all perturbed by the fact that the Imperial Ukase of January 8 said in part: "We consider it necessary to preserve the peasant-class order of existence and the inalienability of peasant allotted lands." A peasant-class organization was not at variance with the creation of an all-class volost organization; but, as to the inalienability of allotted lands, although I considered this law most harmful and one which had done more than anything else to prevent the unification of the peasant class with the rest of the population, I knew perfectly well, not only then but even up to the revolution, that there could be no question of its repeal. Both the government and the progressive elements of the public were, in their blindness, entirely in favor of preserving this law. The government saw in it a guaranty against the penetration of alien elements among the peasants. The public saw in it the peasants' protection against losing their lands to the capitalist element and especially to the petty capitalist element, the kulak—the bogeyman which so terrorized our flabby, sentimental public.

I was much more troubled by the fact that the gubernia conferences included representatives of the nobility, who were elected by assemblies of marshals of nobility and representatives of the nobility, as well as members of the zemstvos, one from each uezd, who were invited by the governors. The differences between these two elements, emphasized by the fact that the zemstvo workers were selected by governors and not elected by zemstvo institutions, could not but antagonize the entire zemstvo element toward the new project. Yet I was unable to make Plehve see my point. He answered that he had learned his lesson from the 1902 example when the members to the uezd agricultural committees were selected by uezd marshals of the nobility, and not by the governors, and that he knew better than to repeat it.

The only thing I could persuade Plehve to do was to instruct the governors not to select only those zemstvo men whose political sympathies were distinctly of a Right persuasion, but to invite prominent zemstvo workers regardless of their political views. Partly to this end, and partly to introduce those of the governors who were to preside over the conferences into the nature of the questions discussed in the projects, I suggested that these governors be invited to St. Petersburg in several groups and be given explanations regarding the technical order of procedure without which the results of the labors of these conferences could not be fully utilized.

Plehve accepted my suggestion, and toward the end of January the first group of governors, about fifteen in number, arrived in St. Petersburg. Plehve presided over their first meeting. He announced that the zemstvo representatives must not be selected on the basis of their political convictions; such selection must be based on the degree of their knowledge of peasant conditions and peasant organization and on this alone. Then he gave me the floor and I explained the fundamentals of the project, insisting particularly upon the project of peasant land tenure which in my eyes constituted the nucleus of the whole question. The peasants, I said, to be useful members of a self-governing class unit, had to be provided for materially. The present system of land tenure did not give assurance of such provision, in fact it robbed the peasant population of any such assurance. As there could be no question of the enforced annulment of the commune, it would be still less just to enforce those peasants to remain in the commune who wish to leave it in order to become economically independent.

Thereupon Plehve suggested that those present express their own views and ask any questions that they wished. Here, alas, the majority of the governors showed their utter unpreparedness, as was revealed by their questions. But the most striking example was presented by the Governor of Kaluga, Ofrosimov. In his gubernia he enjoyed the reputation of being "deaf in ear, mind, and heart." Plehve, who dearly loved to embarrass people, asked him some question which he did not hear and to which he gave the most senseless answer. The most favorable impression was made by the Governor of Kishinev, Prince S. D. Urusov.[39] He talked most sensibly, but it was evident that he was trying to take his cue from the minister. Two years later this Urusov abruptly transferred his allegiance to the Left wing of the Cadet party.

A second group of governors never did arrive in St. Petersburg; for no sooner had the first group departed than the war with Japan began. All governors were ordered to their gubernias to supervise the mobilization of reserves. The matter of peasant legislation was now relegated to a secondary position and the work of revision under Plehve, inasmuch as it was done by the Ministry of the Interior, went no further.

Nevertheless, I was eager to keep in touch with those circles which might have some influence upon the further course of this work and to incline them to that course in the development of the peasant problem which I deemed to be the only just one. To this end I made use of my participation in the so-called economic banquets and offered to speak at one of them on the work done in the Ministry of the Interior on the revision of peasant legislation. At that time social intercourse in the capital was so little developed that any public announcement by a representative of the government concerning a projected reform was quite out of the question. Consequently the economic banquets, which were held once a month, or even less frequently, and were attended by forty or fifty persons, constituted the only social channel through which any pressure could be brought to bear upon the government in the interest of a certain course of action. These banquets were attended by those members of the State Council who were most interested in economic questions and who constituted the nucleus of the banquet group, by some representatives of learning and the academic world including members of the Left socialist group such as Professor Khodsky,[40] and by other more or less prominent persons. Count Rostovtsev was permanent secretary of this group. The banquets were held in a private dining room of the restaurant Donon. They were presided over by the most prominent members of the group. The usual program was about as follows: After a modest dinner there would be a report on some problem of the day, usually an economic one, followed by discussion. There was a general critical attitude toward Witte's economic policy; in fact, one might say that this attitude was the cement which held the members of the group together. It was quite a common occurrence, therefore, to have a discussion of the activities of the Ministry of Finance, as to both its intentions and its actual achievements. At the beginning of the year the state budget was invariably discussed, and the speaker on this occasion was always P. K. Schwanebach.[41]

Sometimes persons who were not members would be invited to the banquets; usually these persons were zemstvo workers who were visiting in the city.

My suggestion that I report on the reform of peasant legislation was gladly accepted, and an unusually large number, including many zemstvo men, assembled to hear what I had to say. As in my explanatory note mentioned above, so in my speech to the banquet group I defended the ministry's project on the revision of peasant legislation. But to the banquet group I based my defense on quite different grounds. I stated directly that the duty of the state was to unify and not to stratify the population, and that therefore legislation based upon class differences should be abolished rather than developed. Yet immediate unification was not always and everywhere possible. Life is not clay and cannot always be molded as seems best, even by legislators. There is need of a certain preliminary process, certain intermediate stages. One of these stages was provided for by the project I had worked out. I pointed out that in substance the project was but a bridge intended to span the gap between general civil law and special peasant legislation. I referred, first, to those legislative innovations which were intended to bring peasant legislation into closer harmony with the country's general code, and, second, to the ease with which the regulation on peasant self-government could be changed into a regulation on the all-class, small land unit, the regulation on peasant land organization into a law which in actuality might very speedily turn all forms of communal ownership into a system of private ownership. All that was necessary, I explained, was to give every peasant the right (provided in the project only for a limited group of peasants) to break away from the commune at any given time. If this were done, the commune, as a group of landholders periodically reapportioning among its members all the commonly owned land area, would cease to exist, for with each reapportionment of communal land those members who received smaller allotments and were, therefore, dissatisfied would leave the commune.

On the subject of the new volost court organization I demonstrated that the project was but a transitory stage toward a general court system and one general judicial system, since the new project on rural contracts and that on inheritance of allotted lands —the first entirely and the second to a great extent—included the principles of the new civil code.

In conclusion, I called on all persons who desired the speedy unification of all classes in the fields of administration, justice, and land organization to do everything in their power to have the new projects made law and at the same time to initiate further changes that would speed up the establishment of one single code applicable to all classes. I also mentioned that the ministry regarded the project not as something definitely settled but as a mere foundation upon which local workers might build.

My explanation of the projects seemed to reconcile a good many persons to them; but at the same time it increased the hostility of the partisans of the commune, about which institution there was much argument in the debates that followed.

I published my rather detailed banquet speech, secured a copyright, and distributed it among those persons whose influence I considered necessary for transforming into law the new projects on peasant legislation. Most curiously my report greatly pleased Stishinsky, who told me that I had chosen a very fine way of *captatio benevolentiae* in favor of these projects. Plehve was much more subtle. He was very much interested in the impression I made by my oral report as well as in its content. After he had read the printed copy, he told me directly: "Here you seem to stress another side of the question, but I myself am not sure which is the right one."

By that time I had had frequent talks with Plehve on the peasant problem and had had an opportunity to point out that the peasantry was no longer a homogenous mass; that the commune, by forcing the most energetic and advanced of its members to range themselves with the least advanced in the cultivation of land, had forced the better peasants to seek an outlet for their energies in other branches of endeavor. Village kulaks, I said, were the most stable peasant element, and it was not their fault that they could not apply their entire energy to the problem of land exploitation. Consequently they had turned their activities in other directions and had become small traders and usurers. Seeking a further outlet for their energies, they had begun to use the labor of their neighbors, and in this they had been helped rather than hindered by the commune. A system which is devised to assist the weak and to protect them from the strong only corrupts the activity of the strong and weakens the weak since it does not develop in the latter the ability to oppose the former. The progress of mankind had resulted from the work of the strong, and improvement in social conditions depends upon the organic strength of a people. Left to themselves, the weak elements might perhaps perish, but their demise would have little significance for human progress and for the vital strength of a people and its government; in fact, their removal might prove even beneficial. It was necessary to give free play to the economic strength and capacities of the people and to their unhampered competition as a means of furthering that natural selection so necessary for the development and strengthening of a sound society. If each individual peasant were given the right to leave the commune, if the deadening law of the inalienability of peasant allotments were repealed, the country population would become a vast and solid force for order and economic progress.

I doubt if my arguments persuaded Plehve. Basing his convictions upon his limited observations of rural life, he continued to assert that our rich peasantry did not possess the germs of moral and cultural progress. He could cite the example of an innkeeper whom he had met in Kostroma Gubernia and who continued to live and keep his family in appalling filth. To Plehve this indicated the degree of his culture. Nor could Plehve forget the agrarian uprisings of 1902 in Poltava and Kharkov gubernias, where all peasants, both rich and poor, had taken part in the looting and all had been individual landowners. From these facts he concluded that as a social factor all peasants—rich and poor peasants, peasant landowners, and members of communes—were alike. By some strange irony Plehve shared the same opinions as were professed by the contributors to the *Russkoe Bogatstvo,* a distinctly socialistic publication. But even if my arguments could not win Plehve to my way of thinking, nevertheless he began to lose his assurance that his point of view was the correct one. Consequently he was without a stable, definite ideology concerning this basic question of public life; and if in some respects he continued to express his former views I am perfectly sure that he did so because of an old habit, for it was ever so much easier for him to express his opinions in familiar, well-practiced formulas and forms of speech. Men often become slaves to phrases, a slavery which increases with the years. Human minds grow torpid with age and incapable of producing new ideas in a clear-cut form. Plehve's mind seemed to be precisely in this condition. Though he spoke the same words and used the same formulas, he was no longer convinced that they were sound; yet he never acquired new ones to take their place. I never lost hope, however, that with his aid, or at least his non-resistance, it would be possible to carry out the serious reform of peasant legislation. At any rate, he did not forbid my propaganda.

As I was eager to see the progress of the work of the provincial conferences called to discuss the new projects on peasant legislation and to propagate my views in provincial society, I asked the Governor of Tver, Prince Shirinsky-Shikhmatov,[42] to invite me as a local landowner to take part in the Tver conference, which he did. This conference left me in a most depressed mood and weakened my hopes that local people might make suggestions and corrections that could be introduced into the law. I tried to console myself with the consideration that I was attending only a few first general sessions devoted to an elementary study of the fundamentals of the projects. I wanted to hope that the work of the commissions, which the conferences were to organize for the detailed examination of different portions of the projects, would be more useful. There were to be three commissions corresponding to the three main divisions of the new projects elaborated by the ministry: social administration, volost courts, and land tenure. Of course, I had no time to take part in their work. But the Tver conference, numbering about fifty participants, revealed the fact that the majority either had not read the projects or had failed to grasp their import. The conference was opened by the chairman, Prince Shikhmatov, who suggested that I outline briefly the projects to be discussed. I did so and was subjected to a sort of cross-examination from those few members, mostly progressive zemstvo men, who had read the projects. Why was this provision introduced? What was the reason for that innovation? Such were the questions asked. It was very apparent that the questioners wanted to expose a St. Petersburg bureaucrat's complete ignorance of the subject which he so lightmindedly had undertaken to explain to the zemstvo workers, and to make him contradict his own statements—which was easy enough to do, since there were about 2,400 separate articles. S. D. Kvashnin-Samarin, an old zemstvo member, once a president of the Tver Gubernia Zemstvo Board and a member of the Left group, was particularly active in this connection. His convictions were those of a typical Narodnik of the 'sixties, and his knowledge of peasant law was unsurpassed. He did not criticize; he was content to cross-examine. But I was not afraid of him; for while I might have made a mistake in many other things, I knew the contents of the projects and their provisions by heart. Kvashnin-Samarin had to end his examination by saying: "Thank you, I am satisfied."

The criticism proper, although it was vague and indefinite, came from another side, from the Right zemstvo group, and an extreme Right group at that. This criticism dealt mostly with the question of the commune and the necessity of preserving it inviolate. Of course, I flared up and answered at length and with some heat that Russia's future, her development and progress, depended upon the success of the plan to abolish the commune and to institute in its stead a system of individual and separate landownership.

When I returned to St. Petersburg I told Plehve what had taken place at the Tver conference. When I had finished my story Plehve took out of his desk a sheet of paper and said: "This is what is being written about you from Tver." It was a copy made by the censors of a letter written by Vladimir Nikolaevich Trubnikov, a pillar of the extreme Right group of the Tver Zemstvo, to A. N. Stolpakov, another Tver Zemstvo man of the same convictions and a member of the Council of the Minister of Ways and Communications. The letter contained a report on the Tver conference and included this sentence among others: "We were visited by Gurko, who had come for the express purpose of edifying us. He is the personification of a liberal St. Petersburg bureaucrat who has no doubts about anything. He made more flashy but empty liberal speeches than we had yet heard from these gentlemen. These St. Petersburg birds will yet bring us harm."

I thought that Plehve would at least ask me what sort of liberal speeches I had made; but to my surprise he merely said with his customary smile: "This is for your own information," and passed on to other matters.

After the projects had been transferred to the local men for examination, the work in the Peasant Section naturally became lighter. The regular office routine was enough to handle the working out of a project for organizing in the most important rural centers rural notaries public with volost boards. The need for such institutions close to the rural population had been felt for a long time, just as the whole rural life needed, in my eyes, many radical reforms.

I decided to use this relatively quiet period to familiarize my-

self with the activities of local peasant institutions and also with
the moods and needs of the Russian villages. With this in view I
asked Plehve for permission to inspect the gubernia and uezd peasant
institutions and other local institutions of the Ministry of the Interior in three gubernias with distinct local characteristics: Nizhnii-
Novgorod, Kursk, and Ekaterinoslav. I told him that my purpose
was not merely to inspect their activities but also to acquaint myself with conditions there and to discover, if I could, any inherent
defects of administration. Plehve consented, and I set out on this
trip in June 1904. I took with me a group of men who—judged
according to the practicability of their opinions and their initiative
and not according to their attainments as editorial clerks in the
bureaucracy—constituted the best working forces in the Peasant
Section. This group included Glinka, Strakhovsky, Baftalovsky,
Znosko-Borovsky, and Petrov, and, in addition, V. I. Kovalevsky,
who was later in charge of the supply and distribution of food
throughout the empire, and Prince N. L. Obolensky,[43] later Governor of Kharkov. They were wide-awake men with a live interest
in problems of state and national life. Kovalevsky, moreover, was
well acquainted with the peculiarities of peasant life. We planned
our work before leaving and determined upon the questions which
we intended to study. Our system was as follows: We would
arrive at a provincial capital together, inspect the three departments
of the gubernia special board—the administrative, the legal, and
the food supply—and then assemble a conference of all local gubernia authorities, both those of the government and those of the local
organizations of the nobility and the zemstvo. I would state the
results of the inspection and then discuss the most insistent needs
of the locality and the means by which they might be met. After
that we would separate into three groups, each of which was to
visit two or three uezds and some sectors of zemskie nachalniki
and volost boards. This trip afforded much valuable and varied
material which I hoped to use for the final edition of the projects.
But the assassination of Plehve on July 15, 1904, put a stop to
our work and left it unorganized and incomplete.

The news of Plehve's assassination reached us in Mariupol on
the shores of the Azov Sea. All of our group were deeply moved
although many did not share his point of view or approve of his
measures. But my colleagues in the Peasant Section had not been
affected by the war which Plehve had waged against every mani-

festation of public thought and activity, which of late had become quite reckless and provoking. The Peasant Section had taken no part in this fight because of the very character of its activity; moreover, many of its workers were where they were because of their ardent desire to take some part in the reform of rural life. They were happy in such work. Now, however, they feared that with a change of minister their work would at least be interrupted.

When I returned for Plehve's funeral I was greatly surprised to find a different reaction among the personnel of the Ministry of the Interior in the capital. When I expressed to Lopukhin,[44] the Director of the Police Department, my horror of what had happened, he said: "It could not have gone on much longer," and added a few more words to the effect that Plehve was stifling everything and everybody.

The fears of my colleagues, that with a change of minister our work of reform would be interrupted, were quite justified. This, however, was due, not to the aims of Plehve's successors, Prince Sviatopolk-Mirsky and A. G. Bulygin,[45] but to the general conditions of the times and to other more complicated reasons of which more shall be said later.

As is well known, the projects worked out in 1902–3 in the Peasant Section were not confirmed; they were not even discussed any further. It would, therefore, seem that there is no object in explaining them in such detail. Yet this is not so, for they played their rather important part in the matter of peasant organization. The work we did was used as a basis and served as a starting point for the Imperial Ukase of November 9, 1906, which conferred upon peasants the right freely to leave the communes. It was also used as a foundation for the regulations on peasant land organization, but the organization as established was in perhaps too strict accordance with the ideas expressed in the explanatory note.

With the exception of a small group of persons, the entire Russian public and even the bureaucratic circles took the Imperial Ukase of November 9 as a wholly unexpected deus ex machina. Yet the ukase was preceded by long and preparatory work and several unsuccessful attempts to apply the principles which it laid down. Of these undertakings and attempts I hope to be able to say more elsewhere. The ukase itself was speedily put into effect only because of the work that had been done on the problem in previous years. The persons who had done this preliminary work could and did become active and able executors of the plan for organizing peasant life upon the principle of private property and of the complete economic independence of each land cultivator.

But the work that had gone into framing the projects for reforming peasant self-government and peasant courts was a loss. I still think that one of two courses should have been adopted: Either to bring the peasants within the general order of administration and legislation; or to introduce substantial changes in our existing laws—for instance, to put the special regulations dealing with the peasant class in harmony with the general code of the empire. To leave the volost courts in the chaotic state in which they remained until the revolution was a grave error on the part of the government—it served to corrupt in the peasant mind the very conception of the right of private property and of those obligations which they had assumed.

CHAPTER XII

SOME OF PLEHVE'S ASSOCIATES IN THE MINISTRY OF THE INTERIOR

When Plehve was appointed Minister of the Interior, that ministry was a poorly organized and archaic institution. It was not even aware of the basic purpose of a central administration, that is, to observe conditions throughout the country and to make improvements where necessary. It did not even possess a well-arranged bureaucratic machine that could handle with dispatch the tremendous amount of business which poured into St. Petersburg. I have already mentioned that in the Peasant Section there were more than eight hundred cases awaiting presentation to the Senate, many of which had been waiting there for a number of years. Most of the other departments of the ministry were in no better condition.

Plehve had preserved his former connection with the ministry and was therefore well informed on the state of affairs there. He had his reasons for dismissing many chiefs of separate sections of the ministry, but his selection of their successors was not always fortunate. He was well acquainted with the working of the state machine. He knew that when the minister and the directors of departments of a ministry were energetic and ambitious men, the position of an assistant minister was dull and insignificant. In such cases, assistant ministers were nothing more than special senior clerks attached to the minister and possessing the legal right to sign documents for him. Neither the sphere of their activity nor the scope of their authority was clearly defined, but depended wholly on the plans of the minister. This may explain why Plehve, who had dismissed nearly all the directors of departments, had at the same time retained all the assistant ministers. He greatly altered their duties, however, and their importance.

Besides A. S. Stishinsky, of whom I have already spoken, these assistant ministers were P. N. Durnovo and N. A. Zinovev.[1] P. N. Durnovo by virtue of his intelligence, his clear understanding of the complex issues of the time, his administrative talent, and his firm and resolute character was undoubtedly superior to the other

men holding responsible positions in the central administration of
the ministry. Durnovo had begun his service in the navy, then after
completing a course in the Military Law Academy he had entered
the Ministry of Justice. In 1864, the year in which new judicial
regulations were passed, he transferred to the civil service. He,
together with a veritable constellation of talented contemporaries,
assisted in creating our new court system, which is distinguished
for its strict adherence to law and its independence of administrative government authority. How much this independence furthered the interests of the state is another question.

For a considerable time our new courts were out of touch with
realities and made their decisions in the interests of abstract truth
alone. They certainly exemplified Montesquieu's[2] theory of the
separation of powers. Count Pahlen, who introduced the new judicial statutes, went to such extremes in his endeavor to raise the
standard of juridical impartiality as to demand that representatives
of the law should have no close relations with the representatives
of any other branch of administration, including local public organizations. In Pahlen's eyes the prosecuting magistrates should be
the watchful eye of the law, always alert to detect deviations from
its exact letter and to expose transgressions committed by representatives of the government. The prosecuting magistrates could
display such impartiality and maintain continuous supervision only
if there was no personal friendship between them and the administrative personnel. This was indeed a worthy ideal; but its practical value to the state was debatable. Such supervision of government officials might easily discredit the administration in the eyes
of the population. The impartial detachment of the prosecuting
magistrate from the administrative personnel has been particularly
manifest in cases of political crimes. It has been and will always
be a matter of individual opinion as to what type of political and
social organization is best. It is not unethical to attempt to effect
a change in the existing order as long as the attempt does not in
itself constitute a criminal offense. Some persons contend that
even the latter is permissible in so far as it aims to achieve not
personal gain but the public good. But a court that is guided by
such abstract moral considerations and not by the provisions of
the existing law, which invariably protects the existing political
and social order, oversteps the limits prescribed by Montesquieu's
theory concerning the separation of powers. For, according to this

theory, these powers, executive, legislative, and judicial, should be separate and independent from each other, but not antagonistic and opposed to each other. And yet Pahlen's system led exactly to the latter condition because it inculcated in the judicial personnel the idea that they were not a part of one state apparatus but the mouthpiece of public conscience and concerned with the postulates of abstract justice and in duty bound to renounce all practical considerations of real life and general plans of the government.

The most perspicacious of the judicial personnel, gifted with a broad statesmanlike understanding of the country's interests, realized the significance of this situation. Durnovo was one of these. But, in addition, he had an eye for his own welfare. He saw that the complete segregation of the judicial personnel from the public would make advancement in its chosen career slow. He did not hesitate therefore to abandon this profession at his first opportunity —a chance to become Vice-Director of the Police Department in the Ministry of the Interior. At that time, 1881, Plehve was director of this department; but later, in 1884, Durnovo was promoted to this higher office. It was then that he displayed his great administrative talent and that great possibilities of a career opened before him. His progress was impeded for a good many years, however, by an incident which led to his dismissal. Wishing to have a positive proof of the infidelity of one Madame Dolivo-Dobrovolsky, an intimate friend of his whom he suspected of being equally friendly with the Brazilian chargé d'affaires, he placed a secret police agent as a domestic servant with his rival. Acting on Durnovo's directions the agent broke into the diplomat's desk and brought its contents to his chief. The Brazilian reported the burglary to the St. Petersburg city police, who, always at war with the Police Department, hastened to investigate the case. The Governor of St. Petersburg reported the incident to Alexander III, and in accord with the Emperor's decision Durnovo was relieved of his post of Director of the Police Department and appointed to the Senate, much to the indignation of the members of that body. But, as time went on, Durnovo's outstanding talents were made evident in the Senate and Sipiagin recalled him to administrative work by selecting him as his assistant and again making him Director of the Police Department. Thus was he engaged when Plehve became minister.

Plehve remembered Durnovo well from their work together in

the Police Department in the 'eighties, but he did not consider it altogether fitting to have him Director of the Police Department. Plehve considered himself a great expert on police organization and wished to have no intermediary between himself and that department. Accordingly he suggested that Durnovo take charge of the Chief Administration of Posts and Telegraphs,[3] a department which was as vast as a whole ministry. Durnovo did so, and carried on this work ably and willingly. Our organization of posts and telegraphs was exemplary; and if it did not develop as speedily as the tempo of public life demanded, this was solely because of the lack of necessary funds. Under the supervision of Durnovo, who defended the department's budget with skill, ardor, and persistence, the organization was considerably improved. But neither his ambition nor his pride was satisfied with this position. His term of service and his rank made him senior assistant minister and, in the event of the minister's absence or retirement, it was he who was entitled to be called upon to take up the minister's duties. Actually, however, he was completely removed from any part in the political activity of the ministry. Legislative projects worked out in the ministry, all general plans, and the political program of the minister himself were entirely unknown to him; and this fact depressed him greatly. It is not surprising, therefore, that he criticized Plehve's activities behind Plehve's back; he even established close connections with Plehve's adversary, Witte, and very likely supplied him with material which could injure Plehve. Durnovo had access to this material; for, even though he had no official contact with offices of the ministry other than that of Posts and Telegraphs, he was in personal contact with many officials in them.

One more word! In the main, Durnovo really profited by being without direct participation in the ministry's political activities, because with the appointment of Prince Sviatopolk-Mirsky as Minister of the Interior, he was able to retain his position as assistant minister and had an opportunity to play a direct part in the administration of the ministry. During the ministry of Sviatopolk-Mirsky he succeeded in divorcing himself so completely from Plehve's reactionary policy that he acquired in upper circles the reputation of being a liberal and progressive. This reputation almost prevented him from obtaining the post of Minister of the Interior in Witte's cabinet in 1905. Yet, in summary, I should hesitate to dub Durnovo a career-maker. He was not outstanding for his pure principles, nor was he overscrupulous in the choice of means he used to advance his own and other private interests; but he was deeply concerned for the welfare of his country. For him, the fate of the Russian Empire was a source of constant thought and anxiety.

Speaking generally, statesmen may be divided into three groups. In the first group—a very small one at all times and in every country—are those who put the interests of the state far above their personal interests and advance the former at the expense of the latter. These few exceptional persons very seldom reach the top of the bureaucratic ladder; in fact, in an autocratic system they attain high positions only under such rulers as William I[4] of Germany and Alexander III of Russia.

To the second group belong those statesmen who have state interests at heart but who seek to advance the interests of the state without doing injury to their own social and political careers. This is characteristic of the tactics of all political parties in all countries with parliamentary government. Of course these tactics include the employment of many means which are not strictly ethical. Both Witte and Durnovo belonged to this group. Each of them in his own way had political ideals which he strove to realize. Each to the best of his ability endeavored to put his ideals into practice. It cannot be said that either of them worked exclusively for his own profit or that either was motivated by purely personal considerations. Witte, by virtue of his stronger personality and the governmental positions he held, had a greater influence on Russian history than did Durnovo; although in suppressing the revolutionary movement of 1905, Durnovo played an important role with decisive effect. Moreover, in mental equipment, in understanding of current conditions, and in political foresight Durnovo was Witte's superior. To the masses of the population he was but a vigorous and pitiless suppressor of all public movements, a reactionary who thought that a great people could be directed and controlled by armed force alone. But in reality, Durnovo's policy was based on a sincere conviction that the great masses of one hundred fifty million people could not be left to their own devices and unsupervised by a strong machinery of state as represented by the administration, the courts, and the police. But never was he a partisan of administrative arbitrariness. His long service in the Ministry of Justice and later in the First Department of the Senate had taught him reverence for the law, and his intelligence showed him that mechanical measures alone were insufficient for governing the country. Had he held high office longer, and especially in more normal times, he would undoubtedly have looked for support in public circles, such as the educated and patriotic circles of the zemstvo. He would have turned his attention to our schools and used his energies to form a numerous, strong, and materially independent teachers' class that would be capable of educating the young generation to take pride in belonging to the great Russian people and to love their country instead of holding it in contempt. For teachers of all classes of the population had for many years indulged in wholesale criticism of everything Russian — Russian system of government, Russian social order, and even Russian history. The result had been to breed contempt for everything Russian.

To the third group belong those statesmen with whom considerations of personal interests invariably overrule considerations of state welfare. To them the value of any political move is determined by the profit they may derive from it. They are of the rabble that follow the chariot of a conqueror no matter over whom he triumphs. It is of such men that General Malet[5] spoke when he was being tried for having attempted to raise an insurrection against Napoleon I. He was asked who had been his accomplices: "All of you," he replied, "had I been successful."

Between these three arbitrary classifications there are several gradations between pure altruism and complete selfishness. Nevertheless, it is possible to make a sharp distinction between career-makers on the one hand and self-sacrificing patriots on the other. Both Witte and Durnovo were patriots, whereas many officials in the Ministry of the Interior thought of nothing but themselves and their own advancement. Certain ones tried to ingratiate themselves with their immediate superiors and gave little attention to circumstances that might, at any time, put their superiors out of office. Others, more subtle, looked ahead and tried to see in what direction the wind might blow in the not too distant future; they avoided open hostility toward their chiefs but did not associate themselves too closely with them, and as soon as it appeared likely that the chief of the moment would be supplanted by another they adjusted their conduct and expression of opinion to meet the probable new situation.

Then there are those career-makers whose political beliefs were determined by the political group which offered the greatest advantages for the moment. Such men are usually called renegades; but this name is not fitting. To be a renegade one has to believe in something, and later to repudiate it. But the members of this group never believed sincerely in anything. They only said they did; so all they had to repudiate were their words and assurances. Their political convictions may be described by an anecdote current in Moscow at the time the Jews were expelled from the capital. According to this story, one Jew, who had adopted the Greek Orthodox faith, was asked by another Jew whether or not he sincerely believed in the principle of Christianity. He answered that he had changed his faith because otherwise he would have been banished from Moscow. This sort of conviction was characteristic of the majority of Russian politicians during the first days of the February revolution of 1917—and it proved their undoing.

The third assistant minister was N. A. Zinovev, a man I did not know very well. I do know, however, that he had received special education—he was either a geodesist or an astronomer—but was lacking in general knowledge. I also know that he was by nature rash and even rude, a trait which caused his transfer from the governorship of Tula to that of Mogilev, for he had created impossible relations with the nobility of Tula. I also know that he exhibited the same bluntness in inspecting zemstvo organizations, a task which Plehve had assigned him. But the inspection was done thoroughly, and his reports contained much valuable material. His colleagues contended that he was slavishly obedient to the instructions and wishes of his superiors and in turn resented all suggestions made by his subordinates. In fact it was said that sometimes persons reporting to him expressed views directly contrary to the ones they wished to have adopted, being sure that Zinovev would adopt the opposite out of contrariness.

Before Plehve became Minister of the Interior, Zinovev had been assistant minister and also Director of the Department of Economy, which was in charge of the entire business of municipal and zemstvo self-government. When this department was transformed into the Chief Administration for the Affairs of Local Economy and S. N. Herbel* was appointed its head, Zinovev was

* Prior to his appointment to this post Herbel[6] had been Governor of Kherson, and before that Chairman of the Kherson Gubernia Board. Plehve selected him to supervise affairs of local economy, hoping that his experience as a zemstvo man would make him an able intermediary between the minister and zemstvo circles; for it was Plehve's purpose to establish friendly relations with the zemstvos. It

removed from direct management of these affairs and was employed almost exclusively in inspecting these local institutions. Under Plehve, Zinovev was entirely in favor of limiting the zemstvos' sphere of authority and of subordinating them to the control of the central government. Later, as a member of the reorganized State Council, Zinovev professed other views. He had joined the Center party,* and seized every opportunity to advocate an increase of power for local self-government. He argued with fervor that the competence of the zemstvos and municipalities should be extended and that they should be protected from the interference and supervision of the government.

I should like also to mention another of Plehve's associates, B. V. Stürmer, who, as Director of the Department for General Affairs of the Ministry of the Interior, played a part of considerable importance and attracted some public attention. Plehve's first appointment to this post had been A. A. Rogovich, a man of high moral integrity, who later became Assistant Ober-Prokuror of the Holy Synod and member of the State Council. But in spite of his extremely conservative views Rogovich had not been on good terms with Plehve, mainly because he was slow and lax in carrying out the minister's orders; consequently, he was replaced by Stürmer.

This career-maker, characterized by lack of scruple, had begun in the office of ceremonies in the Ministry of the Imperial Court. He rose to be assistant head of this office and then profited by an imprudent act of his immediate superior, Count Cassini, to boost himself into the Count's position.† A little later, in the 'nineties, he considered that it would be best for his future career to change

was, no doubt, pursuit of this same purpose that led Plehve to appoint as heads of offices in the Chief Administration for the Affairs of Local Economy, Nemirovsky, former chairman of a gubernia zemstvo board of a southern gubernia, and Psheradzsky, mayor of a gubernia capital. In this way Plehve hoped to be able to establish in the ministry a sympathetic attitude toward the needs of the zemstvos and municipalities and so to establish normal relations between the government and public institutions. These hopes did not materialize; but the fault for this must be shared by both sides. The liberal public strove not toward establishing friendly relations with the government but toward attaining a dominant position in the country.

* Midway between the Octobrists and the Cadets.

† Count Cassini had been given some decoration, probably one of little consequence, for he considered himself worthy of a more important one. In his chagrin, the Count threw the decoration into the office stove. Stürmer witnessed the act and reported it; Count Cassini was dismissed, and Stürmer was appointed his successor.

his field of service. He had set his heart upon becoming a governor. He succeeded in obtaining an appointment as Chairman of the Zemstvo Board of Tver Gubernia, since he was a Tver Gubernia zemstvo member of the extreme Right. The elected zemstvo candidate, Rodichev, had been found politically unreliable by the government and his candidacy had been rejected. Stürmer's appointment to his new post was accompanied with the assurance that after completing his term of office he would be appointed governor.

At Tver Stürmer showed his unscrupulous cleverness in full. He was ignorant of zemstvo business and realized that he himself could not direct it. But he did not wish to be exposed to the criticism of the Gubernia Zemstvo Assembly, the majority of whose members were in opposition to the government and would therefore be glad to discredit the government's appointee; so he made certain arrangements with the leaders of this majority. By these arrangements, Stürmer was to continue the work of the Zemstvo Board as it had been done previously; the majority leaders on their part guaranteed that he would be spared attacks during the sessions of the Zemstvo Assembly. This agreement was carried out by both sides. Stürmer showed the Board's reports to I. I. Petrunkevich, the leader of the opposition, and the opposition criticized the actions of the Board, which represented the government, only enough so that the arrangement would not be revealed to outsiders. In the end it always confirmed and approved all of the Board's undertakings and actions. In this way Stürmer preserved the appearance of a conscientious executive and at the same time acquired the reputation of a man of outstanding diplomatic ability who could fulfill the wishes of the government without antagonizing the public.

In 1895 the promise of a governorship was fulfilled. In that year Goremykin restored to the Tver Zemstvo Assembly the right to elect its chairman; Stürmer was thereupon appointed Governor of Novgorod, and later Governor of Yaroslavl.* And, be it said in

---

* Stürmer's transfer to Yaroslavl was the result of an incident which showed his fondness for display and impressive ceremony. As Governor of Novgorod he gave a formal dinner to the local nobility and their marshal, Prince B. A. Vasilchikov.[7] He planned that it should be a sort of imperial reception; he would wait till all his guests had assembled and then make a majestic entrance. But his guests did not take to this sort of hospitality, and before Stürmer appeared they repaired to the house of Prince Vasilchikov for a "cold snack." This incident apparently taught Stürmer a lesson, for he showed the nobility of Yaroslavl such consideration that they presented him with sufficient land to enable him to become a member of the nobility of that gubernia.

all fairness, in both gubernias he succeeded in establishing friendly relations with the local zemstvos. He held firmly to the banner of the extreme Right for the benefit of the government, yet he avoided all clashes with the zemstvo workers.

The duties of the Director of the Department for General Affairs in the Ministry of the Interior, to which office Plehve now appointed Stürmer, demanded tact and pleasant manners, but also firmness of action. This department dealt with all personal appointments in the ministry, all bonuses and rewards, the granting of vacations and leaves of absence, and the distribution of monetary appropriations for the upkeep and renovation of the ministry buildings, including the residences of governors. Besides, it was upon the director of this department that the Minister of the Interior often imposed the unpleasant task of expressing to local administrators his displeasure at some of their actions and even sometimes of suggesting that they request their retirement. Stürmer's alleged ability to carry out governmental policies and at the same time to win the sympathetic support of the public suggested to Plehve that he would be the right man to perform the delicate tasks of this position. Hence Stürmer's appointment.

But Stürmer never succeeded in establishing friendly relations with Plehve. He submitted meekly to Plehve's sarcasm, so that the latter soon lost all respect for him. Plehve went even so far as to criticize him publicly. During the two years of his work with Plehve, Stürmer drank from a bitter cup indeed. But his new life offered him much with which to console himself: a splendid governmental residence, a good salary augmented with many monetary rewards, a chance to play the role of lord and master before visiting officials of the central government, and an opportunity to satisfy his love for giving splendid luncheons and dinners. All this so attracted Stürmer that he suffered in silence Plehve's sharp and sometimes rude treatment. Just as Witte strove for power as a means to apply his restless creative energy, just as Goremykin strove to acquire a standing that would enable him to surround himself with comforts, so Stürmer strove for power as a means to satisfy his petty ambition and his empty vanity. The outward signs of authority—gold lace on his uniform, decorations, both Russian and foreign, of which he had a great number, and which he kept in a special showcase — the subservience of his subordinates, these things stimulated Stürmer in his pursuit of power. He lacked completely a sense of responsibility toward or of interest in his work. Also, he was tremendously lazy and his chief concern was to find workers who could be charged with all the work under his direction. In the Department for General Affairs all routine work was done by one of the clerks, Shimkevich, and all important work, such as the working out of legislative projects and the compilation of memoranda on complicated matters, was done by Gurland,[8] a professor of constitutional law of the Demidov Lyceum whom Stürmer had brought from Yaroslavl. Gurland possessed a gifted pen, a sound education, and a talent for understanding the moods of his superiors. His brains and ability supported Stürmer in all the posts he occupied in the capital.

One more characteristic of Stürmer must be mentioned—his great patience. He attended the sessions of every conference to which he was appointed; but his presence was purely formal, as he never took any part in the work. He did not seem to be at all interested in the subjects discussed unless they touched upon himself and his own personal interests. He had even developed the ability to slumber gently during sessions while preserving the outward appearance of listening attentively to everything that was being said.

In 1904 Stürmer was appointed a member of the State Council. In the twelve years that followed he searched tirelessly for means to increase his power. Finally, in 1916, he became Chairman of the Council of Ministers, the highest position in the government. He had reached his goal; but the result was his own undoing and the ruin of Russia.

I should like also to mention Professor N. A. Zverev,[9] Head of the Chief Administration for the Affairs of the Press, a department of the Ministry of the Interior. He came from a peasant family of Novgorod Gubernia and had been educated by Khotiaintsev, a landowner of that district, who had seen that the boy had an alert mind and a desire for education. Zverev had abandoned his academic career under the Minister of Education, Bogolepov, a former rector of Moscow University, whose assistant he became. He belonged to that small group of professors who openly admitted their Right-wing political views and were confirmed partisans of autocracy.

Zverev's predecessor as Head of the Chief Administration for the Affairs of the Press had been M. P. Solovev,[10] whom Pobedonostsev had recommended to Sipiagin. Solovev was a man of confused thinking and without any definite policy. During his term of office, the press had found it difficult to determine just what they might and might not do, but on the whole it had enjoyed greater freedom than it did later under Zverev. It was under Solovev, for instance, that *Russkoe Bogatstvo,* a distinctly socialist magazine, came into existence. Zverev, however, made definite demands of the press, so that it knew beforehand what penalties it might expect for certain actions. He also introduced an innovation in this field—although I do not know whether the initiative was his or Plehve's—to the effect that the Right-wing press, which was strongly supported by the government, should bear the same responsibility for its actions as did the Left or opposition press. This was intended to show the public that the government in its impartiality applied the same measures to the conservative press as to the Left-wing opposition press. Strange as it may seem, however, the opposition press took up the cudgels on behalf of the conservative organs and affirmed with some reason that the government allowed no freedom of thought even to its wellwishers and that it suppressed not only that which it considered harmful but also that which was quite agreeable.

All in all, Zverev had little influence upon the press, for he could make no contacts among its leaders. Nor did he figure as a strong personality in the ministry. He stood in awe of his superiors; Plehve made him positively tremble. Under Plehve's successor, Prince Sviatopolk-Mirsky, Zverev was replaced by A. V. Belgard.[11]

Among the persons whom Plehve had transferred from the Imperial Chancellery to the Ministry of the Interior, was D. N. Liubimov,[12] whom he appointed director of the Minister's Chancellery. Liubimov was the son of a professor of chemistry in Moscow University. (His father was one of the closest friends of M. N. Katkov and a regular contributor to the *Moskovskiia Vedomosti.*) His education and the influence of his university environment had made him a decided conservative. He professed openly and cynically, however, that his chief desire was to make his way "to a certain goal." He was a man of recognized talent, and his gifted pen made him of great value to his superiors whose ideas he could express in writing with great speed and brilliance. His inborn courtesy and readiness to be of assistance attracted all who met him. He himself was well aware of this talent and knew how to make use of it. He used to say, with his disarming smile, that he could win the friendship of any dignitary in a half-hour's talk. Liubimov had no influence upon the matters which crossed his desk, but that did not bother him. A fairly long term of service must have shown him that the overwhelming majority of the numerous memoranda and reports which were continually being composed in St. Petersburg bureaucratic circles on all conceivable subjects led to nothing except, perhaps, the advancement of their authors. He treated such reports accordingly and even found entertainment and some excitement in composing them. The brief case in which he carried his own compositions bore an inscription suggestive of his attitude to his work: *"Sic itur ad astra."*

Later, however, Liubimov revealed a strong sense of gratitude to persons who had assisted his career. When Prince Mirsky succeeded Plehve he announced that he strongly disagreed with his predecessor's policies and intended to inaugurate an era of liberalism. Liubimov, disregarding the fact that he might incur the disfavor of his new chief, wrote and published a small laudatory essay entitled *Pamiati Pleve* (*"To the Memory of Plehve"*). Prince Mirsky, however, took no action against him; in fact, Liubimov, thanks to his ingratiating talents, soon succeeded in establishing just as friendly relations with Mirsky as he had enjoyed with Plehve.

Liubimov also demonstrated that he had administrative talent. First as Governor of Vilna, and later as assistant to the Governor-General of Warsaw during the war, he won the confidence of both the Russian and the Polish people. In the period between his incumbency of these positions he was assistant to the Chief of His Majesty's Private Chancellery to Receive Petitions, where he won the friendship of everyone. Mention should also be made of Liubimov's artistic and literary talent and rich imagination. He wrote an essay which dealt with love-making in different periods of history, but because of the nature of its contents it could not be published. In spots it resembled Ovid. One of his stories, *Obed u gubernatora* (*"Dinner at the Governor's"*), depicts a scene in a manner worthy of Leskov,[13] or even of Gogol.[14]

Plehve's selection as Commander of the Gendarme Corps[15] was General V. Wahl,[16] formerly Governor of St. Petersburg and a conservative. Wahl was a typical German. He worked conscientiously in supporting the interests of the state, even though these were purely Russian interests. He showed this during his term as Governor of Vilna, where he did much to preserve the monuments of Russian antiquity in this region, which was falling so much under Polish influence. But Wahl was not a quick nor a profound thinker. He knew police work to perfection and, like the majority of persons who had worked in the Police Department, he was criticized and even reviled. Public opinion said he was a grafter; but this was not true. Wahl was an honest man. Even with his German thrift, his personal fortune remained microscopic. Later, as a member of the State Council, he lived entirely on his salary.

Wahl had no influence upon the policy of the ministry, since he had no direct relation with the political activities of his subordinates in the Gendarme Corps. These activities were directed by the Police Department in pursuit of a policy with which Wahl was not sympathetic, although Plehve unfortunately was. Wahl did not comprehend the Zubatov program. To him it seemed fantastic in conception and harmful in results. He was continually at odds with Lopukhin, Director of the Police Department, a fact which was only natural considering the double subordinance of the Gendarme Corps. Wahl disapproved also of the local policy of the Police Department and expressed himself openly on this subject to Plehve. Yet Wahl could not be called a tenderhearted man. He regarded all political prisoners, even if they had not participated in deeds of a violent nature, as ordinary criminals. He never made concessions in the prison regime for political prisoners. He was a straightforward German who saw no reason to favor persons who had attempted to overthrow the state; their reasons were of no interest or concern to him. When Vera Figner[17] was incarcerated in the Schlüsselburg fortress[18] he would not allow her to wear silk stockings. His education, his theories, and his outlook marked him as belonging to a former epoch and not very sympathetic toward another person's point of view. In the beginning of the twentieth century Wahl was an anachronism. Plehve with all his bureaucratism was much more modern than Wahl, who represented an administrator of the time of Alexander II. Wahl's relations with Plehve were friendly. Plehve appreciated him as a faithful and efficient subordinate who might disagree with the plans of his superiors but would never permit himself to twist the meaning of their orders while executing them. When Plehve finally realized the harm that Zubatov was doing and suspected him of playing a double game, he ordered Wahl to search Zubatov's lodgings and to take away from him all his official papers. This was a plan of action on which Plehve and Wahl were at one.

In conclusion, I should like to say a few words about A. V. Krivoshein, who was Director of the Department of Peasant Colonization when Plehve was appointed Minister of the Interior. What can be said of this man who was later to play so important a part in the government? In my opinion his most outstanding characteristic was a desire to take from life the best that was to be had, regardless of the means by which it was obtained. He had set himself this goal in his youth and had pursued it without deviation. He had soon realized that the best method was to establish extensive and useful contacts in wide and varied circles, not excluding the ladies. In his student days he had succeeded in gaining the friendship of the son of the Minister of the Interior, Count D. A. Tolstoi.* Since then fate had smiled on Krivoshein. Under Tolstoi he was appointed commissioner for peasant affairs in the uezds of the Kingdom of Poland, and a little later was transferred to the central government, namely, to the Peasant Section of the Ministry of the Interior. When the affairs of peasant colonization were taken out of the Peasant Section, a new Department of Peasant Colonization was formed and Krivoshein was transferred to this department, the director of which was Gippius. Krivoshein charmed his new chief and as a result was appointed assistant director of this new department. Later, Gippius lost his mind, but according to law he could not be discharged until a year from the day on which this sad event took place. Meantime Krivoshein became acting director of the department.

Krivoshein was still thus employed when Sipiagin became Minister of the Interior and appointed Stishinsky to be Director of the Department of Peasant Colonization. Stishinsky had made his way up in the world by hard and honest work and by a staunch adherence to conservative opinions. He was no judge of men and

---

* Count Tolstoi's son, the famous "Glebushka," was noted for his tremendous appetite; from morning till night he thought of nothing but food. He was mentally deficient, but his father did not lose hope of developing his intellect and sent him abroad to travel in the care of tutors, one of whom was Krivoshein; another was Prakhov the artist.

was soon charmed by the adroit Krivoshein, who knew how to flatter a superior without appearing obsequious. Before long Krivoshein was appointed director in Stishinsky's stead and was one of the few heads of departments retained by Plehve, Sipiagin's successor. In Krivoshein's case this retention was largely due to the fact that he had cultivated the friendship of Plehve's son, who worked in the same department. But the son's friendship did not save him from the father's criticism and sarcasm. In the summer of 1903 Plehve went so far as to treat Krivoshein with marked rudeness in the presence of several officials of the ministry. Krivoshein, calculating as always,* said nothing at the time, but later that same day he submitted his resignation to the minister. As I have already mentioned, Plehve did not like men who would not stand their ground. On seeing that Krivoshein would not brook rude treatment, even from a superior, Plehve completely reversed his attitude to Krivoshein and asked him to reconsider his resignation. In the autumn of that year, these two men went together on a journey through Siberia. Plehve returned perfectly charmed with his companion. What Krivoshein's attraction was it is hard to say. He had as yet no love for his work and no talent for writing; nor was he eloquent. But he had something, and whatever it was it achieved results.

Meanwhile, Krivoshein had been looking about him and carefully observing the ever growing public discontent. He foresaw the possibility of a sharp change in the course of state policy which would, of course, entail great changes in the governmental circles. He undertook, therefore, to establish personal relations in circles hostile to Plehve and began, in a very mild and cautious way, to criticize the latter's policy. He criticized especially Plehve's attitude toward the zemstvos. Nor did he take pains to conceal his criticisms from Plehve. For instance, when occasion arose to select a new chairman of the Moscow Gubernia Board, Krivoshein told Plehve frankly that it would be very tactless and might cause serious damage not to confirm the election of D. N. Shipov.

---

* Another instance of Krivoshein's cautious calculation is to be seen in his refusal to accept a ministerial portfolio in the cabinet Goremykin formed in 1906 after Witte's resignation. Krivoshein was then Assistant Minister of Finance and a cabinet position meant a considerable promotion. Yet he did not accept the offer because he was not at all sure of the stability of Goremykin and his cabinet, and, perhaps, of the entire regime. He preferred to remain modestly in the background and to conceal his political physiognomy.

Krivoshein took a peculiar stand on the peasant problem. Though he was invited to participate in the debates on the reform of peasant legislation, he refused to take an active part in this work and failed to express any opinion on the basic question, namely, whether peasant courts and self-government should be preserved distinct from those of other classes or whether the peasant class should be made one with other classes of the population. He had more to say on the matter of communal or individual ownership of peasant lands but still avoided expressing a decisive opinion. He realized, however, that in this matter both the government and different public circles seemed to favor the preservation of the commune. As he thought that this policy would finally prove victorious, he expressed himself as opposed to the breaking up of the commune. At the time, this stand seemed to be a most democratic one. The existing law protected the commune, and with conditions as they were it was infinitely more difficult decisively to change the law than to continue the existing arrangement. Later, however, just before his appointment as Head of the Chief Administration of Land Organization and Agriculture, Krivoshein abandoned this point of view. He did it in a very solemn manner. He announced in the Council of Ministers (he was then Assistant Minister of Finance, and, as such, Manager of the Bank of the Nobility and the Peasant Land Bank and had the right to attend the Council's meetings) that he had visited certain rural districts where the peasants were leaving the communes to move to individually owned farms and that he was persuaded that he had been in error in expressing himself as opposed to reforming the commune. He said that he now realized that Russia's salvation, as well as the surest way of assuring the prosperity and even the cultural development of the rural population, lay in carrying out the provisions of the Imperial Ukase of November 9, 1906, which gave peasants the right to leave the communes and move to individually owned farms. One wonders whether he was sincerely convinced of the advisability of this measure or whether he realized that the policy now adopted by the government would be followed for a long time to come, and that to adopt this view would be the easiest way to crown his career with success. I am inclined to think that both considerations are correct. The fact is that, although Krivoshein lacked profound knowledge, especially of peasant conditions, he had an exceptional mind, fine political perceptions, and an ability to orient himself among the most complex political situations. When he saw with his own eyes what a difference there was between individually owned peasant property and property subjected to the constraint of communal management, he could not fail to understand the advantages of the former, even though he had no well-thought-out opinion of peasant welfare. Also his political sense told him that the governmental policy in this direction was a stable one and that Stolypin, as head of the government, intended to continue it.

In further anticipation of later events I should like to describe his transformation after he was appointed head of a large ministry and had thus reached his goal. There was a real metamorphosis. He continued his habitual tactics of making and keeping the most varied personal connections for the attainment of his ends, but he now used them to advance the work entrusted to him. He undertook this work with sincere interest and fervor. His famed restraint in expressing his thoughts and opinions disappeared, at least within the confines of his office. He stated his purposes definitely and clearly, and in effecting them he displayed a power of thought worthy of a real statesman. He also revealed administrative and organizing talents. He made an astute selection of gifted and efficient co-workers and gave them much freedom of action, limiting his control of them to directions of a general character. He had a marked ability to distinguish between the essential and the unimportant. The details he left entirely to the discretion of his subordinates, retaining for himself general leadership and firm control. He was an exacting and serious chief and inspired his subordinates with energy and interest necessary for their work. He could be severe to persons who did not justify his expectations, but he was generous in his praise and encouragement to those who executed his orders with intelligence and skill. He possessed a talent of winning people's favor—a talent which Plehve lacked.

While he was a masterful chief in his own ministry, he became a subtle diplomat outside it. One of his most difficult tasks was to acquire the sums necessary for the work of improving peasant land organization and the technique of Russian agriculture. Kokovtsov was then Minister of Finance, and, as is well known, his chief concern was to draw up a budget without deficits and, if possible, to secure and maintain an accumulation of money in the State Treasury. It was indeed difficult to get from him those tens of millions of rubles which were spent in carrying out Krivoshein's program and almost necessarily caused some friction with Kokovtsov, who became Chairman of the Council of Ministers after Stolypin's assassination in August 1911. Had Krivoshein been moved exclusively by personal considerations and not by a desire to do good for his country, he would not have insisted, year after year, on ever increasing sums for the development of that branch of public endeavor of which he was the director.

Krivoshein was reproached for using every occasion and considerable state sums to advertise his activity.* And it is true that if his efforts to represent the work of his ministry in the most attractive light and to inform the masses of the population of what he was doing are regarded as self-advertising, they will assume a personal and unattractive character. But if his actions are referred to as a scheme for informing the population of intended governmental measures, they acquire the character of sound state policy which seeks to facilitate the realization of proposed measures by winning for them general approval and moral support. A tendency to explain essentially just and useful actions as low personal speculations has, alas, always been a characteristic of the Russian public mind. It resulted in a tendency toward wholesale criticism of government measures. If the government worked in silence, it was said that it was hiding its plans and undertakings from the public whose criticisms it feared. If it tried to apprise the masses of its activity and the results attained, it was accused of self-advertising. Did the public expect the government to represent its own undertakings in an unfavorable light? In the final analysis one must be concerned not with the motives which prompted Krivoshein and Witte, for instance, when they tried to inform the public of the reforms they had undertaken and of the results they had achieved; one must be concerned rather with the degree to which this mode of action proved effective in attaining given state aims. On this basis, there can be no doubt that each of these men chose the proper course of action.

* For instance he published a fine book with many illustrations, describing the course of work for the improvement of the peasant land organization. Another even more splendid publication described Asiatic Russia and its natural resources, a very interesting work picturing the rug industry in our Asiatic territories, especially in Turkestan. But if these works advertised Krivoshein, they advertised Russia much more. They advertised the tremendous processes at work in her land organization, the innumerable natural resources of Asiatic Russia that still awaited exploitation, and the artistic treasures unearthed in studying the products of the Asiatic population of the Russian Empire.

Krivoshein clearly realized that under existing conditions no serious results could be attained unless the proposed government measures were assured of the approval and support of broad public forces. To this end he endeavored to form friendly connections with the Duma members of all parties. He sought popularity with the zemstvos* and the so-called third element.[19] The results were apparent: the Duma invariably supported all of his projects and his requests for monetary appropriations. Furthermore, Krivoshein insisted that all his colleagues show a sympathetic attitude toward the public and tolerance of its opinions and even of its criticisms. He selected as his helpers men with a gift for attracting public sympathy and for smoothing off rough edges. Krivoshein realized, of course, that certain concessions to public desires were not useful to the state. For instance, large appropriations of money to the zemstvos for agricultural needs could not be made when there was no guaranty that these sums would be usefully expended. But he realized that some concessions to the public were necessary if anything was to be accomplished, although he was aware that they might not be justifiable as measures of sound statesmanship. As minister, Krivoshein continued to employ the same methods he had used in making his career, but with the important difference that he used them, not to maintain his personal power, but to apply this power to the needs of the state. If his desires had been limited merely to holding his position, it would have been much simpler and easier for him not to have raised new problems, not to have been fervently active in the welfare of the state; because any activity evokes criticism as well as praise and creates enemies as well as friends. As minister, Krivoshein proved himself to be a statesman of no mean caliber, of courageous initiative and subtle political instinct. As he acquired more and more confidence with the Tsar and the public, he extended his activity beyond the limits of his own ministry. Fortunately, he had connections in industrial circles, so that he did not repeat Witte's error of lending a one-sided support to that branch of public activity which concerned him directly.

I have glanced over the above sketches and have asked myself

---

* In 1913, zemstvo agricultural experts, invited to attend the Agricultural Conference organized by the Chief Administration of Land Organization and Agriculture, addressed to the Assistant Minister, Count P. N. Ignatev,[20] who was presiding over the conference, a warm speech expressing their gratitude for having been given an opportunity freely to express their opinions and desires.

whether I have given an honest delineation of these persons, whether I have over-emphasized petty details, or certain insignificant weaknesses, and have thus distorted the true picture I wished to draw. No one is perfect. All the men I have characterized had their faults. That they were men who did not entirely forget their private interests is also true. But, judged by their intelligence, their general culture, they certainly belonged to our elite. Also, they were men of administrative experience and training. Not for a moment could they be likened to those persons who filled our public organizations, such as the zemstvos and municipalities. The work of government institutions, irrespective of the results achieved, was enormous; and the higher a man's position, the more work he had to do. The majority of the St. Petersburg bureaucrats had no private life at all. Their time was divided between their offices, endless meetings and conferences, and their own desks in their studies at home, where they worked until late at night. Moreover, the Russian inability to separate holidays from week-days gave no time for rest. There can be no question that the best elements of the country were drawn into government service.

Favoritism on a wide scale was never practised. There were positions, it is true, that were simply the expression of patronage; but these were of secondary importance. There was, too, a limited number of sinecures which were filled mostly by persons who had many years of service to their credit but who had only small pensions on which to exist. Our statute on pensions was antiquated and did not provide aged pensioners with means adequate for even a modest living.

Of course, it is possible to draw a picture of the ideal revolutionist. Savinkov[21] did so in his *Memoirs of a Terrorist,* in which he extolled those who carried out the assassination plans he had made and for the results of which he must be held responsible. Indeed, to extol the virtues of his agents was the best he could have done for them. But it is not my purpose to draw any such picture. The upper bureaucrats of St. Petersburg were considered not only by the opposition but also by the entire provincial public as men of little knowledge, who did still less work, and limited their activities to brief appearances in the ministry to hear a few reports and see a few men from the provinces. There was a particularly firm conviction that all advancements in position were the result of patronage, proceeding mostly from the ladies. This idea was patently false. All officials in all ministries were up to their necks in work, nerve-racking work, which did not let up even during holidays. This does not mean, of course, that all work in the ministries was carried on in perfect co-ordination with the actual needs of the population.

The integrity of the overwhelming majority of the high officials is beyond question. Only persons who are absolutely unfair can now accuse our high officials of graft, for all our state archives have been opened and all our secret documents have been published. The Provisional Government, and later the Bolsheviks, conducted most exhaustive inquiries into the activities of our ministers and were unable to detect one compromising fact. (Of course, I do not intend to insult our former government by comparing it in any way with that band of highwaymen who call themselves the Soviet government. I wish to compare it with the governments of Western Europe and to affirm that it was much more honest and disinterested than they.) It is very possible that graft, simple and unadulterated, is practised even less in Western Europe than it was with us, but the desire for enrichment is much more strongly developed there and is attained by other means. To hold a governmental position and at the same time to be connected with large financial and industrial undertakings is not only a frequent but a common occurrence in Western Europe. Under such conditions one does not need to resort to bribery. Bribery, a crude, primitive, and slightly dangerous method, has now been supplanted by a method more subtle and modern, one that is perfectly safe because it is undetectable. A timely notification of some impending act of the government, indirect support of some private enterprise, and a number of other very diverse ways of assisting the profits of some business or bank—these bring much larger returns than primitive, naïve, old-fashioned bribery. In the West, consequently, those who work for the government for some time or who are prominent in a political party assemble tidy fortunes. This phenomenon is well known; but it is little criticized by anyone; in fact, it is taken as a matter of course. Compare this situation with that in Russia, where the law explicitly stated that no civil service position could be filled by a person who was at the same time engaged in private business or who was a director or member of a board of any organization which gave him an income. Our bureaucrats have been accused of striving to obtain positions which permitted the use of governmental houses, of arranging needless trips well paid for by the government, of giving themselves bonuses out of sums left from vacant offices—but how petty these accusations are, and how well they prove that even the higher officials had very little means, and lived on their salaries, which shrank relatively and steadily as the cost of living increased. It often happened, in fact, that men who had held high and responsible positions for a number of years retired to live on miserable pensions and, at death, left to their children as their most valuable possessions only jeweled decorations and silver albums with photographs of their former colleagues.

It is true that, toward the end, these Spartan customs began to change. The rapid development of our industry and banking operations created a new situation. Many of our most prominent officials transferred from civil service to private business. This happened most frequently in the case of men in the Ministry of Finance and particularly in the Credit Office. The salaries paid these men by business concerns often reached fabulous sums. In engaging such a man, private concerns unquestionably took into consideration his official connections and his knowledge of the methods necessary to obtain governmental backing for certain measures, particularly to secure some state concession. Also, after the establishment of elective offices, private enterprises began to include in their directing personnel influential members of the upper and lower chambers.

The customs of Western Europe had begun to penetrate into Russia. The civil service workers now desired to attain not only power and distinction but also wealth, and it is perfectly possible that in a few more years they would have been as successful in this as were their counterparts in Western Europe. But in the main, until the last years of the empire Russian administrators served their country not for money but for honor, and both the bureaucrats and the highest army commanders served not their own interests but those of their country, whose honor and dignity were infinitely dear to them. Even so they could not adequately meet all problems of state—not because of personal deficiencies, but because of several varied and highly complex reasons of which I shall name but one: a rapid increase in population, which served to make ever more marked the changing conditions of life and the difference in national composition, which was becoming ever more noticeable with the raising of cultural levels. No existing authority could cope with all these pressing problems. The rebuilding of the whole governmental structure was inevitable; but this giant task demanded the hand of a genius, another Peter, who, alas, was not at hand.

CHAPTER XIII

PLEHVE'S STRIFE WITH WITTE

For St. Petersburg bureaucratic circles the winter of 1902–3 passed under the sign of strife between Plehve and Witte. This strife had been predicted since the very day of Plehve's appointment as Minister of the Interior. It was caused both by the personal characteristics of these two masterful men and by the radical differences between their political points of view.

Witte was concerned with economic measures and intended to support only those elements of the public which in his estimation were capable of developing the economic life of the country. He realized, and rightly so, that in the twentieth century Russia could not preserve her international standing and her independence from Western Europe without developing her then infant industry. Accordingly he directed all his fiery energy to its development. As a matter of fact Witte was completely under the influence of our famous chemist, D. I. Mendeleev, who urged that support of those branches of our public economy which were least advanced—in this case industry—was the best way to develop Russia's productive forces. But how could industry be aided? A high tariff would only have evoked unbearable tariff reprisals from the powers of Western Europe. There seemed to be but one device: a ready supply of cheap labor. If labor were cheap—even though it were unskilled—the unit production cost in Russia could be kept below that of Western Europe. To keep labor cheap it was necessary to keep down the cost of living, especially the cost of bread. This entailed low prices for grain and thereby took its toll of the Russian landowners. But Witte was not concerned about agriculture, perhaps because he was unfamiliar with its basic principles. He did not consider that it needed any artificial support. He did not realize, for instance, that farming, because of the slowness of production and the consequent slowness of monetary turnover, did not yield high profits. It meant nothing to him that the landowner should suffer from low grain prices so long as industry should benefit therefrom.

Witte had no high regard for the landowning class. He consid-

201

ered its representatives incapable of managing efficiently any productive business or of accumulating capital in the country. He had little sympathy for them also because of their petitions for financial aid and relief: petitions for lower interest rates on loans made by the Bank of the Nobility; petitions for subsidies to the nobility's mutual benefit organizations and for other class needs; and especially petitions from individual borrowers from the Bank of the Nobility who wanted easier terms and deferment of payments. Witte did not and would not see that only in occasional individual cases did these petitions grow out of the fact that the landowners were living beyond their means, and that in the majority of cases the petitions were the result, on the one hand, of an injudicious use of funds raised from mortgaging land and, on the other, of the existing agricultural crisis, which accounted for the very low profit from land.

If funds raised by land mortgages are not used to increase the land's productivity, complications will arise and a burden will be placed upon the very means of production. Now many of our landowners used such funds mainly for the purpose of buying the portions of the inherited estate from co-heirs who were willing to sell, and in so doing failed to develop their land. Even when the mortgage money was used to purchase equipment and otherwise provide for increased production, failure often followed. This was caused by the extremely hard but inevitable crisis which our landowners were passing through. They had been deprived of free serf labor and had had to change from a natural to a monetary system of economy. Conditions were then extremely unfavorable for such a transition, especially since the majority of the landowners had neither theoretical nor practical knowledge of the complicated business of agricultural production. But Witte was unaware of all this. He regarded the landowners as insolvent debtors of the Bank of the Nobility pleading for deferment of payment, as spendthrifts incapable of furthering the well-being of the country or even of keeping themselves out of bankruptcy.

Witte's opinion of the Russian nobility as a civil service class reflected the point of view of the intelligentsia and, more recently, of the industrial class, according to which the nobility were parasites enjoying unmerited privileges. Witte failed to realize that it was not a question of privileges but that the nobility with all its faults was the only class that had an understanding of state problems. Such understanding may not always have been conscious but was the result of many generations of service to the state. The Russian civil service class was steeped in this understanding, which was an integral organic part of it.

And yet, our bureaucrats were not all noblemen. A glance at the high officials of the reign of Nicholas II reveals that the majority of them belonged neither to the nobility nor to the landed gentry: Plehve, Krivoshein, Vannovsky, Kuropatkin, Nebogatov,[1] Kornilov,[2] Alekseev,[3] Bogolepov, Pobedonostsev, Makarov, Rukhlov, Rozhestvensky,[4] Tertii Filippov,[5] Giers[6]—all were commoners; not one was a nobleman.

It is probable that Witte intended to use the industrial classes as the civil service class. But this was an erroneous plan. Even in such merchant republics as Venice and Genoa, the ruling and the civil service class was never fused with and never came from commercial circles. This applies also to modern England. Industrial and commercial circles, by the very nature of their activity, have accustomed themselves to consider all problems from the point of view of personal gain and, taken as an entity, they cannot rise to an all-embracing statesmanlike point of view. Not that individual members of the civil service class did not look out for their own interests as did the rest of the population, but because of a long association with broad-based general problems its point of view was somewhat different. This applies also to the bureaucrats; but they suffered from another complaint: a detachment from everyday life. In Western democracies, the old civil service class has been supplanted rather successfully by representatives of the free professions, mostly practical lawyers, but only after a long, difficult period. In the beginning of the century such a change would hardly have been possible in Russia.

Plehve's attitude toward Russian problems differed from that of Witte. He was not an economist and could not appreciate the positive qualities of Witte's fervent activity. But as an administrator with some understanding of state interests he saw in the landowning class the most conservative elements and the very fabric of the country, although, not being a member of the landed gentry and having no important connections therein, he may have overestimated its significance or rather its power. Neither could he find another class which could have been used to replace the nobility in service to the state. It is possible, however, that he first adopted the stand of protecting the interests of the nobility out of consideration for his career, and later followed this course out of habit.

The struggle between Witte and Plehve, therefore, was essentially a struggle between an economist on the one hand and an administrator and statesman on the other. The economist Witte did not realize that one cannot create a powerful industry in an essentially agricultural country (which is deprived, moreover, of the possibility of exporting her industrial products) by ruining the agriculture of that country. Such a course of action would destroy the only market for industry's products. And because of his deficient understanding of politics the economist Witte did not realize that the agricultural class was the backbone of the state organism and its basic cultural element. The administrator, Plehve, on the other hand, did not understand that without the development of industry which would attract a considerable part of the rural population to factory work Russia could not employ all the labor furnished by the enormous and yearly increasing population and therefore would be doomed to poverty; neither did he understand that this was the only way in which Russia could protect her state and national independence against the pressure of the tremendous industrial forces of the West.

Plehve did not realize that the landed gentry was doomed to lose a part, if not all, of its power by the very nature of things; that there was rising up beside it another class which was acquiring ever more weight in the social structure of the empire, namely the industrial class; that although this latter class was unfit to replace the nobility or to fill the ranks of the civil service, nevertheless, the government had to recognize it and try to win its sympathies and co-operation. . Plehve failed also to take account of the ever increasing number of members of the free professions. But the least understandable phase of his policy was, on the one hand, his desire to win the support of the landed gentry and, on the other, the antagonism which he provoked in zemstvo circles, which were composed, in accordance with the law, mostly of landed gentry.

The assemblies of the nobility were more to the Right than those of the zemstvo, but this can be explained by the fact that the former met once every three years and were attended, in addition to the landed gentry, by noblemen who had actually little to do with local life. There were persons engaged in civil or military service who neither wished nor were able to take part in local social life but were willing to come once in three years in order to keep up their connection with the local nobility. The assemblies of the nobility were given their Right orientation by such elements as the St. Petersburg bureaucracy and the officers of the Guards. The zemstvo assemblies were a truer reflection of the moods of the local landowning class which took part in local activities. To seek the support of the nobility and at the same time to enter into conflicts with the zemstvos was therefore to seek the support of a certain, almost entirely bureaucratic, group, which by its very nature could lend no dynamic support to the existing regime. Consequently, that part of the Russian landed gentry which had some significance and power and could thus give a certain support to the government began to incline toward Witte, who was essentially its enemy, and to oppose Plehve, who sincerely wished to assist it.

By 1902 Witte had sensed the situation and was using every means in his power to attract the zemstvos to his side. He had taken the first step in this direction as far back as Sipiagin's time, when he had formed under his own chairmanship a Special Conference on the Needs of Agricultural Industry.

I will not undertake to explain all of Witte's motives. It cannot now be ascertained whether he realized that without raising the level of agriculture it was impossible further to develop industry or even to maintain the state of development it had reached by that time because there was not a market to absorb its products; or whether it was a diversion, a desire to pacify and to disarm the ever-increasing criticism and opposition of the landowning class to his one-sided economic policy; or whether he was ready to study the problem of agriculture without bias and with an open mind and to examine it in good faith with the help of specialists in order to co-ordinate his further activity with the conclusions deriving from a better acquaintance with the needs of agriculture; or whether he wished to use this conference as a medium for the introduction of certain measures pertaining to the peasant problem, as he affirms in his memoirs, where, however, he misrepresents some facts concerning the actual assembling of this conference. As is well known, the pressure of events soon changed the entire situation under which the conference had been summoned. When it actually assembled, Witte was no longer Minister of Finance. He had become the Chairman of the Committee of Ministers and had lost his extensive power. These conditions render it impossible to judge by the actual results of the conference Witte's intentions in convoking it. Under different conditions Witte might have found it necessary to give the whole affair a direction entirely different from that originally intended.

I am inclined to think, however, that Witte was impelled by all
the motives which I have just suggested, no matter how contradictory they may seem at first glance. It is very probable that he intended to revise peasant legislation in order to abolish, or at least to
modify, the principle by which the peasant class was separated from
all other classes with its own self-government and its own courts;
or, at the very least, to influence to a degree the actual work of revision with which work the Imperial Ukase of January 14, 1902, had
charged the Ministry of the Interior. Undoubtedly it was Witte who
had insisted upon a speedy revision of this legislation, a revision
which had long been considered necessary. But in so insisting, he
probably thought that the work would be given to a special commission presided over by one whose opinions on this subject would be in
accordance with his own. He had even selected for this position, as
he mentions in his memoirs,[7] Prince Aleksei Dmitrievich Obolensky,[8]
who was then Assistant Minister of Finance and manager of the
Bank of the Nobility and the Peasant Land Bank. But Witte's plans
failed. Their failure was probably caused by Sipiagin, who often
acted in accord with Witte's ideas but in this instance had no wish
to release his control of such an important question. In all probability, therefore, the direct reason for assembling this conference
was the fact that the Minister of the Interior had been charged with
the work of revising peasant legislation. In fact, eight days after the
ukase of January 14, another ukase announced that a Special Conference on the Needs of Agricultural Industry would assemble under
Witte's chairmanship and would include many ministers among its
members. It was organized so that, with a capable chairman, it could
undertake the consideration of many questions in any way related to
agriculture. Witte may not only have hoped but also have been certain that by the time the Ministry of the Interior had finished even
a part of its work he, with his customary impetuosity, would have
solved the main points of the entire problem.

The assassination of Sipiagin and the appointment of Plehve
ruined all his plans. Witte knew that under the new minister the
work of the ministry would progress much more swiftly. What could
be done to circumvent this new complication? How was the decisive
role in this question to be retained for himself? To cope with the
situation Witte was obliged to devise new tactics. Accordingly the
Special Conference worked out a program of action, announcing
that it must have the opinion of the local workers on certain ques-

tions included in the program before it could take action. Gubernia and uezd committees to study the needs of agricultural industry[9] were therefore established. They were given the right to discuss in their sessions not only questions which were purely agricultural or pertained to local needs but also "questions pertaining to law and order and to general administration in so far as they have a bearing on agriculture and local life." Witte was perfectly sure that these uezd agricultural committees, since they were formed of the chairman and members of the uezd zemstvo boards and persons invited by the chairman and were under the chairmanship of the uezd marshals of the nobility, would use this right to enlarge upon the original program and to discuss primarily the peasant problem. In this way Witte hoped to bring about the situation which he so much desired. While the Ministry of the Interior was working out the new peasant legislation, the basic points of peasant organization would be discussed locally. Next there would be a sort of "*chassé-croisé*," that is, the project of the Ministry of the Interior would be sent to the provinces for examination by local workers, who would already have discussed the peasant question in agricultural committees, while the resolutions of these committees would go to the conference. The conference, in turn, would immediately start to study those questions which its chairman, Witte, considered most urgent. Of course, Witte would select matters which pertained to peasant organization to be discussed first, and in this roundabout way he intended to regain a dominant position in deciding the vital and interesting peasant problem. At the same time Witte hoped that these committees, which included zemstvo men, would help him to attract to himself the sympathies of the zemstvos and at the same time give him additional knowledge and new perspectives.

At that time Witte was under the influence of two men: Prince A. D. Obolensky, whom he intended to make chairman of the committee for the revision of peasant legislation; and M. A. Stakhovich,[10] the marshal of the nobility of Orel Gubernia. Through these men, who were well acquainted with zemstvo circles, Witte probably for the first time in his life became acquainted with the work of zemstvo organizations; at any rate he learned of the halo with which public opinion surrounded the zemstvos. He realized that his report of 1899, expressing the opinion that zemstvo self-government was incompatible with autocracy, had been erroneous and tactless and that it was not to his advantage to antagonize the entire Russian zemstvo. The stories and opinions of Obolensky and Stakhovich about local public men, their excellent knowledge of peasant life, and their interest in their work as compared with the interest of the St. Petersburg bureaucrats in theirs were a revelation to Witte and impressed him so much that he not only changed his attitude to the zemstvos but considered both Obolensky and Stakhovich extremely intelligent and perspicacious men.

For Witte both Prince Obolensky and Stakhovich were for a long time Egeria's commentators on Russian life, who possessed the gift of explaining the meaning and the essence of the prevailing social currents in the country. This was because of the fact that Witte himself was quite ignorant of Russian provincial life. For a number of years this prevented him from realizing that neither Obolensky nor Stakhovich understood state problems and both were nothing but typical examples of Russian provincial thinkers who had a meager store of definite knowledge and a dilettante attitude toward the most complicated problems of public life. Their close contact with Witte resulted in the advancement of both men, although in different directions. It would seem worth while, therefore, to describe them briefly.

Prince A. D. Obolensky had started his public career as marshal of the nobility of Kozelsk Uezd of Kaluga Gubernia. This experience left its peculiar mark on him for the rest of his career. On the one hand, it made him very self-confident. In the narrow confines of a poor, remote uezd it had been easy for him, a rich man and a graduate of the St. Petersburg School of Law (although only in the third group), to be a shining light, despite the fact that he lacked maturity in education and culture. On the other hand, it left him with a half-scornful, half-supercilious attitude, so prevalent in our provinces, toward the representatives of the St. Petersburg bureaucracy. Local government officials were somewhat envious of the higher bureaucrats in St. Petersburg and stood in awe of their authority. They had no such attitude, however, toward the lesser bureaucrats, whom they were inclined to regard both as hair-splitting clerks and as irresponsible butterflies.

With both these attitudes Prince Obolensky appeared in St. Petersburg early in the reign of Nicholas II. This was hardly a coincidence. Rather was it a result of the intimacy of his younger brother, Prince Nikolai Dmitrievich Obolensky, with the young Tsar, an intimacy which was exploited by the entire Obolensky family. But be that as it may, in a very short time Prince Aleksei achieved a brilliant career. First Ermolov appointed him inspector of agriculture, an office for the whole of Russia; shortly after this he was appointed Assistant Minister of Agriculture; later, in 1897, Goremykin appointed him Assistant Minister of the Interior.

According to the general opinion of all who had the misfortune to deal with him as Assistant Minister of the Interior, Prince Obolensky's complete ignorance of his work and his narrow, provincial outlook became immediately apparent. "In Kozelsk, it would be done so." This was his favorite and harping comment. His contempt for the work in hand and for the very persons of his many subordinates was also apparent. He was not haughty; on the contrary, he behaved like a *Bursch;* but even in this simplicity a certain snobbishness showed through. He was thoroughly convinced that he was alive to and comprehended the real essence of things, whereas his co-workers saw and understood only the externals. In Pushkin's[11] phrase, "he considered everyone else a zero and himself alone an integer." Given these facts, it is easy to understand why he found fault with most documents brought to him for his signature and demanded that they be changed. But he was totally unable to explain with any degree of clarity what change he desired. In the end, after the documents had been recopied several times in an effort to satisfy him, he would sign the first draft. Prince Obolensky's mind was not a creative one; it was incapable of clearness and precision and besides was inclined to paradoxical conclusions and mysticism. In fact he tried to establish this mysticism, probably innate, on a quasi-scientific basis, namely, on the works of Vladimir Solovev[12] for whom he had such great admiration that he had formed a club to study his writings. He especially liked what Turgenev, in *The Diary of a Superfluous Man* (*Dnevnik lishniago cheloveka*), calls "contrasting generalities." This became more pronounced with the years. During the war he favored Germany and rejoiced at the news of every German victory, especially over the English, who were his pet aversion. Still more surprising was his comment on the Brest-Litovsk treaty, which, he said, was perfectly correct and in accordance with the interests of humanity and civilization.*

Such was the man who was so close to Witte and who exercised such great influence upon him for a long time. Only when Witte saw Obolensky at work in his cabinet as Ober-Prokuror of the Synod did

---

* I cannot explain his disgraceful attempts to please the Bolsheviks during their present rule other than by his ill health and the weakening of his will power.

he realize what an absurd dilettante Obolensky was in every respect. Witte says as much in his memoirs.[13] But in the period under discussion, when the conflict between Witte and Plehve was in its early stages, Witte considered Obolensky a veritable oracle.

M. A. Stakhovich, the other person who greatly influenced Witte at that time, was talented, was of great literary erudition, and had a capacity for making friends of people of the most varied views and social positions. He was at home in St. Petersburg's high society, among artists and actors, among zemstvo men, or on a religious pilgrimage with Count Tolstoi. He was a fine reader in parlor groups, an agreeable conversationalist, a merry bottle companion, and a unique and voluminous correspondent. All these social attributes stood him in good stead. He managed to remain the marshal of nobility of Orel Gubernia for a succession of terms, although his political convictions were much more liberal than those of the majority of the Orel nobility. It is very characteristic of him that he was elected member of the First Duma even though service as marshal of the nobility was at that time usually enough to bar a man from a seat in the Duma.*

Stakhovich believed with Prince Obolensky that all the vital and businesslike elements of the country were concentrated in the zemstvos, and that the state apparatus was composed of bureaucrats who deadened everything they managed or even touched. But there was a difference between these two men. It was this: while Obolensky despised and derided the Russian bureaucracy, he endeavored to occupy high positions, to which Stakhovich seemed indifferent. In 1905, for instance, when Stakhovich acted as intermediary between Witte and those public men whom Witte wished to include in his cabinet, he announced at the outset that he wished

* In his further political career Stakhovich again showed his ability to sit on several political chairs at once. When the Tsar received the members of the legislative chambers after the opening of the First Duma, Stakhovich presented himself at the Winter Palace in his Chamberlain's court uniform, in which he presented a striking difference to the other members of the lower chamber, who were dressed with almost deliberate negligence. Also, he managed to make friends with the Cadet members of the Duma without becoming an official member of the party, and he maintained these relations until the very end of the old regime. Later he was elected member (from the Orel Zemstvo) of the State Council and was soon on the best of terms with its Left wing, that is, its academic group, although officially he was not grouped with them. It is typical of Stakhovich that he seldom publicly expressed his views on any subject, although his oratorical gifts were undisputed.

no ministerial portfolio for himself. This absence of ambition can be explained by his unwillingness to impose upon himself any restraint whatsoever and by his hatred of any serious occupation. His inborn laziness was responsible for the fact that, despite his brilliance, he had graduated from the Imperial School of Law at the bottom of his class. He never lost his desire to enjoy all the advantages which the life of a rich bachelor afforded. He was ambitious after a fashion, but he was a bohemian at heart; it was enough if the positions he occupied gave him great outward prestige without restraining him in the pursuit of his slightly gypsy inclinations.

After the February 1917 revolution he accepted the post of Governor-General of Finland; but this can be explained by the fact that he had no intention of governing that country—he wished to serve merely as a living connecting link between Russia and the Grand Duchy and to leave the administration of the latter to the Finnish public men. Like the majority of the members of the Provisional Government he thought that the ties between Russia and Finland could be preserved by showing the widest benevolence toward Finnish public organizations.

Like almost all members of the Provisional Government, Stakhovich was a dilettante. He lacked any deep understanding of state problems, but as compared with Prince Obolensky he was much less unstable and self-confident. These two men were typical products of the time and personify from two angles the flabby Russian zemstvo liberalism, a liberalism which derived from a lack of sound education, superficial intelligence, and an uncertain inclination toward cosmopolitanism. Neither Prince Obolensky nor Stakhovich had a definite political program for solving the fundamental problems of public life, nor were they able to work out such a program; and although each of them had a great urge to criticize, their criticisms usually amounted to nothing but persiflage.

To return now to the story of Witte's struggle to secure the dominating role in the revision of peasant legislation. After he had sent to the local committees the program worked out in the special conference, these matters were temporarily out of his hands and for the time being he was unable to use this conference to realize his intentions. Meanwhile Witte learned that the work of revising peasant legislation was proceeding at feverish speed in the Ministry of the Interior and he began to fear that Plehve would get ahead of him in this matter. So he had recourse to other tactics: he called a special inter-ministerial conference to deliberate with the Peasant Land Bank as to the general policy to be adopted by the bank in selling to the peasants both the land acquired with the special funds appropriated for that purpose and the land transferred to the Peasant Bank by the Bank of the Nobility. He appointed Prince Obolensky chairman of this conference, hoping in this way to have his own views on the peasant problem adopted by the conference. At first glance the plan seemed to be the right one. It was evident that the Peasant Bank could not determine its policy without first working out the basic problems of peasant organization. Moreover, the decisions adopted by an inter-ministerial conference would have carried much more weight than the suggestions worked out by any one ministry.

Plehve saw through Witte's scheme at once; but he had no means of preventing the formation of a conference, whose formal purpose was to determine the policy of the Peasant Bank, an institution subordinate to the Minister of Finance. Plehve was thus forced to accept the role of watchful witness; he appointed as representatives from the Ministry of the Interior: A. P. Strukov, former marshal of the nobility of Ekaterinoslav Gubernia, who was known for his extremely conservative views and who was at that time Chief of the Office for the Affairs of the Nobility attached to the Ministry of the Interior (established by Sipiagin); I. L. Mordvinov, former manager of the Stavropol branch of the State Treasury Department, whom Plehve considered an authority on peasant problems; Lopukhin, Director of the Police Department, who at that time enjoyed Plehve's great confidence; and myself. Plehve thought it necessary to assemble all these persons in his office to decide on a common line of conduct to be followed in this conference; but since no conference agenda had been issued there was no way to determine what tactics we should adopt. Consequently, Plehve merely instructed us to keep him posted and to agree to no important decision without previously obtaining his consent.

On his side Witte mobilized all his most valued collaborators for this conference: the Director of the State Treasury Department, I. P. Shipov;[14] Director of the Department of Direct Taxation, N. N. Kutler; Director of the General Office[15] of the Ministry of Finance, A. I. Putilov.[16] These men were accustomed to represent the Ministry of Finance in all inter-ministerial conferences. These three Ajaxes always appeared together; and although Shipov was a partisan of the commune and Putilov of individual ownership, they voted as one man. The most important debating was usually done by Kutler, who was probably the most able in expressing Witte's views with precision. The general tone of the three was liberal, and in questions pertaining to peasants they invariably defended the views in vogue among liberal zemstvo circles.

Plehve's fears proved to have been unfounded, however, just as Witte's hopes proved to have been in vain. Under Obolensky's chairmanship no conference could ever have arrived at any definite decisions.

I cannot now recall the substance of the violent debates which took place at this conference. But I do know that the questions of the commune and of individual landownership were not even touched upon and all conclusions were general and extremely vague, mainly because Obolensky himself had no definite ideas concerning the peasant problem. He intended that something should be changed and improved; and, as far as could be understood from vague statements, he was even in favor of extending the application of the general civil code to the peasants; but since this question was not included in the program of the conference, he expressed himself guardedly. Kutler was more definite. He directed his fire against the government's policy of protecting the peasants and in particular against the institution of zemskii nachalnik. Kutler was always logical and apparently sincere, but he evinced little readiness to make concessions. During the conference various questions were debated, often simultaneously, although many of them were not supposed to be discussed. But not one final decision was reached.*

* Several specialists in different fields were invited to take part in this conference. There was Kokhtin, the author of a very interesting work on agriculture, a work which was sounder and more intelligible than were his lengthy speeches. There was the famous "nobleman," N. A. Pavlov,[17] known by this sobriquet because he added it to his signature under his articles. Pavlov was intelligent but not profound. He had written a book, the title of which escapes me, which presented a colorful picture of rural and village life but little else. He was impatient to attain fame at one jump; steady and painstaking progress was not to his liking. In his capacity of special duty clerk with the Minister of the Interior—a position which paid no salary—he deluged ministers and other persons of influence with all manner of memoranda on every conceivable subject, and after the Ukase of February 18, 1905, which gave all citizens the right to petition the Tsar directly, Pavlov availed himself of this privilege to a greater extent than anyone else. His motive was the same: to attain immediate fame on the strength of one of his

Nor is this to be wondered at, because it was virtually impossible to reconcile in one unanimously acceptable decision the variety of ideas and suggestions advanced in the conference. All the representatives of the Ministry of the Interior except myself stopped attending the sessions. As I remember, Lopukhin attended only the first session, while Strukov and Mordvinov, even when present, were silent. All the debating was done by Kutler and me. One may ask why I, who on the whole shared the views not of Obolensky, since it was impossible to determine what his views were, but of Kutler, found it necessary to engage him in verbal duels on this subject. There were many reasons. I was loth to let loose my grip on the work to which I had already devoted so much effort and which I hoped to bring to a successful conclusion. Both my professional and my personal pride were at stake. In my own mind I justified my course of action on the ground that no serious reforms in the peasant problem could be accomplished by the methods adopted by the Ministry of Finance. It seemed to me that the peasant problem could be solved only by taking it as a whole and not by separate innovations adopted in the routine course of administration; at the best Obolensky's conference could have had only the latter result. Moreover, I repeat, I did not believe that Prince Obolensky was capable of bringing any business to a conclusion. In his hands it would become *en queue de poisson.* So it was. In fact it was not even possible to record the minutes. Of course, the minutes were written—there was nothing that the skilled pens of the St. Petersburg clerks could not write—but there was no way of getting the necessary signatures.

At the very beginning of this conference Plehve had written an official letter to Witte about certain questions which the conference was to discuss. In this letter he pointed out that some of these questions could not be solved until the Ministry of the Interior had completed its work on peasant legislation and that therefore his Ministry could not assist the conference in its study of these ques-

projects. One memorandum he had submitted dealt with peasant colonization, a subject in which he was interested at the time; and it was this memorandum that gained him admission to Prince Obolensky's conference. When he was asked in the conference how he proposed to carry out his schemes he had nothing constructive to offer. Plehve mentioned him to me as a possible collaborator in the work of revising peasant legislation, but a conversation with him convinced me that he was constitutionally unfitted for practical work. I refused to consider him. Pavlov, however, ascribed my decision to a fear of his talents and knowledge.

tions. Albeit, Witte's attempt to get hold of the peasant problem in this way failed, and he made no more attempts in this direction while he was Minister of Finance.

Witte was defeated even more completely by Plehve on another score: his attempt to dominate the Department of Factory Inspection. Here Plehve worked in agreement with Lopukhin, and their policy was in some way connected with that of Zubatov.

The Police Department had regarded the Department of Factory Inspection with some misgivings from the moment of its establishment. It saw in this department an organization not entirely trustworthy politically and one which was always disrupting the work of the secret police. One would think that the Zubatov policy would have agreed with the policy of this department, but actually the difference was great. The Department of Factory Inspection saw to it that the employers observed the labor laws. Zubatov wished to inculcate in the workers' minds the idea that these laws had no significance. That which was of prime importance was that the government took fatherly care of its children and that it was upon the government that the workers should fix all their hopes, whether or not the law provided for given cases. Under these conditions conflicts between the members of the secret police and the Department of Factory Inspection were inevitable and it was in order to put an end to them that the Police Department strove to subordinate the Factory Inspection to the administrative authority of the Ministry of the Interior. Moreover, the secret police had no confidence in the personnel of the department, which was contaminated by the views of the intelligentsia and not too alert to prevent the penetration of revolutionary ideas into the working masses. But the gendarme organization was above suspicion in this respect. So, by subordinating the Department of Factory Inspection to the Ministry of the Interior there could be introduced, on the one hand, such changes in its personnel as would make it more conservative and more reliable from the government's point of view. On the other hand, there could be created more favorable conditions for carrying out Zubatov's policy.

Plehve did not completely realize his ambitions on this question. The Department of Factory Inspection remained under the Ministry of Finance but, according to the Imperial Ukase of May 30, 1903, which was based on the reports of the Ministers of Finance and of the Interior, all local officials of the department were subor-

dinated to the local governors. The governors were now to supervise the local personnel of the department in the application of labor
laws and regulations regarding the maintenance of law and order
in the factories and the promotion of the well-being of the workers.
Moreover, all appointments of factory inspectors, their distribution
in different districts, and even their bonuses had in the future to
be determined according to an agreement with the local governors.
These latter were given the right to demand periodical and special
reports from the inspectors, and in certain cases could repeal the
orders of the inspectors without first directing that these orders be
examined by local Boards for the Affairs of Factories and Mines.[18]
The scope of the activity of the district factory inspectors was reduced to a minimum; they were simply to inspect the work done by
the individual local officials of the department and to make a preliminary report supplying data for industrial statistics.

The changed status of the Department of Factory Inspection
actually meant its transfer to the Ministry of the Interior and to
local administration and a fundamental change in the character of
its work. The purpose of the institution was to create an intermediary organization between the workers and the employers and
to supervise the enforcement of labor laws for the protection of
life, health, and the well-being of the workingmen. With its transfer to a position subordinate to the administration, it virtually
became not a department of factory inspection, but a factory
police bureau.

One cannot say, however, that Plehve had no reasons for desiring to subordinate the factory inspection to the local representatives of the central government. The fact is that the differences
between the central administrations of the ministries were reflected
in the local branches of these ministries. These differences sometimes
revealed a marked discrepancy between the activities of different
sections of what was essentially the same government. Since the
Minister of the Interior was responsible for the preservation of
order in the country, he could not help wishing to do away with
this lack of co-ordination, which at times amounted to open antagonism between offices and often had deplorable results. The trouble
with the new halfway measure concerning the factory inspection
was that it removed some bad effects but left the source of the
evil untouched. Yet, such as it was, the measure, the result of an
agreement between the two ministers, was essentially a decided vic-

tory of Plehve over Witte. In fact, it was clearly evident that already in the beginning of 1903 Plehve had strengthened his position with the throne and had so undermined Witte's standing that the latter's retirement was only a question of time. Witte, of course, realized the situation but held on to his power even at the price of concessions to which he had theretofore not been accustomed.

An outward sign of the imperial favor to Plehve was seen in the Manifesto of February 26, 1903. This was the first of a series of state acts which consecutively announced, during the next three years, different plans for the improvement of the state structure. The program outlined by the manifesto was hardly noted for its clarity and precision. It contained not so much the substance of the proposed changes in the state regime as the spirit and direction by which they were to be guided. But Plehve was in a hurry to seal his plans by a state act from the throne, even though these plans were only in general outline and not clearly defined in his own mind. In order to make clearer that which follows, I wish to quote from the manifesto.

SOVEREIGN MANIFESTO, FEBRUARY 26, 1903

. . . . To assure the constant observation, by authorities concerned with questions of faith, of the principles of tolerance contained in the basic laws of the Russian Empire, which, while reverently accepting the Greek Orthodox church as supreme and dominant, yet grants to all Our subjects of other creeds and religions the right to profess their faith freely and to conduct religious services according to the rites of their churches.

To continue to carry out the measures designed to lend material assistance to the Greek Orthodox clergy of rural districts, and to encourage them to participate in the spiritual and social life of their parishioners.

To direct, in accordance with the impending efforts to strengthen rural economy, the activity of the state credit institutions, and especially that of the land banks of the nobility and the peasants, in such a way as to support and encourage the development of the basic principles of rural life of the landed gentry and of the peasants.

To transfer the projected work of peasant legislation, after the preliminaries have been completed, to the provinces, where it will be further examined and adjusted to local needs by gubernia conferences attended by deserving persons who enjoy public confidence. This work shall be based upon the inviolability of the communal organization of peasant landownership, and at the same time it shall endeavor to establish means whereby individual peasants may more easily leave the commune.

To take immediate steps to abolish the constraining custom of collective responsibility.

To reform the gubernia and uezd local administration in order to increase the means of immediately satisfying the varied needs of the rural population through the efforts of local men guided in their action by strong and just government officials responsible to Us.

To consider, as the next step in the problem of organizing local life, co-operation between local self-government and the parish wardships of the Greek Orthodox churches wherever possible.

Appealing to all Our faithful subjects to support in the family, in the schools, and in public life those moral principles, which alone under the protection of an Autocratic Power can support the well-being of the people and can assure every person of the stability of his rights, We order Our Ministers and Heads of separate offices whom this may concern to submit to Us their projects concerning how Our plans are to be carried out.

In spite of its vagueness, this manifesto nevertheless included answers to some current questions. In the first place, it rejected the idea of organizing the small zemstvo unit upon principles desired by the progressive zemstvo circles, and suggested instead "co-operation between local self-government and the parish wardships of the Greek Orthodox churches." I could never understand how this co-operation could be accomplished and found no one who could explain it to me. At that time the idea of organizing the rural community on the principle of the parish territorial unit was strongly advocated by the Right press—*Moskovskiia Vedomosti, Grazhdanin,* and at times by *Novoe Vremia*—but I had never encountered any definite scheme for establishing this unit and relating it to the zemstvo organizations. In fact, it was one of the hazy theories of Slavophil ideology.

The manifesto also made it clear that the government intended to strengthen the influence and the authority of the local representatives of the central government over the elected municipal and zemstvo organizations. In fact, it was said that the establishment of this influence was the direct purpose of the reform of the gubernia and uezd local administration.

Finally, on the most important question of the day—the peasant situation—the manifesto stated that it had been found necessary to protect the land commune from compulsory disintegration; yet at the same time individual peasants were to be assisted to leave it. The manifesto also decreed "that the peasants were to be freed from the constraining custom of collective responsibility."*

* It was possible to incorporate this order in the manifesto because when it was published the legislative project on this matter had already been submitted to the State Council and approved by the proper department of the State Council, so that all that was necessary for the publication of a corresponding statute was a formal hearing of the project by the Council's general session and its confirmation by the Tsar. This confirmation took place on March 12, 1903.

The manifesto, however, included a serious innovation, namely, the idea of having gubernia conferences composed of "deserving persons who enjoy public confidence" examine the new projects on peasant organization. It might be of interest to describe here how that idea found its way into the manifesto. It happened as follows. On February 25, Plehve made a report to the Tsar, after which he summoned me and explained that the Tsar wished on the very next day, February 26, the birthday of the late Tsar Alexander III, to issue a manifesto proclaiming the fundamental features of the state program for the future: the support of the landed gentry, the peasantry, and the orthodox clergy; the organization of rural life with the parish wardships as a basic unit and with a further subordination of zemstvo institutions to the central administrative power. The manifesto was also to announce that the projects for the reform of peasant legislation would favor the inviolability of the commune and that these projects would be submitted for examination to local conferences of representatives of the nobility and the zemstvo. Liubimov was preparing the flowery passages; I was to state the essence of the state program. The entire thing had to be finished that evening, as it had to be ready for signing by midnight.

I had never drafted a manifesto before and was consequently somewhat at a loss. Nor did the very general nature of Plehve's instructions lessen my confusion. But fortunately I was familiar enough with Plehve's program to know that his economic policy was directed mainly to the support of rural economy rather than industry as under Witte. I was interested, however, in only two points concerning the proposed new legislation on peasant organization. I thought it most important to construct the paragraph about the future of the land commune so that it would not handicap the adoption at some future time of decisive measures for this natural disintegration of that institution. Second, I wanted as far as possible to predispose public opinion in favor of the revision of peasant legislation—if not in favor of the substance of the work, then at least in favor of the proposed means for carrying it into effect. For a long time I was perplexed; then it came to me: "with the close participation of persons who enjoy public confidence." This was really a repetition of an expression in the Imperial Ukase issued to the State Council on the occasion of its jubilee: "vested with Our own and public confidence," of which the Tsar had scratched out the words "and public."

By 8:00 P.M. I had finished, and then hurried with my draft to Plehve, with whom I found Liubimov and Lopukhin. We spent considerable time reading the beginning of the manifesto which Liubimov had written and left ourselves but little time to discuss what I had written—really the essence of the manifesto. There was little dissension and trouble, therefore, in putting it in final shape. Lopukhin made virtually no comment; he answered all of Plehve's remarks in indifferent monosyllables. Nor did Plehve make any serious changes; discussion centered mainly on the matter of style. I had to defend with considerable energy the words "persons who enjoy public confidence," but fortunately both Lopukhin and Liubimov supported me. Still Plehve was undecided. Finally, we compromised. We added the adjective "deserving" to make it read "deserving persons who enjoy public confidence." The final draft was immediately handed over to be copied on special paper. Plehve went home to change into his uniform and returned about midnight ready to go to the Tsar. All three of us saw him off. I can still see him as he descended the stairs toward the doors wrapped in his fur coat with his brief-case in his hand. At the bottom step he turned to us and said: "Well, shall we retain the 'public confidence' phrase?" I hastened to insist upon its preservation. Plehve turned about and went out. In less than half an hour he was back with the signed manifesto, which he turned over to Liubimov to be printed in the *Pravitelstvennyi Vestnik*.

The manifesto caused much discussion in the press. Each publication tried to read into it the things which it desired, thus indirectly criticizing every explanation different from its own. But those public circles that were interested in questions of government had ceased to attach too much importance to government programs. They had grown accustomed to the fact that what was proposed one day would by no means be realized on the next and probably would be contradicted by some second proposal. This loss of faith in the constancy and stability of the Imperial will robbed Imperial decrees of moral significance, not only among the rank-and-file citizens but also among government officials. It was clear to everyone of average intelligence that Imperial decrees were put into effect only in so far as the persons who inspired them remained in power. Accordingly bureaucratic circles were interested not so much in the contents of a manifesto as in the status of the minister who had initiated it, that is, in the stability of his position at that given moment. The Manifesto of February 26 was discussed from this point of view; the burden of comment was to the effect that it showed Witte's influence to be declining and Plehve's increasing. This opinion was based mainly upon that paragraph which mentioned the credit institutions and their future assistance to the landed gentry and the peasants, that is, to rural economy in general. Witte, indignant that the manifesto had been written without his knowledge, indicated the policy which those institutions subordinate to him as Minister of Finance were to follow, and, of course, decided to pay no attention to it.

Actually, the only influence which the Manifesto of February 26 was destined to have was that exerted by the words which Plehve had hardly been able to bring himself to adopt: "deserving persons who enjoy public confidence." These words were later used without any question being raised in a series of other state acts and manifestoes issued by the Monarch himself.

Meanwhile the struggle between Plehve and Witte went on with increasing intensity, with Plehve striving to influence the Tsar against his antagonist. Here was revealed the tendency of Nicholas II to become captivated by new persons and new ideas. When he ascended the throne, the young Monarch may have desired to dismiss all ministers then in office, but his inexperience in affairs of state and his innate gentleness and timidity prevented him from so doing.* He did not take the initiative, but limited himself to confirming the recommendations of his advisers. As the years went by, however, constant compliance with the desires of his ministers must have proved a strain on him. Yet he could not muster courage enough to oppose the ministers he had inherited. He hoped, therefore, to change these for a new set of ministers with whom he might establish different relations from the outset. This unfulfilled desire to assert his will may also explain his practice of as-

* The young Tsar's timidity in insisting that his wishes be carried out, even in small matters, can be judged by an episode told by Goremykin. It happened in 1896. On one occasion, after Goremykin, then Minister of the Interior, had finished his report, the Tsar, more confused than usual, opened a drawer of his desk and took out a document, saying: "I have been asked to appoint so-and-so vice-governor. Please, Ivan Logginovich, arrange this matter." Goremykin hastened to point out that "so-and-so" had not the slightest right to such an appointment and said that such unmerited appointments might arouse the just indignation of those who had such a right; to make such an appointment would be to establish an undesirable precedent. The Tsar made no objections to Goremykin's argument, but in the same confused manner quickly returned the document to the desk drawer.

signing certain persons special tasks without consulting his ministers. One of the first of these instances was in 1897, when he delegated Khlopov to visit localities hit by the famine and to report on the true state of affairs there. The Tsar himself provided Khlopov with funds for this trip and with a personal note ordering all authorities to comply with Khlopov's requests. Khlopov, traveling in a private railway car arranged for by the Minister of Ways and Communications, made his first stop at Tula or Orel, I forget which, and duly presented his credentials to the local governor. The authorities there immediately reported the incident to Goremykin, who represented to the Tsar the dangers of delegating irresponsible persons to special tasks and arming them with such powers. As a result Khlopov was recalled and deprived of his credentials, and the episode ended. But to Nicholas II it was but another frustration of his desire to take the initiative. Repeated frustrations of this nature tended to make him stubborn, and in the last years of his reign his insistence upon petty matters, usually concerning individuals, assumed a pathological character. The sentence, "This is my wish!" was often on his lips.

Now Witte had dominated the Tsar, and it is not unreasonable to suggest that Nicholas II welcomed a chance to escape this domination. How Plehve succeeded in destroying Witte's prestige with the Tsar, I do not know, but I believe it was done during the discussions on the work of Witte's uezd agricultural committees.

From a political point of view it was a grave error to transfer questions affecting the very foundations of state administration (since Witte's limitless program amounted to precisely this) to the decision of a few hundred small institutions. If Witte had really wished to hear the voice of the people, he should have assembled in the capital local public men elected by the people or even by certain classes of the people, setting the limits, though on a very broad basis, of the problems to be discussed. Of course, this would have been a step toward a constitution but not one from which a constitution would inevitably have resulted. A similar conference had been called by Alexander III early in his reign on the initiative of Count N. P. Ignatev; it was the so-called Conference of Informed Persons and the number and scope of the subjects it examined were quite extensive. But it was fantastic to organize in one country 482 constituent assemblies—for the significance of questions transferred to them made them such—

while leaving the selection of these assemblies to lesser public men who by education, outlook, and political orientation represented a wide variety of types. Nothing could be expected from these bodies but an incomprehensible jumble of decisions in which any manifestations of common sense and real knowledge would be lost in the general chaos of divergent ideas and opinions. More than eleven thousand persons took part in the "work" of these agricultural committees, and their reports comprised more than 28,000 small-type pages—eighteen large volumes which were never read by anyone but the authors. Surely this justifies the conclusion that the only direct result of this move was a very substantial but needless expenditure of state funds.

It is difficult to understand why a man of Witte's undoubted intelligence could have attached any serious significance to the whole affair; yet he did, and sincerely hoped to learn from it something new and important. The explanation lies in the fact of his utter ignorance of Russian provincial life and his blind faith in his accepted oracles—Prince Obolensky and Stakhovich. But such a measure was quite unnecessary as a means of ascertaining the prevailing public opinion. No new information was gained in this way. On the contrary, in some of the uezds where there were some very capable and well-known public men, the uezd committees only repeated what different St. Petersburg publications had expressed and preached for a long time. In each case, however, the discussions and opinions of the committees reflected their respective compositions. In some uezds the committees were comprised of the chairman (the local marshal of the nobility) and the members of the local uezd zemstvo board, as designated in the government's instructions. But in other uezds additional persons were included in the committees: all members of uezd zemstvo assemblies; some local government and zemstvo workers; and, lastly, local peasants elected by the volosts. In some instances selections were made, particularly by the extreme Left and Right, on the basis of political views.

But if there was no concrete gain, as there could not have been from resort to these committees, the ensuing noise was indeed loud. Press organs, according to their respective political party affiliations, seized upon those decisions of separate committees which corresponded to their own hopes and endeavored to use them to prove that local workers held the same views which they had long been professing. The Left press quoted the decisions of Temnikov Uezd of Tambov Gubernia, Sudzha Uezd of Kursk Gubernia, and Ruza Uezd of Moscow Gubernia—which were characterized by a progressive spirit; while the Right press sought its support in the decisions of Chern Uezd of Tula Gubernia, Staro-Konstantinov Uezd of Poltava Gubernia, and Dmitrov Uezd of Kursk Gubernia. The first three uezds had held that the primary cause for the slow development of the peasant masses was the legal status of the peasants. They contended that the personal and civil rights of the peasants should be made equal to those of the other classes, and that they should be subjected to the rule of the general administration and general courts. The second three maintained that it was urgently necessary to increase the rights of the representatives of the central government to supervise the peasant population in order that decisive measures might be taken to check the spread of hooliganism. But was it necessary to organize five hundred committees and to question eleven thousand persons in order to establish the fact that each of these opinions had partisans in the uezds and in the Russian public at large?

It is interesting to note that those very committees which had included all zemstvo members and many other persons complained of the fact that the questions submitted to them had not been placed before the uezd zemstvo boards, "which were the only uezd zemstvo organizations competent to deal with these questions." The Sudzha committee, which included all Sudzha zemstvo assembly members, went so far as to comply with the motion of the Chairman of the Zemstvo Board, Prince Petr Dmitrievich Dolgorukov,[19] later Vice-Chairman of the First Duma, and to petition that the opinion of the local zemstvo assembly be asked. This petition was essentially quite senseless, since it was asked not of more but of fewer than the number of persons who had already been invited to discuss these questions; yet its intention was to discredit the decisions of those uezd committees which had failed to attract all uezd zemstvo members to their work.

The variety of questions raised by separate committees was amazing. For instance, a priest, an invited member of the Tsaritsyn committee, posed the question of increasing the independence of the clergy and of liberating the white (secular) clergy from the domination of the black (regular) clergy, and the committee actually discussed it.

As the composition of the uezd committees and the character of their work and decisions became known, Plehve undoubtedly reported to the Tsar the publicity which this work had achieved and also those measures which he thought should be applied to some of the committee workers. Thus, two members of the Voronezh Uezd committee, Martynov and Bunakov,[20] were banished from the gubernia because they had said that the only way to advance the country along the road of progress and economic prosperity was to adopt a constitutional form of government. Plehve undoubtedly reported also that criticisms of the existing state order could be detected in the very theses advanced by individual members for discussion by their respective committees. The committee of Sudzha, for instance, had introduced into its agenda the examination "of the existing order which almost entirely excluded public elements from participation in the government, and was built upon a basis of bureaucratic organization, police activity, and a spirit of general distrust."

Witte, as chairman of the agricultural conference, had to bear the responsibility for every such utterance. His responsibility seemed the more obvious since he tried to defend the activities of the committees in general, and in particular those of their members who had suffered for their words, because the freedom and breadth of the problems offered for discussion had given them, it would seem, certain guaranties and even encouragement. In my opinion, therefore, Witte, by his defense of the agricultural committees, brought about his own dismissal as Minister of Finance; for in the spring of 1903 the Emperor had not only decided upon his dismissal but had even made the fact known to Plehve. It was supposed that it would take place in the autumn of that year, but it happened in the middle of July. The Tsar told Plehve that he had arrived at this decision suddenly, during a *Te Deum* service at the launching of one of our new battleships. The Tsar said approximately the following: "The Lord put into my heart the thought that I must not delay that which I was already persuaded to do."

This decision did not fully satisfy Plehve, since he had hoped to arrange for Witte to keep his post until the autumn, by which time he hoped to find for this post a candidate of whose co-operation he could be sure. Meanwhile the Tsar made his own choice without consulting Plehve, and the person selected, Pleske,[21] the

manager of the State Bank, was not a person Plehve welcomed
to this post. But at that time fate favored Plehve. Pleske fell
seriously ill soon after his appointment and died in October.

During Pleske's illness, the outcome of which was known to
everybody, Plehve advanced as candidates for the position to be
left vacant D. A. Filosofov, assistant to the State Comptroller,
and V. N. Kokovtsov, State Secretary. Of these two, Plehve favored Kokovtsov, especially after the State Comptroller, P. L.
Lobko, began to support Filosofov's candidacy. The Tsar's choice
fell on Kokovtsov. Plehve's influence had reached its peak.

I can still see V. N. Kokovtsov as he left Plehve's private office
just as I entered the anteroom. He was in uniform, wearing the
ribbon of his decoration, his head bowed in thought. He greeted
me gloomily. Plehve, who was seeing his visitor to the door of the
anteroom, paused at the door of his private office to ask me glee-
fully: "Do you know whom you have just met?" I was surprised
by this question and could not answer, since Plehve surely knew
that Kokovtsov and I were not strangers to each other. "The
new Minister of Finance," continued Plehve. When he had entered his office he added, with a bright smile which seldom appeared on his face, that Kokovtsov had come to him directly from
an audience with the Tsar, where the Tsar had offered him the post
of Minister of Finance. "In your internal policy," the Tsar had
added, "I beg you to follow the suggestions of the Minister of the
Interior."

But even with Kokovtsov Plehve could not accomplish his plans.
The new Minister of Finance expressed himself decidedly against a
complete transfer of the Department of Factory Inspection to the
Ministry of the Interior, and the memorandum which the Ministry
of the Interior composed on this subject and sent to those persons
concerned never reached its ultimate destination, the Committee
of Ministers, to whose authority this question pertained. This circumstance caused a certain restraint in the relations of the two
ministers and they did not become reconciled until just before
Plehve's assassination.

CHAPTER XIV

PLEHVE'S STRIFE WITH THE PUBLIC

If we can say that the winter of 1902–3 was marked, in the field of domestic politics, by the strife between Plehve and Witte, then the winter of 1903–4 was characterized by Plehve's struggle against the growing social-revolutionary movement, on the one hand, and against the liberal public, on the other. During these latter struggles, Plehve became more and more captious and vehement and aroused the indignation of nearly all public circles, even the most moderate and those most devoted to the existing order. It seemed that the government was suspended in mid-air and that its sole support was the administrative and police apparatus—an apparatus which seemed to function without spirit. It worked automatically more or less in accordance with the orders and directions of the government, but even members of the government in ever increasing numbers refused to accept these orders as correct and to share in the program of state policy. The state apparatus was becoming devoid of inner strength.

Strange as it may seem, one of the main reasons why Plehve lost nearly all public support was the retirement of Witte from the post of Minister of Finance. When Plehve was appointed Minister of the Interior, he had hoped to gain the support of the landed gentry and with this support to assure and preserve the internal strength of the Empire. At the same time, counting on the hostility of this class to Witte's economic policy, he had hoped to vanquish Witte. At first Plehve wished to include the zemstvo men in the landed-gentry class and had tried to establish contact with one of the moderate zemstvo leaders, D. N. Shipov, only to meet with a definite refusal on the part of the zemstvos to come to any agreement with the government. Consequently, Plehve was forced to change his policy and to seek support in the more conservative elements of the nobility.

His initial policy in this field was clearly expressed in the Tsar's speeches of September 1902, at Kursk, near which army maneuvers were being held. During the Tsar's reception of the representatives

of the nobility, zemstvo, and volost *starshiny,* Plehve stood immediately behind his sovereign, evidently to show that he, the director
of the government's domestic policy and the faithful executor of the
Imperial will, was learning—together with the persons being addressed—the wishes expressed in the Monarch's words. These
words, however, had been carefully chosen by the Tsar and Plehve
together, and the purpose underlying them had been suggested by
Plehve.

The Tsar said to the assembled nobility: "I know that rural
life demands careful attention. The landed gentry is experiencing
hard times. There are defects also in the peasant organization. It
is in order to do away with these latter defects that the Ministry
of the Interior, in accordance with my orders, is taking much-
needed measures. In due time we shall ask the gubernia committees, attended by the nobility of the zemstvos, to participate in this
work. And as for the landed gentry—the ancient stronghold of
order and of the moral strength of Russia—it will be my constant
concern to consolidate it."

These words are so definite as to make all comment superfluous. For the landowners they meant a change in economic policy
that would affect the direction of rural economy, which up to
that time had been left to its own devices.

No less informative was the Tsar's speech to the chairmen of
zemstvo boards of Kursk Gubernia. This speech contained the
following passage: "Rural economy is of the utmost importance
and I hope that you will apply all your abilities to it. I shall be
glad to assist you for I *desire to unify the activity of all local authorities. Remember that your main task is to attend to local
economic needs.* If you fulfill this obligation you may be assured of my heartfelt favor."

The Tsar's favor was to fall upon the zemstvos only if they
limited their activities to attending to local economic needs or, in
other words, so long as they refrained from meddling in politics.
His words hinted also at the unification of all local administration;
and this, according to Plehve, meant that the impending reform of
gubernia and uezd administration would bring closer together the
functions of the zemstvos and the local branches of the central
government.

The Tsar's remarks to the volost *starshiny* and *starosty* of
several gubernias, remarks which were supposed to be welcomed by

the local landed gentry, were just as significant. The Tsar said: "Last spring the peasants of Poltava and Kharkov gubernias looted several estates. The culprits shall receive deserved punishment, and the authorities, I feel sure, will not permit any such outbursts in the future. I wish to remind you of my father's words to the volost *starshiny* on the day of his coronation in Moscow: 'Obey your marshals of nobility. Put no trust in false rumors.' Remember, one gets rich not by robbing one's neighbor but by honest toil and thrift and by following the Lord's commandments. Convey my exact words to your fellow villagers and assure them that I will never relax my careful attention to their just needs."

The Tsar's remarks at Kursk amounted to the announcement of a program. This announcement the public associated with Plehve's appointment as Minister of the Interior. To remove any doubt of his intention to carry out the program, Plehve, in conversation with the local zemstvo men at Kursk, enlarged upon the Tsar's remarks, especially upon the character of the projected reform of local administration which would leave wide scope for the activity of the zemstvo organizations. He probably attached great significance to this conversation, for he outlined it to the representatives of the press, who hastened to have it published.

At the beginning of his administration, then, Plehve tried to win the support and sympathies of the nobility and the friendship of the zemstvos. Nor were his efforts at first without success. In St. Petersburg a certain group, not reactionary on the whole, acclaimed his actions and lent him support in his fight with Witte. This group was that which met weekly at the home of K. F. Golovin[1] and formed something of a political salon.

This salon occupied a central position among the few political salons of the end of the nineteenth and the beginning of the twentieth century.* Most of those who gathered there were landowners who

* The salon of Prince V. P. Meshchersky, editor of *Grazhdanin,* was much more reactionary. It was made up of St. Petersburg dignitaries and some public men of pronounced reactionary tendencies. It was visited most frequently by persons who sought the help of the prince in obtaining ministerial portfolios or prominent posts in the gubernias, and according to city gossip the search of many was not in vain.

But more liberal than Golovin's salon was the circle of the *Vestnik Evropy,* which usually assembled at the house of A. K. Arsenev. This was a salon of writers, scientists, journalists, and visiting zemstvo men of liberal views. The dominant note here was cultured liberalism, and its aim was to introduce into Russia a regime which would secure a constitutional even though not a parliamentary type of government.

favored the zemstvos. The nucleus of the group was formed of Orel men: N. A. Khvostov, S. S. Bekhteev, A. A. Naryshkin, and A. D. Polenov.

N. A. Khvostov was the Ober-Prokuror of the Second [peasant] Department of the Senate, but a typical zemstvo man of the eighteen-sixties. He had worked in the Orel Zemstvo and in 1882 had been invited by Count N. P. Ignatev to take part in the Conference of Informed Persons. A Narodnik of the 'sixties, Khvostov was an ardent supporter of the commune and of separate peasant courts and administration.   ;

S. S. Bekhteev had been for a number of years chairman of the Eletsk Uezd Zemstvo Board. He was a man of lively intelligence and some knowledge in the field of economics. At this time he was doing research on the growth of prosperity in the country, a study eventually published under the title *Khoziaistvennye itogi istekshago sorokaletiia ("Economic Results of the Past Forty Years")*. The author's unfamiliarity with methods of research is reflected in the rather disorderly arrangement of this work, which contains many interesting ideas and much data. Formerly Bekhteev had been just as fervent a defender of the commune as Khvostov, but by this time he had become an energetic advocate of peasant private ownership. After the revolutionary movement of 1905, when Krivoshein, then Assistant Head of the Chief Administration of Land Organization and Agriculture, was seeking support among other places in the landowning circles, he used his influence in favor of Bekhteev's appointment to the State Council. But Bekhteev, like many other members of this body, had had no bureaucratic experience and played no important part there.

A. A. Naryshkin, who had begun his public career in the Orel Zemstvo and remained a typical zemstvo man of the 'seventies, was distinguished for his high moral principles and his sense of honor. He was organically opposed to every measure that restricted human activity. He was an ardent patriot, but he did not in the least favor the government policy toward the national minorities of the Empire. He was especially opposed to our policy toward the Poles, an opposition which was partly the result of his Slavophil convictions. He demonstrated his loyalty to the Slavophil idea when he enlisted as a volunteer in the Serbian army during the Serbo-Turkish War of 1876. He was wounded and was awarded the soldiers' cross of St. George, the only decoration of which he was really proud. Later he was elected president of the Slavic Charity Society, an organization whose purposes were not so much charitable as political. His Slavophilism made him the apostle of the threefold formula: Autocracy, Orthodoxy, and Nationality. But he put in these words a meaning which had nothing in common with the idea of mere police supervision. He interpreted the principle of authority as a mysterious communion between the monarch and the people. According to him "the people supplied the ideas, but authority belonged to the Tsar." Until the revolutionary movement of 1905 he was considered, and considered himself, a liberal.

A. D. Polenov was intelligent but dull. He saw the world in terms of statistical data. In 1899, Golovin's salon was studying a problem advanced by Assistant Minister of Finance, V. I. Kovalevsky, the substance of which was that because the borderlands, especially the western regions, lived and prospered at the expense of the state, the central districts were becoming impoverished and exhausted. At that time Polenov expressed the views of the salon in a booklet full of statistical data and bearing the high-sounding title: *Izsledovanie ekonomicheskago polozheniia tsentralnykh chernozemnykh gubernii* ("*A Study of the Economic Status of the Central Black-Soil-Belt Gubernias*"). There was a great variety of statistics in the book, but their interpretation was one-sided.

Habent sua fata libelli. Polenov's booklet had two real results. It advanced its author first to the position of Director of Department in the Ministry of Agriculture under Ermolov, and later to that of Assistant Minister of Agriculture. It became apparent, however, that there was some difference between compiling statistical and economic booklets and directing an important branch of public work. Soon after Ermolov's retirement Polenov was placed somewhere else by the new minister. The second result of the booklet was the organization, three years later, of a special conference which became known as the Commission to Study the Impoverishment of the Central Districts. The calling of this conference was partly due to the fact that some of Polenov's data and conclusions had been used by the press and had made a certain impression on the public. Consequently Witte, who was always attentive to public opinion and never failed to rebut any statement which represented his activities in a not too favorable light, charged the Department of Direct Taxation to make a detailed study of the question. The results of this study appeared in a very informative and interesting manual entitled: *Dvizhenie blagosostoianiia s 1861 po 1900 god srednikh chernozemnykh gubernii po sravneniiu s ostalnymi* (*"The Prosperity Movement from 1861 to 1900 in the Central Black-Soil-Belt Gubernias as Compared with the Rest of the Country"*). This study was instrumental also in the calling of the special conference mentioned above.

Besides these constant visitors to Golovin's salon there were many other occasional visitors: Count P. A. Heyden, later a prominent member of the zemstvo congresses and still later the leader of the small Party of Peaceful Reconstruction;[2] A. V. Evreinov, marshal of the nobility of Sudzha Uezd, Kursk Gubernia, who as chairman of the local agricultural committee had clearly shown opposition to the government (he was married to a lady of the prominent Moscow merchant family, the Sabashnikovs, known as liberals and as patrons of the arts); Prince Pavel Dmitrievich Dolgorukov,[3] who later joined the Cadet party; and A. N. Brianchaninov, an ambitious politician who did not succeed in attaching himself to any definite political group.

Among Golovin's guests from the St. Petersburg bureaucracy was P. K. Schwanebach, who became State Comptroller under Goremykin and Stolypin. He was recognized as an authority on economic questions and was renowned for his great erudition, which he loved to display. He was a confirmed and violent critic of Witte's economic policy, though he himself was on the council of the Minister of Finance. His two financial and political essays, "Denezhnaia reforma" ("Monetary Reform") and "Nashe podatnoe delo" ("Our Taxation"), with their clear, concise, informative style—especially the first one—did much to make the reading public understand both sides of Witte's policy. Schwanebach's critical analysis of the annual budget and the accompanying report of the Minister of Finance—a report which always gave a rosy account of the economic and financial condition of the state—was always enlightening and usually devastating. Since conditions did not permit the publication of such criticisms in the form of articles, he made speeches at private and semi-public gatherings such as the so-called "economic banquets," and in the Trade and Commerce Association of which Count Ignatev was chairman. It was at a session of this association that the discussions of Schwanebach's report was interrupted by the order of the authorities.

Such were some of the prominent figures of Golovin's salon. Golovin himself gave a peculiar air to these gatherings. He was blind and paralyzed. He had completely lost the use of his legs and was barely able to move his arms. But his physical disabilities had not dimmed his lively intelligence and his vivid interest in the most varied questions of public and state life. His excellent memory and especially acute hearing enabled him to identify a person by his voice or even by his step; it gave him particular pleasure to welcome a person by name before that person had spoken. Golovin was a novelist and the author of fifteen volumes of belles-lettres, some of which revealed marked ability and a power of subtle observation. He was also a well-informed economist and had written several long articles on economic subjects.

All phases of state and public life were discussed in Golovin's salon, but the most prominent place was given to economic questions. This may be explained by the fact that at that time Witte held the center of the stage and his economic measures were exciting warm comment. Golovin's group, belonging mostly to the landowning class, was naturally opposed to Witte's one-sided policy in support of industry, and acclaimed Plehve's appointment in 1902 as an indication of Witte's downfall. When the agricultural conference was organized, this group, which did not anticipate any beneficial results from the conference, since it was under the guidance of Witte, selected a few of its members to compile a short memorandum on Russia's economic policy setting forth their opinions on this matter. This memorandum was intended for Plehve, in whose hands it was finally placed. In all probability it was used by him in his campaign against Witte. At any rate, Plehve very cordially received those who handed him the memorandum and had a long conversation with them.

This shows that the nobility and the landed gentry supported Plehve warmly because they disliked Witte. But when Witte had been defeated, the landed gentry had no more reason to support Plehve. In fact, Plehve's share in a certain incident tended to make them withdraw this support. The incident concerned the election of a Chernigov marshal of the nobility. As was the custom, two candidates, one of whom enjoyed a majority support, were advanced by the nobility. The minority candidate, in fact, was usually chosen by the nobility after the majority candidate had been selected and stood as a second candidate knowing beforehand that he would get fewer votes than his rival. The final choice was left to the throne, and in no case had the throne failed to choose the candidate who had enjoyed the majority support. But in the instance in question, this customary procedure was violated. Mukhanov, the majority candidate, was passed over by the Tsar in favor of the minority candidate. Plehve opposed the Tsar's selection. Twice he reported to the Tsar on this subject, arguing that such a decision might antagonize the most moderate circles of the nobility which up to then had been a staunch support of the state. But the Tsar was adamant, and Plehve, as a faithful and devoted servant of the throne, took upon himself the odium of the decision. Attempts were made to persuade Plehve to inform the Chernigov nobility of the real authorship of the decision; but Plehve answered firmly: "My duty is to protect the Tsar and not to subject him to the attacks of the public." I can answer for the truth of this statement, as I heard it with my own ears.

Plehve further antagonized the landed gentry by his policy toward the zemstvos. It soon became clear that Plehve desired to limit zemstvo activity to the mere supervision of local economic needs. Nearly all of the landed gentry were zemstvo workers and did not take kindly to these limitations, especially since they felt that they received no material profit from their zemstvo work. In fact strained relations between Plehve and zemstvo men, for which Plehve was not wholly to blame, dated almost from the time he became minister, and derived from events connected with the uprisings in Poltava and Kharkov gubernias. In March 1902 the investigation of these uprisings revealed that they had been stirred up by revolutionary propaganda, in which the statisticians of Poltava Gubernia zemstvo had taken a large and active part.

Zemstvo statisticians were employed to take care of the extensive statistical work done by the zemstvos. Of this work something should be said at this point. Some of the zemstvos had been interested for a long time in determining the value and profit-yielding worth of certain pieces of real estate on which zemstvo taxes were paid. Their work in this field in some of the gubernias, for instance that of Voronezh, provided much valuable information—not so much concerning the value of taxable property as concerning the prosperity of the population and its ability to pay. The determination of peasant household income, as carried out in Voronezh Gubernia by the well-known statistician Vorobev (if I am not mistaken), also had a scientific value and might have had a practical value as well. Because this work involved large expenditures, the government saw fit to assist the zemstvos in it. By the law of January 18, 1899,[4] the zemstvos were apportioned a considerable yearly subsidy. After the promulgation of the law of June 12, 1900, by which limits were set for zemstvo taxation, these yearly subsidies became a permanent policy because the setting of definite limits for zemstvo taxation was directly connected with the completion of the work undertaken by the zemstvo of evaluating taxable property. This work had been carried out according to certain rules, by which it was divided into three parts: (1) the compilation and classification of the statistical material; (2) the determination of the general norms of property evaluation; and (3) the application of these norms to land, city property, and industrial enterprises, including factories and shops. This work, outlined on such a wide scale, was of great importance to the state and by its extensive nature obviously exceeded not only the sphere of interests of separate zemstvos but also their legal competence. Moreover, in most of the cases the zemstvo workers lacked sufficient technical knowledge for such work. Consequently, the results of the work varied in different gubernias, as actually neither the zemstvo assemblies nor the zemstvo boards had control over it. The work passed entirely to the heads of the evaluation offices of the zemstvo boards, that is, to the statisticians, many of whom were not fully qualified to do it. As early as 1902 it became apparent that in the gubernias of Kazan, Chernigov, and Tula the compilations of evaluation statistics were so unsatisfactory that the zemstvo boards and assemblies had been obliged to reject them entirely and have the work done over again. It was learned also that this work was being done extremely slowly and that only a few zemstvos had done more than collect the material. Moreover, work was done differently from gubernia to gubernia: whereas some zemstvos collected barely the material officially demanded, others expanded their activities until they were conducting not a mere statistical evaluation survey but a complicated economic analysis. This explains why in most zemstvos this work was far from completion before the revolution although it had cost the government, or rather the people, tens of millions of rubles.

One may well doubt that such an evaluation of property throughout rural Russia could have any practical significance, both because of the poor qualifications of the hundreds of persons engaged in this work and because of the differences in methods and standards employed.* Yet even supposing that this work had been well done, what was the worth and economic significance of a correct evaluation of property for purposes of direct taxation in a country whose tax system was based upon indirect taxation?

But this needless yearly expenditure of several million rubles was but one side of the question. Much worse and much more important was the opportunity it offered for revolutionaries, acting in the capacity of statisticians, to mingle with the rural population on a perfectly lawful basis, to discuss economic conditions and to spread distinctly socialistic views among the peasants. Neither the administration, because it lacked police supervision in rural localities, nor the zemstvo, which had to accept the services of strangers, could supervise and control the activity of these statisticians in this direction. In some gubernias the number of statisticians was quite large; in 1901 there were 594 in Poltava Gubernia. Most of these statisticians were transients and worked in a given zemstvo only during the summer months.

The government could not be expected to view calmly this revolutionary work carried on among the rural population by such an army of zemstvo statisticians. As indicated above, the investigation of the agrarian uprisings in Poltava Gubernia convinced Plehve that their underlying cause was revolutionary propaganda spread by zemstvo statisticians; accordingly, in his report of June 1902 to the Tsar he petitioned the Sovereign to limit for the current year the statistical work in some gubernias to city and town districts and to city property only. But this report, which was published, did not contain one word of criticism of the zemstvo institutions themselves —it even pointed out that in some localities the statisticians had quarreled with the zemstvo boards and had acted contrary to orders. Nevertheless it provoked much discontent in zemstvo circles, mainly because it mentioned the government's intention to take the entire business of evaluating property out of the hands of the zemstvos and transfer it to the central-government authorities. And although this transfer was never made, the threat to do so contained in the report laid the foundation for zemstvo hostility toward Plehve. As a con-

---

* Yet *Russkiia Vedomosti*[5] averred: "Russia has every reason to be proud before the entire cultural world of her zemstvo statistics."

sequence of a later report by Plehve—March 25, 1904—the Minister of the Interior was empowered to stop all zemstvo statistical surveys at his discretion. In only a few instances did Plehve use this power; but the threat was there and further aggravated the already strained relations between him and zemstvo circles.

During his entire term of office Plehve did not effect one single decisive measure in any field; yet the discontent and grievances he inspired in individual persons, in the public at large, and even in national organizations was very great. He touched almost every phase of public life in some way and in every case he aroused discontent. Threats, leniency, favors—all were intermixed and, in consequence, threats did not frighten and favors did not excite gratitude. The basic principle of state activity—*fortiter in re, suaviter in modo,* was utterly foreign to Plehve, in fact, to all the statesmen who served Nicholas II. Plehve's pinpricks aggravated the people and created a nervous tension without inspiring in them fear of the government. Unlike the Rome of Tacitus' account—*oderint dum metuant*—the Russian government was hated but not feared. The government thunder rolled incessantly; but there was no lightning. And this at a time when Plehve had the Tsar's complete confidence and could have passed any measures. Plehve had assumed the office of Minister of the Interior with great plans, but these dwindled to pettiness or evaporated into thin air. The mountain brought forth nothing but mice.*

In a word, the government behaved like a spoiled woman: it pouted over nothing; it scratched, it cried, and it complained that no one wanted to understand it. But it adopted no decisive, sober,

* In the case of Finland, for instance, contradictory measures and reversals of intention weakened the position of the government and at the same time fired to white heat the anger of the Finnish public. Illustrative of this wavering policy are two state acts proclaimed December 18, 1903, pertaining to the evasion of military service by the Finns. One act, an order to the Governor-General of Finland, stated that those liable for military service in 1904 who failed to appear for service would be made to serve their term in units outside Finland. The second act, a resolution on a report of the Imperial Senate of Finland, stated that the Tsar had "deigned to permit the discontinuance of summoning for further military service the recruits of 1902 who had failed to appear."

Plehve's intentions concerning Viborg Gubernia—so-called Old Finland—are also illustrative. He intended to separate it from the Grand Duchy and bring it directly under the general Russian laws and organization. The proposed measure aroused great indignation among the Finnish people. Soon afterward Plehve modified the plan, proposing now merely to add two volosts to the contiguous St. Petersburg Gubernia. Even this fell through.

stable, and mature measure. That which was forbidden today was allowed tomorrow. That which was repudiated one day was on the next praised and applauded. The prestige of the government, the assurance of the stability of its measures, rapidly diminished. On the one hand, no one could be sure that some innocent action not prohibited by the government would not set one en route, as Pushkin said, "straight, straight to the east"; on the other, the conviction grew that any order of the government could be paralyzed by a display of determined opposition.

That Plehve followed such a vacillating policy was unquestionably the result of his legal and police experience and his lack of contact with the public and its institutions. Plehve desired to establish close and happy relations with the people, but he could no more conquer his formal bureaucratic attitude toward them than he could refrain from sarcasm and irony. *C'etait le doigté qui lui manquait.* It was precisely this shortcoming which was the main reason for his failure to establish friendly or even normal relations with the zemstvo public. It was also to some extent the fault of the persons he had selected as intermediaries between himself and the zemstvos. Thus, his attempt to arrive at some understanding with the Chairman of the Moscow Gubernia Zemstvo Board, mentioned above, failed largely because of the personality of N. A. Zinovev who was charged with the affair. This failure slightly provoked Plehve; so he decided to fight the zemstvo on a business basis by establishing, through an investigation, the defects of the practical economic work of the zemstvo organizations. But the investigators he chose, Zinovev and Stürmer, by their unskilled, rude, and not always honorable conduct, created a final breach between Plehve and the zemstvos.

Zinovev seemed to think that he could deprive these institutions of all public sympathy and justify entirely the policy of the government in regard to them by proclaiming for everyone's information the defects which his investigation revealed. It would have been difficult to commit a graver error. The public was little interested in the economic activity of local self-government, particularly that of the zemstvos. It saw in the zemstvo workers the vanguard of those who were fighting for political freedom, those who were fighting to win for the masses of the population a share in the deciding of state problems. It was for these reasons that the public valued and cherished the zemstvos. Zinovev, moreover, found a good deal of fault with the zemstvo workers. He made accusations against them which were not at all well founded.* This made his entire investigation seem partisan. Consequently, his criticism of other zemstvo activities, which really needed criticism, did not inspire public confidence. Besides, his method of describing the activities of the zemstvos and municipalities was extremely incorrect. His reports enumerated only the defects, made no mention of those zemstvo activities which were carried on satisfactorily, and gave no idea of the growth and expansion of zemstvo work. Thus, in the report on the centennial anniversary of the establishment of municipal self-government, all aspects of municipal economy were criticized with the sole exception of the administration of schools.

The selection of B. V. Stürmer as inspector of the zemstvo boards of Novo-Torzhok Uezd and Tver Gubernia was just as unfortunate. The public considered this inspection a reprisal for the address which the Tver Zemstvo had presented to the Tsar on his accession to the throne, which had stated explicitly the necessity of giving Russia a constitution and which had been inspired by the zemstvo men of Novo-Torzhok Uezd. Under these conditions any inspection, regardless of its results, would have met with public distrust and even hostility. The appointment of Stürmer to the task of revision and his method of procedure only increased these feelings. The fact is that Stürmer himself was a member of the Tver Zemstvo from Bezhetsk Uezd and during his earlier term as chairman of the Tver Gubernia Zemstvo Board, to which he was appointed by the government, he had gained the friendship of the Left-wing circles of the zemstvo. Therefore, when he started the inspection he met with an attitude of friendliness and trust. Stürmer himself would have been the last to wish to change this attitude, and during the inspection he not only refrained from making any criticism but expressed the most liberal views concerning the activities of the zemstvo in general. When his report on the results of his inspection was published, however, it came to the Tver Zemstvo as a blow in the face and caused tremendous indignation. The Tver men were indignant mostly because in his report Stürmer accused the gubernia zemstvo of refusing to apportion certain sums for the support of the schools of the

* For instance, he accused the Moscow Gubernia zemstvo of violating the law in that the gubernia board had organized conferences of chairmen of uezd boards. In reality, however, increased zemstvo work made such conferences necessary. To deny them public and legal existence would have been to drive them into private residences and make them conspiratory. Nothing could have been farther from the intention of the government.

uezd zemstvo, the uezd zemstvo having decided to place all their
zemstvo schools under the competence of the diocesan authorities, in
other words, to turn them into parish schools. Stürmer himself,
when he was a member of the Gubernia Zemstvo Assembly, had inspired this particular decision of the Tver Gubernia Zemstvo.

It also criticized the zemstvo boards which he had inspected for
tolerating the open revolutionary activity conducted by the hired
workers of these boards, the so-called third element, a tolerance
which was not permissible from the government's point of view. Yet
it should be remembered that even those strata of society which had
a statesmanlike understanding of the situation failed to realize at
that time that revolutionary activity undermined not only the existing
form of government but also the very foundations of the existing
order and was directed primarily against themselves. The liberal
elements saw in the revolutionary intelligentsia only a mighty ally
in their fight for the "regime of equity" and abandoned this conception only after the triumph of the Bolsheviks in 1917 when both the
old regime and the very idea of equity and law were demolished.

On January 16, 1904, Plehve made his most humble report to
the Tsar regarding Stürmer's inspection of the Tver Gubernia Zemstvo. Following this, government-appointed zemstvo boards were set
up on January 16, 1904, for the next three years in Tver Gubernia
and Novo-Torzhok Uezd, and at the same time authority was given
to the Minister of the Interior "to prohibit persons found exercising
a harmful influence upon the course of zemstvo administration from
staying in Tver Gubernia or any of its districts." These measures
provoked almost unanimous indignation in zemstvo circles. The deportation from Tver Gubernia of the board member, Petrunkevich,
leader of the liberal party, and of Apostolov and N. K. Miliukov, a
relative of the future leader of the Cadet party, aggravated this
feeling still more. The investing of the Tver governor with the right
"to dismiss from zemstvo service persons dangerous to public order
and peace" had the same effect.

These measures went beyond the provisions of the existing law.
The law permitted the government to appoint the personnel of the
zemstvo board only after it had twice refused to confirm candidates
elected by the zemstvo assembly to this board. Plehve had discussed
this matter in detail with his associates, and all of them except Stürmer expressed themselves in favor of observing the law. Stürmer
explained his stand in a report which he prepared for presentation to

the Tsar and which insisted not only that the government should appoint the personnel of the zemstvo boards but also that the regulation concerning extraordinary protective measures should be applied to Tver Gubernia. When Stürmer had finished reading his report, Plehve took it, tore it up, and threw the pieces into the wastebasket. Then another report was composed in which Plehve provided only for the appointment of new boards. I urged Plehve not to make this illegal and useless move but to no avail. My representations only irritated him. As a sort of *ultimo ratio* of this measure he took out of his brief case a note written in the Tsar's own hand, and showed it to the group. The note said: "I have been thinking a great deal about our conversation concerning the Tver Zemstvo; they must be dealt a severe blow." The note, written in ink and signed by the full name "Nicholas," indicated that the Tsar intended this as an order. Informal notes addressed by him to ministers were generally written in pencil and signed by the initial "N." Only those which were intended as orders were written with this formality.

Was this a justification of Plehve's conduct? Hardly so. It is evident that the Tsar's decision was based upon Plehve's earlier report. Besides, Plehve still had an opportunity to present the position of the Tver Zemstvo to the Tsar in its true aspect and to interpret it on the basis of law. Yet Plehve, a true product of the regime of Alexander III, was not capable of making such a move.

Public indignation was also aroused by the measures intended to limit the scope of the questions discussed by the agricultural committees. It was pointed out, not without reason, that there was little coordination of activities among local authorities. Some governors, as chairmen of gubernia agricultural committees, permitted discussion of any question; others not only arbitrarily limited the scope of questions to be discussed but went so far as to apprise these committees only of some excerpts from the conclusions arrived at by the uezd agricultural committees, withholding everything they considered outside their sphere of deliberation. In Tambov this procedure resulted in the majority of the committee members resigning their posts.

Yet the greatest discontent and indignation was aroused by Plehve's own actions in regard to certain members of uezd agricultural committees. The banishment from Voronezh of Martynov and Bunakov for their speeches in the Voronezh Uezd agricultural committee, and the depriving of Prince Pavel Dmitrievich Dolgorukov, marshal of the nobility of the Ruza Uezd, of the right to participate in the elective public institutions, created discontent among circles of the nobility and gentry that were least opposed to the government.

The relations of the zemstvo organizations to the representatives of the central government, and especially to Plehve, thus became more and more strained. At times the rivalry between the two was like a game. Certain governors, acting through the special boards for zemstvo and municipal affairs, reversed in ever-increasing numbers the decisions of zemstvo assemblies. These assemblies in turn appealed to the Senate against the decisions of these boards, and the Senate often took the side of the zemstvos.

The attitude of the zemstvo circles and their basic hopes were most definitely expressed in the memorandum of the representatives of seventeen zemstvo gubernias who were invited to participate in the work of the Commission to Study the Impoverishment of the Central Districts. This commission had been founded in the spring of 1903, when Witte was Minister of Finance, and, according to his view, was to serve him in his fight with Plehve. It did not meet, however, until October 1903, when Pleske was already Minister of Finance. It functioned under the chairmanship of V. N. Kokovtsov, who was at that time Imperial Secretary and had but recently (1902) retired from the post of Assistant Minister of Finance. He was therefore well acquainted with the question. Plehve looked with disfavor upon the commission and had secured Kokovtsov's appointment as its chairman by representations to the Tsar.

During the first session of the commission, the zemstvo men directed the discussion into general fields and to political rather than economic questions. Naturally enough they stressed the peasant question, as Witte had expected. But times had changed. Kokovtsov had his instructions. Moreover, he had no desire to antagonize Plehve, for he hoped that with Plehve's assistance he would soon become Minister of Finance as successor to the dying Pleske and, therefore, he would not permit any deviation from the outlined work of the commission.[6] He did succeed, however, in handling this matter diplomatically: he did not deny the zemstvo men a chance to express themselves, but suggested that they express their common views in a special memorandum, leaving to the discussion of the commission only the questions outlined in the agenda and not pertaining to politics. To a certain extent, however, the zemstvo men attained their end. Their memorandum appeared in the press and thus helped to spread their views. It included all the slogans which were adopted at that time by progressive zemstvo circles. It advocated that the peasant class be placed on a basis of equality with all other classes, in both rights and responsibilities, and enumerated all the limitations on the peasant status which should be abolished. Next, the zemstvo men pointed out that the measures to improve rural economy could be made effective only if at the same time measures were adopted to improve the cultural education of the peasants. In this connection they expressed the desire that all measures for improving the economic status of the peasants be effected through the zemstvos, and suggested that the zemstvo be provided with state funds, "since the zemstvos, and they alone, could carry out these measures with competence and efficiency." In conclusion the zemstvo men declared in favor of a decrease in indirect taxation on objects of prime necessity and of substituting for it a direct income tax; they were also in favor of lowering the redemption dues and of canceling payments in arrears; in favor of the assumption by the government of village community expenses that directly concerned the state; in favor of having the State Bank and savings banks grant credit in small amounts; in favor of the support of homecraft industries; in favor of the regulation of trades away from home; in favor of the better organization of peasant colonization; and in favor of regulation of land rentals.

I have purposefully cited at length these desires of the zemstvos (the majority of which were adopted by the commission) in order to show once more how the old Russian zemstvo, directed and for the most part composed of representatives of the landed gentry, regarded its duties. When asked their opinion of how to improve rural economy, the zemstvos answered with a series of suggestions directed exclusively toward improving the peasant standard of living and equalizing the rights of the peasants. All this was expressed by the representatives of all zemstvo groups, although the majority of the representatives belonged to the Right group. The most liberal representative was the chairman of the Novgorod Zemstvo Board, Koliubakin;[7] but even he, when speaking of the lack of organization and other defects of rural life, expressed the opinion that these should be done away with as speedily as possible in order to assure the strength of the state and of the existing social order. But such attitudes as these did not—nor do they now—prevent our revolutionaries, and not them alone, from speaking of how the landowners oppressed the peasantry or from stating that the landed gentry was the great evil from which Russia had to be saved.

The Russian landed gentry, as managers of local economic needs, was hardly right in ignoring the interests of all other classes of society but the peasants. Charity may begin at home; but such one-sided action is faulty because the economic prosperity of a state can be assured only by a normal development of all classes of society, albeit such action on the part of the Russian landed gentry must be recognized as extremely unselfish and exalted. Who in the Russia of today will replace this best-educated class which was ready to make any sacrifice for the people's well-being and is now almost entirely extinct?

The zemstvo men were merely trying to protect the independence of zemstvo institutions from interference by the central government. The fact that Plehve was usually the author of the interference made the zemstvo hostile to him. Resistance to the minister's measures developed into open opposition, which irritated Plehve* more than anything else.

The zemstvos and the public were no less indignant because, by Plehve's orders, the activity of the all-zemstvo organization working in the Far East during the Russo-Japanese War was discontinued. Yet one has to admit that in this particular instance Plehve had good reasons for acting as he did. This organization, working under the direction of the deceitful, sly, and weak-willed Prince Lvov,[8] had been flooded with revolutionary elements from the day of its establishment. This became particularly evident when it resumed activity after the murder of Plehve and the appointment of Prince Sviato-polk-Mirsky. It was evident also in the fact that when a lack of discipline appeared in the Manchurian army in 1905 immediately after the termination of the war great revolutionary demonstrations were held in Siberia. During these demonstrations it became known that many of the participants and instigators had formerly worked in the all-zemstvo organization.

Plehve's irritable and angry attitude toward the moderately liberal circles of society had the fatal effect of cementing together all

---

* Evidence of Plehve's irritation was seen when in 1904 he refused to confirm the elections of Kudriaev and Shipov as chairmen of the gubernia zemstvo boards of Vologda and Moscow gubernias, respectively. In the latter case it was really a blunder, because there was no serious reason for opposing the election of Shipov, who enjoyed great popularity in all zemstvo circles.

elements of the opposition, including the extremes. At the beginning of January 1904, for instance, the third congress of representatives of professional and technical education assembled in St. Petersburg. It was closed on the next day by order of the governor of the city and some of the members were banished from the capital. This measure created much indignation; yet the speeches of many of the members had been of a clearly revolutionary character which the government could not tolerate, and the persons banished—Charnolusky,[9] Falbork,[10] and Vorobev—belonged to the Social Democratic group of the Russian intelligentsia. Another instance was the government's refusal to permit the reading at the final session of the Pirogov Congress of Physicians, held January 4 to 11, 1904, of the resolutions adopted by this congress. As a consequence of this prohibition, these resolutions, in formulating which 2,136 members had taken part, were circulated from hand to hand and were much more widely read and attracted much more interest than they would have done had they been read at the congress. The needlessness of this prohibitive measure becomes more apparent if it is realized that the government could have achieved its end by prohibiting the press from printing these resolutions.

Plehve's treatment of the periodical press, and especially his attitude toward individual journalists, also brought down unfavorable comment upon his head. Even the most loyal circles did not approve of the measures which deprived A. A. Stolypin,[11] editor of *Sankt-Peterburgskiia Vedomosti,*[12] of the right to edit his paper, for Stolypin was a moderate journalist and, among other things, had protested warmly against the accusation that the government had organized the Kishinev Jewish pogrom.

As a result of Plehve's indecisive, pinpricking policy, some of the educated circles of society, essentially conservative in character, began to look with a certain tolerance upon the actions of the terrorist revolutionaries and not only refrained from condemning them but even justified their conduct. After the spring of 1903 revolutionary outbursts became more frequent now in one and now in another part of the huge empire. But in liberal circles these did not arouse any fear for the unity of the state. The bourgeois capitalistic structure was considered by an overwhelming majority of well-to-do society to be not only strong but natural, and therefore unshakable. The idea of even its temporary collapse entered the head of no one. What was happening seemed to them to be a mere attack on the political authority for the purpose of gaining for the public a share in the government of the state. Consequently all who took part in this attack, without exception and regardless of the means employed, were acclaimed as allies. It was natural that under these conditions every stern repression of revolutionary uprisings served only to widen the circle of those who were interested in politics and criticized the government.

The public was much shocked by the way the administration handled the uprisings of March 1903 in the Zlatoust works in Ufa Gubernia. In order to maintain order among the workers, the government sent in troops, who fired on the workers, killing forty-five and wounding eighty-three, among whom were several women. The later disturbances in Baku, Batum, Saratov, and Vilna were suppressed without bloodshed and attracted much less attention because the public had become accustomed to consider them as normal and not very dangerous for the state and as warranting no public counteraction. Nor did the Odessa disorders of July 1903 change this attitude, although in this instance the troops, who were then in summer quarters, were called out. Neither was the public shaken by the troubles of the autumn of 1903 in the factories of Ekaterinoslav Gubernia. The uprisings in the Caucasus (in Shusha, Nukha, and Elizavetpol), which public opinion attributed to the stern measures adopted toward the Armenian-Gregorian church, whose property had been placed under government control and whose head, the Catholicos Mkrtich, had been exiled to a monastery, created even a smaller flurry in the public! This measure against the Armenian-Gregorian church had been adopted upon the insistence of Prince G. Golitsyn,[13] Governor of the Caucasus, against Plehve's better judgment; but public opinion ascribed it to the hated Minister of the Interior.

In fact, every action and every incident that aroused public discontent was at that time ascribed to Plehve. This was especially manifest in the cases of the Jewish pogrom at Kishinev and the Japanese War, for both of which the public blamed him.

The Jewish pogrom at Kishinev in April 1903 was associated with Plehve not only in Russian opinion but also in the Western press. This pogrom assumed unusual dimensions. It lasted two days —April 6 and 7. Forty-five men were killed, seventy-one were seriously wounded, and three hundred and fifty suffered minor injuries. The material loss was still greater: seven hundred houses and six hundred shops were demolished, and the number of feather beds—a possession of every Jew, no matter how poor—that were ripped open was so great that the air was full of flying down and feathers.

Censorship prevented the Russian press from printing the silly tale, spread by revolutionary elements, that the government had deliberately let the pogrom run its course unchecked and even that the government was responsible for it. The foreign press, mostly in the hands of Jews, was in a different position. For some time previously the tale that the Russian government not only failed to prevent pogroms but even openly encouraged them had been spread about by international Jewry, which tried in this way to prove that the Russian people, although they indulged in pogroms against the Jewish population, bore no hatred toward the Jewish people with whom they lived side by side. The pogroms, the Jewry argued, were instigated by the Russian government. The Jewish population served merely as a scapegoat by means of which the Russian government could divert the discontent of the Russian people, whose difficult material circumstances were caused by the faulty economic policy of the government itself. The absolute unfairness of this tale needs no proof. The hostile treatment of the local Jewish population by the inhabitants of cities and small towns may be explained in different ways. One may admit or deny the fact that the Christian population was exploited by the Jewish element living among it; but one cannot deny the deep-rooted hostility of the Russian people toward this race, a hostility which easily flared up into wild hatred on the slightest provocation, and which expressed itself in most savage ways. Nevertheless, the tale spread. Even many Russians accepted it in good faith. The pogrom of Kishinev was known throughout the world, not only in western Europe but also in America. In fact, in America there was also published the apocryphal letter, allegedly written by Plehve to the Governor of Bessarabia, von Raaben, dated March 25, 1903, and marked "very secret." "I have been informed that in your region great uprisings are being planned against the Jews as the chief exploiters of the local population. Because of the dangerous spirit of unrest pervading the city population and seeking but a pretext to manifest itself, and also because it is undesirable to arouse by too severe a measure a hostile attitude toward the government among those classes of the population which have not yet become contaminated with revolutionary propaganda, I suggest that Your Excellency seek some means to combat the impending pogroms by means of argument but without recourse to armed force."

It is not surprising that the entire world considered this letter authentic. When Plehve himself saw it in *Osvobozhdenie*,[14] which he read regularly, he at first thought that he had really signed it. He called the director of the Police Department, Lopukhin, and asked him angrily: "How could you have brought this stuff for me to sign?" Only when he learned that there had been no such letter did he calm down. Then he published a special governmental announcement quoting the letter and not only branding it as false but also stating that he had not sent a single letter to the Governor of Bessarabia concerning the expected uprising. Yet the result of this announcement was contrary to Plehve's expectations. One newspaper published the letter and Plehve's announcement but made no comment on either. This served only to confirm among certain classes the belief that the pogrom had been created by the government. This belief was further strengthened by the deportation from Russia of the correspondent of *The Times* (London), Braham,[15] whose dispatches had been full of fictitious information derogatory to the Russian government and who had insisted that the government had had a share in the Kishinev pogrom. But this did not put a stop to the mudslinging at Russia by certain foreign publications; Braham and *The Times* only increased their attacks upon the Russian government and Plehve.

The Kishinev pogrom intensified the hatred of Plehve not only in Russia but also abroad. Yet he had had no part in this sad event. This is proved by the fact that von Raaben, who had not been able to stop the pogrom, was dismissed with the bare pension accorded him by law. I had an opportunity to talk with von Raaben, who, of course, tried to defend himself; he blamed the military commandant in whom he had vested full authority to suppress the pogrom. This was a feeble defense, but it proved that he had no orders from Plehve to avoid "any recourse to armed force" in suppressing the uprising. But the weakness of his argument was apparent and it was pointed out in a circular which Plehve sent to all governors on April 28, 1903, three weeks after the pogrom. The circular reminded them that "during times of unrest civil authorities have no right to transfer their own power to the military commandant in order to suppress uprisings but must personally direct the actions of the armed forces and the police and must exercise energy and intelligence in the whole matter."

Further evidence that the government took no part in organizing

Jewish pogroms appeared a little later. In the autumn of 1904, when Prince Sviatopolk-Mirsky was Minister of the Interior, there were pogroms in Rovno, Volhynia Gubernia, in Aleksandriia, Kherson Gubernia, and in Smela, Kiev Gubernia. In the latter town, one hundred and seventy-two Jewish shops were demolished. To suspect Prince Mirsky of connivance was hardly possible, as was admitted even by the Jewish press.

After a terrible pogrom in Tomsk in 1905, which could not possibly have been ascribed to the government, the publication, *Novosti,*[16] of the Jew, Notovich,[17] published a thundering editorial directed against the Russian people. It said that up to now the Jewry had considered the government of autocratic Russia its chief enemy and it ascribed its misfortunes to the government alone. But now the Jewish people were convinced that the whole Russian people was its enemy. It was against this people that the Jews would have to wage war to the death.

I cannot be silent on the subject of the unfair attitude and wholesale criticism which our progressive press manifested toward the government and its actions. When it was a question of suppressing the uprisings at Zlatoust the people was put upon a pedestal and the actions of the government in trying to establish order were labeled criminal. When the same people took to destroying the Jews it immediately was called "rabble" and the government which failed to have timely recourse to armed force was accused of connivance.

Oh, yes, the position of the Russian government was a difficult one in those days!

PART THREE

The Outbreak of the Russo-Japanese War and the Government's Attempt to Reach an Understanding with the Public, 1904

CHAPTER XV

THE CAUSES OF THE RUSSO-JAPANESE WAR*

The Russo-Japanese War is now history and, moreover, might seem to be of secondary importance. But is it of secondary importance? Has not the Russo-Japanese War a direct relation to the Russia of today? It is possible that this war gave birth to the evils from which Russia has suffered and is still suffering. It was a most unfortunate war in every way. It exposed many of our internal wounds; it stimulated and gave point to criticisms of the existing state structure; it threw into the revolutionary camp many persons sincerely concerned over the fate of their native land; and it not only gave impetus to the revolutionary movement, but even lent it a noble, patriotic character.

Immediately after the war the responsibility for it was laid at Plehve's door, and the person most anxious to encourage public opinion to believe in Plehve's responsibility was the man upon whom the main, but not the whole, responsibility must rest: Witte. Witte, and the public after him, affirmed that Plehve had sought to divert public attention from questions of internal policy by means of an easy, victorious war, thereby to lessen the influence of the revolutionary elements and at the same time to increase the prestige of the existing regime in the eyes of the population. But there was no tangible evidence to support this serious affirmation. I do not intend a detailed analysis of our Far Eastern policy, a policy rich in grave errors; but I would like to emphasize that the causes of this war go back to a former period. They originate in 1895, immediately after the conclusion of the Sino-Japanese Treaty of Shimonoseki, several years before Plehve had become Minister of the Interior.

According to this treaty, China yielded to Japan the entire penin-

---

* The present chapter is based on a concise diary I happened to save, and on the following articles: "Dnevnik A. N. Kuropatkina" ("The Diary of A. N. Kuropatkin"), in *Krasnyi Arkhiv,* Moscow, 1922, II, 9–112; A. M. de Besabrassow [Bezobrazov], "Les premières causes de l'effondrement de la Russie. Le Conflit russo-japonais," in *Le Correspondent,* Paris, 1923, tome 291, 557–615; and B. A. Romanov, "Kontsessiia na Yalu" ("The Concession on the Yalu"), in *Russkoe Proshloe,* Moscow, 1922, I, 87–108.

sula of Liaotung and part of Manchuria. Russia advanced the principle of the territorial inviolability of the Chinese Empire and, with the support of France and Germany, forced Japan to renounce this acquisition and to accept in its stead a monetary indemnity, which China paid with our financial aid. The revision of the Shimonoseki settlement had been Witte's idea, as he himself has revealed in his memoirs, and must be given its due; it was not to Russia's advantage to allow the penetration of the energetic Japanese people into the Asiatic continent and to permit Japan to replace "immobile China" as our neighbor.

Yet within a year the new arrangement was reduced to nothing and through the efforts of Witte himself! In 1896 we reached an agreement with China concerning the construction of the Trans-Siberian Railway through northern Manchuria. This agreement gave Russia sovereign rights over the right-of-way tract in northern Manchuria and thus distinctly violated the principle of the territorial inviolability of China.* But Witte was not content to stop with this. He directed his attention toward Korea.[1]

In 1898 the management of Korean finance was in the hands of the Russian agent, K. Alekseev, whose official title was "Advisor to the Korean Emperor," and Russian officers were employed as instructors in the Korean army. It goes without saying that both the construction of the railway through Manchuria and the position occupied by the Russians in Korea excited grave displeasure in Japan. This displeasure was the more justified since our activity in Korea was not entirely in accordance with Russo-Japanese diplomatic agreements—the Seoul memorandum of May 2, 1896, and the Moscow protocol of May 28, 1896—by which both parties agreed to respect Korean sovereignty and bound themselves to act upon the territory of Korea in perfect co-operation with each other.

At this point another person stepped upon the diplomatic stage to play a part in spreading our influence upon the shores of the Pacific, namely, our Minister of Foreign Affairs, Count M. N. Muravev.[2] Using as a pretext the fact that Germany, after some trifling incident concerning German missionaries in China, had taken by force the Chinese port of Tsingtao (Kiaochow Bay) in November

---

* The idea of constructing the Trans-Siberian Railway through northern Manchuria had first arisen in the Siberian Committee during the preceding reign, but Alexander III had refused to consider it.

1897, Muravev placed before the Russian government the idea of taking over the entire peninsula of Liaotung, including Port Arthur. Such a course of action was in direct contradiction to the Moscow treaty of 1896, according to which we had undertaken to protect China from foreign invasion. By this token we should have opposed Germany's seizure of Kiaochow. We did not do so because six months previously, in July, 1897, the German Emperor, William II,[3] had visited St. Petersburg and had succeeded in obtaining from the Tsar a promise not to oppose a German seizure of Kiaochow. Later the Tsar called this promise "imprudent" and excused himself by saying that William had taken him by surprise.

At any rate, since we were powerless to protest against the penetration of Germany into China, the idea of compensation was bound to follow. If Germany could possess herself of a port on the southern shore of the Bay of Pechili, it seemed but just that we should take one on its northern shore.

A conference was assembled to consider this matter. It met under the chairmanship of Grand Duke Aleksei Aleksandrovich[4] and declared itself opposed to such a move on the part of Russia. The Minister of War, Vannovsky, said that Russia would have to increase her army by half a million rifles if she wished to preserve peace in this far-distant region. The Minister of the Navy, Chikhachev, pointed out that Port Arthur was not at all a good naval base: its roadstead was extremely narrow, and a navy might very easily be trapped there. Witte pointed out very justly that the occupation of Port Arthur would create two enemies for Russia: China, from whom Port Arthur would be taken; and Japan, who would thus be prevented from possessing it. Grand Duke Aleksei Aleksandrovich shared these opinions, but Muravev continued to press his point and in the end won the Tsar to his opinion. In spite of Vannovsky's contention, Muravev proclaimed: *"Un drapeau et une sentinelle—le prestige de la Russie fera le reste."*

Then there began diplomatic negotiations with China concerning a long-term lease of the entire Kwantung province. These negotiations progressed very slowly, and the Celestial Empire refused to grant the lease. The matter might have rested here; but again Witte stepped forward. In agreement with Muravev he suggested that China's consent to the lease might be obtained by bribing influential members of the Chinese government. This business was entrusted to the Russian chargé d'affaires in China, Pavlov, and our financial agent, Pokotilov. Two Chinese dignitaries, Li Hung-chang[5] and Chang Yin-huan,[6] succumbed to temptation. For one million rubles, these Chinese officials agreed to obtain the consent of the Emperor to our plans, and on March 15, 1898, China granted Russia for thirty-eight years a free lease on the Kwantung province with its Port Arthur and Talien-wan Bay, where later was developed the port of Dalny (Dairen).[7]

What was the reason for Muravev's insistence in this case and for Witte's change of front as regards our occupation of the Liao-tung peninsula? In his memoirs, where he has much exaggerated his role, Witte explains his new stand by affirming that he had had information that the Tsar had decided to take Port Arthur by force should the Chinese Empire refuse to let us have the port and the surrounding territory. But it may be doubted that Russia would have undertaken such a crude, unjustifiable violation of international law. Rather may Witte be suspected of having another reason, the same one Muravev had, namely, a desire to please the Tsar and to insure his own position.

To understand how the Tsar figured in these matters, in fact, to understand Russia's Far Eastern policy at the turn of the century, it must be borne in mind that Nicholas II, before his accession to the throne, had had a taste of politics in the Far East. His first personal appearance as representative of the Tsar had been made on the Pacific coast after his sea voyage to the Far East. But this is not all. After returning to St. Petersburg via Siberia, he had been appointed Chairman of the Committee for the Construction of the Trans-Siberian Railway. This committee was also concerned with the general development of Siberia and our Far Eastern possessions. Nicholas II, therefore, even as heir to the throne, had his first experience in Russian administration in matters concerning Far Eastern policy and in questions pertaining to our supremacy in these regions. It was but natural that after his accession these questions should attract his main attention or at least be more familiar to him and therefore more to his liking. He himself was a pioneer in this field, because before him no Russian emperor, even as heir to the throne, had visited Siberia or the Far East. His journey made a lasting and vivid impression upon him. His youthful mind dwelt pleasantly upon the thought of Russian development in the Far East. Some of his companions on this journey also saw great possibilities for Russian expansion on the Pacific, and one of them, Prince E. E. Ukhtomsky,[8] wrote a detailed account of the journey, elaborating these possibilities. Nicholas personally revised this account before its publication.*

When Nicholas II ascended the throne, therefore, he was already deeply interested in Russia's future in the Far East. After his accession other circumstances tended to deepen that interest. Inexperienced as he was in state affairs, he was obliged in the first years of his reign to follow the lead of his ministers, whom he himself was unable to lead because he lacked force of character. Unsuccessful attempts to take the initiative in directing the government of the state and its policy in European affairs left him with a sense of frustration. What was more natural than that he should turn his attention to the Far East, in which he was already interested, and there seek a field for the application of his creative energy and his initiative? Moreover, he was at first encouraged to do so by several of his ministers, especially by Witte. They saw the need of giving the young Tsar some outlet for his personal ideas, preferably in a field of lesser importance where there would be no conflict with the projects they sponsored and where all experiments could be conducted with little danger to the normal course of administration. In their opinions Siberia and the Far East was such a field. Such was the combination of circumstances in Russia which turned the interest of Nicholas II to Russian affairs on the Pacific.†

Outside Russia, William II of Germany was eager to direct the

---

* Later, as Tsar, Nicholas appointed Prince Ukhtomsky editor of the *Sankt-Peterburgskiia Vedomosti,* a government daily, in which Ukhtomsky undertook to demonstrate that Russia had reached the limit of her possible expansion in Europe, where her position was so stable that no further efforts were needed to maintain it. In the Far East, however, Russia's historical mission had not yet been fulfilled. In this direction, therefore, her creative energy should be employed. These ideas found particular favor with the young monarch.

† Witte states in his *Memoirs* that he directed our activities to the east in order to make peace secure in the west. He says that in his conversation with the German Emperor in 1897 (when our Tsar promised not to protest against the German occupation of Kiaochow) he stressed the idea that the countries of Europe, in order to prosper, must live in peace and harmony with each other.[9] In Witte's eyes, therefore, both the interests of the Russian state and his own personal considerations urged him to direct the attention of the young Emperor to the Pacific coast. The same course of action, very likely for this same double motive, was adopted by the Minister of Foreign Affairs. For all his levity, Muravev realized perfectly that all dilettante undertakings in the international relations of Europe, even when such undertakings were inspired by the noblest motives (as, for instance, the idea of general disarmament which led to the Hague Conferences), might entail dangerous consequences. Kuropatkin, too, tried to support his position by adopting the same tactics, when he was appointed Minister of War in 1898.

attention of Nicholas II to the Pacific. In this way, he hoped Russia would be prevented from taking any active part in European international problems while Germany busied herself in that field. Everybody remembers the greeting which William II signaled to the Tsar in June 1897 as he was sailing away over the Baltic: "The Admiral of the Atlantic greets the Admiral of the Pacific."

These words must have been imprinted in the Tsar's memory. Probably he had them in mind when, directly after the outbreak of the war with Japan, he sent to Admiral Alekseev,[10] Viceroy of the Far East, a telegram expressing the hope that he, as newly appointed Commander in Chief of all our naval and land forces acting against Japan, would fulfill the historic mission of establishing Russian supremacy on the shores of the Pacific.

But to return to the main story! Our occupation of Port Arthur received its impetus from Germany's occupation of Kiaochow. Had we limited ourselves to transforming Port Arthur into a naval base, later complications might have been avoided. But Russia had had no overseas colonies. Her colonies, if such they may be called, were territorially connected with Russia proper. It was, therefore, quite foreign to her understanding to keep Port Arthur as a mere naval base, such as England possessed in numbers. Rather did she seek, immediately after the occupation of the Kwantung region, to join the newly acquired territory by land to the rest of Russia.

Once again Witte moved to the center of the stage. He forgot all about his previous apprehensions of Chinese and Japanese hostility toward Russia. He dismissed Vannovsky's claim that peace could be maintained in the new territory only by a large increase in our army. Without any misgivings whatsoever he now undertook to have Russia occupy the whole of Manchuria. First he built through this territory a railway which connected with the Port Arthur line at Harbin. This line was laid through the center of Manchuria by way of Mukden, and the railway right of way actually became Russian territory. On it Russian law was observed and Russian authorities were in control. The large commercial port of Dalny, extravagantly equipped, was developed on a desert stretch of seashore eighty versts from Port Arthur, although the Ministry of War was not asked its opinion as to the expediency of having an unprotected port when there already was the adjacent fortress of Port Arthur. Nor was the Ministry asked if there were enough troops there to defend Dalny against possible enemy landing forces. The Eastern Asiatic Steamship Company appeared as a competitor to the Japanese merchant marine. A society was organized for the exploitation of Manchurian mineral resources. The Russo-Chinese Bank was created to assist Russian industry and commerce in the Far East, including Manchuria. It is true that all this was done under the color of private enterprise, but the camouflage was so transparent that it deceived no one. In a word, Witte built up and directed a veritable kingdom in the Far East. It had its special army known as the Transamur Border Guard, which the inhabitants of the region called Matilda's Guard after Witte's wife. It had a special navy and, what is more important, its special finances, since, owing to the fact that all these enterprises were camouflaged as private business, Witte expended state money for their maintenance without bothering to conform to estimates and other limitations regulating the expenditure of state resources. The extent of these expenditures may be judged by the fact that the building of the Chinese Eastern Railway alone cost four hundred million rubles—that is, more than 150,000 rubles a verst.*

Carried away by his creative drive and his thirst for power, Witte forgot his original motive in supporting the development of our activities in the Far East, namely, his desire to ingratiate himself with the Tsar by finding an outlet for the latter's initiative. In the Far East more than anywhere else Witte managed to substitute for the principle of legal administration his personal or simply arbitrary decisions. The Tsar soon began to see that here, too, he was nothing but a spectator of the fervent activity of a minister. Even so he still wished to find some worthy field in which to apply his own initiative. The ease with which Russia had extended her borders in the Far East prompted him to go still farther in this direction. There arose before him the picture of Russian authority extending over other Asiatic countries, over northern and southern Manchuria and Korea. According to Kuropatkin, the Tsar dreamed even of extending his sway over Tibet and Afghanistan.

At this point the rejected plans of two former project makers, Vladimir Mikhailovich Vonliarliarsky and A. M. Bezobrazov,[11] were resurrected. Both these men were retired officers of the Guards. They had served in the same regiment, but they represented two distinct types. Vonliarliarsky, who had squandered his wife's enormous fortune on various fantastic enterprises, was ever avidly seeking new

* A verst of railway in European Russia cost not more than 60,000 rubles.

adventures that promised fabulous returns. He had absolutely no talent for business, but made up for this deficiency by an utter lack of principle and a readiness to join any combination, in which he usually fell victim to his own inexperience. Bezobrazov, too, was ready to engage in any enterprise; with him, however, the stimulus was not desire to make money but overwhelming ambition and unlimited self-assurance. He was lured by the possibility of playing a prominent role in politics, and he had selected as his stage the Far East, in which field he regarded himself, for some unknown reason, as an expert. These two men became interested in the Far East in somewhat the following way.

In November 1897—that is, before our occupation of Port Arthur—when we were increasing our activity in Korea, a Vladivostok merchant, Briner, had arrived in St. Petersburg with an offer to sell a concession for the exploitation of the enormous forest areas covering the entire north of Korea along the Tumen and Yalu rivers. He himself had acquired this concession from the Korean government. Briner had first addressed himself to Rothstein, the director of the International Bank and well-known as Witte's adviser, but without success. Looking further afield for a buyer he had met Vonliarliarsky, who was immediately interested. A chance to buy for a few tens of thousands a concession to exploit a territory of some five thousand square versts, rich in natural resources, was indeed very tempting. Yet Vonliarliarsky had realized that the exploitation of this territory, far from any means of communication, would necessitate enormous outlays of money and could be accomplished only with government support. With this aspect of the business in mind he had turned to Bezobrazov for advice. The latter had been immediately fascinated by the possibilities and had bent all his energy toward interesting certain influential persons in the matter, and in the end had succeeded in interesting two men: the former court minister, Count I. I. Vorontsov-Dashkov,[12] who was usually unsympathetic to such ventures, and the easily interested Grand Duke Aleksandr Mikhailovich.[13]

With his enthusiasm running high, Bezobrazov had then composed a detailed report on the subject and through the good offices of Count Vorontsov had succeeded in presenting it to the Tsar. The report was designed to persuade Nicholas II to acquire Briner's concession as his personal property; it even outlined a detailed plan for the exploitation of the area.

This was in March 1898, when we were negotiating with China for the transfer of the Kwantung province and Port Arthur. On learning of these negotiations Bezobrazov had depicted in bright colors the importance of the concession as a bond between our Far Eastern possessions (the Ussuri region) and the newly acquired Kwangtung territory. A term of the concession provided that the purchaser would have the right to build railways and telegraph lines. With this in mind Bezobrazov had insisted that a railway be built through the concession territory for the purpose of joining our Far Eastern possessions with Port Arthur. This railway, according to Bezobrazov's scheme, was to pass through northern Manchuria only for a short stretch, touching Kirin.

Now the Russian government had already decided to join European Russia to Pechili Bay by rail, so there was considerable to be said for Bezobrazov's project. In fact, the choice of the route for the railway that would link our Far Eastern possessions with Port Arthur was to determine all our future policy toward the nations of the yellow race. At that time we had to decide whose interests we should ignore in linking Port Arthur by rail to the main line to European Russia. We were bound to go against the interests of either Japan or China. Whose interests should it be? The Minister of War, the Minister of Foreign Affairs, and especially the Minister of Finance, Witte, had thought that it would be more advantageous for us to disregard the interests of weak China. The government had accepted their views and had decided to build the railway through Manchuria. This, it was thought, would be no trespass upon Japanese interests, since these ministers considered that Japanese interests on the continent of Asia were centered in and limited to Korea.

But Bezobrazov had been of another opinion. He had held that for us to build a railway through Manchuria, thus joining its rich southern part to our sphere of influence, would be just as unacceptable to Japan as would be our taking over of northern Korea. He had maintained that it would be impossible to effect communication by rail between Port Arthur and Siberia without incurring the hostility of both China and Japan. Accordingly, we must build our railway through a region which could later be most easily protected from Japan and which would in the meantime hurt the interests of China as little as possible. Such a region, he contended, was the north Korean territory included in the concession. A mountain range, dividing the Tumen and Yalu rivers from the Japanese Sea on the northeast and from the Korean peninsula proper and from the Yellow Sea in the southwest, was a natural barrier protecting the concession territory from a Japanese advance in southern Korea. The range constituted a first-class strategic line of defense for almost the entire length of the projected railway. Moreover, where the southwestern part of northern Korea touched the Liaotung peninsula a mountain pass gave easy access from the seacoast along the Korean Bay into the Kwantung province. By occupying the pass we should, in Bezobrazov's opinion, bar a Japanese approach to Port Arthur. Nor would such a railway irritate China, for it would cross Manchuria for only a short stretch in the north. At the same time, however, Bezobrazov had affirmed that unless we strengthened our military forces in the Far East we should be powerless to protect the land communication between Port Arthur and Siberia against either China or Japan.

Bezobrazov may have been right about the necessity of increasing our military forces in the Far East, but such an increase was out of the question. Consequently it was impossible for us to spread our influence either over Manchuria or over Korea. The state of our national economy did not allow any considerable increase in our army. Moreover, we should have been unable to keep our troops there. Where should we have found a sufficiently large body of trained men to supply army officers for troops located in northern Korea and Manchuria? As a result of the miserable salaries of our army officers, coupled with the slow promotion in the army, there was a steady decrease in the number of capable young men attracted to military service. But when such service involved leaving home, living in the primitive surroundings of the Asiatic east and among a population alien in every respect, thousands of miles away from European Russia, it was reasonably certain that such officer volunteers for this service as the government might secure would be found among those whose cultural and moral level made them unfit to hold a position in Russia proper. What would have been the value of an army trained and educated by such leaders?* But Bezobrazov and his intimates, among whom a prominent place was occupied by his

* The influence of the locality in which an army is stationed upon the commissioned personnel was observed in the 'eighties when some of our cavalry troops were transferred from the gubernia centers of European Russia to the gubernias of the Kingdom of Poland on the German frontier. This transfer was accompanied by a mass retirement of army officers from military service. The cultural level of the remaining officer personnel became much lower.

cousin, Captain, later Admiral, Abaza,[14] did not take these factors into consideration. In fact, they never did consider anything that pertained to the national interests of Russia. They cherished merely the idea of acquiring this immense new territory. The unfortunate Korean concession completely befogged their minds.

But Bezobrazov's opinions were not heeded. It was decided that the railway connecting Siberia with Port Arthur should be built through Manchuria. Witte and the Ministers of War and Foreign Affairs then turned their efforts to achieve an understanding with Japan that would make for peace, and in April 1898 we concluded a treaty with Japan by which we relinquished in her favor the position we occupied in Korea and admitted her preference in developing her commercial and industrial activity there.[15] In consequence we recalled from Korea our military instructors and our financial adviser to the Emperor, and even closed the Russo-Korean Bank, which was ostensibly a private institution but was actually managed by the Russian Ministry of Finance. Bezobrazov's idea concerning the construction of a railway through northern Korea was thus made impracticable, and the idea of exploiting the Korean concession should thenceforth have been forgotten.

Yet, this apparent failure did not discourage Bezobrazov. He continued his efforts to play a role in our Far Eastern policy and, among other things, persuaded the Tsar to send an expedition to examine the territory of Briner's concession, the expedition to be financed by His Majesty's Cabinet.[16] Its purpose was to ascertain the economic potentialities and strategic value of the concession territory. It was headed by Privy Councilor[17] Neporozhnev, employed in His Majesty's Cabinet, and included two officers of the General Staff: Zvegintsev, later a member of the Duma, and Baron Korff, son of a former Amur governor-general, Baron A. N. Korff.[18] When these officers returned from the expedition they were received by the Tsar. Their enthusiastic description of the region and its strategic value (they brought back a detailed topographical map) in protecting our portion of Manchuria from Japan excited the lively interest of Nicholas II. Bezobrazov did everything he could to keep this interest burning bright, and, as a result, on May 11, 1900, the concession was bought in the name of Neporozhnev with money from His Majesty's private funds. The price was the modest sum of sixty-five thousand rubles.

A few comments will not be amiss at this point. It was later affirmed that the concession had been purchased in the hope that it would yield large financial gains. As applied to the Tsar this is simply absurd. The Russian sovereign had no need to have recourse to such means to increase his personal fortune, even admitting his desire to do so. After the Revolution of 1917 it became apparent how little the Russian tsars, including Nicholas II, were concerned with the accumulation of private fortunes; for it then became known that the Russian imperial family had invested no capital outside Russia.

Nor was Bezobrazov following any materialistic aims, despite the general opinion to the contrary. He was deluded by dreams of grandeur. The idea of playing adviser to the Tsar captivated his imagination and the thought of influencing cardinal issues of state policy befogged his weak brain, hid from him the general condition of the country, and led him to conjure up before his mind's eye the chimera of Russian supremacy, perhaps over the whole of Asia. His alter ego, A. M. Abaza, was of a similar type—a good fellow, though of limited intellect. These two were persuaded that possession of the Tumen and Yalu rivers would guarantee protection from what they considered to be the inevitable attack of Japan. They also saw in northern Korea a large field for the development of Russian industry. They dreamed of themselves as pioneers of empire, like those sons of England who with the help of her capital, industry, and trade had secured for the Island Kingdom many attractive colonies. Bezobrazov and Abaza failed to grasp a fundamental difference between Russian and English expansion. England had possessed herself of new lands by her organic force and with the surplus of human energy and monetary resources at her command. The state merely followed the path cleared by this organic force; it consolidated only that which had already been acquired by its sons. Russia's position was quite different if not diametrically opposite. Russia lacked free capital and human enterprise even for the satisfaction of her internal demands, a lack that was keenly felt. The influx of foreign capital and foreign industry into Russia can be explained only by this fact. Any considerable extension of our industrial activity beyond our boundaries would have had to be accomplished by energies that otherwise would have been employed in developing the natural resources of Russia proper. Moreover, such an extension would have had to be the result of state and not private Russian enterprise. It would have had to count, not on private initiative and private capital, but on state resources and government employees, who would have worked simply for their salaries and would have had no personal interest in the practical outcome of their labors. This would have meant following the traditional Russian method of expansion by which, in Kliuchevsky's[19] phrase, "the state grew larger but the people grew poorer." And over and above these considerations was the fact that at that time any Russian of intelligence and firm moral principles could just as easily have used his money with profit in Russia proper, where there were good opportunities close at hand. It became necessary, therefore, to create artificial and exceptionally attractive conditions as a means of interesting private persons in Far Eastern development. Some of the persons thus attracted were those who were in search of thrills and adventure and who preferred the freedom of a pioneer life to the conventions of modern society. But such persons were in the minority. The majority was composed of petty adventurers, men seeking easy profits, and human failures without means and totally unfitted for the steady work necessary to develop a new country. From the point of view of Russian colonial expansion, therefore, the undertaking on the Yalu was not in accord with the organic strength of the Russian people.

Politically this enterprise merely served to complicate our international relations, especially in the Far East. It was obviously a question not so much of acquiring this or that strategic point for our defense against Japan as of the large army which such defense would require. Since we could not provide an army of adequate strength for this purpose, the thing for us to do was to be satisfied with what we already had in Manchuria instead of trying to expand still further, especially in Korea, in direct opposition to Japan's interests.

All plans for the Korean concession were brought to a standstill by the so-called Boxer movement in China. This movement had been planned and was supported by the Chinese government, but outwardly it bore the appearance of an unorganized popular uprising. In Manchuria the movement directed its attack against the Chinese Eastern Railway, then in process of construction, and the workers' settlements along the line. We hurried troops into the affected region and these speedily suppressed the uprising before much harm had been done to our enterprises there. The stretches of railway already completed and other structures suffered but little damage; but the records of the financial expenditures in this work were destroyed.

To the astute observer, the Boxer movement indicated that our position in Manchuria was far from secure, that both the Chinese government and the local population were hostile to our presence and to all our undertakings there, and that consequently we should have to exercise the utmost caution in extending our power and influence in the Far East if we did not wish to incur the bitter hatred of the yellow race. But to some members of the Russian government the ease with which we defeated the Boxers suggested that the yellow race was not a dangerous foe. Kuropatkin, for instance, ignored the warnings of persons well informed on Far Eastern affairs and continued to affirm that as a military force Japan was negligible.[20] Count V. N. Lamsdorf,[21] who succeeded Muravev in June 1900 as Minister of Foreign Affairs, was just as optimistic.

Bezobrazov considered our position in Manchuria unstable, and said as much in his memoranda which he presented to various influential persons, one of whom was the Grand Duke Aleksandr Mikhailovich. Yet to remedy this situation he favored an increase of our military forces in the Far East and our acquisition, for strategic reasons, of northern Korea, that is, the territory in which we had bought the concession. In short, he was really working to the same end as was the government—Russia's expansion on the Pacific.

Accordingly, directly after the suppression of the Boxer uprisings, Bezobrazov again endeavored through his intermediaries to attract the Tsar's attention to a business which he persisted in calling "My Sovereign's private affairs." Nor did he fail, for Nicholas was still intent upon displaying his personal initiative. Bezobrazov's efforts resulted in the drafting of a statute for an East Asiatic Industrial Company. This draft named as founders of the company V. M. Vonliarliarsky, Prince F. F. Yusupov,[22] Count V. A. Gendrikov,[23] M. A. Serebriakov, and A. M. Abaza. Nicholas II consented that the draft should be submitted to the Committee of Ministers. Thus far had the matter gone when it encountered the opposition of the Minister of the Imperial Court, Baron Frederichs.[24]

Baron Frederichs' opposition was incurred in this way. Nicholas II wished to acquire for himself, but in Abaza's name, two hundred of the prospective company's shares and asked Baron Frederichs to make the purchase for him. On June 2, 1900, Frederichs made a report to his Sovereign pointing out that it was by no means certain that the company would be a profit-making concern and that the participation of the Russian Tsar, even though indirectly and anonymously, in Russian commercial ventures, the success of which would be largely dependent upon government acts, was not to be considered. News of it might reach the press, if not in Russia than abroad; at any rate it would not long remain secret. In conclusion Frederichs suggested that the Ministry of Finance should be drawn into participation in this venture.

Count Vorontsov-Dashkov, who had preceded Baron Frederichs as Minister of the Imperial Court from 1881 to 1897, urged the Tsar to participate in the enterprise, prophesying that "if it is not clearly understood that we are working for Your Majesty and under Your Majesty's protection, most of us will probably refuse to give time and energy to increase the fortunes of Messrs. X, Y, and Z, considering the changeability in the views of the ministers."[25] Vorontsov also addressed a letter to Frederichs in which he sharply accused him of hindering an affair of state. Now Baron Frederichs was not noted for his great intellect, but he was known to be scrupulously honest and chivalrous. He was often guided by intuition, and now he felt intuitively that it was not seemly for the Russian Tsar to engage in private business. He refused point-blank, therefore, to comply with his Sovereign's orders and requested permission to resign as Minister of the Imperial Court. He sent in with this request an enumeration of the motives which prompted him so to act, some of which he had already stated in his report of June 2. He pointed out, however, that if the Tsar wished to use his private funds to subsidize the company outright and with no view to personal profit, he, Frederichs, while still considering this an unwise expenditure of the Tsar's private fortune, would consider he had no right to interfere. Nicholas II had the greatest respect for the "old man," as he called Frederichs in the imperial family circle, and heeded his expostulations. He refused Frederichs' request to be permitted to resign and on July 5 issued a statement that the matter of the East Asiatic Industrial Company would not be placed before the Committee of Ministers until after the complete pacification of the Far East. Frederichs' opposition had had its effect.

Still Bezobrazov and his supporter, Vonliarliarsky, were not discouraged. Within a month Bezobrazov, acting in perfect accord with Count Vorontsov, again took up the matter of the company. On July 23, 1900, he presented another memorandum to the Tsar enlarging upon the idea that only Russian influence should be exerted in Manchuria and in all northern China, and "all other foreign influences should be confined to the south of China." "Strike while the iron is hot," wrote Bezobrazov to the Tsar, referring to our success in suppressing the Boxer movement and that apparent accord in Chinese questions which had been expressed in the joint military advance of European forces on Peking.

But once more Bezobrazov met with defeat. This time he ascribed it to Witte's influence. Even so, he was equal to the occasion; he changed his tactics, and instead of continuing his struggle against Witte by criticizing in his memoranda to the Tsar Witte's every move, he tried to come to an understanding with him. In this he must have been at least partially successful, for in a memorandum to the Tsar on April 23, 1901, he mentioned that Witte was favorably disposed toward the idea of forming the company. In fact, in June of that year the statute of the company was confirmed by the Committee of Ministers; yet the founders were not the persons formerly selected from court circles but two figureheads, Albert and Kruse. This did not change matters much, however, since the new company had no funds other than those donated by His Majesty's Cabinet and toward the end of the period the statute had set for the collecting of the company's capital only twenty per cent of the entire amount had been collected. The remainder was never obtained; so that legally the company was dissolved.

Such is the story of the Yalu venture to the end of 1901. Meanwhile our relations with Japan had not been improving. As early as 1900 our diplomatic representatives in Japan realized that our activities in Korea were running counter to Japanese plans. During the years 1897–1899 our representative in Tokyo was Baron R. R. Rosen,[26] one of our best-informed and most farseeing diplomats, who later predicted that our alliance with France and England would bring us into an armed conflict with Germany the outcome of which, even in the event of a German defeat, would be disastrous to Russia. Immediately after our occupation of Port Arthur in 1898 he had tried to tell our Ministry of Foreign Affairs that it was imperative for us to come to some definite understanding with Japan concerning the entire Far Eastern situation and not to limit ourselves to the brief and indefinite agreement which he and the Japanese Minister, Nishi,[27] had signed. At that time Russian prestige in the Asiatic East had been so great that Japan had made considerable concessions in order to avoid any conflict with us on the Asiatic continent or in the waters of the Pacific.

In his reports Baron Rosen returned continually to the subject of our relations with Japan, but in 1900 he became particularly insistent. The reason was this: The Japanese Prime Minister, Marquis Ito,[28] had learned that we had acquired a concession in northern Korea. Also he was alarmed at Russia's failure to withdraw from Manchuria the considerable military force she had moved into that area for suppressing the Boxers. Consequently he had had very serious discussions with Rosen on this subject. Marquis Ito announced that Japan was determined to extend her authority over a part of the Asiatic continent, since her population, because of its natural increase, could no longer be accommodated upon the islands of the Japanese Empire. The part of the continent Japan had in mind, said Ito, was Korea, and preferably its northern part, since the so-called Korean peninsula and the coast regions to the south of it, not counting the Liaotung peninsula already occupied by Russia, were so densely populated that there could be no question of Japanese settlements there. But Japan was ready to recognize the fact that Russia had some claims upon those territories contiguous to her in the Far East. He suggested, therefore, that the two nations, Russia and Japan, map out in agreement respective spheres of influence in that region: Russia to keep the northeastern part of Korea situated beyond the peninsula proper and bordering upon the Ussuri region; Japan to take over the southwestern part on the shores of the Yellow Sea. Such a partition would mean that Russia was to divide the Yalu concession with Japan on more or less equal terms.

Marquis Ito did not conceal from Baron Rosen the fact that Japan had to make a decision either to come to an understanding with Russia and amiably divide with her the eastern shore of the Pacific, or to turn to some other country with which it might form an alliance to oppose further Russian expansion in the Far East. It was understood that Japan's prospective ally would be England, at that time openly hostile to Russia.

Baron Rosen had spent several years in Japan in our diplomatic service and had had an opportunity to study that country at close range. He saw that Japan was growing at a tremendous pace and that her population possessed remarkable fighting qualities. His observations were endorsed by Colonel Vogak,[29] our military agent in Japan at that time, who foresaw that very soon the Japanese army would be dangerous. Rosen was of the opinion that it would be foolish to make an enemy of Japan, especially if she should make an ally of England, the most powerful naval power in the world. He reported in detail his discussion with Ito and urgently advised the acceptance of the Japanese conditions of settlement. However, the idea of taking over not only the concession in Korea but also the entire country had taken root in St. Petersburg. Moreover, the most attractive part of the concession seemed to be that adjoining the already occupied Liaotung peninsula. The Emperor himself noted on Baron Rosen's report that he would never permit Japan to ensconce herself in Korea. Baron Rosen was recalled from Japan and transferred to Bavaria, a secondary post. His successor in Tokyo was A. P. Izvolsky.[30] At almost the same time Colonel Vogak was transferred to China. His successor was Colonel Vannovsky, who later played a rather important part in the Far Eastern adventure.

Vannovsky's reports stated that the Japanese army was of little account as a military force and had very poor technical equipment. These reports laid the foundation for the firm conviction in St. Petersburg governmental circles—a conviction which lasted to the outbreak of war—that Japan would never dare oppose us with armed force.* Izvolsky, too, at first adopted the view that we did not need to consider the Japanese claims, since Japan would be powerless to carry them by force of arms. Yet toward 1901 Izvolsky began to revise his estimate of the situation. Marquis Ito, who had resumed his discussions, continued to insist that Japan had to find an outlet for her surplus population in some part of

---

* Vannovsky himself was so sure of his estimate that even after the beginning of the war he made private statements in St. Petersburg salons which demonstrated conclusively that in the first encounter with the Russian army the Japanese army would be reduced to pulp. Once I was present during such a conversation in the house of S. S. Bekhteev, in April 1904. On returning home, quite optimistic as a result of Vannovsky's announcement, I found an official bulletin from the General Staff announcing our loss of eighteen fieldpieces at Turengchen. The news circulated about St. Petersburg with lightning speed and served to change the attitude of every circle toward the war.

the Asiatic continent and that she had to come to some understanding regarding this either with Russia or with England.

In October 1901 the Japanese government decided to send Marquis Ito to Europe. His first stop was to be St. Petersburg. Should he fail to reach an understanding with the Russian government, he was to go on to London. This development prompted Izvolsky to point out to our Minister of Foreign Affairs, Count Lamsdorf, in a detailed and very convincing letter, that Russia was being given a last opportunity to come to a peaceful understanding with Japan; also that, if we missed this opportunity, a war with Japan would be inevitable, and it would be a hard war.

But St. Petersburg remained blissfully impervious to urgent representations. Witte, Lamsdorf, and Kuropatkin were persuaded that Japan would never dare to declare war on us and, if she did, could easily be beaten. Lamsdorf ignored Izvolsky's arguments, just as Kuropatkin ignored those of Vogak; for Vogak, even after his transference to China, continued to follow the growth of Japan's military might and to report that Japan was preparing for war and that her military resources were very great.* Thus when Marquis Ito arrived in St. Petersburg in November 1901, he experienced a cold reception. Needless to say, he arrived at no understanding there.

Those who directed the government in St. Petersburg had no understanding of the difference in the importance of the Far East to ourselves and to Japan. For us the possession of Manchuria was a matter of secondary importance, if not less, and our penetration into Korea was merely a means of protecting our position in Manchuria. It was nothing but colonial expansion which might be used to advantage some time in the future. For Japan, on the other hand, it was a question of life and death and therefore of great national importance. Japan concentrated her entire attention on the matter, while our government, engaged in many other important and complicated problems, gave it but a passing glance and explained it as a struggle among persons close to the Tsar who were more interested to see which of them would gain the upper hand than to know the outcome of the Korean-Manchurian enterprise.

* On the margin of one of these reports Kuropatkin made a rather harsh comment to the effect that Vogak was writing a lot of nonsense and that his accounts were to be explained by the fact that he was in close touch with Bezobrazov and supported the latter's opinion that our army in the Far East should be increased.

England immediately realized her own advantages in this conflict between Russia and Japan. Accordingly when Marquis Ito reached London he was shown every consideration and succeeded very easily in concluding with the English government, on January 30, 1902, an agreement[31] which assured Japan that in case of war she would have to deal with Russia alone; or, if Russia should secure the aid of some other country—for instance, France—Japan would have powerful naval support from England.

For Japan this alliance was decisive. By it she really settled the question about fighting Russia in case Russia should oppose Japanese penetration on the Asiatic continent. From January 1902, therefore, the whole question from Japan's point of view was one of time.

Japan's alliance with England troubled our government. We decided to restrict our claims in the Far East. On March 26, 1902, we made an agreement with China promising to withdraw our troops from southern Manchuria in a year's time and to evacuate all northern Manchuria within eighteen months, that is, by September 26, 1903.

This agreement was made against the expostulations of Bezobrazov, whose influence was for the moment in eclipse. But this did not mean that he and his plans were no longer a factor in our Far Eastern affairs. One might well think that after his previous failures Bezobrazov would have given up all hope of success and retired from participation in this affair. He might have done so had not Vonliarliarsky been active behind the scenes. It was Vonliarliarsky's persistent belief that with the help of the Korean concession he might escape his own complete bankruptcy, which, despite all his efforts, finally occurred in 1907. Beginning with April 1902—that is after Plehve's appointment as Minister of the Interior—it was Vonliarliarsky who took the lead in this undertaking, using Bezobrazov to present his memoranda to the Tsar. Vonliarliarsky kept in almost daily touch with Plehve and possibly found in him a certain support in their common opposition to Witte.

By the autumn of 1902, the ministers had become greatly concerned about Bezobrazov's schemes,* and ranged themselves in

* Kuropatkin tells of one of Bezobrazov's schemes in 1902 (*Krasnyi Arkhiv*, 1922, II, 12), one to operate in southern Manchuria "by secret means," which was in violation of our obligation not to prevent foreign countries from developing

open warfare against him. Kuropatkin, Witte, and Lamsdorf united to oppose the influence and plans of this adventurer. Their opposition, however, sprang from different motives. Kuropatkin was eager to strengthen our military standing in the west and therefore sought to direct all the limited resources of the Ministry of War to our European frontier. He endeavored to turn the Tsar's attention from the Far East to the West, where thunder clouds of the eternal Macedonian question were beginning to darken the skies. Kuropatkin pointed out that our Far Eastern policy, including the suppression of the Boxer movement, had cost Russia over a billion rubles and had yielded no substantial returns but additional expenditures and losses. The Chinese Eastern Railway, counting the interest on the sum spent to build it, was costing more than thirty million annually, and this figure did not include the fifteen million it cost annually for its military protection by the so-called Transamur Border Guard. Witte's opposition sprang from the fact that he was loth to lose his almost personal control of all his enterprises in Manchuria and on the Liaotung peninsula. He, too, desired to limit state expenditures in the Far East. Lamsdorf was afraid that our noisy activity in southern Manchuria and northern Korea would create international complications not only with China and Japan but also with England and the United States. The possibility of armed conflict with Japan, although that country was still considered negligible, troubled the government. The Foreign Minister held that we could escape such a conflict, not by increasing our military forces in the Far East, but by refraining from aggressive action against Japan.

Bezobrazov, seeing clearly that he alone could not overcome the opposition of these ministers, decided to look beyond them for support. His eye finally rested on the head of the Kwantung province, Admiral Alekseev. Accordingly he obtained for himself an assignment to Port Arthur, ostensibly to ascertain general conditions in the Far East but really to get in touch with Alekseev. Accompanied by a retinue of officials of the different ministries, Bezobrazov left St. Petersburg in November 1902 in a private rail-

---

their economic activities there. "I prevailed upon Bezobrazov," writes Kuropatkin, "to explain what 'secret means' he had in mind. According to him they were as follows: Witte and Lamsdorf were to open all southern Manchuria to foreigners and their enterprises; Alekseev was to allow them to do as they pleased, but, later on, the *hunhutse*, obedient to us, were to appear, the enterprises were to fail, and the men were to disappear."

way car. He carried with him the Tsar's personal letter to Alekseev.* In Port Arthur he played the part of a plenipotentiary representative of the Monarch and investigated the work of all authorities, including the local Chinese. He kept in direct touch with the Tsar by telegraph, the messages being transmitted in a special code. As for Alekseev, at first he seemed somewhat alarmed by Bezobrazov's tactics, especially in regard to our relations with the Chinese; but in the end he was captivated by Bezobrazov's project for reorganizing the administration of Kwangtung province into a Far Eastern viceroyalty, the viceroy to be at the head of all our troops and enterprises in Manchuria. Drawn on by ambition, Aleskseev curried favor with Bezobrazov and supported him in the matter of the Yalu concession. When ordered to evacuate southern Manchuria in accordance with a decision made in St. Petersburg on February 16, 1903, the evacuation to be completed by March 26 and the troops moved to the interior of Russia, Alekseev countered with a request that these troops be moved instead to Kwangtung province. This request was motivated partly by a desire to increase the garrison of Port Arthur but also by a desire to win Bezobrazov's friendship. The request, supported by Bezobrazov, was granted. A detachment of the Chita Cossack regiment was moved to Feng-Hunchun on the Korean border. As for Bezobrazov himself, he utterly ignored our obligation to evacuate southern Manchuria by March 26. In fact, he went so far as to submit to the Emperor a memorandum entitled "An Evaluation of the Situation," in which he not only maintained the necessity of increasing our Far Eastern army by 35,000 men but even drew a sketch of their proposed disposition. He suggested also that we introduce into northern Korea a mounted detachment of 5,000 men equipped with mountain artillery. He even wanted to form military working parties wearing Chinese dress and carrying arms concealed in their supply wagons. Kuropatkin rejected this absurd plan; but the undaunted Bezobrazov formed just such parties of *hunhutse* and armed them with Russian firearms. Of course neither

* In January 1903 two million rubles were placed at Bezobrazov's disposal "for a use known to His Imperial Majesty." Part of this sum was granted out of the twelve-million fund and part out of the secret fund of the Russo-Chinese Bank; but more than half of it came from the profits of the Foreign Department of the Credit Office of the Ministry of Finance. This was indeed a large sum to be placed at the disposal of persons who had not invested one kopeck of their own money in the enterprise they were conducting.

the troops moved to the Korean border, nor were the *hunhutse* bands adequate to defend this region. They were not strong enough to repel a Japanese attack but they were sufficient to infuriate Japan, since they constituted evidence that we did not intend to stand by the conditions of the agreement of 1898 concerning Korea.

Meanwhile Kuropatkin, Lamsdorf, and Witte—with Witte in the van—were able slightly to shake the Tsar's confidence in Bezobrazov by criticizing the latter's activities. Witte had numerous agents in the Far East who, on his orders, kept him posted concerning Bezobrazov. The most important of these agents, perhaps, was the Chief Engineer of the Chinese Eastern Railway, Hirschman, who succeeded in winning Bezobrazov's confidence and learning his plans and hopes, which he reported to Witte. With such exhaustive material at his disposal Witte had the Ministry of Finance compile brief summaries of Bezobrazov's activities in the Far East and then presented these summaries to the Tsar. In vain did Abaza, whom Bezobrazov had left behind as his advocate, explain that Bezobrazov was being handicapped by the ministers' opposition to the Sovereign will to extend our operations in the Far East.

On March 26, 1903, a conference was held to discuss the advisability of transforming the timber enterprise in Korea into a stockholders' company, subject to general regulations for the purpose of exploiting the timber resources on the Yalu. Witte, Lamsdorf, Plehve, Kuropatkin, and Abaza attended the conference. If a company was to be formed capital would have to be raised, because the funds already applied to the exploitation of the Yalu concession had been exhausted. Persons interested in the enterprise, such as Vonliarliarsky, hoped that the capital could be obtained from the State Treasury or from foreign capitalists. They even entertained the idea that Japanese capital might be attracted. They estimated that a capital of two million would be required—a paltry sum for a business of state importance—and looked forward optimistically to a profit of five million in the first year, 1903, and ten million in the year following.*

The four ministers at the conference expressed their fears that our operations on the Yalu might create serious international complications for Russia, not only with Japan but also with Eng-

* Such optimism was hardly justified. In 1903 only one ship was loaded with Yalu lumber, and in order to fulfill contracts lumber had to be bought in America. In place of profits there were considerable losses.

land and particularly with the United States. Kuropatkin was confident that Russia could defeat Japan should it come to war with that country, but such a war would be costly. It would probably last about a year and a half, would cost from seven to eight hundred million, would require an army of at least 300,000 men, and would entail losses of thirty to thirty-five thousand in killed and wounded. Nevertheless, not one had the courage to take a definite stand against continuing our activities on the Yalu. They were concerned only with transforming the enterprise into a strictly private one unsupported by either our land or our naval forces. All agreed to the organization of a shareholding company the activities of which should be strictly commercial and limited to lumbering operations. Witte expressed a desire that the company be headed by really competent business men. All agreed also that the state treasury and foreign capital should participate to a "limited" degree. At Witte's insistence the conference charged the Ministers of Finance and Foreign Affairs to try to obtain from the Chinese government a concession for the exploitation of forest areas on the left bank of the Yalu, the concession to be transferred to this company. At that time Witte seemed to have a certain faith in the strength and worth of the Korean concession.

As a result of this conference a statute was drafted for the formation of such a company, and on May 31, 1903, the statute was confirmed. The company was called The Russian Timber Company of the Far East. Among the founders named, there were, in addition to those mentioned in the statute of the proposed East Asiatic Industrial Company (which had never materialized), Count A. I. Ignatev, P. P. Hesse,[32] and N. G. Metunin. I cannot say if these persons invested any money in the undertaking, for the resources of the company were kept strictly secret. But the subsidy from His Majesty's Cabinet to the enterprise was increased to 250,000 rubles.

It is well to observe once more that the conference of March 26 was unanimous in its decision to create the lumber company. All those in attendance must therefore share responsibility for this creation. Their decision had been prompted by their unwillingness to oppose the Emperor's wishes and also by their assurance that no real danger threatened Russia in the Far East. Certainly Witte did not expect Japan to make war against us; else why did he so bitterly oppose the construction of a dry dock in Port Arthur and refuse to appropriate credit for it.* But Witte's real reason for favoring the creation of the lumber company was his desire to put the enterprise on a formal commercial basis and thereby disassociate it from Bezobrazov. To this end he made connections with those who were interested in the venture for one reason only: profit. One of these was Vonliarliarsky, whose aid he tried to buy in ousting Bezobrazov. But Vonliarliarsky doublecrossed Witte and reported the episode to Bezobrazov, who in turn carried it to the Tsar. These efforts of Witte only increased the Tsar's distrust of him and probably contributed no little to his dismissal as Minister of Finance.

Meanwhile the Tsar had decided to recall Bezobrazov to St. Petersburg and to send Kuropatkin to Port Arthur "to efface the marks left by Bezobrazov." Kuropatkin was also to go to Japan in order to reassure Japanese public opinion, which was very hostile to Russia. As a pacific gesture, on April 10, 1903, the detachment of the Chita Cossack regiment was ordered to withdraw from Feng-Hunchun, where it had been stationed at Bezobrazov's instigation.

Thus far there had been agreement among the ministers. But after Bezobrazov's return from the Far East in April, dissension occurred. He returned with a plan for a viceroyalty in the Far East. Naturally enough, this was not supported by either Witte or Lamsdorf, for the former would have lost direct control of Russian developments in Manchuria and the latter would have lost direction of our Far Eastern international policy. But Plehve viewed the proposal differently. His interests as Minister of the Interior were not endangered by the proposed viceroyalty. Moreover, inasmuch as such a creation would weaken Witte, it appealed to him. These were personal considerations; but he had state ones as well. He saw in the viceroyalty a chance of weakening Bezobrazov's influence and of concentrating all our Far Eastern policy in one person, or rather in one office. In his opinion the institution of the viceroyalty would entail the immediate organization of a Special Committee for Far Eastern Affairs composed of Kuro-

---

* The lack of adequate dry-dock facilities in the Far East caused great delay in repairing our battleships damaged in the first engagement with the Japanese. Witte also refused to advance funds for naval maneuvers at Port Arthur, so that our navy in the Pacific had to go into battle without having had suitable training and experience.

patkin, Lamsdorf, Witte, Bezobrazov, and himself. In this way
the Minister of Foreign Affairs would have a share in the direction of our Far Eastern policy, as had not always been the case,
and Bezobrazov would be officially included in the group of persons concerned with the affairs of the Far East and so made
responsible for his actions. And since the Emperor would preside
over the committee and thereby acquaint himself with its problems,
he would have no reason to listen to Bezobrazov's backstage whis-
perings.

As evidence that such was Plehve's opinion let me mention an
incident which I recall distinctly and in detail. On one occasion
when I called on Plehve on business, he was in the act of seeing a
tall gentleman to the door. As Plehve seldom showed such consideration, I asked the name of the tall man. "What, don't you know
him?" said Plehve. "That was V. P. Meshchersky." "No," I replied, "nor do I wish to know such persons." This began a conversation about persons who attempted to ingratiate themselves with
the Tsar by resort to backstage influences. I remarked that such
influences were possible only because ministers paid attention to
such persons. Were such persons ignored and denied recognition,
their influence would very soon be reduced to naught. Plehve disagreed. He argued that if such irresponsible persons were attached
to some official group, they would be placed on the same level as
other members of the group. "In the case of Bezobrazov," continued Plehve, "once he is appointed member of the Special Committee for Far Eastern Affairs not only am I certain that his attitude
toward the Far Eastern problem will change but I also think that
his word will carry no greater weight with the Tsar than the
word of any other committee member."

The question of the viceroyalty was decided at a conference of
May 7, 1903, attended by Lamsdorf, Witte, Plehve, Chief of the
General Staff V. V. Sakharov[33] acting for Kuropatkin, who had
gone to Japan, Bezobrazov, Abaza, and Colonel Vogak, who had
been recalled from China to manage the enterprise on the Yalu.
The conference opened with reports by Bezobrazov and Vogak
concerning our situation in the Far East. Both pointed out our extreme weakness there and insisted upon increasing the number of
troops in that region. They said that Japan was actively preparing for war. Bezobrazov argued that for Japan our presence in
Manchuria was as little acceptable as was our occupation of a part

of Korea, so that our retirement beyond the Yalu would only weaken our position without preventing a conflict with Japan. He and Vogak both contended that conflict with Japan could be prevented, not by making concessions, but by increasing our military forces in the Far East.

General Sakharov considered that a war with Japan would be highly undesirable for Russia and that if it could be prevented by relinquishing the Korean concession this should be done, especially since our occupation of northern Korea would not be an aid to us in warfare with Japan. Witte also voiced this opinion and suggested that they await Kuropatkin's return before determining our forces in the Far East and the necessity of increasing their number. Lamsdorf, who was hardly capable of articulate speech in any gathering, asked to be permitted to present his opinion later in written form. I do not know what he said. Plehve declared that the reports of Bezobrazov and Vogak threw an entirely new light upon the Far Eastern situation, which seemed to be of such a nature as to demand very cautious treatment. He thought, therefore, that it would be very wise to concentrate in the hands of one person and in one competent central institution the decision of all questions pertaining to that far-distant region.

In the end it was decided to table until Kuropatkin's return the question of increasing our military forces in the Far East. Three other decisions also were arrived at by the conference:

1. To determine the guaranties which we must demand from China before withdrawing all our troops from Manchuria according to the agreement of March 26, 1902.

2. To organize in the Far East a viceroyalty which should have charge of all questions pertaining to that region.

3. To form, under the personal chairmanship of the Tsar, a Special Committee for Far Eastern Affairs; this committee to be composed of the Ministers of War, Finance, the Interior, and Foreign Affairs, State Secretary Bezobrazov,* and Admiral Abaza, the last-named to act as business manager of the committee. The committee's duties were to decide problems pertaining to the Far East.

Such were the resolutions of the conference of May 7, 1903. In June Bezobrazov again went to the Far East to discuss with

* Bezobrazov had been appointed State Secretary on May 6, 1903, the day preceding this conference.

Alekseev the organization of the viceroyalty and the strength of our forces in the Far East. The discussions were held in Port Arthur. Kuropatkin delayed his return to St. Petersburg long enough to participate in them. During the discussions there was a sharp clash between Kuropatkin and Bezobrazov over the desirability of continuing the exploitation of the Yalu. Kuropatkin expressed himself in favor of discontinuing it completely. Bezobrazov, of course, opposed this view. Alekseev refrained from giving his opinion, but immediately after the conference he added his signature to that of Kuropatkin in the latter's telegraphic report to St. Petersburg recommending the discontinuance of our activities in Korea. Alekseev, an ambitious courtier mindful of the fact that he owed to Bezobrazov his high rank as the Tsar's Viceroy, had not dared to oppose Bezobrazov to his face. He was nevertheless in favor of abandoning our Korean projects in order thereby to avoid a war with Japan. These discussions produced no resolutions, however, and the matter was transferred back to St. Petersburg.

Kuropatkin returned to St. Petersburg in July in high spirits. Everywhere he went he declared quite openly that there was not the slightest danger of war with Japan.* Nor did he base this assertion upon any false estimate of Japan's military strength. On the contrary, he had the highest opinion of the Japanese army, its training, its equipment, and especially of the progress it had made during recent years. It was of course inferior numerically to the Russian army so could not hope to endure a conflict with it.†

Kuropatkin also reasserted that we should turn our attention to the West and halt our expansion in the Far East, that we should bend all our efforts to the protection of our western borders instead of wasting our means in the very remote and essentially alien

* Later, in his report to the Tsar on October 15, Kuropatkin again expressed these opinions. He affirmed that Port Arthur was in such perfect condition that it was unassailable either from sea or from land and even by an army ten times as large as the Port Arthur garrison; that the fortress had been supplied with food and equipment for a year; and that our Far Eastern squadron would soon be able to concentrate in the port and even now was in a position to deal successfully with the entire Japanese fleet.[34]

† There was disagreement on this subject between our military and naval agents in Japan. Colonel Samoilov, who had succeeded Vannovsky, estimated the strength of the Japanese army at not more than 350,000 men. Rusin[35] held that Japan, thanks to her system of so-called hidden military cadres, could put into the field a much larger army by duplicating existing regiments and other military units. Rusin proved to be right. Japan's army reached a strength of 800,000 men.

border regions of the Far East, and that we should abandon the Korean concession. But his advice was unheeded. In August 1903, after the Imperial family had inspected the fortress of Libau, Kuropatkin had an opportunity to speak to Her Majesty. He turned the conversation to the weakness of Russia's defenses on the West, a situation resulting from the fact that the Far East was consuming everything. The Empress countered by saying that the danger lay in the Far East, that the main danger was the invasion of the yellow race, and that war was imminent; consequently our greatest strength had to be concentrated in the East and later we could turn our attention again to the West. Kuropatkin argued that there was an ever increasing danger in the West as well, that this was the most important field, and, should Russia be beaten in it, all her successes in fields of lesser importance would count for nothing. But the Empress was adamant. Kuropatkin felt he had argued in vain, and said as much to Her Majesty, who replied: "Yes, indeed. There can be no doubt of that." Nicholas II had heard this conversation, and after dinner he passed Kuropatkin with a smile of triumph as if to say, "Well, you failed that time."[36]

Meanwhile Bezobrazov was becoming increasingly influential. He pushed himself into the conduct of our foreign affairs. He opposed the construction of the Narva strategic railway and argued that the money allocated for this purpose should be used in the Far East. He was instrumental in having the great army maneuvers near Warsaw canceled, and with the money thus saved he had two infantry brigades moved from European Russia to the Transbaikal region.

The creation of the viceroyalty in the Far East was to have distressing results. The statute establishing it was completed toward the end of June and was published on July 31, 1903. In the meantime, however, on July 15, Japan had addressed to Russia a formal note suggesting that negotiations be begun concerning the "condition of affairs in the regions of the Far East, where their interests meet, with a view to defining their respective special interests in those regions." Japan saw in the creation of the viceroyalty Russia's answer to her friendly approach. The organization of a viceroyalty comprising the Kwantung province and the Amur region, two areas separated from each other by the rest of Manchuria, was interpreted by Japan to mean that St. Petersburg meant to include Manchuria in the Russian Empire. This in itself had a bad enough effect on Russo-Japanese relations, but matters were made much worse by the fact that as a consequence of the establishment of the viceroyalty and the Committee for Far Eastern Affairs the conduct of our diplomatic relations with Japan had slipped from the hands of our foreign office into those of Admiral Alekseev, who had been appointed viceroy, and of Bezobrazov and Abaza. This alteration of the traditional channels of diplomatic intercourse offended Japan and made for strained relations. When Baron Motono,[37] Japan's ambassador to St. Petersburg, asked Lamsdorf about certain conditions made with Japan by the viceroy, Lamsdorf replied that he was unable to give any answer, as all questions pertaining to Russia's relations with Japan had been transferred to Admiral Alekseev. Motono pointed out that in that case there was no longer a reason for a Japanese ambassador to remain in the Russian capital.*

Still another circumstance making for strained relations was the fact that our answers to Japan's proposals were given only after considerable delay. This delay is to be explained by the fact that the viceroy was in charge of our relations with Japan only in a formal sense. Actually the course of these relations was determined in close participation with St. Petersburg, not through the Minister of Foreign Affairs, but through the manager of the Committee for Far Eastern Affairs, A. M. Abaza. All this took time, and the Japanese interpreted the delay as a desire on our part to postpone a final statement of intention in order to gain time to increase our fighting strength in the Far East. Japan concluded that Russia intended to solve the argument by armed force.

Certain measures we took to increase our Far Eastern army confirmed this conclusion. It was decided to form four more sharpshooters' battalions which were to be attached to the Vladivostok garrison. In November 1903 Admiral Alekseev under some pre-

---

* This was not the first instance of our faulty diplomacy in our relations with Japan. On a former occasion, when our battleships were visiting the Korean port of Masampo, the Japanese ships also entered the harbor. Admiral Skrydlov,[38] commander of our Far Eastern squadron, was provoked by this Japanese demonstration and immediately telegraphed Admiral Tyrtov of the Ministry of the Navy that the Japanese naval forces should be forbidden to appear in this port while Russian battleships were there. Such a demand was absurd, since the port of Masampo was open to ships of all countries; yet it was supported by Lamsdorf, who advised Izvolsky, our minister in Japan, to take the necessary steps in Tokyo. But Izvolsky refused to do so, and only when informed that he was commanded to do so by Sovereign order did he carry out his instructions. The Japanese, naturally enough, regarded the demand as a deliberate insult.

text or other reoccupied Mukden, a part of southern Manchuria, with military forces. In subsequent negotiations, when we showed more readiness to compromise but would not accept the Japanese conditions in their entirety, Japan continued to see in our readiness to compromise an attempt to gain time to carry on our preparations for war.

Alekseev's attitude at that time was somewhat puzzling. In the middle of 1903 he knew full well that Japan was feverishly preparing for war but undertook no decisive measures to ward off the danger. Japanese preparations were known from information in our possession. In August 1903 our military agent in Japan, Colonel Samoilov, reported that any day might bring an opening of hostilities by Japan. Captain Rusin, more careful in his estimates, confirmed the report that Japan was preparing for war; but in August he reported that after visiting the Japanese ports he was persuaded that Japan was not yet preparing transports to send her forces to the Asiatic continent, since he had not observed the number of commercial vessels necessary for such an enterprise. Later Rusin reported that according to his information Japan was planning to open hostilities toward the end of January 1904 by making a sudden attack upon our fleet. This proved correct.

These reports alarmed St. Petersburg. Alekseev was ordered to show much consideration toward Japan, even to the point of compliance with Japanese conditions. The government and the Tsar himself became especially alarmed when, in the middle of September 1903, Alekseev telegraphed directly to the Tsar that he had been informed that the Japanese intended to land forces in Chemulpo or at the mouth of the Yalu, and that in such an event he intended "to prevent by sea forces a further landing of Japanese echelons." This meant that he intended to attack the Japanese fleet.

The Tsar answered this telegram immediately saying that he did not desire a war with Japan and that he would not permit it to take place. The Tsar's reply ended: "Take all steps to prevent this war."

How are we to interpret these contradictions? How can one reconcile the aggressive intentions of Alekseev, which were expressed so clearly in his telegram to Nicholas II, with his desire to remove the cause of war by renouncing the Korean concession? Persons who were closely connected with Alekseev, who knew him well and were far from wishing to idealize him, proved to me that as the ambitious courtier he had at first tried not to oppose Bezo-brazov, through whom he hoped to obtain the exalted position of viceroy. But as soon as he had reached this post his only desire was to strengthen his position. It was not at all his intention to en-danger it by hazards of war, realizing as he did that a war with Japan would be no joke. But he, like many others, was sure that Japan was afraid of armed conflict with Russia and would stop short of actual warfare. Probably he considered his telegrams to the Tsar a means of frightening Japan and saw to it that Japan learned of the contents of his communications. But if we did not wish war with Japan, neither for a long time did Japan wish war with us. Japan realized that Russia's forces were enormous. Alek-seev was aware of this Japanese feeling and adopted the course of action which Bezobrazov recommended: he attempted to intimi-date the Japanese. According to my information, Alekseev sup-posed that, if Japan could be convinced that at her first attempt to land forces on the Asiatic continent Russia would attack her im-mediately, Japan would give up the idea of such an attack.

The situation about the middle of December 1903 was as fol-lows: Japan wanted us to relinquish all Korea in her favor and to establish a fifty-verst neutral zone on each side of the Manchu-Korean border. Those in charge of our relations with Japan, at the insistence of Bezobrazov, who was supported by Alekseev on this point, were ready to relinquish Korea up to the thirty-ninth parallel; but that meant retaining the mouth of the Yalu, the entire territory of the concession. The members of the government had another view of the situation. Kuropatkin, in his memorandum of October 1903 to the Tsar, had insisted that we limit ourselves to the occupation of northern Manchuria. He even admitted the possibility of returning to China in exchange for this territory the entire Liaotung peninsula together with Port Arthur, on condition that China pay us for the buildings we had erected there. He sent a copy of his memorandum to Plehve (and, possibly, to other min-isters), who had whole-heartedly approved his plans. The Min-istry of Foreign Affairs was of the same opinion. Baron Rosen, who had been reappointed Minister to Japan, thought it necessary to accept Japan's conditions and surrender Korea on condition that we might occupy all of Manchuria.

On December 15, 1903, another conference met under the chairmanship of the Tsar to discuss this subject. This conference was attended by Grand Duke Aleksei Aleksandrovich, Lamsdorf, Kuropatkin, and Abaza. The conference unanimously decided that the negotiations with Japan must go on. Again the Tsar stated: "A war must not be permitted," and added: "Time is Russia's most trusted ally; each year sees her strength grow." But there was no decision to accept Japan's conditions. The concessions we were willing to make were small, and we delayed continually. We continued to take certain steps to increase our forces in the East, but these seldom went beyond the paper stage. We accepted Japan's minor conditions, and we continued to desire peace; but we also kept our hold on northern Korea and protested against the erection of fortifications by the Japanese on the Korean shore. It was decided that the landing of Japanese forces in southern Korea should not be considered as a *casus belli,* but that we would prevent the landing of such forces in northern Korea. And above all we continued to believe in the enormous supremacy of our navy over that of Japan and to reject all ideas that the Japanese might attack us on the sea.

This state of affairs lasted until January 24, 1904 (o.s.), when Japan broke off diplomatic relations with Russia. At that point the Tsar called another conference of several ministers. These favored acceptance of all of Japan's conditions. A telegram to that effect was sent to Baron Rosen. This belated agreement to accept all of Japan's conditions is further evidence that we did not wish war with Japan. But it came too late! The Japanese government probably suspected that even this entire acceptance was nothing but a ruse to secure further delay. Moreover by that time Japan's hostility toward Russia had been brought to a head and the militarist spirit of the Japanese nation was thoroughly roused. Accordingly, the Japanese government detained our telegram to Baron Rosen,[39] and in the meantime suddenly attacked with torpedo boats our battleships in the roadstead of Port Arthur.

Alekseev had been persuaded that the war would not break out as early as January. He had definitely abandoned the idea of attacking the Japanese fleet should the Japanese try to land their troops in southern Korea, since he was convinced that the Tsar did not desire war. The idea that Japan herself might attack us was far from his mind. Until the end of December 1903 our navy had been on guard against a sudden Japanese attack, for as early as September Rusin had warned Alekseev of the possibility of

Japanese aggression. But in January these precautionary measures were gradually abandoned. The result is well known. Our best battleships—"Retvizan" and "Tsesarevich"—as well as the cruiser "Pallada," were disabled for a long time, while at Chemulpo the cruisers "Variag" and "Koreets" perished gloriously in battle. This day was decisive for the entire war, for it left our navy unable to compete with the navy of our adversary.

In the Japanese war, as during all the last years of the old regime, Russia was pursued by a cruel fate. We lost our only talented naval commander, Admiral Makarov,[40] by accident; he perished with the "Petropavlovsk." During the first naval battle with Admiral Togo's[41] fleet our forces considered themselves beaten and signal was given to make for Port Arthur. This occurred just when the enemy had given a signal for retreat. When it was seen that our ships were retreating the Japanese order was immediately revoked. The same ill luck pursued us at Liaoyang. Finally we lost the battle of Mukden because of the terrific sandstorm which blew in the faces of our troops.

What, then, were the causes of the war with Japan? Who was responsible for it?

Obviously Russia was responsible, though the entire Russian government, including the Emperor, was opposed to it. Our government's attitude toward Japan is to be explained by its conviction that Russian strength and prestige were so great throughout the world, especially in Japan, that the latter's vital interests could be disregarded without risk of war. *"Un drapeau et une sentinelle, et le prestige de la Russie fera le reste"*—such had been Muravev's proud declaration, and every member of the government secretly believed it to be true. But belief in it blinded Russian statesmen and Nicholas II to the real facts and led to an overestimation of Russia's might, an underestimation of Japan's strength, and a failure to appreciate the value of Korea to Japan and the significance of our own penetration of Manchuria.

In addition to the government's responsibility, which derives from the unsound appraisal of the situation, there is the special responsibility which attaches to separate individuals, and of these Witte occupies first place. It was he who pushed Russia into the whole Far Eastern adventure. He failed to ascertain to what extent Japan and China would agree to our construction of the Manchurian railway and the organization of a series of commercial enterprises in southern Manchuria. He failed also to find out whether we should be in a position to protect these undertakings *manu militari,* and even refused to allocate the means necessary to strengthen our position in the Far East. Yet he spent Russian money there very freely and thus weakened Russia's organic strength and diverted the attention of the Tsar and the government from the need of strengthening our position in Europe. Had the money spent in Manchuria, which did not belong to us, and in Port Arthur and Dalny, which we did not need, been spent in the center of the empire, it is very probable that we should have met the enemy quite differently in 1914.

Yet the person directly to blame for the Japanese war, the person who had for some time consciously strained our relations with Japan, was Admiral Alekseev. The course he adopted was determined exclusively by personal considerations. He wanted to advance his career, and supposed that his importance and his authority and position would be greater as the situation in his region became more complicated. His culpability is the greater in that he admitted the possibility of armed conflict with Japan and was aware that in such a war naval forces would have a decisive effect on the outcome. Yet he did nothing to improve the fighting strength of the navy. Not only did he fail to attract talented commanders to the Far East but he even consciously surrounded himself with mediocrities. It is true that during the months just before the war he changed his course of action and apparently hoped to prevent an armed conflict with Japan, but by that time it was too late. Japan had spent so much money on her preparations for war and had inspired her population with such militant ideas that for her war was imperative.

After these two men—Witte, who had brought about the situation which led to war, and Alekseev, whose arrogance insulted Japan —we can place the other persons more or less concerned with Far Eastern affairs and more or less responsible for the war. First among these were Bezobrazov and his intimates.

Bezobrazov was responsible in that, with the levity of an irresponsible dilettante and unacquainted with the general needs and conditions of the country, he pushed Russia to the Far East in an attempt to satisfy his boundless ambition and his desire to play a prominent political role. But he did worse than that. He realized the instability of our position in Manchuria and the Liaotung peninsula; he realized also that our very presence there infuriated both Japan and China; and from his insistence on the need of increasing our military forces there he appreciated that our military strength in the Far East was not great. Yet he pursued a course of action which only further irritated Japan and increased her hostility toward us. Members of the government who did not believe Russia was weak in the Far East and assumed that in the event of war with Japan we should be victorious were nevertheless endeavoring to find a peaceful solution of Russo-Japanese problems and were advising Russian concessions. But Bezobrazov, who proclaimed everywhere our weakness in Manchuria and in Port Arthur, insisted upon a curt rejection of all Japanese pretensions. He insistently advised that we should not show any trace of yielding to either Japan or China but rather that we should carry out a policy of aggression in the Far East. No doubt this advice played a fateful role in our relations with Japan, for in accord with it we rattled our sabers and shook our fists although we had not the faintest intention of fighting and even considered war undesirable. Bezobrazov was urged on by his desire to use his famous Yalu concession. The only serious pretension of Japan which we would not accept related to that part of Korea where the concession was situated. Whether or not pecuniary considerations influenced Bezobrazov, it is clear that his restless imagination and boundless ambition—not his concern over Russia's greatness and the future welfare of her people—determined his course of action.

Nor is Kuropatkin to be wholly exonerated; but his motives were of another kind. He realized that Russia could not with her resources support an army on the western border and at the same time maintain a large army on the aggressive against Japan and China. He very justly tried, therefore, to direct the Tsar's attention to the West, so that those rather paltry means which the Ministry of War had at its command with which to protect Russia from her western neighbors would not be still further decreased by expenditures in the Far East. Yet he did not have the courage to face the issue squarely and to insist that Russia was not powerful enough to maintain her standing in Europe and at the same time to conduct an aggressive policy on the Pacific. Instead of saying frankly, "Yes, we are weak in the East, but we cannot become stronger there without endangering our position in Europe," he said that our forces in Port Arthur, Manchuria, and the Amur region were adequate for the protection of our interests there. He believed, apparently, that, before Japan could reach our eastern frontier, forces adequate to defeat Japan could be sent from European Russia. He thought also that the further the Japanese penetrated into Manchuria the more decisive would be their defeat. Kuropatkin's repeated assurances that we could easily defeat Japan in battle influenced the Tsar and explains many of the Sovereign's actions.

Kuropatkin was optimistic even after war had been declared. To the day of his appointment as commander of the Manchurian army he proclaimed that the war would not demand much effort on our part and refused to send to Manchuria certain troops located on our Austro-German border. As commander, however, he changed his point of view radically and immediately demanded that our best artillery, which was concentrated upon our western frontier, be moved to the Far East. Further evidence of Kuropatkin's confidence in our ability to defeat Japan was shown in the plan of campaign which he presented to the Tsar after his appointment as commander. According to this plan, in the first period of war Japan was to be drawn as far as possible into Manchuria and all decisive actions were to be avoided until we could concentrate adequate forces in the Far East. In the second period would come the one or two decisive battles in which the Japanese would be beaten, after which we were to land our forces in Japan and end the war by capturing the Mikado himself. Kuropatkin's responsibility, therefore, lies in the fact that he did not represent to the Tsar the true condition of our military strength. The Tsar was receptive to talk of Russia's great strength, for he himself had an exaggerated idea of her might. This was possibly the result of his trip by coach from Vladivostok to St. Petersburg. The enormous territory and its vast population had so struck his imagination that our generally low level of culture, our economic poverty, our technical backwardness, and the inadequacy of our armament had been completely obscured.*

---

* A striking example of the Tsar's assurance that we would win the war easily is to be seen in the words of the Empress Alexandra Fedorovna to my late mother, who was received by her at the beginning of the war. At that time a rapid construction of the Baikal railway to replace the train ferry over Lake Baikal was being undertaken. The personal supervision of the construction of the railway was undertaken by the Minister of Ways and Communication, Prince Khilkov. My mother expressed to the Empress the hope that Prince Khilkov, with his great

The persons least responsible for the war were those upon whom public opinion fastened responsibility, namely, our diplomatic representatives in Japan and Plehve.

Accusations regarding the war were showered upon our representatives in Japan, whereas they had been the first to advocate and work for a peaceful solution of problems arising from Russo-Japanese conflicting interests in the Far East. The Minister of Foreign Affairs was somewhat at fault in that he failed to insist that we clearly determine what we considered of importance to ourselves in the Far East. In fact, on the eve of the war we had not yet clearly defined the objectives of our policy in the Far East and our future intentions toward Manchuria and Korea. This explains why certain persons in the government at St. Petersburg favored the occupation of the whole of Manchuria and a part of northern Korea, while others advised the occupation of northern Manchuria only. Some, including Kuropatkin, even agreed to return Port Arthur and Kwantung province to China. Baron Rosen, our Minister in Japan, was in favor of relinquishing all of Korea to Japan in exchange for Manchuria; and our Minister to China, Lessar,[42] favored our evacuation of all of Manchuria including the northern part. These differences of purpose were reflected in our negotiations with Japan. They made for delays during our negotiations with Japan which the Japanese interpreted not as the lack of a definite Far Eastern policy but as ruses to gain time to finish our military preparations. Naturally, under such conditions, the Japanese preferred, not to postpone war, but to start it at once.

Plehve's fault lay in the fact that he had, much against his wishes, supported Bezobrazov in his scheme to establish a viceroyalty and a Special Committee for Far Eastern Affairs. In his eyes this measure would diminish Bezobrazov's influence and transfer all questions related to the Yalu undertaking to a joint decision of all the ministers concerned. Actually, the reverse took place; but Plehve had no way of foreseeing this. The Special Committee did not meet once during the eighteen months of its existence, and therefore proved no check upon Bezobrazov, who exerted a strong influence on the viceroy, Alekseev. Bezobrazov concentrated the business in his own hands and went his way without ministerial hin-

energy, would be able to complete this important undertaking in a short time. The Empress answered, "Mais il n'aura pas le temps d'y arriver que la guerre sera terminée."

drance. Plehve had also been interested in Far Eastern affairs as a field in which he might possibly work to undermine the position of his rival, Witte. Bezobrazov's pre-emption of this field precluded such a possibility, and Plehve resigned his interest in our Far Eastern policy. Witte's opposition to Bezobrazov did the Minister of Finance no good, however, and he was dismissed in August 1903. Such was Plehve's position as regards our Far Eastern policy. But it is a far cry from this position to a desire to involve Russia in a war with Japan. Such a desire was attributed to Plehve, but unjustly, because he was definitely opposed to this war. So were all the other ministers and the Tsar himself. Besides, Plehve had had no influence upon those measures concerning the Far East which were adopted before the war. He was not invited to either of the two last conferences, December 15, 1903, and January 24, 1904.

The central government did not desire the war with Japan, but around the state authority there were dreamers, adventurers, and ambitious individuals who played with fire and started a conflagration.

CHAPTER XVI

PRINCE P. D. SVIATOPOLK-MIRSKY AS MINISTER OF THE INTERIOR

After Plehve's assassination, the vacant post of Minister of the Interior again stirred the ambitions of those who considered they were in line for the office or at least had some chance of being appointed. The two camps into which the upper bureaucracy and court circles were then divided came to life and each used every means and influence at its command to win the Tsar to its views. The one affirmed that it was imperative to continue staunchly the course mapped out by the late minister; the other pointed out that it was not possible to continue much longer a policy which had aroused the indignation of all thinking Russia. The former pointed out that a change of state policy after a successful terroristic act would be a direct encouragement of revolutionary activities. The other camp insisted, however, that further irritation of the public during the war, which was going badly and putting an ever-increasing strain on national resources, would endanger the existing regime and prove fatal to success in the struggle with Japan.

The most likely candidate was Minister of Justice Muravev, nominated and supported by the Grand Duke Sergei Aleksandrovich. Muravev himself considered his appointment a certainty. He displayed this assurance at one of the requiem masses for the late Plehve which the Tsar also attended. Muravev demonstratively placed himself at the head of a group of the higher officials of the Ministry of the Interior which had gathered in one of the halls of the ministerial mansion, and when the procession started he boldly assumed the role of leader. As if to strengthen his candidacy by demonstrating his intention of following the policy of the murdered minister he placed himself at the head of the coffin and surrounded himself with the closest collaborators of the deceased.

At the same time other persons of the same conservative group were working to reach the same end by other and devious routes. One of these was the Director of the Department for General Affairs of the Ministry of the Interior, B. V. Stürmer, who had succeeded in gaining the confidence of Count S. D. Sheremetev,[1] who in turn was very close to the court. P. N. Durnovo, who was acting minister, undoubtedly coveted this post also; but he was unable to do much in his own behalf since Witte, his main support at that time, did not even enjoy the imperial favor and was, besides, in the Caucasus, far from St. Petersburg.

At first the conservative group gained the upper hand, but its triumph was fleeting: an Imperial Ukase appointing Stürmer minister was recalled from His Majesty's Private Chancellery, through which such ukases generally passed, before it was published. Its recall was due to the influence of the Dowager Empress Marie Fedorovna, who had always been opposed to Plehve's harsh policy and who had continually advocated a more sympathetic attitude on the part of the government toward the public in general and toward those national minorities inhabiting the borderlands of the Empire, particularly the Poles, who in the persons of their higher nobility had access to the Empress and always endeavored to use her influence to achieve their own national aims. This very circumstance went far to determine the appointment of Prince Sviatopolk-Mirsky who was at that time Governor-General of Vilna and who had won the sympathies of the Poles of that region.

Rumor had it that in order to secure the appointment of her candidate the Dowager Empress used the assistance of Madame E. G. Milashevich, who was Countess Sheremetev by her first marriage and a daughter of the Grand Duchess Mariia Nikolaevna[2] and her morganatic husband, Count G. G. Strogonov. The Tsar had known Madame Milashevich from childhood, was friendly toward her, appreciated her intelligence, and often conversed with her on political subjects. The Dowager Empress knew this, of course, and invited Madame Milashevich and the Tsar to luncheon. Here, it was reported, Madame Milashevich described to the Tsar the growing displeasure even in moderate, loyal circles at the constant repression of hopes and ideas advanced by the public. By way of contrast she portrayed in a favorable light the results of Prince Sviatopolk-Mirsky's mild policy in the Vilna area.

For this reason, or for some other, the Tsar decided to wait a little before appointing Plehve's successor. In the meantime he saw Prince Sviatopolk-Mirsky. The latter was on leave, living on his estate in Kharkov Gubernia. He had no desire to be Minister of the Interior but complied with the summons to St. Petersburg personally delivered to him by the Governor of Kharkov, E. A. Vatatsi.[3] The Tsar received the Prince at Peterhof, at the Aleksandriisky country estate where the entire imperial family was then residing. At first Sviatopolk-Mirsky refused to accept the appointment, pleading poor health and frankly saying that he did not in the least agree with Plehve's policy. It was his opinion that distinction should be made between the secret revolutionary forces and those elements of the public which were not opposed to the existing order as a whole but only to the arbitrariness of the administration.

The Tsar generally saw in refusals to accept high administrative posts the mark of a noble mind and a praiseworthy indifference to the race for office. This was only natural, considering that he was a constant witness of the chase after offices. Consequently, the more stubbornly a person refused a post, the more pronounced became the Tsar's desire to have him accept it. With his remarkable charm, which consisted largely of an engaging simplicity of manner, the Tsar insisted that Prince Mirsky accept the portfolio of Minister of the Interior. He was no longer certain that Plehve's methods had been the right ones and he confirmed in principle the Prince's program. At the end of the interview the Tsar said: "Now I want you to go to the cottage. They will be very happy to learn that you have accepted." The "cottage" was one of the palaces on the Tsar's Alexandriisky estate and at the time was occupied by the Dowager Empress Marie Fedorovna.

What manner of man was this new Minister of the Interior? His outstanding trait was a desire to remain at peace with everyone and live in an atmosphere of friendship. It was not that he sought popularity but simply that by his very nature he could not irritate anyone. He lacked that quality which the French call *la poigne*. His benevolent disposition was the product of a happy life which had been for him one continuous picnic. Pushkin's verse fitted him well: "Blessed is he who was young in his youth and married profitably at thirty; who at fifty was free from debt, personal and otherwise; who attained glory, wealth and high rank peacefully and in due time."

His family had won fame in military service* and life outside

* The Prince's father, a Polish nobleman by birth whose family name was Mirsky, had served in the Caucasus early in the reign of Alexander II as aide-de-camp to the viceroy, Field Marshal Prince Bariatinsky.[4] The Field Marshal was very friendly toward his aide and at the same time was on intimate terms with Alexander II. He petitioned the latter to attach to his aide the family name and title of the ancient house of the Princes Sviatopolk-Mirsky. In the 'nineties the

this service held no purpose for him. He himself had been educated in the General Staff Academy. His main desire in military service was to wear a uniform adorned by imperial monograms and to occupy honorable positions. He had served in the Guards and in secondary positions on the General Staff but had never been over-burdened with work. His marriage with Countess Bobrinsky had brought him great riches and opened the road to preferment: he was appointed a governor, then Assistant Minister of the Interior, then Commander of the Gendarme Corps and, in May 1902, Governor-General of Vilna. In all of these positions he limited his activity to keeping the administrative machinery running smoothly, without exerting himself too much or studying any subject too deeply.

By the time the Prince was appointed Minister of the Interior he had undoubtedly acquired some political opinions, but they were those of the man in the street. He never did realize the responsibility for the peace of the state which his new position placed upon him. It is indicative that he took his own time about assuming the duties of his new office: he was appointed on August 26, but it was September 16 before he began work. Once in office he failed to appreciate the weight of the authority with which he was invested. This, to-gether with his natural lack of dynamic energy, brought it about that although his administration began with smiles for the public, it in-creased public unrest and ended in bloodshed on the streets of St. Petersburg on January 9, 1905, and in his complete estrangement from the active administration of domestic policy. He had entered the office of Minister of the Interior with a light heart. He left it in the same way to make the center of his existence the fashionable Yacht Club.

Prince Mirsky began his ministry by making it known that he would follow a course directly opposite to that of his predecessor. The indicated change was evidenced even before he actively began his administration by the discharge of Assistant Ministers Stishin-sky and Zinovev, General Wahl, Commander of the Gendarme Corps, and Stürmer. All four were appointed to the State Council. Had Mirsky postponed the removal of these men until after his inaugura-tion, he would have been obliged to have unpleasant and disagreeable conversations with them. It was much easier to do it beforehand

Prince's father was ataman of the Don Cossacks. The title of Prince was also conferred on the Prince's uncle, Nikolai Ivanovich; but his two aunts, who lived modestly in Warsaw, bore the name of Mirsky till their deaths.

from behind the scenes and thus spare himself some unpleasant moments. Those who knew the Prince saw in this action one more proof of his weak character and his disinclination to inconvenience himself. This estimate of his character is further borne out by the fact that after his inauguration, when he met the rest of the officials of the ministry, he did not discharge one of them. This fact is especially typical since in some cases pressure was certainly brought to bear on the Prince by persons who exercised an influence upon him.*

* I was among those whom it was considered desirable to remove from the ministry. During my inspection of the peasant institutions of the Nizhnii Novgorod Gubernia, in August 1904, after Plehve's death, I had some trouble with the Novgorod Governor-General, General Unterberger,[5] which was due, I frankly admit, to petty pride on both sides. As a result of the trouble the Assistant Minister, Durnovo, influenced by a letter from Unterberger, telegraphed me to stop my inspection and return to St. Petersburg. But Durnovo, with whom I had been on very bad terms when Plehve was alive, did not stop there. He influenced Mirsky so that at my first report to him, the new minister requested me to tender my resignation. Mirsky explained that he was obliged to take this action because of my conduct in Novgorod; he even refused to listen to my explanations, saying that he had made his decision. I was infuriated and announced that I would not tender my resignation, as I knew of no fault in this matter on my part and considered the accusations baseless. Prince Mirsky was not prepared for such an answer. "What is that you say!" he exclaimed. "In Nizhnii Novgorod you willfully referred to yourself as a person inspecting the gubernia on Sovereign orders. Is this to be tolerated?" Now it was my turn to gasp. My inspection was made as a consequence of Plehve's report to the Tsar, to which Sovereign agreement had been given. Accordingly, I had been given a sort of pass from the ministry in which there was mention of the Sovereign's desire to investigate such and such institutions in such and such gubernias. The pass had been signed by Assistant Minister Durnovo, who had either forgotten all about this document or did not know of its existence, since he was in the habit of signing all such documents without bothering to read them. As for Unterberger, the ministry had forgotten to advise him of my visit to Novgorod.

Durnovo's assurance that I was at fault was based upon the fact that all such inspections conducted by directors of departments were generally undertaken at the minister's orders. In my case an exception had been made because I was inspecting institutions which were not subordinate to my particular department, the Peasant Section. For this purpose the Sovereign's consent was needed and this was equivalent to a Sovereign order. Fortunately I still had the pass in my possession, so that the whole incident was straightened out very speedily and in my favor. Had I lost it, it is very likely that I should have been among those discharged from the ministry before the inauguration of Prince Mirsky, as in this case he was inspired not only by Durnovo but also by Prince Aleksei Obolensky, both of whom had wished my dismissal but for different reasons. Obolensky's motive was a desire to keep me away from the peasant problem. The Novgorod incident seemed to provide an opportunity for removing me entirely from the service. As Durnovo did not have the power to do this, the matter was postponed until after the inauguration of Prince Mirsky. Even then a certain pressure was exercised upon Prince Mirsky to remove me from the ministry and to transfer me to some other position.

By discharging Plehve's official entourage, Prince Mirsky cleared the path for a sympathetic public acceptance of his appointment. He then began his official work by a formal reception of the higher officials of the ministry. At this reception two incidents occurred—a trifling one which nevertheless reflected the influences of the moment, and an important one which received wide publicity. The first was a speech of welcome to the new minister by the "famous" General E. V. Bogdanovich, the highest ranking official in the Council of the Minister of the Interior. In this speech Bogdanovich expressed some extremely liberal ideas which, had they come from any other member of the ministry, would have been in no way remarkable but coming from Bogdanovich, who was known for his bigotry and crude patriotism and who had more than once expressed his admiration of Plehve's policy, amounted to nothing but knavery—and Prince Mirsky accepted them as such.

The second incident was the speech made by the Minister himself, in which he said: "Administrative experience has convinced me that in order to get results the government should base its efforts upon an attitude of sincere trust in public and class institutions and in the people. Only by so doing can it hope for mutual understanding; otherwise a sound organization of the empire cannot be expected."

Following this incident, the Prince made other similar but more definite statements. His intentions were most clearly expressed in an interview with the representatives of the foreign press. He told them frankly that he intended to adopt a decidedly liberal policy, which would be expressed first of all in the decentralization of the administration of the border regions, to which the statute on zemstvo institutions would be extended, and in the abolition of the statutes limiting the rights of the Jews. After the foreign press had published the interview, Prince Mirsky found it necessary to qualify somewhat its meaning and significance. So he informed the correspondent of *Rus* that the foreign journalists had reported his words inexactly. "They interpreted my statements as categorical answers to the questions

Especially insistent, as Mirsky told me later, was none other than Witte, who considered that I was preventing him from taking the matter of peasant legislation entirely into his own hands. I suppose these machinations were not successful because Prince Mirsky could not bear to inflict the slightest discomfort on other people, and particularly on himself. He valued his own peace much more than he valued the state interests entrusted to him, in which he was no different from many other administrators.

they put to me, but I must confess that there are many things on which I cannot now give categorical answers. Heretofore I have not been in touch with many problems, and there are many serious ones with which I am just becoming familiar. Take for example the question of peasant reform, on which subject an enormous amount of material is available. I had become generally acquainted with it mainly from the papers; only recently have I learned the details and, of course, it would be inadvisable to express myself with any degree of certainty on that question because at the present time my opinion as minister is of great importance."*

Prince Mirsky announced that in all his work he would be guided by the principle of confidence, "for without confidence no desirable results can be attained." These words were soon made good in deeds. The Tver Gubernia and the Novo-Torzhok Uezd zemstvos were again given the right to elect boards to administer their affairs. The all-zemstvo organization was given the right to renew its activity at the front. Many persons who had been exiled from certain localities were given the right freely to choose their places of residence. Among these were Bunakov and Martynov, who had been exiled for their speeches in the Voronezh Uezd agricultural committee; N. K. Miliukov, Derviz, Apostolov, and Balavinsky, who had suffered as a result of Stürmer's investigation of the Tver zemstvo; Annensky,[6] Charnolusky, Falbork, Lavrinovich, Vorobev, all of whom were members of the congress on vocational education, and Pereverzev,[7] later Minister of Justice in the Provisional Government; and Volkenstein, Smirnov,[8] Gudz, and others who, for various reasons, had been deprived of the right freely to change their residence. To Prince Petr Dmitrievich Dolgorukov was restored the right to participate in the activities of public men. Among the pardoned were some who had Social Democratic views and were not altogether innocent of revolutionary activity. Zinovev's investigation of the zemstvo institutions was stopped.

The speeches and the announcements of Prince Mirsky were

---

* Although Prince Mirsky said that he was getting acquainted with the "details" of the peasant problem, the fact is that he never familiarized himself even with its fundamental issues, let alone the details. Consequently, he was unable to form a definite opinion concerning it in spite of the efforts of Witte and Prince Obolensky. The latter tried to inspire the Prince with his own slightly mystical ideas on the matter, but since these ideas were not quite clear to Obolensky himself he was not successful in communicating them to Mirsky, who was not very receptive to mysticism.

given wide publicity and evoked almost universal rejoicing throughout the country. Letters and telegrams of congratulation, and addresses from the most varied persons and institutions poured in to
him from all sides. He was addressed by many zemstvo assemblies
and municipal dumas, which invariably quoted his words on the
necessity of an attitude of sincere trust in public institutions and in
the broad masses of the people. In their addresses some of these institutions mentioned that the government's "attitude of sincere trust"
would have a practical significance only if it were expressed in reforms directed toward the establishment of a regime of equity—that
is, the establishment of representative government.

Nor did the press fall behind in this general acclaim. Prince
Mirsky's policy was welcomed by nearly the entire press. In *Grazhdanin,* Prince V. Meshchersky even used the occasion to abuse the
memory of Plehve, before whom, during the latter's life, he had
humbled himself to the point of being contemptible. A. S. Suvorin,[9]
in *Novoe Vremia,* sang of the coming of the spring, but expressed
the fear that this spring might not be lasting and that winter winds
might blow again. Almost the whole press shared this fear. The
fair weather, therefore, should be utilized to the utmost. On this
subject S. V. Yablonovsky even wrote a poem beginning:

"Is this truly spring? The cherry orchard
Stands fairy-like, bedecked with blossoms.
The air is full of warmth and light,
And everything is gowned in the garments of spring."

Only *Moskovskiia Vedomosti* and *Svet*[10] abstained from the general
chorus of approval and both of these papers strove to prove that
Mirsky's words did not necessarily mean a change in state policy,
since Mirsky himself had announced that he would be guided by the
Manifesto of February 26, 1903.

Prince Mirsky tried to retain and strengthen the sympathetic
attitude of the public toward him. He well knew that since the range
of activity of the Minister of the Interior was defined by law it was
by no means limited to spreading sunshine and enchanting the public; in fact, since the Ministry of the Interior had been merged with
the Third Section of His Majesty's Private Chancellery, it had to
perform, sometimes at least, functions quite different from the
spreading of sunshine. He hastened, therefore, to separate the ministry's secret police work from his own work and from the general

political measures undertaken by him. Accordingly, on September 22, 1904, less than a week after his inauguration, there was published an Imperial Ukase, and an instruction approved by the Sovereign, charging the Assistant Minister of the Interior, who commanded the Gendarme Corps, with the general management of affairs for the prevention and combatting of crime and for the preservation of general peace and order, and with the solution of nearly all problems pertaining to the Department of Police which fell within the competence of the Minister of the Interior.*

In this way Mirsky accomplished his purpose—all the unpleasant work was given to General Rydzevsky,[11] who was made commander of the Gendarme Corps. Mirsky himself retained direction of general policy and serenely continued to affirm his confidence in the public. This confidence was expressed in two ways: first, in his presentation to the Tsar of a report concerning Russia's internal political conditions; and, second, in the permission granted to the zemstvo workers to convene on November 6, 1904.

Mirsky's report to the Tsar enumerated all measures which in his estimation could be counted upon to pacify the opposition and to reconcile it to the government. To the report was appended a project of a ukase to the Senate indicating those rather serious changes in the regime which had to be decided upon by the supreme power. The final editing of the ukase was to be done by a special committee presided over by a person honored with the Monarch's complete confidence.

The composition of this report had been entrusted to S. E. Kryzhanovsky,[12] Assistant Head of the Chief Administration for the Affairs of Local Economy,[13] but he had not been given any definite or detailed instructions as to the substance of the reforms to be enumerated in the project of the ukase. Prince Mirsky had only outlined for him his two basic propositions: the first, and in his eyes the more important, was that all governmental institutions and admin-

---

* This was nothing but the revival of the old law which had been in force before 1880 and according to which the political police constituted a separate unit headed by the chief of the Third Section of His Majesty's Private Chancellery, who was at the same time chief of the gendarmes. It is true that the connection of the Gendarme Corps with the Ministry of the Interior still existed, but it was now expressed only in the fact that the commander of the Gendarme Corps was subordinate to the minister and was not given the right to report directly to the Tsar. Under the conditions which Prince Mirsky created, even this connection did not promise to endure. It was actually broken under Mirsky's successor, Bulygin.

istrators throughout the country should be made strictly to observe the law, in other words, that arbitrary governmental action should be abolished. In this way Prince Mirsky probably intended to satisfy the basic desire of the opposition, that is, to establish a regime of equity. I doubt if Prince Mirsky was sincere in supposing that the desires of the public did not go beyond this; perhaps he was only using a popular phrase. By a "regime of equity" the public meant a representative government, and it is difficult to believe that what was clear to the man in the street was not understood by Prince Mirsky. I believe, therefore, that in using this term he wished to represent himself as a man who was trying to assure the country of a strict observation of the law, thereby fulfilling to the fullest extent the desire of the public. Yet he realized that he could not hope to accomplish much with this essentially cheap trick and, therefore, he intended at the same time completely to win the favor of the public by enlarging the State Council, the advisory legislative body of the empire, and by introducing into it representatives elected by important public institutions. This was his second basic proposition. Of course this had little in common with the constitutional organization of the government; it even resembled to a certain extent Plehve's original plans; yet it represented a definite, though timid, step in the direction of constitutional government.

In stating his ideas that were to be put in the report, Prince Mirsky revealed profound dilettantism both in questions of state law and in his knowledge of the problems which were at that time engrossing the public. For instance, he strongly recommended the booklet of Glinka-Yanchevsky[14] as a source from which ideas could be borrowed for the establishing of the regime of equity in the country. This booklet dealt with the reform of the Senate.*

* The author of the booklet—an engineer by education—was at that time a contributor to *Novoe Vremia* and later became editor of the periodical *Zemshchina*,[15] which was subsidized by the government and supported by the Right group of the Third and the Fourth Dumas. This booklet was really the outcome of a very lengthy lawsuit between him and the State Treasury. It pointed out the defects in our legal procedure which provided that, in case of a suit between the State Treasury and private persons, the Treasury, in the persons of its representatives, appeared in the final appeal—that is, in the Senate—simultaneously as a party to the suit and as a participant in making the final judicial decision. Using this instance as a starting point, Glinka-Yanchevsky demonstrated how the Senate was thus partly distorting and partly disregarding the basic duty imposed upon it by its founder, Peter I, namely, the duty of enforcing a strict observance of the law upon all institutions and persons of the empire. Apparently all this seemed the height of state wisdom and almost a revelation to Prince Mirsky.

Prince Mirsky did not directly concern himself with the other questions with which the report had to deal; he was content merely to have repeated a memorandum composed by the Police Department concerning those changes which might be permitted in the regulation concerning extraordinary police protection; these changes were limited to the administrative right to effect arrests and exile.

The personnel of the Ministry of the Interior was very experienced in composing memoranda and reports from the general and usually vague instructions of the higher officials. It was experienced in decoding these instructions, or rather, in applying their generalities to the concrete questions which were the theme of the day and which were engrossing the public mind. The equalization of the civil rights of the peasants with those of other classes, the establishment of a small zemstvo unit, the enlarging of the sphere of activity of zemstvo and municipal institutions, the granting of greater freedom of speech and of the press, and, finally, the betterment of the position of Old Believers and persons of non-orthodox creeds—these were the points upon which the public was insisting at that time.

All these matters were touched upon in the draft of the report and were included in the draft of the Imperial Ukase as basic principles along with Mirsky's two basic propositions. There was also included both in the report and the draft of the ukase a new regulation which at that time only a section of the public approved. This was the very important suggestion to abolish the land commune.

After the report had been drafted it was discussed by Prince Mirsky and his closest collaborators, who did some re-editing of a conservative tendency. Then it was presented to the Tsar. In view of the importance of the measures suggested, the Tsar desired to have the report examined by a special conference under his own chairmanship and including several ministers. The conference met on December 7 and 8, 1904. Only ministers were invited to the conference on the first day, but on the second day it was attended by the grand dukes, Vladimir[16] and Sergei Aleksandrovich, Mikhail Aleksandrovich, and, as I recall, Aleksandr Mikhailovich.

It was in this conference that Prince Mirsky revealed his lack of experience in the methods employed in our upper bureaucratic circles to carry through innovations of some importance. These methods, moreover, are used everywhere and under every regime. He had failed to prepare the ground, so to speak, for a favorable reception of the provisions of his report; he had failed to take the steps necessary

to win the support of the majority of persons invited to the conference; he had even failed to acquaint them beforehand with his ideas.
More than that, he had suggested to the Tsar that Pobedonostsev,
who was well known for his opposition to all innovations, should not
be invited to the conference. Such a request was certain to make the
Tsar distrustful of Prince Mirsky's tactics. Moreover, a desire to
keep persons known to be critical from a discussion of a subject de-
tracts from the value of the discussion. The upshot was that the Tsar
not only invited Pobedonostsev but did so in a personal note, saying:
"We are all confused. Help us bring order out of this chaos."

Given these conditions, it is not surprising that Prince Mirsky,
lacking in statesmanship, unable to present his ideas logically and
convincingly, and incapable of defending his stand, was completely
defeated by his opponents. His weak arguments, which were no
better than those of a commoner and were based not on a profound
analysis of the country's internal conditions but rather on intuition
mixed with a little sound common sense, were answered by his opponents with arguments which were based upon historical facts and
principles of constitutional law and were cleverly designed to influence the Tsar. Grand Duke Vladimir Aleksandrovich expressed
himself in favor of attracting the public elements to the work of
legislation; Grand Duke Sergei Aleksandrovich bitterly opposed this
idea.

Pobedonostsev, as Mirsky had foreseen, took up the cudgels
against the idea of introducing an elected element into the State
Council. In 1882, in a conference assembled by Alexander III to examine the project of the then Minister of the Interior, Count N. P.
Ignatev, concerning the convocation of a *Zemskii Sobor*,[17] Pobedonostsev had hotly accused Ignatev of trying to deceive the Tsar by
affirming that the project would not change the principles of the existing regime, whereas in reality, Pobedonostsev had contended, it
was tantamount to introducing a constitution that would limit the
prerogatives of the Monarch.* Now, twenty-two years later, Pobedonostsev repeated what he had said in 1882. Then he had succeeded
in securing the rejection of Ignatev's project. Now his success was
more limited because of the stand of Witte.

Using the occasion to demonstrate his attachment to the existing

---

* The then Minister of State Domains, M. N. Ostrovsky, made an almost word-
for-word record of this conference. This record was in my possession, but unfortunately has probably been destroyed along with the rest of my archives.

regime, Witte opposed the idea of including elected members in the State Council; he pointed out, however, that the rest of Prince Mirsky's suggestions in the draft and the report were worthy of consideration and that to be properly developed they needed careful study in which the heads of all ministries should assist. Witte's point of view was adopted, and the conference transferred to him, as Chairman of the Committee of Ministers, Prince Mirsky's report and the draft of the ukase for further consideration. Witte was elated. Again he had succeeded in taking into his hands a matter of great state significance, and he intended to make full use of his opportunity.

As for Prince Mirsky, he left the conference completely broken in spirit. He said gloomily to his collaborators: "Everything has failed. Let us build jails." Evidently he understood that his career was at an end, for he tendered his resignation; but the Tsar did not accept it.

As mentioned above, the second way in which Prince Mirsky sought to express his confidence in the public was by granting zemstvo workers the right to convene in St. Petersburg on November 6, 1904.

The history of this convention is as follows. As soon as Mirsky had assumed office, he, like Plehve before him, sought to enter into some sort of agreement with the zemstvo men who were opposed to the government. At that time this opposition was centered in some zemstvo men of Tver Gubernia led by I. I. Petrunkevich. In the 'eighties Petrunkevich had been forbidden residence in St. Petersburg; now the Prince's first step was to lift that restriction. At first, communications with Petrunkevich were made through Lopukhin, the Director of the Police Department who had made the acquaintance of Petrunkevich when Prokuror for the Tver District Court. Petrunkevich admitted frankly that some understanding with the government could be effected but first the government would have to show that it really intended to alter its policy of suppressing all liberal zemstvo thought. This announcement was one reason why Mirsky had undertaken the measures mentioned concerning the zemstvo institutions and their workers over whom some administrative punishment was then hanging. When Lopukhin went abroad, he was succeeded as intermediary by Herbel, the Head of the Chief Administration for the Affairs of Local Economy. Herbel went to Moscow and there established communications with the zemstvo group then headed by D. N. Shipov. This group had been formed and held its first meeting in 1903, when it evolved its general program of action to ensure the success of the progressive wing of the zemstvo in the coming zemstvo elections. This group, thirty to thirty-five strong, included the most prominent of zemstvo workers and members of the city dumas. From Saratov there was N. N. Lvov;[18] from Pskov, Count P. A. Heyden; and from Moscow, Mayor N. I. Guchkov.[19]

As the military situation grew worse, especially after August 1904, and perhaps also because after Plehve's assassination the rumor spread that our internal policy was about to undergo a marked change, this group decided to present a memorandum to the Tsar. This memorandum would point out the unrest which prevailed in the country and emphasize that in order to suppress this growing unrest and at the same time to make our legislation more spirited and useful, elected elements should be drawn into legislative work. Participation in legislation was interpreted to mean participation in a sort of Zemskii Sobor. Steps were taken to have such a memorandum drafted. S. A. Muromtsev,[20] later Chairman of the First Duma, was approached and agreed to make the draft, but on condition that his authorship be kept secret.

So much for outward appearances. Actually, however, this group of moderately liberal zemstvo men was unwittingly directed by the Union of Liberation,[21] which was composed of the zemstvo and municipal workers of the Left and included radical professors and a separate Jewish group. The Union had been formed in 1903 and had its own periodical, *Osvobozhdenie,* published abroad under the editorship of P. B. Struve.[22] Its members assembled from time to time in conspiratory meetings and were in communication with revolutionary organizations. Its purpose was to abolish autocracy and to establish a free democratic regime. In September 1904 the Union participated in the Conference of the Opposition and Revolutionary Organizations of the Russian Empire,[23] held in Paris, and accepted the program of action there worked out. At this conference, the members of the Union, including P. N. Miliukov,[24] sat side by side with representatives of the Socialist-Revolutionists, such as Asef[25] and Viktor Chernov.[26] It was this Union which was convoked in 1904 and adopted the following resolutions:

1. To participate in the coming congress of zemstvo and municipal workers and to urge them openly to adopt constitutional principles;

2. To organize for November 20 a series of banquets to com-

memorate the fortieth anniversary of the new judicial institutions[27] and to adopt a series of radical constitutional and democratic resolutions;

3. To broach at the regular zemstvo conferences the question of introducing a constitutional government and of convoking public representatives for this purpose;

4. To begin an agitation for the organization into unions of zemstvos of the liberal professions and ultimately to unify them into one union which, later, would get into touch with revolutionary parties.

It was not long before the Union achieved the full realization of the program.

The government was completely ignorant of these resolutions. So was Herbel. He had arrived in Moscow and was confining his efforts to dissuading the moderate group from presenting to the Tsar the memorandum which Muromtsev had drafted. In this he succeeded, but he came to no agreement with the group concerning the forthcoming congress. It was Mirsky's intention, of course, to come to some understanding with the zemstvo men, and he had agreed to permit the congress to meet in St. Petersburg. But after Herbel's visit to Moscow it became evident to Mirsky that the congress would be one of public men, including S. A. Muromtsev, who by now had taken his courage in both hands. Mirsky did not foresee, however, that the congress would fall entirely into the hands of the Union of Liberation and thereby take on a pronounced opposition tinge. He became aware of this only after the congress had assembled in St. Petersburg.

The congress, with 104 in attendance, met in private residences: November 6 and 9 at the house of the Tver zemstvo man, I. A. Korsakov; November 7 at that of A. N. Brianchaninov; and November 8 at that of V. D. Nabokov. It adopted resolutions which pointed out in their initial paragraphs the wide differences existing between the Russia represented by Russian officialdom, that is, the government, and the Russia represented by the public elements of the country. The resolutions gave imperative expression to demands never before presented to the government. The demand for freedom of speech, the press, assembly, and organization was here expressed for the first time and until the Manifesto of October 17, 1905, this demand was repeated insistently in the resolutions of various public associations. The inviolability of person and domicile was also emphasized. The resolutions referred openly to the necessity of granting to the public participation "in the work of legislation, in determining state budgets, and in seeing to it that the administration acted within the law." This latter clause (Article II of the resolutions) was adopted by a vote of seventy to thirty, if I am not mistaken. The minority favored "a regular participation of public representatives in legislation" but at the same time advocated "the preservation of the imperial power, one and indivisible."*

Naturally the public attached exceptional importance to this congress, which, in spite of its unofficial character, was considered lawful and under the protection of the Minister of the Interior. This estimate of it was evidenced by the fact that A. S. Suvorin, whose carefulness in these matters was well known, immediately printed its resolutions in his *Novoe Vremia*. Printed copies of the resolutions were thus rapidly spread about and received wide publicity throughout Russia, as did the resolutions of the Union of Liberation.

While the zemstvo congress was in session Prince Mirsky kept in touch personally with its main personages. At the beginning of the congress, however, he had known nothing of the resolutions it would adopt, and without waiting to find out he promised the congress that he would arrange a reception for its members by the Tsar so that they might present their resolutions to him.

Witte of course used this occasion to become more intimate with the representatives of the liberal public. Like a fortune teller, he used language which his audience could interpret as it wished. He continually encouraged the members of the congress to express their own desires and gave them to understand that the government should hear expressed definitely and cogently the desires of the public in matters of state policy. Of course, he was unable to say how he him-

---

* Many civil servants took part in the congress; among these were A. A. Pavlov, of Saratov Gubernia, and V. V. Kovalevsky,[28] of Pskov Gubernia. Both these men were members of the city dumas of their respective gubernias at that time and were employed in the Peasant Section. They told me all that took place at the congress. Nine years afterward, in 1913, N. A. Maklakov,[29] then Minister of the Interior, announced that Kovalevsky could no longer serve in that ministry because he had participated in the congress of November 1904. Of course, this was but a pretext. The real reason was the conflict between Kovalevsky, who was then the business manager of the Office of Provisioning and Supply,[30] and V. E. Frisch, the head of this office. Even so the incident was very characteristic of Maklakov, who was then working with already existing representative institutions. I was obliged to point out to the minister that Kovalevsky had attended the convention not only with my knowledge but even with my approval.

self would react to such a program and whether or not he would support it in full. But this was a question for the future; for the present the most important thing in his estimation was to let the public freely express its thoughts and desires.

Mirsky, influenced by Prince A. Obolensky, the intermediary between him and Witte, shared this attitude and did all he could to arrange the imperial reception of the zemstvo men. But the Tsar refused point-blank to receive even their leaders. One reason for this essentially proper decision was probably the fact that at that time the Tsar had lost faith in the expediency of Mirsky's policy. This policy, it is true, had started the public singing the personal praises of Prince Mirsky; but it had not changed the attitude of the liberal press toward the revolutionists and toward the public uprisings that were occurring here and there under the urge of revolutionary propaganda. The general political atmosphere, partly under the influence of continued defeats at the front and partly because of the greater freedom given the press, not only failed to become more favorable to the government but even became more hostile. The progressive part of the public made more and increasingly sharp demands of the government.

Another reason for the Tsar's refusal to receive the zemstvo men undoubtedly grew out of the fact that he had been informed that the congress did not adequately represent the Russian zemstvos. It was composed not of persons elected by the zemstvo assemblies but of a group of zemstvo members who had united around the Zemstvo Board of Moscow Gubernia, and also of some separate zemstvo men from various gubernias co-opted by the above Moscow Zemstvo Board. It also included public men of definite political opinions who were not connected with zemstvos at all. In a word, the congress was comprised of a group of private individuals possessing no right to speak for anyone but themselves. But even if he admitted that the members of the congress were the real if not the formally chosen champions of the ideas of certain public circles, what answer to their wishes could they have expected from the Tsar? Some of their resolutions demanded a radical change in the existing fundamental laws of the empire, so that any answer the Tsar gave would appear to be a confirmation of these resolutions. Even a simple promise to consider their resolutions would have been an admission that it was possible to put them into effect.

Evidently Prince Mirsky did not realize this. Nor did he realize that his promise to arrange the imperial reception had put the Tsar in a bad light. Here the difference between Prince Mirsky and Plehve was revealed. While Plehve considered it his duty to direct against himself the public discontent aroused by governmental actions, even when such actions had been adopted against his will, Prince Mirsky endeavored to win public sympathy by shifting the responsibility for unpopular decisions directly to the Monarch. This is precisely what he did in this case; he explained to the congress leaders that the Tsar had not heeded his urgent solicitations concerning the reception.

What can we say of Mirsky's policy? Undoubtedly he distinguished justly between avowed revolutionists, who were opposed to the government and the existing order of society, and those public elements which desired only to be allowed to participate in the work of government and which did not demand a radical change in the social or political organization of the state. Wisely, also, he intended to stop the endless caviling, the systematic irritation, and the antagonizing of those elements which not only were not endangering the stability of the state structure but which, cleverly handled, might well have become its most dependable support. Some serious concessions to the liberal public had to be made, and Mirsky's political program had to be based on a willingness to make such concessions.

But the method Prince Mirsky adopted to carry out his program was childishly naive. In the first place, he did not realize that in every country and in every age the existing order has been overturned not so much by direct attack as by the lack of active partisans and defenders. Had he realized this, he would have realized also that the first duty of the government was to create a social class which would support it in its fight with revolutionists of all denominations. It was not enough to stop the direct attacks of the zemstvos, the municipalities, and the liberal press upon the government; Mirsky should also have endeavored to secure their support as an aid to the government in fighting the propaganda of utopian teachings which were perverting the masses and the terroristic acts which were undermining and corrupting government activity.

In both his private and his semi-official conversations Prince Mirsky drew a sharp line of distinction between the revolutionists and the liberal opposition, but he did not have the courage to express this distinction in an official act or public utterance. He did not have the courage to state that the government's confidence in the public and its readiness to permit an extension of the scope of public activity demanded that the public itself should take a stand against revolutionary socialistic propaganda and condemn terroristic acts.

An accord between the zemstvo circles and the government would have had to depend upon a change in the attitude of the zemstvo boards toward the local administration of the government. The government and the zemstvos would have had to work along parallel lines and the latter would have had to discontinue their widespread practice of harboring in zemstvo service both secret and avowed revolutionists of various denominations. This practice was by no means peculiar to the more advanced zemstvo boards; even Right-wing zemstvo men viewed with more than mere complaisance the revolutionary past and the revolutionary convictions of their employees.

In an endeavor to widen the sphere of their activity, all zemstvos, regardless of their political coloring, were eager to secure control of primary education, although actually they could not supervise the work of rural teachers. Nor did the zemstvos see any danger in flooding the country with zemstvo statisticians, who were the immediate directors of revolutionary propaganda among the peasant masses. The duty of the government lay in showing the zemstvo workers what deep revolutionary roots the zemstvo third element had sent down in the village soil, and in declaring that although the government had confidence in the zemstvos it could have no confidence in their third element and that the zemstvos would have to choose with whom they wished to cast their lot—the government or their own employees. Until this had been done, until the leaders of the liberal opposition had announced a complete break with the revolutionary elements, no concessions to the public could have been of any importance in strengthening the existing regime. On the contrary, such concessions would have augmented public unrest and increased public demands on the government.

It may be that the formula, "pacification first—reforms afterwards," was rendered senseless by the fact that public unrest was due fundamentally to the nonrealization of certain reforms and by the fact that the lack of success in combatting the revolutionary movement was mainly due to the liberal public's silent approval of this movement. But there was still another and quite feasible formula: "first an understanding with the liberal opposition, then the necessary reforms." To reach such an understanding, however, the

government first had to determine how far it would go in these concessions and to work out a definite program and have it approved by
the Monarch. When such a solid foundation had been laid negotiations with the liberal opposition (including, I believe, its radical part
as well) could have begun and some quite friendly understanding
could have been reached. P. B. Struve was perfectly right when he
said in his *Osvobozhdenie* that Sviatopolk-Mirsky must face squarely
the question of a constitution. "This he must do," continued Struve,
"out of regard for the Tsar; for if he fails to put this question before the Tsar, he is simply deceiving Nicholas II."

Prince Mirsky's policy was seriously defective because it contained nothing concrete and was based upon no definite program.
Since this was so, the initiative in determining a policy naturally
passed to the public, which hastened to use the government's professed "confidence" to force on it the public's own program. The
public considered, and not without reason, that the revolutionists
constituted the only real force with which the government would
have to contend. The public realized, therefore, that in order to make
its attack on the government successful, it would have to preserve
not only the benevolent neutrality which some of its elements displayed toward the revolutionists but also the actual sympathetic attitude which other of its elements expressed toward them.

At that time two courses were open to the Russian government.
One called for the strict preservation of the autocratic regime and
required the government immediately to enact those organic reforms
made necessary by the development of public life and the economic
development of the Russian people. This involved first of all the reorganization of the social structure: decisive measures to preserve
the remnants of the landowning class, which was disappearing and
losing its political significance, and measures to equalize the representatives of the industrial classes and of the nobility by gradually fusing
the two (a means long since adopted by England). But, together
with these measures, it was also necessary to create a powerful stratum of well-to-do peasantry, with each peasant possessing a farm lot
of from thirty to fifty desiatins as his private property; for the peasant class has constituted the most stable support of the existing order
in all times and in all nations. This course demanded from the
government a display of great energy, extensive reforms, and exceptional tact. But even given all this it was not certain that the revolutionary wave which was sweeping over the country would not

overtake the social reconstruction of the empire. Albeit, this course could not be considered hopeless.

If, however, the government did not consider itself capable of carrying out such an extensive and speedy reform, if it did not consider that such a reform would sufficiently assure the peaceful development of the empire, and if it wished to gain immediately the sympathies of the liberal public, then a second course was open to it. It would have to satisfy that public's most insistent desire: the introduction of a constitutional regime with the election of public representatives by a limited suffrage. If this were done, important reforms could be effected with the help of these representatives. Of course, some radical liberals would not have been satisfied with such a reform and would have attached themselves still more closely to the revolutionary parties. On the other hand, there were considerable educated forces which would have ranged themselves on the side of the government and the fight would not have remained one between the government and all of the progressive public, for the government would have been actively supported by the educated public forces.

It was this latter course that the states of western Europe adopted and followed in proceeding from autocracy to parliamentarism. If, in 1904, after Plehve's death, the Russian government, without abruptly changing its own policy, had asked the leaders of the moderate liberal opposition to express their sentiments, it would have learned that the more progressive public circles, excluding, of course, those already contaminated by socialistic utopias, desired nothing more than a constitutional regime of a non-parliamentary type.*

* I recall here a conversation I had with Professor L. I. Petrazhitsky,[31] editor of *Pravo* and later a prominent member of the Cadet party, about February 5, 1905, the day following the assassination of Grand Duke Sergei Aleksandrovich in Moscow. The public was encouraged by the greater freedom of speech it had been granted and, although its expressed wishes had not been realized, the new freedom had markedly increased its demands on the government as compared with those of November 1904. Professor Petrazhitsky asked me whether or not his publication *Pravo* would be censored if he published an article explaining that when the public speaks of a constitution it really means only participation of representatives of the public in the legislative work of the country. The executive power would remain as before in the hands of the ministerial college, the members of which were appointed and dismissed by and responsible to the Monarch. Some time previously the editors of *Pravo* had agreed to publish the article; but the assassination of the Grand Duke had made them very cautious, since this crime would probably make the government doubly severe and impel it to undertake a series of repressions which would doubtless affect the freedom of publications. I cite this conversation to show once more the moderate pretensions of those who later became partisans of government by the people. It was characteristic that both Stishinsky, who was

These were the desires of the most progressive part of the public; those of the liberal circles of the nobility were even more modest, but even they were in favor of having elected representatives of the people share in the work of state development. Evidence of this was furnished by a memorandum presented to the Minister of the Interior in November 1904 (after the zemstvo congress) by twenty-three gubernia marshals of nobility, including the marshals of the two capitals, Prince P. N. Trubetskoi and Count V. V. Gudovich. The memorandum urged a "reasonable and well-organized participation of the representatives of the zemstvo and municipal organizations in the work of drafting and composing new legislative projects." It was suggested that this task of drafting and composing legislative projects be imposed upon the "State Council and that the sphere of its competence be enlarged accordingly."

Thus it may be said with assurance that about the end of 1904 it would have been quite possible for the government to have reached an understanding with a considerable part of the public concerning a constitutional reform which would have retained the monarchical principle.

Prince Mirsky chose to follow a middle course. Evidently he did not realize that such a course was impossible for the government. He gave the educated public a means of expressing its political ideas and hopes when he permitted (if he did not create) the zemstvo congress; but he omitted to ascertain beforehand what the nature of the program would be and whether or not he would be able to adopt it. It was a characteristic example of "Manilovism":[32] "I shall pat them on the head, and they, in return, will help me not to adopt their own wishes." This was the substance of Prince Mirsky's naïve hopes. Actually the reverse took place. His course of action left him open to the suspicion of provocation, for, obviously, to urge the public to express its wishes and then to fail to carry out these wishes was only to increase its opposition.

Prince Mirsky's light-minded policy, following as it did the harsh and captious policy of Plehve, furnished the first stimulus to the revolutionary movement of 1905, a movement which had found favorable soil for growth in the general dissatisfaction resulting from our

present during this conversation, and I were in favor of publishing the article and expressed our assurance that the *Pravo* would suffer no dire consequences for doing so.

defeats at the front. The first open revolutionary demonstration was the zemstvo congress in November 1904. The resolutions there adopted formed the basis of all later demands which the public made of the government, but with this important difference: the liberal public men anticipated nothing beyond the realization of the resolutions, whereas the Social Democrats and the Socialist-Revolutionists, who adopted the same slogans, regarded the realization of these resolutions merely as a means of getting into their hands a weapon with which to destroy the political and social order of the country.

Prince Mirsky's outward liberalism was not based upon any definite program. It could be reduced to the well-known formula, *"Laissez faire, laissez passer."* But the public, accustomed to administrative domination, proved to be unable to use wisely their newly gained freedom and failed to realize the responsibility which goes with every right, especially a political right. This circumstance gave the Union of Liberation the opportunity to realize its program even more fully than it had itself expected.

The political banquets, proposed by this Union, for celebrating the fortieth anniversary of the judicial reforms were held throughout all Russia and were the occasions of fiery political speeches condemning the existing order and demanding the immediate overthrow of autocracy.

After these jubilee banquets many others followed, for no definite reason. They were arranged by different groups of persons from the liberal professions—lawyers, physicians, civil engineers, journalists—and even by persons without any definite occupation who were known under the general term of public men. Speeches made and resolutions adopted at these banquets became increasingly radical. Interestingly enough, many of those who made speeches at these banquets were civil servants; but they were not reproved or disturbed because of their conduct.

The Union of Liberation was successful also in that part of its program which called upon the zemstvo assemblies to join the constitutional movement. These assemblies, both gubernia and uezd, sent to the government and to the Monarch addresses and petitions which repeated, now in a moderate now in a more forceful form, the resolutions of the November congress. The torrent of these addresses was finally stopped in December by a special Sovereign ordinance. Also the Union of Liberation successfully organized different professional unions; but, since such undertakings demanded a certain amount of preliminary work, concrete results could not be observed until somewhat later, about the spring of 1905. It can be seen, therefore, that at that time the directing initiative force behind public movements was provided by the Union of Liberation.

The Social Democrats, who by then had split into Bolsheviks and Mensheviks, took no organized part in this movement. The Bolsheviks, from Lenin down, were of the opinion that any co-operation with the liberal bourgeoisie would only weaken the stand of the "leaders of the proletariat." But in some cities the "party workers," acting in accord with the instructions of the Menshevik publication, *Iskra,* endeavored to introduce their own particular note into the liberal movement. At Kharkov, Odessa, and elsewhere they burst into the banquets and turned them into public meetings. At Saratov revolutionary elements organized a meeting at which they proclaimed the abolition of autocracy and the institution of a democratic republic.

The result of Mirsky's policy was that the government granted the public some of its demands but refused to grant what it wanted most—a constitution. Thus it not only failed to reconcile the public but strengthened it in its stand and armed it with weapons to attain its end. In the bureaucratic circles of the Right, Prince Mirsky's policy was bitterly criticized as being subtly Machiavellian. It was said that he intended to place the Monarch in a critical position by stating that he, as Minister of the Interior, would not be responsible for the preservation of peace and order throughout the country unless a constitution were granted in accord with the demands of the public and as the only means of avoiding a revolution. These circles even went so far as to nickname Mirsky "Sviatopolk the Accursed."[33]

But Prince Mirsky was not even considering a constitution. His project for introducing into the work of government representatives of municipal and zemstvo organizations who would take part in deliberating on legislation was only the first step toward a constitution; it was not in itself a constitution. His actions were those of a man groping in the dark.

But if Prince Mirsky did not reveal much statesmanship in effecting the desired reconciliation between the public and the government, neither did Witte. It will be recalled that the Tsar's conference of December 7 and 8 had transferred to Witte the task of studying further the suggestions in Prince Mirsky's report. Witte undertook his new work with his customary zeal and accomplished the first part with lightning speed. Ten days after the Tsar's conference, Witte had worked out a new draft of a ukase to the Senate, entitled "Measures for Improving the State Order." This draft contained many suggestions included in Mirsky's report; but there were also important additions, most important of which was the following, by which Witte intended to assure himself of the direction of the entire state policy: "It is the duty of the Committee of Ministers, more than of any other state institution, to bring about a closer unification of the separate parts of the government. Therefore, We order the Committee of Ministers to consider the best way to realize Our desires concerning every question mentioned above and to present to Us as soon as possible its conclusions as to the necessary measures to be adopted in accord with the established order. Concerning all further developments in these affairs, the Committee of Ministers shall report to Us."

Witte inserted the last sentence for a purpose. He hoped in this way to assure himself of regular audiences with the Tsar, of which he had been deprived by his appointment as Chairman of the Committee of Ministers.

The ukase became known as the Ukase of December 12, 1904.[34] It stated, among other things, that the chief concern of the government should be "the improvement of the mode of existence among our numerous peasant class." In this matter Witte was concerned for his own interests. As Chairman of the Special Conference to Study the Needs of Agricultural Industry he hoped to play the principal role in solving the peasant problem. To this end he had included in the text of the ukase a reminder of the commission's work: "at the present time a Special Conference of the most experienced persons in the higher administration is studying the most important phases and problems of peasant life; this study is being made from the information and reports of the local Committees to Study the Needs of Agricultural Industry." Witte intended to carry out his plan, that is, to bring about the unification of the peasant class with other classes, by including in the ukase an instruction to the effect that the Special Conference "should in the course of its work put legislation concerning peasants on the same basis as legislation concerning the other classes and thereby make it easier for the members of the peasant class to enjoy 'the freedom and the full rights' granted them by the statute of the Tsar Liberator."

It was characteristic of the Witte of that day that he made no mention of the measures for abolishing the land commune, although

Prince Mirsky's report had contained a clause on this matter. This circumstance should prove conclusively that in December 1904 Witte did not share the opinion that the first step in introducing a uniform social organization in Russia was to abolish the commune and to transfer to the peasants, as their private property, the lands allotted to them in the commune. The exclusion of this question was all the more significant since Witte made use of all Mirsky's other suggestions except that concerning the introduction of an elected element into the State Council which had been rejected at the Tsar's conference.*

After the publication of the Ukase of December 12 the government tried to use it as a means of putting an end to those public demands which were being widely expressed at that time and which went beyond the reforms suggested by the ukase. A government communiqué of December 14 made it known that all violations of public order and all illegal gatherings would be suppressed by every lawful means at the disposal of the government. It continued: "The zemstvo and municipal organizations, as well as all other organizations, institutions, and societies, are warned not to go outside their proper sphere and not to examine questions for the study of which they have been given no legal rights." The communiqué closed by pointing out that the new public movement was "foreign to the spirit of the Russian people who were faithful to the principles of the existing state order," and it referred to the demands of certain circles as inadmissible and contrary to the inflexible principle of the existing state order made binding by our basic laws.

At first the zemstvo and municipal institutions seemed to heed this communiqué. They neither sent to the government nor published the addresses and petitions which they had prepared. Yet pub-

---

* In his memoirs Witte points out that he included even this suggestion in the project of the ukase but that the Tsar struck it out. This is undoubtedly false. Witte states that he personally presented the project of the ukase to the Tsar and that the Tsar, after striking out the above suggestion, signed it immediately. Now the striking out of some portion of a project submitted to the Tsar for signature would have necessitated copying it over again. But aside from that, it is enough to read the text of this ukase to be convinced that it contained no mention of including public representatives in legislative work, for such a suggestion would have been made the cornerstone of the entire ukase and would have been accompanied by explanations as to its possible interpretation. Witte's statement that he included this matter in the project is all the more strange since he says in his memoirs that it had already been rejected at the Tsar's conference at which he himself had objected to such an innovation.

lic unrest, stimulated to a great extent by the press and maybe to an even greater extent by the Committee of Ministers and its chairman, Witte, was far from appeased. The system of permitting one day that which was forbidden the next infuriated the public more and more.

Very soon after the publication of the ukase Witte feverishly initiated in the Committee of Ministers the work of studying the final articles of the ukase of December 12 so that the general statements contained in them might be developed and a means of putting them into effect might be found. But for all his energy he failed to achieve any definite results. By its very nature the Committee of Ministers could not undertake a task which demanded most painstaking preliminary study and appropriate working machinery. Of course, different ministries could have been charged with portions of this work which pertained to matters within their competence. In fact, this would have been the easiest means; but Witte did not intend to adopt it. On the one hand, he probably feared that to transfer the matter to separate ministries would be to deprive the ukase of the very liberal character that was desired. On the other hand— and this no doubt was the main reason—he desired to advertise the projected reforms as much as possible, to keep them in the public eye as a series of reforms which were not introduced in the regular manner but which he himself had conceived and brought to materialization. At that time Witte had lost his former position of favor with the Tsar and had decided to regain power through the pressure of public demand. Accordingly he strove to win public sympathy in every possible way. With his customary impulsiveness, and utterly unconcerned lest his words be reported to the Tsar in an exaggerated form, he announced to the public men: "I shall drive in the liberal reforms so far that there will be no way of taking them away again."

What method did Witte select to achieve his end? In the Committee of Ministers he had no opportunity to work independently and create appropriate projects of his own but was obliged to transfer this work to others. He therefore adopted a special course of action: he decided to criticize the existing order in all matters touched upon by the ukase. He submitted these matters to the Committee of Ministers for discussion and had all criticism carefully recorded in the minutes. These minutes he published forthwith. In this way the public was officially notified that all previous policy had been a complete mistake if not a disgrace.

The minutes showed that, in its study of the position of the press, the Committee of Ministers had virtually confessed its obscurantism, and in its study of the laws concerning Old Believers it had admitted that the results attained by these laws were directly contrary to the results the government had anticipated when the laws were made. But the Committee's most forceful and insistent criticism had been directed against the regulation concerning the measures for extraordinary police protection. The Ukase of December 12 had stated that the authorities in Russia were not abiding by the provisions of the law and were not being held sufficiently responsible for arbitrary acts, and the Committee of Ministers had enlarged upon this theme. P. N. Durnovo, who had represented Mirsky in the Committee, had drawn a vivid picture of the lack of justice and of administrative arbitrariness in Russia. He had said that the degree to which individual representatives of the administration used the rights given them by the regulation on extraordinary police protection was determined by the personal opinions of these representatives on this subject; in some gubernias the treatment of this matter depended upon the governor and changed with every new one. As time went on, local administrators had begun to apply administrative exile not only to political suspects but also to those whose conduct was considered by the authorities a menace to public peace and order.

Durnovo had then gone on to paint in equally dismal colors the conditions of the population: "There is no citizen," he had said, "who can be assured that his home will not be subject to administrative search and he himself be arrested."*

---

* At that time, as I have already mentioned, Durnovo was professing pronounced liberal views. He openly expressed his opinion that the state could not go on much longer as it was, that the government was becoming more and more like a Tartar horde living in an armed camp. Within the Ministry of the Interior he was directing a revision of the regulation on passports and residence licenses. He held that the old order, according to which no one could go abroad without a special passport, should be repealed; he also insisted on making a law to the effect that every member of a peasant family over eighteen years of age be given an individual residence license without the consent of the head of the family, which the old law required. Such a law would have been in direct variance to the whole order of peasant family organization and would have pertained not to the regulations on passports but to peasant legislation, according to which the allotted land constituted not the property of a householder but the property of the entire family. Such a law would also have endangered family unity, since the existing law merely confirmed the well-established peasant custom whereby members of a family who worked away from home should send a part of their earnings to the family at home. This regulation may be viewed differently; but to repeal it without touching the rest of the regulations on peasant legislation was odd, to say the least. I was

Witte also had expressed himself in terms equally emphatic. He had accused the government of wastefulness and general inefficiency: "It has not paid due attention to the labor problem. It has not alleviated the oppressed condition of the Jews. It has not found a way to pacify the students."

Despite all this criticism of existing conditions, however, there were no immediate changes in the existing laws. There were nothing but hazy promises that the course of the government would be altered at some time in the future. All this served to create the impression that in the government Witte alone sincerely desired to effect changes in the administrative system and that he was powerless to change the old order, since he was not actually at the helm. Witte himself worked to support this impression through his numerous conversations with the representatives of the liberal opposition. The impression was further strengthened by the method adopted for putting into effect the principles proclaimed on December 12. According to this method, special commissions which were not directly connected with government organizations and which were presided over by the most liberal members of the State Council were to work out the required measures. The measures designed to establish the observation of law in the country were to be worked out by a commission presided over by A. A. Saburov. The laws regulating the press were to be revised by a commission under D. F. Kobeko.[35] The commission on religious tolerance was headed by a much less popular person, Count A. P. Ignatev,[36] who was also appointed chairman of the commission to revise the regulations concerning an increase of extraordinary police protection.

The results of the work of these commissions were insignificant. Only the regulations on the press drafted by Kobeko's commission were at all fortunate. The draft for this new press law was acted upon by the State Council on the eve of the opening of the First Duma and remained in effect until the Revolution of 1917. The work of the commission on religious tolerance was in large measure anticipated by a ukase issued on April 17, 1905,[37] before the commission was organized. This ukase repealed almost all restrictions on Old Believers.

Thus, the innovations proposed by the Ukase of December 12

---

decidedly opposed to Durnovo's suggestion. As is well known, however, no changes in the regulations on passports and residence licenses were effected until the revolution, although a revision of some parts of them was very much needed.

were only partially realized. Nevertheless they were essentially just and very necessary. The Russian law on the press was antiquated.* The regulations on extraordinary police protection contained only a few articles which virtually legalized the violation by the administrative authorities of all laws protecting the inviolability of the home and the individual. The laws pertaining to Old Believers had long since outlived their usefulness and were nothing but an unjustified repression of the elements most devoted to national traditions.

Witte states in his memoirs[38] that the Ukase of December 12, 1904, "could have accomplished to a great extent the pacification of the revolutionary spirit had it been put into effect completely and speedily." It is difficult to agree with this, for no matter how far the government was prepared to go in order to carry out the principles expressed in the Ukase of December 12 it was quite powerless to fulfill all the demands which the public made upon it, and had it attempted to do so it would very speedily have brought about its own destruction. This was very convincingly proved both by the attempt of the government to make progress in this direction immediately after the publication of the Manifesto of October 17, 1905, and by the limitless freedom advocated and tolerated by the Provisional Government of 1917, which allowed itself to be exterminated by street rabble led by unprincipled anarchical elements.

The basic mistake in all measures undertaken by Prince Mirsky, and partially carried out by Witte, was inherent not in the measures themselves but in the fact that they were undertaken not to improve the state order but to pacify public opposition. This made the measures appear to be a concession to public demands. Had Prince Mirsky begun his administration with something other than an unjustifiable declaration of "confidence," had he refused to permit the November zemstvo congress, had he taken the initiative in putting into effect the reforms mentioned in the Ukase of December 12— these reforms would have been acclaimed by all elements concerned

* Article 140 of the regulations on the press, dated 1873, states that "The Minister of the Interior may prohibit the publication or discussion by the press of problems of political significance." It explained, however, that "this right is to be exercised only in case of urgent necessity." By January 1905, however, the cases of urgent necessity totaled 564; one had occurred every twenty days, and later they had become more frequent, recurring, on an average, every thirteen days. Even in 1905, when the whole country was in the grip of a revolutionary psychosis, among the problems of political significance was classed the question whether or not ballet dancers should shave their armpits!

for the welfare of the country. But to let the initiative for the reforms slip out of his hands, to give the opposition a chance to work out its own program, and, finally, to limit himself to the partial materialization of the reforms was but to show his own weakness. Such conduct served not to slacken but to speed up the onrush of the opposition.

As a result, public unrest had risen like foam in a glass. This unrest caught up the dregs of society, which until then had been in hiding but now dared to appear freely and openly. University student disorders and demonstrations, which had all but disappeared, now recurred—not so much in St. Petersburg as in Moscow, where they had become so frequent by December 1904 that mounted troops had to be called in to establish order.

In all this the revolutionary elements were not inactive, but their activities and their influence upon the workingmen and the population in general were not very marked at that time. The impetus to the public movement in St. Petersburg at the beginning of January 1905 was supplied by organizations headed by Zubatov's government agents who had been left at their posts after Zubatov's dismissal.

The prestige of the government fell, largely as a result of the publication by Witte of the minutes of the sessions of the Committee of Ministers. It appeared that the government, like a wayward schoolboy, had begun tearfully to admit its many transgressions and all but pledge itself to good conduct in the future. The public very naturally lost all fear and respect for such a government, became more confident of itself, and, feeling itself free, lost its head and unwittingly dragged the country headlong into revolution, despite the fact that the most educated part of the population not only did not desire a revolution but even feared one. In a word, the country was in the grip of a revolutionary psychosis, a grip which no commissions of the government could hope to loosen. It was a question of the government's existence.

The Tsar, who did not lack a talent for observation, was more astute than his counselors. He saw clearly that Witte's activity in the field of political reforms was not pacifying the country but was provoking further disturbances. So, in his customary gentle and indirect manner, he removed Witte from the direction of this work. At the beginning of January 1905 he convoked the Council of Ministers to consider the ever-growing revolutionary unrest. After this meeting was closed, he expressed his desire that in the future all important questions of a general character should be discussed in this council. At the same time he appointed Count Solsky, the senior member, to act as chairman in his stead. Thus the activity of the Committee of Ministers was again limited to debating relatively unimportant questions, and its chairman, Witte, was deprived of his role of director of state policy. Witte had stretched the cords upon which he played too tightly and they had snapped in his fingers.

CHAPTER XVII

PEASANT AND LABOR QUESTIONS DURING SVIATOPOLK-MIRSKY'S TERM OF OFFICE

The lack of a directing force in domestic policy was reflected both in the general course of events and in the Ministry of the Interior itself. The separate departments of this ministry had become virtually independent institutions, not bound together by a single directing will. This was perhaps most clearly evident in the Peasant Section's handling of the peasant problem. Witte had become the guiding force in studying this problem by virtue of being Chairman of the Special Conference, and at first Mirsky intended to follow his lead and that of Prince Obolensky in this question. It was at their instance that he invited N. N. Kutler to replace Stishinsky as his assistant in matters concerning peasant institutions.

I confess I was very much opposed to this appointment. I did not like the idea of having as chief a person against whom I had fought for two years in different commissions. Moreover, I was especially loth to permit Witte to master the field which I had striven for two years to keep free from outside influences. That such was Witte's plan in securing Kutler's appointment I had not the slightest doubt; but I could not persuade Prince Mirsky that such was the case. To my greatest amazement, however, Kutler's appointment (November 20, 1904) did not have the slightest undesirable effect from my point of view. He made no effort to direct the activities of those sections of the ministry of which he took charge; he seemed content merely to sign without argument every document brought to him for signature. This brought much joy to the officials of the Peasant Section, who were somewhat worn out by Stishinsky's meticulous conscientiousness. As for my own relations with Kutler, they were simply nonexistent. He was never present when I reported to the minister, and consequently the problems that pertained to the policy of the Peasant Section passed him by.

I recall a rather typical conversation I had with Kutler during which I mentioned the fact that the Peasant Section did not have sufficient funds to pay for urgent work. Kutler expressed utter amazement at this. According to his information the Section was supposed to administer all sums budgeted for the local peasant institutions of the central government and to appropriate any sums not spent on these institutions. I replied that these unspent sums were taken care of in an item of the ministry's budget other than that which provided for the maintenance of the Peasant Section. Therefore, the Peasant Section could not use these unspent sums. "That does not matter," answered Kutler. "The Department of Direct Taxation of the Ministry of Finance is in precisely the same position as regards the payment of tax assessors; yet those sums allocated for this payment which are unused at the end of the year are generally used by that Department. I shall arrange this matter for you, or rather I shall show you how to go about arranging it yourself."

This conversation had no tangible results, but it showed me that Kutler could easily take on the color of the institution in which he was employed at a given time and that he was quite capable of acquiring a typical ministerial loyalty. In my opinion this was his most outstanding characteristic and can be noted throughout his entire career. He was a conscientious worker and a faithful executor of other people's ideas and instructions, but he had no convictions of his own and adjusted himself easily to every new set of conditions. Later, as Head of the Chief Administration for Land Organization and Agriculture,[1] he at first took the stand of a protector of large-scale agricultural economy and profit-yielding estates; but when he was ordered to compose a project providing for the expropriation of a part of the privately owned land he applied all his talents to this new task. Because of the failure of the project and the perfidy of Witte, who ascribed to him the initiative in composing this project, Kutler was obliged to leave state service. After this he considered himself a Cadet and, when a member of the Second Duma, composed another project on the expropriation of privately owned lands and began to advocate socialist principles. Not having been elected to the Third Duma, he entered the banking business and became a fervent defender of the interests of capital and large-scale industry. Then, after the February Revolution of 1917 he was elected chairman of the permanent council for the congresses of trade and industry. Here he assisted the newly formed union of landowners[2] by apportioning to it a rather substantial subsidy from the sums at the disposal of his council. But his adaptability reached its peak when under the Bolshevik rule he became manager of the State Bank, which he managed in the face of many difficulties, but probably quite conscientiously, until his death.

Mirsky's confidant in the ministry was E. A. Vatatsi, Director of the Department for General Affairs. Mirsky had become acquainted with Vatatsi when Vatatsi was Governor of Kovno and later Governor of Kharkov. Vatatsi had begun his career as commissioner for the affairs of the peasantry in one of the gubernias of the Kingdom of Poland, where he acquired the reputation of being very active, well-informed, and ambitious. My impression of him is that he was intelligent but without any definite political orientation. He was content to execute conscientiously the work assigned to him without setting himself any task of real state significance. He valued his office highly because to him it was the source of his livelihood and a means of advancing his career. Naturally, therefore, he was most anxious to be on good terms with his superiors and his colleagues, and for this purpose his innate good nature stood him in good stead. He was not inclined to intrigue and had made his way by straightforward endeavor and by studying the currents of thought and the ideas predominant among his immediate chiefs. Unfortunately he never showed enough initiative to occupy the position of first rank. He and Mirsky were well suited to each other and their characters had much in common. They were both full of the best intentions, both incapable of serious contention with anyone, and both somewhat acquainted with political "Manilovism." It is easy to understand that Vatatsi was not the man to help Mirsky fight Witte when the latter desired to strip Mirsky of all political importance.

Mirsky was indifferent toward the peasant problem; he was so indifferent, in fact, that he even declined to take a part in the debates on this problem in the Special Conference. This was in marked contrast to the tremendous energy of Witte, who speeded up the compilation of the decisions of local agricultural committees, a compilation which was facilitated by the fact that many of the local committees had not examined the peasant problem because it had not been included in the list of questions submitted to them. Witte also saw the necessity of stating the principles which in his opinion would have to form the basis of the new peasant legislation. In a clever memorandum written by A. A. Rittikh[3] at his direction, Witte expounded the sound opinion that the legislators of a country must strive to have the same legislation for all classes of the population, the same administrative institutions, and the same courts of justice. From this he drew the conclusion that the revision of peasant legislation had at least to aim at unifying the peasants and the other classes by making them subject to the same administration and courts, and not at separating them further.

This memorandum touched but slightly, however, the question of land tenure—that is, of the land commune—and drew no conclusions on this subject. It is evident that at that time Witte was concerned chiefly about the political and not the economic aspect of the peasant problem. This point of view was a strange one for an economist and can probably be explained by the fact that he saw in the proposed change of the civil status of the peasantry a mighty means for reviving the economic life of the masses. This point of view was largely the result of his slight knowledge of peasant life; but it was further strengthened by the fact that, although advanced public opinion was more or less agreed on the question of unifying the peasant class with the other classes as regards administration and courts, there was no agreement on the question of the land commune.

Witte staged the Special Conference debate on the peasant problem with great ceremony. Nearly every man of the bureaucratic circles who considered himself an authority on peasant common law was present. There were the partisans of the existing order headed by P. P. Semenov-Tian-Shansky, who had taken part in the reform of 1861, and including I. L. Goremykin, N. A. Khvostov, Ober-Prokuror of the Second Department of the Senate, and, of course, A. S. Stishinsky. There were also those who strongly favored the abandonment of the principles proclaimed on February 19, 1861. Among these were Senator M. A. Evreinov, who had set down in print his opinion in favor of the all-class volost; A. P. Nikolsky, author of the series of articles "Krestiane, obshchina i X tom" ("Peasants, Commune, and Volume X"); and, of course, Prince A. D. Obolensky, who again displayed the usual chaos of his ideas. Witte even tried to give the conference a certain scholarly tinge by inviting Professors A. S. Posnikov,[4] L. I. Petrazhitsky, D. I. Pikhno,[5] and Gulevich[6] to attend; he had first inspired them with the ideas he desired to have expressed in the conference. Not one of the invited professors spoke in favor of abolishing the commune. On the contrary, Professor A. S. Posnikov, who had written some scholarly works on this subject, defended it. But the professors were in favor of abolishing separate administration and separate courts for the peasants, except when such a step involved the complete giving up of the usages of peasant common law. Here even Professor Petrazhitsky, the eminent authority on civil law, made certain reservations; he held to his favorite theory that civil law must be built up on the intuitive concept of right in human minds.

Great importance was attached to the decisions of the Special Conference, as could be judged by the fact that its sessions were attended by the former Court Minister, Count Vorontsov-Dashkov, who seldom honored even the State Council with his presence, and by Minister of Agriculture Ermolov, Minister of Justice Muravev, and Minister of Finance Kokovtsov. Meetings were held in the great hall of the Council of the Minister of Finance. About sixty persons attended. There was in addition a large secretarial staff of several score. At first the secretary of the conference was I. P. Shipov, Director of the State Treasury Department and later Minister of Finance in Witte's cabinet. But, after Witte had joined the ranks of those who insisted on the abolition of the commune, Shipov, who was a partisan of the commune, was supplanted by A. I. Putilov, an advocate of individual landownership.

Witte himself appeared at sessions only after he had been informed that the rest of the members had assembled. He greeted only those who were seated along his way to the chairman's desk, then opened the sessions immediately. His manner was simple but forceful. His part seemed to be that of host. A crystal cigarette box framed in metal generally stood on the table before him and he wore around his wrist a rosary which he slipped through his fingers slowly but continually. His manner was easy, natural, and informal; he seemed to show a marked consideration for the professors, but he treated the rest impartially, regardless of official position.

It would be an error to say that Witte had a talent for presiding at official gatherings and for directing discussions. But thanks to the nature of the matter discussed and to the rather remarkable composition of the gathering the sessions of the conference were extremely interesting. The peasant question had been divided into three basic parts: self-government, class courts, and land tenure. But, as each part was very complicated and extensive, it often happened that at some one session different aspects of the general question would be discussed. Witte never summarized the opinions expressed. Indeed, this would have been difficult to do, since the discussion dealt not with concrete regulations but with general theoretical principles. The conference appeared more like a political salon discussing world affairs than a state institution seriously debating actual problems of state with the intention of initiating a reform with definite rules and regulations. Such summaries or briefs were made, however, by the secretariat from time to time. These briefs were subjected to another series of short debates and then voted upon.

Witte unquestionably had some influence on the decisions adopted, but he exercised this influence mostly outside the conference room in private conversations with individual members. He seldom expressed himself during the sessions and then briefly. He did not risk engaging in a detailed debate on problems with which he was not too familiar and toward which he had a definite attitude rather than a definite opinion. I mean that he was decidedly against the isolation of the peasants as a class, but he was unable to see how this isolation could be done away with. He did have, however, a clearer idea of how the peasants might be unified with the other classes in the field of local self-government, namely, by the creation of a small zemstvo unit.

It was about this question of introducing a small zemstvo unit that the debates first centered. From the outset the majority favored the all-class small zemstvo unit and the minority opposed it; for although the members of the conference were supposed to have been impartially selected and supposedly represented two diametrically opposed trends of thought, actually there was a majority that would render the final decision in the spirit desired by Witte.

According to the organization of the conference, ministers were supposed to attend personally, since they had been appointed individually and were not permitted to delegate anyone to take their places. In spite of this, however, Mirsky attended only two sessions, if I remember correctly, and even then took no part in the debates. Because of Mirsky's absence the Ministry of the Interior did not participate *de jure* in the conference debates on the peasant problem; but *de facto* it was represented by three persons: Kutler, Krivoshein, and myself. Mirsky gave us no instructions, however; so each of us defended his own personal point of view. Krivoshein expressed his opinion but once, and this did not bear on the peasant problem, properly speaking, but on some related matter of peasant colonization. Kutler and I sometimes expressed directly opposite opinions.

Such a variance of opinion was very little to Witte's liking. He was also disappointed in the fact that Kutler did not justify his expectations and failed to present the opinion of the Ministry of the Interior on the question of peasant legislation in accord with his, Witte's, directions. Witte's desire to bring the Ministry of the Interior to share his views was revealed with particular clarity during the debates concerning the volost courts. As Witte wished to bind Mirsky by a formal declaration that these courts should be abolished, he took pains to ask Mirsky to attend the session in which this matter was to be debated. Mirsky complied with Witte's request but maintained an absolute silence. Finally, Witte asked him directly what stand the Ministry of the Interior took on this matter. Mirsky was in a very difficult position. He had taken no part in the sessions and had no clear understanding of the matter under discussion. In his confusion, he muttered a few words which could have been interpreted to mean anything or nothing at all. Witte, however, hastened to explain them to mean what he desired. This completed the estrangement between Mirsky and Witte which had begun when Witte took it upon himself to carry through the liberal reforms Mirsky had suggested. The next day Mirsky said to me: "Say and do what you wish in Witte's conference, I shall not attend it again. I am quite aware that he wants to corner me; but since I do not yet understand the question, I cannot bind myself by expressing a definite opinion."

Meanwhile the debates on the small zemstvo unit went on. The preceding summer I had investigated the work of the volost boards of several uezds of three different gubernias, and this investigation had definitely shown me that local economic interests would not necessarily benefit from an inclusion in the volost communities of all persons of other classes residing within the volost and possessing real property there. Nor, would the volost communities profit from the combining of small volosts into larger ones; for with the fewer volost centers which would have resulted from such a combination it would have been difficult for the population, because of the poor condition of our roads, to address their individual problems to the volost administrations. Furthermore, the proposed transformation of volost communities, which so far had been purely peasant-class institutions, into all-class communities would in a vast number of cases not effect any favorable results, since many volosts contained no large estates. Therefore the pecuniary means by which such volosts could satisfy various local needs would remain just as paltry as before. I explained to the conference that most small zemstvo units constructed on the principle of all-class organizations would have just enough surplus means to support one volost communal rooster. On the other hand, those volosts which contained either large private properties or industrial enterprises would obtain enough money from volost taxation of these properties to place them in a privileged position as compared with other volosts.

In contrast to this I enthusiastically advocated the English system of the lower branches of local self-government. In England, each of the four main branches of local economy—schools, public health, social welfare, and highways—has its own territorial district whose area is determined by the needs of the sections, the density of the population, and the ability to pay taxes. Thus school districts are tiny territorial units. Public health covers a larger area such as can be adequately served by one hospital. Social welfare may be extended over a still wider territory, since it is manifest mainly in such organizations as orphanages, poorhouses, and similar institutions. Finally, the districts supervising communications are the largest, since, on the one hand, the costliness of road construction necessitates public groups of a rather high capacity to pay, and, on the other, the very nature of the work—the connecting of adjacent and far-flung localities—makes larger territorial units desirable. Other different social needs are satisfied by other larger groupings or counties.

The major part of my report on my investigation consisted of general recommendations which would, in my opinion, assure improved public welfare. The report also contained a scheme of reform which provided that the lower rural unit would be an allclass institution. But I also pointed out that the peasant volost organization would have to be transformed into a purely administrative unit which would attend to the needs both of the local population of all classes and of the state. This new volost unit would have to be under the jurisdiction of the local representatives of the government and would have to be supported by the State Treasury; the offices of the volost, however, would be filled by election as before. My scheme interested several members of the conference but brought no concrete results.

The longer the conference lasted the more convinced I became that it was impossible to expect it to produce any tangible results, and that in such an assembly the reform of peasant legislation would progress at a snail's pace. I saw more clearly than ever that Witte was aiming to secure a wholesale rejection of the projects for the new peasant legislation worked out by the Ministry of the Interior and to have the whole question re-examined by some new inter-ministerial institution which he would dominate. Such an institution might be the Committee of Ministers or this very Special Conference supplemented by a special organization to assist in the work. I did not look forward with pleasure to such a turn of events, because I did not intend to let the problem out of my control. I still thought that the speediest way to solve the peasant problem and to secure the passage of peasant legislation was to let the Ministry of the Interior do more work on it, and to make provision for changes and alterations when necessary. This would have meant, however, that the gubernia conferences[7] which were at that time examining the projects would have had to continue their work energetically.

The Ukase of December 12 had announced that the present question was being examined by Witte's Special Conference from a new angle. As a consequence of this announcement the gubernia conferences mentioned above gave up all desire to examine matters which seemed already to have been rejected. I realized this situation and endeavored to prevail upon Mirsky to address a circular letter to all the governors announcing that the work outlined by the Ministry of the Interior had not lost its importance and that the gubernias should carry it through to its conclusion. I pointed out to him that such a letter was quite permissible in the light of the Ukase of December 12 but would be effective only if based upon a corresponding decision of the Tsar. But Prince Mirsky did not immediately agree, and I had to turn to Vatatsi for help. The latter was attracted by the idea of revenge on Witte, who had deprived Mirsky of the initiative in proposing general political reforms. Both Mirsky and Vatatsi realized, of course, that the circular letter would be a blow against the Special Conference in its study of the peasant problem but primarily against Witte, who was glorying in his victory after a long feud with the Ministry of the Interior. Finally, Mirsky agreed to my suggestion.

We prepared in perfect secrecy a most humble report to the

Tsar and at the same time drafted a circular letter to the governors. Mirsky presented the report to Nicholas II on December 31, 1904, and on the same day the letter, signed by the Minister of the Interior, was dispatched to *Pravitelstvennyi Vestnik*. It was published in the New Year's number, which was always most widely distributed since it contained the list of people granted promotions and decorations on New Year's Day. The circular letter stated that it had been written in accord with the Sovereign's wishes and that the decisions of the gubernia conferences as "expressed by persons especially called in for this task, persons close to the rural population and well acquainted with its peculiar characteristics," would constitute the fundamental material upon which the final edition of the peasant laws would be based. This statement was of particular significance, since by inference it relegated the Special Conference to a position of secondary importance. The letter also explained that the gubernia conferences were to discuss matters freely, since "it is important to obtain from them not a mere confirmation of the projects submitted for their examination but an expression of the opinions prevailing in the circles well acquainted with rural life."

The letter caused quite a shock among the members of the Special Conference; the minority were very much pleased with it, but the majority criticized it vehemently. Witte was very much put out by it. He was very cold toward me during the session following its publication, and I believe he took Kutler to task. The latter had not been initiated into the secret of its composition, but he had taken no exception to it when it was published; in fact, he considered it entirely just that the ministry should try to defend the importance of its own work. After a few days, however, his attitude changed markedly. Nevertheless, the work of the Special Conference went on and finally took up the question of the land commune.*

By making the question of the commune the last item on the agenda Witte showed how little he understood the peasant problem, for a solution of the problems of peasant self-government and

* The discussion of this question took place after the resignation of Prince Mirsky and the appointment of his successor, A. G. Bulygin. As I recall, Bulygin was not even made a member of the Special Conference and certainly took no part in its work. I think it advisable, therefore, to continue the description of the Conference and its work in this chapter dealing with the ministry of Prince Mirsky.

courts, and particularly of the practice by these courts of peasant common law, depended upon the solving of the problem of the commune. This problem, as I have said repeatedly, seemed to me one of fundamental importance, not only because it was closely connected with the organization of peasant life but also because it was bound to affect the whole political and economic future of the empire; and I took advantage of my first opportunity to express my point of view. I made a speech giving in detail all my reasons for thinking that the commune was not something peculiar to Russian peasantry but merely a primitive form of land tenure through which all peoples had passed at some period of their economic development. In conclusion I enumerated the concrete measures which, in my opinion, would have to be adopted in order to facilitate the transition of the peasants from communal to individual landownership and land tenure. These measures were later incorporated in the Ukase of November 9, 1906.

Witte listened very attentively to my speech and after the session he sought me out and shook my hand. "I agree with you perfectly," he said. I must admit that from that day on Witte's attitude toward me changed markedly, and subsequently we had many friendly talks on many different subjects.

But the debates on the question of the land commune went on and on. Professor Posnikov, Stishinsky, Khvostov, and, as far as I can remember, Kolachev,[8] who was considered an authority on peasant common law, argued with particular ardor in favor of preserving the commune. Practically no one favored its abolition. A. P. Nikolsky enumerated in his rasping voice the defects of the commune but did not advance any concrete measures for its abolition.

Public and bureaucracy alike shied at this problem. Many persons admitted the faults of communal landownership, but very few openly favored its abolition. Of the many uezd agricultural committees, for instance, not one had dared to face the question squarely and to propose drastic measures for its solution. The commune seemed to be a sort of fetish. It was represented as a form of land tenure so suited to the Russian population that no one could even dream of doing away with it. For a long time Witte had entertained the latter opinion, and this explains why he made the peasant question a political issue. Socialists of all denominations were also partisans of the commune, and the Russian public, even that part of it which was unaffected by socialist influences, did not have the courage to express itself in favor of measures which in the opinion of some were opposed to the welfare of the population. Many Russians considered socialist teachings unattainable but would concede that should they be partially realized the majority of mankind would benefit therefrom. Only a few understood that the idea of the all-round material equality of man was not only fantastic but positively harmful and conducive not to the betterment, but to the deterioration of the living conditions of mankind. People were unwilling to recognize the justness of the old Roman axiom: *"Humanum paucis vivit genus,"* and that mob rule makes not for progress but for degeneration, both material and spiritual. It was considered especially unseemly in Russia to stand for measures which were anti-socialist in spirit. This goes far to explain the shyness of our public toward the matter of abolishing the commune.

The story of the sudden closing of the conference on March 30 is not without interest. Plehve's death had not rid Witte of all his personal and political enemies. Of these the most powerful, the most steadfast, and the most resolute was I. L. Goremykin, who, thanks to Witte, had in 1899 lost both his position as Minister of the Interior and the Emperor's favor. After 1899 he had continued to serve as a member of the State Council but attended only its general sessions. He was deprived of all means of carrying on an active fight against his enemy, Witte.

Toward the end of 1904 and early in 1905 the tables began to turn. At this time Witte was beginning again to lose the Emperor's favor, and Goremykin, abetted by the Trepov brothers,*

---

* A few words should be said about these two brothers, D. F. and V. F.[9] Trepov. D. F. Trepov's outstanding trait was his unshakable and unbounded devotion to the Tsar. In his mind Russia took second place to the Romanov dynasty. He was poorly educated and of limited intelligence. He had graduated from an institution where, as Shchedrin[10] puts it, the studies were mastered on horseback, and since then he had seldom opened a book other than the Manual of Cavalry Service. He lacked stability of thought and action, and was given to enthusiasms that often brought him face to face with unexpected situations. He would boldly undertake any scheme, since he lacked the foresight to see where it would lead him. In the spring of 1906, for instance, fearful for the dynasty, he negotiated with the Cadets who were attached to the government in the First Duma, although such an action went against the sentiment deeply embedded in his mind: loyalty to monarchism. But with all these shortcomings, he made a good first impression. His manners were good and his tone one of sincerity. On one occasion Prince S. D.

Krivoshein, and some others, conspired to exploit this situation. The first move was to make use of Goremykin's membership in the Special Conference. When this conference tackled the peasant problem, Goremykin began assiduously to attend its sessions. He seldom expressed an opinion, but when he did speak he showed clearly his disagreement with Witte's handling of the problem. It gave him particular satisfaction to point out Witte's inconsistencies

---

Urusov said of him from the Duma tribune that he was "by education a sergeant, by vocation a pogrom-maker"; but this certainly was untrue. Even Witte, who has little good to say in his memoirs of D. F. Trepov, denied the latter allegation.

D. F. Trepov became associated with the Goremykin circle after his appointment as Governor-General of St. Petersburg in 1905. This association was due to the fact that his brother, V. F. Trepov, was a good friend of Goremykin and had been director of a department in the Ministry of the Interior during Goremykin's ministry. It was also due to the fact that Goremykin in his campaign against Witte could make use of D. F. Trepov, who, as Governor-General of St. Petersburg, was able to win the Tsar's confidence. V. F. Trepov was at that time Senator in the First (Administrative) Department of the Senate. He was little better educated than his brother but was a man of innate common sense. In addition, he had an acute business sense, a strong will, and an amazing persistency of purpose. His conservative and monarchist sympathies were as strong as those of his brother; yet to him the monarchy was not an end in itself but a means of developing the welfare of the country. He realized also that it was impossible to preserve the autocratic regime if the basis upon which it was founded was undermined. This basis, in his opinion, was the class structure of society. It was true that the class structure of Russian society was gradually breaking down and was actually preserved only in the form of various regulations scattered throughout the sixteen volumes of the code. At least the outward appearance of this structure, however, was still being preserved.

Consequently, when Witte vociferously criticized the order of things in the empire and proclaimed the necessity of equalizing the peasants with the rest of the classes, V. F. Trepov joined forces with Goremykin to break Witte and, if possible, to take the solution of the peasant problem into his own hands. Krivoshein also joined this circle. As intimated, it was the circle's purpose to work through D. F. Trepov in order to win the favor of the Tsar. But the problem of influencing D. F. Trepov was a real one. Like most weak men, D. F. Trepov resented the feeling that he was being bossed, and had to be handled with care and skill. V. F. Trepov, with his fiery temper and impetuous nature, was not suited to this task. The circle thought that the desired influence might be exerted through memoranda written in an academic and restrained style. Krivoshein persuaded a certain N. V. Plehve to compose these memoranda. N. V. Plehve was a dull individual; but he had a clever pen and could give vivid and pointed expression to other people's thoughts, and in due time the memoranda he prepared for the circle had their effect. When Witte was Chairman of the Council of Ministers and D. F. Trepov was Palace Commandant, the latter was influenced against Witte by Plehve's memoranda and in turn influenced the Tsar also against Witte. The culmination of this anti-Witte campaign came in the spring of 1906 when Witte was dismissed as Chairman of the Council of Ministers and Goremykin was appointed his successor.

and discrepancies, accusing him of now criticizing those government measures which he had approved during his ministry. The particular point in question concerned the repeal in 1895 of Article 165 of the regulation dealing with the redemption of peasant allotments. This article had provided that each peasant member of a commune could make the allotment his private property by completely paying for it within the time limit prescribed by law, and its repeal had erected the main obstacle to the gradual disappearance of the commune. Goremykin pointed out that it was Witte who had most urgently advocated the repeal of this article and had most vigorously defended his stand in the State Council. Now, however, Witte was all in favor of doing away with the commune!

Witte naturally hated to have his inconsistencies and errors revealed. He hotly denied Goremykin's accusations, but to no great avail. Goremykin and his associates were successfully exploiting Witte's loss of favor with the Emperor and within a week the Special Conference was closed by Imperial order and a new conference on the problem of peasant tenure was established under the chairmanship of Goremykin. After almost five years of inactivity Goremykin was recalled to active service; and his recall was at the expense of Witte, his enemy and the cause of his inactivity.

I cannot refrain from relating here an incident which took place at the last session of the Special Conference which was very characteristic of those times and of Goremykin. It occurred at the evening session of March 30, 1905.

Legally, the conference had ceased to exist, for that morning the state acts closing the conference had been signed by the Tsar, the new conference had been ordered, and the rescript had been delivered to Goremykin. But this did not prevent Goremykin from bringing to the session documents proving that in 1895 Witte actually had supported the measures intended to preserve the commune. I can still see the slightly stooped figure of Goremykin as he entered the conference room followed by an orderly carrying two huge folios, the briefs of the State Council containing the papers and documents on the 1895 debates concerning the repeal of Article 165 mentioned above. Goremykin, perfectly composed, opened the folios at places previously marked, and as soon as the conference opened he asked for permission to speak. Stroking his long, silky side whiskers—a familiar gesture—he began to read aloud the arguments which Witte had advanced nine years before in favor of retaining the communal form of land tenure until the end of the term set for the redemption operations.*

To those who knew that the conference had already been closed this spectacle was curious, even painful. Unquestionably Goremykin appeared at the session not only for the purpose of gloating over his defeated enemy but also to avert the accusation that he was responsible for the closing of the conference; he probably intended to convey the impression that the closing of the conference was as unexpected to him as it was to others. Yet, in the eyes of those few persons† who knew what had already taken place, Goremykin's behavior toward Witte smacked of the cruelty with which a cat plays with a mouse. Witte, to be sure, had many faults; but it cannot be denied that he put all his energy and all his strength into whatever matter engaged his attention. He lived in order to advance the interests of the state, and the more important these interests were the more passionately he devoted himself to them. When Witte closed this last session he announced the subject to be considered by the next conference; and, to me at least, his words seemed very tragic.

The purpose of the new conference, stated in the rescript to Goremykin, was to extend peasant land tenure and "strictly to preserve the principle of private landownership from all attempts to undermine it"; and, further, "to define as soon as possible the boundaries of peasant lands" in order "to inculcate in the minds of the people the idea that private property is sacred."

The statement of this purpose in the rescript was in no sense a criticism of Witte. It was the result of the widespread agrarian disorders which had occurred early in April and which were caused by the Socialist-Revolutionist propaganda, which had not ceased since the outbreaks in Poltava and Kharkov gubernias in April 1902. This propaganda had increased since the beginning of the

* In his memoirs[11] Witte states that he was in favor of abolishing peasant redemption payments for the allotted lands. But to what period does he refer? In 1895 he was so little in favor of this measure that he deprived individual peasants of the right to redeem their allotments before the legal term expired, fearing that such redemption would make it easier for the well-to-do peasants to leave the communes, thereby making it more difficult to collect the rest of the redemption dues from the remaining members who were collectively responsible for their payment.

† Among these was Krivoshein, who had told me the sensational news before Goremykin's entrance.

Russo-Japanese War, especially as the fortunes of the war went against us. The general dissatisfaction among the peasants, resulting mostly from the calling to arms of the reserves and the loss of prestige by the state resulting directly from our military defeats, offered fertile soil in which to sow seeds of propaganda for the forced expropriation of land from private landowners. Ordinarily, the transfer of the question of the commune to a conference headed by Goremykin would have been tantamount to sending it to a first-class mortuary, where it might rest in peace to the end of time. But the extraordinary events of these years did not permit this to happen.

If I may return to Prince Mirsky's administration, which had ended, as I have already said, before the close of the Special Conference, I should like to mention two more events which immediately preceded his resignation and which cast long shadows across the turbulent year of 1905.

The first of these took place on Epiphany Day, January 6, when, according to custom, there was a solemn procession of the Imperial family to the house church and an inspection of the troops. This ceremony was marked by its traditional dignity and splendor. A few small units of the guards, quartered in St. Petersburg and its vicinity, and some other troops were drawn up in the halls of the palace on both sides of the Imperial march to the church. The "gentlemen and ladies" privileged to attend the reception were ranged in pairs along the concert hall to form the head of the Tsar's procession. The masters of ceremonies, walking on both sides of this group, were as usual vainly striving to maintain a semblance of order and a straight line. Then they tapped on the floor with their long staffs, adorned with blue St. Andrew ribbons, to announce the appearance of the Tsar. The doors of the Malachite room, where the members of the Imperial family usually gathered before their appearance, were thrown open; and the Tsar, preceded by the Minister of the Imperial Court, made his entrance with the Tsarina. Behind them the rest of the Imperial family walked in pairs to the strains of the Preobrazhensky regimental march.[12]

The brave, open countenances of the giant guardsmen; the slender figures of the cavalrymen standing at attention; the battle-torn, historic colors over the heads of the soldiers; the words of military command rolling from room to room as the Tsar approached; the solemn chords of the military orchestras playing the march, "The Turks know, the Swedes know, the whole world

knows about us"; a clear day, with sunlight flooding the huge splendid halls of the palace; the glimmer of the gold lace on the uniforms
and of the formal court dresses of the ladies—all this made a
wonderful and unforgettable picture, which fascinated even those
who were accustomed to these ceremonies and made one forget
temporarily the unhappy war, its series of defeats, and the troubled,
uncertain conditions in the country.

Indeed, though court ceremonies in all their splendor failed to
arouse any particular emotions in those who attended them at all
frequently, church and military ceremonies favored with the Tsar's
presence always created a feeling of elation. National pride was
awakened. One was made to feel the enormity of the people's
might as represented and symbolized by the Monarch attended by
representatives of the spiritual and physical power of the country.
Those who saw the genuine enthusiasm of the Russian army during
the Tsar's inspections of parades, those who witnessed the elemental
surge of the people toward the Tsar's residence in moments of
crisis in Russian life in the hope of seeing there the personification of the power of the Russian state — these persons ought to
know how truly invincible was the might of Russia when spiritually
allied with her Tsar. Surely this feeling communicated itself to
the Monarch himself. It was but natural, therefore, that on January 6, 1905, the Tsar, whose face since the beginning of the war
had worn a sadder expression than ever before, seemed more composed and cheerful.

Meanwhile the ceremony went on, planned and arranged to the
minutest details. At a given moment, the troops with their colors
left the palace and in resounding measured tread proceeded down
the great Jordan staircase to the quay of the Neva to take their
appointed places there. When Mass in the palace chapel ended,
church processions from all the St. Petersburg churches gathered
by the Neva. Innumerable church banners and the gold-woven,
brocaded robes of the clergy, shimmering in all the colors of the
rainbow, made the palace quay into one huge church gathering
surrounded by military units. It was one of those religious and
military ceremonies which distinguished the Russian Imperial court
from the rest of the European courts and in which the spirit of the
old Muscovite empire, permeated with religious and secular powers,
which complemented each other and formed one whole, was still
alive.

Now the High Mass was ended. The Tsar, surrounded by his family and the higher military and civil authorities, followed the palace clergy and court church procession, descended to the quay, and entered under the canopy built on the ice of the river. While the court choir sang, the clergy lowered a cross into the waters of the Neva, and from the fortress of Sts. Peter and Paul the guns saluted. Detonation after detonation rang out over the river. Then suddenly they were followed by another, more rolling and peculiarly warlike in sound, recognizable to even an untrained ear. Those present looked at each other with anxiety and amazement. Those on the quay and those who had remained in the palace felt that something unexpected had happened. But the ceremony went on in its quiet, measured way. The church and military parade ended in its usual unruffled manner.

Those returning from the river to the palace did not at once learn that the mounted battery of the guards appointed to fire the salute and situated on the Vasilievsky Island near the building of the exchange across from the canopy on the river had fired—some said one, some said several—battle shells. These had killed a policeman, broken the staff of a banner not far from the Tsar, and broken several panes in the upper row of windows in the Nicholas hall. One of the bullets of the old-fashioned large type after breaking a pane had hit one of the golden platters adorning the walls and felled it to the floor. As I happened to be standing near by, I picked it up and passed it to some of the court officials standing by me.

How could this monstrous thing have happened? Was it merely an accident, the result of unforgivable negligence? Or was it deliberate? The investigation showed that the superior officers of the battery were not present at the time of the firing. They had left this matter to ordinary artillerymen; so the matter was explained as negligence. Davydov, the commander of the battery, and Captain Kartsev were court-martialed and sentenced to light punishment, from which they were later freed by the Tsar.

But was it nothing more than negligence? I do not know. It was certainly without precedent for the Imperial Guards, the Monarch's special protectors, to fire on their Monarch during a peaceful ceremony; yet it is interesting to note that the incident aroused no disturbing comment either in public (as I remember, it was not permitted to be published) or administrative circles. But even if it was a simple accident with comparatively negligible results, it showed very clearly that there was "something rotten in the State of Denmark."

But the impression produced by this incident was soon obliterated by another of graver consequence which took place only three days later, January 9. This incident is generally known as Gapon's demonstration.

Early in January 1904, thanks to Zubatov, the St. Petersburg society of factory workers had been formed. This society, whose official purpose was self-education, really aimed at inculcating in the workingmen's minds allegiance to the existing order and educating them to the idea that only the state could protect them from exploitation by capitalists. One of the most active members of this organization was the priest, Gapon, a person certainly above the average. He was ambitious and wanted to play a prominent role at any cost; but these passions were hardly detectable under his real spiritual fervor. During 1904 Gapon had succeeded in acquiring an exceptional influence among the workers. He had accomplished this by a fiery profession of allegiance to the interests of the workers and by explaining to them the extent to which they were being exploited by the capitalists. In this way he aroused in them a class hatred toward their employers and at the same time suggested the idea that the betterment of their lot was entirely dependent on the Tsar. In the meetings which he held in many factories, including the huge Putilov works, and in all of which he had branches of his society, one of Gapon's regular topics was the analysis of the relations between workers and employers.

Did Gapon work with revolutionary aims in view? Had he been connected with revolutionary circles since he began his work among the workers? Apparently not. It seems that at first he obediently carried out the instructions of the gendarmerie. Later, however, he probably became captivated by his role of defender of the interests of the proletariat and developed the opinion that no radical changes could be effected in the class organization of society except by radically changing the entire social structure and that this would be possible only through revolution. He must also have thought that even the unlimited will of the Monarch would be powerless to alter the state of things created by the capitalistic structure of society. With this realization he had come to an understanding with the leaders of the Socialist-Revolutionist party and from that time on not only worked in accord with them but also received their direct assistance. It is also probable that revolution was his main aim when he planned to extend his activity to Moscow and Kiev.

This plan, however, was nipped in the bud. If I remember correctly, Gapon appeared in Moscow in the spring of 1904, allegedly as a representative of the Police Department. But the civil authorities denied him permission to conduct workers' meetings, and the Grand Duke Sergei Aleksandrovich, Governor-General of Moscow, wrote a sharp letter to Plehve, then Minister of the Interior, stating that he could not permit agents of the Police Department to interfere with the work of the Moscow metropolitan gendarmerie. After receiving this letter Plehve issued a very strict order forbidding Gapon, under pain of direst consequences, to carry on his work anywhere outside of St. Petersburg. Nor was Gapon successful in trying to penetrate the Kiev working circles.

Although Gapon did not enjoy the complete confidence of the Police Department and the Minister of the Interior, the St. Petersburg Governor, Fullon,[13] trusted him implicitly. Fullon had been appointed to his responsible post on the recommendation of the Palace Commandant, P. P. Hesse, who had the Tsar's confidence; but the appointment was an unhappy one. He was a very well-brought-up, fashionable man, a pleasant conversationalist and an agreeable partner at whist but other than these he possessed very few accomplishments. As Governor of St. Petersburg he was hopelessly inefficient and utterly without courage.

Gapon had succeeded in charming Fullon to such an extent that the latter allowed his picture to be taken with Gapon at one of the branch meetings of the St. Petersburg factory workers. As the recipient of Fullon's confidence Gapon was in a position freely to disseminate revolutionary propaganda among the workers. In fact, after November 1904, revolutionary propaganda was spread among the members of nearly all of Gapon's workers' societies (twelve in number excluding the Kolomna branch situated outside the city). Besides spreading in these meetings propaganda which he had to camouflage with the formula "The Tsar and the People," Gapon carried on secret propaganda among selected workers. Here he expressed himself more openly and frankly insisted that a radical change of the entire social order was necessary. His closest collaborator in this work was the Socialist-Revolutionist Rutenberg,[14] through whom he kept in touch with the Socialist-Revolutionist party. But Gapon acted independently and never bound himself to follow the directions of the party. The selected workers who attended his special meetings were his own agents. Through them he sowed the seeds of open revolt among the workers and through them he accomplished the workers' strike which led to the events of January 9.

The strike began among the workers of the Putilov plant, who, on December 29, 1904, petitioned the management of the plant to take back four discharged workers and to discharge Tetiavin, the foreman responsible for the dismissal of the four. This was but a pretext, and a poor one at that, since only one of the four workers in question had been discharged; the other three had left of their own free will and not one of them had expressed a desire to be taken back. The management refused to grant the workers' petition. Whereupon the workers of the Putilov plant, prompted by Gapon's agents, announced on January 3 a general strike and at the same time made a series of new demands—the introduction of the eight-hour working day, an increase in rates for piece-work, and so on—and declared that until the demands were met they would not return to work. At the instigation of Gapon's agents nearly all of the St. Petersburg factories joined the strike. Even the printers had been attracted, partly by force, to the movement, so that beginning with January 7, 1905, the newspapers of the capital failed to appear. Finally, Gapon suggested to the workers that they should present a petition to the Tsar.

The strike was as unexpected by the Social Democrats as it was by the police. The latter considered Gapon their own agent and one who enjoyed the special confidence of the governor; consequently they did not supervise his activity. They trusted his reports of the events among the workers and were generally of the opinion that Gapon was carrying on his activities with the knowledge and approval of his superiors. It is interesting to note, however, that what the police did not know was well known to the Union of Liberation, which had tried to reach some understanding with Gapon in November 1904.

But the Social Democrats were more alive to opportunities. As soon as the strike had spread far enough they organized their own propaganda in all factories and came to a definite agreement with Gapon himself. As a result, the petition to the Tsar, composed by Gapon in collaboration with Maxim Gorky, was nothing but the

Social Democratic minimum program; and on January 7, at a conference between Gapon and the Social Democrats, the latter adopted Gapon's suggestion that the "party workers" be put behind the workers in order to keep the latter from retreating before the pressure of the police.[15]

The workers from all factories were to gather before the Winter Palace, coming together from five different directions. On the very eve of the demonstration the gendarmes, realizing that something was amiss and that Gapon was not acting in accordance with the directions of the Police Department, reported the news of the proposed petition to the authorities. By that time, however, Gapon had abandoned all secrecy and had sent a letter to the Tsar and one to Mirsky. In his letter to the Tsar he was still outwardly respectful and begged the Tsar to accept the petition from the workers of the capital, who were to gather from all quarters of the city to present it to him. In this letter he summarized the desires and hopes of the workers as stated in the petition.

Mirsky was caught unawares. In the evening of January 8 he hurriedly called a conference of several persons: the Minister of Justice, Muravev; the Minister of Finance, Kokovtsov; the Director of the Police Department, Lopukhin; the Chief of Staff of the troops, Meshetich; and, of course, Governor Fullon. The conference quickly and unanimously decided to arrest Gapon and to prevent the workers from assembling before the palace. It was suggested that the workers be stopped on the outskirts of the city; but General Meshetich said that this might be difficult to accomplish because of the location of the barracks, the late hour, and the many ways by which detached workers' groups could penetrate from the industrial district to the central part of the city. He suggested that it would be wiser, while carrying out the proposed plan, also to station troops near the palace. This suggestion was adopted.[16]

But Gapon was not arrested, and some of the workers' groups, joined along the way by a crowd of idle onlookers, did succeed in reaching points near the Winter Palace. The main body of workers, however, mostly Putilov workers, was stopped by the troops when it reached the Narva gates. The crowd stopped, too. Then Gapon cast off his mask of secrecy; he harangued the workers and urged them to clear their way by force. "If the Tsar refuses to see us, then we have no Tsar. So let us ourselves defend our rights." At this point the party workers began to work among the demonstrators. Red flags appeared here and there among the crowd, which had started out with church banners and portraits of the Tsar. The excited crowd moved forward. Then the soldiers fired; many victims fell. The crowd hesitated, then dispersed. Among those who fled was, of course, Gapon, whose long priestly hair was cut off by Rutenberg in some doorway. He hid at Gorky's house, where he took off his cassock and assumed the appearance of an ordinary citizen.

As for the rest of the workers' groups, only the one arriving from the Vasilievsky Island showed resistance. Halted at the bridges, it rushed to Schaaf's cold-steel factory, plundered it, then began to build barricades, behind which it took cover with its newly gained arms. But the barricades were captured by the troops and the demonstrators dispersed after only a few hours of street fighting.

The saddest fate awaited those workers' groups, joined by many ordinary curious citizens, which had penetrated to the neighborhood of the Winter Palace. These moved along neither thinking of violence nor expecting any. As they approached the Politseisky Bridge from the Nevsky Prospect, the Admiralteisky Prospect from the Gorokhovaia on one side, and the Troitsky Bridge along the Kamenno-Ostrovsky Prospect on the other side, they were warned and called on to disperse; but they continued to press forward, encouraged by the revolutionaries among them. Unquestionably also the workers were then in an excited state of mind, and many refused to believe they would be fired on from under the very windows of the palace which was their objective. But they were fired on, and after the first salvos they too dispersed.

Why had this demonstration been permitted? Why had Gapon not been arrested in the first place?

The reason for the failure to arrest Gapon is as follows: Gapon realized that the police would learn of his undertaking to present the petition before the undertaking had been carried out; so, making use of his friendship with Fullon, he took care to insure his own liberty. Apparently he assured Fullon that he, Gapon, had many enemies who were working for his undoing. He made Fullon promise on his word of honor that he, Gapon, would not be arrested, no matter what information was received concerning him, as he was working for the good of the country. Fullon, with blind faith in Gapon, gave his word. But Gapon was still not satisfied. "No," he said, "I want you to give me your soldier's word that I shall not be arrested." Why a soldier's word was to be more binding than that of anybody else, I do not know; but evidently Fullon thought it was, for after he had given it he felt he could not go back on it.

This story is almost incredible; but it is the reason which Fullon gave for letting Gapon go free.

All in all, there was something fateful about the whole affair. After Fullon had been ordered to arrest Gapon, why, for instance, could he not have told Prince Mirsky that he found it impossible to carry out the orders himself? Then the task could have been given to someone else. Gapon's arrest would unquestionably have stopped the workers' uprising as nothing else would. Later I had an opportunity to talk with some of the more educated and intelligent of the Putilov workers.* They said that some time previously the management of this factory, where Gapon had his headquarters, had begun to suspect that Gapon was not an agent of the government at all but was working with revolutionary aims in view. On January 8, the eve of the demonstration, this opinion had become so strong that the workers expected Gapon's arrest any minute, and when they came to the factory on the morning of January 9 they asked each other concernedly: "Is the father here? Has he not been arrested?" When they learned that he was there and free, they were convinced that they would be given a chance to see the Tsar and have all the demands of the petition granted.

This assurance of the Putilov workers lasted until they had reached the Narva gates. Here it was hard to stop them. But those comparatively small groups which had approached the Winter Palace could easily have been dispersed without the use of firearms. The military was in charge of the situation; and it had been ordered not to permit the workers to advance beyond a certain point, and to use firearms if need be. It can be said, therefore, that the military merely carried out orders.

There is no doubt that the demonstration of January 9 was arranged by Gapon and his allied revolutionists in order to make the workers hostile to the Tsar. Yet so well had Gapon masked his real purpose that the workers did not suspect it. The incident also showed the solidarity of ideas and the active co-operation be-

* I met these workers in the house of Ippolit Andreevich Hofstaedter [1860–   ], a contributor to the *Novoe Vremia.* He was a very talented and convinced supporter of the Narodnik views of the 'sixties, a fervent partisan of the formula, "The Tsar and the People," who had had relations with the more moderate workers' groups.

tween the more radical bourgeois elements and professed party workers. This solidarity was shown in the delegation which on January 8 waited upon Prince Mirsky, who refused to see it, and upon Witte, who had a long conversation with it. The delegation was composed of future Left Cadets such as Shakhmatov,[17] a member of the Academy of Science, Hessen,[18] Kedrov, and others, on the one side, and on the other, Miakotin, Poshekhonov, and Maxim Gorky, who at that time was taking an active part in revolutionary work and with whom Gapon was closely associated. This delegation insisted that the workers be permitted to see the Tsar. Its purpose was clear: it was eager to have an essentially revolutionary act legalized, and thus to insure its further unrestricted development. Further evidence of this solidarity was furnished on the night of January 9 when all these persons gathered in the rooms of the Free Economic Society[19] and discussed the events of the day with Gapon dressed in civilian clothes.*

The rumors cleverly spread by the revolutionists exaggerated the number of victims that had fallen on January 9. Reports concerning the excesses of the authorities, not only on the day of the demonstration but also later, spread all over the country from St. Petersburg. These reports filled the foreign press and were repeated by the Russian press abroad. An example of such reports of "eyewitnesses" may be found in the rather moderate Paris publication of P. B. Struve, *Osvobozhdenie,* which on January 27, 1905, "hastened to communicate a terrible fact." "On January 13,"

---

* Immediately afterward Gapon fled to Finland. His further activities are well known. He re-established contact with the Russian police and betrayed several party workers and Social Democrats. When the revolutionists learned of this, they enticed Gapon into an empty building on the outskirts of Terioki, where his former friend, Rutenberg, hanged him. His body was discovered several months later. I happened to meet this Rutenberg under most peculiar circumstances. Just before the French troops evacuated Odessa in April 1919 the commander of the Russian forces, General Schwartz, who was forced to leave Odessa after the French had retired, formed a Committee for the Defense of the City. This committee was composed of the Chief of Civil Affairs, Andro; Minister of Finance of the Volunteer Army, Bernatsky;[20] Control Manager, Iliashenko;[21] and Rutenberg. During the evacuation I was for some unknown reason added to this committee thereby becoming a colleague of Rutenberg, and, most surprising of all, found that I had much in common with him. It is interesting that the committee, without even changing its name, continued its activities for a month on the Isle of Halki near Constantinople, where the Russian troops from Odessa had been moved and to a degree interned. Here also were some refugees transported by the English from the Crimea, which the Whites had also evacuated.

said its correspondent, "on the corner of Bolshoi Prospect and Vvedenskaia in St. Petersburg, a horse car occupied partly by girl students of the medical school met some Cossacks. From the passing car the Cossacks caught the word, '*oprichniki*.' Whereupon the bus was stopped, the Cossacks took off two men, and before everybody's eyes began to beat them with their swords and to trample on them, so that in a few moments these men were nothing more than shapeless flesh. A wooden box was produced and the remains were put into it. After this," the correspondent continued, "one may well believe the rumors that on the Vasilievsky Island a Cossack slashed off the head of a student who passed by him in a cab."

The revolutionary press gathered whole columns of such "episodes," and despite their monstrous absurdity many people considered them to be true. The effect of these reports upon the growth of the revolutionary feeling in the country can easily be imagined.

Meanwhile the authorities were completely helpless. On January 9 Governor Fullon, the chief cause of the day's events, had remained in his house on the corner of the Admiralteisky Prospect and the Gorokhovaia and when he heard the firing not far away became panic-stricken. He ran through the reception rooms facing the street and with his own hands turned off all the lights. His fears haunted him during the next few days, when the city, although outwardly calm, was turned into a military camp. Police units were stationed on the street corners and Cossacks patrolled the streets.

On January 10 or 11 I had business with the governor and went to his house, after I had first telephoned to make sure he was in. When I arrived, I observed with amazement that the front door was locked. After much ringing of the doorbell, the door was opened a crack and the face of the porter peered out. I had known the man well in Warsaw, where he had been employed as porter by Chief of Police Kleigels, who had brought him to St. Petersburg when he had been appointed governor of the capital. The porter recognized me, opened the door a trifle wider, and let me into the dark vestibule. But only after he had locked the door again did he turn on the lights.

"What's going on here?" I asked in wonder.

"I have orders not to admit anyone and not to turn on the light. Let me take you to the General."

"You do not have to take me; I know the way."

"I beg your pardon, but the General is in his private rooms and is not leaving them."

He led me through some half-dark hallways and finally opened the door of a small room facing the yard. The only piece of furniture in this room was a large sofa, and upon this sofa I saw the governor of the metropolis, wrapped up in something that looked like a lady's dressing gown and with a skull-cap on his head.

"What has happened to you, Ivan Aleksandrovich?"

"I have a cold, I am not going out. Moreover, I am not governor any more."

"Then why didn't you tell me so when I telephoned you a moment ago?"

"I have not yet given up my duties, but I have been offered the post of Governor-General of Warsaw and Commander of the Forces of the Warsaw Military District."

This announcement stunned me. A miserable coward, who had so recently displayed utter inefficiency and woeful incapacity to preserve order in the city, who was shamefully transferring all his duties to the military command, who was devoid of all administrative talent and incapable of carrying out even police duties—this man was to be appointed commander of the most responsible military post of the empire, commander of a region where most of the Russian forces were concentrated and the administration of which was extremely complicated and difficult.*

From Fullon's place I went directly to Prince Mirsky. I told him in dismay all I had witnessed. But Mirsky's condition was only slightly better. His door was not barricaded, it is true, and he was not overcome with fear; but he lacked energy. When I finished speaking, he said that the post of Governor-General of St. Petersburg was to be filled by D. F. Trepov, who had just been relieved of his duties as Moscow Chief of Police, but that as he himself was not going to remain Minister of the Interior any longer these things did not really concern him.

The government was breaking in every joint. Prince Mirsky's administration, begun as an idyl, was ending in a bloody tragedy. Mirsky had been full of the best intentions; but he lacked even the elementary qualifications of a statesman. When he assumed office,

* As it turned out, however, Fullon was not appointed to Warsaw. He had to be satisfied with a post of commander of an army corps.

this weak-willed administrator had dreamed of pacifying the liberal public and of separating it from the revolutionary elements. But because of his political "Manilovism" all he accomplished was to increase the opposition of the liberal and educated elements of the public and strengthen its solidarity with the revolutionary elements, and to give the latter a powerful weapon with which to arouse the working proletariat against their Monarch. What better opportunity could have been given the underground revolutionists for the propagation of their teachings among the uncultured public masses than the shooting of several hundreds of men going peacefully and in good faith to present to their Tsar the statement of their wants?

The liberal press had its own opinion of Prince Mirsky's administration. The newspaper, *Rus,* speaking for all newspapers of the same orientation, said: "We thought that Mirsky's ministry should be called the ministry of transition from the regime of bureaucratic arbitrariness and brutal force to the regime of equity; from the governing of a great nation by police methods to the intelligent safeguarding of its needs; from discord between the government and the people to their friendly and fruitful co-operation."

Mirsky did strive sincerely to this end; but the methods he adopted were as little suited to his purpose as the purpose was indisputably and fundamentally sound. By pursuing such an aim he should have been able to win the Tsar's admiration for this purpose (the Tsar never had and never could have had any other purpose); but by using the means at his command incorrectly, he achieved deplorable results, discredited in the eyes of the Monarch the methods he had employed, and so prevented their use by other more experienced persons.

The events of January 9 had greatly alarmed the public and caused it to hope for a representative form of government and, if necessary, to call for aid from the forces opposed to the state. These events had also abetted the revolutionizing of the working masses; but they had also created a certain panic among the bureaucrats, convincing them that things could not go on as they were much longer and that a reform of the government was inevitable. This led some of these bureaucrats to look for a quiet haven in which to hide from the coming storm. Among these was Muravev, who gave up his ambition to become Minister of the Interior, although at that time, thanks to the increasing influence of Grand Duke Sergei Aleksandrovich, he had a good chance of getting that appointment.

On January 15, Prince Mirsky was dismissed. He was not even appointed a member of the State Council. On the same day the portfolio of Minister of the Interior was given to A. G. Bulygin, who on January 1 had succeeded Grand Duke Sergei Aleksandrovich as Governor-General of Moscow.

PART FOUR

The Revolution of 1905

CHAPTER XVIII

ALEKSANDR GRIGOREVICH BULYGIN AS MINISTER OF THE INTERIOR

The appointment of Plehve and of Prince Mirsky had aroused much interest and excitement among the bureaucrats as well as among the public; but the appointment of Bulygin as Mirsky's successor created no such stir. Public attention was entirely absorbed by the war with Japan and especially by the ever increasing public unrest, which was daily acquiring a more pronounced revolutionary character. This unrest was no longer manifested in mere demonstrations and resolutions of protest; more and more frequently it involved a violation of public peace and order. D. F. Trepov was appointed to combat this unrest, but his authority did not extend beyond the limits of St. Petersburg Gubernia. Nevertheless, the dictatorial rights assigned to him gave him virtually all control of internal affairs and made it evident that their future course would depend entirely upon him. The appointment of Bulygin as minister, a man whose career up to that time had not been at all outstanding, confirmed this opinion and therefore deprived his appointment of interest.

Bulygin, a landowner of Riazan Gubernia, belonged to that numerous group of local administrators who had been started on their careers by virtue of the fact that Count D. A. Tolstoi, Minister of the Interior under Alexander III, was a Riazan landowner and had selected as governors and vice-governors men of the nobility of his own gubernia who were well known to him. Bulygin had been appointed Vice-Governor of Samara, then Governor of Kaluga, and still later Governor of Moscow. In this last post he had met Grand Duke Sergei Aleksandrovich, who was then Governor-General of Moscow, and had become friendly with him and with D. F. Trepov, then Moscow Chief of Police. These friendships finally brought him his appointment as Minister of the Interior.

Bulygin was a pleasant and honest man. He was even more easygoing than Mirsky—not as a result of a desire to avoid disturbances which would ruffle his peace of mind but as a result of his innate good nature and liking for people. He was a good mixer, and was

355

soon able to find his way about among the complicated relations of court and public life in St. Petersburg. It was these very qualities of his which later won him the position of Manager of the Institutions of the Empress Marie. In this capacity, of course, he did not introduce any improvements in feminine education in Russia; but the principals of women's institutes and schools were charmed to have such a chief.

But Bulygin was no statesman. He was endowed with considerable common sense and had had some administrative experience, but he lacked general knowledge and the capacities for statesmanship. Politically he was a partisan of the autocratic regime, mainly, in my opinion, because he had never stopped to compare the merits of other forms of government; he had been born and raised and had lived and worked under an autocracy and had no clear understanding of any other form of government. He lacked Sipiagin's intuitive understanding of the significance of current events, but otherwise he was of much the same type: a Russian gentleman landowner who deferred to his monarch, regarded the bureaucracy with a supercilious air, and was at home only in his own provincial milieu of the zemstvo and the nobility. He knew this latter class well; he knew both its fondness for opposition to the government and its harmlessness as a revolutionary element. He was unaware, however, of recent changes in this class, of the fact that some of its members had become confirmed partisans of popular government, and that talented persons had appeared in the zemstvos, where they tried to create for themselves a position which for some reason or other they had been unable to reach or had failed to retain in the central government. Nor was he aware of the deep changes which had occurred in the peasant class, such as the appearance in its midst of a large number of people who belonged to it only in so far as it was so stated in their passports but who had absorbed the ideas of city dwellers and who in their outlook on life were far removed from the primitive conceptions of the rural masses of the 'seventies and even of the 'nineties. In the years that had elapsed since the catastrophe of Khodynka[1] in 1896 the masses of the rural population and especially those of suburban areas had undergone a great metamorphosis. In 1896 the crowd on the Khodynka, even with hundreds of dead in its ranks, had enthusiastically acclaimed the Tsar. Had the same catastrophe occurred eight years later this crowd would have given vent to other feelings.

The name of Bulygin is associated with the first project for the creation of the State Duma, a project which planned to give the Duma merely advisory powers. Not that the project reflected Bulygin's ideas, for his only connection with the first draft of the project was as chairman of the commission which accepted it.

At this point I should like to say a few words about this commission. It was composed of A. I. Putilov, representing the Ministry of Finance; Ivanovsky,[2] Professor of Constitutional Law; Fedor Dmitrievich Samarin,[3] a prominent member of a very conservative Moscow slavophile society; and S. E. Kryzhanovsky, Assistant Head of the Chief Administration for the Affairs of Local Economy, who did all the work of the commission.

Bulygin had been given no definite instructions concerning the character of the proposed reform and had no clearly defined ideas as to what form it should take. Professor Ivanovsky neither suggested any scheme for the solution of this important question nor took an active part in the debates on the subject. Samarin expressed some ideas and even put his suggestions in writing, but these were concerned with gubernia and uezd advisory organizations and not with the establishment of a central advisory institution for the empire. F. D. Samarin, like his brother A. D. Samarin,[4] who later became Ober-Prokuror of the Holy Synod, was a man of fine character but without creative imagination. His ideas were those of a typical slavophile of the 'sixties in that he always dealt in general abstractions not unmixed with mysticism. The conception of Byzantine autocracy administered by police methods was entirely foreign to his mind; but he was utterly unable to express in concrete and practical legislative terms the spiritual alliance which he believed to exist between the supreme authority and the masses of the population, and which would justify and sanctify the power of the supreme authority. A. I. Putilov, as representative of the Ministry of Finance, was concerned with protecting the state budget from attacks by the people's representatives. He was the author of those complicated rules and regulations thanks to which, as people used to say later, the state budget was practically armor-plated against the attack of the people's representatives.

Bulygin's commission did not discuss the most important point of all, namely, the system of election to the proposed Duma. It was content to adopt the system suggested by Kryzhanovsky, which was similar to the system in effect for electing the members of the zemstvo assemblies. The whole idea of having a representative body share in the government found no favor in Bulygin's sight. He was in haste to complete the task with which he had been charged and considered the project drafted by his conference as but a preliminary foundation stage of the work to be done by Count Solsky's conference.

This latter conference included, as I have already said, all members of the Council of Ministers. Its duty was to present the final edition of the project to the Tsar. When it began to examine Bulygin's project, Witte propounded at some length the principle, later adopted, that the peasants who actively worked the land should be assured a majority in the Duma. In Russia, he said, this class constituted the majority of the population. It was also the element most reliable for the safeguarding of the existing order. And although Witte was soon delegated to go to the United States to negotiate a treaty of peace with Japan, the opinion he expressed remained the dominant one in the study which Solsky's conference made of the project.

The principle he propounded could very easily have been applied by eliminating the peasant uezd electoral assemblies, as was proposed in the Bulygin project, and by including the volost electors in the all-class gubernia electoral assemblies, so that the peasants would be in a majority in these latter bodies. At the last moment, however, after the third reading of the project, the conference reopened its discussion on this basic question of election. It did so under the influence of a memorandum written by Kryzhanovsky and signed by Bulygin. This memorandum contended that had the question been one merely of ascertaining the sentiments of the population and its relations to the basic questions of national life, the appeal to the representatives of the peasants would have been justifiable, but, since the Duma was to deliberate upon complicated legislative projects pertaining to the most varied questions of national existence, it would be a mistake to leave this responsible task to persons the majority of whom did not possess adequate information. The majority, it continued, would be unable to grasp even the title of a proposed measure, let alone its essence. Solsky insisted that the project undergo a fourth reading; but, in spite of his statement that he too was somewhat confused by the principle advocated by Witte which had been adopted, no serious changes were made. Later, in June 1905, the draft of the statute concerning the State Duma was discussed at Peterhof by a conference over which the Tsar presided; but the unimportant corrections made there did not alter its general character.

Meanwhile Bulygin was little concerned with the whole affair. He took no part in the final revision of the project bearing his name; this revision was done by the Imperial Chancellery. Bulygin did not realize the profound significance of the proposed reform. He thought that a State Duma would be similar to an All-Russian zemstvo assembly and seemed persuaded that its role would be purely advisory. His lack of understanding of the whole matter is revealed by his amazement at reading Kryzhanovsky's memorandum, which pointed out that it was imperative to co-ordinate the new Duma with existing state institutions, and that this could be done by changing the latter. It mentioned that the State Council might thus be reformed and expressed the need of reorganizing the entire central government under the direction of one will and of fostering in it a common understanding of state problems. "Why?" asked Bulygin, "That is the business of the generations to come."

Bulygin had shown that he was not the man to initiate a fundamental change in the state structure. Even in his own ministry he had no influence either upon the tasks in hand or upon the personnel. Under him even more than under Mirsky the departments of the ministry acquired the character of independent institutions engaged in nothing more serious than routine work. There was no trace of any legislative work in any department; initiative in legislation was totally lacking; even the work undertaken by Bulygin's predecessors was abandoned. This situation was the result not only of Bulygin's character but also, and perhaps to a greater degree, of the general spirit of the times. Even the most pressing demands of national existence had been relegated to a secondary position by current events, which were becoming more revolutionary. Everyone, including even the bureaucrats, was anxiously concerned about problems of government organization; and the need of popular participation in the government was increasingly realized. Such preoccupation deprived most of the bureaucrats of energy for anything except routine work; but some of the more alert ones applied themselves to doing something really constructive in this national crisis. The state apparatus had virtually ceased to function as a factor of national life; it had become a mere mechanism serving current public needs. The courts were active; the treasury collected taxes; the institutions which had no organic connection with the state government, such as the liquor monopoly, the post and telegraph, the state railways, and the branches of the State Bank, all continued to function; but the central institutions, which had managed the state for nearly a century, seemed suddenly to lose the very reason for their existence.

Government was really concentrated in the hands of one person, D. F. Trepov, who swayed like a reed in the wind and adopted contradictory measures. On May 21, 1905, Trepov was appointed Assistant Minister of the Interior and Head of the Police Department. This did not mean, however, that his activity was to be directed by Bulygin. It simply meant that the control of the entire secret police had been completely taken away from Bulygin, and that Bulygin was no longer of any political significance. The special ukase issued on this occasion placed Trepov in a position, if not superior to, then certainly independent of his official chief. Bulygin had known nothing of the projected change; he may have learned of it first from the daily papers which reported that the former Third Section of His Majesty's Private Chancellery had been actually restored with the one difference that it remained officially a part of the Ministry of the Interior; therefore at least outwardly the responsibility for its actions would have to be borne by the Minister of the Interior. Bulygin realized perfectly the false position in which he had been placed and submitted his written resignation, which Nicholas II rejected with a sharp comment to the effect that ministers do not tender their resignations but are dismissed by the Tsar. As Bulygin was a gentle soul, and nothing if not a loyal subject, he bowed before the Tsar's will. Later he used to say that he had had so little influence upon the internal policy of the empire that even the news of an important political undertaking reached him only through the papers. Yet from what I knew of Bulygin I suspect he was not overly distressed at being relieved of the routine work connected with the Police Department; for thus he acquired more time to spend on his favorite occupation—whist. As his steady partner in this game he selected Vatatsi, the Director of the Department for General Affairs, who was always on the best of terms with his chiefs.*

* Only once did I see Bulygin indignant at D. F. Trepov's actions, and that was in the summer of 1905 about a month before he was relieved of his post as Minister of the Interior. It was a hot summer day, and when I called at his home on Aptekarsky Island I found him sitting behind a writing desk and, although he was dressed in a light summer suit, wet with perspiration. He appeared to be on the verge of a stroke. His face was purple, his eyes bulged, and there was no sign of his customary good humor.

"What a rascal he is, asking for my advice!" These enigmatic words greeted my appearance.

Under circumstances such as these it is not surprising that nothing startling was done in the Ministry of the Interior during Bulygin's ministry. But in the country at large events of profound importance were taking place. The so-called "liberation movement"[5] was affecting all classes of society. I viewed the course of these events with the eyes of a man who had seen considerable service in the bureaucracy. This fact may have colored my opinion and consequently that opinion may be one-sided, but I do not propose to conceal it on that account. I viewed these events as a man firmly persuaded that Russia and her people were not adult enough to be granted self-government, and that her intellectual classes represented not a constructive but a destructive force. Later I came to believe that the forces of bureaucracy were insufficient to cope with the various problems of our time and that even the form of our government was no longer in step with the varied developments of our people. The form of our government was inevitably doomed, since it had ceased to reflect the opinion of the educated classes of the population, who, after all, form the basis of a nation's existence. In my opinion this was the essence of the tragedy of the Russian government.

On the one hand, the existing government had reason to fear the transfer of control to the public, but those who think that the government's attitude was caused solely by a desire to remain the only force that could determine the fate of the empire are very much in error. During the government's struggle with the public, its decisions were motivated by considerations higher than mere class or personal interest. The government understood very well that the state apparatus had absorbed all that was best in Russia in the way of talent, of loyalty in the rational execution of duty, and especially of ability to

---

"What?"

"Yes, yes, he is asking what should be done about the anticipated demonstration of St. Petersburg workers."

"You mean Trepov?"

"Of course I mean Trepov. He has just telephoned, asking for my advice. Can you imagine it! I told him I would not give him any advice. Since he had undertaken to preserve order and peace in the country, let him do as he pleases without attempting to shift the responsibility on me."

Nor was his indignation a thing of the moment; it took him some time to regain his habitual calm. During our conversation he frequently interjected exclamations expressing his indignation at Trepov's conduct: "We shall come to grief with him! We shall indeed!"

"Then why don't you resign?" I asked.

"I have asked for permission to do so, but they won't let me," he replied, stroking his stomach with a familiar gesture.

understand state problems. Outside this apparatus, with minor exceptions, the only remaining active forces were fanatics befogged with Utopian dreams and theories, or ambitious men who had failed to satisfy their vanity in the civil service, or devotees of abstract theories and light-minded dilettantes who had no doubts about anything and were ready at any given moment to perform any experiment upon the body of the nation. The government realized also that once the election of persons to govern the country was left to an ignorant population, the government would be composed for the most part of depraved and unprincipled persons who would not hesitate to employ out-and-out demagogic methods and make unbounded promises.*

* The period that followed [1917] justified these apprehensions of the government to the fullest extent. The Provisional Government, the creation of the people's representatives, included the best and choicest forces at the public's command. It was headed by a man whom the radical circles of the opposition considered a near genius, yet the genius proved to be nothing but a vacuum and even a crook, who pocketed the public resources at his command. As for the remaining members of his government, many of whom undoubtedly put their whole souls into their work, they proved inadequate to say the least. Later, when the masses actually seized power, their representatives were revealed as men who had promised them great material profit regardless of whether or not or how they could fulfill these promises. Ethically the members of administration raised to office by the people were no better than their bureaucratic predecessors, and technically they were worse. Being amateurs in the technique of administration they had unbounded confidence in themselves. This light-minded self-assurance proved their undoing. The old bureaucratic administrative machine had been functioning for scores of years and could be expected to continue efficient routine work even with ministers of inferior ability. Had the members of the Provisional Government, who were superior in mental capacity to the majority of those ministers whom they succeeded, preserved this old machine, the personnel of which, even after the revolution, was ready to serve Russia faithfully and devotedly under the directions of the new chiefs, they might have lasted longer and preserved order in the country. But they chose to act differently. They will probably try to justify their policy by pointing out the difficult conditions under which they had taken over the government. But were these conditions harder for them than they had been for the old ministers? Scarcely! The position at the front was more stable than it had ever been and the supplies of artillery, ammunition, and all sorts of military equipment had reached dimensions unthought of at the beginning of the war. In addition to this, in the beginning of their regime they enjoyed the unlimited confidence of the people. What a contrast there is between the work of this Provisional Government and that of France in 1870. This French government, which called itself a government of national defense, included really exceptional men and by desperate effort created a new army which stemmed the tide of German invasion. It also prevailed against its internal enemies. Under the leadership of Thiers and Gambetta it overpowered the Paris Commune. The success of this French Government of National Defense is to be attributed to the fact that it represented only national interests. The Cadet-Socialist Russian Provisional Government, on the contrary, represented merely party interests.

On the other hand, when the government found itself not only deprived of public support but actually face to face with an ever increasing public opposition it could not have been expected to cope successfully with the gigantic task of administering 180 million subjects, spread over one-sixth of the inhabited globe, especially at a time when the economic life of the country had collapsed. The many mistakes which the government made at that time were inevitable. The Russian bureaucracy was prey to all the defects and ills common to every bureaucracy in the world: formalism, excessive loyalty to the existing order, routine, insufficient organic connection with public life and therefore an insufficient understanding of the new and complicated needs of a growing society, and a lack of reforming energy. But in the main, especially as a technical administrative apparatus, it worked well, showed continual improvement, and certainly made heroic efforts to fulfill the tasks assigned to it. And as the events of 1905–1906 unfolded, educated and state-minded public circles began to realize that this was true. The liberal opposition was divided into two very different camps. Those of its members who were genuinely concerned for the future of their country and who took part in the progressive movement not merely to satisfy their personal ambition but to assist their country in forming a better government slowly began to range themselves on the side of the government. But those who sought a revolution as a means of salving their wounded pride and attaining power became increasingly radical and allied themselves more and more with the destructive revolutionary forces, because they hoped thereby to achieve success by demagogical methods without considering what price the country would have to pay for their actions.

But to return to the main narrative! The year 1905 can be divided into four periods, the first of which lasted approximately to February 18, when there was published the rescript to Bulygin announcing that representatives from all classes of the population would be called to share the work of legislation. This period was distinguished by many strikes and a steadily growing labor movement.

The second period extended through spring and summer. Its characteristic was an increase of public activity and a series of public conventions. These conventions were held almost exclusively in Moscow, which thus became the center of the liberal all-zemstvo movement. During this period educated public circles tried to decide what attitude they should take toward the events of the day and to work out their political programs. It was during this period, too, that the statute on the advisory State Duma was published. As a result, public thoughts became engrossed in the question of what was the best type of representative body and what the best system of election. In this period also there were agrarian uprisings, labor strikes, and a great many terroristic acts.

The third period, which began about the middle of September and ended with the publication of the Manifesto of October 17, marked the final union of the radical opposition with the revolutionary underground forces. This union made it possible for these forces to organize a general railway workers' strike and to disrupt the normal course of the country's life.

The fourth period, from October 17 to the end of the year, was marked by a series of armed demonstrations by the proletariat. Both the common citizens and the educated classes gradually lost sympathy with such demonstrations. The government, too, altered its program of action. Under P. N. Durnovo's firm hand the government stopped drifting and adopted the plan of decisively suppressing the revolutionary movement.

My purpose in the paragraphs that follow is not to give a detailed account of all the manifestations of unrest but to depict the stages of the swelling revolutionary wave and the government's efforts to hold it in check.

During the first nine months of 1905, that is, well through the third period, the government's efforts were directed by D. F. Trepov. I have already described this man. He was ill-suited for the position he occupied. He was a man of weak will, and this weakness was clearly reflected in his vacillating procedure and in the government's efforts to cope with the revolutionary movement. A good illustration of this is to be seen in the government's treatment of the workers' movement.

Directly after Trepov was appointed Governor-General of St. Petersburg he employed a method to pacify the workers of that city which was virtually Zubatovschina. He arranged that the Tsar should receive a delegation of representatives of St. Petersburg workers. He selected these representatives in collaboration with a worker, Ushakov, who was employed in the state printing office and was a close assistant of Zubatov in organizing workers' meetings. It goes without saying that these representatives had been put through a very fine political filter. When the delegation was taken to Tsarskoe

Selo, the Tsar addressed it to the effect that he would take the interests of the workers to heart; then it was given dinner and sent home.

Were either workers or public deceived by this move? Were the workers pacified? Not at all. Workers cannot be caught by promises alone. Besides, their fellows who were party workers and who were urging them to strike had promised them much more than the Tsar had promised. As for the public, the majority paid no attention whatsoever to the Tsar's address. The only person deceived was Nicholas II, who believed until the very end of his reign that he was opposed by the "intelligentsia" alone and that the masses of the people were backing him. He even considered the factory workers confirmed monarchists at heart, who saw in the Tsar the best protector of their interests. Yet his reception of the workers' delegation did not pacify the workers, who became increasingly fascinated by the revolutionists and permeated by the ideas of socialist Utopias.

Another measure proposed at that time, not by Trepov but by Witte, likewise failed to cope with the situation. I refer to the commission to study the labor question. This commission was instituted January 25, 1905, under the chairmanship of N. V. Shidlovsky, a member of the State Council, and included representatives of factory owners and workers chosen by producers and workers, respectively. The purpose of the commission was as grandiose as it was hazy. The ukase by which it was set up said that it was formed "in order to ascertain immediately the causes of the workers' unrest in St. Petersburg and vicinity and to establish measures designed to prevent unrest in the future."

Generally speaking, this commission was perhaps powerless to eliminate once and forever the causes of workers' unrest; nevertheless, it might have yielded good fruit if—oh, well, there were many "ifs." In the first place it was imperative that the workers' leaders included in the commission, who belonged only partially to the working class, should have sincerely desired the pacification of the working masses. But this was not their desire. They wished not a pacification of the workers but continued unrest. They used every means in their power to hinder the commission and actually succeeded in getting party workers on the commission as workers' representatives.

But the government did not stop with these efforts to appease the workers and to win their sympathies and even gratitude. It also employed its favorite weapon, administrative arbitrariness. Instead of passing suitable legislation whereby the workers might protect their interests by recourse to law—the method adopted in all industrial countries—it began to take part in the direct relations between workers and employers, and, by exercising pressure on the employers, tried to force them to grant some of the workers' demands, such as increased wages and shorter working hours. For instance, on January 24, 1905, the Minister of Finance assembled in his office representatives of the owners and directors of St. Petersburg factories and proposed that they announce what concessions they were ready to make to the workers. As was to have been expected, the factory owners answered that they were not able to state what general concessions could be made. Each enterprise, they said, had its own rules and regulations, and in each wages were paid according to the nature of the work done there. Moreover, the profits of each enterprise varied so that what one factory could do would be impossible for another. But these answers did not satisfy the Minister of Finance, and he made a rather enigmatic statement to the effect that the refusal of the factory owners to satisfy the demands of the workers might have most deplorable consequences for the owners themselves.

But the government took steps more decisive than mere threats. The Minister of War announced to the Putilov works, which had discharged all its workers and had temporarily stopped production until it could find workers who would accept the wages offered by the management, that if the factory did not resume operations he would cancel all government army orders. This ultimatum may be explained by the needs of the war, but really it amounted to a government order to the management to capitulate to the workers.

Another striking example of this attitude on the part of the government was a telegram which Prince Khilkov, Minister of Ways and Communications, had persuaded the Tsar to send to the management of the Libau-Romny railway. In this telegram the Tsar expressed his pleasure and satisfaction upon hearing that the railway had shortened its working day to nine hours and at the same time had increased the wages of its workers.

Clearly, the government intended to play its game at the expense of owners of enterprises and so to earn the gratitude of the working classes. But the workers regarded the government's policy with indifference, for by that time they wished much more than the government had succeeded in granting them by its arbitrary and unco-ordinated actions. As for the employers, the government's policy aroused in them a general indignation and drove them into closer association not only with the opposition but even with the revolutionary elements. They began to flood the government with reports and memoranda sharply criticizing the activities of the government and stating bluntly that the workers' movement, in part, had been created by the government itself and, in part, was the result of the lack of political rights enjoyed by the population in general and the working classes in particular. Such memoranda were presented by the representatives of the railway industry, the Ural mining industry, the St. Petersburg factories, and, finally, a group of factory owners of Moscow headed by Morozov, the chairman of the Moscow stock exchange.

There was also another aspect of the movement. The capitalists hoped, and not without reason, that when Russia was given a representative government the representatives of the capitalists would have a dominating, or at least a very important, part in the government. Accordingly, they had resolved to secure such a government even if they had to use means which might prove dangerous to themselves. Morozov himself, at that time under the strong influence of Maxim Gorky, drew upon his own private fortune to support the revolutionary movement among the workers.

This aspect of the movement was reflected in the memorandum presented to the government by representatives of Moscow industrial circles. "The present labor demonstrations," said the memorandum, "although springing from economic causes, are nevertheless largely political in character. The main reason for these periodical labor uprisings is the lack of political rights enjoyed by the workers." From this it was argued that a sound relationship between workers and employers could be effected only if a political regime of equity were introduced. The memorandum concluded with an almost literal repetition of the resolutions of the November zemstvo congress and the suggestion that the workers be given the rights of free speech, assembly, and organization, and the right to strike.

Another memorandum presented to the government by 198 civil engineers advocated the same program.

Under these circumstances it was very natural that Shidlovsky's commission, which was considering only the workers' economic conditions, could do nothing but increase the irritation of the working masses. The commission was soon brought to an end.

Meanwhile the strikes, which had started early in January, acquired daily a more pronounced revolutionary character and, far from abating, spread steadily to an increasing number of workers' districts. The number of working days used up by strikes in January 1905 rose to the unprecedented and since unequaled figure of 920,000, whereas during the entire year of 1903 there were only 445,000 wasted labor days throughout the empire. Yet it was in these January conditions that Trepov did nothing more effective than to stage a "unification of the Tsar with his people." At the same time serious agrarian uprisings occurred in various gubernias.

The attack on the government was becoming more and more energetic, and the forces conducting it were those of the revolution. In January 1905 the Moscow committee of the Social Democratic Labor party expressed itself sharply against the resolutions of the November 1904 zemstvo congress. It declared that the only way out of the current situation was by an "armed overthrow of the existing government and the convocation of a constituent assembly which would establish a democratic republic and pass legislation recognizing the political and economic demands of the proletariat." It dubbed the attempt of the zemstvos to come to an understanding with the government shameful bargaining and a bargain struck by the bourgeoisie with the government at the expense of the people's rights. At the same time it resolved, "To conduct at every meeting agitation for the rights of the proletariat and against any agreement between the liberals and the Tsarist government; to insist upon a continuance of the revolution;* and to announce that the efforts and demands of the liberals were treason against the people."

In accordance with this resolution, the Social Democratic party, both Bolsheviks and Mensheviks, supported the workers' movement by every means at their command and tried to turn it from economic into political channels. Proclamations were distributed by the thousand; party workers of a hook-nosed, brunette type began to dash back and forth all over Russia. The Socialist-Revolutionists were not far behind. They worked in their favorite medium, the peasantry, and stirred up agrarian disorders. As a result the strike spread from the Moscow factories and printing establishments to Riga, Reval, Libau, and Warsaw. In Warsaw it grew into an armed insurrection that was suppressed by military force. Other industrial centers, such

* The demonstration of Gapon on January 9 was considered its beginning.

as Ekaterinoslav and Kiev, were affected just as severely. The revolutionary movement even reached the Caucasus, where it manifested itself in street demonstrations in Tiflis and Batum. The general slogan called for the convocation of a constituent assembly, elected according to the four-tailed formula. University disorders continued and led to the closing of many universities. Acts of terrorism became more frequent. The Grand Duke Sergei Aleksandrovich, who had retired as Governor-General of Moscow, was assassinated in the streets of Moscow on February 2. Every day brought news of some new source of unrest, some new violation of public peace and order. The government was beginning to lose its head and to become convinced that no cure could be effected for this state of affairs except the making of some concessions to the aroused masses. There was talk of an advisory legislative body elected by the people.

In the highest official circles, however, it was thought possible to retain the autocratic regime and, within its framework, give the people the right freely to express their ideas on questions of state. Nicholas II desired to retain the autocratic principle and at the same time wanted to give all individuals and institutions the right to address the Tsar with their plans; he was even willing to entertain the possibility of an advisory legislative body elected by the people. Accordingly, on the morning of February 18 there were published two state acts: a manifesto "on disturbances and troubles," and a ukase to the Senate on petitions. The manifesto began as follows: "Ill-intentioned leaders of these insurrections, blinded by arrogance, are daring to attack the foundations of the Russian Empire, sanctified by the orthodox church and supported by law. They are seeking to break the chain that connects Us with Our past, to disrupt the existing state structure, and to establish in its place another form of government, foreign to Our country." It continued: "Let all Russians stand firm around Our Throne, true to the traditions of Our past . . . . and support the autocracy for the good of all Our faithful subjects."

The ukase to the Senate bade the Council of Ministers, presided over by the Tsar, "examine and consider the ideas and suggestions presented to Us by private persons and institutions concerning improvements in the state organization and the betterment of the people's existence."

Both these acts were issued from Tsarskoe Selo and took the ministers completely by surprise. In all probability, they had been inspired by the Palace Commandant, P. P. Hesse. Several persons, among them Yusefovich,[6] Hesse's confidant, had had a hand in composing the manifesto from a short outline drafted by the Tsar himself; the final edition had been shown to Pobedonostsev, who had expressed himself whole-heartedly in favor of it.

The manifesto and ukase surprised the ministers all the more since a short time previously the Tsar had more or less agreed to the convocation of an advisory legislative body elected by the people. He had agreed to this largely as the result of the influence of the gentle and retiring A. S. Ermolov. No one had suspected Ermolov of advocating such a move; but on January 17, during his first report after the Gapon demonstration of January 9, he had asked the Tsar's permission to express his sentiments concerning the situation in the country. Then, in a long speech full of sincerity and of love for his country, Ermolov had stated his profound conviction that it was urgently necessary to utilize the aid of public forces in deciding matters of state importance. Ermolov's words, strengthened probably by the events of January 9, had made a great impression on the Tsar. Impulsive as usual, he had suggested that Ermolov talk the matter over with Witte and prepare a written memorandum. But Witte, probably because the initiative had not been his but Ermolov's, whom he considered as less than nothing, had treated the matter with coolness. Ermolov, however, with unusual insistence had continued to strive for the realization of the ideas he had expressed to the Tsar. He had enlarged upon them in subsequent most humble reports, and finally had drafted an announcement of the forthcoming reform as well as the order for working out the appropriate legislative acts. This announcement, he had suggested, might be made in the form of a rescript to the Minister of the Interior stating that the Tsar wished to have persons elected by the population drawn into the work of legislation and charging that minister to work out a statute establishing the method by which this measure should be put into effect.* The Tsar had assigned Ermolov the task of drafting this rescript, but Ermolov's draft had seemed too long and the task had then been entrusted to the Head of His Majesty's Private Chancellery to Receive Petitions, Baron Budberg.[8] Budberg's draft had also been rejected. In the meantime, the Tsar's intention had become known to

---

* This was a deliberate copy of the method employed in announcing the reform of February 19, 1861, the liberation of the serfs: a Sovereign rescript to Nazimov,[7] the Military Governor of Vilna.

nearly all the ministers, and although it had met with no objection from them the preparation of the rescript had gone on in secret. The draft which had finally met with the Tsar's approval had been composed by some person who was near the throne but was not a member of the government. Then, on February 18, Nicholas II asked several ministers to meet to debate the draft he had accepted.

According to Witte's statement in his memoirs,[9] the ministers when they first learned of the manifesto were on their way to Tsarskoe Selo on the morning of February 18 to discuss the projected rescript. They were all indignant that such an important move had been made without their knowledge. It is easy to understand, however, why the manifesto appeared before the rescript to Bulygin was discussed and before it was signed by the Tsar. In the Tsar's mind, the establishment of an advisory elected body would not lead, and was not supposed to lead, to any infringement of the autocratic principle. It was this idea he wished to convey in the manifesto again proclaiming the autocratic principle; also he probably wished to prevent any minister from trying to persuade him in favor of a constitution. But the ministers did not understand the incident in this way, and in order to put an end to the state of uncertainty and hesitation in so far as the project of a consultative legislative body was concerned, they hastened to approve the rescript as drafted without changing a single word; and in order to forestall a possible change of the Imperial mind they asked the Tsar to sign the rescript then and there. Bulygin cut off the word "project" from the drafted rescript, and the Tsar's signature was affixed. Bulygin took the signed rescript with him, and that very evening it appeared in a special edition of the *Pravitelstvennyi Vestnik*.

As is known, the rescript announced the Tsar's intention to "attract most deserving persons, vested with public confidence and elected by the people, to undertake the preliminary examination and consideration of legislative projects." Its concluding sentence was unfortunate: "I foresee complications and difficulties in carrying out this while preserving intact the basic laws of the empire." By this sentence the Tsar evidently intended to point out that the principle of autocracy was not to be violated by the proposed reform. Actually, however, the sentence implied that it was almost impossible to realize this reform because it would be almost impossible to co-ordinate the reform with the basic laws of the empire, that is, the autocracy.

If the ministers were dumfounded by the appearance of the

unexpected manifesto, the public was even more so. In the morning it read the Tsar's appeal to support the autocracy, and in the evening it read his decision to attract the people's elected representatives to the work of legislation. And it goes without saying that the latter, being the first step toward a constitution, completely overshadowed the former, which contained nothing but a few high-sounding words. Of course, the press of the Right, represented by *Moskovskiia Vedomosti* and *Svet*, tried to emphasize the manifesto and to discount the rescript; but theirs was but a cry in the desert. The public almost unanimously acclaimed the decision to draw popular representatives into the work of legislation.

February 18, 1905, thus marks the beginning of the second period mentioned above. It marked a turning point both in the attitudes of different classes and in the character of their activities. On one hand, it gradually stratified the public into different groups; political parties were formed and all the thinking elements of the country found their respective places in these strata. There remained very few mere spectators in this struggle between the government and the public; practically all the educated elements were forced to declare themselves and to attach themselves to one of the four main categories into which public opinion gradually became divided. Beginning with the Right, these were: (1) outright monarchists, who stubbornly insisted that an assembly of people's representatives assisting in legislation must not diminish the authority of the monarch; (2) moderate liberals, who favored a constitutional monarchy but were ready to support the existing government and the structure of the state in all other respects; (3) radicals, who desired to retain a mere semblance of monarchy while striving toward democracy; and (4) revolutionary socialists, who regarded the changes in the forms of government merely as a means of altering the existing economic and social structure. But because of the lack of political education and the inborn lack of discipline among the Russian people these political group lines were not all immediately drawn. The monarchists of the extreme Right and the revolutionary socialists of the extreme Left were already identified, but there came into existence a great many intermediate political organizations representing various trends of political opinion between these two poles, each such group sponsoring its own program and methods of reform. Nevertheless, when the Manifesto of October 17 was issued, two main parties occupying a central position between the extreme Right and the extreme Left were clearly distinguishable. These became known as Octobrists and Cadets, respectively.

These two orientations in the center section of political opinion were not yet evident when the zemstvo congress met in Moscow on February 24–25, with representatives from three-quarters of the zemstvo gubernias in attendance. In fact, it then seemed that all the zemstvo elements had swung to the Left. During this congress the question of a constituent assembly was raised and a new, quite democratic slogan was proclaimed favoring an electoral system based upon universal, equal, direct, and secret suffrage. This frank Left orientation of the February congress may be explained by the fact that preparations for it had been made before the Tsar's decision to include the people's representatives in the work of legislation had been announced in the rescript to Bulygin. Consequently the congress reflected the opinions and attitudes of the zemstvos, the majority of which were still irritated by the government's refusal to make any concessions whereby zemstvo men might be permitted to take part in the work of the central government. It must be borne in mind that the zemstvo congress of that time reflected the attitudes of the gubernia zemstvo assemblies elected in the period 1902–1904, during which the zemstvos were especially oppressed by the administration and were, therefore, very much opposed to it. This factor led to the triumph in the zemstvo assemblies of that period of those zemstvo men who were most radical and most opposed to the government.

Two months after the February zemstvo congress, however, clear-cut differences of opinion became manifest in the zemstvos, and during a second congress held in April two main orientations were sharply defined: the majority (later Cadets) favored a parliament elected according to the four-tailed formula, which was very popular at the time, and the minority (later Octobrists) joined the minority of the November congress of the previous year in favoring an advisory body. D. N. Shipov, who recently had been generally acclaimed the leader of all progressive zemstvo men, joined this minority group and became its leader. This group did not declare in favor of election by class; nevertheless it advocated the 1864 system of elections to the zemstvo.

There was also a third group headed by Kuzmin-Karavaev[10] and Arsenev. This opposed both the four-tailed formula and the old zemstvo system of 1864.[11]

As the revolutionary psychosis enveloped the country, the more radically democratic of these two tendencies dominated the zemstvo circles as well as all liberal professions. Representatives of these professions took their place on the stage of the day by interpreting the ukase on petitions to mean that all Russian citizens were granted the right of public assembly for the discussion of problems of state. This interpretation was patently incorrect. The ukase distinctly mentioned that suggestions "concerning improvements in the state organization and the betterment of the people's existence" were to be presented to the Tsar by *"individuals and institutions";* it did not confer the "right of public assembly." The government tried to confine the application of the ukase to this correct interpretation, but it was practicaly powerless to do so; its authority was gone; it was only partially able to defend the existing order and secure the observance of existing laws.

On March 28 the All-Russian congress of lawyers assembled and unanimously passed a resolution to the effect that the Bulygin commission, which was working out a statute for an advisory State Duma, should limit itself to working out a law convoking a constituent assembly elected by universal, equal, direct, and secret suffrage. This congress was followed by others, one of which was a congress of men of letters which was closed by the police.

At the same time, as provided for in the program of the Union of Liberation, different professional unions were formed. Fourteen had been formed by May, and at the first organization congress, held on May 8, these were united into a Union of Unions.

The destruction of nearly all our navy on May 15 in the straits of Tsushima furnished a new and very powerful impetus to the rise of public excitement. This defeat seemed to be another proof that the bureaucracy was not capable of guiding the ship of state. The public forgot that our Baltic Fleet, especially Admiral Nebogatov's squadron, which was composed of antiquated slow-moving vessels, had been sent to the Pacific in compliance with the public demand and contrary to the opinions of specialists. The specialists had affirmed that to increase Admiral Rozhestvensky's squadron by adding old-fashioned ships would not strengthen but weaken it by hampering and slowing down its ability to maneuver. But that unprincipled career maker, Captain Klado, with the helpful collaboration of *Novoe Vremia,* advocated sending to the Pacific our entire Baltic Fleet, regardless of its fighting ability. The public supported his plan and finally forced the government to carry out this patently absurd venture.

The bureaucracy and the government were to blame for sending to war those antiquated ships, those *"staryia galoshi"* [old galoshes], as Nebogatov's squadron was called; but they were also to blame for not having had enough strength to oppose the demands of the public. This lack of determination only served to confirm the public in its opinion that the bureaucracy was woefully inefficient; and the public attributed all our losses, as well as all our domestic troubles, to the bureaucracy alone, being sure that everything would work smoothly if only control of the government were transferred to the people's representatives.*

Every conference, congress, and public assembly which took place in the spring of 1905 was convinced of its superiority to the bureaucrats. This attitude was most openly expressed by the revolutionary elements or by those closely allied to them. Thus during its second conference, May 25, the Union of Unions mentioned above resolved that the band of highwaymen who were governing the country should be immediately removed and that a constituent assembly, chosen by universal, equal, direct, and secret suffrage, regardless of sex, religious creed, and nationality, should be instituted in their stead. There were in this resolution not only a note of contempt for the bureaucracy but also clearly revolutionary notes. Demands on the government grew daily; the four-tailed formula was extended to include equal opportunity for women and equality of religious creeds and nationalities. At the same time there appeared those centrifugal tendencies which twelve years later brought about the disintegration of the empire—namely, a nationalist and socialist movement in the gubernias of the Kingdom of Poland and a movement for the autonomy of the border regions. In the Caucasus this latter tendency sharpened the relations among the many nationalities there, as was evidenced by a bloody outbreak at Baku entailing the loss of many lives, especially those of Tartars and Armenians.

But in the midst of all this ferment and unrest the patriotic elements held fast to their old ideas. They failed to realize that the danger from the Left threatened not only the existence of the state

---

* In 1915–16 critical public opinion became convinced that the bureaucracy was powerless to cope with the difficult tasks imposed upon it by the World War. There was the same assurance that the public forces, on the other hand, would be able to solve all the pressing problems of war, but 1917 proved the contrary. The bureaucrats of the war period, in spite of an extremely unfortunate group of higher officials, were immeasurably superior to the public forces which succeeded them in February 1917.

government but also those very classes which they themselves represented, and continued with much enthusiasm to add fuel to the all-consuming revolutionary fire.

From May 24 to May 27 a joint conference of representatives of the zemstvos, the municipalities, and the nobility was held in Moscow. It had been assembled as a consequence of the catastrophe of Tsushima, and unanimously adopted a resolution on the necessity of immediately assembling freely elected people's representatives to consider with the Monarch the problems of war and peace and of establishing order in the country. They composed a rather detailed "petition" to the Tsar which was in the main very loyal and permeated with a warm love of country but which declared that the administration would have to be reorganized and that persons enjoying public confidence should be summoned to share in the government. This petition is evidence of the conviction that the bureaucracy was inefficient; it is also the first evidence of that impetuous striving for power which later so strongly colored the activities of the leaders of the Constitutional Democratic (Cadet) party. The Tsushima defeat had temporarily smoothed over the differences of opinion manifested during the April congress, but the May conference, while still preserving a more or less unbroken progressive zemstvo front, showed a great predominance of men who later became Cadets. This was most clearly shown in the persons selected to present to the Tsar the petition we have mentioned. Among these were Professor Prince S. N. Trubetskoi,[12] F. A. Golovin,[13] Prince Pavel D. Dolgorukov, Count P. A. Heyden, N. N. Lvov, Prince G. E. Lvov, Y. A. Novosiltsev, N. N. Kovalevsky,[14] Prince D. I. Shakhovskoi,[15] I. I. Petrunkevich, and F. I. Rodichev. With the exception of N. N. Lvov, Count P. A. Heyden, and Prince S. N. Trubetskoi, the leader of the delegation who did not become connected with the Cadet party, the other members of the delegation were the originators of that party.

Meanwhile, the government had no clearly defined policy. Actually power was becoming more and more concentrated in the hands of D. F. Trepov. Finally, on May 21, he was appointed Assistant Minister of the Interior in addition to being Governor-General of St. Petersburg. All affairs of the Police Department and the St. Petersburg garrison were thus subordinated to him and he became a virtual dictator. At first glance the measures he adopted seemed to lack both rhyme and reason, and substantially they did. But one wonders whether such a program was not one best suited to the existing situation. Supposing the government had desired to act logically and systematically, what was it to do? Two ways of procedure were open to it: either it could take decisive measures to ensure the observance of the law by excited public elements, or it could change or abolish some of the laws and grant the rights of free speech, assembly, and organization. Either course would have been not only wrong but positively dangerous as well. At that time and for a number of reasons—one of which was our military defeats—the government had lost much of its prestige. It could have prevented the population from violating existing laws only by measures so harsh as to be entirely out of proportion to the gravity of the transgressions. Such disproportionate harshness would have been the more offensive since in many instances the law had been violated partly out of great love for country and sometimes under the country's flag. On the other hand, if the government had permitted and legalized public demonstrations by granting the population the right of free speech, assembly, and organization it would have created the necessity of complying with the wishes and hopes which it thereby aroused. This would have involved a transfer of all authority to the people without any assurance that the people would be capable of bearing such great responsibility.

Furthermore, the government was not then in a position to adopt liberal measures of its own free will, as had been possible when Mirsky assumed office. Whatever the government did in this direction would have appeared to be no more than the carrying out of the demands of the public. This would have been interpreted to mean that the public had wrung concessions from the government; it would have been viewed as "a victory for the liberation movement" and considered as a weakness on the part of the government. Nor would it have satisfied anyone. It would neither have strengthened the government's position nor have lessened the hostility of the public; it would merely have increased the demands and the pressure on the government of all opposition forces—both the revolutionary forces and those striving for a reconstruction of the forms of government.

The government had to deal with a population psychically unsound. It could not act according to the dictates of logic which well-balanced persons could understand; rather, it had to give the appearance of giving in to the public and at the same time retain a firm hold on the helm of state. Nor could it hope that measures which would protect the foundations of the state would draw away from the liberation movement a considerable section of the public on which the government could build its future policy. Such a move would have been quite possible in the early fall of 1904; but it was not to be thought of in the spring of 1905. It took the events of the years 1905–1906 to teach the moderately progressive elements upon which Stolypin based his power that civil rights and liberties could be granted only gradually as the educated and half-educated strata of the public became politically enlightened. Yet in the spring of 1905 these moderate liberals were clamoring for civil freedom as insistently as were the radical and revolutionary elements. But even had the government gained the support of the moderate liberals, such a gain would probably have meant that the reactionary circles would have completely lost their influence—provided that the revolutionary wave that was sweeping over the country increased in force. The intolerance of the opposition toward those who represented a conservative point of view had reached such a point that if given an opportunity it would have gone so far as to forbid the conservatives to express their views in public.

It is quite possible, therefore, that the government did not consciously choose to act as it did. Its action was probably determined by many and varied reasons, the chief of which was the fact that it did not know any rational course to pursue. Its salvation lay in this: It had not legalized the right of public demonstration, nor had it granted the population the right to interfere in affairs of state; thus it preserved its right to take severe measures against separate violations of the law, when such violations threatened to have grave consequences for the government. On the other hand, the government did not prevent the advanced classes of society from expressing their pent-up feelings and political opinions, for such expression provided a safety outlet for these feelings and decreased their pressure. This freedom of expression tolerated by the government also aroused the consciousness of that part of the people which was not infected with the revolutionary psychosis, and which thus became the government's powerful ally. Then as always the government feared not so much an increase in the numbers of its enemies and the growth of their attack upon the governmental apparatus as a decrease in the numbers of its partisans and defenders; for no government which controlled the entire state apparatus has ever been overthrown so long as it possessed a sufficiently large number of sympathizers and supporters among the population. Therefore the most urgent task was to attract a part of the public to support the government. The easiest way to do this was to frighten some of the people by persuading them that a change of government would place control in the hands of elements dangerous to public order and peace. The elements openly hostile to the government were becoming more and more insistent in their demands, and the very excesses in which they indulged helped to bring the more balanced and unambitious public men to their senses, and to form that organic force without which no mechanical force can long exist.

The Tsar's decision to receive the delegation of the Moscow conference of the zemstvos, the municipalities, and the nobility referred to above was a wise move in the direction of gaining public support for the government.* Evidently the Tsar realized that although the resolutions of the conference included some points that were unacceptable, the petition and the resolution had been dictated by a sincere love of country and, generally speaking, of the existing regime. In Prince S. N. Trubetskoi's address to the Tsar there was not a trace of anything unbecoming a subject addressing his monarch. The Prince voiced the feelings of a loyal patriot concerned about the future of his country: "We have been brought here by one feeling— that of love for our country and the realization of our duty to you, Sire." These words became known all over Russia and made a most favorable impression on the public. The Tsar's answer was not a direct reply to the petition of the delegation, but it was quite acceptable to all politically conscious Russians. It was not very definite, but it could not have been so at that time. Moreover, the very vagueness of his answer gave the representatives of the less radical revolutionary groups a chance to interpret it any way they desired. The most important part of the reply was: "Have no doubts. It is My will, the will of your Tsar, to assemble representatives of the people. They shall be drawn into state work in a fitting manner. Let there be once more, as there was in the days of old, a communion between the Tsar and the people which shall be the foundation of an organization built upon traditional Russian principles."

The members of the delegation were tremendously impressed by these words, possibly not so much because of their meaning as be-

---

* After the St. Petersburg City Duma had decided to take part in the petition of the Moscow conference, the delegation was joined by M. I. Fedorov, Baron P. L. Korff, and one other representative of the St. Petersburg City Duma.

cause of the charming simplicity with which they were spoken. One thing cannot be denied Nicholas II, and that was his personal charm. It emanated, not from a halo of imperial greatness and might, but from what seemed to be his innate democratic attitude, wholly unexpected in a ruler of one hundred and eighty millions. In some subtle way Nicholas II could convey to persons with whom he was talking the impression that he did not consider himself superior to them or in any way different. His conduct was so unaffected and strangely simple that it won for him the sympathies of all with whom he came in contact. This impression was strongest at first meeting. Persons who were placed in close and continual contact with him in time became immune to this charm and began to have quite different feelings.

After the Tsar's reception of the delegation, the Ministry of the Interior issued a senseless order in the form of a circular letter from the Chief Administration for the Affairs of the Press which forbade the press to comment upon the Tsar's reply and ordered the governors to take steps to prevent excessive comment on it. The stupidity of this order is revealed in the fact that it was issued after most exhaustive comment upon the Tsar's reply had been made.

During the spring months of 1905 there were all manner of conferences and congresses which made ever-increasing demands of the government; but, on the whole, these months were much quieter than the winter months of the year. The strike movement, which in St. Petersburg had resulted in 920,000 wasted working days in January and 506,000 in February, had weakened greatly in April, during which month only 96,000 working days were lost. May 1, despite the efforts of the revolutionary parties, passed very quietly, with factories working at full swing. This fact greatly depressed the party workers, and the liberal Russian press abroad (*Osvobozhdenie*) noted somewhat sadly that no organized forces were as yet leading the masses. There was also a lull in the agrarian uprisings, which had been numerous throughout February and part of March.

These spring months also witnessed the practical beginning of different Right-wing organizations. On March 26, marshals of the nobility—twenty-six in number—assembled in Moscow to discuss a memorandum by Shipov.[16] This memorandum proposed an advisory legislative body and expressed the idea that further changes of governmental forms should be effected in close co-operation with the highest authorities. "The fight with the government is over.

Now we must assist the Tsar!" This was the purport of the memorandum.*

The Tsushima catastrophe also made its impression upon the marshals of the nobility. Under its influence they composed an address to the Tsar in which they implored him not to delay putting the proposed reform into effect. The address was presented to the Tsar on June 15 by Count V. V. Gudovich and Prince Trubetskoi, who, in elaborating upon the statements in the address, pointed out that the Tsar's responsibility for the country's plight might expose him to danger, and that responsibility for the country's welfare must therefore be immediately placed upon the people's representatives. Several assemblies of the nobility arrived at the same conclusion.

At that time, those who represented conservative thought in Russia found it very difficult freely to express their thoughts and sentiments. The old public organizations, the zemstvos and the municipalities, were completely in the hands of the liberal opposition. The assemblies of the nobility convened only once in three years, and a large percentage of their members belonged to the progressive groups. The associations of physicians, lawyers, and journalists were filled with persons whose ideas and actions were not only radical but even openly revolutionary. An expression of conservative ideas in their midst was unwelcome and apt to lead to the unpopularity, even to the persecution, of him who sponsored such an idea. The numerous bureaucratic class, which could boast many men of exceptional minds and formidable in debate, was by the very fact of its official position usually deprived of contact with the public. The *grande muette,* the army, with monarchists constituting a majority in its ranks, suffered even more from lack of contact with the public. In Russian literature the ideology of a republican and parliamentary government, as well as that of different socialistic theories, had been extensively propounded; but a scientifically developed idea of monarchy had not been advanced at all. There were different slavophile works on this subject, but they were so very hazy and indefinite that it was impossible to build upon them anything concrete; moreover,

* Those participating in the composition of the memorandum were: Prince P. N. Trubetskoi, Prince V. M. Golitsyn (former mayor of Moscow), M. A. Stakhovich, V. I. Guerrier,[17] N. A. Khomiakov,[18] Prince G. G. Gagarin, and O. P. Gerasimov, who was its editor. It was entirely in favor of the convocation of a zemskii sobor.

they all were antiquated; they belonged to the preceding epoch and did not take into account those deep economic changes which Russia had experienced during the past ten years. Then, too, it is always harder to justify and defend an existing order with its many defects than to laud unrealized theories, always so perfectly conceived.

The absence of the ideology of the monarchical principle, the events of the day, the defeats on the Japanese front—all these made extremely difficult the task of those who desired to defend the existing order. Not that this existing order was to be blindly praised. Deficiencies in the entire organization of the government, and ills gnawing at the vitals of the bureaucratic regime had been all too clearly revealed by the tragic events of that period. The interests of the state and people demanded that these deficiencies and ills be remedied. The question was, what remedy to use and how to use it? The Right-wing elements did not deny the existence of these ills, but they supposed that the transfer of power to the people would not ease but would aggravate the malady. In their eyes such a cure would have been worse than the disease. They thought that the recovery of the country and the improvement of its government would be more quickly and more successfully accomplished if the existing principle of government were retained and certain reforms granted by the Monarch than if control of the government were to become an objective for the contending political parties.

It so happened that most of the firm partisans of the monarchical principle were members of the governmental administrative apparatus and were engrossed in carrying out their immediate duties. It must also be borne in mind that heretofore the conservatives had not needed to defend their political opinions and to develop their political points of view; hence they had not established a party organization. In the main they were in sympathy with the existing regime and believed that the necessary innovations and reforms would have to be made within its limits.

Not only did the conservative elements lack party organization; they also lacked experience in forming such an organization. They were unaccustomed to public work of any sort and were without the necessary training and practice. In contrast to this, the success of the parties opposed to the government was largely the result of their long-established organization, and the more Left or revolutionary these opposition parties were, the more unified they had become, the stricter was their party discipline and the more experienced they were

in propagating their ideas and winning the sympathy of the public.
The revolutionary hurricane which swooped down upon Russia found
the partisans of the existing regime entirely unprepared and, at first,
deprived of all means of withstanding the ravages of the blast. Only
after the rescript to Bulygin on February 18, 1905, did the conservative elements of the Russian public realize that in order to apply their
ideas and to preserve Russia from forced and untimely experiments
and from a precipitous change in its entire organization, they would
have to take a stand for their opinions and, to that end, would have
to unite into political organizations.

The first of the St. Petersburg bureaucrats to show any initiative
in this direction was none other than B. V. Stürmer. At that time he
held no office other than membership in the State Council, and almost
immediately after the publication of the rescript to Bulygin he began
to invite to his house, for the purpose of studying the political problems of the day, some of his State Council colleagues, and some senators and officials of different ministries, chiefly those of the Ministry
of the Interior. Among these were Stishinsky, Count Toll,[19] A. D.
Zinovev,[20] A. P. Strukov, Count A. A. Bobrinsky,[21] Prince A. A.
Shirinsky-Shikhmatov, L. A. Kireev, A. N. Stolpakov, D. N. Liubimov, A. A. Pavlov, and a number of persons who visited the salon of
K. F. Golovin—about thirty or forty in all. Stürmer's purpose was
to form a group which would assist him to rise to power, and with
this end in mind he behaved very discreetly, rarely committed himself, and was content to play the role of hospitable host. At first there
was at these gatherings merely an interchange of opinions and information on the current situation; there was no thought of forming
any political party. Nevertheless, the number of the participants grew
rapidly, and it was found necessary to assemble at the larger house
of Count Toll. Here the idea arose of forming a definitely Right
political union. The persons present pointed out those who might
form the presidium of the union and outline its political program.
Among those so designated were Stishinsky, Liubimov, Pavlov, and
myself. I not only refused to become a member of the presidium but
expressed my indignation at the category of persons suggested. "Consider!" I said. "You wish to form a public organization, and yet you
propose to head it with officials from the Ministry of the Interior.
You choose a former assistant minister, the manager of his chancellery, his special duties' clerk and a director of a department, and yet
you hope to be able to attract public forces to this organization! Why,

it would seem more like a summons to the police station than an invitation to join a party." Stishinsky and Liubimov, although little flattered by my words, took the same stand. But Pavlov was of another opinion. He argued with much fire that he was an old zemstvo man and a journalist of some renown (he would have been closer to the truth had he said a scandalist of some renown) ; the fact that he was employed as special duties' clerk to the minister, and this as a supernumerary, could not alter the fact that he was still a public man. So, another presidium was elected—whether then or later I do not recall. Count A. A. Bobrinsky, who had been for many years the St. Petersburg marshal of nobility, was made president; his assistants were A. P. Strukov, who had been marshal of nobility in Ekaterinoslav Gubernia, and A. A. Naryshkin, an old and very much respected zemstvo man of Orel Gubernia.

When it became apparent that these new heads of the union were going to make it into a truly public group, some of its initiators left it. These were they who had regarded the union merely as a means of achieving their own private ends. Stürmer was one; Pavlov was another, but his departure did not make anyone particularly sad. On the other hand, the union was joined by many persons more or less associated with the public: Bekhteev, N. A. Khvostov, K. F. Golovin, and others, and some workers of the Slavic Society such as A. A. Bashmakov and P. A. Kulakovsky.[22] Meetings were now transferred to the house of Count Bobrinsky on the Galernaia. A presidium of ten was elected, if I remember rightly, two of whom, Kireev and Shirinsky-Shikhmatov, were not civil service men. This presidium began immediately to work out the union's constitution and political program. The name "Patriotic Union" was adopted. Efforts were made to enlist new members, but these were won slowly. Since the members of the union had little contact with the population in general, recruits could hardly be expected from that source. Nor was there any sense in seeking recruits among the lower ranks of the civil service, for the times were such that even civil service men were concerned for their security and were generally unwilling to reveal their ideas and convictions with definiteness and clarity. No one was sure that the old regime would be able to withstand the ferocious attack being directed against it. Bourgeois instincts and the urge for self-preservation dominated many. Indeed, circles of the Left were drunk with the success which had crowned their efforts to arouse the population, and were sure that in the near future this success would be complete; the conservatives, on the other hand, were depressed and many of them lost all confidence in the security of their position. A compromise! This became the motto of the rank-and-file civil service man.

The leaders of the union were not ready to make public statements. In any event, statements issuing from the Right camp could not have counted upon any considerable success or audience. Therefore, willy-nilly, the union had to content itself with acting through a medium with which bureaucrats were more familiar—attempts to introduce its views not to the public but to the government, by submitting written expositions of its views and suggestions. Bulygin's conference had announced that it would welcome all suggestions pertaining to the project on the State Duma, and this announcement led the union to compose its own draft for the organization of an advisory legislative body and a system for electing its members.

I recall vividly the meetings of the union in Count A. A. Bobrinsky's cozy house on the Galernaia. In a small salon, with its soft rug and a number of cases containing archeological finds gathered from excavations conducted by the Count, the originators of the union assembled around an oval table in the light of several rose-shaded lamps and in all seriousness discussed problems over the final solution of which they had no control whatsoever. Yet here the views of the participants became known; here were defined those points of disagreement which later divided them into different political groups of conservatives; here was composed the union's project entitled: "The Zemskii Sobor and the State Duma." This project provided for two advisory legislative bodies—a larger one to discuss the general problems of state; and a smaller one of about one hundred members, if I remember rightly, elected by the larger body from its own members. The smaller of the two was to draw up the state budget and debate laws of a technical character. The union's project was not taken into account by anybody; but as a result of it two members of the union were invited to the Peterhof conference which, in June 1905, examined the Duma project drafted by Bulygin's conference. In opening this conference the Tsar said: "We have before us two projects: that of the conference working under Aleksandr Grigorevich (Bulygin), and the project of the Patriotic Union." Beyond this the union's project went unnoticed. The Tsar had been notified of it through some members of the union who had connections in court circles.

Another conservative organization called the Union of Russian Men[23] showed more vital activity. This was organized in Moscow. Its originators belonged to the same class as those who had formed the Patriotic Union, but with the difference that they were not employed by the State; also, because of conditions in Moscow, they had broader connections with the public than had the St. Petersburg bureaucrats. The Union of Russian Men had a program of its own and organized meetings of persons of different classes. Soon after the May conference of the zemstvos, the municipalities, and the nobility, members of the presidium of the Patriotic Union had been invited to attend one of these meetings. They accepted the invitation, and at the meeting they attended, an address to the Tsar was composed and persons were chosen to present it to him. The Tsar received these persons soon after he had received the delegation headed by Prince Trubetskoi; but since the press, with the exception of such openly Right publications as the *Moskovskiia Vedomosti* and *Svet,* said as little as possible about it, this latter reception did not acquire any importance.

As yet, however, the activities of the Right circles were having no influence upon the course of events, which became more and more revolutionary. On June 15 a congress* of municipality representa-

* I had occasion to discuss this congress with D. F. Trepov. For some unknown reason Trepov had decided that I was an authority on zemstvo statutes and laws concerning self-government, and shortly after this congress met he had asked me in the presence of a certain Rachkovsky,[24] who was at that time playing a rather conspicuous part in the Police Department, how these congresses of different public organizations could be legally stopped and by what articles of the existing law the participants in these conventions could be made to answer before the authorities. I replied that I had very little knowledge on this subject and could not answer his question. It was my opinion, however, that as soon as a government lost its prestige in the eyes of its people, it could not by partial measures force the people to observe the law. As for bringing the participants in congresses to trial, especially with our slow-moving court procedure, such a measure would be less likely to stop the congresses than to make the arrested members popular heroes and martyrs. The thing to be done was for the government to re-establish its prestige by a display of firmness and resolution. I related an incident which had taken place in the Kingdom of Poland in 1892. In that year there were some labor troubles in Lodz, which culminated in street disorders. The military forces dispatched to restore order had failed to do so. The Governor-General of Warsaw, General I. V. Gurko, sent an open, laconic telegram to the commander of the Lodz garrison: "I suggest that you stop the unrest this very day and don't spare your ammunition." No sooner was the telegram received at Lodz than its contents became known to the workers, who hastened to their own homes. It was not necessary for the soldiers to fire a single shot. (I have related this incident also in my book, *Ocherki Privisliania ("Sketches on the Vistula Region")*, published in 1897 under my initials, V. G.) I cited this incident to Trepov to show the result of a

tives passed a resolution even more radical than the one adopted by
the May zemstvo conference. This new resolution demanded that
home and person be made inviolable; it demanded also the immediate
granting of the rights of free speech, freedom of the press, and freedom of assembly, and the convocation of a constituent assembly
elected on the basis of the principle of universal, equal, direct, and
secret suffrage by all citizens twenty-five years of age or older, regardless of sex, nationality, or religious creed.

The month of July abounded in different congresses. A fourth
zemstvo congress met, July 6–9, in spite of a circular letter to the
Ministry of the Interior forbidding it. The radical elements were
obviously in the majority in this congress, although the presidium included, side by side with such men as I. I. Petrunkevich and F. A.
Golovin, Count P. A. Heyden, the future leader of the advocates of
"peaceful reconstruction." At the same time there were among the
secretaries of the congress representatives of the third element like
Polner, Astrov,[25] and Rosenberg who were close to socialist circles.
The congress debated Bulygin's project on the State Duma, which
had been published in the *Novosti,* July 26, and declared itself against
it. After this Prince Kasatkin-Rostovsky and Govorukha-Otrok,[26]
representatives of Kazan and Kursk zemstvos, respectively, and some
others left the congress with much ado.

The main question placed before the congress was that of issuing
an appeal to the people for the purpose of establishing contact with
them and uniting with them in a fight for a truly popular representative government. The congress was interested, too, in ascertaining
as soon as possible the reaction of the people to Bulygin's project, and
to that end it unanimously voted to organize during the month of
July numerous congresses and conferences throughout the country
to discuss the project. The congress also adopted the text of its appeal
to the people. This appeal contained the following statement: "The
united forces of the Russian people must take a stand to prevent the
threatened ruin of the country; we must fight not one by one, not independently of each other, but unitedly, in order to protect our lives,
our property and our rights."

Yet it was repeatedly stated in the congress that its methods were

firm understanding on the part of the population that the government means business. It was far from my thoughts to advise him to follow suit. Great was my
amazement, therefore, when some three months later I saw the phrase, "and don't
spare your ammunition," in Trepov's historic order to the St. Petersburg garrison.

peaceful methods. "We are endeavoring to solve the present situation by peaceful means." One of the "peaceful means," however, was the call upon the people "to fight, not one by one . . . . but unitedly." The future Viborg Manifesto[27] was to follow the same motif.

The Congress of July 6–9 was closed by the police, and its appeal to the people did not materialize. But this did not prevent many members of the congress from attending the congress of the zemstvo-constitutionalists[28] held the next day. This latter group, including representatives of twenty gubernias, had been formed on November 8, 1903, to persuade the zemstvo assemblies to act in opposition to the government. Now, the zemstvo-constitutionalists decided first of all that Bulygin's project did not correspond to the promise the Tsar had given the zemstvo and municipality delegation on June 6, namely, that elections to the State Duma would be conducted "in a fitting manner," so they resolved that from then on they would consider as purposeless all addresses of caution and admonition and they expressed the hope that such addresses would not issue from zemstvo-constitutionalists.

Later this congress of zemstvo-constitutionalists considered the advisability of joining the Union of Unions, and on this issue the first definite split between the Right and Left wings of the liberal bourgeoisie occurred. In Finland on July 1–3 the Union of Unions had adopted a resolution to the effect that the frequent terroristic acts were justified by the actions of the government. Some members of the congress became indignant at this resolution and would agree to join the Union of Unions only with reservations: "Unanimously acknowledging that Russia is passing through an historic moment in which the means of opposing the government may not and cannot always be based upon the provisions of the existing law but at times may seem to violate them, but not approving every method of waging this fight, such as the method of violence, the zemstvo group of constitutional-democrats joins the Union of Unions." But this formula was rejected and the congress joined the Union of Unions without any reservations. This decision demonstrated the real significance of the congress and marked the beginning of the Cadet party, which day by day drew closer to the Social-Democratic Mensheviks. (As a logical consequence of this earlier radicalism of the Cadets, the coalition of Kerensky, a radical, with Lvov and Miliukov, Cadets, became possible in 1917.) The decision was finally sanctioned in August at the fourth conspiratory congress of the Union of Liberation, but it ended the activity of this Union as a separate organization, which henceforth became the Party of People's Freedom, the Cadet party.

In addition to the congresses of zemstvos and municipalities mentioned above, there were also congresses of newly formed organizations. On July 30 there was a peasant congress which assumed the high-sounding title of All-Russian Congress. Its attendance numbered only about one hundred, one-fourth of whom had no relation whatsoever to the peasant class, and in it the leading part was played by intellectuals close to the Socialist-Revolutionists. The subject discussed was the land problem.

In the meantime the Social Democrats, who in April had failed to come to an understanding on the subject of continuing the labor movement, a failure which explained in part the slight success of the labor manifestations on May 1, were gradually coming to an agreement on how an armed uprising should be prepared. At the third Bolshevik congress which met in May it was unanimously decided that the time had come for the proletarian movement to play a decisive role in the revolution. It called for an armed uprising and to that end charged all party organizations: (1) to explain to the proletariat, by means of propaganda and agitation, the "role of mass political demonstrations and strikes"; (2) to take most energetic steps to arm the proletariat; and (3) to work out a plan for an armed uprising and for controlling it and if necessary to create special groups of party workers for this purpose.[29]

The Menshevik conference, held about the same time, adopted essentially the same resolution. Believing that the general uprising could not be set for a definite date, and supposing that conditions favoring a victorious uprising could be created by supporting constant unrest among the masses, this conference resolved that Menshevik activity among the masses should be increased in connection with current political events and that the masses should be made to realize "the inevitability of the revolution, the necessity of being always prepared to offer armed resistance, and the possibility of this resistance turning into a revolution overnight."

These resolutions show that the essence of the differences between the Bolsheviks and the Mensheviks could be boiled down to this: the Mensheviks desired to use the liberal opposition for their own ends, that is, to co-operate with the radical wing of the liberals, while preparing an armed uprising. The Bolsheviks, on the other hand, attached no importance to the liberal opposition; they intended to sever

all connections with it and to direct all their efforts to preparing an
armed uprising. This difference was demonstrated in the resolutions
which the Bolshevik and Menshevik congresses adopted on the subject. The Bolshevik congress resolved: (1) to explain to the workers
the anti-revolutionary and anti-proletarian character of the bourgeois
movement in all its ramifications, beginning with the moderate liberal
attitude represented by a large majority of landowners and factory
owners and ending with the most radical attitude represented by the
Union of Liberation and many other groups of representatives of the
liberal professions; (2) to prevent at all costs the bourgeois democracy from taking the labor movement into its hands and thus appearing as champion of the proletariat. The Menshevik congress
resolved: "To interest, by means of the widest agitation, large circles
of the population in the proletariat's revolutionary struggle for a
democratic republic, so as to insure the fighting proletariat of the support of non-proletarian groups." These two groups of Social Democrats used corresponding tactics in 1917.

Immediately after the Social-Democratic leaders had adopted the
above resolutions, the party workers began most extensively to spread
propaganda for an armed uprising and directed their special efforts
to sowing seeds of unrest in the army and navy. The results of this
activity became apparent about June. The Social Democrats had
selected the Black Sea Fleet as their first field of operations, and had
succeeded in organizing in Sevastopol a central committee of sailors,[30]
which worked out a plan for mutiny of the whole fleet during the
July maneuvers. This plan was wrecked by the premature mutiny on
June 15 of the crew of the battleship "Prince Potemkin Tavri-
chesky." The sailors arrested all the commanding officers, assumed
command of the ship and for thirteen days roamed the Black Sea
threatening to bombard Sevastopol and Odessa. A short time previously, on June 10, the party workers in Odessa had succeeded in
arousing the local dock workers, who were pacified only with considerable trouble by troops called from their summer quarters.

This success gave wings to the hopes of both Bolsheviks and
Mensheviks. The Menshevik *Iskra*[31] wrote, "The time has come to
act bravely. Courage will win. Take the state banks and arsenals by
force and arm the people."

But these events, like the announcement of the Bolsheviks that
they considered the radicals (i.e., the Cadets) as great an enemy as
the Tsarist government, failed to bring the radicals to their senses.

They continued to attach themselves to revolutionary organizations and even professed admiration for the results of the efforts of the revolutionaries. For instance, an article from Sevastopol published in the *Osvobozhdenie* and entitled "Volnyi Korabl" ("A Free Ship") described with praise the "engrossing, uplifting spectacle" presented by "a free ship sailing the seas under a red flag." "One cannot help admiring the courage, the dash, the epic daring of this free ship," the writer exclaimed and then added in ecstasy: "Thou shalt always be a living example, a proud challenge to freedom, to the light."

But the Black Sea demonstrations and some minor labor strikes in St. Petersburg in June marked the end of the unrest in the summer months of 1905. It was still quieter in August when the number of wasted working days in St. Petersburg fell to 4,000. This is to be explained partly by the season, a very quiet one in every respect, and also by the publication on August 6 of the statute concerning the State Duma and the system by which it was to be elected. Although this system was not exactly what the majority of the most active public men desired, it was acclaimed as a definite and decisive step toward popular government. *Osvobozhdenie* had some reasons for exclaiming, "From the hands of Nicholas II Russia has torn another weapon to be used in her fight against autocracy; she must use it well and to the limit." The majority of the people regarded the future State Duma as a tool with which to fight the government, and discussed the best ways to make such use of it. The young, newly formed parties were getting ready for the elections and directing all their efforts toward securing the greatest possible number of supporters. They turned to the people in an endeavor to train those forces which were to attack the government in the State Duma itself.

For some other unknown reason—perhaps it was the quiet season—the government, which had wavered under Trepov between repression of and concessions to the public, began to favor the latter procedure. It even moderated somewhat its treatment of the revolutionary elements. The bureau of the Union of Unions, which had been arrested in July at the Lesnoi near St. Petersburg during one of its conspiratory sessions, was set free in a body, although the evidence against it presented conclusive proof of its openly revolutionary activity. At the same time an order was issued limiting the arrests of revolutionary workers to the arrest of those who were connected with terroristic acts. The gendarmes continued to ferret out illegal printing establishments but limited themselves to confiscating the presses and other machinery and did not arrest the workers and party men. Public demonstrations were tolerated in so far as they did not become riotous. But the greatest concession to the public was made toward the end of August, when the government suddenly granted autonomous rights to the universities and thereby deprived itself of the right to interfere in the events which took place in those institutions. The revolutionary forces used the new status of these temples of learning to their own advantage.

In July, *Iskra,* speaking of the approaching opening of the universities, said, "The attack [on the government] must go on also in academic halls. The systematic and open violation of all rules established by the police regime, the expulsion of [government] supervisors, inspectors, and spies of all kinds, the opening of the doors of the lecture halls to all citizens who wish to enter them, the transformation of our universities into places of public meetings and political gatherings—all this is the goal that the students must set themselves." "The transforming of universities and academies into property of the revolutionary people! That is the task of the students." "Of course, such a transforming will make the universities a center for the gathering and organizing of the masses."

The government seemed almost to encourage this trend in the universities. The revolutionary elements took to heart the advice of *Iskra* and, as soon as the term had begun, carried it out to the fullest extent. A succession of meetings of the most varied classes of people were held in the universities, and Social-Democratic propaganda, inciting the people to an armed uprising, was circulated very freely. Things reached such a state that the revolutionary students allotted special lecture halls to the meetings of soldiers, officers, clerks, policemen, domestic servants, and secret service agents. These meetings lasted until late at night and were addressed by party orators, who visited the universities for this express purpose. Even specialists were procured to address particular audiences.

The faculties were not in sympathy with this activity, but in most cases they were thoroughly cowed and dared not take any steps to expel from the universities of St. Petersburg and Moscow the motley crowd which controlled them. Only one courageous voice was raised against these vile doings and that was the voice of Prince S. N. Trubetskoi, whom the professors had elected rector of Moscow University. In September he addressed the students in a fiery speech and appealed to them to purge the temples of learning of these incessant disorders. "A university," said the Prince, "is not a place for political meetings. It cannot and must not be made a public square." But soon this voice was silent forever. Prince Trubetskoi died suddenly on September 29. The city and the students of Moscow made use of his funeral to stage a mighty political manifestation; but Trubetskoi's death actually excited much genuine sorrow among the public and among the students.*

With the beginning of September, the year 1905 entered the third period of its revolutionary development. This period ended with the publication of the Manifesto of October 17. It was characterized not only by turbulence—the last months of this year increasingly so—but also by the consolidation of all forces of the opposition and by the total demoralization of the government.

At first the revolutionary movement did not appear in the street; it was concentrated in different official and private buildings, chiefly the universities; but there it raged. By the middle of September there were more strikes and the demands of the strikers were not so much economic as political. The strikes were headed by the best-educated workers, such as the printers. In Moscow the printers' strike began September 23 but lasted only four days and was rather uneventful.

The stimulus to open revolutionary acts was the announcement on October 3 of the ratification of the Portsmouth Treaty. The war was over. The population, which had unconsciously realized that internal strife was not to be indulged in when the country was at war, no longer felt this moral restraint. Beginning with October 4, strikes of an openly political character broke out in St. Petersburg and very quickly spread through all the factories and embraced ever widening groups of the people. Slowly but surely they affected nearly every public utility service such as the streetcars, the power station, and the water works; for although the latter continued to function, they did so with constant interruptions. By October 10 nearly all the working population of St. Petersburg was on strike. Some of the railroads near St. Petersburg had gone on strike on October 7. During the nights the city was plunged in darkness and was usually in a state of

---

* Had Trubetskoi lived a few months longer, things might have been different. Sergei Nikolaevich Trubetskoi had been my classmate at the university and my close friend. He was an exceptionally noble, direct, sincere, and intelligent person. He would not have agreed with the results of the liberation movement in 1906. He would have left the Cadet party, as his brother, Prince Evgenii Trubetskoi,[32] did later. This would have altered the attitude of the befogged Russian intelligentsia toward him.

siege. The banks hastily fixed iron bars to their doors and windows; the stores lowered their metal screens, and those which had no metal screens boarded up their windows and doors. The striking workers crowded the central parts of the city and organized noisy meetings. The Cossack patrols and the mounted police were powerless to prevent such gatherings of the rebellious crowd. Dispersed on one street corner, it would gather on another. Party workers went among the people and inflamed their passions with lengthy harangues, which were made more effective by continual repetition. In some streets barricades appeared and to destroy them the troops were obliged to use arms, as for example on Vasilievsky Island. Agitators even tried to penetrate into the military barracks but were unsuccessful; some sergeants of long service arrested them and delivered them to the authorities. Nevertheless, the general agitation was reflected in the army, which was brought into contact with it when guarding the state institutions and the banks.

News from the gubernias told tales of similar occurrences in many other cities. At Kharkov, Odessa, and Ekaterinoslav the strike turned into an armed uprising, beginning October 10. Barricades erected by the insurgents were taken by the troops only after considerable fighting.

The railroad strike, in accordance with orders from St. Petersburg, spread, beginning October 12, over the entire network and paralyzed the economic life of the country. This railway strike originated in an agreement between the revolutionary parties and the extreme Left wing of public circles embodied in the Union of Unions.

In Moscow the strike movement progressed more slowly than in St. Petersburg; but by October 15 all the Moscow factories were on strike and the normal life of the city was disrupted. There was no electricity, no transportation. The zemstvo and city employees were on strike; some of the government institutions suspended operations; actors of the Imperial Theatre, druggists, physicians, and the students of secondary schools all joined the strike.

The government was at a loss to know what to do. It was not ready to use strong measures, although there was still a possibility of doing so. In St. Petersburg it limited itself to protecting the citizens from the mobs, although on October 14 Trepov issued a detailed order to the garrison announcing that no further assembling of crowds in the streets would be tolerated. It was this order which included the words: "Should the people resist, do not use blank cartridges and do not spare your ammunition." Yet, conditions being what they were, this order had no effect.

On October 15 those already on strike in St. Petersburg were joined by the typesetters of the city, who up to then had continued to work on the newspapers because of their radical tone. The railroad strike virtually isolated the capital; and now, after the printers' strike, the capital was not even in a position to get information of what was happening in the gubernias. The *Pravitelstvennyi Vestnik* and the *Vedomosti Peterburgskago Gradonachalnika*[33] continued to appear but their information was limited and trusted by no one. The wildest rumors were circulated. From somewhere came the information that the workers of the enormous Kolomna factory, situated fifteen versts from the capital, were marching en masse upon the city bent upon destroying everything in sight. This rumor created considerable panic in the fashionable Liteinyi.

Meanwhile, on October 13, there was organized in St. Petersburg the City Soviet of St. Petersburg Workers' Deputies. It consisted of 562 delegates, one for every 500 workers, and represented 147 factories and more than 50 small establishments. Its chairman was an assistant attorney, Khrustalev-Nosar.[34] This Soviet immediately undertook to form workers' shock troops, and in some of the factories the workers, at the instigation of the Soviet, began to make "cold arms."[35]

The bourgeois parties with one exception entirely disappeared from the political stage. This exception was the Cadet party, which assembled on October 14 for its constituent meeting. It adopted the following resolution suggested by Miliukov: "The people demand basic liberties, free election of representatives to a constituent assembly according to the principles of universal, equal, direct and secret suffrage, and a general political amnesty. The Constitutional Democrats support these demands, and therefore this meeting declares its complete solidarity with the strike movement. The meeting welcomes as a most important step of the people the organized, peaceful, and yet formidable advance of the Russian working class, devoid of political rights yet mighty in public spirit." By adopting this resolution, the Cadets demonstrated unprecedented courage and deep political understanding. Then they went to their respective homes and took no further part in the October movement.

On October 15 a committee of publishers assembled in the offices of the *Novoe Vremia* and resolved "to heed no longer the orders of the censors." But they were powerless to carry out their resolution, for without workers they had no means of publishing anything at all.

Meanwhile the government published thundering orders which it was powerless to enforce, and feverishly looked about for a way out of its embarrassment. It concentrated all its hopes upon Witte, who had just returned from America crowned with the laurels of the Portsmouth Treaty and elevated to the rank of Count. But Witte knew his worth and made his own terms. The role he played at that time is very clear: Confident of his ability and bold enough to declare that he knew how to save Russia, he desired to concentrate all power in his own hands in such a way that neither the government nor the crown would be able to deprive him of such new authority. This was easy, and his method obvious. He endeavored to persuade the public that he shared to the fullest extent the desire of the progressives to establish a regime of equity in Russia as a means of promoting the development of the country, a regime in which the population would enjoy all the rights of free citizens. Accordingly, from October 10 to 17 he bargained with the supreme power. The Tsar wished to make him chief executive, but did not want to give him any binding pledges. Witte answered that he could undertake to guide the ship of state only if the basic demands of the people were satisfied. He proposed to meet these demands by having the Tsar confirm his report in which he stated the necessity of immediately granting the people civil liberties. He repeatedly declared at the Tsar's conferences that there was of course another way to insure order in the country: to establish a dictatorship and suppress all uprisings. This latter course, he said, he himself could not adopt; but at the same time he felt he was not in a position to say which course was preferable. This was nothing but an attempt to free himself of all responsibility for the method which would be finally adopted. That the method he desired would be adopted he did not doubt for a moment, so sure was he that the government would not be able to extricate itself from the situation without his aid.

Thus Witte expressed himself before the throne. His attitude and his addresses to the public, however, were quite different. On October 11 he received delegates from the St. Petersburg railway employees, the majority of whom had been on strike since October 7, and spoke to them at length. He prefaced his remarks with the statement that he addressed them not as the chairman of the Committee of Ministers but as a private citizen (!!!). He admitted frankly that military control of the railways, against which the delegates were protesting, was an anachronism and that it was to be wondered why this state of things had not been remedied. Then he spoke of the events of the day and made the following statement—a rather monstrous one to come from the Chairman of the Committee of Ministers: "The government may perish in this fight, but you would perish also,—you, the best of the people. All of which would be to the advantage of that very bourgeoisie against which you are now struggling."

What crude demagogy! What paltry statesmanship! One might justly say that every one of these words was in itself a crime against the state. But by his admission that the government's downfall was possible, and by his attempt to frighten the workingmen with the ghost of the bourgeoisie, Witte meant simply: "Give me power, and I shall satisfy all your wants. I shall guarantee you victory over both bourgeoisie and government." But the result was not what Witte expected. The railway strikers' committee listened to the delegates' story of Witte's remarks and immediately resolved to transform the local strike into a general one throughout the entire country. And this they did.

Meanwhile Witte went on his way seducing the public. On October 13 he telegraphed Professor Yaroshenko[36] in Odessa congratulating him upon his return to the city from which he had been deported by the administration for having made revolutionary speeches at a banquet on November 20, 1904. The news of this telegram was very speedily broadcast by the press, possibly with Witte's connivance.

On the same day, October 13, the Tsar sent Witte a letter empowering him "to unify all government activities." This transformed him from a mere Chairman of the Committee of Ministers, with a limited and clearly defined responsibility, into the head of the ministerial college. Witte, however, answered firmly that he would be unable to comply with the Monarch's wish until his own program was adopted, approved, and published. The die was cast. Witte, confident that the Tsar could not resist this ultimatum, had burned his bridges. The Tsar's position was very difficult indeed. He was then in his summer residence at Peterhof on the Baltic, forty kilometers from the capital, and had no means of communication with it except government steamships. Frightened by his immediate advisers, who feared for the future of the Imperial family, the Tsar hesitated and deferred making a decision. Two days passed. Witte was perturbed. He began to doubt the correctness of his calculations and decided that he would have to have recourse to some other means of influencing the Tsar if he was to gain a complete victory. Accordingly he decided to send to the Grand Duke Nikolai Nikolaevich,[37] whose opinion at that time the Tsar greatly valued, some information which might persuade the Grand Duke that the only way to avert the collapse of the state and the throne was to grant a constitution immediately. To carry out this scheme Witte turned once more to his trusted Ushakov, whom he had received from Zubatov. Ushakov was the state printing-office worker who had assisted Zubatov in organizing workers' meetings. He was a bright fellow with much sound common sense, capable of expressing his ideas smoothly, well informed of the sentiments and moods of the workers, and possessing much authentic information concerning the workers of the St. Petersburg factories. Witte also used the help of Andronnikov, another of his assistants who had some connection with the entourage of the Grand Duke, and on October 16 succeeded in having Ushakov received by the Grand Duke.* Ushakov, acting under instructions, represented the situation to the Grand Duke in such a light as to persuade him that only the granting of the constitution would avert an armed revolution and that the revolutionary movement would cease as soon as the workingmen were given representation in the government.

On the next day, October 17, Witte was invited to present himself to the Tsar. He departed from Peterhof accompanied by N. I. Vuich, Manager of Affairs of the Committee of Ministers, and the devoted Prince Aleksei Dmitrievich Obolensky. On the way he decided that on one point he would have to make a concession. He saw that the people should be apprised of the granting of the constitution not through his own report, confirmed by the Tsar, but by a manifesto issuing from the Monarch himself. He was brought to this decision very likely by the news that on October 16 the Tsar had received Witte's old enemy, Goremykin, who, in company with Budberg, had already composed a manifesto granting the people some of the rights they demanded. Accordingly, on the way to Peterhof, Obolensky

---

* Witte felt so deeply obliged to Andronnikov for his help in this matter that when he returned from Peterhof on October 17 with the signed manifesto he immediately wrote to P. N. Durnovo requesting him to add Prince M. M. Andronnikov to the staff of the Ministry of the Interior. It is a curious fact that the note was addressed not to Bulygin, who was still minister, but to Durnovo, in whom Witte saw Bulygin's successor.

hurriedly outlined a manifesto, with which Witte finally appeared before the Tsar.

This time Witte had calculated correctly. The Tsar was convinced that Witte was the only man who could save the situation, and this conviction prompted him to disregard his personal dislike and distrust of Witte and to give him full power to select Obolensky's draft of a manifesto in preference to that of Goremykin. At the same time the Tsar confirmed Witte's report, which would accompany the manifesto, and which would appear not as the main basis of the manifesto but as an elaboration of it and would point out the necessity of granting liberties without waiting for the necessary alteration of the laws.

The Manifesto of October 17, 1905, was, in essence, a frank capitulation of the government to the public, or rather, to the revolutionary forces. It expressed the "inflexible" will of the Tsar as follows:

"(1) To grant the people the immutable foundations of civil liberty based on true inviolability of person, the freedom of conscience, speech, assembly, and union.

"(2) Without delaying the elections to the State Duma already ordered to summon those classes of the people that have hitherto been entirely deprived of electoral rights to participation in the Duma—in so far as this is possible in the short space of time before the Duma assembles—leaving the further development of the principle of electoral rights to be worked out by legislative order.

"(3) To establish as an unbreakable rule that no law shall go into force without the approval of the State Duma and that those whom the people elect shall have an opportunity actually to participate in supervising the legality of the actions of authorities appointed by Us."

The publication of this manifesto marked the end of the third of the periods into which I have divided the year 1905. It also marked the end of an epoch in Russian history many centuries long. The fourth period of the year 1905 is discussed in the following chapter.

CHAPTER XIX

COUNT WITTE AS CHAIRMAN OF THE COUNCIL OF MINISTERS

October 17, 1905, was undoubtedly a day of rejoicing for the Russian progressives, but different progressive groups experienced different degrees of joy. The revolutionary and socialist elements appreciated the Tsar's manifesto in so far as it granted them civil liberties in which they rightly saw a great opportunity for spreading their ideas unhindered and for extending the scope of their revolutionary activities. But in its entirety the manifesto did not satisfy them. They were glad of the advantages it offered but insisted that it was far from adequate.

The radical liberals, the Cadets, saw in the manifesto the approach of that day of which they had dreamed so fondly, the day when, supported by the masses of the population, they would take the government into their hands. They were really exuberantly happy, but they expressed only moderate joy; they insisted whenever possible that the manifesto was welcome only as the first step toward the transforming of autocratic Russia into a constitutional monarchy, as a means to an end.

Only the moderate liberals, the future Octobrists, acclaimed the manifesto with sincere joy; they saw in it the complete realization of their desires.

But there was one person who rejoiced more than anyone else—Count S. Y. Witte. On October 17, as he returned from Peterhof bearing the signed manifesto and his own confirmed report, Witte felt triumphant. Even though he misconceived both the moods of the lower strata of the population, which demanded not political rights but tangible material gains, and the aspirations of the radical liberals, Witte was happy to have regained authority and a chance to display his customary feverish activity. More than that, he imagined himself to be the idol of Russia and was quite certain that the new state act would bring peace to the country and put a stop to the subversive activities of the revolutionary forces. He seemed totally unaware of the enormous national responsibility which had been placed on his shoulders.

Witte directed all his efforts to carry out as soon as possible the provisions of the manifesto and report so that the St. Petersburg public would be assured that the manifesto was not merely an empty expression but a firm resolve on the part of the government to put the reforms immediately into effect. This is demonstrated by the fact that as soon as he arrived in St. Petersburg from Peterhof he sent the manifesto and report to be published in *Pravitelstvennyi Vestnik*. But he forgot about the vast and excited country beyond St. Petersburg. This was a great oversight which revealed his total lack of administrative talent and even political intuition. Not for a moment did it occur to him that the most elementary considerations demanded that the local branches of the central government be informed before the population as to the new state act and be given certain instructions for announcing the Tsar's manifesto. Nor did it occur to him that precautionary measures should be taken to prevent the demonstrations that might follow such an announcement.* That night, however, he conferred at length with Kryzhanovsky, the author of. Bulygin's project concerning the State Duma, regarding the possible ways of altering the project so as to make it comply with the terms of the new manifesto.

Witte's next concern was to meet the insistent public demand for an amnesty of persons convicted of political crimes. He entrusted to the Ministry of Justice, in collaboration with the Ministry of the Interior, the task of composing a ukase pardoning such persons, and instructed these ministries to extend the pardon to as many categories of political offenders as possible.

Witte also endeavored to establish contacts with different classes of society. In the days immediately following October 17 he seemed to be laboring under the impression that the manifesto and report had won him the sympathies of a majority of the public. This impression was strengthened by the few congratulations which the Tsar received

---

* Other representatives of the government shared Witte's illusions. D. F. Trepov, for example, whom Witte notified of the manifesto by telephone, was transported with joy and said to Gerasimov,[1] chief of the Secret Police of St. Petersburg, "Tomorrow the whole country will celebrate the great patriotic national holiday of the birth of a new, free Russia." On October 17, V. A. Dediulin,[2] Governor of St. Petersburg, assembled in his house all the higher police officials, read the manifesto to them, kissed it, and immediately began to plan, not methods of preserving order in the city, but the manner in which the manifesto should be announced to the city; he even considered having it announced by special heralds.

from some public institutions. The St. Petersburg City Duma sent a rather unceremonious telegram to Nicholas II exclaiming, "Hurrah for the Tsar of a free people!" The greeting from the Moscow stock exchange was more dignified, assuring him of its "unshaken devotion to the Monarch." But the thing that most distorted Witte's perspective in judging the degree of public satisfaction was the multitude of greetings which he personally received, the majority of which came not from institutions or corporations but from individuals. Nor was his illusion shaken by the demonstration on October 18 near the Kazan cathedral, where the demonstrators carried red flags and banners bearing the inscription, "We demand a constituent assembly." Each detachment of the crowd was accompanied by a revolutionary Red Cross unit with physicians and nurses, and thus demonstrated its readiness to fight the army and the police. At first no resistance was made to its progress and when its orators declared that the manifesto was but the first victory of the revolution and that the Tsar would have to pay with his blood for the oppression of the people, the crowd gave vent to its rage by turning against a patriotic demonstration which appeared near the cathedral bearing the tri-colored national flag. There was a short fight. Several shots were fired and the bearer of the Russian flag was wounded; the flag fell from his grasp. The national colors were lowered before the red banners of the International. The crowd moved forward to the accompaniment of its own shouting, but when faced with half a hundred Cossacks it immediately dispersed.

The end of the railway strike on October 22 signified a return to normal life and seemed to justify Witte's assurance that the manifesto was bound to have a pacifying influence. But Witte was not too well informed. It was learned that the railway strike would have ended anyway, chiefly because the rank-and-file citizens were indignant at the inconveniences and material losses which the strike was inflicting upon the people at large. The strike leaders perceived that they might go too far in antagonizing the people, and hastened to use the manifesto as a pretext for an honorable retreat. Nevertheless on October 19 the Moscow strike committee announced that the cessation of the strike was but temporary, that "the railway workers are resuming work only to become better organized, to collect necessary funds, to organize a general armed uprising of the proletariat, and to continue their fight under the banners of socialism"; they would carry on their struggle until they had secured true liberties, a constituent assembly, a general political amnesty, and the satisfaction of their social and economic needs.

Witte's efforts to find support among the radicals and the press were unsuccessful. He asked Prince G. E. Lvov, Kokoshkin,[3] and F. A. Golovin, representatives of the Left wing of the zemstvo congresses and organizers of the Party of People's Freedom, to help him in his work. They answered gently but firmly that what they desired was a convocation of a constituent assembly; this alone would pacify the people. Witte pointed out to them that the introduction of any electoral changes based on universal suffrage would have to rest with the State Duma, but he promised to support the Duma in its efforts to effect such changes. Still they refused to support him. Evidently they were convinced that the government would manage to establish a system of election to the Duma which would insure the government a compliant majority.

Witte suffered a still greater affront from the representatives of the periodical press whom he had invited to interview him. He requested them to help him pacify the public; but in reply the Jew Propper, editor of the sensational *Birzhevyia Vedomosti*,[4] said arrogantly: "Remove your rowdy soldiers. Transfer the protection of the capital from the police to the militia." Witte, who had been in the habit of rebuking aged and venerable members of the State Council, found no courage in his heart to put this impudent trafficker in journalistic trash in his place. The published "interview" with Witte revealed to everyone his lack of firmness and his inability to maintain the dignity of the government.

Witte also encountered difficulties in the all-important matter of selecting the Council of Ministers. It was his plan to choose the members of this body so as to make his selection acceptable to the progressives and to secure men who could be counted on to follow his lead. (For although Witte gladly made friendly advances to the public by allowing it to express its opinions both by word of mouth and in print, he had not the slightest intention of relinquishing to it one particle of his power. He was constitutionally inclined toward enlightened absolutism, a form of government as enticing to an ambitious man as it is difficult of realization.) But from the first he was faced with obstructions to the carrying out of his plan, most of which centered around the person of P. N. Durnovo.

At some time previously Witte had promised Durnovo that if ever he were called upon to form a government he would make

Durnovo Minister of the Interior. Undoubtedly this promise had been given under pressure of some mysterious dependence of Witte upon Durnovo, and probably Witte had never intended to keep it. But Durnovo was now so sure of this appointment that he had already decided how he would arrange his furniture in the official residence of the Minister of the Interior. He even sent someone there, while Bulygin was still occupying the place, to measure a certain room in order to ascertain if it would accommodate one of his bookcases of extraordinarily large proportions. Notwithstanding Durnovo's assurance, Witte was impelled by certain considerations to disregard his promise and to advance as his candidate for Minister of the Interior, Prince S. D. Urusov, a man who as Governor of Tver had won the sympathies of the Left wing of the local zemstvo, which was closely connected with the founders of the Cadet party. These considerations were as follows: First, Durnovo was not the man meekly to execute another person's orders, and Witte no doubt foresaw that he would never obtain perfect obedience from him. Second, Durnovo, because of his political views, was totally unacceptable to the public. The opposition had been far from persuaded of Durnovo's liberalism by his liberal speeches before the Committee of Ministers when it had discussed how to put into effect the Manifesto of December 12, 1904. The progressives intuitively saw in Durnovo a man of strong will and of a distinctly Right orientation, who would make public activities conform to the limits of the law. Third, the liberal press had recalled an incident during the reign of Alexander III which had led to Durnovo's discharge as Director of the Police Department. This affair was interpreted as a blot on Durnovo's character and lowered his standing in the eyes of the public.

Witte not only advanced the candidacy of Urusov as Minister of the Interior as a move to gain liberal support; he also selected as Minister of Justice another man quite acceptable to the Leftist public, Senator A. F. Koni.[5] In 1878 Koni had been presiding judge of the St. Petersburg district court which tried and acquitted Vera Zasulich,[6] who had attempted to assassinate the Governor of St. Petersburg, F. F. Trepov.[7] Since then Koni had been very popular. Witte thought that Koni's appointment, together with that of Urusov, would quash all accusations that he wished to have reactionaries appointed as heads of the administration and the courts. Next he offered several posts in his cabinet to some of the moderately liberal Moscow public men. He offered to D. N. Shipov the position of State Comptroller,

to A. I. Guchkov[8] the Ministry of Trade and Industry, and to Prince
E. N. Trubetskoi the Ministry of Education. On October 26 these
three men arrived in St. Petersburg from Moscow believing that
Urusov was to be Minister of the Interior. Great was their surprise
to learn that Durnovo and not Urusov was to hold that post and that
Urusov was to be Durnovo's assistant. Not seeing their way clear to
become colleagues of the hated Durnovo, they refused to accept the
ministerial portfolios which they had been offered. Trubetskoi bluntly
refused on the ground that in his career as a publicist he had advocated a policy of public education which, as he well realized, the government could not possibly fulfill. Nor would the other two men
yield to Witte's persuasion to accept the positions he offered. In vain
did he assure them that Durnovo was the only official he knew who
could be counted on to hold the revolutionary forces in check. He
kept on negotiating with them until October 30, although both Shipov
and Guchkov assured him that their participation in his cabinet would
not gain him the sympathies of the radical opposition; in fact, they
contended they could be of more use to him by remaining outside his
cabinet, where they could work with him to conciliate a part of the
public. Finally, since he felt obliged to make Durnovo Minister of
the Interior, Witte had to abandon the idea of securing the collaboration of these men and of including in his cabinet men who had considerable public influence.[9]

What had occurred during these few days to make Witte feel
obliged to fulfill his promise to Durnovo, a step which involved losing
the help of prominent public men? The answer is this: Durnovo had
been more resolute than Witte. Witte had suggested that Durnovo
remain assistant minister with the same rights that had been accorded
D. F. Trepov* as independent chief of the Police Department, but
Durnovo had bluntly refused. Witte realized full well that he himself
had had but little experience in the work of administration, and with
revolutionary outbursts becoming more and more frequent he realized
also that words and liberal measures alone could not stop the spread
of the revolt, that other means were needed. Under these circumstances he considered Durnovo's collaboration indispensable; he reluctantly admitted to himself the necessity of fulfilling his promise to
Durnovo and of persuading Prince Urusov to become assistant
minister.

* On October 26 Trepov was appointed Palace Commandant to succeed Prince
Engalychev.[10]

This was the state of things when the Moscow public men named above arrived in St. Petersburg. Desiring above all else to induce them to enter his government, Witte made a second effort to have Durnovo remain assistant minister. While negotiating with Guchkov and Shipov he officially submitted Durnovo's name to the Tsar as candidate for Minister of the Interior, but he characterized Durnovo in such a way that the Tsar refused to make the appointment. Witte was then able to tell Durnovo that he had recommended him for the office of minister, as he had promised, but that the Tsar had rejected the recommendation. Witte assumed that Durnovo would prefer to remain assistant minister rather than to return to the Senate, since by remaining assistant minister he could entertain hopes of being appointed a member of the State Council.

But Durnovo was not to be so easily deceived. He understood immediately that the Tsar's refusal had been prompted by Witte. I happened to see Durnovo just after he had received Witte's letter telling him of the Tsar's decision. He was positively raging. He paced up and down his office like a wild beast in a cage, repeating over and over: "I'll show him! I'll show him!" and he did. What he told Witte, what threat he used, I cannot say. I do know that in a vague way the threat concerned certain of Witte's documents or censored letters which if shown to the Tsar would have ruined Witte's career. Be that as it may, Witte capitulated, and to such an extent that when the Tsar refused a second time to accept Durnovo as minister Witte felt it necessary to report most humbly that unless Durnovo was appointed head of the administration and police of the empire he, Witte, would not guarantee to preserve the existing order from a revolutionary attack. The Tsar's reply was brief: "Very well, but for a short time only." Durnovo was appointed, not as minister, but merely as one in charge of the ministry.

After Durnovo's appointment was assured, Witte gave up Koni as Minister of Justice in favor of S. S. Manukhin.[11] As a departmental director and as assistant minister in this ministry, Manukhin had been a thoroughgoing conservative. Influenced by the spirit of the times, however, he had given up his conservatism and had become an ardent champion of the idea that the courts should be entirely independent of any influence from above. Unfortunately, as Minister of Justice he lacked the strength of will to carry out this idea. In November 1905 there was a need of decisive measures against judicial officers whose dependence on either the administration or certain parts of the public was clearly revealed. Manukhin failed to take these measures and Witte felt obliged to part with him. He was succeeded by M. G. Akimov,[12] on whose appointment, I suspect, Durnovo had some influence. Durnovo was married to Akimov's sister and was on the best of terms with Akimov himself.

Unfortunate in the above appointments, Witte began to exercise greater care in selecting his other ministers. He sought men who were conformable to his wishes. He considered this specially necessary particularly since there were three ministers whose appointment he did not control: the ministers of war, the navy, and the court. These three were selected and appointed by the Tsar himself and in Witte's government were the same persons who had occupied these positions before the Committee of Ministers was reorganized into the Council of Ministers. In these circumstances it was but natural that Witte should make the remaining selections from among his former colleagues in the Ministry of Finance who were accustomed to follow his instructions more or less blindly. He appointed I. P. Shipov Minister of Finance, N. N. Kutler head of the Chief Administration of Land Organization and Agriculture, and Prince A. D. Obolensky Ober-Prokuror of the Holy Synod. In Obolensky's case, however, Witte was mistaken in expecting complete submission. In the final analysis Obolensky always agreed with Witte, but during debates on a subject he presented his own hazy, paradoxical, and amateurish ideas. The speeches of this man—"in whose head three cocks were crowing at the same time," to use Pobedonostsev's neat remark— only served to lengthen the sessions of the Council. Other members soon ceased to pay the slightest attention to him, or even to take the trouble to discuss his ideas. Nemeshaev,[13] formerly manager of the southwestern railways, was appointed Minister of Ways and Communications. He probably knew the railway business quite well, but he was no statesman; his views were those of the man in the street.

Thus Witte's cabinet was divided into three sharply defined groups. The first consisted of Witte's avowed partisans, Shipov, Kutler, and Nemeshaev, who did not dare oppose him. None of these three were really members of the Council of Ministers; they were specialists, as it were, managing special technical branches of the administration, and had nothing to do with state policy. The second group was composed of those who desired to show their own initiative. Within the limitations of their respective offices these men expressed their individual views and policies, but in the Council of

Ministers invariably supported Witte. These were: Count I. I. Tolstoi,[14] Minister of Education; V. I. Timiriazev,[15] Minister of Commerce and Industry; D. A. Filosofov, State Comptroller; and Count V. N. Lamsdorf, Minister of Foreign Affairs. Lamsdorf rarely attended the meetings of the Council of Ministers, and when he did he never uttered a word. As far as I could judge, his was a colorless personality. He was interested in nothing except questions of foreign policy, and had hardly any idea of conditions in his own country, its needs, and the domestic problems which confronted it.

Count Tolstoi and Timiriazev presented a striking contrast. Count Tolstoi was an idealist and a theorist, and although he was upright and well-meaning he was not very intelligent; he was poorly informed about the work entrusted to him and treated it with sentimental dilettantism. Timiriazev, on the other hand, was practical and a materialist. He was familiar enough with problems of industry and trade, but at that time his well-defined aim was to make close connections in the world of industry and finance so that in due time he could enter banking circles with the largest possible salary. In this he was successful, for he later became chairman of the board of directors of the Russian Foreign Trade Bank and until the revolution received an annual salary of several hundred thousand rubles. Timiriazev proved his adaptability most clearly under Bolshevik rule. After the conclusion of the Brest-Litovsk Treaty, he published in some German publication a long article in the form of an interview in which he tried to prove that the conditions of that treaty were favorable to Russia and were quite acceptable. But then Timiriazev's German sympathies were evident even during the war; they were the result of those contacts he had made in Berlin industrial circles when he was there as our financial representative. By making use of these same associations he managed to live quite comfortably even under the Bolsheviks.

Filosofov was a somewhat different type. As I have already said, while speaking of him as a State Secretary of the State Council, he was intelligent, talented, and had made his way very cleverly to a position of high mark and importance. His personality was commanding, almost arrogant. As a member of Witte's government he was concerned only with getting a firm hold on his position as minister, hoping, perhaps, to become in time Chairman of the Council of Ministers, for there was no limit to his ambition. During the October days of 1905 and especially during the months immediately following when street revolutionary disturbances had reached their peak, Filosofov, like many other bureaucrats who were keeping their noses to the wind, concluded that the old regime had breathed its last and that it was about to be replaced by a parliamentary regime. Anxious to prepare a nice niche for himself in this new regime, he endeavored to play up to the public by making almost radical speeches. He also conceived the idea of excluding the State Comptroller, which post he occupied at that time, from the Council of Ministers, thus making him an absolutely independent supervisor of all expenditures of state funds by the ministries. He supposed that this would make his official position much more secure, since it would then be unaffected by changes in the personnel of the government. And, in truth, the idea was sound. It is indeed difficult to supervise and control with any degree of impartiality and steadiness the activities of the members of a body to which one belongs and upon which one depends; it can be done only when civic responsibility has been developed to a high degree.

The third group in Witte's Council of Ministers was composed of those who belonged only formally to the government, and who considered themselves actually independent of it and bound to execute no orders but those of the Tsar. To this group belonged Baron Frederichs, Minister of the Imperial Court; General Roediger,[16] Minister of War; and Admiral Aleksei Alekseevich Birilev,[17] Minister of the Navy. Frederichs rarely attended sessions of the Council of Ministers; he sent in his stead the Head of His Majesty's Cabinet, Prince N. D. Obolensky. Roediger also seldom appeared at the sessions and took no appreciable part in the debates. To what extent he was fitted for his position I do not know, but the outward impression he made was not so much that of a soldier as of a conscientious German professor. This impression was strengthened by his appearance: he wore large glasses, and spoke in measured tones with a marked foreign accent. He was a Swede by descent and a native of Finland. As a military man, his only claim to fame was, as Minister of War, to have abolished the use of drums. Drums, however, were reintroduced soon afterward, as it proved impossible to teach infantry—whose capacity to win victories, according to Napoleon, lay in its marching ability—to march in step without the use of drums. Admiral Birilev was quite different. He was a typical Russian, but with a lively and choleric temperament. He broached all problems with extraordinary simplicity and straightforwardness. He was a devoted and loyal patriot and a decided conservative. He willingly expressed his views

on various subjects and when doing so became easily excited, pound-
ing the table with his fists; but after he had given vent to his excitement he never insisted upon his opinion.

From this sketch of the members of Witte's government it will be
seen that Witte was in a position to command a majority in sessions
of the Council of Ministers. In all questions not directly concerned
with current events and especially in those which had to do with the
economic life of the country, he behaved like an Olympian, not so
much directing the debates as dictating his own wishes. He adopted
the habit of calling certain of his colleagues not by name but by their
official titles. He treated his former collaborators in the Ministry of
Finance as his subordinates. For instance, addressing himself to I. P.
Shipov, he sometimes would say, as if he were giving an order: "The
Minister of Finance will please do so and so in order to carry out my
idea."

But Witte did not dominate all the members of his government.
Durnovo and Akimov paid but scant attention to his opinions and the
decisions of the Council. Nor could Witte do anything to bring them
into line with his wishes, since Akimov, from the very beginning of
his career as Minister of Justice, and Durnovo, from shortly after
he became Minister of the Interior, enjoyed the Tsar's confidence to
a much greater degree than did the Chairman of the Council. Their
personal reports to the Tsar invariably received his approval, regardless of whether or not they coincided with the opinions and ideas
of Witte or of the Council. Their respective attitudes toward Witte,
however, were different. Akimov invariably attended the sessions of
the Council and vigorously defended his ideas, so that Witte had
to take some account of him and make some concessions to him.
Durnovo's tactics were different: except at the beginning of his
ministry he simply did not appear at the meetings of the Council;
instead, he sent some official of the ministry to represent him there.

It was my good fortune to be present at part of a meeting of the
Council of Ministers and I should like to digress long enough to
recall the incident. One evening I was notified from the Council of
Ministers that Witte desired me to come there immediately. If my
memory serves me correctly this occurred during the first half of
November, when the Council was meeting in the Mariinsky Palace.*

* Later the Council met in the building of the Ministry of the Imperial Court
which Witte occupied and which had, up to then, been occupied by the officials of
the Department to Expedite Ceremonies.

When I arrived the ministers were discussing the principles upon which the system of election to the Duma was to be based. All the ministers were present. Witte met me with a civility which he reserved for those he knew but slightly. He asked me to take my place at the conference table and said he had something to discuss with me in a few moments. This gave me an opportunity to listen to a few speeches on the subject under discussion, a subject which was then exciting general interest. Filosofov was the first speaker I heard. He was no orator, but he expressed himself precisely and clearly. His speech could be summed up as follows: For a long time he had considered that universal suffrage was impossible in Russia, but he now felt obliged to express himself in favor of it, since all other systems were foreign to the spirit of the Russian people. "The idea of equality," said Filosofov, "has been so deeply rooted in the consciousness of the Russian people that it is manifest everywhere. A most convincing example may be found in the actions of the peasant mobs during the agrarian uprisings. When appropriating the looted property of the landowners, the peasants observe strict equality in dividing the spoils. These they divide so painstakingly that in the case of objects which cannot be divided they either destroy them or break them into pieces, even if by so doing they deprive the particular object of its value." For instance, he cited cases when the peasants, desiring to divide large objects such as grand pianos, chopped these objects up into fragments and distributed the pieces.

I could hardly believe my ears, for I knew Filosofov well. The evidence he presented showed clearly the people's lack of education if not their primitive barbarism; to argue from this evidence that such people should be given the right to elect a legislative body was to use an unprecedented sort of logic. I had no right to speak at this meeting, but as I sat there in silence I boiled with indignation. Immediately after adjournment I asked Filosofov whether he had no argument to support the granting of elective rights to the Russian people except the one he had advanced, for it was based upon examples best fitted to prove the contrary. Filosofov answered that he believed that the government was powerless to resist the strong public demand for suffrage and that it would therefore be wiser to meet these demands voluntarily than to be forced to submit to them by the revolutionary forces. "But," I replied, "by so doing you are not fighting the revolution but insuring its final triumph." Filosofov resented this; nor did he forget his resentment. Later when Durnovo

proposed to appoint me Assistant Minister of the Interior and submitted this proposal to the Council of Ministers the only person to
object, as Durnovo told me later, was Filosofov. Yet this same
Filosofov had once asked me whether I would not like to be his
assistant in case he should be appointed Minister of Finance.

The next person to speak was Nemeshaev. His speech was just
as amazing. He stated that he had never concerned himself with
problems of popular representation and had formed no definite
opinion on this subject. Some time ago, however, as manager of the
southwestern railway, he had had an opportunity to attend a meeting
of railway employees at Kiev where this subject was discussed. The
speeches he had heard there convinced him that the only rational
thing to do was to grant the population the right of suffrage.

As I recall, Witte himself was the next to take the floor. Evidently he feared that the majority might support the first two speakers with more sensible arguments unless he directed the discussion
into another channel. He hastened to say that he, too, favored a
system which would reflect accurately the people's feelings and ideas
through their representatives, but he believed that such a system had
to be introduced slowly and gradually and at that time it would be
wiser to grant electoral rights only to a limited group of the people,
first of all to the heads of peasant families and not to all members of
their families. At this point he discontinued further debate on this
subject.

Witte then turned his attention to me. He said: "I consider that
the best means of preserving order in the localities away from the
capitals lies in drawing the gubernia and uezd zemstvo assemblies
into the work of preserving order. In order to achieve this purpose,
these assemblies must act continuously and be given definite and
special rights. Then the gubernia and uezd representatives of the
central government, supported by the decisions of these assemblies,
will find it much easier to carry out measures for settling peasant
uprisings, because the support of these assemblies will go far to win
public sympathy. I want you to draft a project," he continued, "for
an immediate convocation of these assemblies, which are to sit permanently until the country is finally pacified, and a project of the
rights with which these assemblies must be vested."

I realized at once that he had been deceived by the name of my
department, the Peasant Section. His error, moreover, was incomprehensible, since he was always in close contact with Kryzhanovsky,

who, as author of Bulygin's project, attended the meetings of the Council of Ministers and had been assigned the task of drafting a project concerning elections to the Duma in accordance with the provisions of the Manifesto of October 17. Kryzhanovsky was also Assistant Head of the Chief Administration for the Affairs of Local Economy, which dealt with the zemstvo institutions. Not seeing fit to call Witte's attention to his error, however, I said briefly that his idea could not be carried out.

"Why not?" asked Witte in surprise.

"Because the personnels of the gubernia and the uezd zemstvo assemblies are almost identical, and when a gubernia assembly is in session the chairmen of the zemstvo boards, who must attend the gubernia assemblies, are unable to attend the uezd assemblies. This applies also to the most prominent and active members of the uezd assemblies, who are invariably elected to the gubernia assemblies."

"Are you positive?"

"I am."

"Well, in that case let's convoke only the uezd assemblies."

This last idea was absurd and impossible of realization. First, it was almost impossible to assemble and keep together in a uezd town a number of persons who had regular occupations and duties elsewhere. Second, no matter what decisions these assemblies made in attempting to pacify the district, these decisions would never be carried out, as zemstvo assemblies had no means of enforcing their decisions. But before I could state these objections, Durnovo joined us.

"Why, Sergei Yulievich," he said, "do you address yourself to an official in my ministry? I do not think you have the right to entrust him with any commissions."

Durnovo's irrelevant and essentially insolent remark ended the conversation between Witte and myself.

This trifling incident illustrates Witte's total lack of information regarding matters of our state life, and particularly regarding the fundamentals of our zemstvo institutions, which he sometimes criticized adversely and sometimes praised. It also showed the lack of respect with which Durnovo treated the head of the "united" government.

I have already said that Durnovo was little concerned with the means he employed to reach a goal. But he had other qualities than this tendency to unscrupulous procedure. The keenness of his intellect enabled him to understand problems and to make decisions, and once a decision had been reached he brought to bear upon its execution a strong and resolute will. This harmonious and working alliance between intellect and will was certainly a commendable characteristic. He also possessed physical courage and stamina. During his term as Minister of the Interior the revolutionists virtually set a price on his head; but Durnovo went his way unruffled. What his inner feelings were I am unable to say, but outwardly he was always calm. Once I walked with him as he went from his house on the Moika to a meeting of the State Council. We crossed the Pracheshnyi bridge over the Moika, but when we reached the Mariinsky Square near the corner where the Ministry of Agriculture building stood, Durnovo abruptly ended our conversation by saying, "Here is where I say goodby." I said that I should like to accompany him to the palace, but he answered with perfect composure: "That is not necessary. So far we have been comparatively safe, but this square has always been dangerous for me. You must not go with me any farther." Of course, I did not comply with his wish, although I must admit I was not too eager to walk with him the remaining short distance. I realized with deeper appreciation his calm and composure.

Durnovo was also without petty pride and vindictiveness. I personally have experienced both of these characteristics. Under Plehve and even more so under Mirsky my relations with Durnovo had been rather strained. Once when officials of the ministry were discussing in the presence of the Minister of Justice, Muravev, the introduction of the new criminal code which entailed some changes in the authority of the zemskie nachalniki, Durnovo requested me to let him have a certain pertinent brief then in the Peasant Section. I refused. When Durnovo said, "As Assistant Minister, I order you to do this," I answered, "Your hands are too short" [i.e., "you have no right to do so"]. When Durnovo was appointed minister, I naturally tendered my resignation to him personally. "Since you, Petr Nikolaevich, have as little sympathy toward me as I have toward you," I said, "we cannot work together." Great was my surprise when he replied: "Neither your personal feelings nor mine matter. We are passing through such difficult times that sentiment cannot be considered. I consider you valuable in your position, and therefore I ask you to remain. Under these circumstances, regardless of your personal feelings toward me, you have no right to resign." Durnovo's views of the general political situation were in sympathy with the opinion I had expressed many times in his hearing: that leniency on the part of the government in dealing with the revolutionary psychosis which had cast its spell over the public would only aggravate the situation. He realized that radical reforms were needed. "We are living in a besieged camp," he said. "We are no longer a national government. We have become Tartar conquerors. But to institute the proclaimed liberties at this point would be to replace one tyranny with another and an infinitely worse one which would be the state's undoing."

Durnovo stood out among the statesmen of that epoch, including Witte, for his great fund of information, his independent ideas, his courage in expressing his opinion, and his statesmanlike understanding of events. His was not a philosophical mind; he could not fathom the psychological depths of the people; but he was a very realistic politician, interested mainly in current problems. His intuitive understanding of the trend of events is to be seen in a memorandum he presented to the Tsar in February 1914, in which he discussed the international position of Russia.[18] He stressed the danger of adding England as a third member of our alliance with France. He contended that as long as Russia was allied with France alone she could remain on friendly terms with Germany; for although Germany might entertain aggressive intentions toward France and Russia, she feared no aggression from these two allies. But as soon as England joined the Franco-Russian alliance the position would radically change. Germany, busy developing her colonial policy and to this end speeding up the development of a mighty navy, regarded England as a bitter adversary in this sphere. But England alone could not cope with Germany. An alliance with Germany's neighbors, however, would place England on another footing. Under such changed circumstances a war between Germany and England, with the participation of Russia and France as England's allies, would be but a question of time. In this event it was to be expected that Germany would prefer to take the initiative and engage in war at the moment she considered most favorable for herself. This moment was then present, when Russia had not yet fully reorganized and equipped her military forces.

Durnovo ranged all European countries in two camps, and later events fully justified his views. He predicted that both Italy and Rumania would at first remain neutral and later would join the Allies, whereas Turkey and Bulgaria would join Germany. Later, he foresaw that no matter who won the war its immediate results would be a social revolution in Russia and Germany, beginning in the country which was the loser and spreading to that one which was the victor. He also pointed out that even in the event of a successful war Russia would gain nothing, since France and England would cast her aside as soon as the great might of Germany had been crushed. England would then resume her plotting against Russia and soon enough would find some means of harming her. Durnovo also pointed out how difficult it would be for Russia to wage war successfully against Germany; for Russia was poorly equipped with ammunition, her industry for the manufacture of military supplies was unorganized, and, most important, she was deficient in large-caliber guns. Durnovo's last point was the more remarkable in that even the greatest French military authorities did not realize the full significance of heavy artillery until a year after the outbreak of war. Only one thing did Durnovo fail to foresee, namely, that England would not wish totally to annihilate Germany on the Continent even though she would strive to destroy Germany's naval strength and to deprive Germany of colonies. England has never considered any one special Continental power as her enemy but has opposed the one which was strongest at a given moment. In the eyes of England, to weaken Germany would be to strengthen France; and England was as little inclined to permit this as to countenance the world dominance of Germany.

In spite of Witte's naive expectations, the Manifesto of October 17 not only failed to pacify the country but even increased the general unrest. Nor was the ukase on amnesty (October 21) more successful. It was very extensive: it pardoned both those who had fought for a constitution and many who had advocated the overthrow of the entire political and social regime, but it did not include those persons who, with political motives, had committed criminal acts. Consequently both the revolutionary circles and the radical public were displeased with it. The opposition press used it as a point of departure for a new and furious attack upon the government. It said, naively enough and even more hypocritically, that the country could not be expected to quiet down until all political offenders, regardless of the nature of their crimes, had been pardoned; for only then would the civil liberties granted by the Manifesto of October 17 be truly realized. This point of view toward political amnesty was adopted by the Provisional Government in 1917, and Russia felt the effects of it to the fullest extent.

The first menacing signs of the effects of the Manifesto of October 17 were the reports from the gubernias telling of the revolutionary excesses which took place immediately after the manifesto was published locally. In many places party workers had learned of the manifesto before the government's local officials and had immediately undertaken to carry out the program laid down by the third congress of the Social-Democratic Bolsheviks and the conference of the Mensheviks. In so doing they adopted the methods advocated by the revolutionary press. *Iskra* had urged: "Seize the prisons! Free the fighters for our cause imprisoned there! Let them swell our ranks." The *Proletarii*[19] proposed that "the municipal institutions be seized and a militia be formed." Accordingly, in many localities the revolutionary elements, protected by the new liberties, came into the open and made a series of demands of the perplexed administration. These included demands for the transfer of the police authority to the town militia, the immediate removal of troops, and, above all, the liberation of all political criminals detained in the prisons. To these ends and with the help of the local workers, they organized numerous demonstrations which were joined by all the scum of the local population and directed, under waving red banners, against the places of detention. If the prison authorities refused to deliver the political prisoners to the crowd, the leaders urged the crowd to break into the prisons. In some places this prison breaking was successful, and all criminals were set free. In Orenburg and Perm the crowd arrested the local governors, Tsekhanovetsky and Naumov, before breaking into the prisons, and forced them to join the demonstration. Tsekhanovetsky was compelled to carry a red flag. Naumov flatly refused to become a red-flag bearer, so the flag was carried over his head by a "comrade."

No sooner was some degree of public order restored in the gubernias than mutinies began in the army. These mutinies were the work of revolutionists of different groupings who were endeavoring to carry out the program proposed to them by the revolutionary center. As early as October 26 the sailors of Kronstadt, future "pride and beauty" of the revolution, mutinied; and in order to suppress the mutiny the government had to summon troops from the capital. Early in November a Soviet of Soldiers' Deputies was organized in Moscow, and immediately a mutiny broke out in the army there which was put down with difficulty. Mutinies attained particularly large proportions in Vladivostok. On October 30 and 31, this city was virtually in the hands of the reservists. At Sevastopol there was a five-day (November 11–15) artillery duel between the mutinying battleships and the coast batteries. In Kiev there was a serious uprising of the sappers on November 18. At Voronezh, about the same day, a battalion in the process of being disciplined revolted and the soldiers barricaded in their barracks withstood a regular siege. When they finally surrendered they set fire to the barracks. Similar outbreaks occurred among the troops situated in Kiev and other localities, but the extent of these latter uprisings was less and they were easily suppressed. In some instances military uprisings were averted by arresting the leading instigators. At the St. Petersburg electro-technical military school, for instance, more than two hundred privates were arrested.

The Manchurian army took on all the symptoms of disintegration. The reserves, returning home through Siberia, held meetings, stirred up unrest, and sowed the seed of revolt, especially at Irkutsk and Chita. In the latter city they organized a Soviet of Soldiers' and Cossacks' Deputies.

There were also many agrarian uprisings. In fact, the results of the "comrades'" work were seen over the entire face of the Russian land. In many industrial centers also Soviets of workers' deputies were formed in pursuance of the St. Petersburg example;[20] all of these Soviets desired to establish contact with their St. Petersburg model, to follow its lead, and to receive instructions from it.

In the borderlands the revolutionary movement was intermixed with a separatist national movement which was most acute in the Baltic gubernias, where detachments of Latvian armed troops looted the castles and the estates of their traditional enemies, the German barons. The gubernias of the Kingdom of Poland were also in the grip of the nationalist movement. Here, in addition to strikes and street disorders, there were popular attacks on the *gmin* (volost) boards, in which the insurgents saw the symbol of Russian domination. Actually the gmin was almost invariably composed of popularly elected local representatives of the people; but as these institutions carried on their correspondence in the Russian language, the insurgents destroyed this correspondence. At the same time there were many assassinations of regular police and of the police for the Kingdom of Poland. In Warsaw conditions became so threatening and acts of terrorism so frequent that the Governor-General, General Maksimovich,[21] who was also Commander of the troops of the

Warsaw Military District, felt it necessary to retire to Fort Zgierz, where he had his summer residence. For this General Maksimovich was dismissed and replaced by General Skalon,[22] who introduced martial law. This circumstance, together with the arrest and indictment of the Kronstadt sailors, gave the St. Petersburg Soviet of Workers' Deputies a pretext for announcing another general strike, which began on November 2.

Once more St. Petersburg was plunged in darkness at night; once more there were no streetcars in operation, no newspapers, and only irregular telephone service. In some districts the bakers also were on strike and these districts were without bread. The strike spread also to the railways, although not to all of them: there was some service on the Nicholas railway, but passengers had to board the trains secretly; the trains did not start from regular terminals and were given a military escort; and the train crews were anxious lest they would have to suffer for violating the decrees of the strike committee. Fear of some new authority, unknown but apparently all-powerful, began to spread over the entire population. The strike movement assumed the characteristics of an epidemic. The extent of the factory strike may be judged by the fact that in Moscow the number of wasted working days for November was 667,000— 150,000 more than in October. But the strike movement included many other classes of people besides the factory workers. One day the barbers would strike; another day it would be the restaurant and hotel employees. No sooner would these strikes end than the newsboys would strike; then it would be the salesmen in stores. This unprovoked and senseless cessation of work became a sort of sport in which everyone indulged regardless of his position or age. Lectures and studies in the universities and colleges were supplanted by meetings where socialists and anarchists conducted fiery debates. Highschool students and even small children followed suit. They presented demands and ultimatums to their principals and left their classrooms in a body. The strike movement also provided some amusement; some conservative newspapers announced that patients in maternity wards had gone on strike and refused to bear children until universal suffrage was granted. Another anecdote concerning the universities had it that a madame of an establishment, the activities of which did *not* include the study of ancient languages, had told her turbulent charges: "This is not a university, thank heaven; this is an establishment."

In the meantime the St. Petersburg Soviet of Workers' Deputies tried to assert itself as an organ of the proletariat controlling the work of the government. It got into direct touch with the Chairman of the Council of Ministers, formally apprised the Governor of St. Petersburg of the unlawful actions of the police which had come to its attention, and demanded that these actions cease. At the same time it organized in the industrial districts of the city a militia which succeeded in overpowering the police. Taking advantage of this situation and its own newly acquired prestige, the Soviet organized a postal strike. It acquired such influence among postoffice and telegraph employees that the government was obliged to use it as a medium for carrying out government orders in this field. The Soviet would co-operate with the government only when it approved the government's orders, such as Witte's telegram repealing the sentence condemning to death the organizers of Kushk republic in Central Asia, after the republic itself had been abolished by military force. The Soviet was even able to organize subsidies for unemployed strikers through the St. Petersburg Municipal Duma, which, partly from sympathy and partly from fear, carried out the Soviet's orders without a murmur.

A correspondent of the *Vestnik Evropy* summed up the situation as follows: "The government has changed. Some persons, particularly formidable because they are unknown and because in the eyes of the people there is something powerful and mysterious behind them, have occupied the place which the people have been accustomed to see occupied by the official government." The same correspondent described how the strikers "closed" a restaurant in Moscow and "took off" the waiters in one of the most important hotels: "Two young men entered the vestibule and demanded to see the waiters. The manager himself ran to comply with the demand. In a few minutes some waiters appeared. The young men said to them 'Close the restaurant.' In a moment the electric lights went out, the employees were gone, and the doors of the dining room were shut. There was not a sound of protest either from the employees, who thus lost their wages for an indefinite period of time, or from the management, which was made to suffer daily losses. This situation was accepted just as meekly by the patrons of the hotel who decided that they could always get something to eat in their stuffy rooms." There were examples of similar "takings off" in St. Petersburg, too, and they took place in government institutions as well as in private concerns. A group of unidentified persons would appear from no-where and in an authoritative manner would demand that work cease immediately. In many instances their demands were complied with, but if their demands met with fairly firm resistance, these persons would disappear and not return.

Even the officials of various ministries became involved in the general movement and organized their own unions, as did the minor government employees. They made collective demands for increases in salary and shorter hours. In some places, alas, these demands were complied with immediately, whereas the feeblest resistance was enough to silence them. I know this from experience. My secretary one day reported to me that some dozens of copyists from the Peasant Section wished to see me to demand an increase in wages. "Tell these gentlemen," I said to the secretary, "that if they are determined to see me they may do so; but advise them that this will be the first and last such occasion." No one appeared, and no more requests of this sort were made of me.

But the average citizen was not prepared to resist. On the contrary, he showed that same boundless passivity, meekness, and docility which later enabled the Soviet plunderers to rob him of everything, even of every vestige of liberty, including the right of free thought, and with the help of a few thousand hired henchmen to conduct all sorts of experiments upon him and make of him a sort of experimental frog. One could have foretold the vivisection to which the Bolsheviks have subjected the Russian people in general and individual citizens in particular by observing the apathy and the spineless meekness of the citizenry in the revolutionary brawls of 1905–6. To use the title of a booklet published by Professor Sergeevsky in 1906, the citizen said to the revolutionists abusing him, "Devour me, you hounds."

A shining example of this submissiveness was furnished by the fact that at the many and varied meetings held during November and December, 1905, some of which were not even political, collections of money were taken for the strikers and sometimes for an armed riot. Hats suitably inscribed were circulated among those present, and even though a few made no contribution none dared express his indignation at the procedure or dared to refuse to pass the hat meekly to his neighbor.

The greater part of the press gave mighty assistance to the revolutionary movement. The strongest support was of course given by

the socialist press, which up to then had appeared in secret and therefore had not been published regularly and had reached but a limited
circle of readers. Now it appeared openly and legally. The newspapers *Nachalo*[23] and *Novaia Zhizn*[24] appeared, bearing the slogan,
"Workers of the World, Unite." The former replaced *Iskra,* the
Menshevik publication, while the second was the continuation of the
Bolshevik publication, *Proletarii.* The Socialist-Revolutionists also
published a paper which they named *Syn Otechestva.*[25] The *Russkoe
Bogatstvo* also cast aside all dissimulations. All these organs openly
discussed the question of armed revolt. They acclaimed the general
strike as "a world phenomenon," and exclaimed enthusiastically:
"Russia is marching at the head of the world revolution." They
lauded the "tact and maturity of the Russian proletariat"; they
pointed out definitely that "the purpose of the revolution is not political reform but radical social change." The dictatorship of the
proletariat! Such was their common slogan; though out of respect
not so much for the government, of which they had no fear, as for
the bourgeoisie, it was as yet camouflaged under the name of democratic republic.

Various publishing houses were established which issued So-
cialist-party literature and, at times, proclamations. This sort of
literature acquired great popularity in both capitals and in the provinces. The newspaper, *Donskaia Rech,*[26] published at Rostov-on-
Don, was particularly zealous in spreading the revolutionary ideas.
The Socialist-Revolutionist *Syn Otechestva,* which advocated the
expropriation of the privately owned lands of the landed gentry, was
supplied free of cost to all the volost boards of the empire.

How did the radical public react to these appeals of the revolutionists and the events which they precipitated? Did it realize where
the socialists of all shades were leading the country? Did it understand to what extent it would lose its own importance in the catastrophe being prepared by the revolutionists, how deeply it would
sink in the sea of lawlessness, unchecked human passions and base
animal instincts? Alas, it did not—not at all.

The chief center of the radical public was the Constitutional
Democratic Party of People's Freedom. This party was not yet
completely organized. Its only executive was the presidium that had
been elected at its constituent assembly in October; but its leaders
were already well known, and it was they who, with a few additions
chiefly from the Jewry, directed its activities from then till the Revo-

lution of 1917. The supreme leader was P. N. Miliukov. The others
were always the same: Kokoshkin, Kizevetter,[27] Rodichev, Manuilov,[28] Nabokov, and Prince G. E. Lvov, together with Prince Dolgorukov and Count Orlov-Davydov, who were being advanced by
them partly as attractive stage decorations and partly because of the
money they brought in.

It was at this time that the main desires of the leaders and the
members of the party became defined. It became known also what
public groups and what national elements would constitute the party's
nucleus and furnish the majority of its members. The purpose of the
party leaders was to establish a regime under which authority would
be concentrated in their hands; and they conceived of such a regime
as a democratic republic. Although they officially advocated a constitutional monarchy and even truly desired to keep the Tsar on the
throne, they needed the Tsar only as a stage setting, as a symbol of
the outward unity of the empire, as a means of attracting to their
side the masses which for centuries had regarded the Monarch as a
source of supreme justice and the dispenser of earthly goods. They
realized full well that the prestige of the imperial name would aid
them both in their contest for power and in their efforts to establish
themselves on a firm basis; but it did not enter their plans to reckon
with the throne.*

It may appear that the Cadet party sprang from the zemstvos;
but this impression is the result of the fact that at that time zemstvo
activity presented the best opportunities for the practice and develop-
men of political agitation. Essentially, however, the Cadet party
was a typically urban party. Soon after its formation it began to
absorb representatives of various liberal professions—professors,
lawyers, and journalists, who kept in constant and close touch with
the party's zemstvo members through the editing staffs of the Moscow papers, *Russkiia Vedomosti* and *Russkaia Mysl*,[29] also *Vestnik
Evropy,* and *Pravo.*

Men in the liberal professions thought that a strictly parliamentary regime, which differed little from a republican one, would
facilitate their rise to power and the concentration of power in their

* This may explain why, in 1917, when the Cadet leaders concluded, rightly or
wrongly, that the Tsar's name no longer had any prestige among the masses, they
easily and speedily adopted the formula of a federal democratic republic: the element of federation was necessary to replace the Monarch as that hub around which
centered all the nationalities and regions of the empire.

hands. Lawyers, journalists, and certain professors have, as is well known, furnished the majority of representatives in the legislative institutions of the parliamentary governments of the West as well as the prominent men of the country. This is the result of the very nature of their activities, through which they establish and maintain contacts with many different sections of society and in this way gain the best information of the currents of thought predominating in the country. By playing upon these currents of thought they can win public sympathy and at the same time direct public opinion as they wish. The Russian Cadets supposed, though without sufficient proof, that this example might be followed in Russia. They seemed to forget that the majority of the Russian people had not yet been sufficiently well educated to follow intelligently the leadership of men of learning and experienced political workers. They disregarded the possibility that once the fate of the country had been placed in the hands of the Russian people, these people would follow not those who could demonstrate the best ways of governing the country but those who could assure them of an immediate improvement of their material status.

I do not mean to imply that none of the leaders of the Cadet party were sincere in averring that the best regime for Russia was a parliamentary one; nor do I wish to convey the impression that they were striving only for their personal gain and the realization of their ambitions. But the fact remains that few people can define clearly the basis of their political and social opinions and the extent to which these opinions are determined by egotistical considerations, such as the protection and advancement of their own personal aims, and by altruistic considerations, such as the development of their country's welfare. As a rule the ordinary man joins that political group which is likely to increase his own material profits. For men of the liberal professions the parliamentary regime promised more than any other because it was founded upon a democratic system of electing popular representatives; consequently, the majority of them joined it.

There was still another reason why men of liberal professions joined the Cadet party. In addition to lawyers, journalists, and professors, the party attracted writers, artists, physicians, and specialists and technicians in various fields. During the past forty years the Russian intellectuals had succeeded in persuading the public that it was inadmissible to defend the existing regime. They had represented monarchy as being synonymous with dire and dark reaction, and their representations had not been in vain; in fact, it took exceptionally strong civic courage to profess openly an adherence to conservative views. At that time, too, a profession of liberalism or a dabbling in politics seldom handicapped one's advancement in government service, whereas an expression of conservative views created obstacles to success in public activity and liberal professions. When writers, journalists, lawyers, and artists manifested their opposition to the government, they were praised by the public. Their writings found many readers, and their artistic efforts a ready market; their help was sought by all who had business with the courts, since not only the juries but also the crown judges showed them profound consideration and respect. Thus material interests encouraged men of the liberal professions to flaunt their liberalism and their defiance of the government and so made it easier for them to become attached to the Cadet party. Was not a man's fitness for a professorship in our universities determined by the political views he professed, views which might have nothing to do with the subject he would have to teach? Did not Moscow University reject the unrivaled oculist, Golovin, who was brave enough to profess conservative ideas, and choose instead some nonentity in science who flaunted his political liberalism? Was the fame of Koni and Tagantsev based wholly upon their skill as criminologists and uninfluenced by their liberal views? Was not Professor Sergeevsky, an outstanding criminologist, persecuted for his conservatism? Was it not common knowledge that one could not propound a thesis expressing conservative views unless it contained some criticism of the existing regime, such as an introductory mention of the difficulties that had to be overcome in autocratic Russia in making any study whatsoever, even a study of mosquito bites?

Of course, the government was much to blame for this situation. Its own activities were not always irreproachable; it often left itself open to very sound criticism. It was also at fault in that it did not try to find partisans among the men of learning and literature. Persons who did receive government support received it in too marked a form—for example, Katkov in the 'eighties and Gringmut[30] in the 'nineties—and could not be considered as constituting a body of government partisans. Persons who were known to enjoy governmental favor lost the favor of the public and were marked as official hirelings, even though they honestly believed in the views they expressed. In order to organize a group of government partisans the government would have had to create for professors and journalists conditions which would have met their academic and material demands and thus would have won them to the support of a regime which had given them their positions and was providing them with a living.

It was these considerations—the ideology of the Cadet program and the chance of material advancement—that attracted the bourgeois intelligentsia to the Cadet party; and in all justice it must be said that the desires of the intelligentsia were natural, legal, understandable, and, in essence, neither anti-governmental nor anti-social.

It is equally hard to condemn the industrialists who joined the party, although they did so rather carefully because of their relationship with the government. Many of these industrialists had amassed considerable fortunes and as a result had become a great organic force in the country. But they did not possess political rights or a degree of economic freedom proportionate to their importance as such a force. They were eager, therefore, to gain greater freedom in their particular economic field and especially to secure political rights and social status equal to those of the landed gentry. In the case of some commercial houses, envy of the political privileges of the landed nobility turned into hatred of this class. Consequently the Cadet party's slogan of expropriating the estates of the landed gentry in favor of the peasants was not only acceptable but highly welcome to such representatives of the commercial world, since it heralded the total destruction of the hated landed-gentry class.

This slogan was regarded by the Cadet party as its highest trump card in attracting the rural masses. But inasmuch as the party was composed of bourgeois elements and some zemstvo elements, it was obliged to introduce into its program a clause providing for the payment of expropriated lands. Now the inclusion of such a clause made it impossible for the party successfully to compete against the Socialist parties among the peasant electors, for the Socialist parties promised to give the peasants all these lands free. The Cadets, therefore, had recourse to action which required trickery: they published their program in two different texts, and in the one intended for the rural population they made no mention of paying for the lands to be expropriated from the landed gentry.

The principle of equal rights for all nationalities which the party adopted and included in its program did more than anything else perhaps toward strengthening its position. It brought into the party

many very active workers—from the provinces, from subject nationalities generally, but especially from the bourgeois Jews who very
naturally were eager to have abolished the restrictions on the Jews.
The support of the Jewish group was particularly valuable for the
party, since the larger part of the metropolitan and nearly all the
gubernia press was concentrated in its hands. The party also gained
wide support abroad in international Jewry.

Let me repeat that it is far from my intention to affirm that the
Cadet party program was merely a political expedient. Undoubtedly
many party leaders and organizers were sincerely convinced that the
principles of the party program were just and for the good of the
state. They were also aware, however, of the fact that these principles were such as to increase the numerical and organic strength
of the party. The fatal error of the party and its irremediable sin
before the country lay in the utterly unscrupulous tactics adopted by
the party leaders. The question of tactics engrossed their entire
attention; their primary interest was in the methods which would
most successfully increase the number of their followers, give the
party greater strength, and so insure the realization of their main
desire, the seizure of power. Thus, what should have been of secondary interest, that is, the possession of power as a means to accomplish reforms, became the dominant one; the avowed aims of the
party were subordinated to the idea of seizing power with the help
of the simple masses of the population who were lured into their
ranks.

Political kitchens, alas, are never renowned for their fastidious-
ness. Goethe once said, *"Ein politischer Lied ist ein garstiger Lied."*
No political party can attain any considerable measure of success
without a dash of demagogy. Yet the political parties of the West,
which work hard to secure power, never sacrifice their political
program for success in the contest for power. How different was the
Cadet party! All its efforts were directed solely toward undermining
the existing government. I repeat that the greatest sin of the party
was its utter disregard of ethical political procedure. I do not refer
to its methods of campaigning, its two-faced programs, the booklets
issued for the use of the agitators it employed, or its method of
fighting its adversaries by spreading insinuations and falsehoods
about the government and public men of the Right. I refer rather
to its utter indifference to the interests of the country and the state.
Had the Cadet leaders shared the theories and the views of the

revolutionary parties, the support which they constantly rendered these parties would have been justifiable. But they were far from sharing these views. They fully realized the destructive effect of the revolutionary theories upon the state, yet they made every effort to keep in step with those who, *per fas et nefas,* tried to realize those theories.

To this it should be added that the Cadet party, like every other party, had never been homogeneous in so far as the opinions of its members were concerned. There were continual conflicts between its central committee, which actually directed party activities, and the party's local branches, especially where the zemstvo element was in evidence. This was but natural. The party leaders had set themselves but one goal, the attainment of power; and they stopped at little to reach it. Obviously, therefore, in their eyes the interests of the party naturally predominated over the interests of the state, whereas the rank-and-file members of the party, even rather prominent ones, had no such aspirations. Thus, the purpose of the leaders was not always identical with that of many other members of the party. The electors who voted for the party were influenced by its program and desired to see carried out the principles proclaimed therein; in the majority of cases they were totally unaware of the back-stage activity of the party leaders and of the agreements the latter reached with the leaders of revolutionary groups.

A fateful role was played in the central administration of the party by its supreme ruler, P. N. Miliukov. He had succeeded in transmitting to the other party leaders and the party itself his own personal qualities—boundless ambition, vanity, self-assurance, doctrinairism, and political amorality. His gross political mistakes were the result, strange as it may seem, of a too perfect thinking apparatus, which functioned with the precision of a clock. His logic, his dialectics were irreproachable and it was precisely this quality that had won him his prominent position in the party. But life has a logic of its own. Just as the heart, as Pascal[31] said, has its own logic that the mind knows not, so life goes on according to its own rules which are perceivable only by persons exceptionally gifted with a special intuitive sense. This gift Miliukov absolutely lacked.

Miliukov's superabundance of formal logic developed in him a stubborn doctrinairism against which nothing could prevail. In 1905 his logic and his study of history had led him to the conclusion that when the government was forced to make concessions to the public it would in the end be forced to fulfill to the fullest extent all the people's demands. By "fullest extent," Miliukov meant the establishment on the basis of universal suffrage of a democratic parliamentary regime in which, he believed, actual power would pass into the hands of the most-educated part of the population, that is, himself and his sympathizers. This theory suggested that popular government is sound and firm only when it has been established by the people themselves through their representatives. This explains Miliukov's firm refusal to make any agreement with the government or to accept any form of constitution granted by the Monarch; it explains also the party's demand in 1905, made under his influence, that a constituent assembly be convoked.

Miliukov was firmly convinced that he would be able to subordinate the people's representatives to his way of thinking and to direct their decisions along the lines he had planned. But he also realized that the radical intelligentsia which he headed was in itself powerless to force the government to surrender all its prerogatives. He realized that his party could break the power of the government and make it tractable only with the help of the revolutionary elements. The revolutionary parties were quite right when, in 1905, they said to the Cadets, "You are trading in our goods; you have appropriated that which we have won." Deep down in his soul Miliukov m. have realized the truth of this statement. But at the same time he had accurately evaluated the strength of the revolutionary forces which leaned upon the masses for support. Without the help of the bourgeois intellectuals, without an initial stirring up of public feeling among the liberal bourgeoisie, the revolutionists were powerless to accomplish anything. Revolution invariably begins at the top, gradually embraces the masses, and ends all too easily in national catastrophe. The Revolution of 1905 trod this road. The public movement began among the zemstvo, municipal, and the various professional congresses which were directed from behind stage by the same elements which had organized the Cadet party. As a result the Cadet leaders, from Miliukov on down the list, thought that it was they who had forced the sovereign authority to yield a portion of its prerogatives to the people's representatives, that it was they who had won for the people the status of free citizens. For these reasons they decided that the executive power rightfully belonged to them. Therefore, they could not be expected to be satisfied with the Manifesto of October 17.

Miliukov and his associates were always conscious of the power and importance of the bourgeoisie as a participant in and leader of the revolutionary movement. But this did not stop Miliukov in the turbulent autumn months of 1905 from making agreements with revolutionary parties and urging them toward active demonstrations. The announcement of the Social Democrats, that at first they would concede all power to the revolutionary bourgeoisie, probably influenced him in favor of acting in harmony with them. He evidently overestimated the strength of the radical bourgeoisie, for he must have known that the masses desired, not a political, but a social and economic revolution and that therefore, unless there was in Russia a force capable of checking in due time the natural development of events, the bourgeois government would not be able to remain at the helm and the power would pass into the hands of the Socialists. He must have considered that his party, in spite of its limited size, constituted such a force. In this case, however, the wish was father of the thought. A strong desire to get into power had evidently blinded Miliukov to a proper appraisal of his support, and his political amorality drove him into the arms of those who considered that the end justified the means.

In this respect there was a great difference between Miliukov and some of the Cadet leaders on one side, and the revolutionary leaders on the other; and the difference was not entirely to the advantage of Miliukov and his colleagues. Most of the Social Democrats were internationalists and from their point of view were justified in conniving for the overthrow of the Russian Empire. Their aims were of a greater magnitude than those of the Cadet leaders; but the latter held in principle to the view of society organized into states, and from this point of view they had no right to risk the fate of their country as an independent unit. By running such a risk, however, the Cadet party and its leader, Miliukov, demonstrated the complete amorality of their tactics and their readiness to risk everything, even the political existence of Russia, for the sake of attaining power.

The Cadets referred to the revolutionists as "our friends of the Left"; and although there were accidental conflicts, the Cadets always supported demands made by the revolutionists. "Remove the police!" "Let the militia preserve order!" "Withdraw the rowdy troops!" "Free all political criminals without exception!" These were the demands of the revolutionists, who at the same time appealed to the population to continue their struggle against the government until a constituent assembly was convoked. These demands were meekly repeated by the radicals. Thus at a meeting of lawyers in Moscow on October 19 under the chairmanship of N. V. Teslenko,[32] a future leader of the Cadet party, it was resolved "to continue the fight for liberation"; and when Prince Lvov, Kokoshkin, and Golovin visited Witte on his invitation they insisted upon the convocation of a constituent assembly. Thus, also, the representatives of the press urged that Witte order the removal of troops from the city limits and the transformation of the police into a militia.

But the peculiarities and tactics of the Cadets were most distinctly displayed during the zemstvo-municipal congress in Moscow, November 6–13, 1905. This was attended by some two hundred and thirty persons, including a few representatives of the moderately liberal groups, who were in the minority on all questions debated. The radicals, headed by Miliukov, dominated the debates at all times. Miliukov with his facile pen drafted resolutions that were phrased so subtly that even persons essentially opposed to them were impelled to support them. He also demonstrated his insistence and his firmness of purpose, so seldom experienced by our soft-willed public and so hard to resist because of our public's laziness and indifference.

The congress regarded Witte's government, or rather Witte himself, as the medium through which results might be attained. Its one aim was to achieve power, and this aim was expressed most clearly by I. I. Petrunkevich, a prominent party worker, who asked the assembly: "Can we at the present time insist on becoming part of the government?" He got no definite answer. Evidently, the congress had come to the conclusion that the government had not yet been sufficiently undermined, and therefore it directed all its attention to finding further means of doing so. It adopted a resolution, a masterpiece of subtlety, by which the functions of a constituent assembly were assigned to the State Duma. The Duma was represented, not as a constituent assembly such as the revolutionists demanded, but merely as a body with constituent functions; and this bait neatly caught many members of the congress. Then followed demands for universal suffrage, the lifting of martial law in the Kingdom of Poland, a general amnesty for political prisoners, abolition of capital punishment, and the removal of restrictions on the Jews. It is apparent that at this congress the basic points of the

Cadet party program were closely interwoven with demands, the realization of which would in the opinion of the leading Cadets of the congress force the government to transfer power to them immediately.

The resolution contained a phrase which spoke of the new popular rights as something wrung from the government by the people. Prince E. N. Trubetskoi tried in vain to substitute a phrase which would refer to these rights as simply "gained by the people." He feared that the former phrase might suggest that the country was in the grip of revolution and this might bring about the crash of Russian securities on the Western exchanges. In vain did A. I. Guchkov, the future leader of the Octobrists, speak of the impracticability of repealing martial law in Poland, "where, as everybody knows, there is armed insurrection." In vain did he attempt to persuade the leaders of the radicals to add to the sentence, "The congress demands the abolition of capital punishment," the words, "and categorically denounces violence and assassination as methods of political warfare." All these suggestions were rejected by the majority, thus revealing that amorality, that lack of patriotism and statesmanship which were the distinguishing characteristics of the Cadet party from the beginning.

The radical press, directed by the Cadets, adopted this same majority attitude. "It would have been an unpardonable mistake," said the *Russkiia Vedomosti,* "for the Russian public to have been opposed to the strike as a method of fighting for the cause of political freedom and social progress." Radical papers enlarged upon the demands for the abolition of the police and the withdrawal of troops. It represented revolutionary demonstrations and acts which would not be tolerated in any country, no matter how much liberty its citizens enjoyed, as "peaceful manifestations of a people expressing its happiness for being granted political rights"; on the other hand, it termed the Cossacks, who were preventing the crowd from becoming openly riotous, a horde of *oprichniki.* This same name was applied to the police when they prevented the revolutionists from setting free the political prisoners in a Moscow prison. A Jew named Bauman, who was accidentally killed during the fighting about the prison, was acclaimed a martyr to the cause of liberty, while the many murders of persons appointed to preserve public order either passed unnoticed or were openly approved. Bauman's funeral, organized by the Social Democrats with much pomp and with many speeches calling the people to arms, was described as a touching manifestation of the people's love for the "fighters for liberty."

The falsification of news from the gubernias by the radical publications was unprecedented. *Russkiia Vedomosti* reported in all seriousness that the authorities at Odessa were "murdering seventy-year-old people and babes in arms." The same correspondent described as follows the strike in the schools: "The school children, moving along in a merry, animated throng, enticed other students from classes everywhere. A horde of policemen, with swords drawn and revolvers spitting fire, attacked the children and killed them. The blood of little children was flowing . . . ."*

The editorials kept pace with the reports of correspondents: "It is the same story everywhere. The demonstrators move peacefully along the street, proclaiming their love of liberty, when suddenly a host of Cossacks falls upon them without the slightest provocation and a savage massacre begins."

This wholesale distortion of facts and events excited the trusting public, which was already suitably prepared, and aggravated the general unrest into a revolutionary fever. People were working themselves up into a state of excitement directed against the existing regime and all its supporters, who were termed either born cretins or depraved rogues, usually both. Some circles became sincerely indignant at the demonstrations of the Right organizations, especially at their patriotic manifestations. The radical press described crowds marching under red banners as "people expressing their love of liberty," and demonstrators bearing the Tsar's portraits as "hooligans drafted from the veriest scum of the population." When the workers formed shock troops the radical press did not mention the fact; but when at Moscow the Union of Russian People planned to form troops for the preservation of order and the clergy announced in the churches that anyone was welcome to enlist, this press furiously demanded that the government "stop these disgraceful activities." And, strangely enough, in the next breath it demanded the resignation of this very government.

Whatever one chooses to call the leaders of the counter-revolutionary movement, one cannot gainsay the significance of the role they played. The work of the Patriotic Union was amateurish, inexperienced, insignificant, and parlor-made, but it did enter the

* *Russkiia Vedomosti,* October 30, 1905.

public arena. One of the public meetings held in the small hall of the nobility club, with only about a hundred in attendance, did not amount to much; but another meeting, organized in the Russian Club to discuss the autonomy of Poland, was more successful and was mentioned in the press. The Union's attempts to secure a press were not very fruitful. At first there was a plan to issue supplements to some established paper. A deal was made with the *Rus,* published by A. A. Suvorin,[33] but after issuing two supplements the paper discontinued the agreement. It was then decided to publish the Union's own weekly paper, although the resources of the Union were but a few thousand rubles. An office was rented, a small office staff was engaged to receive callers, even some newsboys were hired and supplied with special caps proudly inscribed with *"Otchizna,"*[34] the name of the paper. But, as many had foreseen, this plan also failed. There were only a few dozen subscribers, the circulation was small, and the money soon came to an end. After six issues, if I am not mistaken, the paper quietly passed out of existence. Yet this insignificant publication had attracted the interest of several persons, who, in letters and by personal visits to the office, expressed their sympathy with the ideas it had propounded. It is also interesting to note that the chief object of the paper's attacks was Witte, in spite of the fact that its contributors and publishers were almost exclusively rather prominent civil servants and its editor the journalist, Glinka-Yanchevsky.

Another Right group had a more fertile idea. This group was composed of young people, who decided to publish a humorous magazine to counterbalance numerous similar magazines of an openly revolutionary character. These latter were continually changing their names, since the persons selling them were arrested by the police as soon as the true character of the publication became known and the publications themselves were confiscated. The vendors of such magazines had to play a game of hide-and-seek with the police in order to sell this forbidden print, and the price went up accordingly. It reached ten rubles a copy; but sales continued. People bought them mostly in order to round out a collection that would be precious in the future. These journals were insolent and lacking in real humor. Their satire of the government was rude and offensive. In contrast to this the two satirical publications, *Vittova Pliaska*[35] and *Pluvium,* which the young people of the Right established, were truly amusing. They caricatured the government, but in

a manner quite different from that of the scurrilous revolutionary
organs: they criticized it for its spinelessness and lack of courage.
In idea and quality of humor they were superior to the revolutionary
ones, and they sold well. They also stressed the characteristics of the
Cadet party with clarity and acuteness. One cartoon pictured a
Cadet intent upon getting to the throne and a Socialist-Revolutionist
standing behind him with a bomb ready in his hands. The inscription read: "Give in to me, or he will bomb you."

Witte suffered patiently the insults of the revolutionary critics,
but he could not reconcile himself to the criticism of the Right. He
often requested Durnovo to take steps to silence the satirists of the
Right; but Durnovo invariably turned a deaf ear, although he himself was often the butt of the caricatures and knew who their authors
were.

Other sections of the educated and liberal public, who were
concerned for the welfare of the state, also tried to unite in order to
stem the rising revolutionary tide. In St. Petersburg there was
organized a club of public men which attracted about five hundred
persons to its opening meeting. This club expressed a readiness to
support the government and adopted a resolution denouncing the
strikes, but it had no connections among the masses and consequently
made no impression upon the course of events.

The Russian Club, organized a few years previously, showed
little vitality in this period, partly because it was deserted by its
founder and chairman, Prince D. P. Golitsyn.[36] This Prince Golitsyn, under the name Golitsyn-Muravlin, later wrote some dull
novels which no one read. He was almost as stupid as he was
pompous and vain. At the approach of the revolution he was so
terror-stricken that he hastily renounced the chairmanship of the
organization he had founded, an office which was then compromising
him, and suddenly left the metropolis for parts unknown.

But at this time there appeared another Right organization, the
Union of Russian People, which became the butt of all sorts of
attacks. It established the newspaper *Russkoe Znamia,* which it
published until the Revolution of 1917. No matter how one regards
this union and its organizers, one must admit that during the revolutionary days of 1905 it played an important part and caused the
revolutionists much anxiety. The assertion that it was organized
and supported by the police is patently false. Its original capital
backing was donated by Madame Poluboiarinov, a woman with a

fantastic and insufferable disposition but very energetic and intent upon playing a prominent role. She was certainly not allied with the police; on the contrary, as proprietress of a large residence on the Voskresenskaia Quay she had many occasions to quarrel with them.*

The first chairman of this Union, Dr. Dubrovin,[37] displayed quite exceptional energy during this tumultuous period, and somehow established contacts with the masses. Here he found many sincere enemies of the revolutionary aims and many ardent supporters of the monarchy. In later years, it is true, the Union of Russian People had many absolutely indifferent members in both its metropolitan and provincial branches, who were prepared, as the occasion demanded, to work in Soviet Chekas or to take part in patriotic manifestations; but side by side with such members it had members who were its convinced supporters. Later, also, the Union may have been subsidized by the government, although I am not certain of this. Even if these subsidies were made, I suspect that their size was negligible.†

I once attended a meeting of this Union of Russian People. As I recall, it was during the workers' strike in November. The Mikhailovsky riding school, where the meeting was to take place, was in semi-darkness; the only illumination was provided by oil lamps. Admission was free. In the center of the ring was a sort of tribune for the speakers. There were at least two thousand people present. I was interested not so much in the speaker as in the crowd itself, and tried to overhear conversations. I was amazed at the rapt atten-

---

* Madame Poluboiarinov's apartment in her own house was demolished during the first days of the February Revolution, 1917, as were the offices of the newspaper *Russkoe Znamia,* situated in her other house facing the Shpalernaia; the looters attempted to burn down this latter house. Madame Poluboiarinov herself was executed by the Bolsheviks.

† Generally speaking, our government was very parsimonious in subsidizing its supporters. The practice of parliamentary states is much more decisive in this respect. It is true that individual adventurers had always succeeded in getting money from the Russian government, usually by working through their personal connections and under the pretext of pursuing certain political aims. The famous General E. V. Bogdanovich is a fine example of these adventurers. But I know of but one instance when a large subsidy was given to a political organization, and then the money was donated by the Tsar out of his personal fortune. On March 25, 1909, the Tsar donated 100,000 rubles to the Russian Club to pay for a house in Kuznetsky Pereulok. This was only the smaller part of the sum needed; the remainder was donated by club members, particularly by the merchant Puryshev, who was an ardent patriot and a confirmed supporter of Russian historical principles, including autocracy.

tion with which the public listened to the addresses and the animation with which they were received. The speeches themselves were fiery, colorful, and apparently convincing; the atmosphere was charged with electricity. I had the impression that the crowd was ready to commit any excesses; but, as the speeches did not point out any definite object to be attacked, the crowd dispersed peacefully, singing "God Save the Tsar."

Personally I have never sympathized with organizations like the Union of Russian People. I have always thought that certain sentiments such as love of country should be inculcated and strengthened at school and by courses and lectures organized by educational societies, and not by organizing useless tea shops, which decent educated people could not be tempted to enter. In normal times no government should use methods employed by revolutionists, for in its hands such methods become double-edged weapons. But during times of revolutionary unrest, when the people are in the grip of mass-psychosis, the government must support individual organizations that spring up to support it. In 1905 the Union of Russian People was such an organization, even though it did lack sufficiently well-educated supporters. This lack of support on the part of educated Russians was due to the Russian public's deeply rooted fear of appearing reactionary and of being branded as hirelings of the government.

In those days the government was in a precarious position. The revolutionists were already sure of victory. The impotence of the government was increasing at a rapid pace and was accompanied by the usual revolutionary debasing of the people's moral standards. These were boom days for questionable cafés frequented by shady characters and street Venuses. In St. Petersburg there was a deluge of pornographic literature, and the newspapers printed advertisements of books with unmentionable titles and many private advertisements of a very overt nature. The music halls billed cynical little songs, sung by young ladies in extremely scant attire. But what particularly flourished were the gambling houses. Here admission was free for all and they stayed open all night. The same sort of thing was going on in Moscow.

The general demoralization seized many different sections of the public. Civil servants disagreed openly with the opinions of their chiefs. The courts tried to demonstrate their independence either by giving very light penalties to persons indicted for political crimes or by acquitting them altogether. The police seized the occasion to indulge in graft. Even some small children refused to mind their parents. Servants became gruff, and while the menservants drank freely of the master's wine the maids used the perfume and wore the underwear of their mistresses.

In the midst of this chaos and disintegration Durnovo was appointed Acting Minister of the Interior, October 30. He had been managing the affairs of the ministry since October 23, after the dismissal of Bulygin, but as yet had taken no systematic steps to re-establish order. This may be explained partly by the fact that he perhaps considered himself as but king for a day and partly by the fact that he hoped to force Witte, who was in a quandary, to insist before the Tsar upon his appointment as minister. But as soon as he was appointed Durnovo undertook with courage, decisiveness, and intelligence to suppress the revolution. His first task was to raise the prestige of the government. Accordingly, he discontinued the publication of orders which the government could not enforce; but where enforcement was possible he displayed the systematic ruthlessness necessary to show the public that the government did not intend to mince words and was determined to accomplish what it set out to do. But Durnovo had to proceed most carefully. Before he had become minister, he had not clearly realized the country's peril. He once asked Gerasimov, Chief of the Secret Police of St. Petersburg, how many persons would have to be arrested in order to bring peace to the capital. "Nearly eight hundred," Gerasimov replied. "Why not half the city's population?" Durnovo commented ironically. He considered Gerasimov's opinion typical of a policeman's point of view, and said that he would never agree to such a wholesale arrest. Very shortly, however, he changed his own point of view. He called together representatives of different military units garrisoning the capital and was deeply impressed by what these men had to say. All the commanders of the infantry units of the guards, with the exception of General Min,[38] commander of the Semenovsky regiment of His Majesty's guards, announced that they could not answer for the conduct of their units should they be called upon to suppress the revolutionary movement. Nor were the police of certain districts entirely to be relied on.

But Durnovo did not lose his head. He followed without undue haste or nervousness the course he had mapped out, and the effect of the strong will of a central administrator was soon felt both in the capital and in the gubernias. The revolutionary leaders felt it, too, and decided to strike another blow before the government had marshaled its forces, regained its former prestige, and recovered its faith in itself and its power. As I have already pointed out, on November 2 the Soviet of Workers' Deputies announced another general strike on the flimsy pretext of the establishment of martial law in the Kingdom of Poland and the indictment of the Kronstadt sailors. The strike was a fizzle; it was by no means general. Discord in its own ranks stole away some of the Soviet's importance, and the prestige of the government rose accordingly. After five days the strike died a natural death.*

Defeated in organizing a general strike, the revolutionists tried to strike a blow at the state machine by organizing a post and telegraph strike. The pretext was Durnovo's order to dismiss all postal clerks who had joined the postal clerks' union in defiance of the circular letter notifying them that this union was illegal. A congress of delegates of the local unions of postal clerks assembled at Moscow. Under the direction of the Social Democrats, it resolved to

---

* In addition to his other talents Durnovo had a way of impressing on people his own firmness and the inflexibility of his decisions. Of this I was personal witness. During the November strike the city telephone service was partially incapacitated and one evening I had to call on Durnovo in person in order to talk to him. When I arrived at his house he was in conference with the governor, General Dediulin. I waited in the reception room. Almost immediately a young man entered followed by the butler, and said curtly, "I do not care who is with the minister. He has called me here, so let him explain what he wants of me. Tell him that the head of the city telephone service is here." After some hesitation the butler did as he was bid. The newcomer paced the floor, his whole figure radiating defiant courage. Even his cutaway assumed an arrogant air with its tails flying behind him. In a few minutes the butler reappeared and said to the newcomer, "The minister is awaiting you." The head of the city telephone service hurried to the minister's door and swept through it. Five or ten minutes later the same gentleman reappeared. But what a metamorphosis! Where was his arrogance, his proud bearing, his defiant aggressiveness? A gamecock had entered the office; a wet hen walked out.

When I entered the minister's office he was giving the governor orders pertaining to the city telephone service: in case the strike was not stopped immediately, a military telephone detachment was to be held in readiness to replace the telephone operators and the head of the telephone service was to be arrested.

"What did you say to that individual?" I asked Durnovo. "He was a very changed man when he left you."

"Nothing much. I had heard he was conniving with the strikers; so when he announced that he was powerless to force his employees to work when they refused to do so, I told him that neither could I force him to do his work when he refused, but that I had the right and the means of depriving him of any work at all."

declare a general strike of all postal employees until the dismissed employees were reinstated. This resolution was immediately supported by the Soviet of Workers' Deputies, which in fact had inspired it, and on November 17 was carried out in both St. Petersburg and Moscow.

The postal and telegraph strike aggravated the already serious position of the central government by severing its connections with its local branches. At the same time the government was bitterly criticized both by the opposition press, which insisted that the demands of the delegates of the union to the congress mentioned above be met in order to end the strike, and by the metropolitan public, which was very much inconvenienced by the lack of communication facilities. But Durnovo remained firm. In a couple of days and with the help of special military units he succeeded in establishing telegraphic communication with the principal centers of the country. Volunteers, mostly women, achieved some success in sorting and delivering the mail. These measures led the congress in Moscow to demand the immediate removal of Durnovo himself.

This was virtually the central point and peak of the entire revolution. The question was who would stay on his feet in this fight? Durnovo did. In an ordinance of November 21 he announced that all postal and telegraph employees who did not begin work on November 22 would be considered discharged. At the same time he took several steps to protect from the violence of the revolutionists those employees who were willing to return to work. He arrested the leaders of the Moscow congress of delegates. The postal workers, many of whom had been on strike because they feared the reprisals of the Soviet of Workers' Deputies, realized that this time the government was firmer and more powerful than the revolutionists. They returned to work and in so doing dealt a mighty blow to the prestige of the revolutionary center. This proved to be the turning point. Sporadic outbursts, sometimes violent ones such as the armed riot at Moscow, continued until the end of the year; but from November 21 on the revolutionists were beaten. The government had recovered its confidence, while the revolutionists had realized their weakness. The triumph of the government was made more complete when Durnovo accompanied his decisive measures concerning post and telegraph employees with a circular telegraphic order to all local authorities charging them to arrest immediately all revolutionary leaders who had of late revealed their true colors and to transfer such cases to the Police Department. These orders were carried out almost universally. Then, on November 27, Durnovo arrested the Chairman of the St. Petersburg Soviet of Workers' Deputies, Khrustalev-Nosar, who proved to be a mediocre man indeed. He was succeeded in his office by Trotsky (Bronstein).[39]

It was now evident to the Soviet and other revolutionary centers that the government had done with its hesitations and vacillations. They concluded that unless they found some more effective way of weakening the government their plans would come to naught. They selected as this more effective way a pompous address to the population which they called a "manifesto." The Soviet was joined in issuing this address by the Central Committee of the All-Russian Peasant Union, the central and organization committees of the Russian Social-Democratic Labor party, the Central Committee of the Socialist-Revolutionist party, and the Central Committee of the Polish Socialist party. It was published on December 2, 1905, not only by the revolutionary publications, *Nachalo, Novaia Zhizn,* and *Syn Otechestva,* but also by some bourgeois papers (*Rus, Svobodnaia Rossiia, Russkaia Gazeta*).[40] It read in part:

"It is resolved: to refuse to pay redemption dues and all other obligations; to demand that in all business transactions, in the payment of wages and salaries, payment be made in gold and that in transactions involving sums less than five rubles payment be made in full-weight coin; to withdraw all savings from savings banks and the state bank, demanding that they be paid in gold. It is also resolved: to prevent the payment of debts incurred by the Tsarist government when it was engaged in open warfare with the people."

This address was intended to create a panic among the citizens who had their money in savings and, indeed, as a result of it, three hundred million rubles were withdrawn from the state savings banks. Had it been possible to make its terms even partially effective, the direst results might well have ensued and the government might have been placed in a very difficult situation. For one thing, our international credit would have been undermined.

Durnovo realized all this and decided to make a decisive attack upon the revolutionary center. On December 3 he had the Soviet surrounded by police during its plenary session. All its members were seized and put in prison. According to the views entertained by the government at that time, this step, though decisive, entailed certain risks. It had been generally supposed that it might result in

the declaration of another general strike and the rising of the entire working population of St. Petersburg. But Durnovo had insisted that only a hard blow at the revolutionary center could
finally dethrone it in the eyes of the people and thus counterbalance,
at least partially, the "manifesto's" pernicious effect upon the government and the country.

What was Witte's attitude toward these events? When he saw
that the Manifesto of October 17 had failed to pacify the public
and to make him the idol of the multitudes, he was completely bewildered and lost his definite political orientation. Sensitive as he
was to expressions of public opinion and the press, he could not bear
to have himself described by Socialist organs, like *Nachalo* and
Novaia Zhizn, as a "managing clerk of autocracy" or an "ambitious, titled bureaucrat and nothing else." *Russkoe Bogatstvo*
added that as Minister of Finance Witte had ruined the country;
as premier he would flood it with blood, and all this to save his
career. The Right press had only a slightly better opinion of him,
as we have seen above. Under these circumstances Witte endeavored to save his own face before the public, and, while permitting
Durnovo to repress revolutionary demonstrations, he tried at the
same time to make himself out a liberal by practicing his favorite
arts of flattery and deception. He appealed to the excited strikers,
calling them *bratsy* [little brothers], asked for their good behavior,
and promised them all kinds of rewards.

To those who considered they knew Witte well it was apparent that he had experienced a profound change during the days following the October Manifesto. His assurance, his courage, his
aggressiveness had gone. Conversations with colleagues and debates in the Council of Ministers concerning current events and
the measures necessary to cope with them revealed not only that
Witte was without a definite and strong plan but also that he was
utterly bewildered. He was afraid lest he be knocked off the
pedestal of liberalism which he imagined he occupied in the eyes
of the liberal public and at the same time he showed, if he did
not express, his fear of being drowned by the revolutionary wave.
This explains why he played up to all groups of society on the one
hand and on the other allowed Durnovo to suppress the revolution as he pleased, trying meanwhile to convey the impression,
where he saw that he would profit, that he himself was far from
sympathetic to Durnovo's policy, which he suffered merely be-

cause of the support Durnovo found from the throne. It is also possible that by resorting to such measures he tried to protect himself from terroristic attempts, for, alas, Witte had little physical courage. Perhaps this fact also explains his unbalanced confusion during that period of his career.

Nor did Witte's actions speak well for his loyalty to the Monarch. He sought to direct against the Tsar that hostility which resulted from the government's failure to fulfill the demands of the radicals. This is illustrated by his written answer to the resolution of the Moscow zemstvo-municipal congress of November 6–13, demanding that the Duma be empowered with the functions of a constituent body and that elections to this body be based upon universal suffrage. In his answer, which was immediately published by the press, Witte stated that the government's first duty was to execute the will of the Tsar and that "everything which tends to limit the firm and inflexible will of the Tsar must be declined by the government." Witte here said quite clearly that as for himself he was ready to fulfill all the demands of the public, but that the Tsar opposed such demands and was therefore the only obstacle to their realization. No wonder the Tsar had no confidence in Witte.

The panic into which Witte was thrown in these turbulent times was demonstrated most clearly on December 3, when Durnovo ordered the arrest of the Soviet of Workers' Deputies. On that day the Council of Ministers was discussing the question of a project of regulations for the unions, but despite the importance of this issue Durnovo did not attend the session. In his stead he sent an official of the department for general affairs with instructions not to mention the impending arrest of the revolutionary Soviet. No sooner had the Council of Ministers finished the discussion of this matter than Witte was informed that the Minister of the Interior wished to speak to him on the telephone. Witte went immediately to another room to take the call. The other ministers were left in suspense, for it boded something serious for the Minister of the Interior to call the Chairman of the Council of Ministers during a session, particularly at a time when revolutionary excesses in the gubernias, complicated in these days by the mutinies of troops, were at their height. Witte's return did not reassure his colleagues. With a face chalk white and a voice that broke, he announced in great agitation, "All is lost.

Durnovo has just placed the entire Soviet of Workers' Deputies under arrest." These words had the effect of an exploding bomb. Some of the members of the Council sprang from their places; N. I. Vuich began to tremble like an aspen leaf. What happened later I do not know, as Witte discontinued all further debate.

Immediately after the arrest of the Soviet of Workers' Deputies the revolution began to wane, although the revolutionists at once elected another presidium. The arrest of the first Soviet, unaccompanied as it was by any popular demonstrations, destroyed not only in the eyes of the public but also in those of the government and Witte himself the halo which up to then had surrounded this organization. Besides, the persons elected to the new Soviet had neither experience nor influence among the workers and therefore were not very effective. This second Soviet was arrested a month later, on January 2, 1906. This arrest also passed without any demonstrations, even by the workers.

But the party centers of other revolutionary organizations continued to exist. They saw from the arrest of the St. Petersburg Soviet of Workers' Deputies, which had happened so quietly, that the chances of a successful general revolution were waning and that they could hardly count upon a successful armed revolution even in St. Petersburg. They therefore decided to transfer the center of revolutionary activities to Moscow where they thought the size and sympathies of the garrison afforded a situation more favorable for an armed uprising.

Meanwhile the liquidation of the St. Petersburg Soviet of Workers' Deputies had given wings to Witte's imagination, and he conceived the idea of ending the revolution with one blow. He would permit the Moscow revolution to take place, especially since it would occur at a safe distance from his place of residence. The revolutionary leaders would all be dealt with, and the people would receive a convincing object lesson. He explained this idea to some of his closest associates in the Ministry of Finance, such as A. I. Putilov, who expressed his astonishment at the fact that the government should permit overt preparation for an armed revolt.

Durnovo, of course, had no way of personally preventing the events which were about to happen, and on December 8 the Moscow armed uprising did take place and assumed menacing proportions. The Secret Police of the Moscow gendarme corps was very poorly organized, and the Moscow authorities failed to show the necessary firmness and skill in suppressing it. Durnovo, therefore, sent Rachkovsky, Vice-Director of the Police Department, to Moscow to direct the activities of the police and the troops. The instrument of Rachkovsky's success was the Semenovsky infantry regiment of His Majesty's guards under the command of General Min, who later paid for his firmness with his life. In the spring of 1906 he fell victim to a terrorist act. After quieting Moscow, the Semenovsky regiment was sent to the Moscow-Riazan railway, whose workers were on strike and where many prominent party workers were active. Harsh punishment was meted out to the strikers; many of those arrested were executed on the spot.

Yet there was much more to be done than to put down the uprising in Moscow; the government had also to protect the country from the reserves returning from the Far East. These reserves, traveling in special trains, had lost all their military discipline and were nothing but an unruly riotous mob. They got so far out of hand as to wreck a part of the great Siberian railway; they looted the railway stations en route, demanded immediate right-of-way, which on a one-track road caused the stopping of all east-bound traffic, and caused panic wherever they went.

To suppress these returning soldiers Durnovo selected General Baron Meller-Zakomelsky.[41] This general was noted for his firmness and ruthlessness; it was he who had suppressed the Sevastopol uprising in November. He left Moscow for Siberia at the head of a hand-picked punitive detachment. His procedure was simple: When he met a trainload of reservists about whose misdeeds he had been informed, he had his men surround the train; then the reservists were brought out in small groups and straightway given a severe flogging. This treatment had a magic effect. After an encounter with General Meller the reservists behaved "as quiet as water, as meek as grass."

An eyewitness described to me an incident at one of the larger stations near the Urals. The station staff had had word that a train of exceptionally unruly reservists was about to arrive. The café manager cleared out, taking along all the foodstuffs; all his employees went with him. The arrival of the dangerous troops was awaited with fear and trembling. The station was as silent as the tomb. When, after an hour or two, word came that the train had just pulled out of the next station, fear changed to panic. But when the much-feared train finally hove into sight and came to a stop before the station, the carriages were quiet, the doors of the cars were closed—no accordions, no discordant singing, not even a human voice was to be heard. Then a car door opened slowly, a head appeared apprehensively, and was cautiously followed by a body and legs; it was a husky reservist with a teakettle in his hand. He descended slowly to the platform and in a low voice asked a bystander, "May I ask for some hot water?" The bystander showed him where to get it; then, overcoming his trepidations, he inquired, "Why is your train so awfully quiet?" "We met General Meller on the way," was the brief but eloquent answer.*

Yet this was not the end of dealing with the revolutionary forces. The task now was to dispose of the many persons whose connections with revolutionary activities all over Russia had been discovered and were now detained. Their cases were referred to the Police Department, which classified them according to categories; then, depending on the nature of the offense, the accused were brought before the courts for trial or, as was more often the case, were simply banished to remote localities. This classification work was done by a special board attached to the Police Department and composed of the director of that department and an Assistant Prokuror of the court of appeal. This board was presided over by the Assistant Minister of the Interior, the liberal-minded Prince S. D. Urusov, who had unquestionably been given this task by Durnovo because of his, Urusov's, popularity with the Cadets. Urusov had left the civil service in 1905 and had been elected member of the First Duma from Kaluga. Later he became a member of the Cadet party; but now, day after day and in perfect peace of mind, he deported and exiled hundreds of persons, knowing but hazily who they were and what were their offenses. According to the memoirs of A. A. Lopukhin, published by the Soviets in 1923, there was a total of 45,000 persons deported.

This business of classification was very poorly organized in the Police Department, as I had occasion to observe, for after the dismissal of Urusov, Durnovo appointed me to preside over this

---

* It was said of Meller that as a young man, during the Khiva campaign of 1865 when he was attached to Skobelev,[42] who was something of a sadist, he and his chief had amused themselves while drunk by chopping off the heads of Khivan and Turkoman prisoners. This monstrous activity explains the disfavor in which Alexander II held Skobelev at the beginning of the Turkish War of 1877–78, during which Skobelev was attached to the general staff of an army corps and crossed the Danube under Dragomirov,[43] June 13, 1877, as an ordinary volunteer.

board. This appointment was very disagreeable to me. In all my
life I had had no connections with the police or with police affairs
and had no inclination toward this important and very necessary
branch of administration. Had times been normal I should have
refused to accept the appointment; but those were troubled times,
the government was fighting to preserve the existing state order,
and I saw no possibility of refusing to take part in this fight.

The board held its meetings in the building occupied by the
Police Department, of which E. I. Vuich,[44] brother of the Manager of Affairs of the Council of Ministers, was then director.
But as E. I. Vuich was too busy to attend the meetings he sent
in his stead one of the assistant directors, Nil Petrovich Zuev,[45]
who for some reason was nicknamed Crocodile Petrovich, although
he did not resemble a crocodile in any way. He was a very meek,
timid, and browbeaten official, who did his duties conscientiously
but without enthusiasm. I do not remember the name of the other
member, the Assistant Prokuror.

The heads of the offices of the Police Department reported
briefly on inquiries conducted by local gendarme units concerning
those arrested, and accompanied their reports with their recommendations for the term and locality of the prisoners' exile: those
less guilty or less dangerous to be banished to the northern gubernias of European Russia, while those more dangerous to be exiled
to Siberia, the worst places of exile being the Narym and Turukhan
regions. These recommendations were made without benefit of
information as to the age, family status, or education of those
proposed for exile and deportation; for the Police Department
received no such information. Cases arising from a single revolutionary event were not always handled by one person. At one
meeting, for instance, cases concerning the Moscow uprising were
reported by three different persons. Also, differences of opinion
among different officials meant varying degrees of punishment:
the more severe official inflicted the stiffer penalty. It is clear that
under these conditions the Special Board did no more than put
a stamp of approval on the measures proposed by the local secret-
service units and the recommendations of the heads of offices in
the Police Department. The latter were drafted from men trained
in law and were equal in rank to vice-directors of other departments of the Ministry of Interior, and their recommendations,
because of their legal authority, inspired a certain confidence. The

Special Board was little more than an automatic register of cases and decisions.

I realized of course that when one chops wood the chips must fly, that under the present conditions abstract justice was out of the question; yet I would not agree to confirm blindly the decisions of officials reporting on persons of whom I knew nothing, not even their age. Directly after I first attended a meeting of the Board I went to see the Director of the Police Department and asked him to send local gendarme authorities a telegram ordering them to accompany their reports with definite information about the persons whose cases were transferred to the Police Department. We indicated what data we considered necessary, and edited the telegram then and there.

I was not yet satisfied, however. That evening I went to see Durnovo. I described the situation to him and said that, while I did not decline to carry out my new duties and while I was ready to apply the severest penalties to those who were found guilty of undermining the principles of the state, I could not consent to do so blindfolded. The work was complicated; the reports of local administrators had to be carefully considered; in all, it demanded a great deal of time, of which I had none. I was sole manager of the Peasant Section and of the Board for the Affairs of Conscription.[46] I had to sign great piles of documents pertaining to the Department for General Affairs and the Chief Administration of Posts and Telegraphs; twice weekly I attended the sessions of the Senate; I participated in numerous conferences and represented the Minister of the Interior in the Council of Ministers; consequently I had no time to study personally the business of the Special Board of the Police Department. I asked Durnovo, therefore, either to free me from all other work until the hundreds of cases transferred to the Board and pertaining to the administrative exile of revolutionary elements were disposed of, or to appoint someone in my stead. Durnovo did the latter. In a special report to the Tsar he asked permission to appoint V. E. Frisch.[47]

I came in contact with the work of administrative exile only once again. It was during those few days in April 1906 between the dismissal of Durnovo and the appointment of Stolypin when I was in charge of the Ministry of the Interior. The records of the Special Board were to be confirmed by the minister. They were accompanied by the lists of those to be exiled, indicating the place and term of exile. A glance through these lists showed me that the Board and the minister were informed at least of the age, family status, and education of the exiled. Evidently Durnovo had heeded my remonstrances and had ordered the information I suggested.

By 1906 the danger that the existing regime, and even the state itself, would collapse had passed. Terroristic acts directed against individual defenders of the regime recurred now and again, but they did not endanger the state as a whole. But during the last months of 1905 such danger had existed. Then all Russia had been literally on fire. Revolutionary contagion had spread from Vladivostok to Kalish, and from Samarkand to Arkhangelsk; the revolutionists had even formed special fighting units to overthrow the government. These units could easily have been augmented by the reserves returning from Manchuria, infuriated by defeat and by the realization of a fruitless war, had these reserves not been suppressed in time. These units might also have been increased by the propagandized workers of both capitals and of other large industrial centers who secured considerable quantities of firearms and ammunition. The arming of the proletariat had been carried on very vigorously; the revolutionists had at their command whole laboratories of explosives—one was at Vyritsa—but this was not known till later. The troops, including the guards, and even the police had been lax in discipline and offered a far from reliable support.

The Revolution of 1905 had been checked by Durnovo. It was he, and he alone, who had really understood the situation and systematically, even ruthlessly, had taken steps to prevent the break-up of state apparatus. He had checked the flame of revolution in 1905 well enough, but was powerless to prevent its consequences, which proved fatal to the Russian Empire and which became apparent only eleven years later. "Without the 'general rehearsal' of 1905, the victory of the October Revolution, 1917, would have been impossible," Lenin said frankly, and he was right.[48]

This general rehearsal taught the revolutionists two practical lessons. In the first place it showed them how to create a revolutionary administration without having official power. Six weeks' uninterrupted activity of the St. Petersburg Soviet of Workers' Deputies had given them experience and practical suggestions. It is more than coincidence that Trotsky, vice-chairman and later chairman of this Soviet in 1905, headed the Soviet in 1917 also. In the second place, the revolutionists had come to know the Russian radical public and formed a true estimate of its leaders. The revolutionists understood that in the future their first move should be to place these radical leaders in positions of authority. There these leaders would not constitute an obstacle to the final Soviet bid for power but rather would clear the road for such a move.

The leaders of the Cadet party derived no useful lesson from the events of 1905. They continued to build their hopes of success upon the development of the revolutionary activity of the Social Democrats. Years later, however, when it was too late, they had one enlightened moment. An article published in *Rech,*[49] September 22, 1917, stated that unfortunately both the Cadets and Russia had enemies among the Left: "Those who have unchained the lowest instincts of human nature and turned the political struggle into a campaign of general destruction—they are our enemies . . . . We shall be our own enemies as long as we continue, for any reason whatsoever, to carry the ass upon our own shoulders, as the German fable goes."

To return to the events of the end of 1905! In the final analysis the fact that Witte was head of the government aided rather than hindered the pacification of the public. It gave the moderate liberals cause for hoping that the country would gradually adopt a regime of equity as its normal system and that the proclaimed liberties would be assured to the people. To some extent this was what Witte intended, although his intentions did not go as far along this line as those of the radicals. He had not the slightest intention of limiting his own executive power in favor of the people's elected representatives. This was most clearly shown in the law concerning elections to the State Duma. Witte had constructed this law so as to give the dominating role to that part of the population which he considered most conservative, most devoted to the existing regime.

Witte's conservatism was also revealed when the Council of Ministers examined the project of fundamental laws worked out in Solsky's conference, although actually the project was composed by Baron Uxkull-Gyllenband, who had succeeded V. N. Kokovtsov as Imperial Secretary and by Uxkull's assistant, Kharitonov. Later, in 1912 or 1913, I forget which, B. Glinsky[50] wrote some articles for *Istoricheskii Vestnik* based on documents which Witte had given him and in these articles he showed clearly that all Witte's efforts had been directed toward creating a set of conditions by which the Monarch would be enabled to rule the country autocratically and to enact both administrative and legislative measures without the participation of the people's representatives. In his heart Witte was a partisan of enlightened absolutism; he accepted the constitutional regime out of necessity, but the constitution he had in mind was a very limited one in which control would still reside in the Monarch and a government appointed by him. As for the people's representatives, Witte dreamed of winning their favor and then using it as a moral force which would be his chief support before the throne.

As I have already pointed out, Witte also endeavored to confirm and, at the same time, limit those civil liberties already granted the population. It was under his direction, therefore, that there appeared statutes on unions and new censorship regulations which introduced many innovations in this field.

Witte also tried to introduce legislation for certain organic changes. In the first place he tried to secure for the peasants the legal right freely to leave the communes; but in this he was firmly opposed by the State Council which, during the last months of its pre-reform period, conducted itself with extreme caution and correctness. This was seen in the fact that the members of the State Council refused to consider or confirm any question of importance, but deferred it to the consideration of the people's representatives who were about to be elected. In vain did representatives of different ministries point out that for a long time to come the people's representatives would be unable to consider questions even of secondary importance and that this attitude on the part of the Council meant delay in satisfying the immediate needs of part of the population.*

* I recall one incident during one of the last joint sessions of the State Council's departments. It was a question of apportioning supplementary sums for the organization of a gynecological institute. The organization of this institute was supervised by Dr. Otto and was of great interest to the Empress; in fact, the original idea was ascribed to her. The institute was planned according to the latest discoveries of science, and the cost of its construction, equipment, and administration was huge. All original estimates had been greatly exceeded. The supplementary grant requested was for a comparatively small sum—about 100,000 rubles. In normal times this would have been granted with little debate, but now it was opposed most decisively by representatives of the Ministry of Finance and the State Control. S. V. Ivanov,[51] Assistant State Comptroller, objected most furi-

Witte realized his powerlessness to carry important reforms through the pre-Duma legislative machine, but he drew up a detailed program of radical reforms to be placed before the new legislative chambers as soon as they should convene. He intended to have his hands free of administrative affairs when he went before the Duma to lay before it a series of state reforms that would affect all phases of public life. In this intention he was inspired by two forces which attended him throughout his entire career: first, a desire to secure an increasingly firm hold on power; second, an ambition to use power not to direct current affairs, but to push through the reforms he desired. His very nature was comprised of a desire to rule and a desire to create. He could not be content with peacefully perfecting that which existed; his nature drove him to seek something new, and for such a man Russia presented vast opportunities. In Witte's mind the State Duma was to aid him first of all, if not exclusively, to realize his enormous projects which he could never realize under a purely bureaucratic regime.

Another motive which prompted Witte to present his program to the new representative body was the conviction that the representatives should be immediately introduced to problems of state. He thought to occupy the Duma with considerations of national problems and thus divert them from revolutionary orations and fruitless dreaming. A special commission was formed to prepare a list of those legislative projects to be presented at the opening of the First Duma. This commission was presided over by A. P. Nikol-

---

ously. He pointed out that the final decision must rest with the new legislative body. He and the other objectors did not choose to recall that the resulting delay would postpone indefinitely the opening of the institute, and they succeeded in making several members of the State Council agree with them. Ivanov even criticized the very idea of organizing this institute and the great expenditures for what he considered too luxurious equipment. I was attending the session as representative of the Minister of the Interior and could not suffer the expression of this, in my estimation, patent knavery. I argued with some heat that the objections to the organization of the institute and the estimates for its construction should have been made when the estimates were placed before the State Council, and not now when it was only a question of a trifling supplementary grant. The suggestion to leave the final decision with the State Duma, especially if the State Comptroller was correct in assuming that the expenditures had been too great, was equivalent to placing the blame for these expenditures on the Empress, who was so actively interested in the establishment of the institute; in fact, some details of interior decoration were executed according to her sketches. Perhaps I should not have spoken as I did, but my words had effect: the grant was confirmed unanimously.

sky, who had succeeded Kutler in March 1906 as Head of the
Chief Administration of Land Organization and Agriculture, and
was composed of representatives of all ministries except the ministries of war, the navy, and the Imperial court. This commission
soon discovered what an enormous quantity of legislative material
had been accumulated only to be waylaid in inter-ministerial correspondence. I can still visualize the huge typewritten folio which
contained nothing but the titles of legislative projects awaiting their
turn for consideration by this commission. Future historians would
no doubt be interested in studying this list.

Witte himself was keenly interested in the work of the commission and discussed it with representatives of different ministries. In discussions with me he reviewed mainly the question of
giving the peasants the right freely to leave the communes.

In order to speed up even more the preparation of projects for
the Duma, Witte also did away with inter-ministerial correspondence concerning these projects and submitted them directly to the
Council of Ministers.

At the same time Witte realized full well that to meet the Duma
with an empty treasury was equivalent to becoming its slave, since
he would be placed in the role of a petitioner for funds. But the
revenues of the state were seriously depleted by the terrific expenses
of the Japanese War; consequently, as soon as conditions in the
country were sufficiently stable to make it possible to secure a foreign loan, Witte opened negotiations with a group of Paris bankers. After some effort he made a preliminary arrangement with
it for a loan larger than any country in the world had ever made
—something like eight hundred million rubles in gold. Then, at
the last moment, the agreement all but failed. V. N. Kokovtsov
had been sent to Paris to sign the agreement, and there he met
other envoys who had gone to Paris with the intention of preventing the deal. These envoys, alas, were Russians. One of them
bore an illustrious name and represented the Cadet party. This
Cadet interference was unquestionably a great inconvenience to
Kokovtsov in executing the task with which he was charged, not
so much in effecting the loan as in preserving the conditions to
which Russia's creditors had agreed.[52]

Among the dark deeds of the Cadet party this sending of emissaries abroad for the purpose of undermining the credit of their own
country was perhaps the darkest and most disgraceful, even though

such action was represented as directed against the Russian government and not against Russia herself; and the fact that the Cadet party felt it necessary to seek help abroad instead of in its own country is proof of its weakness. This, moreover, also stamped the caliber of the Cadet statesmanship; the educated circles of Western Europe could not understand how a patriotic organization could plot against its own country and seek support for its plot from foreigners.

The successful completion of the foreign loan untied Witte's hands and left him sure of victory. He was prepared to steer his course between the supreme power and the people's representatives, assuring each that his reforms would be highly acceptable to the other and so he would carry out his own will without hindrance or delay. In these rosy expectations he was supported by the entire Council of Ministers. Also the first reports of the Duma election returns were encouraging: the majority of those elected belonged to the peasant class; many of the clergy were also elected. Not only Witte but also the public was certain that the peasant deputies were the most respectable and intelligent of their class, something like our volost heads (*starshiny*), and would be as wax in the hands of the government. This was the main reason why the revolutionary and opposition elements demanded that the system of election be changed to the four-tailed formula. Socialists of different denominations even decided to boycott the elections; they hoped thus to lessen the position of the Duma deputies in the eyes of the workers.

I attended a session of the Council of Ministers held directly after the first election returns had come in. Everyone present was pleased; Witte expressed a common feeling when he said: "Thank heaven! The Duma will be predominantly peasant." The Ober-Prokuror of the Synod, Obolensky, added: "And a clerical one, too. Not bad at all." The Council of Ministers was in the best of humor as it passed on to consider other current affairs. During the ensuing discussion many remarked: "Now it will be easier; now we shall pass this measure through this Duma." It occurred to no one that the fact of being a peasant did not constitute a guaranty of political loyalty.

Later reports had more to say about the party affiliation of the new deputies. It soon became known that the majority called themselves Cadet men. This meant that the peasant majority would be more an obstacle than an aid to the government, for it was generally realized that such a majority would be but a herd led by a few Cadet intellectuals.

As the final composition of the Duma became certain, Witte's face clouded. He again began to show signs of extreme nervousness and irritability. He ascribed the results of the elections to Durnovo and those harsh measures with which the latter had suppressed the revolutionary movement. This charge was unjust. Durnovo's measures had been applied mostly to cities, and could not have influenced the attitude of the rural masses which constituted the majority of the electors. The real reason for the election results was the widespread Cadet propaganda which had promised the peasants as much land as they wished but had maintained a discreet silence as to how the promise was to be fulfilled. Witte was convinced, however, that the fault was Durnovo's alone. This conviction was strengthened by information he received at about that time concerning the administrative exile of forty-five thousand persons.[53] It may be asked, however, what would the results of the elections have been had these forty-five thousand agitators been left alone. When Witte said that he was continually asking Durnovo to slacken his repressions, he was right; but he forgot to mention that he did not do so until January 1906, that is, after the revolution had been driven under cover.

After the beginning of 1906, when Durnovo was at last appointed Minister of the Interior (up to then he had been merely Acting Minister), relations between Durnovo and Witte became strained. The Tsar's favor toward Durnovo made Witte suspect that Durnovo might be the next Chairman of the Council of Ministers. From that time on Witte did everything he could to get rid of Durnovo. Witte thought that the revolution, as a danger to the state, was ended; therefore, he saw no more need of Durnovo. Moreover, he realized that it would be difficult to appear before the Duma with the unpopular Durnovo as a member of his government. The press significantly designated Witte's government as that of Witte-Durnovo, and in order to reclothe himself in the white garments of liberalism Witte had to remove this associate who had now become so hateful to him.

But how was this removal to be effected? In October the Tsar had given Witte free choice in selecting the members of his government. Since then, however, the Monarch had changed his policy and it was possible that he would refuse Witte's wish to replace Durnovo by someone else. Under these circumstances Witte decided to act directly. He tendered his resignation to the Tsar, giving as his reason the differences between his and Durnovo's political views. Witte was firmly convinced that the Tsar would ask him to remain and would discharge Durnovo.* But Witte was mistaken. He had already lost the Tsar's confidence when he was dismissed from the post of Minister of Finance in 1903, and during his term as Chairman of the Council of Ministers the Tsar's sentiments toward him had become definitely unfriendly. The Tsar had come to the conclusion that Witte was not as loyal to his Sovereign as was to be expected of a first minister.

I became convinced of Witte's imminent dismissal about two weeks before it actually occurred. During the first part of April I had occasion to present myself before the Tsar. In conversing with His Majesty about the opening of the Duma I expressed the opinion that successful co-operation with the Duma would depend largely on absolute harmony among the ministers. I took the liberty of saying, with a suitable gesture, that the ministry must be one and firm, like a fist. But the Tsar was not much impressed. "Indeed, yes," he answered, as if waving aside something secondary, "but the main thing is to have the ministry in the right hands. You understand of whom I am speaking." These words filled me with consternation. For if the Tsar, who knew me but slightly and saw me but very seldom, would say such a thing to me, his unfriendly feeling toward Witte must have reached a high point indeed. At any rate, it was apparent that Witte would be dismissed before the opening of the Duma.

Witte himself had no inkling of what was in store for him until the very last. Three days before his dismissal he spoke in the Council of Ministers about the government's relations with the Duma and, full of his everlasting optimism, expressed the opinion that an understanding with the Duma could be reached without much effort. In the meantime His Majesty's Private Office was preparing a farewell rescript to Count Witte.

A decisive part in Witte's dismissal was played by that small circle which I have mentioned above, and which centered around Goremykin, V. F. Trepov, and A. V. Krivoshein. As Commandant of the Palace, D. F. Trepov had an opportunity to see the Tsar daily, and working through him the circle did not let a day pass after Witte's appointment as Chairman of the Council of Ministers with-

---

* In his memoirs Witte presented this matter in quite another light. On my side, in my article, "Chto est i chego net v vospominaniiakh grafa Witte" ("What is and what is not said in the Memoirs of Count Witte"), *Russkaia Letopis,* Vol. II, Paris, 1922, pp. 59–153, I pointed out those reasons which made clear to everybody that Witte's account, like many other parts of his memoirs, was entirely untrue.

out representing Witte's activities to the Tsar in an unfavorable light. Through V. F. Trepov the circle had connections with Durnovo, who was often the source of valuable information. But the affair brought no gain to Durnovo himself. The results of the Duma elections and the open hostility of the public toward Durnovo prompted the circle to suggest to the Tsar the advisability of dismissing both Durnovo and Witte. In this way the public would be shown that the dismissal of Witte did not mean a definite turn of state policy toward reaction. Also, the removal of these two persons by one ukase would show the public that they were considered as one; this would lower Witte's reputation in the eyes of the progressive public and deprive him of that halo of liberalism which he had so painstakingly built up. But there was not perfect harmony of opinion in the circle. Goremykin and V. F. Trepov believed that the Duma members must not be made to seem too important. D. F. Trepov, on the other hand, held that the government must come to an understanding with the Duma, or at least avoid antagonizing it, so as not to aggravate its opposition or to arouse public excitement. He was especially insistent that all factors which were provoking the hostility of the population must be removed, and among these he very sensibly classed Durnovo. According to D. F. Trepov, Durnovo had already played out his role of suppressor of the revolution, and state need no longer demanded his further association with the government. He advocated that Goremykin be made head of the government, because he saw in this old statesman a man whose outstanding characteristic was calm rationality. Besides, Trepov was close to Goremykin personally and saw that it would be most convenient to have an understanding with the latter and in general to preserve his influence upon the Tsar.

The result of these different opinions was a compromise, which was finally adopted by the Tsar. By the ukase of April 20, six days before the opening session of the First Duma, both Witte and Durnovo were dismissed, and Goremykin was appointed Chairman of the Council of Ministers.

This ukase was a complete surprise not only to those whom it directly concerned but to bureaucratic and public circles as well. Witte was positively furious at seeing himself thus identified with Durnovo, and could never forget the association. Moreover, enforced inactivity was not to Witte's liking, especially at a time when great vistas for his creative plans were opening up. Later, he tried to return to power, even to positions of secondary importance. To this end he addressed himself to persons such as Krivoshein, for whom he entertained hostile rather than friendly feelings; but all in vain. In the eyes of Nicholas II, Witte was a traitor. When Witte passed away in 1915 and the news of his death reached the Tsar's headquarters at the front, the Tsar expressed himself to the effect that now, finally, a dangerous source of revolt had been removed.

Stolypin also distrusted Witte. When Krivoshein, acting on Witte's behalf, asked Stolypin to appoint Witte chairman of a special railway commission which was to reorganize the entire railway system in Russia and to draw plans for the construction of railways throughout the country, Stolypin said jestingly: "I must, Aleksandr Vasilevich, refer your request to the prosecuting magistrates to have you indicted for state treason."

As for Durnovo, he had had no reason to suppose that the hour of his dismissal was drawing near. The Tsar had always given him a cordial welcome and expressed confidence in him; he was on the best of terms with both the Trepov brothers and could not have expected any tricks from them. Of course, he was well aware of the public's attitude toward him and therefore expected no welcome from the Duma. But he hoped to cope with it all. He was preparing for the Duma and on the eve of his dismissal had said to P. M. Kaufman: "They (the State Duma) shall see what sort of a reactionary I am." His plan was to present the Duma with a liberal program and then to submit the necessary legislative projects. Then, suddenly, all his plans were frustrated. I read of his dismissal in the papers on April 20 and immediately went to see him. I found him at his desk, sorting some papers. Outwardly he was calm and gave no sign of indignation; but he was depressed and sad, and made no effort to conceal the fact. "Indeed, it is a great blow to me," he said frankly. "For those of us who have devoted our lives to serving the state it is most painful to attain the height of authority and then to be deprived of it. You will experience it yourself some day." He gave me a slightly ironical look, then added: "In the meantime, take over my duties." He spoke to me about some urgent matters pertaining to the Police Department. He suggested that the exiled Professor Gredeskul,[54] who had been elected member of the Duma from the city of Kharkov, should be recalled from Arkhangelsk. Then, when saying goodbye, he exclaimed with sudden animation: "Just think of Witte! How furious he must be to be dismissed along with me!"

CHAPTER XX

GOREMYKIN'S MINISTRY AND THE FIRST STATE DUMA

Goremykin's ministry lasted only two and a half months. It determined upon the dissolution of the First Duma and then followed that body off the political stage. This ministry was especially marked by the multiformity and diversity of its membership. With the exception of Izvolsky it included no sincere champion of the constitutional regime. It contained men who had become resigned to the reform, who saw in it something that could not be revoked, and whose one desire was simply to establish an acceptable *modus vivendi* with the people's representatives without making needless concessions to them, especially in the field of authority. Other members of the new ministry refused to renounce the old principle of an absolute monarch and aimed, therefore, not so much at collaboration with the Duma as at widening the chasm between the people's representatives and the crown in order to end the constitutional experiment and return to the old regime of unlimited arbitrariness.

Goremykin assumed a strange attitude. He disliked all decisive measures and was inclined to let events take their natural course. He did not wish to annul the Manifesto of October 17; he intended to face the aggressive public, not with an active, lively opposition, but with a quiet, stubborn, passive resistance. He intended to preserve the existing system of government in its entirety and to effect reforms only when absolutely necessary. He wished to keep the State Duma within the confines established by law. His attitude was: "You Duma members may consider the new legislative projects; if you reject them, the old ones will do."

For his ministers he wanted men obedient to his will, fairly well informed concerning their respective fields, not inclined toward liberalism, and still less inclined toward the idea of radical reform. Least of all did he want men with initiative and enthusiasm. He was little concerned with the attitude of his ministers toward the change in government effected by the October Manifesto. He himself decided to ignore the Duma and to establish no relations with its chairmen or its individual members. He had decided at the outset that no understanding with that body could be reached, and concluded that all efforts in this direction would be fruitless, even harmful, since they might be construed as a capitulation of the government. He shied sharply from such a possibility; for he was firmly persuaded that the least concession by the government would in the end lead to the destruction of all state authority.

For a long time Goremykin had been interested in problems of foreign affairs—apparently his dream was to be appointed ambassador to one of the most important European capitals—and now he intended to concentrate his attention upon such problems and to permit no interference in them from the people's representatives. He considered Count Lamsdorf's policy fundamentally unsound. But, being incurably lazy and hating reports, he did not intend to take any portfolio himself; hence his first act was to find a Minister of Foreign Affairs who would carry out his ideas. Believing that the Tsar valued Count Lamsdorf highly, Goremykin decided that the only way to get rid of Lamsdorf was to persuade the Tsar that he should appear before the Duma with an entirely new ministry except for the three ministers who were appointed directly by the Tsar. To Goremykin's surprise, as he himself told me, the Tsar showed no reluctance to appoint a successor to Lamsdorf.*

Goremykin succeeded easily in removing the old ministers; but this did not signify that the selection of a new cabinet would depend upon him alone. Stolypin, the new Minister of the Interior, for instance, was selected by Nicholas II. Goremykin learned of the Tsar's intention to make this appointment when he first reported to the Tsar after his appointment. Goremykin did not know Stolypin and asked me what I had to say about Stolypin's possible appointment. I told him that I had little to say about it, as I knew Stolypin only slightly; the only time I had had business with him was when he had come to St. Petersburg with a project for transferring to other lands the

* This is but one illustration of the peculiar indifference of Nicholas II to the personnel of his closest and most important assistants. He lacked the capacity of becoming attached to those who surrounded him, and parted with them without any sorrow. V. I. Mamontov[1] is another example of such treatment. When he was Head of the Chancellery of the Imperial Household he was very close to the Tsar and the Tsarina. Later, after his appointment as Head of His Majesty's Private Chancellery to Receive Petitions Addressed to the Emperor, he was totally cut off from the Imperial family and never again invited to the Imperial dinners or even to the Imperial hunts.

peasants of the villages in the Belovezh forest area so that their continuous protests to the government against the alleged damage done by the buffaloes preserved in this area might be brought to an end. On this occasion he had impressed me as a man of intelligence but not outstanding in any respect; he had not even expressed his facts and ideas smoothly. His character, however, was beyond reproach.

A few days later Goremykin told me that the Tsar had in mind another candidate, N. I. Zvegintsev, Governor of Smolensk. "Now," said Goremykin, "I must choose between Stolypin and Zvegintsev. What do you think?" I answered that there could be no hesitation in choosing between these two men. "Zvegintsev is known as a clever and shrewd man, but in monetary matters his reputation is extremely bad. While marshal of the nobility of one of the uezds of Voronezh Gubernia he was accused of embezzlement, and now, as Governor of Smolensk, he has the name of being a grafter." As a result, Goremykin then and there sent a telegram calling Stolypin to St. Petersburg.

I met Stolypin immediately after his arrival in the capital. I explained to him the purpose of his trip and that he was to present himself to the Tsar the next day. I also availed myself of the opportunity to attempt to show him that Russia could not develop peacefully until the commune was abolished, and that it was most important that he should obtain the Tsar's consent to this measure at once. But it seemed to me that Stolypin knew little about this subject; he seemed to lack even a clear understanding of what the land commune was.

The next day, however, after he had returned from the Tsar, Stolypin told me that he had expressed to His Majesty the desirability of transferring the peasants from communal to individual landowner-ship and that no objections had been made. Stolypin also told me that at first he had refused to accept the post. Then the Tsar had said that it was his express desire that Stolypin should accept it, whereupon Stolypin had declared that to him as a subject the Tsar's wish was sacred. He had then kissed the Tsar's hand. The prestige and power of the Monarch was still alive and strong at that time among those who lived away from the capital.

Stolypin played an important part in the history of Russia during the few years he was head of the government. His rather extensive experience had been gained in the field of provincial administration, but actually he was much more a politician than an administrator. He had no talent for understanding men and consequently none for selecting his assistants. Those of his Saratov colleagues whom he selected were of limited intellectual ability (as, for example, A. A. Makarov, his Assistant Minister, who later became Minister) or were noted for their two-faced flattery (for example, I. I. Knoll, Manager of his Chancellery), or for their mediocrity (for example, Golovachev, his special duties clerk, or Beletsky,[2] his Director of the Police Department and formerly Vice-Governor of Samara). Nor was he much more fortunate in selecting associates from the St. Petersburg bureaucracy (for instance, A. I. Lykoshin, an absolute nonentity without initiative or will power, and P. G. Kurlov,[3] an intelligent and able but unprincipled go-getter, who not only succeeded in deceiving Stolypin but also undermined the Tsar's confidence in him). Even as a politician Stolypin lacked a definite and complete program. He had a vague desire to effect a reconciliation between the government and the people but no definite plan for carrying it out, although he had tried to carry out such a policy while Governor of Saratov Gubernia, where he had been popular with the zemstvo. He brought with him to St. Petersburg his provincial way of doing things and evidently hoped to apply it in his relations with the Duma with which he endeavored to establish personal contacts through men, now Duma members, whom he had known at Saratov, especially N. N. Lvov. But if Stolypin lacked knowledge, he had intuition. With astonishing speed he found his bearings in the complicated bureaucratic and court atmosphere of St. Petersburg, and with the assistance of his numerous relatives soon succeeded in establishing contacts with the most influential circles and persons. He did this not so much to fortify his personal position as to aid the successful realization of his political plans. Later, spoiled by a long stretch of office, he took a deathlike hold upon his power and was ready to sacrifice much to retain it. But for a considerable time after he became minister he manifested no readiness to make any concessions in order to retain his office. At first he showed none of that self-assurance which he later developed.

Stolypin understood well enough the significance of public opinion, just as he realized also that the stability of the state and internal order depended upon the attitude of the people toward the government. He knew nothing, however, about the needs of the people and those organic reforms which were necessary for the normal development of the country. What is more, he hardly concerned himself with them. Since he lacked definite ideas and plans of his own, he listened to those of other people and selected those ideas which he thought would best realize the hopes of the more state-minded public elements. Even so, he was less concerned with the reforms themselves and their actual results than with the degree in which they would be approved by the people and would thus strengthen the position of the government; for during his entire ministry his main concern was to strengthen the position of the government. Albeit, Stolypin was an exceptional statesman. His remarkable intuition went far to make up for the shortcomings which have been mentioned. Among the many contradictory suggestions that came to him, he could detect those which would be most likely to win public support. These he adopted firmly and courageously and carried out without hesitation. The outstanding example of this was his adoption of the idea of changing the land organization of the Russian peasantry, which I shall describe later. His intuition also prompted his gradual change from an understanding with the Right wing of the Cadets to a firm support of the Octobrists and, later, of the Nationalists. He perceived that as the position of the Duma grew stronger the educated and patriotic elements of the people were inclining more and more toward some gradual change of government with definitely national characteristics.

Stolypin also had a talent for arousing in everyone with whom he dealt a feeling that he was sincere in everything he said. He inspired confidence and even affection. Had he been born in a country with an established parliamentary regime, he would probably have become the leader of a political party, for he was a fiery orator, even though his speeches were written by other men. His lack of ability in selecting assistants would have been no handicap, for the party organization would have performed this function. But in a country like Russia, still in large part an absolute monarchy, Stolypin's inability to pick the proper assistants explains why his success was confined to strengthening the position of the central government and raising its prestige and influence; he accomplished little in reforming local administration and justice, and still less in reforming local economy.

In Goremykin's ministry Stolypin kept in the background. During the sessions of the Council of Ministers he was absolutely silent, realizing perhaps his inexperience in matters of state. In fact, during this period, his speech, as well as his arguments and illustrations, bore the stamp of provincialism. This was shown especially when his immediate collaborators made reports to him. Often he would say: "In Saratov," or "In Grodno" (where he had been governor before his transfer to Saratov), "we used to do thus and so." It required time for him to adjust himself to the national scope of the affairs he was called to manage. Even so, he was never a really efficient minister; under him the departments of the Ministry of the Interior were left to their own devices.

At the very beginning of his new work Stolypin decided to become head of the government. He pursued this course subtly and intelligently, outwitting even that sly Ulysses, Goremykin. It is my profound conviction, however, that he desired to become Chairman of the Council of Ministers not because of ambition, but, first, because of his critical attitude toward Goremykin whose inactivity he noticed immediately, and, second, because he realized that the successful administration of internal policy, nominally under the direction of the Minister of the Interior, depended upon the united activities of all the ministers and, therefore, could be achieved only by having the Minister of the Interior become head of the government. He was encouraged in his course by his relatives and by members of the Duma. But more of Stolypin later.

For Minister of Finance Goremykin selected V. N. Kokovtsov to replace the rather colorless and unstatesmanlike Shipov. Kokovtsov answered perfectly the demands which Goremykin made of his associates. Goremykin could be quite sure that Kokovtsov would remain imperturbable and quiet, present no disagreeable surprises, and suggest nothing that deviated even slightly from the established routine. The state of Russian finances after the Japanese War and the turbulent revolutionary period made it necessary to treat the resources of the State Treasury with extreme care and to permit no risky economic or financial operations. For this Kokovtsov was the right man; so Goremykin selected him without the slightest hesitation, and this selection met with the Tsar's entire approval.

Kokovtsov managed Russian finances for a period of eight years, during the latter part of which—from the autumn of 1911 until February 1914—he was also Chairman of the Council of Ministers. His general characteristics are well known. He was moderate, exact, and conscientious. In all the positions he held he tried to acquaint himself with all the details of his work, always orienting himself according to the established order. He was without initiative. As Assistant Minister of Finance under Witte, he had been in charge of those departments of the ministry whose duty it was to accumulate and protect the resources of the Treasury. In this capacity his main work had been to present to the State Council those objections which the Ministry of Finance invariably made to all demands of other ministries for increased appropriations. Witte realized that the increase in the resources of the country and the influx of money into the State Treasury depended not so much upon careful expenditures as upon a skilful encouragement of those branches of public economy which were in process of development or were likely to develop; but he himself attended to this phase of his work and supervised the distribution of subsidies, loans, and donations. These were handled by departments with which Kokovtsov had nothing to do. Kokovtsov had the difficult and thankless task of making cuts in the appropriations to those departments and ministries which were outside Witte's competence. And now, as Minister of Finance, Kokovtsov continued to play the role of watchman over the country's coffers.

I should like to say a few words about Kokovtsov's nature and ability. He had a logical mind. Also, he had had a literary training and could deliver a smoothly worded and detailed speech. By nature, however, he was pettifogging. He lacked that imagination that makes for creative thought. Nor was he a man of great daring, although on more than one occasion he demonstrated that he was courageous. Though he was disinclined to endanger or sacrifice his own private interests, he defended firmly and steadily the state interests entrusted to his care. For instance, in December 1913 he objected stubbornly to the measures proposed by the State Council to diminish the use of strong liquor in Russia, measures which were bound to diminish also the revenues derived from liquor sales. Despite the opposition of Witte and of Krivoshein, who at that time enjoyed the Imperial favor, and despite the knowledge that Nicholas II himself was then in favor of increased temperance, Kokovtsov opposed the measures to the bitter end, and in so doing incurred his own dismissal. On another occasion Kokovtsov demonstrated his political courage by refusing to comply with the wish of the Empress to sell or give a piece of state land to some protégé of hers. This is a testimony to his official honesty but also to the narrowness of his state views, for what harm would there have been in allowing a bit of land to pass into private hands?[4]

In general, however, Kokovtsov preferred to avoid conflict with any force which he considered strong. This is to be explained by the fact that he was very ambitious to make a successful career. At the beginning of his government service he had hardly expected to reach those heights which he eventually attained, but he accepted as his due the success that came his way; he expanded his demands upon life accordingly and came to consider any non-materialization of his wishes as a patent infringement on his rights and an unmerited personal offense. One incident may serve as an illustration.

In the spring of 1902 Kokovtsov was appointed Imperial Secretary. Soon afterwards I happened to visit Filosofov, who was at that time Assistant State Comptroller. I found him looking through a sort of civil service "Who's Who." "I have just parted with V. N. Kokovtsov," he said. "He expressed his joy at leaving the 'garbage-heap,' as he called the Ministry of Finance. I was interested to learn how working in that Ministry had affected Kokovtsov himself. I see by this book that during the six years of his work as Assistant Minister of Finance he was made a senator, promoted to the rank of privy councillor, decorated with the cross of Alexander Nevsky (or was it the White Eagle?) and received a yearly award[5] of two thousands rubles. The 'garbage-heap' has yielded its all; now it can be abandoned," concluded Filosofov.

Through his entire life Kokovtsov was attended by a lucky star which made him, a man without extraordinary abilities, Minister of Finance and later Chairman of the Council of Ministers and brought him all manner of honors and distinctions including the title of count. Yet it must also be noted that during the turbulent periods through which Russia passed when he was in office, he managed by some quirk of fate to avoid prominence in the civil service, so that he escaped being made the butt of the public's attacks. In 1905 he was Imperial Secretary and, therefore, even though he had some relation to politics, this was not well known to the general public; and in 1917 he was an ordinary member of the State Council, thus happily avoiding persecutions from the Provisional Government. Fate smiled upon him still further. He left Soviet Russia in good time and found a comfortable position as head of one of the Russian banks in Paris with a large salary, which enabled him to carry on without any marked changes in his standard of living. His is a case most exceptional in the history of the Russian emigration.[6]

The man selected as the new Minister of Justice in Goremykin's ministry was I. G. Shcheglovitov.[7] He was an unprincipled career-maker, a former contributor to the liberal periodical, *Pravo,* and not averse to making use of his reputation as a liberal. He was not at all sure, however, that the government would be victorious over the public, a victory which he personally very much desired and which he did as much as possible to win; hence he was careful not to burn his bridges and was ready to make all sorts of compromises.

The other ministers, except Prince Shirinsky and Stishinsky, were colorless persons. Men like Kaufmann and Schaufuss[8] were hardly noticeable in the Council of Ministers upon whose decisions they had no effect. But Prince Shirinsky and Stishinsky, who represented the Right wing of the Council, adopted a stand which in my estimation was quite sound: they held that all further concessions to the public and to the progress of the revolution would be conducive to the fall of the government. Nevertheless, they were short-sighted and narrow-minded. Shirinsky was a fanatical partisan of absolute monarchy. His mind could entertain only a limited number of ideas; he contended that the existing evils arose from the weakness of the government. To him, a regime employing police measures in government was almost perfect. Neither Shirinsky nor Stishinsky was well-informed on economic questions; the enormous importance of economic freedom was quite beyond their comprehension.

Goremykin's calm stood in marked contrast to the turbulent activity of Witte. When Witte was head of the government the waiting room of his office was filled at all hours of the day and till late at night with all sorts of people with whom Witte had lengthy conversations at great cost to his own energy. Goremykin, however, avoided current problems of administration from the outset and concentrated his interests upon a few issues of general significance. His first act was to study the draft of a revision of the Fundamental Laws of the Empire contained in the revised text of Volume I of the Code, which had already been prepared and accepted by the Council of Ministers. This he did with great care, without assistance from anyone, as far as I know. The changes and additions he made were determined by a desire to give the supreme power, even under the new regime, an opportunity to rule the country independently, even though this should lead to a conflict between it and the people's representatives. This revised Code was confirmed by the Tsar; but after it had been sent to be printed and published, Nicholas II made known his wish that the budget of the institutions of Empress Marie should be fixed at a certain sum which was to be exempt from debate by the legislative bodies, just as the budget of the Ministry of the Imperial Court, fixed at eleven millions, was so exempt. Here, however, Goremykin displayed unexpected firmness and announced that no further changes could be introduced in the laws of the empire, once they had been transferred to the Senate for publication.

The fact that Goremykin's ministry assumed office on the eve of the opening of the new legislature put it in a very embarrassing situation. The fact that our government had never had a definite political program made it impossible for the new government to appear before the Duma with anything approaching finished legislative projects for the various reforms which the progressive public was demanding. All work of this nature planned by Nikolsky's commission had been stopped. It is true that the Chairman of the Council of Ministers had instructed the members of that commission to prepare for presentation to the new legislature those projects which had already been approved by the Council of Ministers; but there were not many such projects, and even those that had been approved were of secondary political significance. Consequently, when the Duma was opened there were only two legislative projects ready for it to debate. These were introduced by the Minister of Education: one dealt with the organization of a laundry at some university (Dorpat, I believe), and the other concerned a proposed winter garden at some other school. These were trivial matters, indeed, with which to greet the Duma, which had every reason to pass over them in order to compose an address to the Tsar expressing a thorough condemnation of governmental activities. I suppose it would have done the same thing even had it had worthy legislative projects to work on, but in that event the position of the government would have been different.

As already mentioned, Goremykin had decided to ignore the Duma's very existence. This was a great mistake; for to ignore an institution established by Sovereign will and consisting of representatives of the people only served to emphasize the fact that the government did not favor the new constitution and was merely yielding to the insistent public demands. This attitude on the part of the government deprived the public of all assurance that the rights given today would not be withdrawn tomorrow; also it suggested that the public might obtain still wider rights by continuing its attacks. Success in having once prevailed against the government roused hopes of being able to repeat the process.

Goremykin also became involved in a question of etiquette. Should the Chairman of the Council of Ministers make the first official visit to the Chairman of the Duma, or vice versa? Muromtsev, haughty and supported by the example of the West, especially that of France, where the Chairman of the Council is preceded in rank by the President of the Republic, the Chairman of the Senate, and the Chairman of the Chamber of Deputies, considered it beneath his dignity to call upon Goremykin. The latter, however, considered it quite impossible that the head of the government, who was appointed by and responsible to the Monarch alone, should call upon the head of an elected body. This trifling circumstance made for strained relations between the government and the Duma from the very start. Each side assumed a hostile attitude toward the other, and neither desired to effect an understanding.

The First Duma was dominated by the Cadets, who did not even take the trouble to conceal the fact that they intended to use the Duma not for the good of the country but as an instrument to overthrow the government. Their attitude is illustrated by an interesting incident. On the occasion of the opening of the State Duma, it was suggested in the Moscow municipal Duma that felicitations be sent to the new national representative body; but the Cadet members of the municipal Duma (twenty-six out of one hundred and fifty) opposed the suggestion. Their leader, Professor A. A. Manuilov, even went so far as to say privately to Mayor N. I. Guchkov: "You wish the Duma to do good work, but we desire only to overthrow the government."

This Cadet attitude was certainly known to Nicholas II, as is revealed by what he said to Witte. On December 6, 1905, when Witte presented the statute on the elections to the Duma for the Tsar's signature (in the presence of S. E. Kryzhanovsky, author of the statute, whom he had taken along in case the Tsar should ask technical questions to which Witte would have no ready answer), he said to the Monarch: "The Duma will be as an assistant to Your Majesty in your difficult work." "Oh, come now, Sergei Yulevich!" the Tsar answered, "I know perfectly well that I am agreeing to the establishment of an institution which will be my enemy. Yet I am thinking of the future; I am thinking of my son. I wish to create a new center of authority in the country to insure the strength of the country at large."

The attitude of the underground revolutionary elements toward the Duma was one of opposition. This was no secret. They feared that the bourgeois elements in the Duma would realize that their main enemy was not the government but the revolutionists—the militant

Socialists who dreamed of overthrowing the entire social structure—and that they would therefore come to some understanding with the government and ally with it in war upon the really revolutionary movement. But, alas, neither the government nor the progressive public realized that their mutual conflicts profited only that *tertius gaudens* which, eleven years later, was to seize power, overthrow the political regime, undermine the social structure, and ruin that same progressive public.

The hostility of the majority of the First Duma toward the throne was shown clearly on the first day of its sessions. All the Duma members attended the Imperial reception in the throne room of the Winter Palace dressed in a deliberately careless fashion. Be it said, however, that there was a certain lack of tact on both sides. The court had decided that this reception was to be particularly solemn and brilliant. The Imperial regalia had been brought from Moscow, and these were to be borne by the highest officials, ranged on both sides of the throne. The throne was draped in the Imperial ermine mantle; it was said that the Tsarina herself had draped the mantle so that it would hang in artistic folds. Velvet ropes down the center of the room formed a sort of corridor through which the Imperial suite was to pass. On one side of this corridor were members of the State Duma and on the other members of the State Council, senators, and the other higher civil and military officials. The contrast was striking. The court and the government, flourishing gold-laced uniforms and numerous decorations, was set opposite the gray, almost rustic group representing the people of Russia. Naïvely believing that the people's representatives, many of whom were peasants, would be awed by the splendor of the Imperial court, the ladies of the Imperial family had worn nearly all their jewels; they were literally covered with pearls and diamonds. But the effect was altogether different. This Oriental method of impressing upon spectators a reverence for the bearers of supreme power was quite unsuited to the occasion. What it did achieve was to set in juxtaposition the boundless Imperial luxury and the poverty of the people. The demagogues did not fail to comment upon this ominous contrast. Nor did the Tsar's address of welcome improve matters. It was intelligently composed and clearly delivered with a certain Imperial dignity, but the Tsar especially emphasized the fact that he was welcoming *the best* representatives of the people.[9]

In the Duma itself, the leaders of the people's representatives, who had outlined in their minds the whole program of their proposed attack upon the government, turned the Duma tribune into a pulpit for the preaching of revolution. This began when I. I. Petrunkevich, one of the most malicious enemies of the government and the existing order, touchingly demanded of the government an immediate and general amnesty for all political prisoners, including those who had committed civil crimes from political motives. If I remember correctly, Petrunkevich's motion was adopted unanimously. Then the Duma composed an address to the Tsar stating all the points of the Cadet program and demanding their immediate acceptance. These points included political amnesty, universal suffrage in elections to the State Duma, and the expropriation of state, udel,[9a] church, and private lands in favor of the peasantry.

Unwilling as Goremykin was to have anything to do with the Duma, the government was obliged to break its silence and make some sort of answer. But the preparation of this answer produced extensive wrangling in the Council of Ministers.

The sessions of the Council were held in the Ministry of the Interior building near the Tsepnoi Bridge, in the residence occupied by Goremykin. Here in the large study, with which I was so familiar in Plehve's time, the ministers met daily. At first the sessions lacked organization. The members did not sit around a common table but distributed themselves about the room; this gave the sessions the air of a social gathering. Nor did the members attend the sessions too punctually. Izvolsky, for instance, was late almost every day as he came from dinner at some foreign embassy, wearing a dress coat, *une fleur à la boutonnière*. For some unknown reason he preferred to sit astride his chair, facing its back, a position not altogether in harmony with the tone of the gathering and the seriousness of the discussion. His face reminded one of a pug dog, and he wore a monocle. He was anxious to pass as an authority on parliamentary practice and procedure; but his influence was negligible. Kokovtsov made lengthy and seemingly businesslike speeches, but evidently had not yet come to any definite decision concerning what attitude the government should assume toward the Duma; certainly it was very difficult to follow the trend of his ideas. Stolypin maintained an obstinate silence. Discussion went from one topic to another, as there was no prepared government program and, generally speaking, the opinions expressed were not clearly thought out. Only Stishinsky and Shirinsky had definite views concerning the State Duma, and these could be summed up thus: the State Duma was a revolutionary institution; therefore, it would be well to dismiss it, or still better, to abolish it completely. Goremykin did not appear to be master of the situation at all. He presided over the sessions without giving them direction, and with an air which seemed to say: "Babble as you will, for I shall act as I see fit."

In discussing the Duma's address to the Tsar, Izvolsky suggested that it be answered by an address from the throne, as was done in Western states. The objection was made that this would bring the Tsar directly into conflict with the people's representatives. Goremykin was inclined entirely to disregard the Duma's address, but some ministers protested that that would only embarrass the government in the long run. Stolypin was still silent. It was finally decided that the government would stand between the supreme power and the people's representatives and answer the Duma's address in its own name. The Duma's address was discussed in summary fashion, and it was decided which of the Duma's demands might be realized even partially; then the Council charged Shcheglovitov and myself each to compose an answer. I suppose that I was chosen for this task because I had urgently advised that the government break its silence and express its real opinion.

The Council examined our drafted answers on the next day. Shcheglovitov read his first. It was humble, ingratiating, and remarkably vague. Then, with no intervening discussion, I was asked to read mine. The answer I had prepared was written in the language of authority; it stated definitely the government's views on all issues mentioned in the Duma's address. Goremykin generally took a long time to make up his mind, but once he had made a decision he carried it out with unwavering resolution. On this occasion he decided for my project, which was then discussed in detail. A few unimportant changes were made in it, which softened its tone; then I was given the task of re-editing it and sending copies to all members of the Council of Ministers, so that they might make whatever objections and observations they might have. I was then to check these observations and prepare the final edition for printing and for forwarding to the members of the Duma. All this had to be done within twenty-four hours.

As usual the session of the Council of Ministers lasted until a late hour; but with the aid of a typist with a hectograph I sent out the copies of the revised draft and by about five the next afternoon these copies had been returned with comments. I have to trust to memory to recall these comments, but if I am not mistaken they were made mostly by V. N. Kokovtsov and A. S. Stishinsky, who, with their customary thoroughness, had read and commented upon my text. Happily, their remarks were not at variance, so that it was easy to incorporate them into the text and prepare the final edition, which Goremykin read the next day from the tribune of the Duma.

When Goremykin rose to deliver the government's answer there was dead silence in the Duma; but he had a feeble voice and hardly anyone heard what he said. Fortunately and wisely copies of the government's reply were distributed among the Duma members. Only once did Goremykin raise his voice, and that was when he read the passage regarding the impermissibility of expropriating privately owned lands in order to increase the land allotment of the peasants; then he even lifted his finger as a threat.

The leaders of the Duma were infuriated not so much by the ministers' disagreement with their program—they had had a premonition on that score—as by the finality of its tone. Concluding, with reason, that the government intended actively to resist their pretensions, they raised their own demands according to the adage: "Behold the lap dog! What a mighty animal he must be to bark thus at the elephant."

The tone of the government's answer was all the greater surprise since all previous statements by individual members of the government had been remarkably humble in spirit. Shcheglovitov had been especially meek before the Duma.* His readiness to make concessions to the revolutionary public was revealed in the legislative projects which he was going to present to the people's representatives. One of them dealt with the responsibility of government officials, and the other proposed the abolition of capital punishment even as a sentence of courts-martial. The former was essentially just. The existing order of things by which officials could not be indicted for civil-service offenses without the approval of their chiefs was quite intolerable. Shcheglovitov's remark to me when the Council of Ministers was debating this project was quite sound. He

---

* Later, in the Third Duma and as Chairman of the State Council, when he had sensed that the government had gained the upper hand, Shcheglovitov changed his attitude and became insufferably harsh and insolent in addressing the legislative chambers. Like all cowards, he was insolent when he considered himself invulnerable and humble when he was not sure of his position.

whispered in my ear: "Well, if even this reform is impermissible, then we had better return to the practices of Genghiz-Khan." I do not recall whether or not this project was adopted; if it was, nothing definite came of it, for the existing order of indicting officials for civil-service offenses remained unchanged until the end of the old regime.

Shcheglovitov's other project—the abolition of capital punishment—found no support in the Council, if I remember correctly. Although Stolypin had voted for Shcheglovitov's other project, he opposed this one because he considered it untimely. He left the further elaboration of his attitude to his assistant, A. A. Makarov, a typical prosecuting magistrate, whom I met now for the first time. Other members of the Council of Ministers argued that it would be strange indeed to abolish capital punishment at a time when the revolutionists were making a system of murdering state officials and employees.

Since various projects were being advanced I tried to persuade the Council of Ministers to present to the Duma the project of a statute allowing the peasants freely to leave their land communes, a project which had been rejected by the State Council for formal reasons during Witte's ministry. Stolypin placed this project before the Council of Ministers, but Goremykin took a definite stand against it. Stolypin did not utter a word in its defense, and it was again rejected. But inasmuch as the project was at variance with the desires of the Cadet party and therefore would have been turned down by the Duma, Goremykin's stand was probably the right one at that time.

While the Council of Ministers was thus discussing projects but approving none, the Duma continued its attack upon the government. This attack was concentrated on the agrarian issue. The main points of the agrarian reform it proposed were stated in a document signed by thirty-three Duma members. These points were set forth very briefly as in a proclamation. They were designed simply to increase public unrest and to risk nothing, since their authors were sure that neither the government nor the State Council would agree to them. They were not accepted even by all the Duma members. Such progressive public men as N. N. Lvov and Prince Volkonsky opposed them.

Nevertheless, these demands provoked the Council of Ministers to break its silence on the agrarian issue. The ministers decided to take exception to the essential points of the proposed reform. They even selected Stishinsky and myself to expound these exceptions from the tribune of the Duma, but they gave us no instructions concerning the nature of the remarks we were to make. I had not been present at the session where this decision was taken and learned of it from Stishinsky. I asked him what was the government's positive program on the agrarian question, for I considered it impossible merely to criticize and reject the Duma's suggestions. Stishinsky replied that this matter had not been discussed. "You are to go to the Duma in the morning," he said, "but it is for you to decide what you will say."

What was I to say? I was bound by no instructions, but I could not ignore the fact that a few days previously the Council of Ministers had summarily declined to present to the Duma a project permitting each member of the commune freely to leave it. But inasmuch as this project had been presented to the Council of Ministers over Stolypin's signature, thus making official his agreement to it, I resolved to end my speech to the Duma by pointing out that the only means of improving peasant well-being was not to abolish private landownership but to strengthen it by abolishing communal landownership. I worked almost the entire night on my speech and at about eleven o'clock the next morning went to the Taurida Palace.[10] News of the governmental move had traveled far and wide, so that almost all members of the Duma were present. In the ministers' room (the ministers' pavilion was built much later) Stolypin accosted me. "Please, do not speak today in the Duma," he said. His agitation showed through his habitual calm and composure, and I was completely dumfounded by his words. In the first place, I was vexed to think that I had spent the entire night to no purpose; and, in the second place, I was anticipating with pleasure a chance to pit myself against those dilettantes who had spoken on this subject in the Duma. The land question was highly complicated and I was sure that I should not meet with any serious refutation of the material I had collected. This material proved beyond doubt that the transfer to the peasants of all fertile lands of European Russia would not improve their well-being, since it would not increase to any perceptible degree the amount of land already in their possession; for the majority of the peasants such an increase would be expressed in fractions of a desiatin per capita. I asked Stolypin why he wanted me not to speak.

"Because the land question and all suggestions connected with its final solution must come from me, the Minister of the Interior. In this basic and most important question I cannot allow any person but myself to speak in the Duma."

"You must address your objection, Petr Arkadievich, not to me but to the Council of Ministers, which has charged me to speak today. I cannot comply with your wishes unless the Council, or at least its chairman, advises me to do so."

"Yet you cannot act contrary to my desire."

"I have already explained my stand and I cannot change it. Here is a telephone. Call up Goremykin, and if, after talking with you, he himself tells me not to speak today, I shall not do so."

But Stolypin would not agree to call Goremykin. For some time we continued to walk back and forth. Stolypin continued to state reasons why I should not appear, and I replied stubbornly: "Here is the telephone! Call up Goremykin."

At last, seeing that he could not prevail upon me, he said: "Well, in any event, please keep to the facts and make no generalizations." But I paid no heed to this admonition. My speech was written out and I had no desire to change it. But Stolypin had also asked me to speak in my own name and not in that of the Minister of the Interior, and with this request I felt obliged to comply—with what results we shall see later.

The session opened about midday. Prince Petr Dolgorukov, a vice-chairman, was presiding. He was reputedly a specialist in peasant problems; but his knowledge of the subject was elementary, and his treatment was that of a Russian intellectual who absolutely ignored the economic consequences of the measure proposing the expropriation of private lands. Unlike the majority of the Cadets, however, he was sincerely persuaded that this measure would be beneficial to the state and he supported it even though it would injure his own interests. At about four in the afternoon the land question was taken up. The long hours since the session had begun not only had proved trying but also had increased the agitation which I naturally felt at making my first appearance before the representatives of the Russian people.

Stishinsky spoke first, for about an hour. His speech, smoothly and calmly delivered as usual, was essentially a formal report, full of many references (as the press was quick to note) to prove that neither the existing laws nor the decisions of the Senate permitted the allotment of any additional land to the peasants. Then came my turn. As I was beginning to speak I noticed Stolypin leave the assembly; but in view of his request I said to the assembled Duma: "Permit me to step outside the boundaries of the ministry in which I have the honor to work and to explain the matter as far as my intelligence and abilities allow, as one who has made the study of it his specialty." I ended the speech with these words: "Not by abolishing private ownership, not by repealing the right of private ownership of land, but by giving the peasants full possession of that land which they are now using shall the State Duma—a gathering of state-minded persons—earn the deep gratitude of the Russian people."

I had spoken in a voice clear and strong and commanding. It was the voice of a representative of the government, and the Duma had listened very attentively. If I may say so, my speech made a tremendous impression. However, the data I had used were just as important as the manner of speaking in making the speech effective. The leaders of the Duma, and especially the leaders of the Cadet party, saw immediately that their task of overthrowing the government was not to be so easy—that the government was still able to fight for itself. I believe they realized then the futility of their attempts to lower the prestige of the government, to overthrow it, and to take power into their own hands. From this realization it was but one step to personal hatred of the ministers comprising the government, and against these ministers they decided to concentrate their attacks.

After I had spoken, a Trudovik[11] (the name adopted by the Socialist-Revolutionists in the Duma) requested the Chairman of the Duma not to permit speeches by "outsiders." Dolgorukov evidently did not understand what I had said to evoke this remark, for he answered in a puzzled tone that as far as he was aware no outsider had been permitted to speak.

The next speaker was Herzenstein[12] (if I remember rightly), a Cadet. His arguments were so very weak and based upon intentional perversions of points I had made that I was eager to answer him. But as I waited for an opportunity to do so I became increasingly excited. My head went suddenly empty, and despite every mental effort I could not decide what I should say or how I should deliver my counter-attack. I was seized with a premonition of certain failure, and such failure would have destroyed completely the impression made by my first speech. It would seem, however, that the Duma leaders feared what I might say in rebuttal to Herzenstein, lest it should ruin them completely in the eyes of the many peasant representatives. Fortunately for me, therefore, they proposed and carried a motion of adjournment, although it was quite early and the sessions usually ended much later. My lucky star and my adversaries had saved me from failure. The land question was not discussed again in the Duma till four days later, and by then I had recovered my composure.

Because my speech had made an impression upon the Duma, Stolypin was displeased with me for making it and considered himself insulted. He went directly from the Duma to see Goremykin and announced that he wished to tender his resignation, since he could not permit that his assistant and not himself should appear before the Duma in matters under his direction. He was especially hurt, as Goremykin explained to me the next day, because the Council of Ministers had chosen me to speak on the land problem over Stolypin's opposition. In my opinion Stolypin had some grounds for feeling as he did. In the first place, Stishinsky, the other person who addressed the Duma on the land question, was the head of the Chief Administration of Land Management, that is the head of a ministry and not its second ranking representative; second, Stolypin himself had not yet spoken from the tribune of the Duma; third, the land problem was the most important problem of the time. Goremykin did not accept Stolypin's resignation; he managed to pacify him in some way and, in speaking of the matter to me, asked me to do all in my power to smooth over the misunderstanding.

Meanwhile the State Duma had learned of the incident and had decided to permit representatives of the ministries to speak only as acknowledged spokesmen of the ministers. The leaders of the Duma probably intended by this regulation to prevent me from speaking and answering criticism. I learned of this turn of affairs in the Duma itself from a clerk of the Ministry of the Interior who was on duty in the Duma during its sessions. He also told me that Stolypin would not attend that particular session and charged me to speak for the ministry.

My first speech had been published, and in the intervening three days the leaders of the Duma had had a chance to study it and to prepare their replies. Even so the criticism of it by Petrunkevich, a Cadet leader, was neither clever nor eloquent. For my own part,

I had remembered my previous confusion when faced with speaking impromptu and had prepared my answers to speeches as yet unmade. In this I had been unexpectedly helped by one of my former colleagues in the Peasant Section, Baron A. F. Meyendorff (later Vice-Chairman of the Fourth Duma), who sent me a magazine containing a speech Herzenstein had made at a zemstvo convention in Moscow in April. This speech had dealt with the agrarian question, and in it Herzenstein had tried to prove the patent absurdity of expropriating private lands; he had pointed out that the presence of representatives of landowners in legislative institutions was important, since it facilitated the fight against representatives of capital and industry. In further preparing myself I had made use of petitions to the Peasant Land Bank from some Cadet members of the Duma who were in favor of land expropriation; the petitioners had requested the Bank immediately to purchase their lands. One of these petitions was especially insistent. It had been sent in by D. D. Protopopov,[13] a member of the Duma and marshal of the nobility of one of the uezds of Samara Gubernia; his signature was conspicuous among the thirty-three who had signed the Duma project for agrarian reform. Thus armed, I faced the Duma with confidence.

When I mounted the tribune, I was greeted with cries of "Retire!" (Stishinsky was usually accorded a similar welcome.) I can still see the member Zhilkin[14] in one of the upper seats shouting, "Retire! Retire! Retire!" and, as he finished, hiding his head under the desk with which all seats were supplied. His shouts let loose a terrific din and yelling, so that I was obliged to fold my arms and make it apparent that I would wait until quiet was restored. I was just as little inclined to renounce my right to speak as I was willing to speak while they were so noisy. In the end I was given a good hearing. My remarks were brief but successful. When confronted with the fact that he had changed his views, Herzenstein declared that at the zemstvo convention he had been discussing theories, whereas now the Duma was engaged in practical work. He sought a way out of his dilemma by saying something to the effect that at any rate his writings were read, which in itself was a victory.

After the debates on the agrarian question the Duma changed its methods of carrying out its program. At first it had acted with a measure of outward decency and propriety toward the government. After the government's answer to the Duma address, the Duma's attitude had become hostile. But now, after the debates on the land question, it adopted definitely a revolutionary course of action. This was undoubtedly due to the fact that the Duma had become convinced that by opposition alone it would not be able to seize power from the crown and that in order to force the Monarch to make further concessions, the events which had led up to the Manifesto of October 17 would have to be repeated. In short, the Cadet party wanted to have the Socialists pull its chestnuts out of the fire. The Cadets did not realize that once the revolution began it would not stop until it had run to extremes which would claim them and the entire bourgeois intelligentsia for its victims. This was proved by the Revolution of 1917.

So the Trudoviks came to the fore—as did persons of shady reputation, such as Aladin,[15] once a guide in the low dives of London and later, during the war and the Revolution of 1917, a hireling of the English secret service. This individual, who spent much of his time in flagrant, open debauchery, made fiery speeches from the tribune of the Duma, denouncing the government and going so far as to say: "Blood is flowing in the shadow of the Imperial mantle." But even this did not cause the chairman of the session to call the speaker to order.

It is difficult to say what the government should have done. Anything, I suppose, but play the silent game it played. Not being a minister, I was unable to do anything except to laugh openly in the faces of orators who stormed from the tribune of the Duma. It was quite convenient to do so, as the government's seats were right next to the tribune. On one occasion, before the opening of the session, I said to a minister sitting next to me, and loudly enough so that several Duma members in the passage separating the government seats from the places of the deputies could hear me: "Let us listen to the ravings of these hooligans." This, together with my speech on the agrarian question, made many members of the Duma, especially their leaders, hate me. I was aware that neither Goremykin nor Stolypin approved of this course of action. They, especially Stolypin, thought that the government should preserve an Olympian calm toward the Duma; but I could not bear to conduct myself in that way. I continued to act as I saw fit, especially since no member of the government said anything to me about it.

Soon after the debates on the agrarian question the Duma debated the government's suggested appropriation of funds to provide relief for regions suffering from famine. On this issue the Duma was placed in a difficult position: it had either to approve the appropriation—that is, to agree with the government—or to risk arousing the discontent of the population by refusing the appropriation for relief and for assistance in sowing the winter crops. Stolypin decided to speak to the Duma in person on this matter, and thus I was deprived of a chance of giving the Duma a piece of my mind.

I confess that I had some misgivings regarding Stolypin's success before the Duma. He was not too well acquainted with the organization of relief and, besides, I suspected him of being a poor orator because of a certain defect in enunciation, if for no other reason. But I was mistaken. From the tribune, Stolypin spoke loudly, distinctly, and masterfully. Also his appearance was a great asset: he was tall and slender and looked not only dignified but even majestic.

His speech was somewhat deficient in factual material, but was permeated by an inner conviction and sincerity and contained some happy phrases and figures of speech. He endeavored to separate the Socialist orators from the Cadets, with whose leaders he was at that time on friendly terms. He created no ill feeling on the part of the Duma toward himself. All this certainly must be construed as marking a successful speech. The suggested appropriation was granted, even though accompanied by several resolutions denouncing the government.

But things could not go on as they were. The government had either to come to some agreement with the Duma or to dismiss it altogether. On this issue the members of the government entertained different views. The minority, including Izvolsky and D. F. Trepov, were inclined to compromise with the Duma, but for different reasons. Izvolsky, for instance, was completely ignorant of conditions in Russia, largely as a result of prolonged sojourns abroad. He was fascinated by Western European customs and was openly sympathetic to parliamentary forms of government. In the interest of such a form of government he conducted conversations with the Cadet leaders and workers—Miliukov and Company—and tried to persuade the Tsar that the only sound course of action was to transfer all authority to the Cadets. When the question of dissolving the Duma was discussed by the Council of Ministers he opposed the measure, as was to be expected, and pointed out that, in the West, legislative chambers had been dissolved because of a refusal to approve budgets or legislative projects considered necessary by the government but that no legislative body in the West was ever dissolved because of its members' speeches or resolutions. However, as the Duma became more and more radical and increased its revolutionary propaganda, thus demoralizing the country, and as Izvolsky saw more clearly that he was likely to lose his ministerial portfolio under a Cadet regime, he experienced a change of mind. One evening he appeared in the Council of Ministers, late as usual, and, getting astride a chair, solemnly announced that he now considered the dissolution of the Duma possible in principle, since "a few days ago the Portuguese legislature was dissolved for no reason except its general revolutionary spirit." This incredible reasoning made the action of tiny Portugal a criterion of political procedure. According to this logic Russia was permitted to adopt this or that measure only on condition that an analogous measure had been adopted by a foreign country, no matter how insignificant. Yet such reasoning did not provoke even a smile in the Russian Council of Ministers. Those who favored the dissolution of the Duma were evidently so glad that Izvolsky had at last been able to see their point of view that they were willing to overlook the reason for his change of opinion.

Goremykin's behavior in this matter was peculiar. Openly, he neither opposed nor supported the dissolution, and gave the general impression that he would take no action. Secretly, however, he painstakingly prepared the ground at Peterhof for such a move.

Stolypin also kept his own counsel. He had no direct dealings with the Cadet leaders but was apprised of the steps which Izvolsky had undertaken. Also, through the Duma members from Saratov Gubernia (mainly through N. N. Lvov), he tried to persuade the Cadets that he personally held liberal ideas and ideals.

The Cadets, headed by Miliukov, were perfectly sure that they had won their game. They thought it was no longer a question of securing power but only of becoming sole masters of the situation. Accordingly they announced that they would not have Stolypin as a member of their government; his portfolio would be given to one of their own men, the famous Prince Lvov, who in 1917 became the head of their government and used his position to effect the destruction of all authority in the country.

Meanwhile the Right wing of the Council of Ministers used every means in its power to hasten the dissolution of the Duma. It endeavored to enlist the assistance of D. F. Trepov, who continued to enjoy the confidence of the Tsar; but all its efforts in this direction were in vain. Trepov's political convictions were founded not on reason but on sentiment and were therefore unstable. He was concerned with only one thing: to protect the person of the Tsar and his family. He belonged not to the government but to the court, and considered himself beyond the reach of any political party as long as the Tsar's power existed. Trepov was no longer interested—or so he thought—in leaving state power in the hands of the bureaucrats. Hence he negotiated with the Cadet leaders. This circumstance caused the Cadet party leaders, who overestimated the importance of Trepov, to believe that very soon complete power would fall into their hands. Meanwhile the Duma continued its government baiting. Prince Shirinsky and Schwanebach were most anxious to have it dissolved. They called on me one day and suggested that I go with them to Goremykin. We found Goremykin at home and, as usual, unengaged. What means he used to prevent anyone from disturbing him I do not know, but the fact remains that he was usually alone.

It was a hot day in July. Goremykin was sitting on a sofa near a window looking out on the Fontanka on whose other bank stood the Engineer Palace. He was dressed in a pongee suit but was wet with perspiration. His smooth, round, pale face and his pale, protruding, expressionless eyes really reminded one of a whitefish; in fact, in some senatorial circles he was so nicknamed. On a small table at his elbow stood a dish of milk curds which he was eating lazily and mechanically. He listened with the greatest indifference to the expostulations of Shirinsky and Schwanebach to the effect that the Duma had to be dissolved immediately. He did not even trouble to argue the point. In vain did Shirinsky unleash his favorite incomprehensible metaphors. In vain did Schwanebach proudly quote examples from the history of the French Revolution. Goremykin remained unmoved.

I was sitting aside near the window. Goremykin's impassivity made me furious. I had a great desire somehow to ruffle his calm.

"Ivan Logginovich," I suddenly exclaimed, pointing outside, "do you see that?"

"Where? What?" Goremykin woke up, evidently supposing that I had detected some danger from which he was not entirely protected.

"Over there, on the other bank."

"Well, what about it?"

"The Engineer Palace."

"What of it?" asked Goremykin, composed again.

"This of it! Had the event which took place there on March 11, 1801 [the assassination of Emperor Paul I],[16] been postponed until March 12, it would not have taken place at all, for on the 12th Arakcheev,[17] especially called to St. Petersburg by Paul, was already at the gates of the city and would have been able to break up the plot. The same holds true of the Duma. Today it may be possible to dissolve it. Whether this will be possible in a week's time, we do not know."

"You are right," said Goremykin, slightly moved.

I doubt if what I said had any influence on bringing Goremykin to a decision, for he was a man who arrived at decisions quite independently and as a result of his own deliberations. However, on the next day the Council of Ministers adopted a resolution calling for the dissolution of the State Duma, and on the day following Goremykin went to Peterhof with the minutes of the Council of Ministers.

When the members of the Council learned of this they (with the exception of Stolypin) assembled at Goremykin's house to await his return. About eight o'clock he arrived. He entered the room, in which the ministers were waiting, with a notably cheerful air and quoted a sentence from a letter of Madame de Sévigné to her daughter : " *'Je vous le donne en cent, je vous le donne en mille, vous n'avez pas idée de la nouvelle que je vous apporte!'* I am no longer Chairman of the Council." Then he announced that the ukase dissolving the Duma had been signed and that the new Chairman of the Council was to be Stolypin, who was then at the palace but was expected any moment. Shortly after Goremykin's announcement Launits,[18] Governor of St. Petersburg, arrived and announced that no demonstrations were expected when the Duma was dissolved but as a precaution he had recalled several cavalry regiments of the guards from their summer quarters to St. Petersburg. He also suggested that some of the ministers, such as Stishinsky, who resided in private houses, should move for the time being to official buildings in order to make easier the work of the police. Stolypin soon arrived, but as he had no further news the ministers dispersed.

This is what had happened. Goremykin had twice reported to the Tsar on the necessity of dissolving the Duma and had twice secured the Tsar's approval. But when he had eventually presented the text of a ukase for the Tsar's signature, he had learned that the Tsar had changed his mind. When he left for Peterhof on July 8

Goremykin had resolved to get the Tsar's signature at any cost. So he took with him the text of a ukase dissolving the Duma and also his own resignation, which he intended to tender to the Tsar should the latter refuse to sign the ukase. Somewhere on the way he learned that it had already been decided that he should resign in favor of Stolypin, and that Stolypin had had orders to appear at Peterhof.

At Peterhof, however, Goremykin received another surprise. He was met by Court Minister Frederichs, who suggested that he ought to go to the Duma and express the Tsar's disfavor with its activities. Goremykin realized the absurdity of such a move and refused point-blank to make it; and once he was in the Tsar's presence he saw that the idea of such a move was not the Tsar's but had been suggested to him, probably by Frederichs working through D. F. Trepov and the latter's brother-in-law, Mosolov,[19] who was in charge of the Chancellery of the Court Ministry. Goremykin easily persuaded the Tsar that such an address to the representatives of the people would result in an open conflict between the throne and the representatives. The Tsar then agreed to the dissolution of the Duma and signed the ukase immediately. But Goremykin did not stop at that. He realized that the dissolution made inevitable his own dismissal and the appointment of a Chairman of the Council of Ministers with a stronger reputation for liberalism. He was also aware of the Tsar's fondness for adopting simultaneously two measures of a somewhat contradictory nature, so that one might seem to soften the other. Consequently Goremykin decided to anticipate the march of events, and as soon as the Tsar had signed the ukase he tendered his own resignation and suggested as his successor that person whom, as he knew, the Tsar had already chosen—Stolypin. This was a clever move, especially as it made it unnecessary for the Tsar to say that he had already resolved to put another in Goremykin's place. One is inclined to think that it always pained the Tsar to dismiss a minister—not because Nicholas II was innately kind, for actually he was indifferent to the feelings of the person dismissed, but because it disturbed his own peace of mind and obliged him to make an effort of will which he always found difficult. His gentleness of disposition and weakness of character were clearly manifest upon such occasions. In this instance he agreed immediately to Goremykin's resignation and approved the appointment of Stolypin.

As he left the Tsar's study Goremykin met D. F. Trepov, who asked anxiously what the Tsar had decided. Pointing to his brief case Goremykin said shortly: "I have here the signed ukase for the dissolution of the Duma."

"This is terrible!" exclaimed Trepov. "We shall have all St. Petersburg here in the morning."

"Those who come will not go back," Goremykin answered calmly. He inferred, however, from Trepov's words that all efforts would be made to have the Tsar revoke his decision before the ukase was published. Accordingly he took every possible precaution to forestall such an occurrence. As soon as the session of the Council at his house was ended, he sent away all clerks and officials, including the gendarmes officer, who at first refused to leave his post because his duty was to see to the safety of the Chairman of the Council of Ministers. Then Goremykin announced to his family that he was tired, gave orders that he was not to be disturbed under any conditions, and went to bed. As a further precaution he locked the door of his bedroom and the room next to it, so that he would not hear anybody knock.

Goremykin's forebodings were well founded and the measures he took not superfluous. A few hours after he had barricaded himself in his bedroom a special courier brought him a letter from the Tsar. But he did not get the letter till the next morning with his coffee and the *Pravitelstvennyi Vestnik*. The letter from the Tsar commanded that the ukase be postponed, but the *Pravitelstvennyi Vestnik* had already published it. This incident demonstrated not only Goremykin's resourcefulness and sagacity, but also his courage. The taking upon himself of all responsibility for the dissolution of the Duma when it was really no concern of his, since his resignation had already been accepted by the Tsar, was the act of no ordinary man. It would have seemed more rational to let his successor untangle the situation.[20]

The *Pravitelstvennyi Vestnik* of July 9 also contained news of the dismissal of Stishinsky and Prince Shirinsky, of which I was already aware, and a manifesto explaining why the Duma was dissolved and stating that the dissolution did not mean the repeal of the liberties granted by the Manifesto of October 17.

Stishinsky's dismissal was a great surprise to me. In spite of our many disagreements on different questions, he and I were great friends. I went to him to express my sympathy. I met him in the office of the Chief Administration of Land Organization and Agriculture, to which he had just moved from his private residence at the insistence of Launits. He was calm, as usual, but obviously depressed. He told me that he had learned of his dismissal not from the *Pravitelstvennyi Vestnik* but from one of his colleagues, A. A. Rittikh, manager of the Committee for Land Affairs. Stishinsky had telephoned to give the agenda for the next session of that committee, and Rittikh, who had learned of his dismissal, had had to tell him that he was no longer empowered to set the dates of the sessions.

Stishinsky had been expecting his dismissal but was extremely offended at the way in which it had been effected. The previous evening, when Goremykin had announced that Stolypin would be the next Chairman of the Council, Stishinsky had said that he would immediately tender his own resignation; but Goremykin had advised him not to do so, arguing that Stolypin was not likely to change the personnel of the Council of Ministers. Stishinsky was especially furious at Stolypin, who, when he returned from Peterhof to join the ministers, not only knew of the forthcoming dismissal of Stishinsky and Shirinsky but very likely was carrying the ukases for their dismissal in his brief case at the time. He had not said a word, however, to the persons concerned, and neither Stishinsky nor Shirinsky ever forgave him for this lack of consideration. They became for all time his political and personal enemies.

From Stishinsky I went to see Goremykin. The old man was in the best of humor. Evidently, he was not a bit sorry at having lost his position. I asked him whether he had known beforehand of the dismissal of Stishinsky and Shirinsky and also, when it had been decided to accompany the ukase on the dissolution of the Duma with an explanatory manifesto, and who had written the latter. To all these questions Goremykin answered that he had not known anything.

While we were talking the telephone rang. I could not follow the ensuing conversation, except to ascertain that Goremykin was displeased with something. Later he explained it to me. It seemed that there was a possibility of dissolving the State Council as well, although no mention of this had been made in the ukase concerning the Duma. "We had better keep the State Council," said Goremykin, "for, should it be necessary to issue an important state act, such as a change in the statute on elections to the Duma, it could be done through the State Council, which now includes public representatives." It dawned on me that the sly Ulysses had not resigned at his own wish, that in planning the dissolution of the Duma he had also planned the next steps of the government, namely, the introduction of changes in the electoral law; these changes were to be enacted with the help of the State Council.

Not till much later did I learn of the circumstances attending the composition and appearance of the explanatory manifesto. The Tsar had suggested to Stolypin that he accept the post of Chairman of the Council of Ministers even before Goremykin had tendered his resignation; but neither the Tsar nor Stolypin had at that time any intention of dissolving the Duma. Stolypin's only condition had been the dismissal of Stishinsky and Shirinsky, to which the Tsar had agreed. Stolypin's plan, supported whole-heartedly by D. F. Trepov, was to show the public in general and the Duma in particular that the government had adopted a more liberal course. Stolypin hoped to replace Stishinsky and Shirinsky with Duma members. He hoped this change would satisfy the Duma and that he would then be able to retain it and come to some understanding with it. But he had reckoned without Goremykin. Immediately after the Tsar had signed the ukase dissolving the Duma Stolypin was apprised of what had transpired, but could not change the Tsar's decision; in fact, he did not even attempt to do so. All he could do under the circumstances was to try to soften the impression which the dissolution of the Duma was bound to make by having the ukase followed with a special manifesto in which the Tsar expressed his intention of preserving the principle of popular representation. After obtaining the Tsar's approval of his plan, Stolypin had then returned to Goremykin's house, where the ministers were waiting. Thence he went to his own house accompanied by Shcheglovitov, his friend at that time, S. E. Kryzhanovsky, second Assistant Minister of the Interior, and F. D. Samarin, at that time a highly esteemed public man. The purpose of the meeting in Stolypin's house was to draft immediately the mollifying manifesto. Shcheglovitov's draft, heavy and indefinite, was rejected unanimously. That written by Stolypin himself was also criticized. Samarin, a slow-moving person, incapable of finishing anything in a short time, wrote a few disconnected sentences in which occurred the phrase, "knights of word and deed." This phrase struck Stolypin's fancy and he insisted that it be included in the final draft of the manifesto which should be drawn up on the basis of his own draft. This work on the manifesto continued nearly all night, and not until early morning was the final edition presented to the Tsar for his signature. Then it was sent to the offices of the *Pravitelstvennyi Vestnik* to be published in a special edition.[21]

PART FIVE

The Constitutional Regime, 1906–1914

Part III

The Constitutional Regime 1900–1911

CHAPTER XXI

STOLYPIN'S MINISTRY AND THE SECOND AND THIRD STATE DUMAS

During the six years of his premiership, P. A. Stolypin's policy underwent marked changes. At first he dreamed of securing as his ministerial colleagues many prominent representatives of the Cadet party, which had enjoyed a majority in the First Duma and with which he had not been able to come to an understanding while the Duma was in session. But after the dissolution of the Duma the leaders of this party went to Viborg, where they published the well-known Viborg Manifesto, calling upon the people to stop paying taxes and to stop serving in the army. This killed all Stolypin's hopes of coming to an understanding with them. The Chairman of the Council of Ministers could hardly include in the government persons who had openly summoned the people to rebellion against the existing order. Stolypin, therefore, turned for help to those leaders of the opposition who stood politically to the right of the Cadets. These men headed the small Party of Democratic Reforms[1] and were distinguished from the Cadets not so much by their program as by the methods by which they hoped to put their program into effect. Whereas the Cadets did not renounce revolutionary tactics and, therefore, kept in close touch with the Socialist parties, the Party of Democratic Reforms renounced revolutionary methods altogether, rejected terror as a political device, and wished to have nothing in common with those parties who worked underground. The Party of Democratic Reforms was not averse to effecting a compromise with the government; it was even willing to enter the government on condition that the major points of its program were carried out. Also representatives of the Party of Peaceful Reconstruction, Count Heyden and N. N. Lvov, were quite ready to come to an understanding with Stolypin. Especially was this true of N. N. Lvov, a Saratov landowner, who was under moral obligation to Stolypin. At some time previously Stolypin had gone to Balashov in order to save Lvov's life, which was threatened by the population in a burst of somewhat unexpected reactionary excitement.

The ensuing negotiations began happily, but soon became complicated. Of the negotiations proper I can say nothing, as I was not taken into the confidence of those concerned.[2] I only know that Stolypin was ready to go far in making compromises. He intended to fill with public men the two posts left vacant by the dismissal of Stishinsky and Shirinsky. There was talk of A. F. Koni as candidate for the post of Minister of Justice. Stolypin was also prepared to choose a public man for the post of State Comptroller.* At one time it was thought that the public men and Stolypin had reached an understanding. Then suddenly everything collapsed. I don't exactly know why, but in my opinion the main reason was as follows: it was at first believed that the bringing of public men into the ministry would soften the effect which the dissolution of the Duma was bound to produce. The idea of making such a concession to the public grew out of the same fear which prompted D. F. Trepov to compromise with the Cadets and to oppose the dissolution. Everyone feared the results of the dissolution, but whereas Goremykin and his supporters thought that to retain the Duma would be even more dangerous than to dissolve it—believing as they did that any understanding with the Duma was out of the question and that sooner or later it would have to be dissolved anyway—the persons opposed to the dissolution did not stop to consider the future; they merely shut their eyes and shrunk from the present danger. The immediate entourage of Nicholas II succeeded in inspiring in him also a fear of the serious effects that would result from the dissolution. Goremykin's procedure, therefore, aroused the Tsar's profound displeasure. (He sent an officer to Goremykin to ascertain the exact time the Tsar's letter had been delivered to him.) But as the days went by and no untoward event occurred, both the Tsar and the government became convinced that the country was in no danger. The dissolution of the Duma had provoked no excesses and the government gradually re-

---

* I believe this to be true because of the following incident. About a week after Stolypin's appointment, Schwanebach visited me and told me that he had just been told by Stolypin that, according to an understanding between Stolypin and some public men, Stolypin had agreed to give the post of State Comptroller to D. N. Shipov (or was it Heyden?) and that he, Schwanebach, would therefore be obliged to leave this post. It so happened that the next day Goremykin was leaving Russia for a trip abroad, and many ministers, Schwanebach included, went to see him off. At the station Schwanebach approached me beaming and said: "Mort et resuscité dans les vingt-quatre heures." He explained that Stolypin had summoned him and told him that the agreement between himself and the public men was off, hence that he, Schwanebach, would not have to leave his post.

covered confidence in its ability to rule without regard for the revolutionary and reform demands of the different classes of the population. As this feeling of confidence and security grew, so the desire to include in the government outsiders who were not connected with the bureaucratic classes began to wane.

The Tsar's change of attitude toward the dissolution of the Duma was very soon evident. It was seen, for instance, in the fact that D. F. Trepov lost all influence with him, whereas Goremykin received increasingly gracious treatment. Goremykin was called to Peterhof and warmly thanked both by the Emperor and by the Empress for his services. The little Tsarevich appeared also, and the Tsarina asked Goremykin to bless him.

The leaders of the First Duma also helped to effect a change in the court's attitude. Their Viborg Manifesto was intended to place the government in a critical position; but it evoked no response from the country. This revealed at once that the Cadet influence was negligible upon those popular elements in which this party hoped to find support. It was not in vain that Durnovo had exiled forty-five thousand agitators. The terrorists, too, were quiet. They had resolved to suspend all terroristic acts during the session of the Duma and as yet were not prepared to resume them. Under these circumstances the government felt strong enough to reject the additional petty demands which the public men stipulated as a condition for entering the government, and to abandon all negotiations with them.

For this step Stolypin was less responsible than was the Emperor himself, who was always averse to making any concessions to the public. I wish to emphasize, however, that here the Tsar's motive was not so much the desire to keep autocratic power in his hands (this desire was strongly developed in the Empress, but not with the Emperor) as it was the profound conviction that Russia was not ready for self-government; that the transfer of the work of the government to the public would endanger the country. As the years went by the Tsar had gradually became accustomed to his role of absolute ruler; but by nature he had no appreciation of the unlimited authority he possessed. The ease with which he abdicated in 1917 and his subsequent life and actions conclusively prove this.

During this time, especially after the removal of Trepov's influence, the influence of persons of not merely conservative but even reactionary orientation grew steadily at the Imperial Court. Among these were persons whose limited intellectual powers left them incapable of understanding political problems. Such a man was Prince M. S. Putiatin[3] (Assistant to the First Chamberlain of the Court, Count Benckendorff).[4] Inspired by Prince A. A. Shirinsky-Shikhmatov, formerly Ober-Prokuror of the Holy Synod, who had succeeded in making connections among the court entourage, Putiatin had managed to ingratiate himself with the Empress. Both she and the Tsar saw that the political troubles of the time were endangering not only the country but also the dynasty; she could hardly escape being concerned with political questions and looked about her for persons who seemed entirely trustworthy and capable of shedding true light upon the situation. She very naturally chose such persons from the immediate entourage of the Imperial family. It was at that moment that Putiatin appeared on the court scene. The Empress had lengthy conversations with him and he was perhaps the first to involve her in affairs of state. This is apparent from her letters to the Tsar.[5] At first she entered into state problems rather timidly; but with the years her participation in these problems grew in assurance and, as everybody knows, attained such proportions that every important decision and the selection of high officials depended solely upon her.

Although the Emperor dreamed only of reducing as far as possible all liberties granted the people, Stolypin was of an entirely different opinion. He had set himself the task of reconciling public and government. He believed steadfastly that even the most malevolent representatives of the public were opposed to the government because of its continuation of certain out-of-date practices of the past. He was thoroughly convinced that as soon as the government proved its sincere desire to heed the voice of the people by effecting certain liberal reforms and by repealing certain regulations which caused the most exasperation, the opposition would be disarmed and public sympathy would be his. In particular, he believed that the government would have to make certain important concessions to the Duma's demands concerning the land question.

His first remark to me, after his appointment as head of the government, was: "There are 180 days before the Second Duma assembles. We must make good use of them so that when the Duma meets we may appear before it with a series of reforms already realized. This will demonstrate the government's sincere desire to remove from the existing order all things incompatible with the spirit of the times."

He repeated these words on several later occasions, and I am sure that he said the same thing to all members of his government and to his collaborators in the Ministry of the Interior. His chief objective, however, was not to improve the well-being of the people, not to perfect the method of governing the country, but to strengthen the power of the government, to increase its prestige, and to conciliate the public. This aim he followed firmly and resolutely during his entire term of office, and with important results. Reforms interested him not in themselves, nor in the effects they might have upon the development of the country, but in the degree to which they were likely to be approved by the public and to create a halo around the supreme power whose strength would thus be consolidated.

Almost from the start he very correctly divided Russian public circles into two distinct groups: those who would not be contented with any reforms, since their only purpose and desire was to gain power for themselves; and those who were concerned for the future of Russia and could appreciate the efforts the government made to heal Russia's wounds and cure her diseases. In the first group he classed the leaders of the Cadet party, especially after the Viborg Manifesto; in the second, the liberal public circles which had become crystallized politically in the Octobrist party. At first he was not completely averse to the idea of securing the co-operation of many persons belonging to the Cadet party. This was the reason for his first serious measure transferring all state lands, all udel lands, and a part of the tillable cabinet lands[6] to the competence of the Peasant Land Bank in order that these lands might be sold to the peasants. Stolypin considered this measure extremely important and supposed that it would be favorably received by the peasantry and would steal the thunder from the Cadets. I was of a contrary opinion. To me this measure seemed of no great significance. These lands were already used almost entirely by the peasants, who rented them on very easy terms. If the measure were enacted, it would only increase peasant hopes of some day gaining all privately owned lands. "We have partially realized the Cadet program," they would say; "therefore, we can realize it completely."

Stolypin's greatest difficulty in effecting this measure was to obtain the consent of the Imperial family for the transfer of the udel lands. The Tsar realized that these lands were the property of the Russian Imperial house and did not wish to decide upon the matter alone. Accordingly he consulted Grand Duke Vladimir Aleksandrovich and his wife Mariia Pavlovna. These reluctantly consented to the measure. A Sovereign ukase transferred to the peasants the state and udel lands.

Interestingly enough, this measure had not been discussed by the Council of Ministers, at least in my hearing. Stolypin, knowing I was opposed to the measure, kept me ignorant of his doings until he had accomplished his end. It was only by accident that I learned from Count A. A. Bobrinsky that Stolypin's designs went even farther than the transfer of state and udel lands to the peasants and included the expropriations of other lands as well. Soon after becoming head of the government Stolypin had once said to Bobrinsky: "You will have to part with a portion of your lands, Count." This made it clear to me why Stolypin had so opposed my appearance in the Duma to speak on the agrarian question and especially why he did not want me to speak for the Ministry of the Interior. Evidently, he was at that time conducting negotiations with some of the Duma leaders and it is quite probable that he was ready to confirm the Cadet-party program concerning the land question. Stolypin was an absolute ignoramus in economic questions. He did not understand that the abolition of private land ownership in Russia would mean economic collapse, from which the peasant class would be the first to suffer. I repeat, however, that Stolypin was little concerned with the real results which might ensue from the measures he proposed.

I could not bring myself to look upon the government's procedure merely as a means of *captatio benevolentiae;* at the same time I could not discount the general psychological importance of the government's attitude. Stolypin and I had few points in common, either in temperament or in way of thinking. With Stolypin, theories always occupied the foreground, and in the field of theory he was a master. Intuitively he saw which political line to follow in order to acquire popularity; and, I hasten to add, he sought this popularity not for himself personally but for the entire regime as represented and directed by him. Besides, in the beginning of his career he was personally modest and realized full well that he was not entirely prepared to deal with many of the fundamental problems of state life. Later he changed—but more of this anon.

After the Sovereign ukase transferring to the peasants the state and udel lands, Stolypin tackled many other important reforms. For instance, a project to introduce compulsory primary education in Russia was discussed by the Council of Ministers. It was presented and defended, not by the Minister of Education, Kaufmann, who seemed to be not too well acquainted with it, but by his assistant, Gerasimov. As usual, Stolypin gave each speaker his turn but took no part in the discussion. (He was really a rather poor chairman, for he was totally incapable of giving résumés of debates and resolutions.) The project was really childish. It proclaimed the principle of general compulsory education but provided no program for putting it into effect. (The Bolsheviks were another government prematurely to proclaim this principle.) I pointed out to the Council of Ministers this lack of necessary preparation, and that the Ministry of Education would have done much better to busy itself preparing teachers for primary and secondary schools. Kokovtsov also opposed the project because of the expenditures it would entail. In the end it was suggested that the Minister of Education alter the project—a suggestion which amounted to rejecting it altogether.

The meeting then adjourned and the members of the Council went their several ways. None had realized how narrowly he had escaped a great danger. The meeting had been held at Stolypin's country house on Aptekarsky Island on the evening of August 11. We learned later that the terrorists who made an attempt to assassinate Stolypin the next day had passed by his house that evening intending to throw their bombs through a bay window into the room where the meeting was being held. Fortunately for us, a small garden lay between the window and the street. The terrorists, thinking that the bomb would fall short of its mark, gave up their plan at the last moment. This at least was the story told, although I have never been interested enough to verify it.

About three o'clock the next afternoon I had occasion to telephone Stolypin from the ministry, and asked a secretary to get the connection. In a few minutes the secretary came rushing into my office, pale and agitated, and told me that the clerk on duty at Stolypin's country house had asked him to hang up, saying he, the clerk, had to call a doctor. There had been an explosion and a fire at the country house, and there were a few casualties. I hurried to the scene of the disaster and was one of the first to arrive. The only other person there was Launits, the Governor. The sight that greeted me was terrible. A hired landau was standing at the curb before the house, the horses dead in their harnesses. The house was in ruins; the façade was entirely demolished. The front wall had fallen, exposing to view the large vestibule and the little reception room. The ceilings of both these rooms had crashed, and had carried with them the furniture of the two rooms above occupied by Stolypin's children. Stolypin's daughter had had both legs broken and had been carried to a neighboring house. (She finally recovered entirely.) Stolypin's small son had fallen with the ceiling but was found safe among the debris. The several persons who had been in the anteroom had been killed by the explosion and their bodies were lying there under some sort of covering.

Stolypin's courage was equal to the occasion. He himself carried his son from under the debris. In spite of the shock of the whole affair he maintained his composure. The force of the explosion had thrown him and his visitors, Polivanov, the marshal of nobility of Simbirsk, and Beliakov, Chairman of the Gubernia Board, to the floor even though they had been two rooms removed from the center of the explosion. A falling inkpot had smeared Stolypin's neck and the back of his head.

Kokovtsov arrived soon after I did. How vividly I recall the scene that followed. In a tiny washroom that faced the garden Stolypin was trying to remove the ink from his neck. Kokovtsov was standing on one side of him, I on the other. Wet and with water streaming from him, Stolypin exclaimed with animation: "This shall not alter our program. We shall continue to carry out our reforms. They are Russia's salvation." Nor was this by any means a pose, for Stolypin was at that period of his ministry in the first flush of creative effort and sincerely devoted to the idea of reform.[7]

A few days after this tragic occurrence, a session of the Council of Ministers was held in Stolypin's house on the Fontanka. It was being held in the chapel *avant-salle,* which had windows facing the court, for after the country house incident the front rooms were not considered quite safe. Certain formalities were also established for persons wishing to enter Stolypin's house. The project under discussion was one prepared by Peterson, Chief of Office of the Viceroy of the Caucasus, and concerned the land organization of the peasants of Transcaucasia. During the heat of the debate a messenger entered with a letter for Stolypin. Stolypin read it immediately and then announced that he had a very important communication to make to the Council, so that he was forced to postpone to the next day further debate on the subject under discussion. He then asked the clerks to withdraw and read the document aloud. It was a rather long, personal note from the Tsar, which began something like this:

"I desire the immediate institution of courts-martial to pass judgment according to military law." It stated also that certain types of political crimes—terroristic acts, armed rebellion, etc.—were to be put under the authority of these courts. This note created an enormous impression. The measure it proposed was obviously at variance with Stolypin's policy of coping with the revolution by constitutional means. As I recall, Shcheglovitov was also opposed to the Tsar's proposal, although later he introduced his own arbitrary methods into the administration of justice.

Next day I was obliged to go abroad to join my mother of whose critical state of health I had just received news. When I returned some two weeks later, I read at the frontier that the regulations on the courts-martial had been confirmed and had been immediately put into effect. I also learned that in my absence a new means of fighting the underground terrorists had been discussed, a means which I thought most effective, namely, the system of hostages. According to this system, political criminals condemned to death were not executed but were held as hostages against the commission of more terroristic acts. This system was adopted by the Bolsheviks from the outset of their regime, and of all their measures was the least illegal in so far as it dealt with persons convicted of counter-revolution. The 1906 revolutionists were fighting the government openly, and, to my way of thinking, the government was not only justified but even duty bound to take every step to prevent the break-up of the state and to insure a normal course of administration in the country. False sentiment and mock liberalism toward the enemies of the state affected the entire workings of the state apparatus and consequently violated the interests of millions of people.

But Stolypin thought differently. He rejected with horror the proposed new method of fighting the revolution, and stood firm upon his resolution to have the government work out an extensive program of reform. He must have had great faith in his own lucky star. And, in truth, fortune seemed to smile on him at that time. The explosion at his country house did more than all his liberal measures to win him the sympathy of all classes who were not utterly sunk in the depths of revolutionary psychosis. In view of all this, I decided to try to take advantage of the situation to realize my constant dream: to make it legal for the peasants freely to leave the commune.

As a result of my efforts an inter-ministerial commission was organized under my chairmanship to revise and reconsider the project on this subject, which had already been placed twice before a higher body: the State Council in March 1906, and the Council of Ministers in May 1906. This commission prepared for the consideration of the Council of Ministers a covering memorandum to accompany the project. This project I brought to Stolypin to be signed; but at the last moment he decided to have me countersign it for the Minister of the Interior. He said that he was not thoroughly acquainted with the matter and if the Council of Ministers should object to some detail of the project he would be in a more favorable position to make necessary changes if the project did not bear his signature.

As the day set for the debate drew near, I awaited it with trepidation. For four years I had strained all my efforts to free the Russian peasantry from the yoke of communal ownership, but so far all had been in vain. Then the day came. When I arrived at the session of the Council of Ministers I saw present, to my greatest consternation, the aged member of the State Council, P. P. Semenov-Tian-Shansky, who had participated in the reform of 1861 and was a fervent champion of the commune. "Can it be," I thought, "that Stolypin invited him to discuss the plans for permitting peasants to leave the commune? This can only mean that he himself is against this project." At that moment Stolypin came up to me and said, "Do not say anything about your project until Semenov leaves. He would be in our way. He is here on business for the Alekseevsky Committee."[8] The matter which concerned Semenov took but little time and, as soon as he had left, the Council took up the examination of the land project.

The first to speak on my project was Prince B. A. Vasilchikov,* who had succeeded Stishinsky as Head of the Chief Administration of Land Organization and Agriculture. He said that he was wholeheartedly in favor of the project in all its details but he saw no possibility of realizing it immediately through the application of Ar-

---

* Vasilchikov was a typical Russian gentleman of European Russia and a confirmed constitutionalist. He was an honorable and intelligent man, but neither a good worker nor a statesman. He represented a type of minister of the period of Nicholas I; he was upright, honest, and could speak openly and frankly even to the Monarch, yet he had no knowledge of any problem; he relied simply upon his own common sense but was utterly incapable of handling skillfully any complicated matter. He occupied his post as Head of the Chief Administration of Land Organization and Agriculture for only a short time and was succeeded by Krivoshein. I believe his retirement was occasioned by some trouble with Kokovtsov, who refused him monetary appropriations. His own enormous fortune and the social position into which he was born gave him a certain independence and permitted him to "tell the truth to kings" without even a smile.

ticle 87 of the Russian civil code.[9] "I consider myself a constitutional minister," he said. "Consequently, in my opinion such important measures must not be determined without the participation of the legislative chambers."

I replied that such procedure applied only to normal times. In the turbulent days in which we were living it was a question, not of such formalities, but of whether or not the proposed measure was necessary. The vital interest of the country must be placed above this or that provision of the law. I was absolutely convinced that the abolition of the commune was the only means of preserving in the country the principles of modern society, such as the right to individual ownership of land; at the same time, it was the most rational means of insuring the well-being of the peasantry.

The next speaker was Kokovtsov. His speech was prolific in words and poor in ideas, and it was very difficult to ascertain whether he was for or against the project.

We debated each article in turn and, although nearly every one evoked some objection from some minister, all of them were adopted in the end. The article abolishing the principle of family ownership[10] among the peasants occasioned the most debate, and, while there were no objections to establishing the principle of individual ownership of the allotted lands held by peasants according to hereditary household tenure, the extension of the same principle to peasants holding land according to repartitional tenure was opposed, my arguments notwithstanding. Stolypin gave me no support in defending the project and, as a result, the principle of family ownership was retained for peasants who were members of communes. It was not until three years later, on June 11, 1910, that regulations issued under Article 87 of the civil code were considered by the legislative bodies and made law and my original idea of establishing the right of private ownership of land for members of communes was at last realized. Actually, however, its realization had but little significance, since in real life the Russian peasant families considered inviolable the principle of *patria potestas*.

Be that as it may, as I left the session, which had approved my project in principle, I was overjoyed. "Now lettest thou thy servant depart in peace," said I to myself. This thought proved to be prophetic, for some three months later I was virtually removed from all participation in government activities.

Before it debated the project on the commune, the Council of

Ministers had considered another project, signed by Stolypin, worked out in a commission under my chairmanship. The materials involved had been assembled in the Peasant Section a long time previously, when the new peasant legislation was being prepared, so that the commission had not worked long. It was made law in the ukase of October 5, 1906. This law abolished nearly all restrictions upon persons belonging to the peasant class and practically equalized the rights of all classes of the empire. It also repealed the discretionary power of the zemskie nachalniki (three days' arrest or five rubles fine), which had evoked continual criticism from the opposition press.*

The Council of Ministers devoted September, October, and November, 1906, to the examination of many different legislative projects which were to be carried out under Article 87. Of these projects I remember several, two in particular, pertaining to the Ministry of the Interior: one from the Department for Ecclesiastical Affairs of Foreign Religions, the other from the Department for General Affairs. The first concerned the freedom of religious beliefs. The project was based upon the American system and advocated the following: every group of people (at least twenty, I believe) of similar religious beliefs, provided the beliefs held did not violate the moral code, was recognized as a religious community, regardless of how much its beliefs were at variance with the dogmas of the Greek Orthodox Church. This extraordinary breadth of view, following on the heels of the intolerance practiced for centuries even in regard to denominations so closely related to the Orthodox Church as were the Old Believers, seemed to me both dangerous and untimely. The pro-

---

* While this project was being discussed by the Council of Ministers, Gasman, Assistant Minister of Justice, objected to some article dealing with the volost courts. His objections were of a conservative nature, for Minister of Justice Shcheglovitov had by then thrown off the cloak of liberalism he had worn at the time of the First Duma and had instructed his collaborators accordingly. To meet Gasman's objections I employed a method which I had used as far back as Plehve's time: I defended my project by the arguments not of a liberal but of an ultra-conservative. Among other things I referred to myself as a Black Hundred[11] man in good standing. This phrase was most unpleasant to Stolypin who was at that time defending his liberal reputation and could not permit it to be said that his closest assistant was a Black Hundred man. He took no active part in defending the project, however, even though it bore his own signature, and after the Council had adopted the project without any changes, he suddenly announced, "My Black Hundred assistant has been so liberal today, that I am afraid if he goes any farther in these Black Hundred activities of his, he will suggest that we abolish government altogether."

posed measure afforded great opportunity for the development of all sorts of sects which could easily have created great confusion in the religious consciousness of the people.

I was never backward in objecting sharply to different projects which Stolypin placed before the Council, but I realized that one man alone was powerless to accomplish anything. Accordingly, before the discussion on this project, I found P. P. Izvolsky,[12] who had succeeded Shikhmatov as Ober-Prokuror of the Holy Synod, and expressed to him my hope that he would oppose certain provisions of the project to be discussed. I knew that he was poorly informed on church and religious problems and that by nature he was shallow, hesitating, and kind, and consequently incapable of any counter-action.* But it seemed to me that he had a clear-cut reason for opposing the measure, namely, the impossibility of adopting such a project without ascertaining the opinion of the Holy Synod. To my great amazement he said that he saw no reason to object to the project. After some conversation with me, however, he announced that there were certain points against which he was going to speak.

During the discussion in the Council of Ministers, Stolypin, according to his custom, let article after article pass when there were no objections from any side. Izvolsky, despite what he had said to me, was silent. I therefore felt obliged to speak. I stated the principal reasons why I could not accept the idea of establishing religious anarchy in the country, then addressed myself to Stolypin in words something like these: "You are striving to win for the government the sympathies of the public and to weaken the opposition, but you might just as well face the fact that the real opposition, the one that lies at the root of all revolt, cannot be won over by any concessions. If it demands all sorts of liberties, it demands them only to this end: that it may use them to overthrow the existing regime. The parts of the public whose support could be won are the moderate liberal and moderate conservative circles. Do you really think that those circles would welcome your new regulations tending to undermine the

---

* P. P. Izvolsky was included in Stolypin's government because of the influence of his brother, A. P. Izvolsky, Minister of Foreign Affairs, who had been Stolypin's ally during the First Duma. At one time P. P. Izvolsky had been inspector of schools in Kiev. He had once joined the circle of Prince E. N. Trubetskoi, who was a professor in Kiev University, and had become permeated with radical liberalism. Later he had become head of public education, first in Kiev School District, then in St. Petersburg School District, and in these offices he had displayed no remarkable ability.

prestige of the Orthodox Church? I do not know the views of the
Ober-Prokuror of the Holy Synod on the matter, but I do know that
even if by this measure you gain a measure of approval from the
radicals you will at the same time antagonize not only the extreme
Rights, with whom you are even now in conflict, but also the moderate Rights, and the support of these two groups is not to be
despised."

At this Stolypin's attitude changed with amazing alacrity. He
became quite excited and answered with spirit that no one could suspect him of desiring to undermine the prestige of the Orthodox
Church. P. P. Izvolsky also made some objections. As a result the
project was rejected.

The second project, the one compiled by the Department for
General Affairs of the Ministry of the Interior, granted new privileges to the Jews. This called forth interesting differences of opinion. It provided further concessions in exempting the Jews from
military service on physical grounds, in admitting the Jews to
schools, and in widening the classes of persons of Jewish extraction
who had the right to reside outside the Jewish settlements. On
the day fixed for the examination of this project, I met P. K.
Schwanebach in the vestibule of the Winter Palace.

"Have you read the Jewish project?" he asked me. "It is perfectly impossible. I hope that you will object."

"Yes, I do find it premature and ineffectual. But I do not think
it quite fitting to object; for, after all, it is signed by my chief,
Stolypin. But you raise the objection and I will support you."

In this instance, too, the articles of the project were passed one
after another without question. No one objected, not even Schwanebach, despite my signs to him, meaning, "Well, why don't you do
something?" Once more I felt obliged to speak.

The project was defended by Kokovtsov, who often considered
matters from the point of view of their reaction upon the stock exchange. He began by saying that he personally did not like Jews and
realized the great harm they were doing. "But," he continued, "I
have come to the conclusion that all measures directed against them
are ineffective. The Jews are so clever that no law can be counted
upon to restrict them. It is useless to lock a door against them, for
they are sure to find a passkey to open it. Moreover, a policy of restrictions only irritates the Jews unnecessarily and creates conditions
favorable to all sorts of abuses and arbitrariness on the part of the

administration and the police. The laws restricting the Jews have accomplished nothing except to create sources of revenue for various agents of the administration."

I could not let such a statement pass unchallenged. "For the first time in my life," I said, "I hear that because locks do not accomplish their purpose, because someone uses a passkey, therefore the locks must be taken off altogether. One thing is certain: either the Jews are harmless, in which case the government must abolish all restrictions against them, especially that concerning the Jewish settlements; or their presence is a pernicious influence, in which case, since locks are ineffective, we must use bolts or anything that will serve the purpose. The first course may be the wiser one. The population of the country, including our intelligentsia, deprived of any legal protection against the preponderance of the Jews, would have to develop in itself some resistance to them, as actually has taken place within the Jewish settlements. Once it has experienced what Jewish dominance really means, as for instance in matters of education, our intelligentsia might cease to be so sympathetically concerned for the fate of the Jews. As for adopting partial measures to equalize the rights of the Jews with those of the rest of the population, this course can have only negative results. It will not pacify the Jews or diminish their revolutionary sympathies; on the contrary, it will put into their hands a weapon which will facilitate their fight against the government. Everybody knows what part the Jews played during the recent upheaval. Now, as a reward, the government is about to give them privileges!"

After my speech other members joined the debate, ranging themselves for and against the project. Stolypin seemed at first to side with its defenders; then he became confused and postponed the debates to a later date.

My objections seemed to irritate the ministers, especially since I was actually not a member of the Council and attended its sessions because of a custom introduced first by Goremykin. I sensed this and told Stolypin next day that I feared that my participation in the debates on this subject might have a result totally contrary to the one I had desired; therefore, I had decided not to attend the next session devoted to this matter. I also restated to him in detail all the reasons why I considered it most harmful to adopt this project.

When this matter was next debated, the members of the Council, at Stolypin's suggestion, first resolved that the majority opinion would be accepted by everyone so that the record of the session would show the Tsar a unanimous decision.* The reason for this resolution was to avoid placing upon the Tsar all responsibility for either decision. If the Tsar had adopted a decision to grant the Jews certain rights, it would have antagonized all the Right circles of the public; on the other hand, if he had declined it, it would have increased the antagonism of the Jews, which was not to be disregarded. The affairs of the Council were supposedly kept secret, but the persons concerned usually managed to learn of everything that occurred there.

In the end a majority of the Council approved the project. Curiously enough Stolypin himself was among the minority, although he himself had placed the project before the Council. Despite the unanimous decision of the Council, however, the Tsar refused to confirm it, thus acting against the entire government and assuming full responsibility for the rejection of the project.[13]

Different versions circulated in St. Petersburg concerning the rejection of this project. It was said that the principal role in its rejection had been played by that same Yusefovich who was one of the authors of the manifesto for strengthening the autocracy. Some said that Stolypin had advised the Tsar in his decision. There were many other versions, and which was correct I do not know.

Of discussions on other projects debated in these months, I remember those on the project concerning the income tax, a reform which was carried out in 1915. N. N. Pokrovsky,[14] Assistant Minister of Finance, reported on the project, but the matter seemed to be beyond the grasp of the Council of Ministers. Besides Kokovtsov, who had initiated the project, and State Comptroller Schwanebach, no member of the Council was familiar with the principles of income taxation or of economic questions in general. Consequently the debates were extremely chaotic, owing to Stolypin's inability to conduct them, and the opinions expressed presented a strange mixture of the opinions of the man in the street and out-of-date notions.

Here ends my intimate knowledge of the work of the Council of Ministers under Stolypin and of his plans for facing the Second Duma which was to assemble February 20, 1907. In December 1906 I was indicted for having drawn a contract with a man named Lidval

---

* Usually when a division of votes occurred the Tsar was shown the record stating the resolution of the majority and that of the minority, and confirmed the one he chose.

who was thereby to supply a certain amount of grain for the relief of certain areas stricken with famine. Lidval had failed to live up to the contract; the government had suffered some losses, and as a result I was excluded from further participation in its work.

The Gurko-Lidval affair, as the press called it, was a very notorious one. The press covered me with all sorts of mud. The radical press attacked me not only because by so doing it sought to lower the prestige of the government but because it was glad of an opportunity to give vent to all its hatred of me which had been pent up since my first speech in the Duma and which my general attitude toward the Duma majority had inspired.

It is not my intention here to recite the details of this lawsuit or to try to exculpate myself, for of what value is evidence presented by the person accused? I shall say only a few words concerning Stolypin's part in this affair.

At the time, and later, my friends and some others said that Stolypin let the affair go ahead because of his personal unfriendliness for me. They went so far as to assert that he saw in me a possible rival whom he wished to destroy. I deny these assertions most vigorously. My relations with Stolypin had not been smooth and I doubt if he was fond of me, but in all matters that concerned me he was governed only by considerations of the good of the state as he understood it. He wished to show the public that he would not shrink from most rigorous measures concerning officials of his ministry, no matter what their position, should the slightest suspicion appear as to the legality of their actions. For myself, I was only too eager to have the affair brought into court, since the courts alone could represent it to the public in its true light and cleanse my reputation of all the mud which was being laboriously flung upon it from all sides.

Stolypin desired not only my indictment but also my condemnation, for he was sure that should the courts acquit me the press would say that the trial had been nothing but a farce and that the acquittal had been decided beforehand. He supposed that only my condemnation would prove to the public that the government allowed no preferences toward its officials of any rank. His logic was quite sound, for if at the cost of one man's reputation, the government could benefit the entire country, no statesman should stop at exacting such a sacrifice. But in my soul I blamed Stolypin for one thing and I still do. He did not choose to appear in person at the trial and to testify there. He demanded on the contrary that the court appear before him at his residence in the Kamenno-Ostrovsky Palace. There he testified in secret audience and gave the most splendid characterization of my work. But the very fact of a court appearing before a, witness was unprecedented, although the law made provision for such procedure in the case of persons of a certain position and of a certain class of service. This circumstance showed clearly, however, the presumption Stolypin had acquired merely a year after his appointment as head of the government. I have always thought that it was Stolypin's duty to attend the entire trial in person, not only out of consideration for me but also in the interests of the government, in order to find out for himself whether or not I was guilty and then either to call down on my head all the thunder and lightning of justice and to point out that the government had not hesitated to indict one of its workers as soon as the public had suspected him of illegal practices or to point out that the government, once convinced of its servants' honesty and loyalty, considered it its duty to protect those servants from slander and mud.

I cannot refrain from mentioning the odd—to say the very least—accusation of the Ober-Prokuror of the Senate, Kempé. He accused me of acquiring grain for relief purposes at a low price and charged that this had led to the lowering of the price of grain on the market. My contract with Lidval, like many others I had drawn with other persons and executed successfully, was actually concluded at prices somewhat lower than the market price; but when it is the duty of a representative of the government to guard the interests of the treasury, it is utterly ridiculous to object to his efforts to make contracts profitable for the government. It is equally ridiculous to imply that the lowering of grain prices in a year of famine is contrary to the interests of the population. In my opinion all this was but a reflection of the discontent on the part of grain-merchants' and landowners' circles which I had provoked by endeavoring to lower the price of grain. As a result I brought myself under cross fire: the opposition was indignant with me for my speech in and my attitude toward the Duma, and unprincipled dealers and agricultural circles of the Right were also against me.

I have no intention of writing here in my own defense, but I hope that my readers will not resent or deny me the assertion of my natural right and desire to quote the opinion of another man who was not without interest and authority in this matter. During the years of my émigré life in Paris, I met the former mayor of the city of

Moscow, N. I. Guchkov, who had been one of the body which conducted my trial. Here is a copy of his letter to me.

Paris, July 20, 1924

Much Esteemed Vladimir Iosifovich:

I have learned that you are writing your memoirs in which you will probably mention your so widely known indictment for overstepping your official rights. I consider it my duty to apprise you of a fact which pertains to this affair and which cannot fail to interest you.

During my term of office as mayor of the city of Moscow I was appointed by Sovereign order in November 1907 a member of the special Senate Board before which you were to appear as a person accused of a civil service offense. At that time, I confess, my attitude toward you, whom I have never met, was rather unfavorable. The attacks the press had directed against you throughout that entire year could not have failed to make a certain impression on anyone not thoroughly familiar with the matter concerned in your case.

From the first day of the trial the entire affair appeared to me, as well as to other members of the Special Board, in an entirely different light from that accepted by the press. I saw clearly that you were a victim of the opposition, which was at that time slandering the government and its individual representatives. Concerning you, this opposition seemed to harbor the most violent hatred and to display unusual bitterness.

As the trial unfolded, my first impression was strengthened, and finally culminated in a firm conviction of your innocence. Some other members of the court—representatives of the public, such as Count Gudovich, marshal of nobility of St. Petersburg, and the starshina of a volost of St. Petersburg Gubernia (whose name escapes me)—evidently had the same experience, for when the jury was debating the case we three declared ourselves for your innocence and acquittal. But the senators, of whom there were five, thought otherwise, and despite our remonstrances they remained unshaken in their opinion.

This unusual firmness of the senators and especially the fact that, while the points of the verdict were being discussed they opposed certain corrections which I tried to introduce into the text in order to make it easier to reach a verdict of not guilty, brought me to the painful conclusion that their conduct was inspired by directions from above.

The day after the case closed, troubled and agitated, I went to the Chairman of the Council of Ministers, P. A. Stolypin. I considered it my duty to tell him my exact opinion of the injustice of the verdict and of the fact that the Ministry of the Interior had had no grounds for convicting you.

I told him that I believed there was a desire to throw Gurko as a bone to the dogs in order to pacify the opposition and so to attract its sympathies to the government. But, I asked, was this just? Was this in harmony with the ultimate good of the government and its representatives?

To my words, P. A. Stolypin answered nothing definite.

Please accept the assurance of my profound esteem.

N. Guchkov

In describing further the events and personalities of this epoch, I shall do so as a mere sideline spectator and ordinary citizen. The connections which I preserved in St. Petersburg bureaucratic circles sometimes gave me an opportunity to enter backstage, so to speak, and to post myself on events not known to the general public. I believe that I am in a position, therefore, to continue these reminiscences beyond the period of my tenure of office. In so doing, I shall limit myself to a few brief sketches.

As is known, the Second Duma proved to be even more radical than the first. It was composed to some extent of militant socialists who, after the experience of the First Duma, had decided that the existing electoral law gave them a chance to work among the masses of the population and, therefore, had discontinued their boycott of the Duma.

For four months Stolypin withstood the Second Duma's fierce attack upon the government. This Duma was so openly revolutionary in character that it could not have hoped to attract the sympathies of any educated groups. Stolypin decided correctly that the Duma was its own worst enemy, that its course of action had antagonized all state-minded persons, and so had made it possible for the government to introduce some changes into the electoral law without arousing the indignation of the people. Changes in this law would be based upon such principles as would ensure the country of educated and loyal representatives.

On June 3, 1907, therefore, the Second Duma was dissolved and simultaneously, by Imperial ukase, some changes were introduced into the electoral system. This act was certainly unconstitutional, a *coup d'état,* yet it was inspired by Stolypin, who really intended not to violate the constitution but to strengthen and preserve it. The government was on the horns of a dilemma: either to abolish popular representation altogether, or, by changing the electoral law, to obtain representatives who would be a constructive factor in public life. Of course, there was still another way out: to comply with the demands of the opposition and to establish a parliamentary form of government. This might have been ultimately possible during the First Duma; but during the Second Duma such action would have been sheer madness, for by that time it had become clear that the Cadet party was not concerned with the interests of state.

The extreme Right circles made full use of these circumstances to influence the Sovereign to put an end to all attempts at constitutional reform and to return to the old form of absolutism. But Stolypin realized the danger of such a reactionary step. He realized that in order to strengthen its position, the government would have to attract the co-operation of at least some educated classes. To this end it should not abolish the constitutional form of government but should support it. This was feasible only with a system of election to the lower chamber which would ensure a majority of representatives loyal to the state. Stolypin also realized that it would be desirable to have not only the opposition but even revolutionary elements represented in this chamber, so that the country, through its bourgeois elements, might be able to judge for itself of the anti-social demands presented by the revolutionists.

Accordingly, a new system of elections was proclaimed, based upon the law of June 3, 1907. This new system answered the purpose mentioned. The composition of the Third Duma was in perfect harmony with the expectations of the government and the intentions of Stolypin. Its most influential group was the Octobrists, which numbered some 170 out of the total 480. They had stated upon their banners that they were firmly in favor of having the people's representatives participate in the legislative work of the country but that beyond this their constitutional hopes did not go.

The Third Duma proved in all respects more productive than its predecessors, and this fact gave promise of strengthening a constitutional regime suitable to the cultural level of the Russian people. True, the Third Duma did not produce many prominent Russian statesmen. This seemed partially to justify the affirmations of the bureaucracy that outstanding statesmen were not to be found outside bureaucratic circles, which had absorbed those elements of the population that were most educated and best understood state affairs.

During the five years of its existence the State Duma was unable to lay down a solid, logical foundation for state policy. Nevertheless, it studied in detail some basic questions of state life and indicated the general direction in which progress was to be made. In the realm of international affairs, however, the Duma had no deciding voice. This realm was considered the prerogative of the throne, and the Minister of Foreign Affairs had always to secure the permission of the Tsar to inform the Duma of anything pertaining to it. The only thing in this field that the Duma could do was to increase our military power by voting credits, and this is, after all, the mainstay of a state in the deciding of international matters.

The period of the Second Duma and the first year of the Third saw Stolypin at his best. With the Second Duma he displayed a remarkable force of character and unruffled calm. "The Duma is rotting on its stem," he used to say, and, fearless of its passionate outbursts, he pursued relentlessly his own policy of preserving the constitutional guaranties at the same time as he strove to win the sympathy of those strata of society which were loyal to the state and thereby to strengthen the prestige and power of the government. "You cannot frighten me," he said to the revolutionists in the Duma. This remark became known throughout the entire country and increased his popularity. His remark to the Second Duma, later inscribed upon his memorial at Kiev, was also to the point: "You desire a great upheaval. We desire a great Russia."

Stolypin's selection of Krivoshein as head of the Chief Administration of Land Organization and Agriculture was a very successful move. Stolypin finally came to realize fully the significance of the land reform which established the right of commune members to leave the commune. He had also come to realize the importance of khutor and individual landownership in general, and generously assisted Krivoshein in his work in this field, especially by appropriating sums necessary for this expensive undertaking.

Stolypin was also successful in establishing good working relations with the majority of the Third Duma. In this he was aided by A. I. Guchkov, the leader of the Octobrists. Under Stolypin's leadership also harmonious relations developed between the Ministry of the Interior and the zemstvos, although the person most responsible for this was not Stolypin but S. E. Kryzhanovsky. It was thanks to the latter's care that the Ministry of the Interior established as one of its offices an information bureau where newly arrived zemstvo men could obtain necessary information and where special clerks of the ministry assisted them in their efforts to see that the zemstvo petitions, which they came to present, received due consideration. In a word, under Stolypin's direction, and to a great extent owing to his clever policy, calm and peace spread over the country. After the tumult of recent years, Russia once again trod the road of enrichment and progress. Prosperity increased rapidly. It is enough to say that while in 1900 the average income of a citizen was 98 rubles yearly, in 1912 it was 130 rubles, an increase of over thirty per cent.

As the country calmed down and as Stolypin's personal position became more secure, he himself underwent a marked change. Authority went to his head, and the flatterers surrounding him did the rest. He who had been so modest upon his arrival from Saratov, who had realized so clearly that he was not sufficiently prepared to deal with many problems of statewide significance, and who had so sincerely welcomed criticism, came to think of himself as an outstanding historical figure. Some knavish souls from the Ministry of the Interior whispered in his ear that he was Petr Stolypin, a second Peter the Great, a Reformer; and while he did not subscribe to this characterization of himself, it did not arouse his indignation. He became intolerant of adverse criticism and difference of opinion. Finally he parted with the Octobrist party because he considered it not meek enough. Now the great merit and entire significance of the Octobrist party was precisely this, that while it recognized the necessity of supporting the Russian government in order to strengthen the position of the lawful authority, it judged all matters upon the basis of their usefulness to the country and did not hesitate to oppose the government when its party opinion differed from the official one. To the Stolypin of 1910 this situation was unacceptable. He needed men who would be subordinates in word and deed, and so transferred his sympathies to the Nationalist party[15] and began to look to these for support. This party, if not because of its program then because of the purpose of many of its members, was ready to follow in whatever direction the government might lead.

Stolypin also engaged in open conflict with the party of the Right. For all its shortcomings, this party was not a *governmental* one; it considered itself the party of the state, and to its mind everything that tended to lessen the imperial authority was to be sharply opposed. It goes without saying that all personal enemies of Stolypin who had conservative opinions had joined this party. They flaunted their devotion to the throne and, playing thus upon the weakness of Nicholas II, used every pretext to blacken Stolypin's reputation in the eyes of the Monarch. This is illustrated by an incident concerning the confirmation of the personnel of the naval general staff. The list had been confirmed by the Duma and was transferred to the State Council. Here the question was raised whether the Chairman of the Council of Ministers was infringing upon the Monarch's prerogatives, since such military and naval lists were not subject to approval by the legislature; they were supposed to be confirmed by the Tsar himself after they had been studied by the Military Council.[16] For this reason the State Council refused to confirm the lists submitted to it. Stolypin immediately tendered his resignation, but Nicholas II would not accept it. Really, however, Stolypin was obliged to give in; the lists were finally confirmed by the Tsar, although it is more than doubtful if this manner of settling the question was in accord with the provisions of existing laws.[17]

In this as in other cases there was evidence of an intrigue against Stolypin on the part of a group of State Council members, among whom were Durnovo and V. F. Trepov. In such intrigues Durnovo, the very popular leader of the Right group of the Council, was prompted by feelings of personal hostility toward Stolypin and by other private considerations. This was illustrated, for instance, by opposition in the State Council to the legislative project dealing with the establishment of the zemstvo institutions in the nine western gubernias. This project had been initiated by the government and had already passed the Duma, but under Durnovo's leadership the Right wing of the State Council used every means in its power to have the project rejected. This positively enraged Stolypin. He announced to the Tsar that with the systematic opposition to his program which he found in the State Council he saw no possibility of continuing any fruitful work. Once more he tendered his resignation. For several days the situation was uncertain. The Right wing of the State Council, especially Durnovo, was already celebrating a victory; but Stolypin's prestige in the eyes of the thinking public was still great and the Tsar appreciated him so much that he did not desire to let him go. Stolypin, too, stood his ground firmly. He agreed to remain Chairman of the Council of Ministers on three conditions: (1) an enforced leave of absence of an indefinite period for Durnovo and V. F. Trepov; (2) the appointment of new members to the State Council by the crown but with his, Stolypin's, knowledge and approval; and (3) the prorogation of the Third Duma for a period of several days, so that the statute on the western zemstvos might be confirmed by Sovereign power under Article 87.

When Stolypin made these conditions he also made the following interesting statement to the Tsar: "If Your Majesty generally approves of my policy for gradually introducing the people into the work of government, be good enough to agree to my conditions, without which I cannot carry through my policy. If, on the other hand, Your Majesty finds that we [the government] have gone too far and desires to make a definite step backwards, then you should dismiss me and appoint P. N. Durnovo in my stead. There is still a third line of conduct, which is in my opinion the least efficient: to move neither forward nor backward but to stay in one place. I may be mistaken, of course, but if Your Majesty believes that this policy is the one to be adopted, appoint Kokovtsov in my stead."

The Tsar agreed to Stolypin's conditions. Durnovo and Trepov were each given a prolonged leave of absence, the legislative chambers were prorogued for three days, and the statute on the western gubernias was confirmed by the Sovereign.

But Stolypin's victory was a Pyrrhic one. The Tsar never forgave him for having forced his hand. As early as the spring of 1911 Nicholas II had decided to part with Stolypin. The latter's assassination and the resulting necessity of appointing his successor as Chairman of the Council of Ministers did not find the Tsar unprepared. Even before he left Kiev Nicholas II asked Kokovtsov to wait on him and not only offered him the post of Chairman of the Council of Ministers but also said that he had in mind a candidate for the position of Minister of the Interior.[18]

Stolypin was the only outstanding man of all the collaborators of Nicholas II to whom one could apply that embracing epithet of the Romans, "Felix." Generally speaking, both the late Tsar and the majority of his collaborators had been born in the dark of the moon; their fate had followed them throughout their lives and also had affected Russia. Stolypin's luck was with him continually until his death; he died at his post and, what is more, almost on the eve of his natural death: the autopsy revealed the fact that all his vital organs had been severely overstrained and the medical men were unanimous in affirming that his end was at hand.[19]

CHAPTER XXII

KOKOVTSOV'S MINISTRY AND THE FOURTH STATE DUMA

As the country calmed down after the tumult of 1905–6, and as the apprehensions caused by the recent revolutionary movement disappeared, the government tended more and more to return to its former methods of administration. This was most clearly reflected in the appointment of ministers. Nicholas II was little inclined to respect the order established by the Manifesto of October 17, which had entrusted all power to one person, the Chairman of the Council of Ministers. The first ministry had been selected by Witte. The second had been selected according to a plan worked out by the Tsar and Goremykin, by which the Tsar's personal choice of ministers was more evident. The third Chairman of the Council, Stolypin, had succeeded in selecting the personnel of his government; but his struggle to preserve this state of things became increasingly difficult. A few months before Stolypin's tragic death, the Tsar had decided to let him go, and one reason for this decision was the Tsar's opinion that Stolypin's selection of his own men was an encroachment upon the prerogatives of the Monarch. After Stolypin's death these prerogatives were reasserted. One reason was that when Stolypin's successor, V. N. Kokovtsov, assumed office outward conditions did not necessitate any changes in the government. Kokovtsov, therefore, was placed at the head of a government some members of which were politically unsympathetic toward him and disinclined to follow his directions. He succeeded, it is true, in opposing the appointment of A. N. Khvostov,[1] Governor of Nizhnii Novgorod and the Tsar's candidate for the vacant post of Minister of the Interior, and in securing the appointment of A. A. Makarov, his own candidate. But the fact remains that Kokovtsov never succeeded in creating a united government that would follow his directions. Every subsequent change in the personnel of his government was made, if not against his wishes, then certainly not in accordance with them. As far as I know, Kokovtsov made only one other attempt to secure the appointment of a candidate of his own selection and that ended in utter failure. I refer to his efforts to effect the dismissal of Sukhomlinov,[2] the Minister of War, and the appointment of A. A. Polivanov in his stead. This took place in the autumn of 1911. The Tsar was at Livadia. Here Kokovtsov suggested to him that Sukhomlinov be replaced by another person. Kokovtsov had weighty reasons for this suggestion. He had learned that among Sukhomlinov's immediate entourage there was a person, Altschuler, who was connected with the Austrian intelligence service. I do not know the details of what Kokovtsov said to the Tsar, but according to what was later known at St. Petersburg the Tsar at first agreed to his suggestion. When Sukhomlinov learned of the danger threatening him, he departed in all haste to Livadia and there succeeded not only in strengthening his own position but in obtaining the dismissal of Polivanov, his assistant and his rival candidate. When Sukhomlinov returned to St. Petersburg some days later, he was met at the station by all his assistants. Walking up to Polivanov and without extending his hand, he said sharply: "By Sovereign orders you are no longer Assistant Minister of War."[3]

Sukhomlinov was not the only member of the government who was in direct opposition to Kokovtsov. Krivoshein and Kokovtsov had been on bad terms ever since they had been colleagues under Stolypin. Their conflict was really the outcome of Krivoshein's annual demands of Kokovtsov for ever increasing amounts of money to meet the needs of the Chief Administration of Land Organization and Agriculture.

I have previously discussed Krivoshein at the beginning of his career. When he at last achieved his ambition and was appointed head of a large independent ministry, he changed radically. His modesty, his concealment of his political opinions, his readiness to execute all orders of his superiors—all these disappeared. To reach his ends he still used his old method of acquiring and cultivating wide connections; but now he used these connections, not to further his private ambitions, but to develop the business in his charge— the management and the development of rural economy. This task demanded all his attention, and he conducted it with affectionate enthusiasm.

Krivoshein was also ambitious to become head of the government, and the ambition grew as he acquired greater influence with the Tsar and certain agricultural and industrial circles. To this end he followed his established method of making valuable connections.

Even though at that time the Empress had no influence, he used every means in his power to win her favor, which he did very successfully.* He contrived to have established a special committee for the encouragement and development of peasant handicrafts and suggested that the Empress be made chairman of the committee. In discussing other subjects with her, he touched upon many state matters and undoubtedly succeeded in captivating her mind and imagination. Soon his influence began to be manifest in different directions, such as in the appointment of ministers.† In fact, he and not Kokovtsov soon became the most important person in the Council of Ministers.

Meanwhile, Kokovtsov, though head of the government, remained precisely and exclusively the Minister of Finance, and even in this realm the great influence he enjoyed was negative and deadening. Had it not been for the Duma with which he had to contend, the economic development of the country and the development of our military and naval forces would have been stopped altogether. He never became anything but a watchman guarding the interests of the State Treasury. He systematically hoarded gold in the state coffers, and while he was so engaged one could almost hear him talk to his accumulated treasures in the lines of Pushkin:

> Come, you have roamed the world enough,
> Serving the passions and the needs of man.
> Sleep here a sleep of strength and rest,
> The sleep of gods in deep heaven's span.

When Kokovtsov became Minister of Finance in 1906 his principles were suited to the condition of Russian finances, but in 1908 they were at variance with national interests. It is wise to be very saving of public funds and to limit credit during periods of economic depression; but when the country's productive forces are developing rapidly such a policy is unsound. From 1907 to 1914 Russia was experiencing exceptionally great economic development. In part

---

* In his relations with the Empress Krivoshein was handicapped by his ignorance of all foreign languages. The Tsarina spoke Russian, of course, but it was difficult for her to conduct conversations in this language on subjects of a complicated nature. It was much easier for her to explain her ideas in detail in some Western European language. But Krivoshein managed somehow.

† For instance, Count P. N. Ignatev, who succeeded Kasso[4] as Minister of Education, was advanced by Krivoshein, whose assistant he had been up to that time in the Chief Administration of Land Organization and Agriculture.

this was due to the fact that industry had improved its markets by increasing the well-being of the population, and this in turn was due to the fact that the peasants were farming the land under different forms of land tenure and were employing different methods in exploiting the productive forces of the soil. In my opinion it was a misfortune to have in charge of the state coffers at such a time a man who considered it his chief duty merely to fill them, and who evidently did not understand that, given a prosperous population, a state may exist without large gold reserves.* Moreover, the main object of this hoarding—the stabilization of the ruble—was not attained. The experience of the World War showed that under extraordinary conditions a large accumulation of gold in the State Treasury does not prevent the depreciation of a country's monetary unit. At the beginning of the war we had the greatest accumulation of gold that had ever been in the possession of any one country; yet our ruble fell farther than the monetary units of other countries, although their gold resources were much less than those which backed our paper currency. Ultimately the hoarding of gold by the Russian State Treasury actually enabled the Bolsheviks to lengthen the period of their crazy experiment—the abolition of all individual public economy—by living on the work of the old bureaucracy and spending for the needs of their state the gold funds that had been accumulated during the preceding period.

The appointment of A. A. Makarov as Minister of the Interior cannot be considered very successful. Makarov was a typical legal worker; he was accustomed to analyze the past but lacked the ability to anticipate the future. Yet it was said long ago: *"Administrer— c'est prévoir."* Furthermore, the habit of dealing with persons as if they were either under judicial examination or on trial brings about a specific attitude toward the human race in general and its institutions in particular. This attitude manifests itself, first of all, in a sort of formalism expressed in everlasting protocols and other written records. This was precisely Makarov's attitude toward the numerous representatives of the government subordinated to him as Minister of Interior and toward public institutions. The Tsar showed much perspicacity in nicknaming him a notary public. As successor to Stolypin, who had possessed vivacity, ease of manner, and an under-

* See also my *Nashe gosudarstvennoe i narodnoe khoziaistvo* (*"Our State and People's Economy"*), published in 1908. I expressed the same ideas in the State Council in analyzing the budget for 1914.

standing of the psychology of the zemstvo men, Makarov showed from the very beginning his somewhat dull and indifferent, if not hostile, attitude toward them. Consequently, that living contact, which had been established between the zemstvos and the Ministry of the Interior, was broken.

Makarov displayed his callousness and lack of political tact in his speech in the Duma on April 11, 1912, in response to the Duma's inquiry concerning the shooting of workers at the Lena Goldfields. There had been more than a hundred casualties, and the Duma had been informed that the shooting had not been caused by any aggression on the part of the workers. The affair had created much excitement and was being played up by the opposition press. Without conducting any inquiry, and relying entirely upon the report of Captain Treshchenkov,[5] the gendarme officer who had ordered the shooting, Makarov declared from the Duma tribune that the captain had been quite right in giving such orders and that these had been caused by the crowd's attack on the troops. But the facts were different. A later inquiry revealed that the economic conditions of the Lena workers were extremely bad, that their strike had been entirely justified, and, finally, that the strike had been a peaceful one, so that the troops had had no provocation whatever for shooting. As a result, some local administrators, such as the local governor, whose name I do not recall, Kniazev,[6] the Governor-General of Irkutsk, and Treshchenkov, the gendarme officer, were dismissed from their posts. The matter was then hushed up and no others were indicted. The government's treatment of the Lena incident was basically wrong and, of course, did much to shake public confidence in the justness of the Tsar's decision. Alexander III would not have acted thus.[7]

No important measure was carried through by the Ministry of the Interior under Makarov. The projects for reforming gubernia and other branches of local government, prepared under Stolypin, remained in blissful repose in the different departments of the ministry. But Makarov did not last long as minister. He stumbled over Rasputin. He learned through the Police Department that certain individuals had in their possession letters from the Empress to Rasputin, and he used every means in his power to acquire them. For a considerable sum he succeeded in doing so. Then he presented them to the Tsar. What his purpose was in making this presentation one hesitates to say. The letters of the Empress were of a very innocent nature; they concerned the health of the Tsarevich and asked for Rasputin's advice and blessing. It was, of course, the duty of a minister of the Tsar to remove them from private hands and thus to prevent them from becoming an object of barter, but there his duty would seem to have ended. Evidently, however, Makarov wished to win promotion from them as well as to show his devotion to the Imperial family and his ability to protect it from all annoyance. He could not grasp the fact that to transfer these letters to the Tsar could not bring anything but unpleasantness to both the Emperor and the Empress. Great must have been his stupefaction, therefore, when a few days later he learned that he had been dismissed and no explanation offered.

Makarov's successor was N. A. Maklakov, a former Governor of Poltava. In appearance Maklakov presented a striking contrast to Makarov. He was a fat, rubicund, cheerful man, a typical provincial dandy, a ladies' man, a highly diverting raconteur and reputed to be an inimitable anecdotist. He was less like a provincial administrator than a special duties clerk whose type was well known in the gubernias and whose special duties were generally imposed less by the governor than by the governor's wife and concerned household and social affairs. As manager of the Tambov local branch of the Treasury Maklakov had succeeded in captivating the heart of the local philanthropist, Aleksandra Nikolaevna Naryshkina,[8] née Chicherina,* the aunt of the man who was later the Bolshevik Commissar for Foreign Affairs.[9] She was well connected at court, so that Maklakov was soon appointed Governor of Poltava. There he met the Tsar in 1909 during the ceremonies of the bicentennial anniversary of the Battle of Poltava. The Tsar liked him very much, and it was to the Tsar himself that Maklakov's selection as minister was due. Kokovtsov had nothing to do with it. When Maklakov was appointed minister he immediately realized that in order to keep his position he had to make friends with the extreme Right group and to parade Right convictions. He considered that the best way of showing these convictions was to be distrustful of the zemstvo, to remain on strictly official terms with the Duma, and to avoid every close contact with its most prominent members. This course he followed until the end of his ministry, and in the process he probably convinced himself that he was an ardent partisan of absolutism, although I doubt if he had any definite inclination in

* It is believed that this lady was later tortured to death by the Bolsheviks at Tambov.

that direction. However, when he was arrested by the Provisional Government and later when he was imprisoned and murdered by the Bolsheviks, he conducted himself with dignity and noble courage.

Like his predecessor, Maklakov did not concern himself with any serious state problems, and under his administration no legislative projects of any importance were laid before the Duma, with the exception of the project for establishing the small zemstvo unit, a project worked out under Stolypin.

Maklakov resembled Stolypin in that he regarded the position and duties of his office as those of an All-Russian governor. For instance, he spent his nights visiting the police stations of St. Petersburg. Later he realized that the duties of a minister are somewhat different from those of a governor, and abandoned these excursions.

Before sketching briefly the activity of the Fourth Duma, I wish to say a few words about the election of its members and of governmental interference in these elections. A. N. Kharuzin,[10] the Assistant Minister of the Interior, who was once my colleague in the Imperial Chancellery, was charged with the task of supervising them. Kharuzin was intelligent, very ambitious, and inordinately pleased with himself. He did not hesitate to break both the letter and the spirit of the law if he could further his career by so doing. He used every means in his power to make the results of the elections favorable to the government. I wish to stress the term favorable. Any government has the right to strive to secure a majority in the legislative chamber to support its policies. Any government which believes that its program answers the interests of the country not only has this right but is in duty bound to exercise it. But there is a difference between a desire to secure a majority sharing the views of the government and a desire to have a legislative body without one man who can think and act independently. During the reign of Nicholas II the government desired to make of its supporters and agents pawns who did not dare to have minds of their own. Yet, curiously enough, this intolerance of contrary opinions was not accompanied with firm enforcement of the Sovereign will. The Supreme Power was not strong enough to exact strict obedience, and at the same time it was too weak to risk permitting independent thought. "Do as you like, but do not dare to criticize me." Such seemed to be its motto.

During the elections to the Duma the government did not limit its activity to supporting certain parties. It studied individual candidates and painstakingly removed those from whose lips it feared criticism of its actions. It was forgotten that legislatures of sycophants are a government's least secure support in times of crisis. *"La Chambre retrouvée"* of Charles X,[11] so called because of its extraordinary submissiveness, dethroned Charles X after a few days of street revolution.

The list of Third Duma members was studied and the government decided to prevent the re-election of those who had been foremost in expressing their dissatisfaction with governmental measures. Among such undesirables* were A. I. Guchkov, Prince Shakhovskoi, who had succeeded Guchkov as chairman of the Duma's commission for national defense, and Kamensky,[15] who in the Third Duma had raised the very disagreeable question of renting the lands, rich in coal, of the Aleksandro-Severskaia Church situated in Ekaterinoslav Gubernia. I, too, was included in this group, evidently because I had criticized during the All-Russian Congress of the Nobility in 1908 the financial and economic policy of V. N. Kokovtsov.

Different means were employed to remove different undesirables. Some were indicted on some pretext or other, so that they lost the right of being elected; some were eliminated by the exertion of pressure upon the electors, others by an artificial combination or separation of electors' *curiae* in the uezds. Special use was made of the clerical *curia,* which, according to the law, could either act or remain inactive.

The government's desire to make the Duma a docile instrument was well illustrated in the 1912 elections at Tver. In this gubernia it was a contest between two parties: on the one hand, the Cadet party, which included as usual the Left wing of the zemstvo and the representatives of the liberal professions; and, on the other, what

* The government's interference in the Duma elections was not confined to removing undesirable persons. The Police Department went much farther, though evidently it did not apprise the Minister of the Interior of its actions. During the investigation by the Extraordinary Commission of Inquiry[12] in 1917, Makarov emphasized these actions of the Police Department. For instance, in the elections to the Fourth Duma this Department had secured the election of Malinovsky,[13] one of its agents and an avowed provocateur, as representative of a workers' *curia* in Moscow. Later, however, Malinovsky had become a leader of the Social Democratic party in the Duma and had made very provocative speeches from the tribune. He had been denounced by Burtsev,[14] who made it his specialty to discover among the revolutionists the agents-provocateurs who had sold themselves out to the police, and was obliged to leave the Duma. Later Malinovsky was executed by the Bolsheviks.

might be called the Octobrists—because there was no organized Octobrist party in Tver Gubernia. This latter party included extreme Rights who were too weak to appear independently, moderate Rights, and Octobrists proper. The clergy, obedient to the diocesan authorities, was also an important element in this group; in fact the clergy had furnished the Third Duma with three of the eight members from Tver Gubernia.

As for my own election to the Duma I considered that the most difficult step would be to get myself chosen by the Tver Uezd zemstvo assembly as an elector to the gubernia electoral assembly, because only two such electors were to be chosen from Tver Uezd and one of these was to be chosen from the clergy. Moreover, there were many peasant representatives in the uezd electoral assembly who were eager to become members of the Duma in order to secure the four-thousand-ruble salary. But as the peasant representatives could come to no understanding among themselves, their tactics were simple: to vote against all candidates, even when they were their own representatives.

At an early stage in the elections I learned that the Central Government's gubernia administration, that is, the governor, N. G. Biunting,[16] had done everything in its power to prevent my election to the gubernia electoral assembly. To this end the governor had addressed himself to Archbishop Anthony,[17] with whom I was in close touch, but without success. The uezd electoral assembly elected a priest and me as electors to the gubernia assembly which would elect the members of the Duma. In this gubernia assembly there were about sixty electors, of whom from twelve to sixteen were clergymen. These, together with Octobrists proper, headed by Shubinsky,[18] seemed to indicate a certain victory for the Right. After lengthy negotiations in the gubernia electoral assembly an agreement was reached: the clergy were to have two seats and Shubinsky's election as a representative of the landowners' *curia* was to be assured.* On their part the landowners' *curia* agreed to accept for the other five members of the Duma the list of the Right group. In this list I was included. But before the election proper I received information that the governor was still trying hard to prevent my election.

---

* All gubernia electors took part in electing members from the landowners' *curia,* but the candidate had to be a landowner possessing a full quota of land. Consequently peasant and clergy electors had no interest in voting against a candidate nominated by a majority of the landowners, and willingly accepted him.

He even made it known that this was the attitude of the government and especially of its head, Kokovtsov.

I was aware that Kokovtsov had been very much displeased by my speech to the All-Russian Congress of the Nobility, yet this had taken place three years previously. Moreover I had no idea that either the government or Kokovtsov would attach any importance to my election to the Duma, much less take steps to prevent it. As, nevertheless, I wished to find out how matters stood, I went to St. Petersburg. First I went to see Makarov; but he could tell me nothing definite except that Kokovtsov was particularly interested in the elections and that it was alleged that he was giving directions to gubernia authorities.[19] I saw then that Biunting had spoken the truth when he said that the government was opposed to my election. I saw also that although Makarov was indifferent, he had received his instructions from Kokovtsov and would not take it upon himself to act contrary to them. Next I went directly to Kokovtsov and asked him frankly if it were true that he had given orders to prevent my election to the Duma. Kokovtsov had greeted me courteously and now answered with a frankness and directness which did him honor.

"Yes," he said, "I should prefer the election of a Cadet rather than your election. You understand, do you not, that it would be much easier for me to reply, say, to Shingarev[20] (his constant opponent in debates on the state budget), who sits on the Left, than to you, who would sit on the Right."

I thanked him for his frankness, after which we chatted in friendly fashion for some time, discussing other matters. Kokovtsov told me that a few days previously, in accord with the Tsar's express desire, he had summoned Rasputin. Later, the Tsar had asked him what impression Rasputin had made upon him. Kokovtsov had answered: "Your Majesty, such individuals never make any impression upon me."[21] We talked as if we belonged to the same political group, or even like two members of the central government.

Kokovtsov might have changed his attitude toward my candidacy had I promised to refrain from criticizing his financial and economic policy. He did not make any such offer, however, and I saw no possibility of binding myself by any promises or obligation.

At last the day of the Duma elections arrived. All sixty electors of Tver Gubernia gathered in the nobility assembly hall. It was apparent from the start that our Right wing had a clear majority.

From one of the electors I learned that all electors from the clergy had been called to the Archbishop's house, where the Archbishop had presented to them N. N. Lodyzhensky, special-duties clerk with the Ober-Prokuror of the Holy Synod and at the same time one of the electors from Kashin Uezd. The Archbishop announced that the electors were to act in perfect accord with the instructions he had received from the Ober-Prokuror and the government in general. It soon became known that Lodyzhensky had brought the Archbishop a letter from St. Petersburg (some said it was from Sabler,[22] some from Kokovtsov), stating that the electors from the clergy were to be instructed to vote against me. Evidently Archbishop Anthony had not wished to take it upon himself to put obstacles in the way of my election.

It so happened that our party had made it clear to the clergy electors that unless they voted for me none of them would be elected to the Duma. They felt, however, that they could not disobey their instructions. As a result, no candidate of the clergy was elected. As for myself, I withdrew my candidacy.

My visit to St. Petersburg had taken place before the zemstvo assemblies elected members to the State Council, and as soon as I had realized that, under the circumstances, I had little chance of being elected to the Duma, I had decided to submit myself as candidate for election to the upper legislative chamber. This candidacy had been successful. It now occurred to me that it would be rather awkward for me to appear in the State Council if it were known that I had been defeated in the Duma elections. It would have seemed to imply: "I have come to you because they would not have me in the other place, which I consider superior to this one." Consequently, as I have said, I withdrew my candidacy for election to the Duma.

Instead of the clerical candidate and myself we hastened to select as candidates two persons on whom the Octobrists and the Lefts could agree.

A few days later, I met the entire clerical group of electors descending the main stairs of the nobility assembly hall. "Well, what now, my fathers?" I said. "This is the result of being a mere herd driven by a clerk."

"This is not our fault," they answered to a man, literally gnashing their teeth. "It is the fault of accursed St. Petersburg."

The results of the government's attention to the elections to the Fourth Duma showed themselves not only in the composition but also in the work of this body. In party composition the Fourth Duma differed but little from its predecessor; but it was deprived of its most talented and energetic members, advocates of a middle-of-the-road policy. Without them the Fourth Duma lacked that initiative so prevalent in the Third Duma. The government evidently intended to make the majority party in this new Duma its docile tool. But persons who bow before authority are likely to change their allegiance as soon as this authority changes hands. During the World War, when the government was at odds with the public and as the latter grew in strength to become the dominating force in the country, the Duma meekly followed the public's lead and was finally enslaved by the Duma's minority, the Cadets, who were the mouthpiece of the public.

Cadet tactics in the Fourth Duma were very different from their tactics in the Third Duma. They abandoned the idea of discrediting the Duma and of systematically obstructing its work. Evidently they realized that in order to attain their primary goal of introducing the principles of democracy into Russia it would be much more efficient to take part in the work of the Duma, and, in this perfectly legitimate way, to do that which they could no longer hope to accomplish by means of obstruction. These changed tactics helped the Fourth Duma considerably and as a result all the complicated legislative projects introduced by the government were debated in commission and, with some changes, passed on to the State Council.

Between Duma and government, however, there was no unity—only temporary alliances between Duma and separate ministers such as Krivoshein of agriculture, Count Ignatev of education, and Grigorovich[23] of the navy. As a result all appropriations requested by these ministers were approved by the Duma and eventually granted.

Kokovtsov's attitude toward the Duma was formally correct but by no means friendly. For quite a long period he had no relations whatever with it. This was the result of a trivial episode. Once, during the Duma debates (if I remember rightly the debate concerned the statute on the Amur border patrol), N. E. Markov,[24] a member of the Right group in the Duma, suddenly exclaimed, "Above all, one must not steal." This was not addressed to anyone in particular, but from the trend of his speech it was obvious that he meant it for the government. Evil tongues attributed Markov's unexpected and savage outburst to the fact that a short time previously Kokovtsov

had restricted the state subsidy made to the ultra-conservative publication, *Zemshchina,* published by the Right faction. Be that as it
may, Kokovtsov was insulted and left the Duma, taking with him
all the members of the government present, and for some months
neither he nor the other members of the government, evidently at his
request, appeared in the Duma.

It is hard to imagine anything more absurd. The government
could have requested the Chairman of the Duma to repress any member whose conduct was unbecoming to a Duma member. It would
have been still simpler immediately to demand from the tribune that
Markov explain himself. This would probably have ended the matter. But for the government to break off relations with the people's
representatives because of a few words of one Duma member was as
unexpected as it was unstatesmanlike. The attitude *"Ich bin beleidigt"*
is not one to be assumed by a government. But the most peculiar
feature of the entire incident was the fact that for some time the
Duma did not know the real reason why the members of the government were not attending the sessions and paid no particular attention
to their absence. When it finally realized that the government was
boycotting it, it very easily put a stop to the boycott. The presidium
of the Duma simply omitted from the agenda all legislative projects
for new appropriations to the government. The effects of these
tactics were felt most acutely by Grigorovich, Minister of the Navy,
who inquired as to the cause of the delay, and asked the Chairman
of the Council of Ministers for permission to appear before the
Duma in person. As this permission was denied, he asked the Tsar
himself for this permission, and this request was granted. He immediately asked the Duma when he could expect it to discuss his
project, which had long since been approved by the military commission. He said that he would be there to defend it in person. His
project was immediately put on the agenda and approved by the
Duma in his presence. His example was followed by other ministers.
Finally, Kokovtsov himself deigned to honor the Duma with his
presence.[25]

A few words now about the work of the Fourth Duma. Slowly
but surely a regime of equity was introduced into the country, and
gradually the separate branches of the state administration were
improved. Gradually also the Duma's conflicts with the government
became less frequent, and open warfare gave way to peaceful negotiations. During the two years of the Fourth Duma's work under

normal conditions before the outbreak of war it debated and decided many legislative projects of primary importance, especially in matters concerning legal procedure and criminal law. It approved the project for establishing courts of justices of the peace; it made government officials responsible for their actions by giving prosecuting magistrates the right to indict them without the consent of their superiors; it established the practice of the so-called suspended sentence; and, finally, it approved a new statute, which, when it became law, increased the independence of the Ruling Senate by establishing a new method of filling vacancies through co-option subject to imperial approval. This reform was of considerable significance in reducing the element of arbitrariness in the administration.

During the seven years before the war the economic life of the people enjoyed a prosperous development. A few remarks on this general subject will not be amiss. Let us first consider state economy in so far as it was reflected in the state budget. When the Third Duma met we had just concluded peace with Japan after a serious defeat. The treaty did not call for any indemnity, but we had to pay reparations to Japan for her indirect losses. According to the computations of A. Rafalovich,[26] our financial agent at Paris, the Japanese War cost our State Treasury two billion, three hundred million (2,300,000,000) rubles. The Revolution of 1905–6 had also undermined our finances, so that at the beginning of 1906 the State Treasury was without ready money and owed the State Bank for an issue of six per cent State Treasury notes. Our yearly budget showed a considerable deficit, which was covered by foreign loans, an expedient which was necessary to prevent the depreciation of the Russian ruble. In two years' time, however, despite increased expenditures, our budgets began to show an increase of revenues over expenditures. The result was a great cash reserve in the State Treasury. On January 1, 1910, this reserve amounted to 107 million rubles, in 1911 to 333 million, in 1912 to 477 million, and in 1913 to over 600 million.

If our state economy thus grew in strength, accumulating tremendous but perfectly useless sums, it was only because the people's economy developed by leaps and bounds. There was no branch of production which did not show marked growth. But there was one knotty problem that had to be faced. Our budget, as everybody knows, was based mainly on the liquor monopoly. It was natural that those in charge of Russian finances should treat with utmost caution all measures likely to curtail this source of state revenue. This point of view was held by Kokovtsov. Krivoshein, who was not directly concerned with the condition of Russian finances and who realized how much the sobriety of the Russian peasant would improve peasant economy, was of another opinion. He enjoyed the complete confidence of both Emperor and Empress, and so decided to take the bull by the horns and somehow to carry through decisive measures against the spread of the strong drink habit. The Tsar was always fascinated by big ideas for improving the conditions of the masses, and he not only accepted but even championed Krivoshein's point of view. He suggested to Kokovtsov that the latter should immediately introduce before the legislative chambers a project of measures to reduce the use of liquor. Kokovtsov was not very enthusiastic about this, but he was obedient to the Tsar's wishes and carried out his orders. A legislative project was laid before the Duma bearing the modest title, "Some changes in the statute on the state sale of strong drink." This project provided for merely a mild palliative and caused great debates in the Duma. Chelyshev,[27] the member from Samara, made a speech which lasted about four hours; he was a self-appointed apostle of temperance and was warmly in favor of totally prohibiting the manufacture and sale of liquor. Other measures for abolishing the use of intoxicating liquor were proposed, but the Duma finally approved the original project adding some provisions for limiting the use of drink.

In the State Council, however, a series of decisive measures against the use of strong drink were introduced by none other than S. Y. Witte, the creator of the liquor monopoly. In a long speech he described how, when he had established the liquor monopoly in accordance with the instructions of Alexander III, his idea had been to regulate the use of strong drink. This idea had been perverted by his successors to such an extent that now the Chief Administration of Indirect Taxation and Liquor Trade[28] in the Ministry of Finance had become a corrupter of the people's morals. Witte was always seeking a return to power, and perhaps he thought that the best way to regain the favor of the Tsar was to advocate the prohibition of strong drink. In his speeches he advocated curtailment of the revenue from the sale of state liquor but without disrupting the state budget. The idea of overthrowing Kokovtsov, whom he heartily disliked, also appealed to him, especially since it would have left vacant the post of Minister of Finance for which Witte had never ceased to yearn. But Kokovtsov was firm. Surely he must have realized that in defending the liquor monopoly as the main source of state revenue, and in answering each radical suggestion by a firm *non possumus,* he was jeopardizing his position; yet he remained adamant against every suggestion of the State Council for limiting the use of liquor.[29]

So deeply did Nicholas II distrust the Manifesto of October 17 that Witte could never have emerged victorious from his duel with Kokovtsov had not a third party, A. V. Krivoshein, joined the contest. Krivoshein's relations with Kokovtsov had been strained for a long time. I have already mentioned the latter's steady opposition to appropriations requested by the Chief Administration of Land Organization and Agriculture. This opposition irritated Krivoshein, even though in the end he usually overcame it. Krivoshein had abundant initiative; he dreamed of great reforms and could not tolerate the steady, deliberate precision of Kokovtsov. Moreover, Krivoshein was near the realization of his ambition to become director of state policy. In fact, the matter had already been decided in principle. Kokovtsov was to be dismissed[30] from his post as Chairman of the Council of Ministers and as Minister of Finance, and the former post was to be offered to Krivoshein. But here fate intervened to cheat Krivoshein. He fell suddenly and dangerously ill. He had contracted angina pectoris, and its attacks threatened his life. As I recall he fell ill early in November 1913, and toward the middle of December his condition was very critical. There could be no question of his assuming any new responsibility. Toward the end of December, however, he began to recover. All immediate danger had passed, but he could not yet assume any official duties. The doctors prescribed a long rest and a trip to the south. A temporary successor to Kokovtsov had to be found, and the Tsar selected I. L. Goremykin to be Chairman of the Council of Ministers. P. L. Bark[31] was appointed Minister of Finance. He was a man who did not shrink from rubbing elbows with Rasputin. Krivoshein said that it was he who had selected Bark. Witte claimed that Bark had been selected on his, Witte's, recommendation; but of this I have grave doubts. Witte always wished to give the impression that he was a very influential statesman, and was fond of taking credit for any government measure.

With these changes in the administration the project for a reform of the liquor laws, which was still being violently discussed by the

State Council, lost interest for everyone, Witte included. It was rumored in the State Council and then in public that Bark had promised to take measures to limit the sale and use of liquor and to change the entire state budget. This news killed any desire to fight the Minister of Finance on this ground. Nevertheless, the State Council introduced a series of changes in the project which limited further the use of liquor and it was in this form that the project became law. It is hard to decide now how effective these measures would have been. The World War started six months later and the sale and purchase of vodka was then strictly prohibited, so that there was no chance to ascertain the efficacy of the new law.

Of the other problems which excited St. Petersburg political circles during the first half of 1914 I recall the problem of the small zemstvo unit, the volost zemstvo. A legislative project, worked out under Stolypin, had been sidetracked in the Council of the Chief Administration for the Affairs of Local Economy, which was composed of representatives of the zemstvos and the nobility. Under pressure from the Duma and Krivoshein, N. A. Maklakov, who was not very favorably inclined toward this project, introduced it into the State Duma *à son corps défendant*. It passed that body despite the vigorous opposition of the Cadets, who argued that they too wished the small zemstvo unit but not the kind proposed in the project. In May it was placed before the State Council. Here it was bitterly opposed by the Right wing of the Council, led and inspired by P. N. Durnovo. In vain did those of the State Council who were zemstvo representatives defend the idea of the volost zemstvo. The most active defender was Count F. A. Uvarov,[32] member of the State Council from Moscow zemstvo. All their arguments could not prevail against the stubborn "We do not want it!" of the Rights. I, too, participated as actively in this business as I was able. I can still hear myself pronouncing a sentence from the tribune of the State Council, a sentence which proved to be prophetic. I said to the great landowners: "Go to the volost zemstvo while you still have time, while they are still ready to take you." The project asserted the principle that landowners possessing a certain area of land were *ipso facto* to be included in the volost zemstvo without the necessity of being elected. It is interesting to note that even such avowed Cadet men as Moshnin and Petrunkevich, members of the Tver Gubernia assembly, supported the project and argued that the principle it contained was both natural and necessary, at least until the population should learn in practice that the participation of the landed gentry in work directed to improving the well-being of the peasants was useful, and that local welfare must be built not upon the welfare of separate villages but upon the sound basis of the prosperity of all classes. In the end, the State Council rejected this project by one vote.

N. A. Maklakov's conduct on this matter had been peculiar. He had not only failed to defend the project but had expressed openly his lack of sympathy with it, whereas he was in a position to see to it that the project was passed by the State Council; for the Right wing of the Council, numbering about one hundred members, consisted for the most part of government appointees and included many who were quite ready to do as they were bidden. Evidently, however, a hint had been given that the government would not support the project.

Goremykin also had nothing to do with the project. He was lazy at best, but now he was seventy years of age. Many were the anecdotes told in the lobbies of the Duma as to his pastimes. It was said that his hours were distributed among night-time sleep, daytime naps, and the reading of French novels. Of course, this was an exaggeration. It was true, however, that with the years Goremykin had become firmly resolved to let events take their course. His appointment had not caused any demonstration of public sympathy or discontent. In the spring of 1914 the opposition of the Cadet party and its ambitious leader was silent, at least outwardly. The Cadets continued to dally with the Socialist leaders and, in secret, evidently still cherished the criminal desire to seize power by revolutionary methods. The Miliukov Cadet paper, *Rech,* used every pretext to arouse public dissatisfaction with the government, but it did so carefully. It had learned that a wholesale discrediting of the regime and persons connected with the government did not pass unpunished. The censorship became more and more daring, so that at times it lost all sense of proportion; now and then it even prohibited the discussion of certain permissible topics, confusing fundamental and grave matters with trivial ones.

Meanwhile the agitation of the revolutionary elements went on and with results. The workers of the many St. Petersburg factories, recovered from the tumult of 1905–6, and organized in revolutionary cells, were again becoming as wax in the hands of the revolutionary leaders. This became clear in the spring of 1914, when there were serious uprisings in the factories and riotings in the streets. But neither the bureaucrats nor the man in the street, who was always ready to criticize the government but was hostile to revolution, were a bit alarmed. The successful suppression of the 1905–6 movement had given an assurance of the stability of the regime and deprived the newly awakened workers' movement of any dangerous aspect.

The British navy, and then the French navy with the President of the French Republic, were expected to arrive in St. Petersburg in the middle of the summer. On these occasions St. Petersburg put on her holiday dress and the court held a series of official receptions and banquets. There were references to the eternal Anglo-Russian and especially Franco-Russian friendship. The political skies were cloudless, and the members of the legislative chambers, closed in June for the summer vacations, had no foreboding of the storm on the horizon. I, too, went for the summer to my family home a few versts from the city of Tver.

PART SIX

The World War, 1914–1915

CHAPTER XXIII

THE PUBLIC AND THE GOVERNMENT IN THE FIRST MONTHS OF THE WAR

The July days were sunny and fair. As had happened during recent summers, the peat bogs of the gubernias of Tver, Novgorod, and St. Petersburg caught fire and the air for many miles around was filled with an acrid smoke. Russia, particularly rural Russia, was under the spell of its customary summer torpor.

On July 12, the twenty-fifth anniversary of the institution of the zemskie nachalniki, the zemskie nachalniki of Tver Uezd assembled for a reunion dinner, which I attended as the marshal of nobility of Tver Uezd. We had already received news of the assassination of the Austrian heir apparent at Sarajevo, but most people did not consider it an incident of international significance. Those present at the reunion dinner, including the vice-governor, who was present in Governor Biunting's absence, expressed extreme amazement when I pointed out in a dinner speech that Europe was on the eve of serious events.

Through the days that followed the provincial public was as calm as ever, though the papers were filled with the news of Austria's arrogant ultimatum to Serbia and the probable approach of a world conflict. This serenity was interrupted only by the orders for partial and then general mobilization. At Tver the examination of the reserves began on July 19. Mobilization was carried out in absolute order. The reservists (younger classes) arrived in full number and seemed to accept with composure their entry into the ranks. Because liquor shops had been closed there were no street brawls. The regular troops showed more nervousness. They moved to the border regions two days after the proclamation of mobilization. Troop trains were loaded in exemplary order. Women bidding their relatives farewell wept freely, and the faces of the soldiers registered emotion but their bearing was confident and composed.

The requisitioning of horses for army service, occurring as it did after mobilization, encountered some difficulties. In many peasant households women were now the heads of the families and they

537

displayed much displeasure and at times despair when the government began to requisition their best horses. I supervised some of this requisitioning and could describe many painful incidents in which women literally howled. At times I could not bear it and I must confess that on several occasions I left a family with a perfectly good horse by pronouncing it unfit for army service.

The sudden removal of the male population at first almost completely stopped operations in some industrial enterprises, but as regards agricultural work in Tver Gubernia it made no great difference. Those tasks which the men performed, such as haymowing, had already been finished; the harvesting of the crops, which were not extensive in Tver Gubernia, had always been the work of the women. Moreover, there were still some male laborers available, though wages for their work rose at once. The building trade, which required experienced workers, suffered somewhat, as the middle of July marks the height of the building season in northern Russia.

It cannot be said that the war was popular with the peasants. They experienced no patriotic exultation. The war aroused among them a muffled, submissive, sullen discontent, although the distribution of subsidies to the families of the soldiers about a month after the outbreak of hostilities greatly helped to dissipate this feeling. This business of subsidies was widely but poorly organized. No definite instructions were given as to what members of a family were entitled to subsidies. No mention was made of the age at which the male members of a household were to be considered incapable of work. Accordingly there were many discrepancies. Amounts given out as subsidies differed from uezd to uezd. The commissions formed to distribute these subsidies were attached to the zemstvo boards but had different attitudes toward their task; some of them were very careful of state or, rather, public money, while others distributed it freely. There were cases when a soldier's family, especially if it was large, would receive as much as thirty or even forty-five rubles a month, a sum which the man himself could not have earned. In such cases the women did not seem to mind the fact that their men had been drafted.

Although the war excited neither patriotism nor indignation among the peasants and factory workers, it deeply stirred the patriotic sentiments of the educated classes. It immediately welded the zemstvos into unity. All political differences disappeared. Cadets of all shades showed as great patriotic spirit as did persons of the

Right. Young scions of Left-wing Tver families, such as Bakunin,[1] went as volunteers to the front. The intelligentsia were not far behind; the zemstvo third element showed a readiness to work to the utmost for the needs of the country. Party aims, as far as could be judged from the politically articulate elements of Tver Gubernia, were temporarily abandoned.

The inveterate intriguers among the zemstvo ranks took another attitude. Prince G. E. Lvov immediately took steps to resurrect the All-Russian Zemstvo Union of which he had been the head during the Russo-Japanese War. When zemstvo workers gathered in Moscow to decide upon the organization of this body, it appeared at first that Count F. A. Uvarov, who was put forward by the Moscow zemstvo men, might defeat Prince Lvov as head of the All-Russian Zemstvo Union. But Russia's fate seems to have been foreordained. Count Uvarov declined the nomination. He had decided to go to the front with his Cossack troops in which he was a reserve officer, and all the entreaties of the Moscow zemstvo and others proved unavailing. Prince Lvov's supporters carried on an active campaign, and when the election was held no electors opposed to his candidacy were present. I was an elector from the Tver Gubernia zemstvo, and certainly I was not notified and was not present.

It is difficult to estimate the tremendous significance of Prince Lvov's election. Had Uvarov accepted the nomination, certainly a different story would have to be told. Uvarov was an old zemstvo man, careful and thorough, forceful and persevering. He would not have allowed the All-Russian Zemstvo Union to develop beyond his control. Prince Lvov, on the other hand, did not care whether or not the union became unwieldy. Among the zemstvo third element it was generally believed that the bureaucrats spent public funds inefficiently and even dishonestly. But in all Russian history there is no institution whose resources were spent so wildly as were those of the All-Russian Zemstvo Union. Had the war not ended in revolution, the heads of this union would surely have been called to account. As far as I know, Prince Lvov had at first no thought of leading a revolution. He enlisted renowned agitators in the ranks of his collaborators; but he did this, not to create machinery for the conducting of well-organized propaganda, but because his motto was to let all persons do as they wished. These anarchistic principles were later demonstrated to the full, and Russia paid and continues to pay for them dearly.

The government's attitude toward the All-Russian Zemstvo Union was incomprehensible. On the one hand, it treated the union with utter, complete, and sometimes open distrust; and, on the other, it supplied it with tens of millions of rubles and exercised no control over their expenditure. Under the pretext that zemstvo institutions were not subject to state control but were inspected by their own officers, Lvov persuaded Maklakov and his colleagues that the government should not control the All-Russian Zemstvo Union's expenditure of state funds, that such control by the government would be misconstrued by the zemstvos and the public and taken as an insult. This argument was ridiculously naïve and cannot stand criticism. The zemstvos had their own organs for controlling the expenditure of funds raised by zemstvo taxation. Such local control of local funds was theoretically quite understandable, but in practice it was hardly permissible. Not only has a state the right but it is even duty bound to supervise the expenditures of all sums used for public needs irrespective of their source. Any other arrangement is not to be tolerated where state funds are involved. When it is considered that the inspection commissions of the gubernia zemstvo assemblies convened for only ten or fourteen days yearly and had barely time to glance through the expense sheets of the zemstvo executive organizations—the boards—it becomes clear that these commissions could not supervise the spending of many millions by the All-Russian Zemstvo Union. Such supervision was a task with which the State Control alone could have hoped to cope, possessing as it did a large, well-organized, experienced, and permanent special personnel. It is true that a commission to inspect the activities of the All-Russian Zemstvo Union was elected by zemstvo deputies, but to what purpose? In the first place, and contrary to all zemstvo traditions, it was elected exclusively from the ranks of the zemstvo Left wing. Every member elected was sure to sing the praises of the Union's Central Committee. V. D. Kuzmin-Karavaev, an old Tver zemstvo man, about whose political convictions there was no doubt, was elected chairman. The commission's only achievement was a very superficial inspection of some institutions situated near the front. It made no audit of real expenditures, for it had decided quite correctly that even if its members (five or six) spent the rest of their lives auditing these expenditures they would not get through half of them. No report of the inspection was published, nor were the special deputies, who could report to the zemstvos, informed of it. The only report made was an oral one by Kuzmin-Karavaev during a special deputies' meeting and it made no reference to expenditures or statistics in any form; it was merely an eloquent eulogy of the work done by certain zemstvo detachments at the front. According to Kuzmin-Karavaev every private at the front knew that government institutions never had anything the soldiers needed, while the "All-Russian," as the Union was called at the front, had everything. This oral report was greeted with general applause and never again was there any question of audit or inspection. In the final analysis, the expenditures of the All-Russian Zemstvo Union were never once efficiently checked by any controlling agency.

But the All-Russian Zemstvo Union was something more than a body which included a multitude of revolutionary agitators on the one hand and many who desired to avoid active military service on the other. (The famous "Zemstvo Hussars" were a popular laughing-stock despite the general regard for the zemstvo organization.) Undoubtedly zemstvo detachments working at the front were well equipped. Certainly they had greater resources than corresponding government organizations. The zemstvo union did not care how much money it spent and was not bound by any maximum rates and fixed regulations. Government organizations, on the other hand, worked under different conditions and could not have worked otherwise. Money was appropriated to them according to a definite plan and all expenditures had to be made according to the normal prices set by the ministries in charge. Nevertheless, it must be said that the All-Russian Zemstvo Union did some good work and, to its credit, it did not engage in open revolutionary activity until the February revolution. By contrast, the activity of the All-Russian Union of Towns was revolutionary from the outset.[2]

Meanwhile the war was going on. At its outset, party conflicts among the zemstvo and nobility circles suddenly disappeared. Everyone threw himself with enthusiasm into work that was within the scope of the zemstvo and nobility organizations. Base hospitals were organized on a large scale; the cost was not counted. All-Russian Zemstvo yearly budgets were revised and all items not concerning immediate and indispensable needs were excluded. Little attention was paid to expenses that would be entailed by the efficient upkeep of the new hospitals, as it was firmly believed that the war would be short. For instance, an extraordinary assembly of the Tver nobility at first decided to appropriate all its reserve funds for the organization of a hospital in the nobility assembly hall; but it did not consider expenses of maintenance. It was difficult to persuade these gentlemen to consider the possibility of a lengthy war. About the time of this special assembly, news arrived announcing that England had joined the Allies and that Italy, Germany's ally, would remain neutral. Some prophesied that the war would be over in six weeks. Some recalled the Franco-Prussian War of 1870–71 and foretold that this war would be just as short but with opposite results. In vain did level-headed persons try to point out that presumably Germany was not unprepared for this international conflict she had brought about, and that even though the eventual victory of the Allies, given their harmonious co-operation, could be considered certain, yet the struggle would be hard and long. "To Berlin, to Berlin!" was the general optimistic outcry. Thoughtful people were very much alarmed by this attitude for they recalled that in 1870 the French had entered the war with just such bravado but with tragic results.

Assurance of the immediate triumph of the Allies and the brevity of the war reigned also in the upper administrative circles of St. Petersburg. On one occasion, after the Tsar had received the members of the legislative chambers in the Winter Palace, Shcheglovitov and Krivoshein addressed some of the members. Both men expressed their assurance of a quick victory over Germany. Shcheglovitov said with characteristic pleasantry: "Vasilii Fedorovich (Emperor William II) has made a mistake; he won't be able to hold out." Krivoshein was of the same mind; he made it evident that he considered this war almost a boon for Russia. When the conversation turned to a discussion of resuming the sessions of the legislative bodies, Krivoshein insisted upon waiting until the following February. The members of the Duma, on the other hand, desired to have the sessions opened on November 1. Rubbing his hands nervously, which was with him a sign of self-satisfaction, Krivoshein said to them: "You should rely on us [the government], gentlemen, and everything will be fine." The government was quite persuaded of our military preparedness.

In the first days of the war many were carried away and filled with high hopes by the sight of the people's demonstration before the Winter Palace. An enormous crowd had filled the entire square adjoining the palace, and, when the Tsar appeared on the balcony, had gone down upon its knees and sung "God Save the Tsar." This impressive manifestation had inspired the government to issue a special act proclaiming the unity of Tsar and people. The government even decreed a new flag symbolic of the union of public and official Russia. Alas, this spirit waned all too soon! But even while it lasted some saw fit to explain that the new symbolic flag could not be used as an ordinary flag and must not exceed a certain number of square inches in size. The emblem of unification became a toy, lost all significance, and was soon entirely forgotten.

As the war went on, the desire of the public to participate in the country's great tasks had to be recognized by the government for psychological reasons if for no others. The Russian public forces had so far matured by 1914 that it was impossible to restrict their role to that of mere onlookers, as had been possible during the war of 1877–78. Now they had to be given an active share in the common tasks. This was done, but with bad grace and with much bickering. To be sure, the government was in a difficult position. Its shortcomings were pointed out by the opposition, which was supported by the revolutionary elements. This criticism of the government had a considerable effect upon the public, which tended to forgive public organizations everything—even the defects in their work which were disclosed—such defects the public generally ascribed to the government's evil activity and calumnies. The government suffered greatly from its inability to use publicity and the press to strengthen its own position. Military successes would have aided greatly in this direction, but after the first victories—the invasion of East Prussia and the capture of Lvov[3]—our military successes ended.

The progress of events at the front was reflected in the reactions of people in the provinces. At Tver, where I passed the first six months of the war, the news of our capture of Lvov made a tremendous impression. The wounded arriving at the Tver hospitals were mainly from the Austrian front and were in fine spirits. They all spoke of the "masses and masses of our men over there" and said "our success is sure." This feeling infected the population and rumors of a near peace became widespread. But the mood soon changed. The unexpected annihilation of Samsonov's[4] army near Soldau created utter consternation. It was a bolt from the blue. To make matters worse the communiqué issued on this was poorly worded. It concluded with an assurance that this defeat did not necessarily mean the loss of the war. At that time no Russian dreamed that the war would end in our defeat; the very mention of such a possibility created a feeling of anxiety and shook the people's firm conviction in a speedy victory for Russian and allied arms. Dark rumors of treason were spread about. Where they originated or to what degree they were initiated by our revolutionary elements or German agents, it is difficult to ascertain. At any rate many people who were certainly not anti-national became pessimistic. Many who before Soldau had sung hymns to the tune of "Thunder on, O Victory" now mourned "Everything is lost."

When the war of movement and maneuver gave way to trench warfare and a war of position, the people lost some of their acute interest in news from the front. To them the war became something like a protracted, ever painful illness, foreign to their everyday life and threatening unexpected developments. Any other attitude could hardly have been expected. The enthusiasm of the first days had vanished. The purposes of the war were not clear, and the government did nothing to explain to the people the real meaning and significance of the struggle or to show to what extent the welfare of the country and the people would depend on its favorable outcome. The people grew indifferent and this indifference was fed by the scarcity of news from the front. The official bulletins included little but general information pertaining either to the entire front or to a large sector of it. Mention of what troops were engaged in a certain battle and of their commanding officers was prohibited.* As a result the people lost interest in the official communiqués, which soon stopped altogether. This withholding of news had another effect: the war did not produce one national hero. In the Russo-Turkish War of 1877–78, for instance, I recall that the names of Skobelev and my late father were heard all over Russia. The people need heroes. Hero worship uplifts the people, gives them faith in their power and future success. It may be said that there were no heroes to produce; but a hero can always be created. What was needed was not to conceal the names of the commanders but to make known the names of those who distinguished themselves, so as to create an interest in the war and stimulate hopes for its success. The Empress Catherine realized this full well. So did Napoleon. Were all Catherine's eagles and Napoleon's marshals really so exceptional? Yet the very fact of their glorification created an atmosphere of heroism and enthusiasm.

* In spite of this prohibition the Germans always knew what Russian forces were opposing them and with what commanding officers they would have to deal.

In November the legislative chambers resumed their sessions for a few days. The examination of the state budget had lost all meaning; the state expenditures it listed were the same as for the preceding year; the tremendous expenses connected with the war were outside the budget and were not to be appropriated by the legislature. Nor was there any important legislative measure put before the Duma, and its work was reduced to making efforts to raise the people's morale. In this it achieved some success; but, in contrast, the State Council demonstrated once more its deadness and senile impotence.

Early in 1915 came rumors of a lack of ammunition and rifles at the front. These were vigorously denied by the War Ministry and especially by the Chief Artillery Administration.[5] The State Council readily ascribed them to Russian impressionability.

At the same time there were rumors of embezzlements in the ministries in charge of providing the various supplies for the army. For a long time the Ministry of the Navy had had a reputation for embezzlement, and when war broke out it was said that this ministry evinced its patriotic feelings by suspending all graft in the making of large contracts. Soon, however, it was reported that graft was again being practiced in the high places of the Ministry of the Navy. All this excited Duma circles, and by the time the news reached the masses it had become exaggerated to the proportions of a nightmare. The public was further indignant at the fact, petty in itself, that automobiles carrying ladies, many of whom were well-known courtesans, were seen in the streets of St. Petersburg, whereas all private cars had been requisitioned for military use. "So this is what our cars were taken away for?" said former car owners. The military authorities issued orders to all officials provided with automobiles for service needs not to let ladies use these vehicles. But the order was not strictly enforced. The courtesans disappeared, but the wives of the officials continued to use the military cars. This matter provoked the people and augmented the distrust and irritation that grew out of the bad news from the front.

Then, about March 1915, the St. Petersburg factories producing munitions ran short of coal. In normal times all our coal came from England in ships which took away in exchange our grain brought to St. Petersburg over the Mariinsky Canal system. With the closing of the port of St. Petersburg coal had to be brought from the Don Basin. This presented a novel problem for our railways. The increased transportation of coal to St. Petersburg retarded the transportation of foodstuffs to the capital and the prices for certain food commodities began to rise. Just at that time some members of the State Council who were interested in economic problems, including members elected by industrialists, organized a so-called Economic Conference to study current economic problems. A. S. Ermolov, former Minister of Agriculture, was elected chairman. But no sooner had the conference finished studying its first problem—the ways and means of getting an adequate supply of coal to St. Petersburg and of increasing the output of coal in the mines*—than it was dissolved by the government. On the very day when the results of the studies were to be reported to a wider circle of the State Council, Ermolov was summoned before the chairman of that body and told that the members of the State Council had no right to enter the Mariinsky Palace except to attend the sessions of the legislative chambers; as for the Economic Conference, it was to discontinue immediately all meetings and debates.

Of all the government's prohibitive measures at that time this was an outstanding example of a suspicious and critical attitude toward manifestations of public activity which were not only perfectly harmless but even capable of achieving desirable results. With one hand, the government gave to questionable persons the uncontrolled disposal of hundreds of millions of rubles, and with the other it forbade the meekest members of the State Council to assemble under the leadership of a minister of many years' standing to discuss problems having no relation whatever to politics.

Every revolution begins at the top; and our government had succeeded in transforming the most loyal elements of the country into critics, if not of the regime, then at any rate of those at its head and of their administrative methods. Criticism of the government's activity spread in ever widening circles to affect increasingly larger masses of the population. Meanwhile the government did nothing to influence public opinion in its own favor. Goremykin, the Chairman of the Council of Ministers, gave no sign of his existence. To his innate aversion to any kind of activity was now added senile

---

* This problem of coal output was studied very thoroughly by the conference, with the close participation of N. F. Ditmar, who was a member of the State Council and also Chairman of the Permanent Council of Mine Owners of South Russia with headquarters in Kharkov, and who in his latter capacity was in a position to know exactly the conditions in the Don Basin.

helplessness. He had moved to the enormous residence on Mokho-
vaia, and there he locked himself up and saw no one but his closest
colleagues in the Council of Ministers. As during the First Duma,
he had no communication with the members of the legislative
chambers.* In February, 1915, however, Goremykin decided to
give a reception for the members of the Duma and the State Council.
Evidently he desired to show that he was not hostile to them but
would like to be on good terms with them.

The reception was ridiculous. The members of the extreme
Left wing of the Duma did not accept the invitation, but almost all
other members felt it their duty to be present. A great crowd gathered, filling the rooms of Goremykin's residence. The rooms were
almost devoid of furniture, since nearly all the furnishings had been
ordered in Italy before the war and could not be brought to Russia
after war broke out. Goremykin was lost in the crowd. Soon he
went to his study on the lower floor, where were gathered a few of
his intimate friends. Most of the other guests, tired of elbowing
their way about, soon departed. Only a few ministers remained.
Then a telegram arrived announcing our retreat in the Avgustovo
woods and our army's great losses. Goremykin, perspiring and worn
out by the reception, sat on the upper landing of the main staircase. Before him stood several ministers, Krivoshein, Rukhlov, and
others, discussing the news with great animation and some apprehension. Goremykin took no part in the discussion; apparently he was
utterly indifferent. Suddenly he seemed to come to his senses. He
raised his head and repeated several times: "N'est-ce pas que c'est
très spacieux ici?"

---

* Individual members of the Duma visited him at times, but these were few.
The most frequent such visitor was his relative by marriage, P. N. Krupensky,[6]
who became so famous in the days of the Provisional Government when an investigation of the records of the Police Department revealed that this department had
paid him 20,000 rubles.[7] Krupensky could not deny this fact and was obliged to
surrender his title of deputy. During the Third Duma this nimble man was a sort
of mediator between the government and the lower legislative body: a spy for
both sides. He played openly a double game. He was a past master of backstage
negotiations and intrigue and possessed an uncanny capacity for forming or dissolving different groupings in the Duma, undoubtedly according to the instructions of
his government. He was also a specialist at organizing political clubs. Apparently
he pursued this specialty for personal gain, as these clubs were generally organized
with government money. During the war he also obtained large sums from banking and industrial circles for the organization of the so-called Economic Club in
the large house which he rented on the Moika near the Tsaritsyn Lug.

This may have been a ruse to divert the conversation from an unpleasant subject, or it might have been his way of saying "Oh, never mind." Those present saw in his outburst a senile weakness of mind.

One thing was clear: Goremykin was no longer the calm, level-headed, resourceful man of 1906; he was a weak, old man, capable at best of petty, childish tricks, avidly clinging to power, or, rather, to those material goods which power brought him.

CHAPTER XXIV

THE GROWTH OF OPPOSITION TO THE EMPEROR AND HIS ADVISERS

Perhaps the first event of the war which made the public fear seriously for the successful outcome of the struggle was our retreat in the Avgustovo woods in February 1915, which left the Germans in possession of the entire border region near Verzhbolovo. It was at the same time that the first definitely alarming news of the shortage of ammunition reached St. Petersburg. Against Austria, however, our advance through the Carpathians was still pushing forward and the capture of the Austrian fortress of Przemysl in March served somewhat to appease the fears of the public. But the true conditions at the front were not generally known until May 1915 when news arrived of our forced retreat from Galicia after the defeat on the Dunajec. Then it became known that as early as December 1914 our troops situated on the Bzura and defending the approaches to Warsaw had been ordered by the Stavka (General Headquarters) to fire no more than sixty shells per field piece per month, that is, one shot in the morning and one in the evening of each day.

Other facts also became known then for the first time. It was learned that at the very beginning of the war the Putilov works had inquired whether there would be need of an increased output of guns and ammunition; if so, the works would have to increase their technical equipment. The Chief Artillery Administration had replied that there would be no need of any extra output. The Chief Artillery Administration had also refused to place an order for shells with the "Pulemet" Company. This had occurred in November, when the shortage of ammunition was already being felt and when the Stavka was demanding insistently that the Ministry of War increase the supplies of ammunition for the front.

It was but natural that the fears created by our losses in battle and aggravated by the above-mentioned knowledge of the ammunition shortage should sharpen the discontent of the public with the government. The ominous word "treason" ran like an electric current through all strata of society and with the assistance of the revolutionists finally reached the masses. Among the workers the cry of "treason" became a veritable battle-cry and an excellent pretext for riots and various demands.

Political circles also took alarm. Their attacks upon Minister of War V. A. Sukhomlinov, if not upon the entire government, began with a very sensational report made in St. Petersburg by P. P. Riabushinsky,[1] the leader of the Moscow merchants and a member of the opposition. Riabushinsky had just returned from the front and in his report declared that the soldiers in the front lines had neither ammunition nor arms, that whole units were without rifles and were armed only with clubs. This report was made in a very excited, almost hysterical tone and ended in a general appeal to start manufacturing firearms and ammunition. I cannot say to what extent Riabushinsky intended to sharpen the general indignation at the government, but his words conveyed a profound patriotic feeling and created a tremendous impression. The facts he quoted spread with lightning speed over the city and over the country. The permanent council of the congresses of industry, finance, and commerce immediately summoned a special congress of all representatives of these three branches of public activity and resolved at once to organize central and local military-industrial committees which would mobilize Russian industry for the work of defense.

The leaders of the Duma also became excited. Rodzianko,[2] its chairman, with the consent of the Stavka moved that a special commission be organized to discuss the needs of the army and that this commission be comprised of representatives of the government and of representatives from both legislative chambers.

The government saw that in so grave a moment it was impossible to protest against the desires of the public and made some concessions. It permitted the organization of the War Industry Committees. It even allowed the inclusion in them of representatives of factory workers. It also agreed to the election of Guchkov as head of the new committees. Guchkov was chosen for this position by the Special Congress of representatives of industry, finance, and commerce mentioned above. Also, in accord with a suggestion by Rodzianko, a conference on defense was organized. Both of these organizations, especially the second, played a great part in providing the army with what it needed.

In June 1915, and after prolonged effort, the public secured the dismissal of Sukhomlinov, Minister of War, and three other ministers: Maklakov, Minister of the Interior, who had become notorious for his hostility to any public activity; Sabler, Ober-Prokuror of the Holy Synod, who was trying to ingratiate himself with Rasputin; and Shcheglovitov, Minister of Justice, who was allegedly working against the independence of the courts. The fact that the Duma was soon to meet had something to do with effecting these dismissals, but the main influence to this end was exerted by a group of progressive ministers, headed by Kharitonov. In May 1915 these progressive ministers had told Goremykin that they would not work any longer with Maklakov, Sabler, and Shcheglovitov. They had asked him either to dismiss these three or themselves. Goremykin had reported this to the Tsar, who had been very much displeased; but the general excitement, reflected in the debates of the Duma, had forced Nicholas II to agree to the demands of the Kharitonov group. The supreme power evidently preferred to have a renovated ministry appear before the Duma in the hope of lessening its attacks on the government.

As for Sukhomlinov, matters did not stop with his dismissal. At the instance of the Duma, which convened on July 9 for the summer sessions, a special commission, including representatives of the legislative chambers, was organized to ascertain who was really responsible for the failure to send supplies to the army. This commission investigated Sukhomlinov's activities and finally demanded that he be indicted before the courts. Sukhomlinov's trial[3] was accorded so much publicity and discredited the existing regime to such a degree that it may be fitting to pause and analyze his personality.

Sukhomlinov had begun his career as a cavalryman in the guards. Then, after graduation from the General Staff Academy, he soon gained a reputation as a brilliant, well-educated, and resourceful cavalryman. He had a clever pen and a sense of humor, and made a name for himself by his articles on military subjects published in the military journal, *Razvedchik*,[4] under the pseudonym, "Ostap Bondarenko." He was a good mixer; he knew how to meet and charm people; consequently he passed swiftly through the first ranks of service as General Staff officer. He became principal of the officers' cavalry school and later, still a young man, commander of a cavalry division with headquarters at Kharkov. At that time he was married to a fine, much-respected woman and both his official and family life proceeded normally. His salary was then quite adequate for the life he was leading. Unfortunately his wife soon died. He then fell in love with and married the widow of a civil engineer. Sukhomlinov's second wife had had a rather Bohemian past. She had been closely connected with the theatrical world of Kharkov, Kiev, and Odessa and had been accustomed to merry suppers in restaurants and drinking parties at home. Sukhomlinov's life now changed radically. His house was open to all kinds of people. There was a round of dinners and suppers where wine flowed freely. The expenses entailed greatly exceeded his salary. Financial difficulties became increasingly acute and Sukhomlinov fell into the hands of men who supplied him with money but bound him with something stronger than promissory notes. Outwardly, however, everything remained the same and Sukhomlinov continued to advance in his brilliant career. He was appointed commander of the troops of the Kiev Military District and Governor of Kiev. The salaries of these combined posts, it might be thought, should have freed him of the shady characters who surrounded him at the time; but such was not the case. His expenses continued to exceed his income. He became more and more dependent upon all sorts of questionable persons. Among these there was one in particular with whom Sukhomlinov would not part. When Sukhomlinov was appointed Chief of the General Staff and, later, Minister of War, this man, whose true character has since been ascertained beyond a doubt, followed him to St. Petersburg. This man was Altschuler, an Austrian Jew and a spy of the Austrian General Staff. While Sukhomlinov was Minister of War he was often warned against Altschuler. He was also warned against the suspicious relations of one of his subordinates, Miasoedov,[5] with the German authorities. Miasoedov was a former chief of the gendarme station at Verzhbolovo. He had gained Sukhomlinov's confidence to such an extent that the General had had him restored to the gendarme corps on the Tsar's order and against the will of the Police Department. He was even detailed to serve Sukhomlinov himself. His ultimate fate is well known. During the war he was suspected of being a German spy, tried by court-martial, convicted, and executed.

Altschuler and Miasoedov were not the only persons who possessed Sukhomlinov's confidence and were at the same time somehow engaged in military espionage. But it seems highly improbable that Sukhomlinov himself was consciously accessory to the activities of these shady personages, as was later affirmed. His personal

interests as a minister who enjoyed the confidence and favor of the
Tsar were too much at variance with such conduct. The large sums
(about 700,000 rubles) discovered in his possession at the time of
his arrest were not large enough to be considered as pay for treason.
Treason would unquestionably have brought him a much larger
amount. Besides, the origin of this money was established at the
inquiry. It had been made from stock-market speculations conducted
for him by one of the St. Petersburg banks which was connected
with various enterprises working for the army and which hoped by
being useful to the Minister of War to obtain more war orders.
Sukhomlinov was guilty of masked bribery but of no more than
that, and the basic cause of it all was his inordinately large expenses.
These had continued even after the death of his second wife; for he
had married again, and his third wife, formerly Madame Butovich,
was as lavish and improvident as his second. She had spent large
sums on her clothes, for which purpose she had often gone to Paris.
This expense, together with the continued round of receptions, had
been more than Sukhomlinov's ministerial salary, doubled at the
orders of the Tsar, and his very considerable traveling expenses to
remote spots like Turkestan or Vladivostok, could cope with. So he
had had recourse to stock-market speculations conducted by a bank
without any risk to himself.

Sukhomlinov was neither a traitor nor a deceiver. Nevertheless,
the fact that he was at all times surrounded by spies has been firmly
established. Perhaps this can be explained by his exceptional light-
mindedness. He did not believe that either Altschuler or Miasoedov
could be a spy; but for some obscure reason, in which the friendship
of his third wife for the wife of Miasoedov played a part, he did
not wish to ascertain officially what sort of persons these men were.
Nor did Sukhomlinov consciously confide any secret information to
them, but inasmuch as he babbled about everything of a confidential
nature that he happened to know he must have betrayed many a
secret. Never, however, was he a cold-blooded or a willful, and still
less a mercenary, traitor.

Sukhomlinov's trial was one of the outstanding events of Russian history during the World War. Just how wise it was to hold
this trial at such a time is open to debate. While the opposition
demanded his trial both in the interest of abstract justice and for
the purpose of discrediting the existing order, the Right blamed the
government for holding it. The Right argued that a scandalous trial

that revealed in time of war our military defects would not correct these defects but would merely undermine the confidence of the people and the army in ultimate victory.

However that may be, the people acclaimed Sukhomlinov's dismissal just as unanimously as they acclaimed the appointment of A. A. Polivanov[5a] as his successor. The Cadet party, which was then most influential in forming public opinion, considered Polivanov more or less its member. Polivanov was on the best of terms with Guchkov. The Right, however, doubted Polivanov's loyalty and would have preferred to have a Minister of War better known to it. It had no candidate of its own, however; so it accepted Polivanov. Polivanov's appointment was a patent concession to the demands of the public and was accepted as such by the Duma.

Polivanov was undoubtedly superior to Sukhomlinov as Minister of War. He was well-informed, serious, industrious, conscientious, and experienced in the problems of that office. His talent for being on good terms with the legislature also served him well. Later, however, as chairman of the Provisional Government's commission which worked out the "rights of the soldier"[6] he became the object of deep scorn. Polivanov not only failed to direct the commission's work so as to preserve the necessary military discipline but even sided with those who worked out a project under which the army was bound to become an unruly mob of hooligans. This conversion of the army into a mob actually occurred after the project had been confirmed by Guchkov's successor as Minister of War—Kerensky.[7]

The offices left vacant by the dismissal of Maklakov and Sabler were filled by two public men: Prince N. B. Shcherbatov,[8] who became Minister of the Interior, and A. D. Samarin, who became Ober-Prokuror of the Holy Synod. Both these men enjoyed a blameless reputation. Samarin, the marshal of the Moscow nobility, belonged to a venerable Slavophile family. It was known that he would not compromise, and there was confidence that with him as Ober-Prokuror of the Holy Synod Rasputin, of whose role all Russia was talking, would not be permitted to influence the affairs of the church. Samarin's extreme Rightist convictions were hardly acceptable to the opposition, but his public work and the halo of integrity which surrounded his name precluded any criticism of his entry into the government.

Prince Shcherbatov had won fame as an agriculturist. As chairman of the agricultural society of Poltava, he had succeeded in making the work of this organization extremely fruitful. He had been the marshal of the Poltava nobility, and later a member of the State Council elected by the Poltava zemstvo. Before the war he had been appointed head of the Chief Administration of State Stud Farms and, according to the reports of specialists, had organized this branch of stock raising extremely well. Straightforward and honest, he accepted his new post of Minister of the Interior very unwillingly. He felt that the educated classes of Russia—the nobility and the zemstvo—were not revolutionary, and that their opposition to the government was the result of a long misunderstanding. In short, he seemed to be a proper person for the post of Minister of the Interior.

But, alas, neither Samarin nor Shcherbatov was equal to his tasks. The Russian bureaucracy had its defects, but at least it knew administrative technique. Samarin and Shcherbatov were dilettantes and their dilettantism showed itself very soon. Shcherbatov decided to effect a "clean-up" of the administrative personnel in gubernias, and to this end he discharged a number of old-time governors and replaced them with zemstvo men. But once in office these latter immediately absorbed all the defects of the bureaucracy without assimilating its technical training. Shcherbatov also failed to display the energy and the moral strength which his office demanded.

The dismissal of Shcheglovitov was also acclaimed by the public, for he had acquired fame as a perverter of the statutes of Alexander II. His successor, Aleksandr Alekseevich Khvostov,[9] was little known to the public, however, but was very popular in legal circles.

The dismissal of Sukhomlinov, Maklakov, Sabler, and Shcheglovitov was an act which was not influenced by Rasputin and which was carried out not at the insistence of the Empress but even against her will; and the selection of their successors was the result of an agreement between the Stavka and Krivoshein, who enjoyed at that time special influence with the Emperor and Empress. Polivanov was advanced mainly by the Stavka, Samarin and Shcherbatov by Krivoshein, and Khvostov by his friend Goremykin.

Krivoshein regarded these changes as a preliminary step by which he could oust Goremykin. In his estimation, the new ministers would soon see for themselves the impossibility of having as their chief the elderly cunctator who desired less and less to face the new conditions of political life in the country. Early in 1915 Krivoshein had become persuaded that with Goremykin as its head the government could never meet the demands of current events. Striving, as usual, to smooth out the differences between the bureaucracy and the public, Krivoshein dreamed of organizing a governmental body whose members should be, as far as possible, representatives of the public. He was also concerned with winning for the government the support of Moscow business circles and with planning to appoint as Minister of Commerce and Industry a prominent Moscow manufacturer, G. A. Krestovnikov,[10] who was very influential among the Moscow business men.

Krivoshein considered himself the natural choice to succeed Goremykin. So did the Tsar, but at the last moment Krivoshein seemed to shy from the enormous responsibility he would have to assume and persuaded the Tsar to form for the duration of the war a government headed by Polivanov. Krivoshein would then become Vice-Chairman of the Council of Ministers and take charge of the civil administration. This was a tactical error on the part of Krivoshein. The Tsar did not like Polivanov and had little confidence in him. This may explain why the Tsar's confidence in Krivoshein began to wane. At any rate, the Tsar refused to discharge Goremykin, whose profound loyalty he had no reason to doubt. Later changes in the personnel of the Council of Ministers were inspired by Rasputin.

In May our situation at the front had indeed been serious, but during July and August it became steadily worse. The people's fears grew as our army retreated, and in the middle of July after the abandonment of Brest-Litovsk and Grodno without resistance, these fears reached their peak. It was rumored that our capital was in danger of capture by the enemy and that steps were being taken to remove the art treasures from the city. The government was just as panic-stricken as the people, if not more so. On July 16, 1915, Polivanov made a report on the situation at the front. "I consider it my duty as a citizen and an official to announce to the Council of Ministers that our country is in danger." So he began. Then he proceeded to draw a terrifying picture of the conditions in the Russian army. "The army is becoming steadily demoralized. Cases of desertion and surrender are assuming tremendous proportions. The Germans are pursuing us with artillery alone; their infantry takes no part in the action; we are powerless to withstand their gunfire, deprived as we are of ammunition. Moreover, the Germans are suffering no losses, while we are losing men by the thousands."

This report greatly overdrew the picture at the front and struck terror into the hearts of the ministers. This terror was intensified by the fact that the retreating army was spreading in the rear that disorganization which accompanies every retreat; the situation was made worse by the lack of co-ordination between the orders of the civil authorities and the orders of the Stavka. According to the statute on the field administration of the troops (*polevoe upravlenie voisk*) the Stavka had supreme authority in all regions situated near the front. This statute had been adopted on the supposition that the army would be under the supreme command of the Tsar. As early as the third day of the war Nicholas II had intended to assume the supreme command, but under pressure from his ministers he had abandoned this plan. Subsequently the Stavka was declared to be in command not only of the rear but also of the capital of the empire, and in this way the civil government became subordinated to changing military commanders of secondary abilities, since the best ones were sent to the front. The power these second-rate commanders enjoyed went to their heads. They imagined themselves great potentates and lectured the government as if it were a presuming subordinate. Often they carried out their own private policies in matters concerning the maintenance of law and order in the country in regard to the press, labor problems, and public organizations. The Governor of St. Petersburg became subordinated to the Commander of the St. Petersburg Military District and reported to the Minister of the Interior only the things he chose to report. This situation was bound to be reflected in the general state of affairs. From the start the Stavka had used all of its extraordinary prerogatives and had become a sort of dictator.

The question of the relations between the civil government and the Stavka constituted a frequent subject of discussion in the Council of Ministers. All the ministers complained about the arbitrary actions of the rear military commanders. In July, Shcherbatov painted a vivid word picture of the situation before the Council of Ministers. He made it clear that both General Yanushkevich,[11] Chief of Staff of the Commander, and General N. A. Danilov,[12] commander of the rear of the Northwestern Front (nicknamed the "Red" to distinguish him from General G. N. Danilov,[13] the "Black," who was Quartermaster General of the Stavka) had acquired dictatorial habits which were imitated by all their subordinates, including even lieutenants. The civil authorities were obliged to comply with the most absurd demands. "It is impossible to understand," they said, "whose orders are to be executed, and whose are not. Orders fall upon us in torrents and frequently contradict each other. Consequently the chaos and turmoil is beyond conception, and the least objections of the civil authorities are met with shouts and threats, almost with arrests. It is under these conditions that the army is retreating, followed by refugees who have left their homes, some of their own will but most of them on orders of the military command." Shcherbatov's remarks caused Krivoshein to observe bitterly: "We are being beaten by the Germans at the front and by lieutenants in the rear."

Meanwhile there were tens and hundreds of thousands of refugees. Many of these had left their homes to escape the rumored savageries and brutalities of the Germans, but most of them had been moved by orders of the Russian military command in order that the regions surrendered to the enemy might be laid waste. People had been torn away from their homes with but a few hours in which to settle their affairs. Their stores of food and at times even their houses had been burned before their very eyes. It is easy to imagine the frame of mind of these refugees. Homeless and hungry, beset with hardship and privation, they were intensely hostile to the authorities. Slowly they moved eastward, blocking all roadways with a solid mass of humanity and carts filled with all sorts of household possessions, hindering military transport, and introducing chaos into the life of the rear. It was impossible to feed and shelter these multitudes. Hundreds died of hunger, exposure, and sickness. The highways were strewn with unburied dead. And while tens of thousands dragged themselves along the railway tracks, they were passed by trains filled with all sorts of rubbish, including cages containing canary birds belonging to officials of the department of army supply. The refugee wave aggravated the hardships of war throughout all Russia, increased the food shortage, and created housing and other problems.

On August 4 Krivoshein said at a session of the Council: "The masses of refugees moving eastward in an unbroken front are trampling the crops, ruining the hayfields, and destroying the forests. Curses, illness, misery, and poverty prevail over the face of Russia. The starved and ragged refugees are creating panic wherever they appear. Where they have passed the land is like a desert. Not only the rear, but the homeland itself is being put to waste and ruin."

The situation became particularly acute about the middle of August. The Council learned that the Stavka was discussing a project to widen the rear to the Tver-Tula line; it learned also that the Commander in Chief of the Southwestern Front, General Ivanov,[14] intended to remove the population of the front a hundred versts inland and to evacuate Kiev. The Council held that for many reasons the population should not have been removed nor its belongings destroyed. Besides, the evacuation was being conducted ruthlessly and as a result the peasants were arming themselves to guard their property. The military authorities were also destroying factories and their supplies of raw materials and manufactured goods and taking no steps to move such supplies inland. "We cannot permit 'Red' Danilov and his horde of rear heroes to devastate the central provinces," exclaimed Prince Shcherbatov.

Early in August the Council had to face another very acute problem. This concerned the Jewish population deported by the military command from the entire front and sent far inland. The Stavka, perhaps for a good reason, did not trust the Jews, who were suspected of spying and signaling to the enemy. But to base the removal of the entire Jewish population, even though it included many traitors, upon this assumption was wholly unjustifiable.

The senseless and ugly treatment which the Jews received from the military command had troublesome results. The foreign press and foreign Jewish banking circles were indignant; the former criticized us in the papers and the latter threatened to discontinue all credits. The Minister of Finance announced that he had been visited by the bankers Kamenka, Varshavsky, and Ginsburg, who had practically delivered an ultimatum, demanding that this shameless persecution of their people be stopped.

The situation in which the Jews were placed was further complicated by the fact that legally they had no right to move inland to territories outside the pale of Jewish settlement. In some places the local population met them with everything but physical violence. Under these conditions the Council decided that the government should grant the Jews the right to reside in all parts of the empire except in the Cossack territories, where the hatred toward the Jews was so great that such a move would have had serious results, and in other regions such as those situated near the residences of the Tsar—"the regions under the competence of the Ministry of the Imperial Court."

There was a short debate on the means of carrying out this measure. It could not be put into effect through Article 87 while the Duma was in session, but to pass it through the Duma would be a slow process and possibly difficult. It was problematical whether the Fourth Duma would adopt so radical a measure. The Council finally decided to put the measure into effect through the agency of the Minister of the Interior, based upon Article 158,[15] dealing with the establishment of the ministries, which gave ministers the right to transcend the existing laws in cases of acute necessity. The only person who voted against the measure, although he refused to have his vote officially recorded, was S. V. Rukhlov, an ardent Russian nationalist. "I do not wish to cause any discord," he said, "but I cannot support this decision. It means that while the entire country is suffering, the only ones to get privileges are the Jews." Prince Shakhovskoi (the only protégé of Rasputin in the Council of Ministers at that time) moved that the Jews be permitted to reside wherever they wished, not only in cities but also in rural districts; but this motion was not seconded.

In the meantime conditions at the front were going from bad to worse. Yanushkevich's greatest concern was to shift all blame on the rear and the civil authorities. He laid the blame for the shortage of firearms and ammunition upon those branches of the government which were responsible for provisioning the army, and in doing so he overlooked the fact that the Stavka had known the exact amount of supplies on hand and in the Carpathian adventure had disregarded the necessity of sparing our ammunition, of using it for defense and not for extending the front lines, until such time as these supplies should be increased. It would seem that the military were less eager to have the public assist in making up deficiencies in military supplies than to save face before public opinion, which had forced the Stavka to court the favor of public organizations to such a great extent. The military realized that it was these public organizations and not the government and its agents that made public opinion.

This play for the favor of public opinion was in a measure permissible, but the Stavka went much farther. Toward the end of July it telegraphed to the military censors who were then controlling the press and ordered them not to concern themselves any longer even with matters which were not necessarily military secrets. The design here was as simple as it was cynical. All military activities were to be considered as secret; therefore the press was not to dwell upon them. The government, however, could be criticized without restraint. The entire blame for the state of affairs might thus be placed upon the government. This was what actually occurred. Prince Shcherbatov mentioned many times in the Council of Ministers that these military orders made it impossible to handle the press, but the Council did not help him to correct this situation and he lacked the personal courage to act alone. Yet as Minister of the Interior he had considerable power. All he needed to do was to summon the editors of various publications and tell them that, although he had no right to subject their publications to preliminary censorship (as a matter of fact, he could have done even that in time of war; it could be done even in republican France, not to mention monarchical countries), he still had the right to banish them.

To crown it all, Yanushkevich invented a method, monstrous in theory and ineffective in practice, to improve the fighting strength of the Russian army. In a letter to Krivoshein he wrote: "Fabulous heroes, idealists, and altruists are few; they constitute perhaps not more than one per cent of our soldiers; the rest are selfish and ordinary. The Russian soldier," continued this surprising estimate of Russian military valor, "must be given a material interest in resisting the enemy. . . . . He must be induced to do so by a promise of additional land; surrender must be punished by deprivation of land allotments now owned." Yanushkevich suggested that the size of the additional allotments should be six to nine desiatins per soldier.

This letter made the ministers indignant. Such wholesale discrediting of the Russian soldiers, who were without arms and were being killed by the thousands and who, according to Napoleon's estimate, had no equal in the world—this, together with the business of making heroes of them by bribing them, brought the ministers to despair. Besides, Yanushkevich's idea was utterly impracticable, since there was not enough land in the entire empire to make such additional allotments to the several million soldiers. The transformation of any army into so many *Landsknechte* was a novel idea indeed! As Prince Shcherbatov correctly observed: "No one has yet been able to buy heroism. Love of country and self-sacrifice have no market value." Krivoshein exclaimed excitedly: "Why should poor Russia be made to suffer all these tragedies? I can be silent no longer, regardless of the consequences for myself." The majority of the other ministers expressed similar sentiments.

What was to be done? The ministers were aware of the appalling conditions at the front and in the entire country. Several times they had petitioned the Tsar to permit the organization of a Military Council, which should include the Ministers, to co-ordinate civil and military activities. To achieve this end, they had negotiated with General Frolov,[16] Commander of the St. Petersburg Military District, but their efforts had been of no avail. The Tsar's autocratic power was still unimpaired, but he was becoming increasingly less inclined to use the power that was legally his. He put off the petitioning ministers with a "Wait a while!"* As a result, they got excited and wrangled among themselves. They pictured the situation in even more sinister aspect than was really the case. Beyond this, however, they did nothing. In their excitement they only marked time. Samarin exclaimed hotly: "Is it possible that even the Tsar's closest servants, who enjoy his personal confidence, cannot make the Tsar listen to them?"

The Council of Ministers suffered from lack of political unity. Its Left wing was composed of men like P. A. Kharitonov and S. D. Sazonov,† who were always inclined to make concessions to the public. There were also such determined partisans of bureaucratic methods of administration as S. V. Rukhlov and A. A. Khvostov. Neither of these trusted the public; they regarded all its demands as evidence of a desire to overthrow the existing regime. Goremykin was essentially a member of this group. He was no longer a liberal. On the contrary, his devotion to the Tsar, whom he always strove to protect from all excitement and unpleasantness, steadily increased.

Perhaps the main reason for the Council's impotence lay in the fact that, as Sazonov said, it hung "in mid-air, without support from above or from below." The government had lost its prestige among progressive circles and even among the masses, which were generally little concerned with politics. Nor did it enjoy the confidence

---

* The well-known psychiatrist, Karpinsky,[17] had observed the Tsar and was positive that Nicholas II was suffering from a mental complaint known as negativism. The afflicted patient is markedly weak in resisting the wills of others and extremely stubborn in refusing to make any decision or to take any action. The disease is generally accompanied by the development of a suspicious and distrustful attitude toward all persons who do anything for the patient and are in contact with him.

† Sazonov[18] was a man of simple thought; all issues were clear to him, but he did not understand the complexity of the international situation and the internal conditions of Russia; like most of our diplomats, he had only a hazy idea of Russia; he was Anglophile in sympathy, a trait totally unsuitable in a Russian Minister of Foreign Affairs.

of the sovereign power which had appointed it. But without the confidence of the Tsar it could do nothing. Ultimate failure seemed inevitable. The ministers realized this. They saw no way to remedy the situation and consequently were in despair.

The worries and fears of the government were not confined to events at the front and in the rear; there was also public unrest in the country. What had happened during the last months of our war with Japan was happening again. Patriotic conservative circles, anxious for the future of the country, had united with the opposition to criticize the government and to swell the tide of discontent. The demands of the public were essentially not revolutionary, and the government realized that it could not treat them as revolutionary acts. Yet the real revolutionary forces, under cover of seemingly patriotic motives, worked to attain their destructive ends. It was extremely difficult to decide which demands were prompted by anxiety for the country and which were prompted by a desire to overthrow the regime. Every measure directed against the revolutionists while they were camouflaging their activities under a patriotic flag was bound to appear in the eyes of the public as an attack upon civil rights and a chance to work for the welfare of the country. Examples of such camouflaged revolutionary activities were found in the All-Russian Zemstvo Union, whose agents were engaged in a strenuous propaganda in the rear as well as at the front, and in the Duma when many ultra-patriotic speeches delivered therein were essentially nothing but battering-rams shattering the prestige of the government.

Meanwhile the work of the patriots and that of the revolutionists, outwardly similar but with different aims, went on. As early as the beginning of August 1915 there were in Moscow allegedly patriotic street manifestations which turned into riots, the pacification of which resulted in bloodshed. At about the same time there were serious riots at Ivanovo-Voznesensk where the workers made a series of demands allegedly prompted by the fact that the plants had not been sufficiently used to provide means for defending the country. These riots were suppressed with the aid of troops at the cost of sixteen dead and thirty wounded. It was very difficult to contend with these riots, for they were the work of revolutionists who, in order to intensify the unrest among the workers, rallied them round the slogan of the safety of the state.

The government's concern about the increased public unrest is all the easier to understand if it is recalled that on August 11, 1915, the Minister of the Interior told the Council that he was powerless to fight the growing revolutionary movement because he could not rely upon the troops in the event of armed conflict with the crowds: "The ranks of the police are being depleted," said Shcherbatov, "and the population is being excited daily by the speech-making in the Duma, the lies of the press, the endless defeats on the front, and the rumors of disorders in the rear."

On another occasion, he pointed out that conditions in Moscow were serious: "There are no troops except a *sotnia*[19] of Cossacks, one reserve battalion of eight hundred men, half of which is doing daily patrol duty, and two rather unreliable militia companies on the outskirts. On the other hand, there are about 30,000 privates convalescing in hospitals, an unruly and willful element with respect for no one. In case of disturbances this horde will range itself with the crowd." Conditions were serious also in St. Petersburg, where riots and strikes had already occurred at the Putilov works and the metal factory.

"Quos vult perdere Jupiter dementat!" The government and the Minister of the Interior were aware that there was a revolutionary movement brewing in the country. They realized, too, that they had no forces to combat it; yet during all the time that elapsed between then, August 1915, and the revolutionary uprising in St. Petersburg in 1917, they took no steps to secure such a force. Surely they did not know what they were doing. Ten thousand men from the front, distributed among the main administrative and industrial centers and subjected to a military discipline which they had lacked at the front and which makes troops an effective instrument in the hands of commanders, would have been force enough to accomplish the task in hand.

There were soldiers' mutinies in nearly every country participating in the World War, but in the Western countries measures were taken to deal with the mutineers. Italy, despite difficulties, recalled from the front a large part of her cavalry, concentrated it inland, and tempered it by that iron discipline which is gradually lost by military forces situated at the front for a long time. This move practically saved the existing regime in Italy. The little-known revolt of 1917 at Milan, organized by the revolutionists, was so successful that for six days a republican administration ruled the city; but it was suppressed by this cavalry, several thousands of insurgents being killed.

Our government, however, did not think of such preventive measures; or perhaps it was not able to execute them. It antagonized nearly all thinking Russia, seeming to have no regard for public opinion; but it took no measures to protect either itself or the country. Even the extreme Rights did not think of such measures, though their favorite method of enforcing authority was by the use of bayonets. Instead of preparing a force capable of coping with revolutionary outbursts by improving the military discipline of those troops in the rear, conditions and military units were created in the capital itself which were just what was needed to insure the triumph of revolutionary action. This at least was General Kornilov's opinion of the reserve battalion of the guards then stationed in St. Petersburg, an opinion expressed after he had been appointed commander of the St. Petersburg Military District by the Provisional Government and had become acquainted with the training and education of these troops.

Popular unrest was also manifest in the organization of meetings which conspired to force the government to change its ways and to create conditions which would oblige the Monarch to put persons vested with public confidence in charge of the government. In March 1915, party aims had been submerged in the desire to win a victory over the enemy. This led naturally to a desire to have in the government men who could guide the ship of state safely through the storm that had broken upon it. The future was to prove, however, that a man who enjoyed public confidence was not necessarily a man able to cope with the exigencies of the situation.

In August 1915 a congress of progressive public men assembled in the house of Konovalov[20] in Moscow. It decided that pressure by the public directed to a definite goal would be the best means of influencing the government. It decided to have the different zemstvo and municipal organizations adopt unanimous resolutions—a device which had been used in 1905. The first step was taken by the Moscow Municipal Duma. Its resolution was dominated by sentiments of patriotism; there was not a hint of revolutionary activity in it, as was proved by the fact that it was signed even by the extreme Right of this body, including such a confirmed Black Hundred man as Shmakov.[21] The Moscow Duma sent a telegram to the Sovereign declaring its loyalty and stating that victory depended upon having a government that enjoyed the confidence of the people; it petitioned the Tsar to receive its delegation. It also sent a telegram of greetings to the Grand Duke Nikolai Nikolaevich, the Commander in Chief, emphasizing the fact that the people looked to him as their national military leader.

The telegram to the Grand Duke Nikolai Nikolaevich and the resolutions of the congress in Moscow evoked some debate in the Council of Ministers, and for the first time sharp discord appeared between the majority of the Council and its chairman. Goremykin saw in the resolution of the congress and the Moscow Duma nothing but a desire to change the existing regime and to limit the power of the Tsar. Almost all the ministers, especially Samarin and Krivoshein, opposed such an interpretation. They held that the public anxiety and demonstrations were nothing but the "wail of a suffering soul." After lengthy debates, the Council of Ministers decided that the telegram of the Moscow Duma should be graciously answered by the Tsar but that the Sovereign should refuse to receive the delegation. And so it happened.

Meanwhile the dark forces which surrounded Rasputin and which had made of him a tool for the attainment of their own ends had become infuriated at the appointment of Polivanov and especially of Samarin. They had also been striving to diminish the influence of the Grand Duke Nikolai Nikolaevich upon the Tsar. The first move of the Rasputin band was to implant in the mind of the Empress, and through her in the mind of the Tsar, a suspicion as to the Grand Duke's loyalty to the throne. At first by innuendo and then openly they tried to persuade the Empress that the Grand Duke, relying on his popularity with the army, was thinking of forcing the Tsar to abdicate in order that he himself might occupy the throne. The only means of averting such a coup, they insisted, was to remove the Grand Duke immediately, and this was possible only if the Tsar himself would assume command of the Russian forces. Playing as usual upon the mysticism of the Imperial pair, Rasputin and Company succeeded in persuading the Tsar that his duty was to share with his army its joys and hardships. To such an idea the Tsar's mind was very receptive. At the very beginning of the war he had intended to place himself at the head of his army, and only with great difficulty had the government dissuaded him from doing so. Under the pressure from Rasputin, and especially from the Empress, he now resolved to carry out his original purpose, and nothing could shake his decision.

It was during a meeting on August 6 that the Council of Minis-

ters learned that the Tsar had decided to remove the Grand Duke
Nikolai Nikolaevich. Polivanov made the communication. During
most of the session he was silent and preoccupied, but toward its
close he suddenly announced that he had decided to violate his pledge
of secrecy and reveal a decision the Tsar had made. He said that he
considered it his duty to inform the Council of Ministers that His
Majesty intended in the very near future to take over the command
of the army. The ministers were astonished and confused, but they
expressed themselves unanimously against such a move.

The public reacted to the Tsar's decision in the same way but for
different reasons. Some were anxious for the outcome of the war;
some were afraid of the enormous risk to the Tsar entailed in his
assumption of all military responsibility at a moment when our situation was going from bad to worse and there was danger that the
enemy might seize one of the two capitals; others were displeased
with the removal of the Grand Duke Nikolai Nikolaevich, who had
won the sympathies of the progressive public by his famous order
concerning the future re-establishment of an independent Poland,[22]
by his sympathetic attitude toward the public, and by his alleged
desire that it should participate widely in the work of national
defense. The All-Russian Zemstvo Union, which had won for itself
a privileged position at the front, feared that it might not be able
to keep this position if the command were changed. The entire press
advertised the activities of the Grand Duke and played up to different
groups of the people.

The ministers were grieved that the Tsar had adopted such a
grave decision without first consulting them. It transpired, however,
that Goremykin had been apprised of the fact before the rest of the
ministers. When they reproached him for having withheld this most
important information, he answered: "I could not tell that which the
Tsar had revealed to me as a secret. I am a man of the old school.
To me a Sovereign order is law. I must say also that all attempts
to dissuade His Majesty will be fruitless. He made this decision a
long time ago. He feels that the duty of a Tsar is to be with his army
in moments of danger, and now that the situation at the front is so
bad he considers it his sacred duty to be with his troops, either to
conquer or to perish with them."

The ministers were not convinced. "We must protest, beg, im-
plore, insist, do everything in our power," said Samarin. He added
that since the Khodynka affair and the Japanese War the people

considered Nicholas II a bearer of ill fortune. The popularity of the Grand Duke, on the other hand, was well established. He was the beacon around which the last hopes of the people had rallied. To change the commander at such a moment would be to create a most painful impression upon the masses and the army. The ministers considered that further retreat, possibly the evacuation of St. Petersburg and Moscow, after the Tsar had assumed full responsibility for military actions, would weaken and perhaps shatter the prestige of the Monarch's name; it might even cause the fall of the dynasty. They also feared the effect the Tsar's decision might have upon the tone of speeches in the Duma.*

Meanwhile the Tsar had taken steps to carry out his decision, a decision in which he had been encouraged by members of his entourage.† He had sent General Polivanov to the Stavka with a letter to Grand Duke Nikolai Nikolaevich suggesting that the Grand Duke accept the posts of Viceroy of the Caucasus and Commander in Chief of the Army of the Caucasus.

During the sessions of August 10 and 11 the Council again discussed this subject. It hoped at least to delay the execution of the Tsar's decision or to moderate its consequences. Accordingly, Sazonov reported to the Tsar the ministers' anxiety concerning the grave step the Tsar had decided to take; but Nicholas II refused to alter his decision. Whereupon the Council, trying to make the best of what they considered a bad move, charged Krivoshein to compose a rescript to the Grand Duke paying tribute to his great military talents and explaining the Tsar's reasons for placing himself at the head of his army: for example, the need of unifying the civil and

---

* The excitement in Duma circles is illustrated by the following episode. On August 11, during a session of the Council of Ministers, Rodzianko, Chairman of the Duma, arrived at the Mariinsky Palace and demanded that he be received. When Goremykin went out to see him, Rodzianko announced in great agitation that the Tsar must not be permitted to remove the Grand Duke and to assume command himself. He called upon the Council to take all possible steps to prevent this. Goremykin answered calmly and coldly that the government was doing what it considered to be its duty, and that he could do without Rodzianko's advice. At this Rodzianko rushed unceremoniously from the room and swept like a hurricane through the vestibule. The doorman handed him his cane, but Rodzianko shouted: "To hell with the cane!"

† Shcherbatov reported to the Council of Ministers that General Voeikov[23] had not only refused to try to dissuade the Tsar from carrying out his decision but even had stated that he favored the idea. Voeikov, a selfish courtier, had no desire to fight Rasputin, under whose influence, as the letters of the Empress clearly reveal, the Tsar had made his decision.

military administration, and the Tsar's Imperial duty. Samarin continued to insist, however, that another plea be made to the Tsar to renounce his pernicious decision. He exclaimed with great feeling: ."The Russian Tsar is our last trump card." The ministers also considered once more the idea of organizing a military council in which they and the Grand Duke should participate, and charged Polivanov, now returned from the Stavka, to convey this idea to the Tsar. But Goremykin, who best knew the disposition of Nicholas II, declared firmly that nothing would result from all this. The differences between the ministers and their chairman were becoming more pronounced every day. The ministers continued to insist upon making a most energetic appeal to the Tsar; the majority even favored the establishing of good relations with the legislative chambers and the public. But Goremykin was adamant. He insisted that all attempts to influence the Tsar would be of no avail and, as for relations with the Duma and the public, he held the same opinion that he had held for nine years: that the government should neither fight nor conciliate the Duma, but ignore it.

Then came the important session of August 16. Samarin again insisted that the Council appeal *in corpore* to the Tsar to abandon his idea of assuming command of the army. "Lately," said Samarin, "it has been rumored that some secret influence has played a decisive part in this question of command. I shall ask the Tsar about this: I have the right to do so. When His Majesty offered me the post of Ober-Prokuror of the Holy Synod I agreed to accept it only after he had told me that all rumors against him were the inventions of enemies of the throne. But these rumors have become so persistent that I shall remind him of our conversation at that time and if there is now any substance in the rumors I shall tender my resignation. I am ready to serve my lawful Monarch to the last drop of my blood, but I shall never serve a ———."

Rasputin's name was mentioned more and more frequently in the Council of Ministers, especially in connection with the Tsar's decision. It was said that the spreading rumors of Rasputin's influence had undermined the monarchical principle much more effectively than all the revolutionary riots together. According to Samarin, Rasputin had even had the impudence to say that he had removed the Grand Duke. This made it all the more imperative for the Grand Duke to retain his command. But Goremykin droned everlastingly: "It is impossible to dissuade the Tsar. We must not unnecessarily torment a man already upon the rack." Nevertheless, after many petitions from individual ministers acting as emissaries of the Council but unsupported by Goremykin, Nicholas II finally consented to hear the opinion of the entire government.

The session with the Sovereign in attendance was held August 20 at Tsarskoe Selo. The subjects discussed were: first, the command; second, future domestic policy—whether it would be one of firmness —that is, a sort of dictatorship—or one to meet the desires of the public. "The golden mean," Krivoshein said at this session, "would only infuriate everybody." But the results were not what the ministers had hoped. The Tsar's conviction remained unshaken, and on the next day he left for the Stavka to assume command of the army. Nor was any decision reached on the question of domestic policy. It was apparent that the Tsar had accepted Goremykin's reactionary point of view but at the same time did not intend to stop the criticism of the government which flowed from the tribune of the Duma, as he had no wish to quarrel with that body.

During the session on the following day, many members of the Council reproached Goremykin for not having supported them in trying to dissuade the Tsar from assuming the supreme command; it had seemed to them that Goremykin thought the Tsar right, although previously he had expressed himself differently in the Council. Once more the ministers petitioned the Tsar in a letter, imploring him not to assume the entire responsibility for the future of the war. This petition was signed by all the ministers except Prince Shakhovskoi, A. A. Khvostov (this fact once more revealed Prince Shakhovskoi's nearness to Rasputin; Khvostov had at that time joined the camp of Goremykin), the Minister of War, and the Minister of the Navy. The last two were prevented by military rule from signing, but they took steps to apprise the Tsar that in this question they were in sympathy with the majority of their colleagues.

The insistence of the ministers can be explained only as being the result of some strange psychosis. They all realized and often mentioned the impossibility of preserving the dual control in government. This dualism was the result of the fact that dictatorial rights had been given to the Commander in Chief. Modern warfare is by no means limited to military events. All the vital forces of a country and all branches of administration participate in it. Under such conditions, if the supreme commander is not specifically limited to the exercise of military control, he must perforce assume control of the entire government, civil and military. It is a mystery why the Russian ministers of the summer of 1915 failed to grasp this fact.

At the session of the Council of Ministers on August 21, the day the Tsar left for the Stavka, the Council discussed the advisability of proroguing the Duma until the autumn. All the ministers were in favor of prorogation, but some were anxious to part with this body on friendly terms. They were afraid that otherwise the prorogation might provoke workers' disturbances. Some of the ministers even affirmed that they would rather have a "plotting Duma" than prorogue it without a preliminary understanding. Goremykin again expressed a definite and contrary opinion. "The labor movement will go on as always," he said. "The workers' movement and the prorogation of the Duma are two entirely different matters."

There was also the problem of appointing a government which would enjoy the confidence of the country and which the public was demanding so insistently. Some of the ministers thought the Council should petition the Tsar in the interests of such a government; but Goremykin refused to consider such a move. "If that is your stand," Sazonov said to Goremykin, "we [meaning those who differed with Goremykin] consider ourselves free to act as we see fit. You, Ivan Logginovich, and we do not agree." Goremykin answered quickly, "I earnestly beg you to report this to the Tsar and to ask him to replace me with a man better fitted to perform the duties of my office."

At one time Goremykin had considered it desirable to come to some understanding with the Duma leaders before proroguing that body and to accompany the ukase of prorogation with a pleasant message from the government to the legislative chambers. By September he had in his possession the necessary ukase; but by then he had changed his mind about having it accompanied by a message of good will from the government. The change in his attitude was due to the organization in the middle of August of the so-called progressive bloc in the Duma.

The power behind the formation of this bloc was, I believe, Krivoshein, who was anxious to become head of the government. He thought that if he could effect a union of the moderate Right elements, especially the Octobrists with whom he had long been sympathetically and closely connected, and those elements of the opposition, which at the beginning of the war had declared themselves ready to support the government in the work of defense, he would have support in his campaign to become head of the government. Once he had achieved this goal he thought such a bloc would continue to support him, and this would mean co-operation, not friction, between government and legislature.

I base this estimate of Krivoshein's plans and procedure on the following evidence. In the first place, as long as the bloc existed, Krivoshein was sympathetic toward it. Second, and most important, the platform which the bloc adopted immediately after its formation—namely, the creation of a ministry enjoying public confidence —was precisely the program that Krivoshein desired. Later the majority of the bloc interpreted this phrase, a "ministry enjoying public confidence," to mean a ministry responsible to the legislative chambers; but immediately after the organization of the bloc, and through the winter of 1915–16, it interpreted the phrase to signify a government which enjoyed the moral if not the formal support of the Duma and the masses of the people. Of course it is quite possible that some members of the bloc, such as Miliukov, had from the beginning understood the phrase to signify the establishment in Russia of a parliamentary regime of Western European type which would insure their own participation in the government— really, their main concern—yet they had not said so openly; the bloc had never once raised the question of changing the country's constitution. Even though Miliukov and his group were striving for this form of parliamentary regime, I suppose they understood the phrase to mean a government whose personnel would not provoke the hostility of the Duma and the public. Everyone realized that it was but a short step from such a government to one responsible to the representatives of the people.

To return, however, to the actual formation of the bloc itself! The engineering of the union was done by P. N. Krupensky, a specialist in political combinations. He visited and interviewed all the prominent representatives of the Duma groups, from the Cadets to the moderate Rights, as well as a few members of the State Council, and suggested that they dine together to discuss the ways and means of co-ordinating the activities of the two chambers. This suggestion was favorably received, and early in August all the representatives of the Duma center and the academic group of the State Council gathered at the "Contan" on the Moika. Among those present from the State Council were Baron Meller-Zakomelsky,

M. M. Kovalevsky,[24] and M. A. Stakhovich; and from the Duma,
Miliukov, Count V. A. Bobrinsky,[25] Efremov,[26] Shulgin,[27] and, of
course, Krupensky himself. At first the conversation was of a
general character; but toward the end of the dinner Krupensky,
who had left the room for a short while, rushed back in great agitation and announced that the Tsar had decided to take over the command of the army. The news created a tremendous sensation, especially among the members of the opposition. The Duma members
present were all monarchists, opposed to and afraid of revolutionary
movements during the war; and among them the Tsar's decision
aroused many fears. They regarded the Stavka, headed by the Grand
Duke Nikolai Nikolaevich, as a sort of corrective to the extreme
Right policies of the Tsar, but they felt that under Nicholas II the
Stavka would lose its corrective influence. Krupensky's news seemed
to draw together all present, despite their varying political opinions.
They decided to meet again in the house of M. M. Kovalevsky. Later,
they met several times at the home of Baron Meller-Zakomelsky, who
was elected chairman, and there the bloc continued to hold meetings
until the Revolution of February 1917.

Soon after the first meetings this group of men undertook to
draft a program for the bloc which would be acceptable to all factions
of the legislative chambers. This task was delegated to Miliukov,
Shulgin, and myself; Baron Meller-Zakomelsky, as the host of the
house where the meetings were held, also was to participate. When
the program had been drafted, a copy of it was printed for each
organizer of the bloc, ten of us, I believe. It was then discussed in
the different groups of the Duma and State Council. As I remember,
the program was adopted by all the groups without any serious
change, and on August 25 was signed by the representatives they
elected to the central committee of the bloc. For the progressive
nationalists of the Duma Count V. A. Bobrinsky signed; for the
Center, V. N. Lvov;* for the Octobrists, the zemstvo men, Dmitriukov;[28] for the Left Octobrist progressives, S. Shidlovsky,[30] I. N.

---

* Lvov[29] was a man of bold ambition and devoid of all restraint. At first he
joined the extreme Right of the Duma but later drifted more and more to the Left.
As a member of the Provisional Government he said he belonged to the extreme
Right of the Duma groups represented in the Provisional Government but expressed himself always in the spirit of the extreme Left and always voted in favor
of the most revolutionary measures. Finally, however, he allied himself with the
Bolsheviks and obtained an important post among the so-called *zhivotserkovniki*
(members of the living church).

Efremov; and for the Cadets, Miliukov. For the academic group of the State Council, D. Grimm[31] signed; for the Center, Baron Meller-Zakomelsky; and for the provisionally non-party group, myself.

Of the State Council only the academic group joined the bloc without any reservations. The Center did not definitely decide whether or not its activity was to be guided by the decisions of the bloc. It was sympathetic toward the bloc, but was unable to join it openly because many of its members had been appointed to the State Council by the Sovereign. Nevertheless, they chose a representative, namely, Baron Meller-Zakomelsky.

The position of the non-party group, to which I belonged, was even less definite. This group was only twelve or fourteen strong, and consisted mostly of former ministers, most of whom were progressive or liberal but who considered that it would be rather awkward to join any definite party group. As former members of the government they were rather opposed to the men who were their successors, but their conduct was quite correct throughout; they made no personal remarks from the tribune, and considered it impossible to join the bloc openly. In view of these circumstances this group did not formally elect a representative, and I had no formal credentials. Nevertheless, its majority was sympathetic to the organization of the bloc and to its program.

The attitude of the extreme Right of both the Duma and the State Council was different. Almost from the start they suspected that the bloc had revolutionary aspirations and feared, not without reason, that once the opposition elements were united with those more moderate elements which considered that the existing regime was the proper one for the country the elements farthest to the Left would, by virtue of their political experience and energy, take the upper hand and acquire the greatest influence. And as events unfolded the committee of the bloc did incline more and more to the Left, the Leftist swing being due to changes of opinion not so much on the part of representatives of the opposition as on the part of those who were generally more conservative.

These representatives of the parties and groups of the Duma and State Council were convinced that only a firm, strong, and active government could lead the country to victory, and that such a government must enjoy public confidence and be capable of organizing the active co-operation of all citizens. They came to the unanimous conclusion that the immediate and supreme requisites for the creation of such a government were: (1) the organization of a government of persons who enjoyed popular confidence and who had come to an agreement with legislative institutions regarding a definite program for the immediate future; (2) a radical change from the previous methods of government which were based upon a distrustful attitude of independent public activities. This change was to be effected by the introduction of the following measures: (a) a strict observance of the law in the administration; (b) the removal of a dual control in carrying out measures that did not concern military operations; (c) the introduction of new elements into local branches of the central government; and (d) a logical and coherent policy for preserving internal peace and removing differences in the rights of nationalities and classes.

The following measures were to be adopted to carry out this program: a partial amnesty of political criminals and the return of exiles banished by administrative order; complete religious tolerance; the solution of the Russo-Polish problem; the taking of preliminary measures for the removal of restrictions on the Jews; a conciliatory policy toward Finland; the resumption of trade union activity; the equalization of the rights of the peasant class with those of all other classes; the introduction of the volost zemstvo; the establishment of zemstvo institutions in Siberia, Arkhangelsk Gubernia, the Don Cossack region, and the Caucasus; the reform of the zemstvo statute of 1890 and of the municipal statute of 1892; and also a number of other less important legislative measures.

When the members of the Council of Ministers learned of the formation of the progressive bloc and had acquainted themselves with its program, most of them considered it possible to establish normal and even friendly relations with the representatives of the people by coming to an agreement with the bloc. Even a man as conservative as was Samarin said that it was not possible to reject the public elements during such a great war and that a unification of all strata of society had to be effected. Goremykin thought differently. He saw in the bloc nothing but a revolutionary enterprise. He viewed the bloc as an "unacceptable" organization, outside the law. "The ill-concealed plans of the bloc," he said, "seek merely to limit the power of the Tsar. I shall fight it to the last." The majority of the ministers, however, considered that five-sixths of the bloc's program could be accepted by the government; and after many heated debates it was decided to negotiate with the representatives of the bloc. Goremykin's consent to this move had been reluctantly given and only on condition that the negotiations be private and informatory. The Council of Ministers then selected four of their number—Prince Shcherbatov, A. Khvostov, Prince Shakhovskoi, and P. A. Kharitonov—to confer with the leaders of the bloc at Kharitonov's house.

This conference took place on August 27. The bloc was represented only by Duma members: Miliukov, Dmitriukov, Efremov, and Shidlovsky. The ministers asked what was to be understood by the phrase "a ministry enjoying public confidence." The Duma men answered that it meant simply that His Majesty should freely appoint someone who enjoyed the confidence of the public and charge that person to select a cabinet and to establish definite working relations with the Duma. The representatives of the bloc showed themselves quite ready to compromise.

On August 28 Kharitonov reported to the Council of Ministers on the desirability and feasibility of coming to some arrangement with the bloc. As if he had not heard what Kharitonov said, Goremykin submitted for the Council's consideration the question of proroguing the legislative chambers; he himself favored immediate prorogation. Sazonov and some other ministers admitted the desirability of proroguing the Duma in the very near future but suggested that the date of prorogation be determined in agreement with the bloc. The Council then returned to a discussion of the bloc's program. The views expressed by the members of the Council were hazy and were leading to nothing definite, when Krivoshein intervened. He maintained that the real issue lay not in the selection of programs but in the selection of persons. "Let the Monarch decide," said Krivoshein, "how he desires internal policy to be directed: whether to ignore the expressed hopes and wishes of the public or to effect some understanding with them. If he desires the second course, let him select some person who enjoys public confidence and charge that person to form a government. Unless this choice is made we shall get nowhere. Personally I heartily believe that the Tsar should select such a man and permit him to form a government that will meet the needs of the country."

Krivoshein's words, immediately backed by Sazonov, Kharitonov, and Count Ignatev, forced Goremykin to declare himself.

"This means," he said testily, "that in your estimation the question of proroguing the Duma ought to be postponed until government portfolios are distributed and the right of the Tsar to select his own ministers is limited?"

"We, the Tsar's old servants, take it upon ourselves to prorogue the Duma," Krivoshein answered, "and at the same time tell the Tsar that general conditions in the country demand a change both of government and of general policy."

"That is to say," Goremykin insisted, "you present the Tsar with an ultimatum: the resignation of the Council of Ministers and a new government."

In the end the Council resolved, "To prorogue the Duma immediately and to petition the Tsar for a change of ministry."

"I shall report in detail to His Majesty and shall do what he bids me," Goremykin said irritably, and closed the session.

The Council of Ministers did not meet again until September 2. In the interval Goremykin visited the Stavka, where he had a lengthy interview with the Tsar. The Council never knew what Goremykin had to say in this interview, but the Tsar's decision which Goremykin brought back was short and to the point: "To prorogue the Duma not later than September 3. The ministers to remain at their posts." Goremykin added that the Tsar intended to see the ministers at the Stavka in the very near future.

This decision horrified all the ministers. Sazonov almost fainted, and in leaving the session he exclaimed: "Il est fou, le vieillard!" Krivoshein expressed himself with unusual directness and courage: "Our discussions have shown, Ivan Logginovich, that the differences existing between you and the majority of the Council have gradually increased. You reported to the Tsar, and he seemed to agree with you. You carry out the orders of the Tsar, but your colleagues have objected to the efficacy of your policy. Permit me one question! What is your plan of action in view of the fact that representatives of the government are convinced that new measures are necessary, that the entire government apparatus is in opposition to you, that both internal and international conditions are becoming more and more threatening?"

"I shall fulfill my duty to the Tsar," answered Goremykin, "no matter how much opposition and resistance I meet. I reported everything to His Majesty and asked to be replaced by a more up-to-date man. The Sovereign orders followed, and to me they are law."

The records of the Council of Ministers make it clear that Goremykin was at least consistent, firm, and deeply loyal to his Sovereign during the summer of 1915, even though his policy brought harm to Russia.

Additional light is thrown on Goremykin's conduct during these days between August 21, when the Council announced its disagreement with Goremykin's policy, and September 16, when the Council sat in session presided over by the Tsar at the Stavka, by the lengthy letters of the Empress to the Emperor. These letters reveal Goremykin's desire to remain in power and his wholesale criticism of those ministers who opposed his views. Goremykin was certainly entitled to hold opinions that differed from those of his colleagues, but he had no reason for seeing in their actions some sort of intrigue or a lack of loyalty to the Tsar. He can scarcely have avoided realizing that his colleagues were deeply shaken by the events in Russia and differed with him, not because of petty personal grievances and ambitious plans, but because they estimated differently the forces then at work in the Russian Empire. The real motives which governed Goremykin's policy during those critical days cannot be accurately ascertained at this moment. One thing is certain, however, namely, that one of these motives was a desire to retain his position.

When the ministers failed to prevail upon the Tsar to remove Goremykin, they sought by clandestine measures to do so by using the Duma progressive bloc. Through outside persons they apprised the bloc of the Tsar's stand on the matter and suggested that the leaders of the bloc address themselves to Goremykin directly. Accordingly, early in September the bloc's committee elected a delegation to point out to Goremykin that the conditions of the times demanded exceptional energy, which he lacked; therefore he should surrender his place to some person with more youthful vigor.

This delegation's report to the bloc's committee makes it appear that the interview with Goremykin had been conducted in gentle and peaceful tones. Goremykin, however, had not been able to see the delegation's point of view. He had taken refuge in the Sovereign's orders and stated that as long as the Tsar saw fit to retain him as head of the government, he could not possibly refuse to bear the heavy burden thus imposed on him.

Actually, however, the Tsar had not yet reached a definite decision. Krivoshein had reason to suppose that the ministerial crisis might be solved as the public desired. Even the Empress realized, as is revealed by her letters, that it was impossible to retain Goremykin as Chairman of the Council when everybody was against him;

but she insisted that Nicholas II postpone his removal until such time as it would appear to be effected at the Tsar's own instance and not in conformity with a demand of the Council. Alexandra Fedorovna even considered possible candidates for this post, one of whom was Polivanov. At that time only the dismissal of Prince Shcherbatov had been decided upon, though not yet carried out. His successor was to be Aleksei Khvostov,* who had been eagerly seeking this post through the help of Madame Vyrubova[32] and Rasputin. The Tsarina was also eager to secure the immediate removal of Samarin, whom she regarded as a personal enemy.

As the day set for the meeting of the ministers at the Stavka approached, the letters of the Empress seem to be more decisive, more insistent upon having the Tsar retain Goremykin and reprimand if not dismiss the other ministers. Apparently different factors had influenced her. She was probably influenced by conversation with Goremykin. Also the change of supreme commander had provoked no outbreaks, and the conditions at the front had improved markedly since the Tsar had placed himself in command. Now this change had been especially insisted upon by Rasputin; consequently her faith in him had been strengthened. Rasputin had also suggested that Goremykin be retained as head of the government and that the rest of the ministers be replaced. In all her letters Alexandra Fedorovna strikes the same note: "You must put your foot down. You stood firm for the removal of Nikolai Nikolaevich; now continue to stand firm."

On September 14 Goremykin again visited the Stavka. The letters of the Empress had so well prepared his way that Goremykin had no trouble in persuading the Tsar to bring matters to a head immediately; to assemble the ministers at the Stavka and tell them firmly that he did not approve of their course of action and that he considered it necessary to retain Goremykin as head of the government.

The desperate efforts of the ministers to change the course of state policy not only had failed but also had made their task more difficult. By the time they assembled at the Stavka the Tsar had become so unfavorably disposed toward the majority of them that he addressed the session with unusual sharpness and directness. He

---

* Khvostov was the nephew of the Minister of Justice, a son of the former Ober-Prokuror of the Second Department of the Senate, of whom I have spoken earlier.

referred to their petition, either to remove Goremykin or to accept their resignation, as a ministers' strike. The ministers listened patiently to this angry speech. It was followed by a lengthy and rather painful silence. Finally, Goremykin said to the Tsar: "Let these gentlemen explain to Your Majesty why they do not desire to work with me. Let the Minister of the Interior, for example, give his reasons." Shcherbatov was caught unawares. He could only mutter a few insignificant sentences, although he did draw out his speech in order to give the others time to recover their senses.

When Shcherbatov was finished, Krivoshein asked for permission to speak. Evidently he had determined to have his say. Very courageously he pointed out the impossibility at such a critical time of totally disregarding public opinion: "Unless the public actively participate in the war, unless there is co-operation between government and people, we shall not be able to conquer our enemies. Goremykin has not only adopted the directly opposite point of view but is even ready to oppose persistently the desires of the people and thus systematically irritate them. Under these conditions, naturally, he is not acceptable to them."

Samarin spoke next, and with even more force and eloquence. He said that his forefathers had bequeathed to him the duty of serving his Monarch not in fear but in sincerity; that he was ready to give his all to this service, but that he could not reconcile his collaboration with Goremykin with the dictates of his conscience.

Shcherbatov, now master of himself, spoke again. He spoke in a conciliatory manner, evidently desiring to smooth down the strain created by the preceding speeches and to lower the feverish temperature of those present. He pointed out that differences among individuals were of two sorts. First, there were differences among those working in different fields or embracing different political opinions: these might be bridged over. Second, there were unbridgeable differences among representatives of different generations. For instance, he himself was a respectful son and had the greatest consideration for his father, but couldn't work with him. The same thing had now happened between the ministers and the Chairman of the Council. The ministers had the greatest esteem for Goremykin, a contemporary of Shcherbatov's father, but were unable to work with him. (To this Goremykin muttered *sotto voce:* "Yes, indeed, I could have come to an understanding much better with his father.") Shcherbatov also pointed out the extreme danger of trying to stem a stream by building a dam without outlets; the water will eventually rise over the dam no matter how high it is, and the higher the dam at the moment of collapse, the greater the damage. It was much more rational, he contended, to provide outlets for the water and, by directing it correctly, to use its power at will.

But this session in the Stavka was without result. Neither did the Tsar alter his decision nor did the ministers change their opinions. Such a state of things could not last, and the ministers who had expressed themselves most violently against Goremykin were soon removed. Shcherbatov was supplanted by Aleksei Khvostov, a member of the Fourth Duma; Samarin by Volzhin,[33] Director of the Department for General Affairs; Krivoshein by A. N. Naumov,[34] a member of the State Council elected by the Samara Zemstvo; and Kharitonov by N. N. Pokrovsky, Assistant Minister of Finance. Under these changed conditions a compromise with the progressive bloc was out of the question. A split between government and public was inevitable.

Krivoshein, the most talented and intelligent of the Tsar's advisers, was henceforth regarded by the Empress as her personal enemy. This obliged him to leave St. Petersburg, and he accepted the position of Chief Plenipotentiary of the Red Cross on our western front. Here, as elsewhere, he showed his energy and initiative, but he had no further influence upon the course of events. Thus ended Krivoshein's work under the old regime. He played some role in the Volunteer Army: just before the evacuation of Novorossiisk he was head of two branches of administration; but of this I know nothing specific. I met him in the Crimea, where he was civil adviser to General Wrangel, but he was no longer the composed, resourceful, and resolute Krivoshein I had once known. New conditions demanded new songs and new birds. At that time Krivoshein was a broken man, both physically and spiritually. During the last year of his life he worked in all sorts of public organizations in Paris but exerted little influence. He himself complained also of having lost the will power to make even the most commonplace decisions.

As mentioned above, the September changes in the government were bound to bring further differences between government and public. Not that the progressive bloc itself was so important, but an agreement with it was necessary in so far as it would bring nearer an agreement with the public. At that time the public was discussing very widely the bloc's activities. In fact, the extreme Rights ascribed too much importance to its formation and, later, accused it of responsibility for the February Revolution, whereas, in reality, the inception of the bloc had no formal effect on the future course of events. I do not recall a single instance when a resolution adopted by the bloc influenced the decision of the legislatures or an individual member thereof. This does not mean, of course, that it was without psychological significance; for its attitude during the winter of 1915–16, and especially in the autumn of 1916, was reflected in the Duma if not in the State Council.

The bloc held weekly and very lively sessions at which the many important questions of the day were discussed and information was exchanged on the backstage influences which were making themselves felt with increasing acuteness. One regular topic of discussion was the increasing influence of Alexandra Fedorovna and Rasputin, if not upon the course of events, then certainly upon the selection of the government personnel. V. N. Lvov, who later became Ober-Prokuror of the Holy Synod in the Provisional Government, often reported sensational revelations of Rasputin's interference in the affairs of the church and the Holy Synod.

I wish to repeat that the committee of the bloc did not favor, but feared and sought to forestall, revolutionary outbreaks. For instance, in the fall of 1916, Prince G. E. Lvov and M. V. Chelno-kov,[35] Chairman of the All-Russian Towns organization and also Mayor of Moscow, attended the session of the bloc and expressed their opinion that Russia was powerless to end the war victoriously under the existing regime, and that the only salvation of the country lay in a revolution. The members of the bloc's committee who replied to them were very much opposed to this suggestion and pointed out frankly that to agree to a revolution during war was to be guilty of treason against one's country.

Although the bloc was very much concerned with the harmful influence of Rasputin, it never alluded to the persons of the Emperor or the Empress. Neither did it discuss the ever increasing rumors of the latter's sympathy for the Germans or her secret communications with them. I do not know where Miliukov gathered the data, on the basis of which he spoke from the tribune of the Duma in November 1916, hinting boldly at the Empress' treason,[36] for during the sessions of the committee he never mentioned this subject— although the informal tone of these sessions afforded him ample opportunity to do so.

Unfortunately I do not recollect the details of the bloc's activities and debates. I kept no notes, and even had I done so I should not have been able to preserve them to this moment. Two of the members, however—Efremov and Miliukov—made notes on the activities of the committee. Efremov was chairman of the group of progressists whose main purpose was to surpass the liberalism and opposition of the Cadets. During the sessions of the committee I usually sat next to them and therefore had an opportunity to notice in what detail they made their notes. If they have preserved their memoranda it would be interesting to have them published. By the speeches and discussions of the conferences one could, for instance, note how the public moods, at first slowly and then with increasing speed, rose to a higher and higher pitch of excitement; one could prove not only that the bloc did not prepare the revolution but also that when the specter of the revolution arose the bloc did everything in its power to remove it.

Today, after what has happened, one wonders whether there was any way out of the situation or whether the collapse of the old Russian regime was inevitable. It is my opinion that August 1915 was the last moment at which a possible understanding might have been reached between government and public. I believe that at that time the public would have been satisfied with the removal of Goremykin and the establishing of the Krivoshein-Polivanov combination, and that a government organized by them would have been capable, without jeopardizing public order and peace, of effecting some understanding with the representatives of the people and of transforming them from a force of opposition into one of friendly co-operation.

There was always the danger, of course, that such a government would have been dissolved by the intrigues of Rasputin and Company, who would then have succeeded to power. But if we exclude this possibility, the discord between the patriotic part of the public and the Supreme Power in August 1915 could have been removed without transferring power to persons advanced by the public who were totally unprepared for their task, as the future was to prove. After August 1915 it was no longer possible to satisfy the demands of the public simply by a change of bureaucrats, regardless of their political convictions, for the public came to regard Prince Lvov, the Chief Plenipotentiary of the All-Russian Zemstvo Union, as the only man capable of heading the government. Anything but his appointment would not have satisfied the public or the Cadet party, which had a tremendous influence at that time.

Had the weak Prince Lvov been placed at the head of the government, his first move would probably have been to carry out a series of radical reforms of a demagogic nature. Yet regardless of whether these reforms would have been in the best interests of the country, it is absolutely certain that the attempt to put them into effect would not have solved the most urgent and insistent problem of the moment —namely, how to achieve victory. Internal reforms would have attracted the entire attention of the public and the conduct of the war would have been relegated to a secondary position with increasingly bad results. The war, already hateful to the population, would have become doubly insufferable. Desertion from the army, as after the February Revolution, would have been widespread. This would soon have led to an open demonstration against the war itself. Such a demonstration would have been supported by the Bolsheviks, who, in turn, were supported by German money. Nor must we forget that the Cadet program included complete political pardon for all political offenders, indicted, exiled, or banished. Bad conditions would have been made worse by the orgy of subversive propaganda in which these gentlemen would have freely indulged. They would have sown their evil seed on a soil made more fertile by the fact that the country had been deeply shaken by the long and exhausting war.

But the opportunity of August–September, 1915, was missed; and by the end of 1916 it had gone. By then the public had been irritated by a series of senseless measures, which were all the more aggravating in that they did not deal with urgent problems of state. It could no longer be pacified with half measures. The only possible way out would have been the formation of a government formally chosen from above but actually elected by a preliminary arrangement with the leaders of the Duma. Even so, the Cadets, who at that time had subordinated the Octobrist and the nationalist groups of the Duma (recall how the speeches of Shulgin in the special conference for defense reflected Cadet methods!), might have insisted upon the appointment of Prince Lvov as head of the government, in which case the subsequent course of events would not have differed greatly from what actually took place. Conditions were lacking even for an agreement between the Supreme Power and the leaders of the Duma whereby a government could have been formed which would have met the needs of the time. First of all, to effect such an agreement both parties to it would have had to be frank in their statements and faithful in executing their promises. Personally, I do not believe this was possible. Each party would have harbored secret intentions of double-crossing the other. Secondly, a strong and inflexible directing will was needed. Michelet[37] was right when he said in his *Histoire de la révolution française* that kings who were not responsible to the people need stronger will power to keep promises made to the revolution than they do to protect their own sovereign rights. In Russia there was no such strong will. Consequently that which was conceded and granted today was curtailed or repealed tomorrow.

For the conflict which began between government and public and political forces six months after the beginning of the war and reached its peak late in 1916, both sides must bear some responsibility; but the harvest was reaped by a *tertius gaudens*. It is a well-established fact that revolutions begin from above; and the Russian Revolution was no exception to this rule. In running its course it became what Pushkin had already termed "a Russian revolt, senseless and merciless."

EDITORS' NOTES

EDITORS' NOTES

INTRODUCTION

Page 5, note 1. **Nicholas II** (1868–1918). Eldest son of Alexander III; last Emperor of Russia, 1894–1917.

2. **Alexander III** (1845–1894). Emperor of Russia, 1881–1894; second son of Emperor Alexander II and father of Nicholas II.

3. **Count Sergei Yulievich Witte** (1849–1915). Born at Tiflis; attended Novorossiisk University (Odessa); entered the service of the Odessa State Railway in 1870; general traffic manager of the Southwestern Railways of Russia, 1886–1889; member of an Imperial commission to study railway questions, 1878; head of the railway department in the Ministry of Finance under A. I. Vyshnegradsky and chairman of the tariff committee, 1889; in 1892 became Minister of Ways and Communications and in 1893 succeeded Vyshnegradsky as Minister of Finance; by drastic measures put a stop to the great fluctuations in the value of paper currency and had specie payments resumed; introduced the gold standard in Russia on the basis of the laws of 1897 and 1899; organized government monopoly of the sale of alcohol; in 1903 was transferred from his post as Minister of Finance to that of chairman of the Committee of Ministers; chief of the Russian delegation which signed the peace with Japan at Portsmouth, September 1905; on his return to Russia was made a count and chairman of the first Council of Ministers under the new constitutional regime set up in accordance with the Manifesto of October 17, 1905, for the drafting of which Witte was largely responsible; dismissed from office in 1906 and appointed member of the State Council.

Page 6, note 4. **Nikolai Pavlovich Bogolepov** (1847–1901). Graduated from Moscow University, 1872; professor of Roman Law and, from 1883 to 1895, rector of that University; supervisor of the Moscow educational district, 1895–1898; Minister of Education, 1898–1901; on February 14, 1901, was shot by Petr V. Karpovich, a Socialist-Revolutionist and former university student, who considered Bogolepov's policy as Minister of Education reactionary; died the following March 2.

5. **Dmitrii Sergeevich Sipiagin** (1853–1902). Graduate of St. Petersburg University; served in the Ministry of the Interior; Marshal of Nobility of Moscow Gubernia, 1884; Vice-Governor of Kharkov, 1886; Governor of Kurland, 1888–1891, of Moscow, 1891; Assistant Minister of State Domains, 1893–1894; Assistant Minister of the Interior, 1894–1895; Head of His Majesty's Private Chancellery to Receive Petitions, 1895–1899; Acting Minister of the Interior, 1899–1900; Minister of the Interior, 1900–1902; assassinated by the Socialist-Revolutionist Balmashov.

6. **Viacheslav Konstantinovich Plehve** (1846–1904). Of Lithuanian family; graduate in law of St. Petersburg University; after serving in the judicial institutions of the provinces and St. Petersburg became Director of the Police Department in the Ministry of the Interior and later Assistant Minister of

589

the Interior, 1881–1894; Imperial State Secretary, 1894–1902; appointed State Secretary of the Grand Duchy of Finland, 1899; Minister of the Interior, 1902–1904; as a promoter of the "Russification" of national minorities he was bitterly hated in Poland, in Lithuania, and especially in Finland; credited by the opposition press with being accessory to the Kishinev massacres, an accusation which others held to be unjust and unsupported by fact; a determined opponent of Witte's policies; escaped an attempt made on his life early in 1904; assassinated on July 15 of the same year by Igor Sazonov, a Socialist-Revolutionist. (Boris Savinkov tells how this assassination was accomplished in *Memoirs of a Terrorist* [New York, 1931], pp. 58–70. See also Sazonov's own account in a "letter to his comrades" quoted by I. Steinberg, *Spiridonova Revolutionary Terrorist,* translated and edited by Gwenda David and Eric Mosbacher [London, 1935], pp. 123–27.)

7. **Prince Petr Dmitrievich Sviatopolk-Mirsky** (1857–1914). Graduate of His Majesty's School of Pages and later of the Nicholas Academy of the General Staff; served in the Russo-Turkish War, 1877–1878; Governor of Penza, then of Ekaterinoslav; Assistant Minister of the Interior, commander of the Gendarme Corps, and Director of the Police Department, 1900–1902; Governor-General of Vilna, Kovno, and Grodno Military District, 1902–1904; after the assassination of Plehve in 1904 became Minister of the Interior, from which office he was dismissed in January 1905, being succeeded by A. G. Bulygin.

Page 7, note 8. **Socialist-Revolutionists.** The repressive measures taken by the Imperial Government after the assassination of Alexander II, March 1, 1881, succeeded to such an extent that the surviving members of the *Narodnaia Volia* party, a terroristic organization formed in 1879 (see note 2, chapter x, p. 623), in the last issue of their periodical of the same name, October 1, 1885, acknowledged their defeat. During the following years many attempts were made to restore the party organization, and while these efforts failed, many circles and groups were formed in which the traditions and ideas of the earlier revolutionary generation were preserved. Some of these circles called themselves *Narodnaia Volia* groups, others had no particular designation, and others called themselves Socialist-Revolutionists in order to distinguish themselves clearly from the Social Democrats and at the same time, by avoiding the name *Narodnaia Volia,* not to commit themselves to a definite method of struggle—the terror. In 1896 K. Breshko-Breshkovskaia and other former members of the *Narodnaia Volia* returned from exile and joined in the work of the Socialist-Revolutionist groups. Certain of these groups held conferences in 1897, first at Voronezh and later at Poltava, to work out a common program. (S. Sletov, in *K istorii vozniknoveniia partii sotsialistov revoliutsionerov,* pp. 76–78, calls these the first and second congresses of the S.R. party in its original composition.)

Raids by the police delayed the development of a united organization, but late in 1900 a congress was held in Kharkov and a Manifesto of the Party of Socialist-Revolutionists was printed and circulated. After this certain groups began to call themselves Committees of the Party of the Socialist-Revolutionists. In the meantime the nucleus of another organization, called the Union of Socialist-Revolutionists, had been formed at Saratov in the years 1894–1896, and in the latter year it issued a program which was re-issued in 1898 in Russia and in 1900 abroad. This organization, which was mainly terrorist and conspiratory in its methods, began to publish *Revoliutsionnaia Rossiia* in January 1901. Later in this year the Union and the Party of Socialist-Revolutionists united, adopting the name of the latter and designating *Revoliutsionnaia Rossiia* as the official organ under the control of the Central Committee of the party abroad. The first official congress of the reorganized party met at Imatra, Finland, December 29, 1905, to January 4, 1906.

The S.R. party accepted terrorism as a supplement to mass revolution as a method of political struggle, and this terrorism was carried on by the so-called Fighting Organization, which, though subject to the party Central Committee, was strictly secret in its composition and independent of other party bodies in its activities. The Fighting Organization began its activities in 1902 under the direction of Grigorii Andreevich Gershuni and after his arrest in 1903 it was directed by Asef, who was later exposed by Burtsev as being in the pay of the police. Among its victims the Fighting Organization claimed such prominent persons as the Grand Duke Sergei Aleksandrovich, uncle of Nicholas II, and two Ministers of the Interior, Sipiagin and Plehve.

Like the activity of other revolutionary parties, that of the S.R.'s diminished in the years following 1907, when its Central Committee was again transferred abroad. During the war some of the S.R.'s were "defensists" and some "internationalists"; but when the Revolution came in Russia in 1917 the S.R.'s enjoyed the greatest numerical strength of any single socialist party. The events of 1917 accentuated, however, the divisions within the party: the Right and Center S.R.'s supported the Provisional Government; the Left S.R.'s opposed it and co-operated with the Bolsheviks in its overthrow.

9. **Manifesto of October 17, 1905.** Guaranteed to the Russian nation the fundamental principles of civil liberty—inviolability of person, and freedom of thought, speech, assembly, and organization; a democratic franchise; the principle that no law could henceforth be made without the consent of the State Duma, which had been created, with consultative power only, by the Manifesto of August 6.

10. **Petr Nikolaevich Durnovo** (1845–1915). Graduate of Naval School and Military Law Academy; at sea, 1860–1869; after serving in army, navy, and provincial judicial institutions entered the Police Department of the Ministry of the Interior, 1881–1884; Director of this Department, 1884–1893; appointed Senator, 1893; Assistant Minister of the Interior, 1900–1903; Head of Posts and Telegraphs in the Ministry of the Interior, 1903–1905; appointed member of the State Council, 1905; Minister of the Interior, 1905–1906. Durnovo believed that Russia's interests would be best served by close and friendly relations with Germany, and in February 1914 warned the Emperor of the dangers of a conflict with Germany to the monarchical principle and the autocratic regime. (A translation of this warning is given in F. A. Golder, *Documents of Russian History, 1914–1917* [New York, 1927], pp. 3–23.)

Page 8, note 11. **Ivan Logginovich Goremykin** (1839–1917). Graduate of the Imperial School of Law; in the First Department of the Senate, 1860–1864; Commissioner for Peasant Affairs in the Kingdom of Poland, 1864; Vice-Governor of Plotsk, 1866, of Keletsk, 1869; member of the Provisional Commission for Peasant Affairs in the Ministry of the Interior, 1873; Assistant Ober-Prokuror of the First Department of the Senate, Ober-Prokuror of the Second Department of the Senate, 1884; Assistant Minister of Justice, 1891; Senator, 1894; Assistant Minister and then Minister of the Interior, 1894–1899; appointed to the State Council, 1899; chairman of the Council of Ministers, May–July, 1906, and 1914–1916.

12. **Council of Ministers.** A Committee of Ministers (*Komitet Ministrov*) had been established in 1802 by Alexander I, who in the previous year had reorganized the government departments as ministries on the Western European model. In addition to the ministers, the Committee included the Imperial Secretary and the heads of the departments of the State Council. The Committee was merely an advisory body, in which the ministers had an opportunity to discuss measures within their competence and to co-ordinate them in the interests of the state before presenting them for the sanction of the Emperor. The chairman was not a prime minister but merely the presiding officer.

There was also a Council of Ministers (*Sovet Ministrov*), established in 1861 at the suggestion of Prince A. M. Gorchakov for the purpose of considering questions which required not only the approval but also the presence of the Sovereign in council. It included the ministers and other officials enjoying ministerial prerogatives and two others specially appointed by the Emperor. The Imperial Secretary also attended the meetings, which were called at the pleasure of the Sovereign.

On October 19, 1905, the Council of Ministers was reorganized in such a way as to unify the work of the various ministries; and on April 26, 1906, the Committee of Ministers was abolished.

13. **Petr Arkadevich Stolypin** (1862–1911). Graduate in physics and mathematics, St. Petersburg University; entered the Ministry of State Domains, 1885; Marshal of Nobility, Kovno, 1899; Governor of Grodno, 1901; Governor of Saratov, 1903, where he acted with great firmness and tact during the disturbances of 1905; Minister of the Interior, April 1906; succeeded Goremykin as chairman of the Council of Ministers in July of the same year; held these offices till his assassination in Kiev, September 1911.

14. **Peasant Land Bank.** Established, 1882, for the purpose of assisting peasants to purchase land; began operations in April 1883, with nine branches; in 1888 its activity was extended to include the Kingdom of Poland; by 1891 it had thirty-nine branches; was under the supervision of the Ministry of Finance; was managed by a council consisting of a manager, an assistant manager, and three others appointed by the Ministry of Finance and another member representing the Ministry of Agriculture; the local branches were managed by a council consisting of a manager, appointed by the Ministry of Finance, one member appointed by the local governor, and two members elected by the local gubernia zemstvo assembly.

15. **land communes (*pozemelnaia obshchina*).** See note 5, chapter i, p. 595.

16. **law of December 11, 1905.** The Manifesto of October 17 laid down

the general principle that those classes of the population which had previously been deprived of electoral rights should be drawn into participation in the work of the Duma. On December 11, 1905, while the Moscow riots were still going on, the government, as a concession to popular feeling, issued an electoral law which gave the suffrage to a majority of the people. This suffrage, however, was neither equal nor direct.

17. **new law . . . . promulgated on the authority of the Monarch.** This law was issued on June 3, 1907, in the form of a ukase to the Senate setting forth new regulations for the election of the Third Duma. These regulations were such as to give the larger landowners a predominant influence in electing the members of the Third Duma. (See Sir Bernard Pares, "The Reform Movement in Russia," in *The Cambridge Modern History* [New York, 1910], Vol. XII, chapter xiii, pp. 373–74; also H. H. Fisher, ed., *Out of My Past: The Memoirs of Count Kokovtsov* [Stanford University, 1935], pp. 177–78.)

18. **Aleksandr Vasilevich Krivoshein** (1858–1921). Graduate in law of St. Petersburg University; in the Ministry of Justice and later in the Ministry of the Interior, 1884–1896; Assistant Head of the Department of Peasant Colonization, 1896–1904, and Head, 1904–1905; Assistant Head of the Chief Administration of Land Organization and Agriculture, 1905–1906; member of the State Council, 1906; Assistant Minister of Finance, 1906–1908; Head of the Chief Administration of Land Organization and Agriculture, 1908–1915; participated in the organization of the Anti-Bolshevik Right Center and the Council of National Union of Russia, 1918; an important member of Baron Wrangel's anti-Bolshevik government in South Russia, 1920.

Page 9, note 19. **Count Vladimir Nikolaevich Kokovtsov** (1853–   ). Graduated from the Imperial Alexander Lyceum, 1872; in the Ministry of Justice, 1873–1890, at first in its statistical, then in its legislative office, and after 1879, Senior Inspector and Assistant Head of its Central Administration of Prisons; in the Imperial Chancellery, 1890–1896, as Assistant State Secretary, State Secretary, and Assistant Imperial Secretary; Assistant Minister of Finance, 1896–1902; Imperial Secretary, 1902–1904; Minister of Finance, 1904–1914, and also chairman of the Ministers' Council, September 1911–January 1914; created count, 1914; in emigration since 1918.

20. **Grigorii Efimovich Rasputin (Novykh)** (1871–1916). Son of a poor Siberian peasant; uneducated, and to the end of his life unable to write correctly; acquired a lasting reputation for dissolute behavior; in 1904 he left his family and devoted himself to religious exercises, declaring to his people that he was inspired by God; adopted the views of the Khlysty sect, made various religious pilgrimages to holy places, and spent some time in different monasteries, but did not become a monk; in 1907 became acquainted with Archimandrite Feofan, confessor of the Empress, and through him, and with the assistance of Grand Duchesses Militsa and Anastasia, was introduced at the Court; acquired great influence with the Empress and thereby exercised an increasing influence on political appointments; an unsuccessful attempt on his life was made by Guseva in 1914. A small group of men, including Grand Duke Dmitrii Pavlovich, Prince Yusupov, and Purishkevich, determined to get rid of Rasputin, and he was killed in the Yusupov Palace, December 15, 1916.

21. **Empress Alexandra Fedorovna** (1872–1918). Last Empress of Russia; born Princess of Hesse-Darmstadt; granddaughter of Queen Victoria of Great Britain; shot with her family in Ekaterinburg by the Bolsheviks.

22. **Boris Vladimirovich Stürmer** (1848–1917). Graduate of St. Petersburg University; in the First Department of the Senate, 1872–1875; in the Ministry of Justice, 1875–1878; in the Department of Heraldry of the Senate and in the Office of Ceremonies (*Tseremonialnaia ekspeditsiia*) of the Ministry of the Imperial Court, 1878–1892; chairman of the Tver Gubernia Zemstvo, 1892–1894; Governor of Novgorod, 1894–1896, and of Yaroslavl, 1896–1902; Director of the Department for General Affairs in the Ministry of the Interior, 1902–1904; member of the State Council, 1904; chairman of the Council of Ministers, January–November, 1916; Minister of the Interior, March–July, 1916; Minister of Foreign Affairs, July–November, 1916.

Page 10, note 23. **Aleksandr Dmitrievich Protopopov** (1866–1918). An Octobrist; member of Third and Fourth Dumas; Marshal of Nobility of Korsunsk Uezd, 1912, and of Simbirsk Gubernia, 1916; vice-chairman of the State Duma, 1914–1916; member of the progressive bloc; Minister of the Interior, September 1916–February 1917.

CHAPTER I

Page 13, note 1. **Committee to Supervise the Construction of the Siberian Railway (*Komitet po sooruzheniiu Sibirskoi zheleznoi dorogi*).** The construction of the railway from Cheliabinsk to Vladivostok was begun in 1891 and was practically finished by 1899, although a line around Lake Baikal was not constructed until 1906.

Page 14, note 2. **Nikolai Matveevich Chikhachev** (1830– ?). Adjutant General; Admiral; graduate of the Naval School; served in the Russo-Turkish War, 1877–1878; Chief of the Naval General Staff, 1884; Minister of the Navy, 1888–1896; member of the State Council, 1897; member of the Special Conference to Study the Needs of Agricultural Industry, 1902; director of the Russkoe obshchestvo parokhodstva i torgovli, a large steamship concern.

Page 15, note 3. **Emperor Alexander II** (1818–1881). Emperor of Russia, 1855–1881; eldest son of Emperor Nicholas I; called the "Tsar Liberator" because of the many reforms he introduced, particularly the emancipation of the serfs, February 19, 1861; in his later years his policies disappointed both liberals and revolutionists; several attempts to take his life failed, but on March 1, 1881, he was killed on the streets of St. Petersburg by a terrorist bomb.

4. **Anton Pavlovich Chekhov** (1860–1904). Grandson of a serf; graduated in medicine from Moscow University, 1884; did not practice medicine but continued his literary career begun as a student; author of many comic sketches, short stories, and several plays produced with great success by the Moscow Art Theater; wrote in 1891, *Ostrov Sakhalin*, a thorough and impartial report of convict institutions on Sakhalin Island; died in Germany.

5. the reform of February 19, 1861. By this reform of Alexander II the right of bondage over the peasants settled upon privately owned estates was forever abolished. Household serfs were freed within a period of two years. Peasant serfs received their personal freedom and allotments of land as well. These allotments varied in size from district to district, but in general the peasants as a whole received from the landlords more than half of their cultivated land. This land did not immediately become the property of the peasants, however; it still belonged to the landlord, whom the peasant had to pay for its use. But if peasant and landlord wished to terminate this relationship, the land might be sold to the peasant. In that event the landlords were paid by the state for the land turned over to the peasants and the peasants were to repay the state by payments over a period of forty-nine years. These peasant payments were the so-called "redemption dues." As the years passed, the peasants were not always able to make these payments, which were therefore reduced by decree in 1881. But arrears continued to accumulate until the Ukase of November 3, 1905, cut redemption dues in half for the year 1906 after which they were to be canceled outright. Within twenty years after the Act of Emancipation approximately 85 per cent of the landowners had sold to the peasants the land allotted to them by the Act of Emancipation. Peasants on udel and state lands were emancipated in 1863 and 1866, respectively, and arrangements were made for redemption payments by which these peasants also could purchase the land allotted them.

Extensive though these changes were, they left much to be desired. The individual peasant still did not enjoy complete personal ownership of the land he cultivated. This land, whether acquired from the state or from a private landowner, was held in communal ownership by groups of peasant families living in village communities, which exercised a far-reaching control over the individual peasant. Within the practice of communal ownership, there were two types of tenure: household tenure (*podvornoe zemlepolzovanie*) and repartitional tenure (*obshchinnoe zemlepolzovanie*). In the former system, which was particularly typical of western and some Ukrainian gubernias, where the traditions of the Polish and Lithuanian states were stronger than those of Moscow, tracts of land were distributed among the peasant families and held in heredity. If a family died out its land became village land and could be distributed among other families or given to some family in heredity. In some gubernias (Ekaterinoslav, Taurida, and Kherson) the peasants were allowed to decide immediately after the reform of 1861 which type of tenure they wished to practice. In the system of repartitional tenure, which was typical of most Great Russian gubernias, those of Central European Russia, the tracts of cultivated land might be redistributed among the peasant population if two-thirds of the peasant holders agreed to such repartition. A similar two-thirds vote might also effect a change from repartitional to household tenure.

Many of the complications pertaining to rural administration and land organization arose from the fact that there existed two institutions directly concerned with the peasants and the land. One was the village community (*selskoe obshchestvo*), a unit of local government which dealt with administrative matters; the other was the land commune (*pozemelnaia obshchina*), an economic unit which was largely the outgrowth of peasant custom and which dealt with matters relating to the communally owned land. In some instances, these two institutions were co-extensive and in some cases not. It was apparently the intention of the drafters of the statute of February 19, 1861, that there should be one institution exercising both administrative and economic functions and that the members of a village community should at the same time be members of a single land commune; but when it came to applying the statute it was found necessary in some cases to permit the registration in a given village community of certain inhabitants who did not participate in the ownership of communal land and were not, therefore, members of a commune. It was also found necessary in certain cases to include in a single village community several land communes each possessing a separate tract of land. This was especially true when members of a single village community had previously been serfs of two or more landowners.

The governing body of the village community was the village assembly (*selskii skhod*), which was not elective but was made up of all householders belonging to the village community without regard to property status, age, or sex. The village assembly elected the village elder (*starosta*) and other officials, who, with the exception of the tax collectors who served for one year, were elected for three years and were exempt from corporal punishment and from the performance of the so-called natural services. They were, however, until 1874, when the office was abolished, under the administrative and police supervision of representatives of the central government, the peace mediators (*mirovye posredniki*), whose primary function was to adjust differences between landlord and peasant arising out of the sale and purchase of land. After 1889 they were under the supervision of the *zemskie nachalniki*, who were empowered to remove officials from office.

In addition to the election of officers the village assembly appointed members of the volost assembly (*volostnoi skhod*) (see note 5, chapter xi, p. 629), passed judgment on members of the community who violated laws and ordinances, dismissed members of the community and admitted new ones, appointed guardians and trustees, applied to the government for aid for education, etc., and performed other local administrative functions. Under the statute of February 19, 1861, the village community was responsible for each of its members and for the collection of all levies and dues; but by the regulations of June 23, 1899, regarding the collection of taxes—state land taxes, redemption dues, etc.—this collective responsibility was abolished in villages with household land tenure and in 1904 in villages with repartitional tenure in most gubernias. The village community also maintained by self-taxation the organs of peasant self-government of both village and volost, such as village *starosty*, volost *starshiny*, and even police and judicial officers. In addition there was a tax, paid in natural services (*naturalnyia povinnosti*), for the maintenance of roads, performance of police duties, extinguishing of fires, etc.

As for the land commune (*pozemelnaia obshchina*), the term *obshchina* legally denoted the communal ownership of arable, pasture, and other land periodically repartitioned among the peasants belonging to the commune. The word *obshchina* was, however, never used by the peasants, who referred to the group collectively owning a given tract of land as a *mir* or, in the Ukraine, as a *hromada*. Three types of commune were generally recognized: (1) "simple" (*prostaia*), in which one village community constituted a single land commune; (2) "composite" (*sostavnaia*), where one commune embraced several villages; and (3) "divided" (*razdelnaia*), where several communes were included in a single village community. The great majority of the communes were of the "simple" variety. As a rule in the "composite" type the commune owned pasture and forest lands while the arable land was separately owned by the several village communities. A single land commune sometimes included as many as thirty village communities; and the assembly which regulated land tenure, the size of allotments, etc., might include several thousand members.

The land commune was, naturally, concerned with matters pertaining to communal landownership: the periodic repartition of the land among the member households, the levying of assessments, the apportioning of dues and natural services, and so forth. In the "simple" type of commune these functions were performed by the village assembly; in the "composite" type land questions were settled at a joint assembly of the several villages concerned; and in cases where a village community included several land communes the members of these different land communes held separate assemblies, which came to be called *selennye* and which were permitted by the Senate though not provided for by law.

Local peasant institutions in different parts of the empire showed other variations from the types mentioned here.

The fact that each peasant was obliged to share in the responsibilities of the community made it generally difficult for him to leave. Means of effecting a personal separation varied; but during the process of collective redemption with state aid, which was the general practice, the peasant holder could give up or transfer his allotment only with the consent of the village assembly; he could withdraw from the land commune only after he had paid half the debt due on his holding, and even then the other holders could refuse to assume the remaining half of his indebtedness and thereby prevent his withdrawal; also arrears in taxes charged against his household had to be paid up; as a rule evidence had to be produced that he would be accepted into membership of some other commune; moreover, a junior member of a household had to have the consent of his father.

After the turn of the century there was an intensification of effort to improve the general situation among the peasants. The Ukase of November 9, 1906, was a big step in this direction. It took away from the village community its authority over the peasants and gave each householder the right to own, bequeath, or sell that portion of land which the household had been allocated at the last distribution. This ukase also provided that upon the demand of two-thirds of the communal assembly each household might consolidate its scattered strips of land into a single plot; by a law of June 14, 1910, such consolidation might be effected by the vote of a simple majority; and a law of May 29, 1911, provided for the permanent division by a majority vote of that land which had not previously been divided even temporarily for individual use.

6. *raznochintsy.* Originally a legal term applied to individuals who did not belong to the merchant class, to a guild, or to the hereditary nobility; in this strict sense the term became obsolete, but in common usage it was applied to persons of various social origins whose education and occupation gave them a status different from that of the traditional classes of Russian society: i.e., nobility, clergy, townsmen, peasants. The *raznochintsy* came virtually to constitute a new social class of which the so-called intellectuals made up a considerable part.

Page 16, note 7. *kramola.* An old Russian term meaning a disturbance or revolt; in general, a political crime.

8. **redemption dues.** See note 5, chapter i, p. 595.

Page 17, note 9. **The Russo-Turkish War [and] the Treaty of Berlin.** The Treaty of San Stefano, April 21/March 3, 1878, which closed successfully for Russia her war with Turkey, 1877–1878, provided among other things for the creation of a greater Bulgarian state. But the treaty met with objections: Greece, Serbia, and Rumania feared the power of a "Greater Bulgaria"; Austria and England feared the proposed new state as a Russian vassal and as an extension of Russian power. These latter two powers insisted on a revision of the treaty. This was achieved in the Treaty of Berlin, July 1/13, 1878, which provided, among other things, that there would be no "Greater Bulgaria." This revision caused deep resentment in Russia.

10. **Nikolai Karlovich Giers** (1820–1895). Graduate of Tsarskoe Selo Lyceum (in 1844, this institution was transferred to St. Petersburg and re-named the Imperial Alexander Lyceum); in Asiatic Department of the Ministry of Foreign Affairs, 1838–1841; held various diplomatic positions, 1841–1875; Senator, Assistant Minister of Foreign Affairs, and Head of the Asiatic Department, 1875–1882; Minister of Foreign Affairs, 1882–1895.

11. **Count Nikolai Pavlovich Ignatev** (1832–1908). Graduate of His Majesty's School of Pages, 1849, and of the Nicholas Academy of the General Staff, 1851; military attaché to London, 1856–1857; head of the military and diplomatic mission to Khiva and Bokhara, 1858, and later Envoy to Peking; Head of the Asiatic Department of the Ministry of Foreign Affairs, 1861–1864; Envoy to Constantinople, 1864; Governor-General of Nizhnii Novgorod; member of the State Council, 1877; Minister of State Domains, March 1881; Minister of the Interior, May 1881–1882; chairman of Slavic Society of Charity, 1888.

12. **Count Dmitrii Andreevich Tolstoi** (1823–1889). Graduate of Tsarskoe Selo Lyceum; in the Department of Ecclesiastical Affairs of Foreign Creeds in the Ministry of the Interior, 1848–1853; Director of the Chancellery of the Ministry of the Navy, 1853–1861; Acting Director of the Department of Education in the Ministry of Education, 1861; later, appointed Senator; Ober-Prokuror of the Holy Synod, 1865–1866; Minister of Education, 1866–1880; member of the State Council, 1880; Minister of the Interior and Chief of the Gendarme Corps, 1882–1889; famous for his reactionary policies.

13. **Ivan Nikolaevich Durnovo** (1830–1903). Attended the Artillery School and served for a short time in the army; Marshal of Nobility of Chernigov Uezd and then of Chernigov Gubernia; Governor of Ekaterinoslav, 1871–1882; Assistant Minister of the Interior, 1882–1886; Chief of the

Fourth Section of His Majesty's Private Chancellery, 1886–1889; member of the State Council, 1886; Minister of the Interior, 1889–1895.

14. **Petr Semenovich Vannovsky** (1822–1904). Adjutant-General; served in the army, 1857–1861 and 1868–1880; Minister of War, 1881–1898; resigned and was appointed member of the State Council, 1898; Minister of Education, 1901–1902.

Page 18, note 15. **The foreign policy of Alexander . . . . able to maintain.** Although this statement may fairly represent the Russian opinion of Alexander III's success in foreign affairs, it is not strictly true. From 1881 to 1887 there existed the so-called Alliance of the Three Emperors, between Russia, Austria, and Germany. This broke up because of Russia's distrust of Austria in the Balkans. Russo-German friendship was preserved, however, in the Reinsurance Treaty, 1887–1890. The non-renewal of this treaty after its first three-year term left the field clear for the formation of a Franco-Russian alliance which was finally completed in January 1894, more than half a year before the death of Alexander III. Note the author's comments on this alliance on p. 21.

Page 19, note 16. *Vestnik Evropy.* Historical-political magazine; founded in 1802 by A. A. Karamzin and published bimonthly until its discontinuation in 1830; renewed publication, 1866, appearing four times a year until 1868, when it became a monthly; after the 1905 revolution the collaborators formed the Party of Democratic Reform, which, however, was soon dissolved; closed in 1917.

17. *Istoricheskii Vestnik.* Historical-literary monthly; founded by A. S. Suvorin, 1880; editor, S. N. Shubinsky; discontinued under the Soviet regime.

18. **zemstvo assembly.** The realization of Russia's internal weakness, so vividly revealed in the Crimean War, together with the emancipation of the serfs in 1861, called forth a reorganization of the entire system of local administration. This reorganization was effected in 1864 when the zemstvos, units of local government since the middle of the sixteenth century, were reformed. The act of 1864 established the reorganized zemstvos in thirty-four of the central gubernias of the Empire, thus excluding Siberia, Turkestan, the Caucasus, Trans-Caucasia, Poland, the Baltic provinces, the Cossack territories, and nine gubernias in the west where many of the large landowners were Poles.

In each of these thirty-four gubernias there was a gubernia zemstvo as well as an uezd zemstvo for each uezd. Each of these zemstvos had an assembly (*sobranie*) and, as an executive organ, a board (*uprava*). The uezd assemblies were elected by the local population voting in three curiae according to property qualification: the first curia represented the nobility or gentry, who owned real estate outside city limits; the second curia represented the urban bourgeoisie, who owned real estate in cities; the third curia represented the peasantry, whose ownership of real property was in most cases vested in the commune. Members of uezd assemblies elected from among their own number the members of the gubernia assemblies. Each uezd and gubernia assembly elected the members of its own board, but in each case the selection of the chairman of this board had to be confirmed by the central government.

The zemstvo assemblies were elected every three years and met regularly once a year and occasionally for a special session. These meetings usually lasted several days. The members of the boards also were elected for a three-year term and acted for the assembly between meetings of the larger body.

According to the act of 1864, the zemstvos enjoyed wide competence in local affairs and within these limits were independent of central-government interference. The only supervision of them was exercised by the governor of the gubernia, an appointee of St. Petersburg, who saw to it that zemstvo decisions did not violate any law.

The spheres of uezd and gubernia zemstvos were not sharply delimited by law. Practice and usage tended, however, to mark off broadly their respective fields. By and large the uezd zemstvos were concerned principally in the supervision of local schools, libraries, hospitals, roads, and postal and agricultural services. The gubernia zemstvos were concerned with similar matters but on a larger scale. They maintained and supervised institutions such as hospitals for the treatment of special diseases, orphanages, insurance organizations, commercial warehouses, agricultural experimental stations, etc.—institutions which are usually located in the more important centers of population. They maintained also special staffs of experts upon which uezd zemstvos might call for aid and guidance.

The revenues of the zemstvos were largely derived from zemstvo taxation of real estate, chiefly lands and forests, but also of industrial enterprises. The rate of taxation was determined annually according to the expenditures contemplated in the coming year's budget. Every increase in a zemstvo budget carried with it, therefore, an increase in that zemstvo's taxation.

The zemstvos attracted many progressive and unselfish workers, including a large number from the landlord class, and zemstvo achievements in health, educational, and agricultural services were indeed noteworthy, even though uneven from zemstvo to zemstvo. These achievements were made in the face of considerable misunderstanding and opposition. The peasants particularly tended to view zemstvo enterprises with distrust and even to regard zemstvo workers as agents of the central government. But even greater obstacles to zemstvo work were created by the St. Petersburg government and its representatives, neither of which could refrain from interference in zemstvo affairs. Frequently the zemstvos were carried into opposition to the government merely by defending their independence, and this opposition was interpreted by the government as an attack upon the principle of autocracy. The government, therefore, sought to extend its control over the zemstvos by new legislation. According to a law of August 19, 1879, the appointment of all zemstvo employees had to be confirmed by the local governor, who was also authorized to remove zemstvo employees whom he considered politically undesirable.

More drastic legislation was approved by Emperor Alexander III on June 12, 1890. This legislation altered the system of zemstvo elections in such a way as to give the landowning gentry a dominant position in the zemstvos, and this in spite of the fact that the landholdings of the gentry had decreased greatly since 1864. The curia of the nobility now elected a majority of deputies to the zemstvo assemblies; the second curia was not greatly affected by the change; but the peasant curia was abolished and the peasants deprived of the right to elect directly the peasant deputies: the peasants elected candidates for membership in the zemstvo assemblies and from these candidates the local governor appointed the peasant deputies, the number of whom, moreover, was greatly reduced. The independence of the zemstvos was further limited when the governors and the Minister of the Interior were empowered not only to approve or reject chairmen and members of zemstvo boards but also to make their own appointments to these posts after they had twice failed to approve elected candidates. The governors were also authorized to quash not only those resolutions of zemstvo assemblies which violated a law but also those which, in their opinion, were not in accord with the general interests of the state and the needs of the local population.

In spite of these restrictions the zemstvos continued their very considerable services to the people. Many zemstvo leaders hoped that out of these institutions would evolve a system of representative government adapted to Russian conditions, and zemstvo-constitutionalists sponsored resolutions in zemstvo assemblies calling for the replacement of autocracy with a constitutional government. In November 1904 the first all-Russian congress of zemstvos met in St. Petersburg and adopted such a resolution. In the following May a delegation, headed by S. N. Trubetskoi, from the third all-Russian congress of zemstvos actually submitted to Nicholas II an outline program of constitutional reforms.

There had been some talk in the 'nineties of introducing zemstvos into the western gubernias, and in 1903 a restricted type of zemstvo—members of assemblies and boards were appointed by the government from persons of the requisite property qualification—was introduced into six of these: Kiev, Volhynia, Podolia, Vitebsk, Minsk, and Mogilev. But it was only in 1911 that these gubernias received zemstvos.

In 1912 a law extended zemstvos to three other gubernias—Astrakhan, Orenburg, and Stavropol. There were plans for a still further extension of zemstvos, but these did not mature. Moreover, these acts of 1911 and 1912 did away with a special curia for the nobility and gentry, and established in addition to the peasant curia a curia embracing landowners of all classes. In the zemstvos of the six western gubernias property qualifications for voting were reduced and there were created Russian and non-Russian landowners' curiae. The Russian curia enjoyed the larger representation in the assemblies. These provisions were designed to keep the zemstvos free from the domination of the Polish landowners, who were numerous in these six gubernias.

19. **Ivan Ilich Petrunkevich** (1844–1928). Graduate in law of St. Petersburg University; member of Chernigov Gubernia Zemstvo, 1868; Justice of the Peace (*mirovoi sudia*), 1869; chairman of the Congress of Justices of the Peace (*mirovoi sezd*), 1879; deported to Kostroma Gubernia for participation in the zemstvo address to the government, 1879; returned to Chernigov Gubernia, 1886, elected zemstvo member and again deported; settled down in Tver Gubernia, elected member of Novo-Torzhok Uezd Zemstvo; deported from Tver Gubernia, 1894; allowed to return to public activity, 1904; an organizer of the Union of Liberation (*Soiuz Osvobozhdeniia*), and later

one of the organizers of the Cadet party; participated in town and zemstvo congresses as a member of the Left wing, 1905–1906; member of the First Duma; floor leader of the Cadet party in the First Duma; signed the Viborg Manifesto; in emigration after 1920.

20. **Fedor Izmailovich Rodichev** (1854–1933). Graduate in law of St. Petersburg University; volunteer in the Serbian War, 1867; Marshal of Nobility of Vesegon Uezd, 1877–1890; Justice of the Peace, 1878; elected chairman of Tver Gubernia Zemstvo Board, 1891, but his election was not confirmed by the government; one of the initiators of the Tver Zemstvo address to the Tsar, 1894, for which he was deprived of electoral rights; barrister in St. Petersburg Court of Appeals, 1898; exiled, 1901–1904; a member of the deputation to the Tsar, June 6, 1905; member of the Union of Liberation; one of the founders of the Cadet party and a member of its Central Committee; member of all four Dumas; after the February Revolution, member of the Provisional Committee of the Duma and later Commissar of the Provisional Government for Finland; after the October Revolution, in emigration.

21. **I. A. Korsakov.** One of the founders and a prominent member of the Cadet party.

22. **the Cadet party.** The Constitutional Democratic party; also known as the Party of People's Freedom; organized in October 1905 by Russian liberals under the leadership of Professor P. N. Miliukov and I. I. Petrunkevich. The party program included, among other things, equal and universal suffrage, civil liberties, equality before the law, and the allotment to peasants of lands of the Imperial family, of the state, and of private proprietors, who were to be fairly compensated.

23. **a most humble address.** On the occasion of the accession of Nicholas II a number of zemstvos sent delegations to read addresses of welcome to the new Emperor. Of these, the address of the Tver Zemstvo Assembly, expressing the hope of liberal political reform, has become most famous because of the blunt rebuke it evoked from the young monarch. Rodichev, the author of the address, was forbidden to live in St. Petersburg for a year and some of his associates received lighter punishments. (See F. Rodichev, "The Liberal Movement in Russia [1891–1905]," in *The Slavonic Review* [December 1923], pp. 249–62. A translation of the text of the address and the Emperor's reply is given in A. Kornilov, *Modern Russian History* [2 vols., translated by A. S. Kaun, New York, 1917], II, 276–78.)

24. **Dowager Empress Marie Sophia Frederika Dagmar Fedorovna** (1847–1928). Second daughter of King Christian IX of Denmark; first engaged to the heir to the throne, Nikolai Aleksandrovich (eldest son of Emperor Alexander II), who died in April 1865; later married the new heir to the throne, Aleksandr Aleksandrovich, who became Alexander III; after the February Revolution she was permitted to live with other members of the royal family in Crimea under close guard; in 1919 left the Crimea for England, and spent the last years of her life in Copenhagen.

Page 20, note 25. **Bank of the Nobility.** Established in 1885 for the purpose of issuing long-term loans to the landed gentry on the mortgage of their estates. It was placed under the direct supervision of the Ministry of

Finance and the credit institutions of the State Council. The management of the bank consisted of a manager and an assistant manager appointed by the Ministry of Finance, and of a Council of which not more than eight members were to be appointed by the Ministry of Finance and not more than three elected by the assemblies of the nobility. Branches of this bank were established all over Russia except in the Kingdom of Poland, the Grand Duchy of Finland, and the Baltic regions.

26. *zemskie nachalniki* (land captains). The office of *zemskii nachalnik*, created by the law of July 12, 1889, gave to its holders, who were members of the gentry class, administrative and judicial authority over the peasants, thus subordinating the peasant communities to agents of the central government. The *zemskie nachalniki* were supervised by the Gubernia Special Board (see note 21, chapter ii, p. 607).

Page 21, note 27. **Iosif Vladimirovich Gurko** (1828–1901). Father of the author and of General V. I. Gurko of World War fame; educated in His Majesty's School of Pages; distinguished himself in Russo-Turkish War, 1877–1878; Assistant Commander in Chief of the troops of the St. Petersburg Military District, 1879; Acting Governor-General of St. Petersburg, 1879–1880; Governor-General of Odessa and Commander of the troops of the Odessa Military District, 1882; Governor-General of Warsaw and Commander of the troops of the Warsaw Military District, 1883–1894; dismissed from this post at his own request.

28. **relations with France . . . . toward Germany.** (See note 15, chapter i, p. 599.)

29. **State Council** (*Gosudarstvennyi Sovet*). Established by Alexander I in 1801 under the name *Nepremennyi* (Permanent) *Sovet;* in the text of the oath taken by the members of the newly established council it was called *Gosudarstvennyi* (State) *Sovet,* and so it was subsequently called. The solemn opening of the State Council took place on January 1, 1810. It was reorganized on the hundredth anniversary of its establishment by an Imperial Ukase of 1901. After this reorganization the Council consisted of a chairman and an unlimited number of members appointed by the Emperor. It had four departments: (1) Legislation; (2) Civil and Ecclesiastical Affairs; (3) State Economy; (4) Industry, Science, and Commerce. Each department was comprised of a chairman and at least three members, all appointed by the Emperor for half a year; a minister could not be chairman of a department. Each department met separately, but there were also general sessions of the entire Council. The Council examined projects of laws proposed by the ministers, who were members ex-officio, discussed the budget and all state expenditures, but had no authority to propose modification of the laws. In 1906 the State Council was again reorganized to form the second chamber of the bicameral legislative system set up after the Revolution of 1905. According to this reorganization half the members were appointed and half elected by certain public bodies, including the zemstvos, the Synod of the Orthodox Church, the Academy of Sciences, chambers of commerce, the nobility, etc.

Attached to the State Council was the Imperial Chancellery (*Gosudarstvennaia Kantseliariia*) consisting of several sections, four of which corresponded to the four departments of the State Council. At the head of the

Chancellery was the *Gosudarstvennyi Sekretar,* assisted by a *Tovarishch Gosudarstvennago Sekretaria,* translated in the text as "Imperial Secretary" and "Assistant Imperial Secretary," respectively, in order to avoid confusion with the titles of the heads of the four sections, each of whom was called a State Secretary (*Stats-Sekretar*) and was assisted by an Assistant State Secretary (*Pomoshchnik Stats-Sekretaria*). Officially, a "State Secretary" was called a "State Secretary of the State Council." Business went first to the proper section of the Imperial Chancellery, thence to the State Council. State Secretaries or their assistants reported on matters under consideration to the departments of the State Council, whence these matters were brought before the Council in general session.

In addition to these four sections there were in the Imperial Chancellery a Section for the Affairs of the Imperial Secretary, a Section in Charge of Archives, and a Section for the Codification of Laws. The functions performed by this last section had originally been performed by a Commission to Draft Laws attached to the State Council in 1810; in 1826 this Commission was reorganized and became the Second Section of His Majesty's Private Chancellery; in 1882 another reorganization transferred its functions to a Codification Section established in the State Council; in 1893 this section was discontinued and its functions were taken over by the newly created Section for the Codification of Laws in the Imperial Chancellery. (See also chapter ii of the text, and note 13, chapter iii, p. 609.)

CHAPTER II

Page 23, note 1. **Mariinsky Palace.** Originally the Leuchtenberg or Mariia Palace, built in 1844 in the Italian style by Stakenschneider and presented by Nicholas I to his eldest daughter, Mariia, Duchess of Leuchtenberg, and her husband. Served as the hall of the State Council until 1917; under the Soviets occupied by medical offices.

2. **Ilia Efimovich Repin** (1844–1930). Great Russian painter; well known for his portraits, many of which were of celebrated contemporaries, including the author Tolstoi, the historian Solovev, and the composers Glinka, Borodin, and Musorgsky; of his other paintings the following are among the best known: "The Haulers of the Volga," "The Procession of the Cross," and "Cossacks Writing an Insulting Letter to the Sultan of Turkey."

Page 24, note 3. **Grand Duke Mikhail Nikolaevich** (1832–1909). Fourth son of Emperor Nicholas I; father of Grand Duke Aleksandr Mikhailovich; in the army during the Crimean War, 1854–1855; made a member of the State Council in 1855; head of all military schools, 1860; Viceroy of the Caucasus and Commander in Chief of the Caucasian Army, 1863–1881; participated in Russo-Turkish War, 1877–1878; left the Caucasus in 1881 and was made chairman of the State Council, which position and others he held until his illness in 1903; left for the south of France, where he remained most of the time until his death.

4. **Dmitrii Martynovich Solsky** (1833–1910). Graduate of the Imperial Alexander Lyceum, 1852; Assistant Head of the Second Section of His Majesty's Private Chancellery, 1852–1867; Imperial Secretary, 1867–1878; State Comptroller, 1878–1889; member of State Council and chairman of its Legislative Department, 1889–1893, and of its Department of State Economy, 1893–1902; made a count, 1902; chairman of the State Council, 1904–1906.

5. **Nikolai Fedorovich Deriuzhinsky** (1855–   ). Graduate of Moscow University; after service in provincial legal institutions was appointed to Codification Section of the State Council, 1883–1892; Assistant State Secretary, 1892–1901; member of the consultative body in the Ministry of Justice, 1901–1903; State Secretary of the State Council, 1903–1904.

Page 25, note 6. **Dmitrii Nikolaevich Nabokov** (1827–1904). Graduate of Imperial School of Law; made a Senator, 1864; Chief of His Majesty's Office for the Affairs of the Kingdom of Poland, 1867; appointed to the State Council, 1876; Minister of Justice, 1878–1885.

7. **Ivan Stepanovich Ganetsky** (1819–1887). Adjutant General; fought against Polish rebels, 1863; won fame at Plevna in Russo-Turkish War; member of the Military Council, 1879; Commandant of Peter and Paul Fortress, 1881–1887.

Page 26, note 8. **Nikolai Vasilevich Kleigels** (1850– ?). Served with distinction in Russo-Turkish War, 1877–1878; Assistant Chief of Police in Warsaw, 1888; Governor of St. Petersburg and then Governor-General of Kiev, Podolia, and Volhynia; Adjutant General to His Majesty, 1903.

9. **Board of Weights and Measures** (*Palata mer i vesov*). Established in 1863; supervised by the Ministry of Finance.

10. **Dmitrii Ivanovich Mendeleev** (1834–1907). Russian chemist; graduate of Central Pedagogic Institute in St. Petersburg; entered St. Petersburg University, 1856; studied under Regnault in Paris and Bunsen in Heidelberg, 1859–1861; professor of chemistry at the Technological Institute in St. Petersburg, 1863–1866, and at the University of St. Petersburg, 1866–1890. After resigning his professorship in 1890, became Director of the Board of Weights and Measures, a position he held till his death; famous for his "Periodic Law," a generalization to the effect that "the properties of the elements and the properties and compositions of compounds vary periodically with the atomic weights of the elements." (Patterson Muir, *History of Chemical Theories and Laws* [New York, 1907], p. 361.)

11. **Public men.** The term here so translated, *obshchestvennye deiateli*, has no exact parallel in English. It refers to persons not state officials but yet active in public affairs.

Page 27, note 12. **Baron Yulii Aleksandrovich Uxkull-Gyllenband** (1852–1918). Graduate in law, St. Petersburg University, 1875; in the Senate and later in the Chancellery of the State Council; Assistant State Secretary and State Secretary (1878–1899) of the Legislative Department of the State Council; Assistant Minister of Agriculture and State Domains, January–November, 1899; Assistant Imperial Secretary, 1899–1904; Imperial Secretary, 1904–1909; member of State Council, 1909.

Page 28, note 13. **Mikhail Nikolaevich Ostrovsky** (1827–1901). Graduate of Moscow University; an active assistant of State Comptroller V. A.

Tatarinov, 1863–1871, in the latter's reform of the Russian State Control; Assistant State Comptroller, 1871–1878; appointed Senator, 1872; member of the State Council, 1878; Minister of State Domains, 1881–1893; later, chairman of the Legislative Department of the State Council.

Page 29, note 14. **volost courts.** In 1838 special peasant courts were established in Russia. Although these courts were intended for state peasants only, they seem to have served as prototypes for the volost courts for peasants established by the reform of February 19, 1861. The volost courts were really class courts; that is, they tried peasants alone, and almost all peasant offenses came under their jurisdiction. The judges of these courts were elected from among the peasants, and no government confirmation of such elections was required. The courts were founded on the principle of peasant judicial autonomy and they used customary law. Those responsible for the reforms of 1861 considered them but temporary institutions in the process of giving the peasant class legal equality with the other classes; but the law of July 12, 1889, which established the office of zemskii nachalnik, seemed to make the volost courts permanent and to deprive them of their peasant autonomy. Thereafter the judges were elected merely as candidates from which the zemskie nachalniki might make the final selection. The volost courts also lost their class character, and their jurisdiction was extended to all inhabitants of the countryside except those who, like the nobility, belonged to the privileged classes. These changes tended to make the volost courts mere offices of the central government rather than autonomous judicial institutions of the peasant class.

15. **State Control** (*Gosudarstvennyi kontrol*). In the reign of Alexander II, V. A. Tatarinov was sent abroad (1856) to study foreign methods of state control, and the result of those studies served as a basis for the reform of 1863–1866, simplifying the management of the Russian treasury. In 1892 the State Control was organized as a ministry, with the following offices: State Comptroller, Assistant State Comptroller, the Council of the State Comptroller, a chancellery, three departments each headed by a general comptroller, a central bookkeeping office, two auditing commissions, and local branches throughout the country.

The State Control checked the estimates which all ministers sent to the State Control office at regular intervals. The opinions of the State Control were communicated to the ministers in question and to the State Council. If the ministers did not agree with these opinions, the estimates were examined by the State Council in the presence of the State Comptroller. The State Control also audited the books of all government institutions, with the following exceptions: (1) the Ministry of the Imperial Court; (2) His Majesty's Private Chancellery; (3) state credit institutions and the Special Credit Office of the Ministry of Finance; (4) the special administration of the Holy Synod which supervised special funds for the maintenance of ecclesiastical schools; and (5) the Ministry of Foreign Affairs in regard to special expenses which were known only to His Majesty; and a few others. The State Comptroller had to submit to the State Council, no later than October 1, a report of the expenditures for the preceding year.

Page 31, note 16. **Department of Factory Inspection.** An Imperial

Commission on factory conditions had been appointed as early as 1859, but nothing came of its deliberations until 1882, when legislative measures were taken, under the ministry of Bunge, for the protection of women and children in factories. Factory inspection was established under the supervision of the Department of Commerce and Industry in the Ministry of Finance. A little later (1886) other grievances were dealt with and partly removed by regulating contracts for hire and by providing that the money derived from deductions and fines should not be appropriated by the employers. At the same time local factory organizations entitled Boards for the Affairs of Factories (*Prisutstviia po fabrichnym delam*) were established; these were given the right to issue orders for the carrying out of "measures to safeguard the life and health of, and to render medical assistance to the workers." However, zemstvos and municipal dumas had similar rights and soon began to clash with the Boards. To obviate these difficulties there was promulgated the law of June 7, 1899, establishing a Special Board for the Affairs of Factories and Mines (*Glavnoe prisutstvie po fabrichnym i gornozavodskim delam*). This was attached to the Ministry of Finance and was given complete authority to issue regulations pertaining to factories and mines; the local boards became merely executive organs of the Special Board.

Page 32, note 17. **Sergei Vasilevich Zubatov** (1863–1917). Active in radical and revolutionary groups in the 'eighties in Moscow, he soon began to report them to the police; in 1889, became Assistant Chief and later Chief of the Moscow Secret Police Department; as the inspirer and organizer of the "Zubatovshchina," or "police socialism," he promoted in 1902 workers' unions in Moscow and St. Petersburg for the purpose of diverting the workers from revolutionary activity; resigned, 1903, and was later exiled to Vladimir; again connected with the Police Department during Trepov's administration, 1905; committed suicide shortly after the February Revolution of 1917.

18. **Chief Administration for the Affairs of the Press** (*Glavnoe upravlenie po delam pechati*). Founded in 1862 in the Ministry of the Interior.

19. **His Majesty's Private Chancellery to Receive Petitions** (*Sobstvennaia Ego Imperatorskago Velichestva Kantseliariia po priniatiiu proshenii na Vysochaishee Imia prinosimykh*) Formed in 1895, taking over some functions formerly performed by the Imperial Household (*Imperatorskaia Glavnaia Kvartira*), which had been established in 1883 and which carried out the Emperor's personal orders and instructions.

20. *Otechestvennyia Zapiski.* First appeared as two symposiums (*sborniki*) of literary and contemporary materials; published in St. Petersburg, 1818–1819; became nonpolitical monthly under Pavel Svinin, 1820–1830, when it closed for lack of funds; reappeared in 1839 under A. A. Kraevsky as an important literary and political journal with Belinsky in charge of the literary section, 1839–1846; under Saltykov and Nekrasov, 1868–1884, assumed radical tendencies and became a legal organ of the Narodniki; suppressed, 1884; Lermontov, Koltsov, Hertzen, and P. L. Lavrov were among its contributors.

Page 33, note 21. **Gubernia Special Board** (*Gubernskoe Prisutstvie*). An institution established July 12, 1889; was composed of the governor of the gubernia who was its chairman, the vice-governor, the gubernia marshal of the nobility, the local *prokuror* (public prosecutor) and his assistant, and two other persons from the local nobility appointed by the governor in agreement with the gubernia marshal of nobility and confirmed by the Minister of the Interior; supervised the activity of the zemskie nachalniki and the uezd congresses; responsible to the Ministry of the Interior.

CHAPTER III

Page 36, note 1. **Ivan Yakovlevich Golubev** (1841–1918). Graduate of the Imperial School of Law; in the Chancellery of the Fourth Department of the Senate, 1860–1864; in the Ministry of Justice, 1864–1866, where he participated in the drafting of the judicial reform of Alexander II; later served in the St. Petersburg District Court, the Senate, and the Ministry of Justice; member of the State Council, 1895; chairman of the Department for Civil and Ecclesiastical Affairs of the State Council, 1905; vice-chairman of the State Council after its reorganization, 1906; opened the Second, Third, and Fourth Dumas as the Tsar's representative.

Page 38, note 2. **Petr Mikhailovich Kaufmann-Turkestansky** (1857–1926). Graduate of the Imperial Alexander Lyceum, 1877; served in the secretariat of the Committee of Ministers and later in the Ministry of the Interior under Loris-Melikov; Assistant State Secretary in the Imperial Chancellery, 1886–1892; Secretary of the Fourth Section of His Majesty's Private Chancellery, 1892–1896, and Assistant Chief, 1896–1903; in the First Department of the Senate, 1903–1904; in charge of the Red Cross during the Russo-Japanese War; after the conclusion of peace, was appointed member of the State Council; Minister of Education, 1906–1908; on the staff of the Commander in Chief, and in charge of the Red Cross, 1915.

3. **Petr Alekseevich Kharitonov** (1852[6?]–1916). Graduate of the Imperial School of Law, 1873; in the Ministry of Justice, 1873–1883; consulting jurist in the Ministry of Justice, 1883; in the Codification Section of the State Council, 1888–1892; in charge of the State Printing Office, 1891–1893; in 1893 Assistant State Secretary of the Legislative Section of the Imperial Chancellery and in 1897 Acting State Secretary of the Section for Civil and Ecclesiastical Affairs of the Imperial Chancellery; Assistant Imperial Secretary, 1904; member of the State Council, 1906; State Comptroller, 1907–1916.

4. **Sergei Vasilevich Rukhlov** (1853–1918). Graduate of St. Petersburg University; served in the Ministry of the Interior and later in the Imperial Chancellery as State Secretary of the Section of State Economy; appointed Assistant Manager of Navigation, 1903; member of the State Council, 1905; one of the founders of the All-Russian National Union, 1908, and its first chairman; Minister of Ways and Communications, 1909–1915.

5. **Dmitrii Aleksandrovich Filosofov** (1861–1907). Graduate of St. Petersburg University in mathematics, 1883, in law, 1885; entered the Minis-

try of Education, 1886; in the Imperial Chancellery, 1887; appointed State Secretary of the Section of State Economy, 1899; State Secretary of the Section of Industry, Science, and Commerce, 1900; Assistant State Comptroller, 1901; State Comptroller, 1905; member of the State Council, 1906; in the same year became Minister of Commerce and Industry in Stolypin's cabinet.

6. **Aleksandr Fedorovich Trepov** (1862–1926). Educated in His Majesty's School of Pages; in the Ministry of the Interior, 1889–1892; Marshal of Nobility of Pereiaslavl Uezd, 1892–1895; Assistant State Secretary, 1899; member of the special commission to draft a plan for a State Duma according to the rescript of February 18, 1905, and the Manifesto of October 17, 1905; later, sent abroad to study the legislative institutions of Western Europe; Senator, 1906; member of the State Council, 1914, where he belonged to the Right group; Minister of Ways and Communications, 1915; chairman of the Council of Ministers for six weeks in 1916; died in emigration in France.

Page 39, note 7. **Ivan Ivanovich Shamshin** (1835–1912). State Secretary; member of the State Council; Senator.

Page 41, note 8. **"four-tailed"** (*chetyrekhvostka*) **formula of election.** This refers to universal, direct, secret, and equal suffrage.

Page 44, note 9. **Aleksandr Aleksandrovich Polovtsev** (1832–1912). Graduate of Imperial School of Law; began service in the First Department of the Senate; Senator, 1873; Imperial Secretary, 1883; member of State Council, 1892; one of the founders, secretary, and chairman (1878) of the Imperial Russian Historical Society.

10. **Nikolai Valerianovich Muravev** (1850–1908). Nephew of the famous Count Muravev-Amursky, Governor-General of the Far East; graduate of St. Petersburg and Moscow universities; lecturer in criminal law at Moscow University; Assistant Prokuror of St. Petersburg Court of Appeals, 1879, Prokuror, 1881; Prokuror of Moscow Court of Appeals, 1884; Ober-Prokuror of the Cassation Court for Criminal Affairs of the Senate, 1891; Imperial Secretary, 1892; Minister of Justice, 1894–1905; Ambassador to Rome, 1905.

Page 45, note 11. **Ivan Trofimovich Tatochka.** In the Imperial Chancellery, 1893–1902; Special Duty Clerk in the Ministry of the Interior, 1902.

12. **Prince Petr Mikhailovich Volkonsky** (1776–1852). General Field Marshal; served in the wars against Napoleon; accompanied Alexander I to the Congress of Vienna; on return to St. Petersburg was appointed His Majesty's Chief of Staff; at coronation of Nicholas I (1826), was appointed Minister of the Imperial Court, which position he occupied till his death.

13. **His Majesty's Private Chancellery** (*Sobstvennia Ego Imperatorskago Velichestva Kantseliariia*). Established in 1812 as one section, to which were added:

Second Section. Formed in 1826 to replace the Commission to Draft Laws attached to the State Council. Under the leadership of Speransky, who was put in charge of it when it was formed, the Second Section performed a colossal work in preparing for the publication in 1832 of both the Complete Collection of Russian Laws and the Code of Laws. In 1882 its functions were taken over by the Codification Section of the State Council, which, in turn, was closed in 1893 (December), when its functions were taken over by the Imperial Chancellery.

Third Section. Formed in 1826; supervised police affairs; in 1839 the Gendarme Corps was attached to it; discontinued in 1880, its functions being transferred to the Police Department in the Ministry of the Interior.

Fourth Section. Established in 1828 to replace the Chancellery of Empress Marie Fedorovna and to take charge of the institutions of that Empress; in this capacity administered, in the reign of Nicholas I, 365 schools for girls and various charity organizations; later was known as "Vedomstvo Imperatritsy Marii"; in 1890 took charge of over five hundred educational centers and charity institutions.

Fifth Section. Established in 1836 to supervise affairs concerning state peasants; in the next year it was reorganized into the Ministry of State Domains; this Ministry, though reorganized from time to time, continued in charge of Russian agriculture, whereas the Fifth Section was formally abolished in 1856.

Sixth Section. Established in 1842 to introduce civil rule in the Transcaucasian region; discontinued in 1845.

Page 46, note 14. **Nikolai Dmitrievich Sergeevsky** (1849–1908). Graduate in law of St. Petersburg University; professor of Demidov Lyceum in Yaroslavl, and of criminal law in St. Petersburg University (1882) ; one-time lecturer in the Military Law Academy; publisher and editor of *Iuridicheskaia Letopis,* 1890–1892; Head of the Section for the Codification of the Fundamental Laws of Finland, 1893; member of the Consultative Board in the Ministry of Justice and editor of *Zhurnal Ministerstva Iustitsii,* 1894; State Secretary of the Section for Codification of Laws of the Imperial Chancellery, 1895.

15. **Nikolai Mikhailovich Korkunov** (1853–1904). Graduate in law of St. Petersburg University; professor there and in the Imperial Alexander Lyceum and Military Law Academy, 1879–1904; member of the Section for the Codification of the Fundamental Laws of Finland, 1893.

16. **Kronid Ivanovich Malyshev** (1841– ?). Son of a clergyman, received an ecclesiastical education; in 1864 entered St. Petersburg University to study law; sent abroad for two years by the university and upon his return lectured there until 1882; in the Codification Section of the State Council, 1882–1895, which became in 1893 the Section for the Codification of Laws in the Imperial Chancellery; later member of the Consultative Board in the Ministry of Justice.

Page 49, note 17. **confirmed by the Russian Emperor.** The controversy is discussed at length by J. R. Fisher, *Finland and the Tsars, 1809–1899* (London, 1899). See also John H. Wuorinen, *Nationalism in Modern Finland* (New York, 1931), pp. 187–203.

18. **Eduard Nikolaevich Berendts** (1860–   ). Professor of law in the Demidov Lyceum and in St. Petersburg University, 1901; Director of the Demidov Lyceum, 1904–1905; professor at the Imperial Law School, 1907; member of the Chief Administration for the Affairs of the Press, 1908; Senator, 1914.

19. **Mikhail Mikhailovich Borodkin** (1852–   ). Lieutenant General; graduate of Alexander Military Law Academy; assistant to the chief military prosecutor (*Glavnyi voennyi prokuror*), 1909; appointed head of the Alexander Military Law Academy, 1911; Senator, 1911; member of the State Council, 1916; wrote extensively on the Finnish question.

20. **Kesar Filippovich Ordin** (? –1892). Graduate in mathematics of St. Petersburg University; author of a number of articles on Finland.

21. **Fedor Pavlovich Elenev.** Served in the Ministry of the Interior as a member of the Chief Administration for the Affairs of the Press and of the Council of the Minister of the Interior; wrote on the peasant question and on the Polish and Finnish questions.

22. **Nikolai Stepanovich Tagantsev** (1843–1923). Well-known criminologist; graduate in law of St. Petersburg University, 1862, when he was sent abroad to study criminal law; on his return collaborated on *Zhurnal Ministerstva Iustitsii* and *Sudebnyi Vestnik;* professor at St. Petersburg University and Alexander Lyceum, 1868; editor of *Zhurnal Ugolovnago i Grazhdanskago Prava,* 1873–1878; member of the Consultative Board of the Ministry of Justice, 1881; Senator, 1887; chairman of the Commission to study the project of the new Finnish legislation, 1890; chairman of the Commission to study Russian legislation, 1894, and chairman of the section to study criminal law; member of the State Council, 1906; principal author of the new Russian penal code of 1903.

Page 50, note 23. **The law incorporating Finnish soldiers into Russian army units.** The law, passed June 29/July 12, 1901, disbanded the existing Finnish army organized under the military service law of 1878 and provided that thereafter the Finns should do their military service with Russian troops under Russian regulations. The Finns declared the act unconstitutional, and over half of those liable for service did not report for examination. Two or three years later the Imperial government released the Finns from military service in lieu of an annual payment of ten million marks to the Russian treasury. In the meantime, however, during Plehve's term as State Secretary for Finland, several other measures regarding the use of the Russian language and employment of Russian officials in Finland were adopted to the great irritation of the Finns. (See Kustavi Grotenfelt, "The Legal Struggle, 1899–1906," in *Finland, the Country, Its People and Institutions* [Helsingfors, 1926], pp. 186–88.)

24. **Count Carl Aleksandr Armfelt** (1850–1925). Chief of His Majesty's Chancellery for Finland, 1895; ceremonial master of the Finnish Diet, 1894 and 1897; inspector for the Finnish banks, St. Petersburg Control, 1895–1900; Finnish State Secretary in St. Petersburg, 1902; member and founder of the academic institute in Åbo, 1923; retired from politics, 1923.

Page 51, note 25. **constituted Viborg Gubernia.** This represented part of the territory won by Peter the Great (1682–1725) in 1721 at the Treaty of Nystad which concluded his wars with Sweden.

26. **Aleksei Nikolaevich Kuropatkin** (1848–1925). Entered the army in 1864; in 1875 engaged in diplomatic work in Kashgaria and in 1876 took part in military operations in Turkestan, Kokand, and Samarkand; served with distinction as Chief of Staff to Skobelev in the Russo-Turkish War of

1877–1878; in 1882 became a Major General and in 1898 Minister of War; in 1904 he was given command of the Russian army then mobilizing in Manchuria for the conflict with Japan; after the defeat of Mukden and the retirement of the army to Tieling, he resigned the command to General Linevich, and took the latter's place as commander of one of the armies in Manchuria; served in the World War on the Russian Western front and in 1916 became Governor-General of Turkestan; after the Bolshevik Revolution became a village clerk near his former estate in Pskov Gubernia; died at Shemshupino (Pskov). (See also chapter xiv of text.)

27. **at Port Arthur.** For Witte's account of this incident, see S. Y. Witte, *Vospominaniia Tsarstvovanie Nikolaia II* (2 vols., Berlin, 1922), II, 228 ff.; also the abridged English edition, *The Memoirs of Count Witte,* translated and edited by A. Yarmolinsky (Garden City, 1921), p. 259.

CHAPTER IV

Page 53, note 1. **State Bank.** Established by statute in May and opened on July 1, 1860, with a capital of fifteen million rubles, later increased to twenty-five million; performed two functions: financial and commercial; supervised by the Minister of Finance and the Council of State Credit establishments; minor matters concerning the bank were under the supervision of three deputies, two from the St. Petersburg nobility and one from the State Control; the direct control of the bank's operations was entrusted to a board made up of a manager, his assistants, six directors, and three deputies. Branches of the bank were established in other Russian cities. (See also Margaret Miller, *The Economic Development of Russia, 1905–1914* [London, 1926], pp. 82–88.)

2. **Prince Aleksei Borisovich Lobanov-Rostovsky** (1824–1896). Graduate of Tsarskoe Selo Lyceum; Envoy to Constantinople, 1859–1863; Governor of Orel, 1866; Assistant Minister of the Interior, 1867–1878; Ambassador to Constantinople, 1878–1879, to London, 1879–1882, to Vienna, 1882–1895, to Berlin, 1895; Minister of Foreign Affairs, 1895–1896.

3. **Pavel Lvovich Lobko** (1838–1905). General of Infantry; graduate of the General Staff Academy, 1861; in the Chancellery of the Ministry of War, 1867; professor in the General Staff Academy in 1870; appointed tutor to the future Emperor Nicholas II, 1885; member of the State Council, 1898; State Comptroller, 1899–1905.

Page 54, note 4. **voted for it.** For Witte's account of this incident see S. Y. Witte, *op. cit.,* I, 230; also the English edition, p. 77.

5. **Konstantin Petrovich Pobedonostsev** (1827–1907). After graduating from Imperial School of Law, was employed in the Moscow Department of the Senate; professor of Russian Civil Law, Moscow University, and tutor of the sons of Alexander II, 1860–1865; member of the Consultative Board of the Ministry of Justice, 1865; Senator, 1868; member of the State Council, 1872; Ober-Prokuror of the Holy Synod, 1880–1905; as an uncom-

promising reactionary opposed the application of Western institutions in Russia; an advocate of repressive policies against national and religious minorities.

6. **The Holy [All-Russian Ruling] Synod** (*Sviateishii Vserossiiskii Pravitelstvuiushchii Sinod*). After the death of the Patriarch Adrian in 1700, Peter the Great did not permit the election of a successor. Instead he abolished the Patriarchate and in 1721 established a collegiate body, the Holy Synod, as the supreme institution for the administration of ecclesiastical affairs. The executive of the Synod, the Ober-Prokuror, in later times held the rank of minister and reported on church affairs to the Emperor, who appointed the members of the Synod. The Provisional Government of 1917 reorganized the Synod, abolished the office of Ober-Prokuror, and set up a Ministry of Confessions. Later, after the Bolshevik Revolution, the Patriarchate was restored for a short time but was subsequently abolished in the Soviet Union.

Page 55, note 7. **the commercial treaty of 1894.** A treaty of commerce and navigation between Germany and Russia, signed at Berlin, January 29/ February 10, 1894. Ratifications were exchanged at Berlin, March 8/ March 20, 1894. This treaty concluded a tariff war between the two countries; it reduced German duties on Russian grain and Russian duties on German manufactured goods; it was to remain in force for ten years and to continue after that time unless notice to the contrary was given by one of the contracting parties twelve months before the expiration of the ten-year term. The complete text and annexes of the treaty are given in: Great Britain, Foreign Office, *British and Foreign State Papers, 1893–1894* (London, 1899), Vol. 86, pp. 442–83. See also Witte, *op. cit.,* I, 269–73 (English edition, pp. 62–72).

8. **Witte . . . . Minister of Finance.** Witte has written his own account of his work as Minister of Finance. (See Witte, *op. cit.,* Vol. I, chapter v [English edition, chapter iii].)

9. **Mikhail Nikiforovich Katkov** (1818–1887). Publicist; graduate of Moscow University; in his student days a friend of Belinsky and Bakunin; began early to write bibliographical notes, translations of Heine, Shakespeare, and others, and to contribute to *Otechestvennyia Zapiski* and other periodicals; attended Heidelberg University, 1840; professor at Moscow University, 1845–1850; editor of *Moskovskiia Vedomosti,* 1851, and of *Russkii Vestnik,* 1856; became conservative in his political views, particularly after the Polish revolts and the activities of the revolutionists, 1862–1863; conducted written polemics with Chernyshevsky and Herzen.

10. **Nikolai Khristianovich Bunge** (1823–1895). Graduate in law of Kiev University, 1845; appointed professor there, 1850, rector, 1859–1862, and elected rector, 1871–1875, 1878–1880; Assistant Minister of Finance, 1880; Minister of Finance, 1881–1886, during which time among other things the "soul-tax" was abolished for most of the population, the Peasant Land Bank was established (1882), and factory regulations were promulgated (1883); chairman of the Committee of Ministers, 1887.

11. **Ivan Alekseevich Vyshnegradsky** (1831–1895). Graduate in physics and mathematics of the Pedagogic Institute, 1851; taught in St. Petersburg

cadet school and in 1858 in the Mikhail Artillery Academy; studied abroad and after his return to Russia in 1862 lectured again in the Mikhail Artillery Academy and in the Institute of Technology; director of this Institute, 1875; member of the Council of the Ministry of Education, 1884; member of the State Council, 1886; Minister of Finance, 1887–1892.

12. **Afinogen Yakovlevich Antonovich** (1848–1915). Graduate of Kiev University and later professor of economics there; editor of *Kievskoe Slovo,* 1887–1892; Assistant Minister of Finance, 1893–1895; later, member of the Council of the Ministry of Education.

Page 56, note 13. **Finance Committee.** Established by Alexander I as a part of the general reorganization of the central legislative and administrative institutions of Russia. In view of the fact that most of the members of the recently formed Committee of Ministers were not in direct contact with the affairs of the Ministry of Finance, Alexander I, at the suggestion of Count Vasilev, then Minister of Finance, decreed on October 13, 1806, the formation of a Finance Committee, entirely independent of the State Council and the Committee of Ministers. The chief duty of the Committee was to discuss questions concerning the raising of state loans and other matters relating to the credit of the state. It was of a consultative nature and its deliberations and conclusions came into force only after receiving Imperial sanction. The chairman of the Committee and its members were chosen by the Emperor himself from among the highest state dignitaries. The Minister of Finance was always a member, and the management of the affairs of the Committee was incumbent upon the Ministry of Finance. The Committee continued without interruption until the Revolution of 1917, when it, like the State Council, was suppressed.

Page 57, note 14. **Friedrich List** (1789–1846). German economist; professor of administration and politics at the University of Tübingen, 1817–1819; as deputy to Württemberg chamber he was active in advocating administrative reforms; expelled from the chamber and imprisoned; after his release he emigrated to America, where he lived from 1825 to 1832, and achieved success as a journalist, as a speculator in coal and railways, and as a writer on political economy; in 1832 became United States consul at Leipzig; played an influential part in the establishment of the German *Zollverein.*

15. **Aleksandr Ivanovich Chuprov** (1842–1908). Graduate in law of Moscow University, 1866; sent by the university to study abroad, 1872; returned to lecture on political economy and statistics at Moscow University, 1874; invited to attend, as a specialist, Count Baranov's commission to study Russian railways, and in 1888 took part in the commission to study the decline in agricultural prices; contributed to *Russkiia Vedomosti.*

Page 61, note 16. **Special Conference for the Affairs of the Nobility** (*Osoboe Soveshchanie po delam dvorianskago sostoianiia*). Established in 1897 by Imperial order under the chairmanship of I. N. Durnovo, chairman of the Committee of Ministers; after five years its functions were taken over by a Special Chancellery for the Affairs of the Nobility established in the Ministry of the Interior. (See also Witte, *op. cit.,* I, 460–64 [English edition, pp. 208–10].)

Page 62, note 17. **Aleksei Sergeevich Ermolov** (1847–1917). Graduate of the Imperial Alexander Lyceum and the St. Petersburg Agricultural Institute; entered the Ministry of Finance, 1871; Director of the Department of Indirect Taxation, 1883; Assistant Minister of Finance, 1892; in charge of the Ministry of State Domains, 1893, and commissioned by Alexander III to reconstruct this ministry into the Ministry of Agriculture and State Domains; Minister of Agriculture and State Domains, 1894–1905; member of the State Council, 1905; member of the International Agricultural Institute in Rome, and an honorary member of the Academy of Science, 1899. (See also chapter v in the text.)

18. **Grand Duke Mikhail Aleksandrovich** (1878–1918). Son of Emperor Alexander III; designated as his successor by Nicholas II at the time of the latter's abdication, March 2, 1917, but refused the succession; killed by the Bolsheviks.

19. **Special Conference . . . . and . . . . the agricultural committees.** The Special Conference on the Needs of Agricultural Industry (*Osoboe soveshchanie o nuzhdarkh selsko-khoziaistvennoi promyshlennosti*) was founded January 22, 1902, under the chairmanship of Witte, who was empowered to invite for consultation various individuals, including the Minister of Agriculture and State Domains and the Minister of the Interior. Twelve commissions were established for preliminary work. Secretarial work was done by the Chancellery of the Minister of Finance. Special local committees were established throughout the Empire: gubernia committees, of which there were 82, were presided over by the governors of gubernias; uezd committees, numbering 536, by the uezd marshals of nobility. The committees were composed of some zemstvo men, local officials of the institutions concerned, representatives of agricultural societies, etc. They were not to attempt to draft the required measures—this was actually the task of the Special Conference—but rather to make clear the most important local needs. The work done by the local committees was completed and published in 58 volumes. The Special Conference was unexpectedly brought to an end, March 30, 1905. For Witte's account of this work, see Witte, *op. cit.*, I, 476–81 (English edition, pp. 215–19). (See also chapters xiii and xvii of text, and Stuart B. Tompkins, "Why Witte Failed to Solve the Peasant Problem," in *The Journal of Modern History*, IV [June 1932], 235–39.)

Page 63, note 20. **zemstvo institutions in the western gubernias.** See note 18, chapter i, p. 599.

Page 64, note 21. **dissatisfaction of the public.** See Appendix 1, especially pp. 697–700.

Page 65, note 22. **Novoe Vremia.** Daily St. Petersburg newspaper founded in 1868 by Kirkor and Yumatov, passed over to F. N. Ustrialov in 1871; published by O. K. Notovich, 1873–1874, and edited by M. P. Fedorov; bought by A. S. Suvorin and V. I. Likhachev in 1876, Fedorov continuing as editor; A. A. Suvorin became editor in 1896; in 1897 added a Wednesday illustrated supplement which included belles-lettres and bibliography; after 1881 had two issues daily; at first progressive, under A. S. Suvorin became conservative; was widely circulated, with outstanding men of letters as contributors; ceased publication after the October Revolution.

23. **Russkoe Delo.** Edited and published in Moscow by S. F. Sharapov,

1886–1890 (with interruptions); discussed political, literary, and agricultural topics.

24. **Sergei Fedorovich Sharapov** (1856–1911). Editor and publisher of *Russkoe Delo, Russkii Trud, Svidetel.*

25. **Ilia Faddeich Tsion.** Well-known physiologist; graduate of Warsaw Medico-Surgical Academy and Kiev and Berlin universities; professor at St. Petersburg University, 1870–1875, when he was dismissed after student demonstrations against him; engaged in journalism and study of financial problems; wrote for *Moskovskiia Vedomosti;* agent of Ministry of Finance in Paris, 1880; in 1891 published a leaflet criticizing Vyshnegradsky, Minister of Finance; also wrote critical leaflets on Witte; recalled to Russia but refused to return.

Page 66, note 26. **Prince Vladimir Petrovich Meshchersky** (1839–1914). Graduate of the Imperial School of Law; special-duty clerk in the Ministry of the Interior; editor of *Grazhdanin,* 1872–1914; collaborator of *Russkii Vestnik* and *Moskovskiia Vedomosti;* author of several novels and his memoirs.

27. *Grazhdanin.* Weekly (1872–1887), daily, and then semi-weekly; published by Prince V. P. Meshchersky, 1872–1914; among its early editors were G. K. Gradovsky, F. M. Dostoevsky, and V. F. Putsykevich. At first moderately conservative, it became under Meshchersky's editorship more conservative, reflecting the views of conservative nobility and bureaucracy. The paper received an annual government subsidy of about eighty thousand rubles.

28. **Evgenii Vasilevich Bogdanovich** (1829–1914). General of Infantry; member of the Council of the Minister of the Interior; in 1914 sent a letter to Nicholas II requesting the removal of Rasputin; author of a number of patriotic and religious works, including *Rossiia na Dalnem Vostoke ("Russia in the Far East").*

CHAPTER V

Page 69, note 1. **Minister.** The Ministry of Agriculture was organized originally as the Ministry of State Domains, 1837 until 1894; reorganized as the Ministry of Agriculture and State Domains, 1894–1905; by the Ukase of May 6, 1905, reorganized as the Chief Administration of Land Organization and Agriculture.

2. **Count Pavel Dmitrievich Kiselev** (1788–1872). In the army; participated in the Battle of Borodino in the war with Napoleon and in the later campaigns of 1813–1815; Adjutant to Emperor Alexander I; Chief of Staff of the Second Army, 1819; participated in Turkish War, 1828–1829, after which he took charge of the administration of Moldavia and Wallachia until 1834; member of the State Council, 1835; appointed member of the Secret Committee for Peasant Affairs, following a talk with the Emperor on the necessity of liberating the peasants, but the committee was much opposed by the higher circles of society and accomplished little; as Minister of State Domains, 1837–1856, took over (1837) from the Fifth Section of His Maj-

esty's Chancellery (created 1836) the supervision of the special administration for state peasants; created count, 1839; Ambassador to Paris, 1856–1862, when he resigned; remained in Paris until his death.

Page 73, note 3. **Count Petr Aleksandrovich Heyden** (1840–1907). Graduate of His Majesty's School of Pages and Mikhail Artillery Academy; became member of District Court, 1868, in Voronezh and then in St. Petersburg, later becoming vice-chairman of the St. Petersburg District Court and member of the Court of Appeals; Chief of His Majesty's Chancellery to Receive Petitions, 1886–1890; a uezd marshal of nobility in Pskov Gubernia, 1895; chairman of the Imperial Free Economic Society, 1895; active participant in zemstvo movement, 1904–1905, representing moderate liberal tendencies of the nobility; presided over a zemstvo and town congress in defiance of the government, 1905; after the October Manifesto he joined the Union of October 17 (Octobrists); later when this party became more conservative he left it and organized a new group called the Party of Peaceful Reconstruction (*Partiia mirnago obnovleniia*); active member of the First Duma.

Page 74, note 4. **Mariia Gavrilovna Savina.** Well-known actress; from 1874 to 1915 in the Alexander Theater in St. Petersburg.

5. **St. Isaac's Cathedral** (dedicated to St. Isaac of Dalmatia). The largest church in St. Petersburg, built on the same spot as two previous churches. The original one was of wood, erected by Peter the Great in 1710, and subsequently destroyed. Catherine II commenced another which was finished in 1801. The existing edifice was begun under Alexander I, in 1817, and finished in 1858. It was built according to plans by the French architect Ricard de Monferrand and at great cost; such materials as granite, marble, porphyry, jasper, lapislazuli, bronze, and gold were used in its construction and decoration. The building is in the form of a cross and is crowned by an enormous golden dome. After the Revolution of 1917 it was transformed into an antireligious museum.

CHAPTER VI

Page 75, note 1. **the [Ruling] Senate** (*Pravitelstvuiushchii Senat*) was established by Peter the Great in 1711 with extensive administrative and judicial powers. During subsequent reigns its functions were considerably altered, its administrative activities were curtailed, and it became primarily concerned with the promulgation and execution of laws. According to the Code of Laws published in 1857 (third edition) there were twelve departments of the Senate: Departments I–V, the Land Surveying Department, and the Heraldry Department were located in St. Petersburg; Departments VI–VIII (abolished in 1871) were in Moscow; Departments IX–X (abolished in 1876) were in Warsaw. As the judicial reforms of Alexander II were put into effect, Departments II–V and the Land Surveying Department were consolidated into one, and by the end of the nineteenth century the Senate was organized as follows: First Department took charge of administrative matters which could not be finally dealt with by any other institution; Second

Department, established 1882, dealt with peasant administration; Legal Department, established 1898, assumed the duties of the former legal departments (II–V) and of the Land Surveying Department; Department of Heraldry; the remaining two departments were Courts of Cassation, one for civil and one for criminal affairs. An Ober-Prokuror presided over each department. The Minister of Justice, as General Prokuror and the highest officer of the body, presided over plenary sessions. Members of the Senate were appointed by the Emperor. The Senate was abolished by decree of the Soviet Government, November 24, 1917.

Page 77, note 2. **Tver Gubernia Zemstvo Board.** See note 18, chapter i, p. 599.

Page 78, note 3. **King George [I] of Greece** (1845–1913). Born Prince Christian William of Schleswig-Holstein; second son of King Christian IX of Denmark; his election to the throne of Greece was recognized by the powers of Europe in 1863; assassinated at Salonica.

4. **Sir Basil Zaharoff** (1850–1936). Financier and politician; born in Constantinople of Russian father and Greek mother; educated in London and Paris; became one of the world's richest men, his fortune being built up from munition plants, shipbuilding, oil, and other enterprises; exerted a strong if indirect influence during the World War and at the Paris conference through his connections with important political personages; during this period extended considerable financial aid to the British and French governments and later was honored by these countries for his war services; established chairs of aviation at the universities of Paris, Petrograd, and London and endowed the Marshal Foch professorship of French literature at Oxford University and the Field-Marshal Haig chair of English literature at the University of Paris.

Page 80, note 5. **reform of 1864 in the Kingdom of Poland.** In the early months of 1864 there was formed in St. Petersburg a committee of five persons, presided over by the Emperor, to study the affairs of the Kingdom of Poland. The Committee gave its attention first of all to the peasant question, the investigation of which was assigned to N. A. Miliutin, Prince Cherkassky, V. A. Artsimovich, and Y. F. Samarin. By the ukases of February 19, 1864, Polish peasants were given the land which they were then cultivating; they also retained the right to use the landlords' pastures. The landlords were compensated for the loss of land by payments from the State Treasury in so-called liquidation paper bills (*bumagi*). An all-class *gmina* (volost) was created as an organ of self-government.

6. *Narodniki.* In the first years of the reign of Alexander II when emancipation and other reforms were being widely discussed, many of the younger generation broke with the traditions and ideas of their seniors in the revolutionary camp and enthusiastically espoused more radical ideas on social and political questions as expressed by Chernyshevsky, Dobroliubov, and Pisarev. The emancipation act fell far short of the demands of the young intellectuals, as it did of the anticipations of the peasants. There were riots and disorders in the universities to which the government responded with wholesale expulsions and arrests. To the expelled students Herzen addressed his famous appeal to go "To the people!" (*V narod!*) and hundreds

of the young intellectuals of both noble and humble birth, their numbers increased in 1867–1868 by fresh expulsions from the universities, heeded Herzen's summons and participated in the "To the people" movement. This movement reached the peak of its intensity in the early 'seventies; its participants were referred to as the *Narodniki* (men of the people), a term which came later to be applied to those liberals and revolutionists who were interested chiefly in the problems of the peasant, who were hostile to industrialism.

The *Narodniki* were non-Marxist in their revolutionary thinking. They were for the most part disciples either of Lavrov, who advocated a program of peaceful propaganda, persuasion, and education among the people, or of the anarchist Bakunin, who urged a program of insurrection; but the government made no distinction between propagandist and insurrectionist groups and took steps to stamp out the entire movement. Numerous arrests, mass trials like that of the "50" in 1876 and of the "193" in 1877, and many sentences of imprisonment, together with the sad lack of peasant response to the efforts of the *Narodniki,* evplain the decline of the "To the people" movement. (See note 2, chapter x, p. 623.)

Page 81, note 7. **President of the French Republic.** François Félix Faure (1841–1899). French statesman; successful tanner, shipbuilder, and merchant; elected to National Assembly, 1881; Under-Secretary for Commerce and the Colonies, 1881, 1883–1885, 1888; Vice-President of Chamber of Deputies, 1893; Minister of the Navy in Dupuy's cabinet, 1894–1895; succeeded Casimir-Périer as President of the Republic, 1895–1899; paid a visit to Russia, 1897, during which references were openly made to the secret Franco-Russian alliance.

8. **Goremykin's dismissal.** See Appendix 1, especially p. 695.

CHAPTER VII

Page 82, note 1. *Oprichnina.* Originally the bodyguard of Ivan the Terrible, later known for its merciless robberies; comprised mainly of young men of noble birth who swore to renounce every other tie and family connection and to serve the Tsar alone; the insignia—a dog's head and a broom— was intended to convey the idea that its bearers would bite and sweep away every traitor; an institution very much hated by the people for its cruelty and acts of injustice.

Page 84, note 2. **Ananii Petrovich Strukov** (1851–   ). Graduate of St. Petersburg University; in the Legislative Section of the Imperial Chancellery; in 1882 transferred to the Ministry of the Interior; elected Marshal of Nobility of Ekaterinoslav Gubernia, 1882; elected member of the State Council, 1906; appointed member of same, 1912.

3. **Dmitrii Gavrilovich Bibikov** (1792–1870). After military service under Alexander I became vice-governor of Vladimir, Saratov, and Moscow gubernias, successively; Director of the Department of Foreign Trade in the Ministry of Finance, 1825–1835; Governor-General in Kiev, Volhynia, and Podolia, 1837–1852; made Adjutant General, 1845; General of Infantry and member of State Council, 1848; Minister of the Interior, 1852–1855.

4. **Nicholas I** (1796–1855). Son of Emperor Paul; brother of Alexander I; Emperor of Russia, 1825–1855.

Page 85, note 5. **Gubernia Special Board for Zemstvo Affairs** (*Gubernskoe po zemskim delam prisutstvie*). These boards were established in 1890, and in 1892 were re-named Gubernia Special Board for Zemstvo and Municipal Affairs (*Gubernskoe po zemskim i gorodskim delam prisutstvie*). Each was made up of the governor of the gubernia (chairman), gubernia marshal of nobility, vice-governor of the gubernia, manager of the local branch of the State Control, public prosecutor (*prokuror*) of the district court, mayor, chairman of the gubernia zemstvo board (*uprava*), and one member elected by the gubernia zemstvo assembly (*sobranie*).

6. **Aleksandr Semenovich Stishinsky** (1851–1920). Graduate of Moscow University, 1872; worked in the Department for General Affairs of the Ministry of the Interior; transferred to the Imperial Chancellery, 1873; Assistant State Secretary, 1882–1886, when again transferred to the Ministry of the Interior; Head of the Peasant Section, 1893; Assistant Imperial Secretary, 1896–1899; Assistant Minister of the Interior, 1900–1904; member of State Council, 1904; Head of the Chief Administration of Land Organization and Agriculture, April–June, 1906; chairman of the Committee to Fight German Domination [in Russia], 1916.

7. **Police Department.** In the Ministry of the Interior; before 1880 its functions were performed by the Third Section of His Majesty's Private Chancellery.

Page 86, note 8. **uezd congresses (*uezdnye sezdy*).** Established by the law of July 12, 1889, which also established the office of zemskii nachalnik; replaced the uezd Boards for Peasant Affairs and the Congresses of Justices of the Peace; were permanent bodies, one for each uezd; each was presided over by the uezd marshal of nobility and had two sections or boards (*prisutstvie*): an administrative board and a judicial board; the administrative board was composed of the uezd marshal of nobility as chairman, all zemskie nachalniki of the uezd, the *ispravnik* or uezd police officer, and the chairman of the uezd zemstvo board. The Judicial Board consisted of: uezd marshal of nobility (chairman), uezd member of the district court who acted as chairman when necessary, town judges, honorary justices of peace, and zemskie nachalniki.

Page 87, note 9. **the Fontanka Palace.** The palace on the Fontanka by the Tsepnoi Bridge, formerly the residence of the Chief of Gendarmes; rebuilt and magnificently redecorated and refurnished by Sipiagin, it became the official residence of himself and his successors.

10. **Michael Fedorovich Romanov** (1596–1645). First Tsar of the House of Romanov; elected to the Russian throne by the *Zemskii Sobor*, February, 1613.

CHAPTER VIII

Page 89, note 1. **Prince Mikhail Ivanovich Khilkov** (1843–1909). Graduate of His Majesty's School of Pages; traveled in Europe and America, where he worked in railway shops and engine works; after his return to

Russia held responsible railway positions; Head of the Bulgarian Ministry of Public Works, Ways and Communications, Trade and Agriculture, 1882–1885; took charge of a number of Russian railways, 1885–1895; Minister of Ways and Communications in Russia, 1895–1905; member of the State Council, 1905.

CHAPTER IX

Page 92, note 1. **Eduard Vasilevich Frisch** (1833–1907). Graduate of the Imperial School of Law; Assistant Ober-Prokuror and Prokuror of the Senate's Court of Cassation for Criminal Affairs; Assistant Minister of Justice, 1876–1883; member of the State Council, 1883; head of the Codification Section of the State Council, 1883–1893; chairman of the Department for Civil and Ecclesiastical Affairs of the State Council, 1897–1900; chairman of the Legislative Department of the State Council, 1900–1907; chairman of the State Council, 1906.

Page 93, note 2. **Aleksandr Nikolaevich Ostrovsky** (1823–1886). Writer of realistic plays picturing the life of the merchant class and petty bourgeoisie; studied law at Moscow University; employed as a minor clerk in Moscow courts, 1843–1851; dismissed from service and put under police supervision for some of his writings which were taken by Moscow merchants as personal offense; later, under a more liberal regime, sent into the provinces to report on the condition of the people; this mission inspired several historical dramas; under Alexander III received a pension of 3,000 rubles a year; with the help of Moscow capitalists established a model theater and school of dramatic art in that city; also founded the Society of Russian Dramatic Art and Opera Composers.

3. **Vladimir Ivanovich Kovalevsky** (1848– ?). Graduated from St. Petersburg Institute of Agriculture, 1875; while still a student was imprisoned in Peter and Paul Fortress, 1875–1877, for his connection with the Nechaev affair; entered the Ministry of State Domains, 1879; Director of the Department of Manufacture and Trade in the Ministry of Finance, 1892–1900; Assistant Minister of Finance, 1900–1902; resigned and for fourteen years engaged in private business; chairman of the Imperial Technological Society; chairman of the Scientific Agricultural Committee, 1920; after 1923 honorary chairman of the State Institute of Applied Agriculture.

Page 94, note 4. **Valerian Alekseevich Tatarinov** (1816–1871). In the Second Section of His Majesty's Private Chancellery, 1842; Assistant Director of the Chancellery of the State Control, 1850; General Comptroller of the Department of Civil Accounting, 1852; sent abroad, 1855, to study other systems of state control; on his return five of his studies were published, 1858–1861; Head of the Commission to Study the Basic Principle of State Accounting, 1858; the subsequent recommendations of his commission were adopted and were of great benefit to Russia; acting State Comptroller, 1863.

Page 96, note 5. **Nikolai Vladimirovich Shidlovsky** (1843–1907). State

Secretary in the Imperial Chancellery, 1865–1892; later member of the Senate, the State Council, and the Finance Committee.

6. **Fedor Gustavovich Terner** (1833–1906). Director of the Department of Direct Taxation in the Ministry of Finance; Assistant Minister of Finance; member of the State Council; Senator.

7. **Count Nikolai Alekseevich Protasov-Bakhmetev** (1834–1907). Graduate of His Majesty's School of Pages and in 1856 of the Nicholas General Staff Academy; served in Russo-Turkish War, 1877–1878; Governor of Astrakhan and Ataman of Astrakhan Cossacks, 1880–1882; Head of His Majesty's Special Chancellery to Supervise the Institutions of the Empress Marie, 1890.

8. **Institutions of Empress Marie.** See note 13, chapter iii, p. 609.

Page 97, note 9. **Count Konstantin Ivanovich Pahlen** (1833–1912). Graduate in law of St. Petersburg University; worked in the Chancellery of the State Council, 1855; during the Crimean War (1853–1856) was a member of the commission to help the wounded, organized by the Empress; assistant director in the Police Department in the Ministry of the Interior; Governor of Pskov, 1864; Assistant Minister, then Minister of Justice, 1867–1878; member of the State Council, 1878.

Page 98, note 10. **Dmitrii Grigorevich Derviz.** Ober-Prokuror of the Senate's Court of Cassation for Civil Affairs, and member of the State Council.

11. **Treaty of Aigun** (May 16/28, 1858). In the spring of 1858, China was threatened by the Taiping rebels from within and by foreign powers, especially England and France, from without; Russian troops held fortified posts on the north bank of the Amur, where there were established Russian colonists. Under these conditions China recognized the futility of struggling against Russia's demands to negotiate a new treaty concerning the frontier. Chinese officials, therefore, requested that Muravev confer on this question with Prince T-shan, Commander in Chief of the forces on the Amur. The conference was held at Aigun (beginning May 11, 1858) and the treaty was signed five days later. Russia was conceded the entire northern bank of the Amur, while the territory between the Ussuri and the sea was to be held in common by the two powers until a final settlement should be reached; furthermore, navigation on the Amur, and on the Ussuri and Sungari, was to be confined to Russian and Chinese vessels. This opened to Russia the trade of all northern Manchuria and thus strengthened her position in the Far East. The news of the treaty was received with great satisfaction in St. Petersburg, and Muravev, for his services, was created Count of the Amur. The treaty was ratified by the Emperor of China on June 2 and by the Tsar on July 8.

12. **Petr Petrovich Semenov-Tian-Shansky** (1827–1914). Geographer and writer; member of the Russian Geographical Society, 1849, and vice-president, 1873; organized an expedition to Tian-Shan, 1856–1858, visiting places unknown to the Europeans; organized a second expedition in 1888, this time to Turkestan and the Transcaspian region.

13. **Yakov Ivanovich Rostovtsev** (1803–1860). Adjutant-General, known for his activity in peasant reform; graduate of His Majesty's School of Pages; warned Emperor Nicholas I of the coming Decembrists' conspiracy

of December 12, 1825; as aide-de-camp to Grand Duke Mikhail Pavlovich accompanied him to the front in the Turkish War, 1828, and the Polish War, 1831; appointed Chief of Staff of the Grand Duke for the Supervision of Military Schools, 1835; appointed member of the Committee to Study Peasant Affairs, 1857; at first skeptical of the peasant-liberation reform, became ardent advocate after his journey abroad in 1858; chairman of the Editing Commissions instituted for the same purpose, 1859, but died without seeing his work completed.

Page 99, note 14. **Egor Abramovich Peretts** (1833–1899). Graduate in law of St. Petersburg University, 1855; in the Second Section of His Majesty's Private Chancellery; participated in the drafting of the judicial reforms of 1864 and the projects of municipal self-government, 1870; State Secretary, 1869–1879; Imperial Secretary, 1878–1883; member of State Council, 1883.

15. **Matilda Feliksovna Kshesinskaia.** Ballerina; daughter of a Warsaw ballet master; left the stage in 1903.

16. **Andrei Aleksandrovich Saburov** (1838– ?). Graduate of the Imperial Alexander Lyceum; in the Chancellery of the Committee of Ministers, 1857, and in the Ministry of Justice, 1859; held various positions in the Senate, 1864–1872; member of the Consultative Board of the Ministry of Justice, 1872–1875; Supervisor of Yurev (Dorpat) educational district, 1875; Minister of Education, 1880–1881; back in the Senate; member of State Council, 1899.

CHAPTER X

Page 107, note 1. **Baron Roman Aleksandrovich Disterlo.** Graduate in law of St. Petersburg University in the early 'eighties; one-time lecturer in law at the Mining Institute; State Secretary of the State Council, 1897; literary critic.

Page 108, note 2. *Narodnaia Volia* (**Will of the People**). In the winter of 1876–77 several narodnik (see note 6, chapter vi, p. 618) revolutionary circles in different parts of Russia joined in the formation of a society, which took the name Zemlia i Volia (Land and Freedom), the name of an earlier but short-lived society of the early 'sixties. Certain members of the society believed that terror was the only effective answer to the repressive measures with which the government was trying to crush the revolutionary movement. Three terroristic acts in 1878 and the early months of 1879, Vera Zasulich's wounding of General Trepov and her trial and acquittal, Kravchinsky's assassination of General Mezentsev and his escape, and Solovev's unsuccessful attempt to kill the Emperor, caused great excitement in public and revolutionary circles. In the summer of 1879 the members of Zemlia i Volia met in a congress at Voronezh and debated the use of terrorism as a revolutionary tactic. The result was a split in the society: those members who opposed terrorism united under the name Chernyi Peredel (the Black Partition); those who favored terrorism united under the name Narodnaia Volia. One of the early decisions of the Narodnaia Volia was to assassinate the Emperor, a decision which was carried out March 1, 1881. After this assassination the revolutionary societies were broken up by the police or driven underground. In the last number of the publication *Narodnaia Volia,* October 1, 1885, the remaining members of the party acknowledged their defeat. Repeated efforts to revive the party failed, though its traditions were kept alive by certain revolutionary groups which in the late 'nineties developed into the Socialist-Revolutionist Party. (See note 8, introduction, p. 590.)

3. **Petr Vasilevich Orzhevsky** (1839–1897). Assistant Minister of the Interior and Commander of the Gendarme Corps, 1882–1887; Senator; Governor-General of Vilna, Kovno, and Grodno, 1893–1897.

Page 110, note 4. **auditor of a military district court.** An office instituted by Peter the Great; the auditor was a member of the so-called Auditoriat, that is, the military court, and combined the duties of prokuror, secretary, and examining judge; after the military judicial reform of 1867 the office of auditor was retained only in two Siberian and the Turkestan military districts, being finally abolished in 1890.

5. **Department for General Affairs of the Ministry of the Interior.** Attended to various matters such as those concerning the personnel of the Ministry and the elections of the marshals of nobility; its functions overlapped to a certain extent those of the Minister's Chancellery.

Page 111, note 6. **Council of the Minister.** In Imperial Russia the various ministries, excepting the Ministry of Justice, had a Council of the Minister presided over by the Minister and including the assistant minister, the directors of all departments, and members specially appointed by the Sovereign. The Minister could invite other individuals, business and professional men and others, to the sessions of his Council.

7. **Count Mikhail Mikhailovich Speransky** (1772–1839). Son of a clergyman; received a clerical education; private secretary to Prince Aleksei Borisovich Kurakin, General Prokuror of the Ruling Senate in the reign of Paul I; in the Chancellery of the Senate, 1797; in the Ministry of the Interior, 1802; prepared for Emperor Alexander I a plan for the reorganization of Russia's judicial and administrative institutions, but this draft was neither finished nor published; appointed Assistant Minister of Justice in charge of the Commission to Draft Laws, 1808, and began drafting a new Code of Laws, studying the Napoleonic Code as he progressed; proposed far-reaching financial reforms which aroused great opposition; exiled to Nizhnii Novgorod, 1812; restored to favor in 1816 and appointed Governor of Penza; Governor-General of Siberia, 1819–1821; returned to St. Petersburg and was made member of the State Council; his main work was accomplished under Nicholas I when the complete Code of Laws was published in 1833; created a count in 1839, the year of his death.

Page 113, note 8. **Dmitrii Fedorovich Trepov** (1855–1906). General *"à la suite";* second son of General F. F. Trepov and brother of A. F., V. F., and F. F. Trepov, Jr.; Chief of Police, Moscow, 1896–1905, and close collaborator of the Governor-General, Grand Duke Sergei Aleksandrovich; Governor-General of St. Petersburg, Assistant Minister of the Interior and Chief of Police, 1905; Commandant at the Imperial Court, October 1905.

9. **"To the People" movement.** See note 6, chapter vi, p. 618.

Page 115, note 10. **Moscow Board for Factory Affairs.** See note 16, chapter ii, p. 606.

11. **Grand Duke Sergei Aleksandrovich** (1864–1905). Son of Emperor Alexander II and uncle of Nicholas II; assassinated, February 1905, by Koliaev, a Socialist-Revolutionist.

12. **Jean Baptiste Colbert** (1619–1683). French statesman; as Comptroller-General of Finance, 1661–1683, under Louis XIV, he reformed the financial administration of France, making war on grafters and improving the system of taxation; a practising mercantilist; aided industry by subsidies and protective tariffs, but at the expense of agriculture; established the French merchant marine.

Page 116, note 13. **Lev Aleksandrovich Tikhomirov** (1852–1922). Revolutionist; participated in the "Group of Seventy," the Chaikovsky Circle, and the Zemlia i Volia; chief literary force and member of the Executive Committee of the Narodnaia Volia party; emigrated, 1882, and lived in Paris; changed his views as revealed in his *La Russie politique et sociale* (1888) and his *Pochemu ia perestal byt revoliutsionerom* and in 1888 sent his recantation to Alexander III, obtained pardon, and returned to Russia, 1889; later wrote for *Russkoe Obozrenie* and, as is stated in the text, was editor of *Moskovskiia Vedomosti*.

14. **Werner Sombart** (1863–   ). German economist; professor at University of Breslau, 1890–1906, Berlin Commercial High School, 1906–1917, at University of Berlin since 1917; his best-known work, *Der moderne Kapitalismus,* first appeared in 1902 and was enlarged and brought up to date in edition of 1926.

15. **Friedrich Otto Hertz** (1878–   ). Austrian Social Democrat; economist; one of the critics of Marxism; his best-known book is *Die agrarischen Fragen im Verhältnis zum Sozialismus* (Wien, 1899), which was translated into Russian in 1900.

16. **Karl Kautsky** (1854–1938). German Marxist and historian of socialism; friend of Marx; member of the Second International; founder and editor of *Die Neue Zeit* (1883–1917); opposed Eduard Bernstein and revisionism; one of the creators of the Erfurt program of 1891; pacifist during the World War; rejected invitation to the Zimmerwald conference; one of the founders of the Independent Social Democratic party of Germany, 1917; one of the organizers of the Vienna "Two-and-one-half" International and was in favor of its joining the Second International in 1922; refused to join the German Communist party and criticized the Soviet system as set up by the Russian Revolution; rejoined the Social Democratic party; collected the documents which were edited by Professor Walther Schücking and Count Max Montgelas and published as *Die deutschen Dokumente zum Kriegsausbruch, 1914* (Berlin, 1919), English edition, *Outbreak of the World War* (New York, London, 1924).

17. **Sergei Nikolaevich Prokopovich** (1871–   ). Russian economist and publicist; in the Provisional Government as chairman of the National Economic Council; Minister of Commerce and Industry, August–September, 1917, and Minister of Food, September–October, 1917; after 1918 professor of National Economy, Moscow University; in 1921 one of the founders

and members of the board of the committee for famine relief; imprisoned by the Bolsheviks and exiled abroad; professor of National Economy in the Russian Institute of Science in Berlin, 1923–1924, which was later transferred to Prague; edited *Russkii Ekonomicheskii Sbornik* (Prague, 1925–1928) and *Biulleten Ekonomicheskogo Kabineta* (Prague, 1924–1930).

18. **Georgii Valentinovich Plekhanov** (1856–1918). One of the earliest and most brilliant theoreticians of Marxism in Russia; began revolutionary activity as a narodnik, 1875; member of Zemlia i Volia and later of Chernyi Peredel; emigrated 1881; one of the founders of the Emancipation of Labor Group, 1883; took part in the formation of the Second International, 1889, in which he later represented the Russian Social Democratic Labor party; advocated party unity after Bolshevik-Menshevik split, 1903; criticized Bolshevik tactics, 1905; pro-Entente defensist during World War; returned to Russia, 1917, and opposed Bolshevik seizure of power; his collected works are published in twenty-four volumes.

Page 117, note 19. **Grigorii Porfirevich Sudeikin** (? –1883). Inspector of Secret Police, 1882–1883; used the services of Degaev, 1882, as an agent-provocateur; assassinated in Degaev's apartment by Degaev and two members of the Narodnaia Volia party, Starodvorsky and Konoshevich. (See note following on Degaev.)

20. **Sergei Petrovich Degaev** (1854–1908). Army officer; member of the Narodnaia Volia party; participated in the plans for the assassination of Alexander II (March 1, 1881); set up a secret printing office in Odessa, 1882, and was soon afterward arrested; while in prison agreed to the offer of Sudeikin, Inspector of Police, with whose help he escaped, to act as agent-provocateur; as such he betrayed many revolutionary leaders, including Vera Figner and L. A. Volkenstein; soon suspected by his comrades and left for Paris, where he revealed his activity to the political emigrés; the revolutionists promised to spare his life if he would assassinate Sudeikin, which he, with others, did in 1883; escaped abroad and lived the rest of his life in the United States under an assumed name.

21. **Maxim Gorky** (Aleksei Maksimovich Peshkov) (1868–1936). Son of poor people; received little formal education and spent early years doing odd jobs, wandering about Russia; his first story published in Tiflis paper, 1892; a collection of his stories, published in 1898, gained wide recognition; became a Marxist and throughout his life made financial and other contributions to the Russian Social Democratic cause; elected to the Russian Academy, 1902, but election annulled by the government; arrested for his part in the events of Bloody Sunday, 1905; settled in Capri, 1906, where he founded a school for workers of the R. S. D. L. party; returned to Russia, 1913; founded *Letopis,* 1915; edited *Novaia Zhizn,* 1917–1918, in which he criticized Bolshevik seizure of power; organized aid for writers and scientists during the civil war; abroad for his health, 1921–1928; returned to Russia as strong supporter of Soviet regime; edited *Nashi Dostizheniia;* member Communist Academy; adviser and friend of many Soviet writers.

Page 119, note 22. **Georgii Appolonovich Gapon** (1870–1906). Ukrainian priest who led the procession of workers to the Winter Palace, January 9, 1905. (See also pp. 342–51.)

Page 121, note 23. **Third Section.** See note 13, chapter iii, p. 609.

Page 122, note 24. **Count Petr Aleksandrovich Valuev** (1814–1890). Writer and statesman. In 1834 in the First and later in the Second Section of His Majesty's Chancellery; aided Speransky in his work on codification; special-duty clerk attached to the Military Governor-General of Riga, 1845; Governor of Kurland, 1853; Director of the Second Department of the Ministry of State Domains; Secretary to the Committee of Ministers, January–April 1861; Minister of the Interior, 1861–1868; member of the State Council; Minister of State Domains, 1872–1877; chairman of the Committee of Ministers, 1877–1881; created count, 1880.

25. **Count Mikhail Tarielovich Loris-Melikov** (1825–1888). Born in Tiflis of Armenian parentage; attended the Lazarev Institute for Eastern Languages and the Military School of the Guards; served with distinction in the Caucasus, 1853–1856; Military Governor of Southern Daghestan, 1861; Governor of Terek region, 1863; served with distinction in the Russo-Turkish War, 1877-1878, with the rank of a general; made a count at the conclusion of the war; Provisional Governor in Astrakhan, Saratov, and Samara with unlimited powers during the plague, 1879; Provisional Governor in six gubernias with unlimited powers to fight treason, 1879; Minister of the Interior, 1880–1881, and trusted adviser of Alexander II; author of the so-called "Constitution" which the Tsar was about to promulgate when he was assassinated; resigned, May 1881; spent the last years of his life in Nice, France.

26. **Dmitrii Nikolaevich Shipov** (1851–1920). Graduate of St. Petersburg University; chairman of Volokolam Uezd Zemstvo Board, 1891, of Moscow Gubernia Zemstvo Board, 1900; one of the leaders of the Union of October 17; joined the Party of Peaceful Reconstruction, 1908; elected member of the State Council, 1907–1909; after the Bolshevik Revolution, 1917, member of the National Center; imprisoned by the Bolsheviks in Butyrskaia prison, where he died.

Page 123, note 27. **Plehve in particular.** See Appendix 1, especially pp. 695–96.

Page 124, note 28. **Gubernia Special Board for Municipal Affairs** (*Gubernskoe po gorodskim delam prisutstvie*). Established by statute of 1870 to settle differences between Mayors and Municipal Boards, between the city Dumas and Municipal Boards, and between Governors and city Dumas. Local municipalities could appeal directly to the Senate against the decisions of the Gubernia Special Board. In 1890 there was established a Gubernia Special Board for Zemstvo Affairs (*Gubernskoe po zemskim delam prisutstvie*) and in 1892 these two boards were fused into a Gubernia Special Board for Zemstvo and Municipal Affairs (*Gubernskoe po zemskim i gorodskim delam prisutstvie*). (See also note 5, chapter vii, p. 620.)

Page 126, note 29. **"informed persons" (*sveduiushchie liudi*).** This term was first used in connection with the establishment of the State Council, the departments of which were permitted to invite to their sessions non-members whose practical experience or special knowledge might be of value. This practice of benefiting from the participation of "informed persons" was continued through the nineteenth century, notably in the discussions, committees, and conferences preparatory to the reforms of 1861, the zemstvo reforms of

1864, and the municipal statute of 1870. "Informed persons" were invited also to discuss with Valuev's commission in 1872 the condition of Russian rural economy and with Plehve's commission in 1880 the fall of agricultural prices. In 1881 such persons were called to discuss the lowering of redemption dues, the liquor question, and the problem of peasant colonization; in 1894 they participated in a commission to study judicial legislation, and in 1900 in a conference to study the condition of the coal-mining industry.

30. **Hugues Félicité Robert de Lamennais** (1782–1854). French priest; philosophical and political writer; his conviction that religion was of paramount importance as the basis of social philosophy led him gradually from a position of ultraconservatism to the idea that only in a completely free society could the church be really free; in his paper *Avenir,* founded in 1831, he championed freedom of the press, freedom of conscience, and adult suffrage (a complete contradiction of papal policy); after the publication in 1834 of his most revolutionary work, *Paroles d'un croyant,* he was excommunicated; elected deputy to the National Assembly, 1848, where he sat on the Left; other works: *Livre du peuple* (1837), *De l'esclavage moderne* (1839); for his *Le Pays et le gouvernement* (1840) he was imprisoned for a year.

Page 127, note 31. **Peasant Section (*Zemskii Otdel*).** By the Imperial Ukase of March 4, 1858, there was formed within the Ministry of the Interior a Central Statistical Committee, which, in view of the forthcoming peasant reform, was divided into two sections: a Statistical Section and a Peasant Section. After the reform of February 19, 1861, the Peasant Section supervised the carrying out of this reform in the different localities and of peasant affairs in general. On June 27, 1861, the Peasant Section was separated from the Central Statistical Committee and made an independent section, which assumed, in time, the proportions of a department in the Ministry of the Interior. The head (*upravliaiushchii*) of the Peasant Section was vested with the full powers of a director of department. The section came to have charge of local self-government, economic organization, and military conscription among the rural population. By the decision of the Ministry of the Interior, governors-general, gubernia and uezd marshals of the nobility, members of gubernia boards for peasant affairs, peace mediators (*mirovye posredniki*) and other individuals could be invited to sit permanently or temporarily in the sessions of the Council of the Minister of the Interior, when it discussed the affairs of the Peasant Section.

Attached to the Peasant Section was a board for the peasant affairs of the gubernias of the Kingdom of Poland (*Prisutstvie po krestianskim delam gubernii Tsarstva Polskago.*)

Page 129, note 32. *statskii sovetnik.* Literally, State Councilor; the fifth highest rank for civil servants in the Table of Ranks (*Tabel o rangakh*) issued in 1722 by Peter the Great, according to which all state servants were divided into fourteen classes or *chins.* State servants, regardless of birth and lineage, began on an equal footing and were promoted on the basis of individual merit; the order of promotion was defined in the Table of Ranks, which contained four categories of service: civil service, military service, naval service, and service in the Imperial court. As the years passed the term *chinovniki,* that is, those included in the *chins,* came to be commonly applied to the members of only one of these categories, the civil servants.

CHAPTER XI

Page 131, note 1. **Imperial ukase of November 9, 1906.** See note 5, chapter i, p. 595.

Page 132, note 2. **village communal taxation (*mirskie sbory*).** See note 5, chapter i, p. 595.

3. **Board of Peasant Affairs in the gubernias of the Kingdom of Poland.** Decisions from this board might be appealed to the central government's Special Board for Peasant Affairs of the Kingdom of Poland in the Ministry of the Interior, of which the Head of the Peasant Section was chairman ex-officio.

4. **Georgii Georgievich Savich.** Graduate of the Imperial School of Law; Assistant State Secretary, 1884; Acting Head of the Peasant Section in the Ministry of the Interior, 1896.

Page 134, note 5. **an all-class volost or a small zemstvo unit.** The volost unit had been introduced for state peasants in 1838, but the reform of February 19, 1861, established it as an administrative unit of self-government for all peasants. In the administrative structure it stood between the uezd zemstvo and the village community. A volost was comprised of several villages, and its government was organized as follows: (1) volost assembly (*volostnoi skhod*); (2) head (*starshina*); (3) volost board (*volostnoe pravlenie*); there was also a special volost peasant court. (See note 14, chapter ii, p. 606.)

The volost assembly was made up of elected volost and village officials, such as volost starshina, assistant volost starshina, collectors of dues, volost court judges, and one representative elected by the village population for every ten peasant households.

The volost starshina was elected by the volost population (after the introduction of zemskie nachalniki in 1889 this election had to be confirmed by one of these officials). The starshina's duties were as follows: he was to see that order was maintained in the volost; he had a number of police duties, such as the maintenance of passport regulations and the execution of court decisions; and he supervised minor officials, the maintenance of roads, etc.

The volost board consisted of the starshina, village starosty, and collectors of dues; it was the executive office of the volost community.

But the volost failed to fulfill the expectations of the men who framed the statute of 1861 and of workers for peasant reform. It was an artificial creation and never well understood by the peasants. The powers of its assembly were small by comparison with the powers of its executive officers, who came to be increasingly dominated by local officials of the central government; this was especially so after the institution of zemskie nachalniki in 1889. Instead of becoming an organization of peasant self-government, therefore, the volost gradually became a small administrative unit of the St. Petersburg government.

Parallel to this development, there was also an alienation of the peasants from zemstvo institutions. The peasants saw in the zemstvo organization not an agency to serve peasant interests but a government device to exact from them money for the upkeep of doctors, teachers, and engineers who, the peasants thought, were more interested in their own subsistence than in the satisfying of peasant needs. To a number of Russian public men these tendencies in local self-government were disturbing, and in the 'nineties some of them advanced the idea of a small zemstvo unit which should be a unit of truly democratic self-government. This unit would represent all classes, would operate within certain limits, but within those limits would be independent of all outside influence. It was hoped that such a unit would serve as a political training ground for the rural population. Legislation providing for the introduction of a small zemstvo unit was actually passed by the Third Duma but was defeated in the State Council. The debates in the State Council on the small zemstvo unit are briefly described in the text, chapter xxii, pp. 532–33. (See also Appendix 1, p. 699 and Appendix 5, p. 722.)

6. **law of June 12, 1900.** This law set limits to zemstvo taxation in order to protect the population from too burdensome tax obligations. It stipulated that zemstvo taxes on real estate were not to be increased more than three per cent yearly. So strong were the demands on the zemstvos, however, that zemstvo budgets increased beyond the limits set by this law. (See Appendix 1, pp. 699–700.)

7. **Yakov Yakovlevich Litvinov** (1852– ?). Zemstvo physician, 1876–1901; special-duty clerk and Assistant Head of the Peasant Section in the Ministry of the Interior, 1901–1906; Head of the Peasant Section and chairman of the Special Board for Peasant Affairs of the Kingdom of Poland, 1906–1907; brought to trial, along with Gurko, in connection with the Lidval affair, 1907; Senator, 1915.

8. **Grigorii Viacheslavovich Glinka.** Graduate of Moscow University; Assistant and, in 1905, Head of the Department of Peasant Colonization; Assistant Head of the Chief Administration of Land Organization and Agriculture, and plenipotentiary to supervise the provisioning of the army, 1915; Senator, 1916.

9. **Department of Peasant Colonization** (*Pereselencheskoe Upravlenie*). Established in 1896 in the Ministry of the Interior to take over the work of settling peasants on new lands, work which had previously been done by the Peasant Section; in 1905 this department was transferred to the Chief Administration of Land Organization and Agriculture.

10. **village as a whole.** See note 5, chapter i, p. 595.

Page 137, note 11. **volost boards (*volostnoe pravlenie*).** See note 5, chapter xi, p. 629.

12. **Prince Nikolai Dmitrievich Golitsyn** (1850–1925). Graduate of the Imperial Alexander Lyceum; entered the Ministry of the Interior, 1871; Governor of the gubernias of Arkhangelsk, 1885, Kaluga, 1893, Tver, 1897; appointed Senator, 1903; plenipotentiary of the Red Cross in Turgai and Uralsk oblasts and Saratov Gubernia to organize help in the famine-stricken areas, 1907–1908; member of the State Council and chairman of the commission to render assistance to the Russian prisoners of war abroad, 1915; chairman of the Council of Ministers, December 1916–February 1917.

Page 138, note 13. **tax-paying classes.** According to the General Statutes published in Volume IX of the *Code of Laws of the Russian Empire,* every inhabitant of Russia was arbitrarily placed in one of four classifications:

(1) nobility, (2) clergy, (3) town population, and (4) rural population. Each of these divisions did not necessarily represent a homogeneous class. There was a hereditary and an honorary nobility. The clergy was separated according to creeds. The town population comprised four categories: honorary citizens, merchants, *meshchane* (a manifesto of March 17, 1775, designated as *meshchane* all town inhabitants who did not possess 500 rubles and therefore were not permitted to become members of the merchant class; later the term *meshchane* included all who did not belong to the other three town classes), and guild members—a statute of November 1799 established three guilds for all forms of handiwork: (1) artisans, (2) servants, seamstresses, and laundresses, and (3) artisans of little training.

Independently of these four main classifications, the Russian population was divided into a so-called taxable condition or class (*podatnoe sostoianie*) and a nontaxable condition or class (*nepodatnoe sostoianie*). The division was originally made on the basis of those who paid and who did not pay the soul-tax introduced by Peter the Great. On this basis the taxable class included all peasants, Russian and foreign artisans, Jews (after the annexation of Polish territory by Catherine II), colonists settling in Russia after the reign of Catherine II, national minorities (*inorodtsy*), and *meshchane* (exempted in 1863). In 1775 merchants were exempted from payment of the soul-tax but were obliged to pay a one per cent capital tax. The nontaxable class included the hereditary and honorary nobility, the clergy (with some exceptions), princes and nobles of Tartar origin, medical men, brokers, honorary citizens, and persons holding advanced academic degrees.

Membership in the taxable class carried with it certain other liabilities and limitations: taxable persons were registered as residents of a certain place and could travel from that place only with a passport; this regulation was designed to prevent escape from tax paying. Persons of this class were also obliged to perform natural services, including emergency work such as the cleaning of railway lines after storms, etc. Membership in the nontaxable class, on the other hand, carried with it the rights of free movement and exemption from natural service and corporal punishment.

The soul-tax was by no means a satisfactory form of taxation, and steps were taken in the nineteenth century to adopt a new system. On May 18, 1882, a Sovereign order exempted as from January 1, 1883, meshchane, landless peasants, and laborers from paying the soul-tax. On May 15, 1883, all tax arrears of taxable classes were canceled and peasants working in factories were exempt from the soul-tax. On May 28, 1885, the Emperor, acting on a recommendation of the State Council, decreed the abolition of the soul-tax as from January 1, 1886, for all peasants who had been emancipated in 1861 (peasants in privately owned estates) and 1863 (peasants on udel lands), for all Baltic peasants not on state lands, for the Ukrainian Cossacks, and for some other elements of the population. On January 1, 1887, this abolition was extended to all persons in European Russia, and on January 19, 1898, also to the most of Siberia. The abolition of the soul-tax did not carry with it the removal of the other liabilities and limitations of the taxable classes.

Page 139, note 14. **Russkoe Bogatstvo.** Founded under the name *Zhurnal Torgovli, Promyshlennosti i Estevoznaniia* ("*Journal of Industry, Agricul-*

ture, and Natural Science") in St. Petersburg in 1876; until 1878 was edited by N. F. Savich and appeared three times a month; in March 1879 resumed publication as a monthly, edited and published by D. M. Rybakov; in the same year became the property of S. N. Bashina and was renamed *Russkoe Bogatstvo;* discontinued, 1882, after publication of eight numbers; later as the property of L. E. Obolensky appeared from January 1883 to 1891; after that date changed hands several times; suspended for three months in 1899 for its articles on the then current Finnish measures; after 1891, when the editorship passed to the circle of the former collaborators in *Otechestvennyia Zapiski,* became one of the most influential and widely circulated organs of the press, many well-known writers and historians collaborating on it; reflected Narodnik tendencies and conducted bitter polemics and theoretical struggles against Marxism; suspended by the government, 1906–1907, but continued publication under the names of *Sovremennyia Zapiski* and *Sovremennost;* after 1907 resumed its former name; closed again September 1914, but continued publication until March 1917 as *Russkiia Zapiski;* closed finally in 1918.

15. **Emancipation of Labor Group** (*Gruppa osvobozhdeniia truda*). One of the first Russian Social-Democratic organizations, founded September 1883 in Switzerland by G. V. Plekhanov, P. B. Akselrod, V. I. Zasulich, L. G. Deitch, and V. N. Ignatev, who had previously been members of Chernyi Peredel; 1890–1892, published *Sotsial Demokrat* and issued a number of other publications, and translated some of the writings of Karl Marx and Engels; in 1889 was represented by Plekhanov at the first Congress of the Second International in Paris; in 1895 joined the Union of Russian Social Democrats, and in 1900 some members of the group joined the editorial board of *Iskra* and *Zaria;* ceased to exist after the second Congress of the Russian Social Democratic Labor party in 1903.

Page 140, note 16. **Prince Petr Alekseevich Kropotkin** (1842–1921). Served in the army in the Amur Cossack Voisko; described his impressions of the Amur region and North Manchuria in *Russkii Vestnik,* 1862, 1863, 1865, 1867; secretary of the physical geographical section of the Russian Geographical Society and participated in an expedition to investigate glaciers of Finland and Sweden; in 1872 visited Switzerland and joined the International Workingmen's Association at Geneva; later adopted the philosophy of anarchism and on returning to Russia took an active part in revolutionary circles; arrested and imprisoned in 1874, but escaped in 1876 and went to England, then to Switzerland, where he joined the Jura Federation; in 1877 worked in the socialist movement in Paris, returning to Switzerland in 1878; expelled from Switzerland, 1881, and spent some time in England and France, where he was sentenced to five years' imprisonment for his membership in the International Workingmen's Association; released in 1886 and settled near London, where he wrote his *Memoirs of a Revolutionist,* 1899; returned to Russia, June 1917, taking no part in politics.

Page 141, note 16*a*. **Chief Administration of Land Organization and Agriculture.** See note 1, chapter v, p. 616.

Page 142, note 17. **Nikolai Nikolaevich Kutler** (1859–1924). Graduate of Moscow University; practiced law and worked in the Ministry of Finance,

1882–1892; Assistant Director, 1892–1899, and Director, 1899–1904, of the Department of Direct Taxation of the Ministry of Finance; Assistant Minister of the Interior, 1904–1905; Assistant Minister of Finance and Manager of the Bank of the Nobility and the Peasant Bank, 1905; Head of the Chief Administration of Land Organization and Agriculture, 1905–1906; Cadet; member of the Second and Third Dumas; after the Bolshevik Revolution worked in the People's Commissariat of Finance; member of the Board of the State Bank of the U.S.S.R., 1922–1924.

18. **Baron Petr Nikolaevich Wrangel** (1878–1928). General; born of a noble family of Swedish descent; graduate of the Mining Institute and the General Staff Academy; worked as a mining engineer in Siberia; served as an officer in a Cossack regiment during the Russo-Japanese War; afterward was transferred to the horse guards with the rank of captain; during the World War he commanded successively a squadron, a regiment, and a division of Cossacks; after the October 1917 Revolution escaped to the Crimea and then to the Don; later served with Alekseev and Denikin; in April 1920 was appointed commander in chief of the Volunteer Army which he reorganized and led against the Bolsheviks; in November 1920 he and about 130,000 refugees were forced to leave the Crimea and dispersed in the Balkans and other parts of Europe; worked as a mining engineer in Brussels from 1926 until his death.

19. **famous estate of Falz-Fein.** In 1856, "Askania Nova," about 600 square kilometers of land granted to German colonists by an Imperial Ukase of March 3, 1828, was purchased by Friedrich Fein, a landed proprietor. Fein added considerably to the "Askania Nova" property and his family came to be one of the wealthiest of South Russian landowners. His interest in scientific farming and stock breeding drew him into association with Gottlieb Pfalz, a famous sheep-breeder and wool expert who subsequently married Fein's daughter Elizabeth. Emperor Alexander II honored this young couple by endowing them with hereditary honorary citizenship and permitting them to use the double name of Falz-Fein. Their descendants and heirs continued to make advances in agriculture and animal husbandry, and to set aside vast tracts of their estates for the preservation of the natural flora and fauna of the steppes and as a sanctuary for other types of wild life which they brought there. It became a spot of beauty and of naturalist scientific interest with its artesian wells, botanical gardens, and zoölogical park. In the spring of 1914 it was honored by an Imperial visit, and shortly thereafter its part owner and manager was the Emperor's guest at Livadia, who at that time ennobled the Falz-Fein family. The ravages of revolution and civil war took a severe toll of the property and the animal life of the estates, and the Falz-Fein family emigrated in April 1919. Much that had been done to beautify the estates was destroyed, but "Askania Nova" has been preserved. It is now called "Chapli" and is operated by the government. (See Waldemar v. Falz-Fein, *Askania Nova. Das Tierparadies* [Berlin, 1930]; the author of this book is the youngest brother of the last owner of "Askania Nova," Friedrich v. Falz-Fein, who died in 1919.)

20. **N. N. Kupriianov.** Member of the Special Board for Peasant Affairs of the Kingdom of Poland (see note 3, chapter xi, p. 629); later, until the

World War, held the post of Governor of Suvalki, whence he was expelled by the German troops in February 1915.

Page 143, note 21. **Pravo.** Weekly St. Petersburg newspaper; founded by I. V. Hessen, who was also editor-in-chief during its entire period of publication, November 8, 1898—December 22, 1917. Among the collaborators were: V. M. Hessen, A. I. Kaminka, N. I. Lazarevsky, V. D. Nabokoff, L. I. Petrazhitsky, Prince Petr Dolgorukov, Ya. G. Frumkin, V. B. Eliashevich, G. N. Stilman, I. M. Strakhovsky. It was devoted chiefly to the technical discussion of legal questions; from the autumn of 1905 dealt also with political matters and became the leading organ of the liberation movement.

Page 145, note 22. **Vikentii Ivanovich Baftalovsky** (1864–   ). In 1910 became member of the Council of the Chief Administration of Land Organization and Agriculture, and assistant to the Head of the Department of Peasant Colonization; in 1916 became member of the Council of the Minister of the Interior.

Page 147, note 23. **special renting of land (***chinshevyia dela***).** The custom of the permanent and hereditary use of land in return for a payment to the landowner in money or services; derived from the French *cens,* which was introduced into Poland when the Duchy of Warsaw was formed; retained after Poland came under Russian rule and practiced in the western gubernias until the early twentieth century.

Page   148,   note   24. **Baron   Aleksandr   Feliksovich   Meyendorff** (1869–   ).   Graduate   of   St.   Petersburg   University;   Octobrist;   vice-chairman of the Third Duma.

Page 150, note 25. **Aleksandr Ivanovich Lykoshin** (1861–1918). Graduate of the Imperial School of Law; entered the Ministry of Justice, 1882; assistant to an Ober-Prokuror in the Senate's Court of Cassation for Civil Affairs, 1901; member of the Consultative Board in the Ministry of Justice, 1904; member of the Council of the Ministry of Interior, retaining his previous position, 1907; Assistant Minister of the Interior and Head of the Peasant Section, 1907–1914; Senator, 1911; member of the State Council, 1914.

26. **A. A. Bashmakov.** A conservative publicist; appointed by Stolypin about 1911 as editor of the *Pravitelstvennyi Vestnik;* took active part in the Pan-Slavic revival in St. Petersburg during the Balkan wars, attacking the government for its moderation, and was obliged to resign his post as editor of the official paper; in emigration.

Page 151, note 27. **Committee for Land Affairs.** Established by a ukase of May 6, 1905, in the Chief Administration of Land Organization and Agriculture to supervise matters concerning peasant land organization.

28. **Rudin.** The first novel of Ivan Turgenev (1818–1883); published in 1856; its central character, Dmitrii Rudin, represents Turgenev's portrayal of a typical educated Russian idealist of the 'forties.

Page 152, note 29. **Pravitelstvennyi Vestnik.** Official daily newspaper, published in St. Petersburg from 1869 to 1917 in accordance with the Imperial order of October 27, 1869; continued as *Vestnik Vremennago Pravitelstva* from March 5 to October 27, 1917; in addition to official government communiqués it published scientific, historical, and bibliographical information and news.

30. **Aleksandr Aleksandrovich Makarov** (1857–1919). Graduate of St. Petersburg University; entered the Ministry of Justice; served as prokuror and chairman of various district courts; in 1906 chairman of Kharkov Court of Appeals and some time later appointed Assistant Minister of the Interior; Imperial Secretary, 1909; after the death of Stolypin, 1911, became Minister of the Interior, and in December 1912 was appointed member of the State Council; Minister of Justice, July 1916–January 1917.

Page 153, note 31. **Sergei Dmitrievich Rudin** (1860–   ). Assistant Head of the Land Surveying Office of the Ministry of Justice, 1904–1915; appointed Senator, 1915.

32. **Ministry of Justice.** Founded in 1802; consisted of the following departments: First Department, which dealt with legislative matters, statistics, etc.; Second Department, which dealt with the personnel of the Senate, the judicial institutions, etc.; Third Department, the land surveying office; Fourth Department, Moscow archives of the Ministry of Justice. Attached to the Ministry of Justice was the Consultative Board. The Ministry had to supervise the Imperial School of Law, the Constantine Institute of Land Surveyors, and other schools of land surveying. The Minister of Justice was also General Prokuror of the Senate.

Page 161, note 33. **special servitudes** (*servitutnyia prava*). Limitation of the rights of landlords in favor of the peasants. This custom dated back to the period of serfdom. At that time, owing to the shortage of land in the possession of the landlords of western gubernias for cultivation by the peasant serfs, a practice had been established whereby the peasants were allowed to use at certain periods of the year some of a landlord's lands, particularly the forests, where they could graze their cattle, cut and gather wood, mushrooms, berries, etc. With the abolition of serfdom, these special privileges of the peasants remained, and later became a source of continuous dispute between peasant and landlord.

Page 162, note 34. **Manifesto of February 26, 1903.** This manifesto was concerned with measures for improving the state order. Among other things it stated that gubernia conferences, in which worthy public men enjoying public confidence should participate, would be called to study the proposed revision of peasant legislation. The Ukase of January 8, 1904, definitely called for the organization of such conferences in all gubernias in which the office of zemskii nachalnik had been established.

Page 164, note 35. **Count Emmanuil Pavlovich Bennigsen** (1875–   ). Graduate of the Imperial School of Law; special-duty clerk in the Chief Administration of Land Organization and Agriculture; member of the Third Duma; Octobrist.

Page 165, note 36. **Leonid-Ludwig Zinovievich Slonimsky** (1850– ?). Journalist. Graduate of Kiev University, 1872, after which he wrote in legal and other periodicals, including *Vestnik Evropy;* one of the editors of the small encyclopedia of Brockhaus and Efron.

37. **Aleksandr Petrovich Nikolsky** (1851–1919). Graduate in law of St. Petersburg University; worked in the Commission to Study Russian Railways, established by Imperial order in the late 'seventies; transferred to the Ministry of Finance, 1886, where he remained for twenty years, serving in

various positions, including Director of the State Bank, Manager of the Savings Bank, and Director of the State Savings Bank; Head of the Chief Administration of Land Organization and Agriculture, 1906; appointed Senator, 1906, and member of the State Council, 1908; represented the Viceroy of the Caucasus in state institutions, 1910; member of the Finance Committee, 1914.

Page 166, note 38. *Moskovskiia Vedomosti.* Moscow University publication; appeared twice and then three times a week from 1756 to 1859, and after 1859 daily; from 1756 to 1779 contained only official news, such as Imperial orders and court news; after 1779 gradually widened its scope; edited by such distinguished men as M. N. Katkov, 1850–1855, and V. F. Korsh, 1856–1862; put out supplementary editions such as *Ekonomicheskii Magazin,* 1780–1789, and *Sovremennaia Letopis,* 1863–1871.

Page 168, note 39. **Prince Sergei Dmitrievich Urusov** (1862–   ). Graduate of Moscow University; uezd marshal of nobility in Kaluga Gubernia; member of the gubernia zemstvo and chairman of the justices of the peace; in the Ministry of the Interior, 1900–1902; Vice-Governor of Tambov, 1903; six months later, Governor of Bessarabia; Governor of Tver, 1904; Assistant Minister of the Interior, 1905–1906; Cadet member of the First Duma; sentenced to three months' imprisonment for signing the Viborg Manifesto; Assistant Minister of the Interior in the Provisional Government, 1917.

Page 169, note 40. **Leonid Vladimirovich Khodsky** (1854–1918). Economist; professor; graduate of Mining Institute in Gatchina in 1883; Doctorate in Political Economy, 1891; professor at St. Petersburg University, 1895–1918; editor and publisher of *Narodnoe Khoziaistvo,* 1900–1905, and of the Left Cadet paper, *Nasha Zhizn,* 1904; after the October 1917 Revolution, emigrated.

41. **Petr Khristianovich Schwanebach** (1846–1908). Graduate of the Imperial School of Law; attended universities of Leipzig and Paris; Assistant Director of the Credit Office; Assistant Manager of the State Bank; member of the Council of the Minister of Finance; appointed Assistant Minister of Agriculture and State Domains, 1903, and Head of the Chief Administration of Land Organization and Agriculture, 1905; member of the State Council, October 1906; State Comptroller, April 1906–June 1907.

Page 173, note 42. **Prince Aleksei Aleksandrovich Shirinsky-Shikhmatov** (1862–1929). Graduate of the Imperial School of Law, 1884; in the Ministry of the Interior as adviser to Esthonia Gubernia Special Board (*Pravlenie*); on the staff of the Holy Synod, 1900–1903; Governor of Tver, 1903; appointed to First Department of the Senate, 1904; Assistant Ober-Prokuror of the Holy Synod, 1905, and Ober-Prokuror, 1906; member of State Council, 1906; Acting Governor of Saratov, 1913; member of the Council of the Minister of the Interior, 1915.

Page 175, note 43. **Prince Nikolai Leonidovich Obolensky** (1876–   ). Graduate of St. Petersburg University; entered the Peasant Section of the Ministry of the Interior, 1901; Acting Director of the Chancellery of the Governor-General of Warsaw; member of the Council of the Minister of the Interior; chief for civilian matters in the office of the Commander in Chief of the Stavka; Governor of Kursk, September 1915, and Governor of Kharkov, December 1915; chairman of a special conference in the Ministry of the Interior to fight high prices, 1916; became Governor of Yaroslavl, November 1916; in emigration, where he was secretary to Grand Duke Nikolai Nikolaevich.

Page 176, note 44. **Aleksei Aleksandrovich Lopukhin** (1864–1927). Graduate of Moscow University; in judicial institutions since 1886; assistant prokuror and prokuror of various district courts and courts of appeal, 1890–1902; Director of the Police Department in the Ministry of the Interior, 1902–1905; Governor of Esthonia, 1905, but removed from office in same year after disturbances in Reval; in 1908 revealed to Burtsev, a Socialist-Revolutionist and to other members of the Socialist-Revolutionist party in London that Asef was an agent-provocateur; on his return from London was arrested, tried for rendering assistance to the Socialist-Revolutionist party, and sentenced to five years' exile, 1909; was granted amnesty and restoration of civil rights, 1912; assistant director, Moscow branch, St. Petersburg International Commercial Bank, 1913.

45. **Aleksandr Grigorevich Bulygin** (1851–1919). Graduate of the Imperial School of Law; began work in the Tambov district court, 1871; held various administrative offices including that of Governor of Kaluga, 1887, of Moscow, 1893, and assistant to the Governor-General of Moscow, Grand Duke Sergei Aleksandrovich, 1902; appointed to the State Council, January 1, 1905; Minister of the Interior, January–October 1905, when he returned to the State Council; Chief of the Fourth Section of His Majesty's Private Chancellery, 1913.

CHAPTER XII

Page 178, note 1. **Nikolai Alekseevich Zinovev** (1840–1917). Graduate of the Lazarev Institute of Foreign Languages; began work in the Land Surveying Department, 1856; chairman of Belostok-Belsk congress of peace mediators, 1865; member of the Gubernia Board for Peasant Affairs in Grodno, 1866; attached to the Ministry of the Interior, 1869; manager of State Domains in Vilna Gubernia, 1876; Governor of Suvalki, 1882; later Governor of Tula and Mogilev consecutively; Director of the Department of Economy in the Ministry of the Interior, 1901; Assistant Minister of the Interior, 1902; Senator, 1903; member of the State Council, 1904.

Page 179, note 2. **Charles Louis de Secondat, Baron de La Brède et de Montesquieu** (1689–1755). French political philosopher and historian; his *Lettres persanes,* published in 1721, satirized existing political, religious, and social institutions; admitted to the French Academy, 1728; on the basis of intensive study of past institutions and careful observation of existing ones he wrote *L'Esprit des lois,* published in 1748; his doctrine of the separation of powers here set forth stems from the political philosophy of John Locke (1632–1704), but he gives to the doctrine a great and original development; he characterizes the powers in a state as legislative, executive, and judicial and sees in the separate operation of each of these powers as a check and balance on the others the guaranty of political liberty.

Page 181, note 3. **Chief Administration of Posts and Telegraphs in the Ministry of the Interior** (*Glavnoe Upravlenie pocht i telegrafov*). Existed for a short period as a ministry, but in 1868 was made a section in the Ministry of the Interior.

Page 182, note 4. **William I** (1797–1888). Succeeded his brother, Frederick IV, as King of Prussia, 1861; first German Emperor, 1871–1888.

Page 183, note 5. **Claude François de Malet** (1754–1812). Joined the King's musketeers, 1770; on the outbreak of the French Revolution joined the National Guard and fought in 1792 on the Rhine; subsequently saw service in Italy and attained the rank of Brigadier-General, 1799; in 1808 was charged with conspiracy and thrown into prison, where with other prisoners he planned the overthrow of the Emperor; during Napoleon's Russian expedition (1812), escaped from prison, spread the rumor of Napoleon's death, gained control of two regiments of Napoleon's guards, but failed in his attempt to win over the commandant of Paris, and the following day was court-martialed and condemned to death; executed on October 29.

Page 184, note 6. **Sergei Nikolaevich Herbel** (1858– ?). Graduate of Elizavetgrad Military School, 1878; served in the army until 1883, when he became member of Kherson Uezd Zemstvo and honorary justice of the peace; chairman of Kherson Uezd Zemstvo Board, 1892, and of Kherson Gubernia Zemstvo Board, 1900; Vice-Governor of Kherson, 1902, and Governor, 1903; Head of the Chief Administration of Local Economy in the Ministry of the Interior, 1904; member of the State Council, 1912; in charge of supplies of the Southwestern Army, 1915–1917; Minister of Food Supply in the Ukraine under Skoropadsky and chairman of the Council of Ministers, 1918; after the fall of Skoropadsky, left for Germany.

Page 186, note 7. **Prince Boris Aleksandrovich Vasilchikov** (1863–1931). Graduate of the Imperial School of Law; entered the Ministry of Justice, 1881; Marshal of Nobility of Staraia Russa Uezd, 1884, of Novgorod Gubernia, 1890; Governor of Pskov, 1900–1903; Head of the Red Cross for the Northeastern District during the Russo-Japanese War; chairman of the Russian Red Cross Society; member of the State Council, 1906; Head of the Chief Administration of Land Organization and Agriculture, July 1906–May 1908; died in emigration.

Page 188, note 8. **Ilia Yakovlevich Gurland** (1868– ?). Graduate of the Yaroslavl Demidov Lyceum, 1891; professor of constitutional law there, 1902–1904; special-duty clerk in the Ministry of the Interior, 1904; member of the Council of the Minister of the Interior, 1907; became editor of the government official paper, *Rossiia,* 1907; director of the newly formed "Bureau of the Press," 1916; emigrated after the February 1917 Revolution.

9. **Nikolai Andreevich Zverev** (1850–1917). Graduate in law of Moscow University; professor there in 1884 and again after his return from abroad, where he was sent in 1885 to study philosophy of law; Assistant Minister of Education, 1898; Senator, 1901; Head of the Chief Administration for the Affairs of the Press, 1902–1904; in the Second Department of the Senate, 1904–1909; member of State Council, 1909.

10. **Mikhail Petrovich Solovev** (1842–1901). Graduate in law of Moscow University, 1864; chairman of the Belostok-Belsk Congress of peace

mediators, 1866–1867; member and editor of the Warsaw juridical commission, 1867–1873; in the Chancellery of the Ministry of War, 1873–1896; Head of the Chief Administration for the Affairs of the Press and member of its Council, 1896–1900.

Page 189, note 11. **Aleksei Valerianovich Belgard** (1861–   ). Acting Governor of Esthonia Gubernia, 1902; Head of the Chief Administration for the Affairs of the Press and chairman of its Council, 1905; Senator, 1912.

12. **Dmitrii Nikolaevich Liubimov** (1864–   ). Graduate of St. Petersburg University; entered the Ministry of State Domains, 1887; in charge of the Chancellery of the Minister of the Interior, 1902; Governor of Vilna, 1906; Director of the Department of State Domains in the Chief Administration of Land Organization and Agriculture, 1912; Head of His Majesty's Chancellery to Receive Petitions, 1913; Senator and assistant to the Governor-General of Warsaw, 1914.

Page 190, note 13. **Nikolai Semenovich Leskov** (1831–1895). Russian novelist; assistant to a steward of several estates; in connection with his work traveled and thus became acquainted with Russian life; about 1862 settled in St. Petersburg, where he spent most of the rest of his life; first important novel, *Nekuda* (*The Blind Alley*), 1864, was fiercely criticized by the radicals as was his *Na Nozhakh* (*At Daggers Drawn*); best known in Western Europe for his *Soboriane*, 1872 (English title, *Cathedral Folk*, 1924).

14. **Nikolai Vasilievich Gogol** (1809–1852). Educated at Nezhin Gymnasium, where he started a manuscript periodical, *Zvezda;* in 1830 published *Vechera na khutore bliz Dikanki* (*"Evenings on a Farm Near Dikanka"*), a series of stories about Ukrainian rural life; 1834–1835, lectured in history at University of St. Petersburg, meanwhile continuing his writing; 1836, published his comedy *Revizor* (English translation by C. Garnett, *The Government Inspector*, 1926); lived abroad, 1836–1848; while in Rome wrote his classical novel, *Dead Souls*, which began to appear in 1842; returned to Russia, 1848, and died in Moscow.

15. **Gendarme Corps.** Founded in 1827; its first chief was Count A. Kh. Benkendorff, who had been appointed in the previous year as Head of the Third Section of His Majesty's Private Chancellery; in this way the Gendarme Corps became the executive organ of the Third Section. All Russia was divided into five, later into eight, gendarme districts (*okrugs*), each of which was under a general, subordinate to the Chief of Gendarmes; in 1875 the name of the corps was changed to the Special Gendarme Corps. In 1880, the Third Section was abolished and the Gendarme Corps was placed under the Minister of the Interior, but in military matters it continued to receive orders from the Minister of War. By the Ukase of June 22, 1882, an Assistant Minister of the Interior became the head of the corps, while the Minister of the Interior continued as its chief; the Assistant Minister assumed the title of Commander of the Special Gendarme Corps; he was also in charge of police. Gendarme divisions and mounted city detachments did active police work at the call of civilian authorities, such as dispersing gatherings, maintaining order, etc. Other units of the corps were employed in the detection and investigation of political crimes, the supervision of railways and political prisons (Schlüsselburg and Kara). Gendarme officers were responsible for

their actions directly to their chiefs, and a local prokuror could do no more than report their actions to the Ministry of Justice. Any disagreement between such a prokuror and a local chief of gendarmes was reported to the First Department of the Senate. (See also note 13, chapter iii, p. 609.)

16. **General Viktor - Karl - Konrad - Wilhelm von Wahl** (1840–1915). Governor of St. Petersburg, 1892, of Vilna, 1901; Assistant Minister of the Interior and Commander of the Gendarme Corps, 1902; member of the State Council, 1903.

Page 191, note 17. **Vera Figner** (1852–   ). Of noble birth; an outstanding revolutionary leader; member of the Narodnaia Volia party, and in 1879 became a member of its Executive Committee; participated in preparations for the assassination of Emperor Alexander II, 1881; escaped arrest and engineered the spreading of revolutionary propaganda among the army in Southern Russia; arrested in 1884 with her entire organization; tried in St. Petersburg and condemned to death, but the Emperor commuted the sentence to life imprisonment; in 1904 was exiled to Arkhangelsk Gubernia; as a result of the Ukase of October 21, 1905, was amnestied and set at liberty; was abroad, 1906–1915; elected honorary chairman of the First All-Russian Congress of Peasants' Deputies, May 17, 1917. (See her memoirs, *Zapechatlennyi trud*, 2 vols. [Moscow, 1921–1922]; authorized English edition, *Memoirs of a Revolutionist* [New York, 1927].)

18. **Schlüsselburg fortress.** On a small island in the Neva River near Lake Ladoga, taken from the Swedes by Peter the Great in 1702. After 1884, and at the suggestion of Alexander III, it became exclusively a prison for serious political offenders. From 1908 to 1917 it was used for both criminal and political prisoners.

Page 197, note 19. **third element** (*tretii element*). The salaried staff of the zemstvos (doctors, teachers, nurses, statisticians, etc.). (See also Appendix 1, especially pp. 696–97.)

20. **Count Pavel Nikolaevich Ignatev** (1870–1926). Graduate of Kiev University; entered the Ministry of the Interior, 1892; chairman of the Kiev Gubernia Zemstvo Board, 1904; Governor of Kiev, 1907–1908; Director of the Department of Agriculture in the Chief Administration of Land Organization and Agriculture, 1909; Assistant Head of the Chief Administration of Land Organization and Agriculture, 1912; Minister of Education, 1915–1916.

Page 198, note 21. **Boris Viktorovich Savinkov** (1879–1925). Writer and revolutionist; joined the Fighting Organization of the Socialist-Revolutionist party, 1903; was involved in the assassination of Plehve and Grand Duke Sergei Aleksandrovich; volunteer in the French army during the World War; Assistant Minister of War under Kerensky; active in anti-Bolshevik movement, 1918–1921; arrested and sentenced by a Soviet court to ten years' imprisonment, 1924; alleged to have committed suicide in prison, 1925; author of three novels under the pseudonym "V. Ropshin" and of *Memoirs of a Terrorist* (New York, 1931).

CHAPTER XIII

Page 203, note 1. **Nikolai Ivanovich Nebogatov** (1849–1912). Rear Admiral; commander of the Third Squadron of the Baltic Fleet at Tsushima; tried to save four surviving ships but was surrounded by twenty-eight Japanese ships and surrendered; later tried by a naval court-martial, 1906, and sentenced to death; this sentence was commuted to ten years' imprisonment, deprivation of all rank, and expulsion from the service.

2. **Lavr Georgievich Kornilov** (1870–1918). Russian General of Cossack and Mongolian extraction; graduate of the Nicholas Academy of the General Staff; served on the Afghanistan border, in Central Asia, and in the Russo-Japanese War; Military Attaché in China, 1907–1911; rendered distinguished service during the World War; was taken prisoner by the Austrians but escaped, 1916; Commander of the Southwestern Front, July 23—July 31, 1917; Commander in Chief of the Russian Armies, July 31—September 11, 1917; in the subsequent break with Kerensky was arrested and imprisoned at Bykhov; released on December 2, 1917, and made his way to the Don, where, with Alekseev and Kaledin, he formed the triumvirate which conducted the early activities of the Volunteer movement against the Bolsheviks; led the First Kuban campaign; killed at his headquarters, April 13, 1918, by a shell.

3. **Mikhail Vasilevich Alekseev** (1857–1918). Graduate of the Nicholas Academy of the General Staff; served in Turkish War, 1877–1878; Chief of Operations of Third Army, Russo-Japanese War, 1904–1905; Chief of Staff of Nicholas II, 1915–1917; Commander in Chief, 1917; founder of the Volunteer Army, 1918.

4. **Admiral Zinovii Petrovich Rozhestvensky** (1848–1909). Selected in 1904 for the difficult command of the Baltic Fleet on its voyage to the Far East; wounded and captured by the Japanese in the battle of Tsushima, May 1905; on his return to Russia was tried by a naval court-martial in which the prosecution demanded the death penalty; acquitted and retired.

5. **Tertii Ivanovich Filippov** (1825–1899). Graduate of Moscow University; teacher in a Moscow high school; special-duty clerk in the Holy Synod, 1856; transferred to the State Control, 1864; Assistant State Comptroller, 1878; State Comptroller, 1889.

6. **Mikhail Nikolaevich Giers** (1856–1924). Minister to Brazil, 1895, to Peking, 1898, to Munich, 1901, to Bucharest, 1902; Ambassador at Constantinople, 1912, at Rome, 1915–1917; member of the Russian Political Conference in Paris, 1919; chief diplomatic representative of the Wrangel Government abroad, 1920.

Page 206, note 7. **mentions in his memoirs.** See Witte, *op. cit.,* I, 472.

8. **Prince Aleksei Dmitrievich Obolensky** (1855–1933). Graduate of the Imperial School of Law, 1877, after which he worked in the First Department of the Senate; chairman of the Congress of Justices of the Peace in Kozelsk Uezd, Kaluga Gubernia, 1881; Marshal of Nobility of same uezd, 1884–1894; rural inspector for the Ministry of Agriculture and State Domains, 1894; Manager of the Bank of the Nobility and the Peasant Land Bank, 1894; Assistant Minister of the Interior, 1900; Senator, 1901; Assistant

Minister of Finance, 1902; member of Special Conference to Study the Needs of Agricultural Industry, 1903; again Manager of Bank of the Nobility and Peasant Land Bank, 1905; became member of State Council, June 1905; Ober-Prokuror of the Holy Synod, October 1905–1906.

Page 207, note 9. **Gubernia and uezd committees to study the needs of agricultural industry.** See note 19, chapter iv, p. 615.

10. **Mikhail Aleksandrovich Stakhovich** (1861–   ). Graduate of the Imperial School of Law; Marshal of Nobility of Orel Gubernia, 1895–1897; actively participated in various government and public conferences and, in 1903, together with Shipov was reprimanded by the Emperor for participating in a zemstvo congress forbidden by the government; chief representative of the detachment of the nobility in Manchuria during Russo-Japanese War; with Count P. A. Heyden, D. N. Shipov, and A. I. Guchkov formed from the minority of zemstvo congresses the "Union of October 17" (1905); member of the First and Second Dumas; elected member of the State Council, 1907 and 1912.

Page 209, note 11. **Aleksandr Sergeevich Pushkin** (1799–1837). Attended Tsarskoe Selo Lyceum, 1811–1817, where he began to write verse; banished in 1820 for poems and epigrams critical of the regime; traveled in the Caucasus and the Crimea; employed in government service in Kishinev and Odessa, whence he was dismissed and banished to his estate in Pskov Gubernia, 1824, where he remained until 1826, thus escaping being involved in the Decembrist affair in which were many of his friends; pardoned by Nicholas I, 1826; mortally wounded in a duel, 1837. Among the works which have given Pushkin his place as one of the very greatest figures in Russian literature are: *Ruslan and Liudmila* (1820); *The Captive of the Caucasus* (1822); *Boris Godunov* (1831); *Eugene Onegin* (1823–1830); *Poltava* (1829); *The Bronze Horseman* (1833); and, in prose, *The Queen of Spades* (1834) and *The Captain's Daughter* (1836).

12. **Vladimir Sergeevich Solovev** (1853–1900). Russian idealistic philosopher, critic, and poet; son of the historian, Sergei Solovev; studied theology at the University of Moscow, in England, and in Egypt; reader of philosophy at Moscow University, 1877, but a short time later his criticism of the government lost him his post and later his professorship at St. Petersburg University, where he had gone after leaving Moscow; devoted the rest of his life to writing; the chief tenet of his theology favored a union of Eastern and Western beliefs in a universal church; upheld the Christian ideal of universal brotherhood as opposed to Slavophilism.

Page 210, note 13. **says as much in his memoirs.** See Witte, *op. cit.,* II, 107–8 (English edition, p. 349).

Page 212, note 14. **Ivan Pavlovich Shipov** (1865–1919). Graduate of the Imperial Alexander Lyceum and St. Petersburg University; in the Department of Direct Taxation in the Ministry of Finance; tax inspector in Tver Gubernia, 1891, and the same year in the Chancellery of the Committee of Ministers; Assistant Director of the Special Credit Office in the Ministry of Finance, 1894; Director of the General Office, 1897; secretary to the Special Conference to Study the Needs of Agricultural Industry, 1902; Director of the Department of the State Treasury, 1902; accompanied Witte to Portsmouth, 1905; Minister of Finance, October 1905—April 1906; sent to the Far East to study various economic problems in Manchuria, Japan, and China, 1907; Minister of Commerce and Industry, 1908–1909; member of the State Council, 1909.

15. **General Office** (*Obshchaia Kantseliariia*). A department of the Ministry of Finance, made up of a committee of specialists for the consideration of financial projects. Another department, the Special Credit Office (*Osobennaia Kantseliariia po kreditnoi chasti*), was concerned with credit matters.

16. **Aleksei Ivanovich Putilov** (1866–   ). Graduate of St. Petersburg University; entered the Ministry of Finance, 1890; Director of the General Office, 1902–1905; Assistant to the Minister of Finance, October 1905—April 1906, when he resigned to become director of several financial and industrial enterprises, including the Russo-Asiatic Bank, of which he remained chairman until the Bolshevik Revolution; in emigration.

Page 213, note 17. **Nikolai Aleksandrovich Pavlov.** Publicist; contributor to *Moskovskiia Vedomosti* and *Grazhdanin;* active in the association of the "United Nobility" and in political circles and salons of the Right wing.

Page 216, note 18. **Boards for the Affairs of Factories and Mines.** See note 16, chapter ii, p. 606.

Page 224, note 19. **Prince Petr Dmitrievich Dolgorukov** (1866–   ). Graduate of Moscow University; well-known zemstvo man and for many years chairman of Sudzha Zemstvo Board; for his radical pronouncements at the sessions of Sudzha Uezd Committee to Study the Needs of Agricultural Industry was removed from his post by Plehve but reinstated under Sviatopolk-Mirsky; one of the founders of the Union of Liberation (*Soiuz Osvobozhdeniia*) and of the publication *Osvobozhdenie;* participated in zemstvo congresses, 1904–1905; one of the founders of the Cadet party; member and vice-chairman of the First State Duma, 1906; was imprisoned for three months and deprived of his rank for signing the Viborg Manifesto; reinstated in 1909 and re-elected chairman of Sudzha Uezd Zemstvo Board.

Page 225, note 20. **Nikolai Fedorovich Bunakov** (1836–1904). Well-known pedagogue; graduate of St. Petersburg University; lectured at normal schools; as a zemstvo member participated in the work of Voronezh Committee to Study the Needs of Agricultural Industry, 1902, and insisted on social and political reforms; for this insistence he was forbidden to continue his lecturing and was banished to his native village, Petitino.

21. **Eduard Dmitrievich Pleske** (1852–1904). Educated at the Imperial Alexander Lyceum; Assistant Director and Director of the Special Credit Office and Manager of the State Bank; Minister of Finance, 1903–1904; appointed member of the State Council, 1904.

CHAPTER XIV

Page 229, note 1. **Konstantin Fedorovich Golovin** (1843–?). Belles-lettres writer and publicist; pseudonym, K. Orlovsky.

Page 232, note 2. **Party of Peaceful Reconstruction** (*Partiia mirnago* *obnovleniia* [*Obnovlentsy*]). Founded in 1906; favored a liberal constitutional monarchy; occupied a place between the Right Cadets and the Union of October 17; headed by Count P. A. Heyden, M. A. Stakhovich, D. N. Shipov, and N. N. Lvov.

3. **Prince Pavel Dmitrievich Dolgorukov** (1866–1927). Graduate of Moscow University; member of the Union of Liberation; active participant in zemstvo and town congresses, 1904–1905; one of the founders of the Cadet party and the first chairman of its Central Committee; candidate from the city of Moscow to the First State Duma; member of the Second State Duma; supporter of the anti-Bolshevik movement in the south; emigrated 1920; returned to Russia in 1924 and was arrested, but escaped to Poland; went again to Russia in disguise in 1927 with a forged passport, was arrested, imprisoned, and shot.

Page 235, note 4. **law of January 18, 1899.** This law superseded the earlier regulation of June 8, 1893, concerning the rules by which the value of immovable property was estimated for the purposes of taxation. The 1893 regulation had placed this work of assessment in the hands of the uezd zemstvo boards, but these had proved incapable of handling the work efficiently. The law of June 18, 1899, transferred this work from the uezd to the gubernia zemstvo boards and transferred the chairmanship in the Gubernia Commission for Assessments from the gubernia marshal of nobility to the governor. Besides, a yearly subsidy of one million rubles was assigned from the State Treasury to gubernia zemstvos for the continuation of the work of assessing immovable property.

Page 236, note 5. *Russkiia Vedomosti.* Daily newspaper; organ of Russian liberals; founded in Moscow in 1863 by N. F. Pavlov; edited by N. S. Skvortsov, 1866–1882, and by V. M. Sobolevsky, 1882–1912; after Sobolevsky's death, 1912, became the organ of the Right-Wing Cadets; suppressed by the Bolsheviks in 1918.

Page 242, note 6. **work of the commission.** For Kokovtsov's account of the events preceding his appointment as Minister of Finance, see Kokovtsov, *op. cit.,* pp. 11–14.

Page 243, note 7. **Aleksandr Mikhailovich Koliubakin** (1868–   ). Cadet; member of Third Duma; chairman of the Novgorod Zemstvo Board.

Page 244, note 8. **Prince Georgii Evgenevich Lvov** (1861–1925). Graduate of Moscow University; entered the Ministry of the Interior, 1886; member of the Special Board for Peasant Affairs in Epifan, Moscow, and Tula; member of Epifan and Tula Zemstvo assemblies; chairman of Tula Uezd Zemstvo Board, 1903–1906; Head of the All-Russian Zemstvo Union to render assistance to the sick and wounded at the front in the Russo-Japanese War; elected to the First State Duma, 1905, and joined the Right Wing of the Cadet party; organized medical and food assistance to the settlers in the Far East; member of the Moscow Gubernia Zemstvo Assembly and Moscow Municipal Duma; in 1913 elected Mayor of Moscow, but his election was not confirmed by the government; Head of All-Russian Zemstvo Union to render assistance to sick and wounded soldiers, 1914–1917; chairman of the Council of Ministers and Minister of the Interior of the Provisional Government, March–May, 1917; arrested after the Bolshevik Revolution and imprisoned in Ekaterinburg but escaped to Siberia and then to Paris, where he spent the remainder of his life; member of the Russian Political Conference in Paris, 1919.

Page 245, note 9. **V. I. Charnolusky** (1865–). Narodnik; active worker in the St. Petersburg committee to promote literacy and in the congresses on people's education; member of St. Petersburg Soviet of Workers' Deputies, 1905; arrested and exiled several times; after the October Revolution, 1917, continued to work and write on educational problems.

10. **Henrich Adolfovich Falbork** (1864–). Writer; promoter of popular education; member of the committee to promote literacy; walked through famine regions, 1891, and submitted a report on the conditions to the Free Economic Society; with V. I. Charnolusky organized first statistical investigation of popular education in Russia; on his initiative the League of Learning and the Pedagogic Academy were established.

11. **Aleksandr Arkadevich Stolypin** (1863–). Graduate of St. Petersburg University; journalist; editor of *Sankt–Peterburgskiia Vedomosti;* forced by Plehve to give up his position because of his "undesirable views"; after 1904, on the staff of *Novoe Vremia;* one of the active members of the Union of October 17; emigrated.

12. *Sankt-Peterburgskiia Vedomosti.* One of the first Russian newspapers; founded in 1728; attached to the Academy of Sciences with academician G. F. Miller as its first editor; later other academicians edited it; in 1863 the paper became an important organ of public and political thought, with V. F. Korsh as its editor; in 1878 its management was transferred from the Academy of Sciences to the Ministry of Education; Prince E. E. Ukhtomsky became editor in 1896, after which the newspaper advocated freedom of religious belief, respect for national traditions, freedom of speech, and development of public initiative. *Russkaia Gazeta* (a supplementary edition of *Sankt–Peterburgskiia Vedomosti*) was published from 1886 to 1890.

Page 246, note 13. **Prince Grigorii Sergeevich Golitsyn** (1838–1907). Graduate of His Majesty's School of Pages and the Nicholas Military Academy of the General Staff, 1860; participated in wars against the Caucasian mountaineers, 1860–1861; Military Governor of the Uralsk Region and Ataman of the Uralsk Cossack Voisko, 1876; acting commander of the troops of Orenburg Military District and Governor-General of Orenburg, 1880; Senator, 1885; member of State Council, 1893; Governor of the Caucasus, 1897–1904.

Page 248, note 14. *Osvobozhdenie.* Organ of the liberals; established by P. B. Struve in 1902 in Stuttgart and later in Paris; in the summer of 1903 members of this liberal group met in South Germany and founded a political group known as the Union of Liberation, which included zemstvo leaders, university professors, lawyers, journalists, etc.

15. **Dudley Disraeli Braham** (1875–). English journalist and editor; joined Berlin office of *The Times* (London), 1897; correspondent in St. Petersburg, 1901–1903, in Constantinople, 1903; became assistant to Sir Valentine Chirol, Head of the Imperial and Foreign Department of *The Times,* 1907, and succeeded to that office, 1912; elected same year a director of The Times Publishing Company; traveled for *The Times* in Europe, Asia Minor, the Far East, and America; left service of *The Times,* 1914; editor of

the *Daily Telegraph,* Sydney, New South Wales, 1914–1922; founded and became first editor of *Forum* (Australia), 1922; editor of *West Australian,* Perth, Western Australia, 1924–1930; returned to London, 1930, to rejoin *The Times.*

Page 249, note 16. *Novosti.* Daily newspaper; founded in St. Petersburg, 1872, by Yu. Schreider; purchased in 1876 by O. K. Notovich, who built it up from an insignificant daily to an important political organ; defended the interests of large-scale industrialists; in the national question defended the rights of separate nationalities to cultural autonomy and freedom of conscience; in foreign affairs assisted in effecting the Franco-Russian rapprochement.

17. **Osip Konstantinovich Notovich** (1849– ?). Son of Kerch rabbi; graduate of St. Petersburg University; published and edited *Novoe Vremia,* 1873–1874; purchased (1876) and edited *Novosti;* sentenced to one year's imprisonment, March 1906, for publishing news of the Belostok pogroms.

CHAPTER XV

Page 254, note 1. **attention toward Korea.** See Witte, *op. cit.,* I, 38–39 (English edition, pp. 82–83).

2. **Count Mikhail Nikolaevich Muravev** (1845–1900). Studied in Heidelberg University; in the Ministry of Foreign Affairs as secretary to various embassies; in the Red Cross at the front during the Russo-Turkish War, 1877–1878, after which he returned to diplomatic service; Minister in Copenhagen, 1893–1896; after the death of Prince Lobanov-Rostovsky, 1896, became Minister of Foreign Affairs; represented Russia at the Hague Conference in 1899.

Page 255, note 3. **William II** (1859–   ). German Emperor and King of Prussia from 1888 until his abdication in November 1918; since then in Holland.

4. **Grand Duke Aleksei Aleksandrovich** (1850–1908). Fourth son of Alexander II and uncle of Nicholas II; entered naval service in his youth; succeeded Grand Duke Konstantin Nikolaevich as head of the Ministry of the Navy with the rank of General Admiral, 1882; relieved of his post in 1905, when the rank of General Admiral was abolished.

Page 256, note 5. **Li Hung-chang** (1823–1901). Chinese statesman; attended Hanlin University; for his part in putting down the Taiping rebels, created an earl and made governor of Kiangsu, which post he held from 1864 to 1866; called upon to suppress the rebellion of Nienfei (a remnant of the Taipings), 1866; viceroy of Hukwang, 1867–1870; later appointed viceroy to province of Chihli, where he actively suppressed anti-foreign sentiment. To his duties as viceroy were at length added those of superintendent of trade, and from that time until his death, with a few intervals of retirement, he practically conducted the foreign policy of China: concluded the Chifu convention with Sir Thomas Wade (1876); arranged treaties with Peru and Japan and (1886) with France; represented the Emperor at the Shimonoseki

Conference, 1895, and at the coronation of the Tsar, 1896; in 1900 appointed viceroy of the two Kwang Provinces; recalled to the capital at the outbreak of the Boxer trouble; the peace of September 1901 was largely secured through his efforts.

6. **Chang Yin-huan.** When the agreement was made in March 1898, Chang chose not to accept the 500,000 lan the Russian government was to pay him, because he was already under suspicion of accepting bribes. He preferred to wait until such rumors had subsided, and by September he had not been paid anything. Later in that month, however, he asked for 15,000 lan (it is not clear whether this sum was a part of or in addition to the 500,000 lan) the payment of which was authorized by the Russian government. Here the available record stops. (See "Perepiska o podkupe kitaiskikh sanovnikov Li-Khun-Chzhana i Chzhan-in-Khuana" ["Correspondence regarding the bribing of the Chinese high officials, Li Hung-chang and Chang Yin-huan"] in *Krasnyi Arkhiv* [1922], II, 287–93, especially pp. 292–93.)

7. **port of Dalny (Dairen).** See Witte, *op. cit.*, I, 128 (English edition, p. 103).

8. **Prince Esper Esperovich Ukhtomsky** (1861–   ). Publicist and poet; graduate of St. Petersburg University; in the department of Ecclesiastical Affairs of Foreign Religions in the Ministry of the Interior; studied Buddhist tribes in Siberia and Central Asia and published accounts of them in *Russkii Vestnik* and other magazines; became head of the Russo-Chinese Bank and of the Chinese Eastern Railway Board in the late 'nineties; became editor of *Sankt–Peterburgskiia Vedomosti*, 1896.

Page 257, note 9. **with each other.** See Witte, *op. cit.*, I, 110–11 (English edition, p. 409).

Page 258, note 10. **Admiral Evgenii Ivanovich Alekseev** (1843–1909). Adjutant General; graduate of the Naval Cadet School, 1863; naval agent to France, 1883–1888; accompanied the Heir to the Throne to the Far East, 1891; Assistant Head of the Chief Naval Staff, 1892–1895; Commander of the Pacific Ocean Squadron, 1895–1897; Chief Flag Officer of the Black Sea Fleet, 1897–1899; Chief and Commander of the Troops for Kwantung region and Naval Forces of the Pacific, 1899–1903; Viceroy for the Far East, 1903–1905; Commander in Chief of the Army and Navy during the earlier part of the Russo-Japanese War, after which he was replaced by General A. N. Kuropatkin; member of the State Council, 1905.

Page 259, note 11. **Aleksandr Mikhailovich Bezobrazov.** Officer of the Guards; in the 'nineties was known in stock exchange circles of St. Petersburg and gained the confidence of the Tsar; appointed member of the Special Committee for the Affairs of the Far East, 1903.

Page 260, note 12. **Count Illarion Ivanovich Vorontsov-Dashkov** (1837–1916). Distinguished army service in the Caucasus and in Turkestan, 1865; became Assistant Governor of Tashkent, 1866; returned to army service, 1869; took part in the Russo-Turkish War, 1877–1878; Minister of the Imperial Court, 1881–1897; appointed Viceroy for the Caucasus and Commander in Chief of the Troops of the Caucasian Military District, 1905.

13. **Grand Duke Aleksandr Mikhailovich** (1866–1933). Son of Grand Duke Mikhail Nikolaevich, who was a brother of Emperor Alexander II.

Page 263, note 14. **Rear Admiral Aleksei Mikhailovich Abaza** (1853–   ). In charge of the detachment of the naval cadet school, 1902–1903; Manager of the Special Committee for the Affairs of the Far East, 1903–1905.

15. **activity [in Korea].** The treaty here referred to is the Rosen-Nishi Agreement of April 13/25, 1898, relative to independence of Korea and neutral rights. The text is as follows:

"Baron Rosen, State Councillor, Chamberlain, Envoy Extraordinary and Minister Plenipotentiary of the Emperor of All the Russias, and Baron Nissi, Minister for Foreign Affairs of His Majesty the Emperor of Japan, in order to give effect to Article IV, of the Protocol signed at Moscow on May 28/June 9, 1896, between the Secretary of State Prince Lobanoff and the Marquis Yamagata—being duly authorised to that effect, have agreed to the following Articles:

"ARTICLE I. The Imperial Governments of Russia and Japan recognise definitely the Sovereignty and entire independence of Korea, and pledge themselves mutually to abstain from all direct interference in the internal affairs of that country.

"II. Desiring to remove all possible cause of misunderstanding in the future, the Imperial Governments of Russia and Japan pledge themselves mutually, in the event of Korea having recourse to the advice and assistance, either of Russia or of Japan, to take no measure in respect to the appointment of military instructors or financial advisers, without arriving beforehand at a mutual agreement on this subject.

"III. In view of the wide development taken by the commercial and industrial enterprise of Japan in Korea, as well as the large number of Japanese subjects residing in that country, the Russian Government will not hinder the development of commercial and industrial relations between Japan and Korea.

"Done at Tokyo in duplicate the 13/25 April, 1898.

"ROSEN.
"NISSI."

From W. W. Rockhill (ed.), *Treaties and Conventions with or concerning China and Korea, 1894–1904* (Washington, 1904), p. 433, where it is translated from the French text as printed in *British and Foreign State Papers,* XCII, 1068.

16. **His Majesty's Cabinet** (*Kabinet Ego Imperatorskago Velichestva*). Established by Peter I. With the formation of the Ministry of the Imperial Court (1826), it became a section of this ministry and was headed by the Minister of the Imperial Court. The Cabinet took charge of the Emperor's property and of the wills of members of the Imperial family. In 1888 it assumed the functions of the former Chancellery of the Imperial Court.

17. **Privy Councilor** (*tainyi sovetnik*). The third highest rank in the civil-service category. See information on the Table of Ranks, in note 32, chapter x, p. 628.

18. **Baron Andrei Nikolaevich Korff** (1831–1893). Graduate of His Majesty's School of Pages; took part in the struggle against the mountaineers in the Caucasus, 1859; continued in military service; appointed Governor-

General of the Amur and Assistant Chief of the troops of the Amur Military District, in which capacity he distinguished himself as an active administrator and politician, 1884–1893.

Page 265, note 19. **Vasilii Osipovich Kliuchevsky** (1841–1911). Eminent Russian historian; professor at the University of Moscow, 1879–1911; closely connected with Liberal circles and one-time member of the Cadet party.

Page 266, note 20. **as a military force Japan was negligible.** In his *Zapiski generala Kuropatkina o russko-iaponskoi voine; Itogi voiny* (Berlin, 1909), the English edition of which is *The Russian Army and the Japanese War* (2 vols., New York, 1909), Kuropatkin quotes from a special memorandum to the Tsar written in October 1903 in which he points out that Japan would be able to oppose Russia on the continent with an army of at least from 300,000 to 350,000 men. He adds, referring to the memorandum: "From the above lines it will be seen how seriously the War Department regarded such an antagonist as Japan, and how much anxiety it felt concerning possible complications with that Power on account of Korea" (pp. 151–53 [English edition, I, 164–66]). Later in this book Kuropatkin insists that he was a "convinced opponent of an active Asiatic policy," that he had the greatest respect for the Japanese Army and that: "Everything that I saw and studied concerning the country [Japan]—its armed forces, and its work in the Far East—convinced me how necessary it was to come to a peaceful agreement with Japan, even at the expense of concessions which might at first appear to be derogatory to our national self-esteem" (pp. 177–78, 194–97 [English edition, I, 197, 217–21]).

21. **Count Vladimir Nikolaevich Lamsdorf** (1845–1907). Of a Westphalian family, one branch of which in 1817 received the title of count in Russia; accompanied Gorchakov to the Congress of Berlin in 1878; assistant to the Minister of Foreign Affairs, Muravev, 1897; Minister of Foreign Affairs, 1900–1906.

22. **Prince Feliks Feliksovich Yusupov [Count Sumarokov Elston]** (1856–   ). Father of F. F. Yusupov, who took part in the assassination of Rasputin; in the Ministry of the Interior, 1883–1885; Adjutant to Grand Duke Sergei Aleksandrovich, 1886–1904; Commander of a Cavalry Regiment, 1904–1908; Commander of the Second Cavalry Division of the Guards, 1908–1911; Chief of the Moscow Military District and Chief Representative of the government in Moscow City, 1915; in emigration.

23. **Count Vasilii Aleksandrovich Gendrikov** (1857–1912). In military service, 1876–1884; Marshal of Nobility of Volchansk Uezd, 1885; Master of Ceremonies, 1889–1896; Steward of the Imperial Household and attendant upon the Empress Alexandra Fedorovna, 1896–1900; Chief Master of Ceremonies and attendant upon the Empress, 1908.

24. **Baron Vladimir Borisovich Frederichs** (1838–1922). Lieutenant General and later Aide-de-Camp General to the Tsar; Assistant Minister of the Imperial Court, 1893–1897, and Minister of the Imperial Court, 1897–1917; in 1913 received the title of count; in 1921 obtained permission from the Soviet Government to go to his estate in Finland, where he died soon after.

Page 267, note 25. **views of the ministers.** See B. A. Romanov, "Kontsessiia na Yalu" ["The Concession on the Yalu"] in *Russkoe Proshloe* (1922), I, 100.

Page 268, note 26. **Baron Roman Romanovich Rosen** (1849–1922). Graduate of the Imperial School of Law; entered the section for civil affairs in the First Department of the Ministry of Justice, 1868; in the Asiatic Department of the Ministry of Foreign Affairs, 1872; Vice-Consul in Yokohama, 1875, and later secretary of the Russian Mission in Yeddo (Tokyo), in which capacity he remained until 1884; Consul-General in New York, 1884–1890; Minister to Mexico, 1890–1895, to Belgrade, 1895–1897, to Tokyo, 1897–1899, to Munich, 1900–1901, to Athens, 1901–1904; returned to Tokyo in 1904 but was obliged to leave in January when diplomatic relations were severed; Minister to the United States, 1905–1911; second plenipotentiary at the peace negotiations at Portsmouth, 1905; member of the State Council, 1911.

Page 269, note 27. **Baron Tokujiro Nishi** (1847–1915). Studied law in St. Petersburg University, 1873–1874; Secretary to the Japanese Legation in Paris, 1874; also St. Petersburg, 1878; Secretary to the cabinet; Minister Plenipotentiary to St. Petersburg, 1886–1896; created baron 1895; Privy Councilor, 1897; Minister of Foreign Affairs, 1897–1898; Minister Plenipotentiary to Peking, 1899–1900, during the Boxer trouble.

28. **Marquis Hirobumi Ito** (1841–1909). Japanese statesman; went to England as a student, 1861; Governor of Hiogo, 1868; Vice-Minister of Finance, 1869; junior plenipotentiary with Iwakuri mission abroad, 1871; served in Ministry of the Interior, 1878; in 1882 sent abroad with others for almost two years to study constitutional systems in foreign countries; Prime Minister, 1886–1889; in 1888 engaged in preparing a written constitution which was promulgated February 1889; President of the Privy Council, 1889; as Prime Minister for the second time carried his country through the Sino-Japanese War, resigning in 1896; again Prime Minister from January to June, 1898, and from October 1900 to June 1901; President of the Privy Council, 1903; in 1905 negotiated convention with Korea by which the foreign affairs of that country were placed under control of a Japanese resident general, in which capacity Ito served from 1906 to (July) 1909; assassinated by a Korean at Harbin, October 1909. (See Kokovtsov, *op. cit.,* pp. 229–43.)

Page 270, note 29. **Colonel Konstantin Ippolitovich Vogak.** Military agent in China and Japan.

30. **Aleksandr Petrovich Izvolsky** (1856–1919). Graduate of the Imperial Alexander Lyceum; entered the diplomatic service, holding junior appointments at Bucharest, Washington, and the Vatican; subsequently became Minister at Belgrade, Munich, Tokyo, and Copenhagen; in 1906 succeeded Count Lamsdorf as Minister of Foreign Affairs, and from 1910 to 1917 was Russian Ambassador at Paris.

Page 272, note 31. **Marquis Ito . . . . an agreement.** The negotiations leading up to this agreement were conducted for Japan by Baron Hayashi, Japanese Minister in London, and had progressed far before Marquis Ito reached England early in January. The treaty was signed on January 30, 1902, by Baron Hayashi for Japan and by Lord Lansdowne for England. (See Great Britain, Foreign Office, G. P. Gooch and Harold Temperley, eds., *British Documents on the Origins of the War, 1898–1914* [11 volumes, London, 1926–1938], II, 89–137, especially pp. 96–123.)

Page 276, note 32. **Petr Pavlovich Hesse** (1846–1905). Lieutenant General; graduate of His Majesty's School of Pages; served in the army; Commandant of the Imperial Household, 1888; General on duty to His Majesty, later receiving the title of Palace Commandant, 1896–1905.

Page 278, note 33. **Viktor Viktorovich Sakharov** (1848–1905). Lieutenant General; graduate of the Nicholas Academy of the General Staff; served in the Russo-Turkish War, 1877–1878, after which he was Assistant Chief of Staff of Warsaw Military District, then Quartermaster General of the General Staff of the Warsaw Military District, and then Chief of Staff of the Odessa Military District; Chief of the General Staff, 1898; Minister of War, 1904–1905; killed in Saratov Gubernia, where he had been sent to restore order during agrarian disturbances.

Page 280, note 34. **entire Japanese fleet.** Concerning this report Kuropatkin says: "I presented to the Emperor a special report on the Manchurian question, in which I showed that, in order to avoid complications with China and a rupture with Japan, we must put an end to our military occupation of Southern Manchuria, and confine our activity and our administrative supervision to the northern part of that territory" (Kuropatkin, *op. cit.*, p. 169 [English edition, I, 188]).

35. **Aleksandr Ivanovich Rusin** (1861–   ). Graduate of Nicholas Naval Academy; naval agent in Japan; Head of Nicholas Naval Academy and Naval School, 1908–1913; Head of the Chief Naval Staff, 1913–1914; Chief of the Naval General Staff, 1914; Assistant Minister of the Navy, 1915.

Page 281, note 36. **"Well, you failed that time."** See the entry for August 24, 1903, "Dnevnik A. N. Kuropatkina," in *Krasnyi Arkhiv* (1922), II, 66–77.

Page 282, note 37. **Baron Ichiro Motono** (1862–1919). Japanese diplomat; graduate of the University of Lyons; translator in the Japanese Foreign Office, 1890; Councilor, 1893; Private Secretary to the Foreign Minister, 1895; Secretary of the Legation at St. Petersburg, 1896; Minister Resident in Belgium, 1898; a Japanese representative at the Peace Conference at The Hague, 1899; Minister to France, 1901–1906; created baron, 1907; Ambassador to St. Petersburg, 1906–1916; Minister of Foreign Affairs, 1916–1918; created viscount, 1918; member of the Permanent Court of Arbitration at The Hague.

38. **Admiral Nikolai Illarionovich Skrydlov** (1844– ?). Graduate of Naval School; served in the Russo-Turkish War, 1877–1878; chief inspector of mine laying, 1894–1898; commander of the squadron of battleships engaged in the pacification of the Island of Crete, 1898–1900; chief of the Pacific Squadron, 1900–1902; Commander of the Black Sea Fleet and Black Sea ports, 1902–1904; after the death of Rear Admiral Makarov, Commander of Pacific Squadron during the Russo-Japanese War, 1904–1905; again appointed Commander of the Black Sea Fleet, 1906.

Page 285, note 39. **our telegram to Baron Rosen.** In Russia's note to Japan on January 22/February 4, a note which had not reached its destination when diplomatic relations were severed two days later, Russia did not accept

Japan's important condition that the territorial integrity of China in Manchuria be respected (*British Documents on the Origins of the War, 1898–1914,* Vol. II, No. 286, Scott to Lansdowne, February 4, 1904, and Vol. IV, No. 66, Hardinge to Lansdowne, April 4, 1905). There is at hand no record of a conference called by the Tsar at the time diplomatic relations were broken, nor of any telegram sent to Baron Rosen with a belated acceptance of all of Japan's conditions. It is true, however, that even after the severance of diplomatic relations Russia was interested in coming peaceably to an agreement with Japan on all points of difference (*ibid.,* Vol. II, No. 295, Lansdowne to Scott, February 8, 1904, and No. 297, Lansdowne to Scott, February 9, 1904) ; but the outbreak of hostilities on January 26/February 8 precluded such a possibility.

Page 286, note 40. **Admiral Stepan Osipovich Makarov** (1848–1904). Participated in the Russo-Turkish War, 1877–1878, and the Turkestan campaign, 1881 ; carried on extensive hydrological studies in the Mediterranean and Black Seas, the northern Pacific, and Far Eastern waters ; designer of the "Ermak," first and largest of Russian ice-breakers, built in England in 1899, in which Makarov made a voyage to Franz Joseph Land in 1901 ; Commander of the Baltic Fleet, 1897, and Commandant of Kronstadt, 1899 ; appointed commander of all naval forces at the outbreak of the Japanese War ; perished in the explosion of the "Petropavlovsk" on a Japanese mine off Port Arthur, March 31, 1904.

41. **Admiral Heihachiro Togo** (1847–1934). Joined the Japanese Navy in 1863 ; studied naval science and navigation in England, 1871–1878 ; in 1894, as captain of the cruiser "Naniwa," sank the Chinese troopship "Kowshing" en route to Korea, thus precipitating the Sino-Japanese War ; at opening of Russo-Japanese War in 1904, was put in command of the combined squadrons of the Japanese Navy and for his brilliant service was made Chief of the Naval Staff and given the title of count ; was created a marquis while on his deathbed.

Page 290, note 42. **Pavel Mikhailovich Lessar** (? –1905). Engineer and diplomat ; political agent for Asiatic affairs in London ; Minister to China, 1901.

CHAPTER XVI

Page 293, note 1. **Count Sergei Dmitrievich Sheremetev** (1844– ?). Honorary member of the Academy of Sciences ; member of the State Council ; chairman of the Archeographic Commission and of the Society of the Lovers of Old Russian Letters and Promoters of Russian Historical Knowledge in Memory of Alexander III ; author of a number of historical and archeological works.

2. **Grand Duchess Mariia Nikolaevna** (1819–1876). Daughter of Emperor Nicholas I ; married to Duke of Leuchtenberg ; participated actively in the management of girls' schools and directly supervised the Patriotic Institute ; after the death of her husband (1852) became chairman of the Academy of Arts and later chairman of the Society to Promote Arts ; married Grigorii Aleksandrovich Stroganov in 1856.

Page 294, note 3. **Emanuil Aleksandrovich Vatatsi** (1856–1920). Graduate of the Imperial School of Law; attended Berlin University; Governor of Suvalki, Kovno, and Kharkov consecutively, 1898–1904; Director of the Department for General Affairs of the Ministry of the Interior, 1904; Assistant Minister of the Interior, 1905; Senator in the Second Department of the Senate, 1906; Assistant to the Viceroy of the Caucasus from 1909 till his resignation in 1915.

4. **Prince Aleksandr Ivanovich Bariatinsky** (1814–1879). Entered the army at seventeen; distinguished himself in the wars against Caucasian tribes; Major General, 1848; General of Infantry, 1856; as Viceroy of the Caucasus, 1856–1862, subdued all Caucasian tribes; member of the State Council, 1862.

Page 296, note 5. **Pavel Fedorovich Unterberger** (1842–1921). Graduate of Nicholas Military Engineering School and Academy, 1864; held various positions in the army in Siberia; Military Governor of the Maritime Province, 1888; Ataman of Ussuriisk Cossack Voisko, 1889; Commander of the troops of the Maritime Province, 1895; Governor of Nizhnii Novgorod, 1897; Senator, 1905; Commander of the troops of the Amur Military District and Governor-General of Amur Province, 1905; Ataman of Amur and Ussuriisk Cossack Voiskos, 1906–1910; member of the State Council, 1910.

Page 298, note 6. **Nikolai Fedorovich Annensky** (1843–1912). Narodnik; publicist; statistician; took charge of statistical work of Kazan Gubernia zemstvo, 1883–1887, and of Nizhnii Novgorod zemstvo, 1887–1895.

7. **Pavel Nikolaevich Pereverzev.** Lawyer; Socialist - Revolutionist; Prokuror in St. Petersburg Court of Appeals under the Provisional Government; Minister of Justice, April 24—July 7, 1917.

8. **A. V. Smirnov** (1873–   ). Zemstvo statistician in Yaroslavl and Vladimir gubernias; traveled in the United States, 1908; on return settled in Tambov and practiced law; wrote for the Cadet organ, *Russkiia Vedomosti*.

Page 299, note 9. **Aleksei Sergeevich Suvorin** (1834–1912). Journalist and publisher; founder of *Novoe Vremia* and a large publishing establishment; in his youth a moderate liberal, later of more conservative views.

10. *Svet.* Nationalistic St. Petersburg daily; founded, 1882; V. V. Komarov, editor and publisher.

Page 300, note 11. **General K. N. Rydzevsky.** Assistant Minister of the Interior, 1904–1905, and Chief of Police and Commander of the Gendarme Corps.

12. **Sergei Efimovich Kryzhanovsky** (1862–1934). Graduate in law of St. Petersburg University; in judicial institutions, 1885–1896; transferred to the Ministry of the Interior, where he occupied various posts, 1896–1911; Assistant Minister of the Interior, 1906; Imperial Secretary, 1911; member of the State Council, January 1917; played an important part in preparing the drafts of the law of August 6, 1905, on the consultative Duma, and of that of June 3, 1907, revising the electoral law of December 11, 1905.

13. **Chief Administration [and Council] for the Affairs of Local Economy** (*Glavnoe upravlenie i Sovet po delam mestnago khoziaistva*). Organized in 1904 from the Departments of Economy and of Medicine in the

Ministry of the Interior; supervised national food supply, public charities, municipal self-government, and so forth.

Page 301, note 14. **Stanislav Kazimirovich Glinka - Yanchevsky** (1844– ?). Graduate of Nicholas Military Engineering School and later student at the Nicholas Military Engineering Academy; before graduating was arrested and imprisoned for two years and eight months for "failing to report on the criminal intentions of his comrades"; served in a sapper company in Turkestan, 1866–1875; established a number of commercial enterprises in Central Asia; publicist; editor of *Zemshchina,* the organ of the Right group in the State Duma.

15. *Zemshchina.* Published in St. Petersburg, 1909–1917; organ of the extreme Right of the State Duma with such collaborators as Markov II, Purishkevich, Zamyslovsky, and others.

Page 302, note 16. **Grand Duke Vladimir Aleksandrovich** (1847–1909). General; third son of Alexander II; Commander of the Twelfth Army during the Russo-Turkish War, 1877–1878; after 1876 president of the Academy of Art; Commander in Chief of the Guard and of the St. Petersburg Military District, 1884–1905; member of the State Council; Senator.

Page 303, note 17. *Zemskii Sobor.* The Russian national assembly of the Muscovite period; representative of all classes; called irregularly by the Tsars in times of crisis. Ivan the Terrible is said to have summoned the first Sobor in 1550; certainly he summoned one in 1566. The last Sobor met in 1653.

Page 305, note 18. **Nikolai Nikolaevich Lvov** (1867–). Zemstvo worker and member of the First, Third, and Fourth Dumas; member of the Cadet party and later one of the organizers of the Party of Peaceful Reconstruction (*Partiia mirnago obnovleniia*); after the Bolshevik Revolution a supporter of the White movement in the South.

19. **Nikolai Ivanovich Guchkov.** An active member of the Moscow commercial community; Mayor of Moscow, 1905–1913.

20. **Sergei Andreevich Muromtsev** (1850–1910). Professor at Moscow University; editor of *Iuridicheskii Vestnik,* 1879–1892; active in zemstvo congresses in the early 'nineties; one of the founders and leaders of the Cadet party; member of its Central Committee; member and chairman of the First Duma, April 1906; signed Viborg Manifesto; wrote and lectured at Shaniavsky University, 1908–1910.

21. **Union of Liberation.** See note 14, chapter xiv, p. 645.

22. **Petr Berngardovich Struve** (1870–). An exponent of "legal Marxism" in Russia in the 'nineties; author of the Manifesto of the First Congress of the R.S.D.L. party, 1898; editor of *Novoe Slovo,* 1897, of *Nachalo,* 1899; joined the Union of Liberation and in 1902 established its organ, *Osvobozhdenie,* in Stuttgart and Paris; member of the Central Committee of the Cadet party; Cadet member of the Second Duma; edited *Russkaia Mysl* in Petrograd; member of Denikin's and later Wrangel's government; emigrated; edited *Russkaia Mysl* in Prague in 1924 and *Vozrozhdenie* in Paris in 1925.

23. **Conference of the Opposition and Revolutionary Organizations of the Russian Empire.** In the summer of 1904, a number of Russian revolu-

tionary parties and organizations of the liberal opposition, convinced that a propitious moment had arrived for the achievement of reform, determined to overlook the differences which had divided them and to unite in a co-operative effort to establish a democratic regime in Russia. In September and October the *rapprochement* of these parties and organizations was realized at meetings in Paris attended by representatives of three opposition and five revolutionary organizations. The three opposition parties were the Finnish, Russian, and Polish constitutionalists. The five revolutionary groups were the Russian Socialist-Revolutionists, the Polish Socialist party (P.P.S.), the Georgian Socialist-Revolutionists and Federalists, the Armenian Revolutionary Federalists, and the Lettish Social Democratic Labor party. From this conference there issued the following declaration:

"None of the parties represented at the meeting, in uniting for concerted action, thinks for a moment of abandoning any point of its particular program, or of the tactical methods of the struggle, which are adapted to the necessities, the forces, and the situation of the social elements, classes, or nationalities whose interests it represents. But, at the same time, all declare that the principles expressed below are recognized by all of them:

"1. The abolition of the autocracy; revocation of all the measures curtailing the constitutional rights of Finland.

"2. The substitution for the autocracy of a democratic régime based on universal suffrage.

"3. The right of every nationality to decide for itself; freedom of the national development, guaranteed by the law; suppression of all violence on the part of the Russian government, as practiced against the different nationalities.

"In the name of these fundamental principles, the parties represented at the conference will unite their efforts in order to hasten the inevitable fall of absolutism, which is equally incompatible with the realization of all the ulterior purposes pursued by each of the parties." (See Paul Milyoukov, *Russia and Its Crisis* [Chicago, 1906], pp. 523–28; also Konni Zilliacus, *The Russian Revolutionary Movement* [London, 1905], pp. 345–47.)

24. **Pavel Nikolaevich Miliukov** (1859–   ). Historian; professor at Moscow University; professor of history in Sophia, 1897–1898; editor of *Mir Bozhii* and *Bolshaia Entsiklopediia,* 1899; lectured on Russia and southern Slavs in the United States, 1902–1905; collaborated in *Osvobozhdenie* in Stuttgart; one of the organizers of the Union of Liberation, 1905; participated in the liberal congresses, 1905; chairman of the Union of Unions; initiator and chairman of the Central Committee of the Cadet party; editor of *Svobodnyi Narod* and *Narodnaia Svoboda,* 1905, both of which were suppressed; member of the Third and Fourth Dumas; Minister of Foreign Affairs in the Provisional Government, March–May, 1917; active in the anti-Bolshevik movement; after the Bolshevik Revolution, in emigration; editor of *Posledniia Novosti;* author of many historical works.

25. **Evno Fishelevich Asef** (? –1918). Well-known agent-provocateur; son of a tailor; engineer by profession; began his work for the Police Department, 1893; joined the Union of Socialist-Revolutionists abroad in 1899; together with G. A. Gershuni joined into one party various Socialist-

Revolutionist groups; after Gershuni's arrest in 1903 assumed leadership in the Fighting Organization of the S.R. party; organized some successful terroristic acts, including the assassination of Plehve, July 15, 1904, and of the Grand Duke Sergei Aleksandrovich, February 4, 1905; responsible for the arrest of many S.R.'s; some S.R.'s were suspicious of him as early as 1902, but it was only in 1908 that his associations with the police were finally proved by Burtsev and confirmed by the Head of the Police Department, A. A. Lopukhin; the party Central Committee condemned him to die, but he succeeded in escaping and settled down in Germany in 1910 under an assumed named; arrested by the German police, 1915, and imprisoned until 1917. (See Boris Nikolaevsky, *Azef, the Spy* [Garden City, 1934].)

26. **Viktor Mikhailovich Chernov** (1876–   ). A founder of the Socialist-Revolutionist party and member of its Central Committee; in emigration, 1899–1917; Minister of Agriculture in the Provisional Government, May–September, 1917; chairman of the Constituent Assembly, 1918; opposed Bolsheviks and Whites, 1918–1919; in emigration since 1921; member of the Executive Committee of the Second International; author.

Page 306, note 27. **fortieth anniversary of the new judicial institutions.** The anniversary of the judicial reform of Alexander II, November 1864. This reform separated the administrative and judicial functions of government, between which no distinction had been previously drawn. It established to a considerable degree the independence of judges, equality of all classes before the law, public trials, and the jury system, although certain cases, such as those concerning treason and the press, were withheld from the competence of juries. Provision was also made for the trial of minor cases by justices of the peace elected by zemstvos and municipal dumas.

Page 307, note 28. **Vladislav Vikentevich Kovalevsky** (1862–   ). Graduate of St. Petersburg University; Justice of the Peace in Novorzhevsk Uezd, 1887, Zemskii Nachalnik in the same uezd, 1890; Assistant Head of the Peasant Section, 1908; member of the Statistical Council, 1914, and later Assistant Director of the Central Statistical Committee of the Ministry of the Interior; member of the Council of the Minister of the Interior, 1915, and in charge of the food supply of the Empire; Acting Assistant Minister of the Interior, 1916.

29. **Nikolai Alekseevich Maklakov** (1871–1918). Graduate of Moscow University; special-duty clerk in the Moscow Branch of the State Treasury; tax inspector of Suzdal, 1894–1900; Head of a section of the Tambov branch of the State Treasury; Head of Poltava branch of the State Treasury, 1906; Governor of Chernigov, 1909; Acting Minister of the Interior, 1912; Minister of the Interior, 1913; member of the State Council, 1915; shot by the Bolsheviks.

30. **Office of Provisioning and Supply** (*Kantseliariia Prodovolstvennoi Chasti Imperii*). Established in 1900 in the Peasant Section of the Ministry of the Interior; its functions had formerly been performed by the Department of Economy in the same ministry; it was placed under the supervision of the Assistant Head of the Peasant Section.

Page 312, note 31. **Lev Iosifovich Petrazhitsky** (1866–   ). Of Polish descent; jurist; professor of law at St. Petersburg University; one of the editors of *Pravo* and *Vestnik Prava;* Cadet; member of the First Duma; after the October Revolution (1917), professor at Warsaw University.

Page 313, note 32. **"Manilovism."** A term derived from Manilov, in Gogol's *Dead Souls,* a sentimental and weak man, fond of professing high ideals but incapable of realizing them.

Page 315, note 33. **"Sviatopolk the Accursed."** A reference to a Sviatopolk of the eleventh century who put three of his brothers to death, in order to gain the throne of Kiev. For this he was likened to Cain and was known as "Sviatopolk the Accursed."

Page 316, note 34. **Ukase of December 12, 1904.** This ukase directed the Committee of Ministers to work out measures which should reduce the restrictions in the regulation of the press, provide state insurance for factory workers, provide for greater religious toleration, define the scope of local self-government, reduce the degree of disfranchisement of the national minorities, and do away with all manner of exceptional laws. The Committee was to consider each point separately, work out the best method of putting the measures into effect, and inform His Majesty of the progress of this work. Witte states (Witte, *op. cit.,* I, 299–301 [English edition, pp. 220–22]) that Mirsky had opened his campaign for reform by submitting a report to the Tsar, appending to it the draft of a ukase which included the measures to be enacted. The Prince's report was discussed by a conference presided over by the Emperor. No decision was reached and the Tsar ordered Baron Nolde to draft under Witte's supervision a decree reflecting the views of the conference. This draft was then to be considered by the Committee of Ministers. At a second conference on December 6 or 7 there was a discussion of a definitive text which included a rather vaguely worded provision for the admission of elected representatives to participate in the legislative activity of the government. The Tsar changed this article in the sense that these representatives were selected by the government rather than elected by the people. Witte advised the Emperor to strike out the article altogether, and this was done.

Page 320, note 35. **Dmitrii Fomich Kobeko** (1837–   ). Graduate of the Imperial Alexander Lyceum, 1856; in the Chancellery of the Ministry of Finance, and in 1865 was appointed its manager; member of the Council of the Minister of Finance; Director of the Department of Direct Taxation; member of the State Council, 1901; Director of the Imperial Public Library, 1902; chairman of the commission to study the drafting of the new law concerning the press, 1905; writer on historical subjects.

36. **Count Aleksei Pavlovich Ignatev** (1842–1906). Graduate of the General Staff Academy, 1862; Commander of the Horse Guards Regiment, 1873; Chief of Staff of the Guards Corps, 1881; Governor-General of Irkutsk, 1885; appointed Assistant Minister of the Interior, 1889, but en route to St. Petersburg was ordered to Kiev as Governor-General, where he served from 1889 to 1896; in 1896 appointed member of the State Council; chairman of the Conference to Examine Special Regulations concerning the Safeguarding of the State Order and chairman of the Special Conference on Religious Toleration, 1905; killed by a Socialist-Revolutionist in Kiev.

37. **ukase issued on April 17, 1905.** The Ukase of April 17, 1905, elabo-

rated the principles of religious toleration laid down in two previous laws: the Ukase of December 12, 1904, which provided for a re-examination of regulations concerning Old Believers and persons of other non-orthodox creeds; and the statute of the Committee of Ministers confirmed by the Emperor on February 11, 1905, which instructed the Minister of the Interior to see to it that all restrictions of non-orthodox religious creeds which interfered with the freedom of religious conscience and which were not directly based on law were removed within three months.

Page 321, note 38. **in his memoirs.** Witte, *op. cit.*, I, 302–3 (English edition, p. 225).

CHAPTER XVII

Page 325, note 1. **Chief Administration for Land Organization and Agriculture.** See note 1, chapter v, p. 616.

2. **union of landowners.** The author, V. I. Gurko, uses the term *"soiuz zemlevladeltsev."* An organization called *soiuz zemelnykh sobstvennikov* was formed in the summer of 1917, mainly of large landowners, headed by Krivoshein and with the active participation of the author and others. In all probability it is to this organization that the author refers. When the Right Center, a fairly conservative anti-Bolshevik group, was formed in 1918, it was joined by the Union of Landowners.

Page 326, note 3. **Aleksandr Aleksandrovich Rittikh** (1868–   ). Graduate of the Imperial Alexander Lyceum; Director of the Department of State Domains and Manager of the Affairs of the Committee for Land Organization in the Chief Administration of Land Organization and Agriculture, 1905–1912; Assistant Head of the Chief Administration of Land Organization and Agriculture, 1912–1916; Senator, 1916; Minister of Agriculture, January–March, 1917.

Page 327, note 4. **Aleksandr Sergeevich Posnikov** (1846– ?). Economist; graduate of Moscow University; studied agrarian conditions in Western Europe; wrote in defense of the land commune (*obshchina*) in Russia; lectured in Novorossiisk University, 1876–1882; resigned and became active in zemstvo work in Smolensk; an editor of *Russkiia Vedomosti,* 1886–1897; in 1902 Dean of the Economic Section of the St. Petersburg Polytechnical Institute, where he lectured on Political Economy; one of the founders of the Party of Democratic Reforms, 1906.

5. **Dmitrii Ivanovich Pikhno** (1853–1913). Graduated from Kiev University and became professor there, 1877; after the death of V. Y. Shulgin, the founder of *Kievlianin,* became its editor in 1879; member of the State Council.

6. **Vladimir Sergeevich Gulevich** (1867–   ). Graduate in medicine of Moscow University, 1890; professor of medical chemistry at Kharkov University, and later at Moscow University, 1899–1918; member of the Academy of Sciences since 1929; author of a number of scientific works.

Page 332, note 7. **gubernia conferences.** These were organized by Plehve and Gurko in opposition to the committees of Witte's Special Conference. (See note 19, chapter iv, p. 615, and text, pp. 166–68, 217–25.)

Page 334, note 8. **Viktor Vasilevich Kolachev** (1864–   ). Director of the Department of Agriculture and Rural Industry in the Ministry of Agriculture; Senator.

Page 335, note 9. **Vladimir Fedorovich Trepov** (1860–1918). Educated at the Imperial Alexander Lyceum; Governor of Taurida, 1902; Senator, 1905; member of the State Council, 1908–1911; chairman, Supervisory Council of the International Commercial Bank of St. Petersburg until 1917; arrested by the Bolsheviks in July 1918 and shot in August of the same year.

10. **Shchedrin [Mikhail Evgrafovich Saltykov]** (1826–1889). Novelist; graduate of Tsarskoe Selo Lyceum, 1844, when he entered the Chancellery of the Minister of War; began to write for *Otechestvennyia Zapiski;* published two stories, 1847–1848, displeasing to the authorities; was transferred to Viatka until 1855; special-duty clerk in the Ministry of the Interior, 1856–1858; Vice-Governor of Riazan, 1858–1860, of Tver, 1860–1862; one of the editors of *Sovremennik,* 1863; Manager of the Penza branch of the State Treasury, 1864–1866, and of the Tver branch, 1866–1868, when he resigned from government service; contributor to *Otechestvennyia Zapiski,* under Nekrasov, and in 1868 after Nekrasov's death became its editor, which position he held until it was suppressed, 1884. Among his best known works: *Gubernskie Ocherki ("Gubernia Sketches"),* (1856), *Gospoda Golovlevy ("The Golovlev Family"),* (1880–1883).

Page 338, note 11. **in his memoirs.** Witte, *op. cit.,* I, 455–74 (English edition, pp. 387–88).

Page 339, note 12. **Preobrazhensky regimental march.** The march of the famous Life Guards Regiment, originally formed by Peter I in 1687 from his playmates in the village of Preobrazhenskoe, after which the regiment was named.

Page 343, note 13. **Ivan Aleksandrovich Fullon** (1844–1918). Adjutant General and General of Infantry; Chief of Gendarme Corps in Poland; succeeded General Kleigels as Governor of St. Petersburg, 1904–1905; Commander of the Eleventh Army Corps, 1905–1911.

14. **Petr Moiseevich Rutenberg** (1874–   ). Member of the Fighting Organization of the Socialist-Revolutionist party; planned the assassination of Gapon, 1906; author of *Ubiistvo Gapona ("The Assassination of Gapon"),* published abroad, 1909; civil governor of Petrograd, 1917; in emigration in Palestine.

Page 345, note 15. **the pressure of the police.** Maxim Gorky knew Gapon and was associated with him in the events of January 9; but it is not established that he collaborated with Gapon in composing the petition to the Tsar. On the evening of "Bloody Sunday" Gorky did prepare for publication in Russia and abroad a declaration telling how a deputation (initiated by him) had approached Witte and Sviatopolk-Mirsky to ask them to have the troops kept in barracks on the day of the demonstration and to induce the Emperor or his representative to receive the delegation of workers. It is possible that the author has in mind Gorky's authorship of this declaration and not a collaboration with Gapon in composing the famous petition. For an account of

Gorky's participation in the events of January 1905, see Alexander Kaun, *Maxim Gorky and his Russia* (New York, 1931), pp. 353–69.

Gapon's petition was similar in many respects to the Social-Democratic minimum program; but there were certain differences. Gapon's petition was the less sweeping of the two. Both called for the freedom and inviolability of person and freedom of speech, press, meeting, organization, and religious conscience; both called for free and compulsory education, for separation of church and state, and for absolute equality before the law. But whereas the Gapon petition called merely for the responsibility of ministers and a guaranty that the government would be law-abiding, the S.D. minimum program demanded the overthrow of the autocracy and the establishment of a democratic republic with extensive local self-government; the latter also called for the replacement of the standing army by a general arming of the people. In economic matters the Gapon petition listed measures to overcome the poverty of the people, such as the abolition of indirect taxes, the institution of a progressive income tax, the abolition of redemption dues, and the gradual transference of the land to the people, also measures against oppression of labor, including the establishment of an eight-hour working day. The S.D. minimum program suggested similar measures but called for the confiscation of large landed estates.

A translation of the Gapon petition is given in James Mavor, *An Economic History of Russia* (2 vols., 2d ed., London, 1925), II, 469–73. The S.D. minimum program is given in V. I. Lenin, *Sochineniia* (2d ed., 30 vols., Leningrad and Moscow, 1929–1932), V, 386–87.

16. **This suggestion was adopted.** For accounts of this meeting and of the events of "Bloody Sunday," see also Kokovtsov, *op. cit.,* pp. 35–38; Alexander Gerassimoff, *Der Kampf gegen die erste russische Revolution. Erinnerungen* (Frauenfeld, 1934), pp. 41–44; and Witte, *op. cit.,* I, 306–9 (English edition, pp. 252–53).

Page 348, note 17. **Aleksei Aleksandrovich Shakhmatov** (1864–1920). Graduate of Moscow University; scholar and writer on Old Russian letters and language; became member of the Academy of Sciences, 1894; chairman of the Academy's Section to Study Russian Language and Old Russian Letters; editor of the Academy's publication entitled *Izvestiia Otdeleniia russkago iazyka i slovesnosti ("News of the Section on Russian Language and Letters")* ; famous for his work on western Slavic languages and their connection with the history of the western Slavs.

18. **Vladimir Matveevich Hessen** (1868–1920). Graduate of Novorossiisk University; professor of law in St. Petersburg University, 1896, and lecturer at the Imperial Alexander Lyceum; one of the editors of *Pravo* and *Vestnik Prava;* Cadet; member of the Second Duma.

19. **[Imperial] Free Economic Society** (*Imperatorskoe volnoe ekonomicheskoe obshchestvo*). One of the oldest scientific institutions in Russia, founded in 1765, apparently upon the suggestion of Catherine II, to speed up the dissemination of useful and practical knowledge to the people. From the beginning the Society considered the question of organizing food stores for the peasants and other peasant problems. It also discussed, at the instigation of Empress Catherine, such problems as communal and individual land tenure,

free and bondage labor, etc.; and many of these discussions were published in the Society's publications among which was *Trudy Imperatorskago Volnago Ekonomicheskago Obshchestva*. The Society continued to develop, and in 1872 adopted new regulations dividing it into three sections.

Page 348, note 20. **Mikhail Vladimirovich Bernatsky** (1876–   ). Professor of Economics in St. Petersburg Polytechnical and Technological Institutes; collaborated on *Obrazovanie* and *Sovremennyi Mir;* Minister of Finance in the Provisional Government, September–October, 1917; member of the governments of Denikin and Wrangel; in emigration.

21. **Ilia Efimovich Iliashenko** (1859–   ). Entered the Ministry of Justice, 1883; Assistant Ober-Prokuror of the Senate's Court of Cassation for Civil Affairs, 1904; chairman of a department of Kharkov Court of Appeals, 1906, of St. Petersburg Court of Appeals, 1909, of the Kazan Court of Appeals, 1910; Senator, December 1910; Assistant Minister of Justice, 1914.

CHAPTER XVIII

Page 356, note 1. **the catastrophe of Khodynka.** As part of the festivities attending the coronation of Nicholas II in Moscow in May 1896 the populace was invited to the Khodynka field near the city to receive souvenirs of the coronation of a new Tsar. The authorities failed to make adequate arrangements for managing the vast crowd that assembled and in the rush to secure the mementoes many lost their footing on the uneven ground and fell under the feet of the surging throng. Their cries added to the confusion, and in the resulting panic hundreds of men, women, and children were crushed or trampled to death. Despite the catastrophe, the coronation festivities proceeded as planned.

Page 357, note 2. **Viktor Viktorovich Ivanovsky** (1854–   ). Graduated in law from Kazan University, 1878; studied abroad, 1883; became professor of constitutional law in Kazan University, 1886.

3. **Fedor Dmitrievich Samarin.** Graduate of Moscow University; elected member of the State Council, 1907–1908.

4. **Aleksandr Dmitrievich Samarin** (1872–   ). Graduate of Moscow University; served in the army, 1891–1893; zemskii nachalnik in Bronnitsy Uezd of Moscow Gubernia, 1893–1899; marshal of nobility of Bogorodsk Uezd, 1899–1908, of Moscow Gubernia, 1908–1915; member of State Council, 1912; in the beginning of the World War held important positions in the Red Cross; Ober-Prokuror of the Holy Synod, July–September, 1915.

Page 361, note 5. **"liberation movement."** See note 14, chapter xiv, p. 645.

Page 370, note 6. **Georgii Feliksovich Yusefovich [Iosefovich]** (1885–   ). Graduate of the Imperial School of Law; entered the Ministry of the Interior, 1906; Assistant Secretary in the Police Department in the Ministry of the Interior, 1910.

7. **Vladimir Ivanovich Nazimov** (1802–1874). Participated in the Turkish campaign, 1828–1829; appointed Vilna Military Governor and Governor-

General of Grodno, Minsk, and Kovno, 1855. In 1857 Alexander II, who was passing through Brest-Litovsk, expressed to Nazimov, as a friend, his disappointment in the backwardness of the Great Russian nobility in the matter of liberating the serfs. Nazimov offered to start such a reform in the western gubernias. Soon afterward the nobility requested Nazimov to raise the question of freeing the peasants; this request was forwarded to St. Petersburg, and in answer to it there followed an Imperial rescript to Nazimov, November 20, 1857, which provided for the study of the peasant problem in Lithuania and actually served as a beginning of the peasant reform. Nazimov was appointed member of the State Council, 1861; dismissed from the post of Governor-General, 1863.

8. **Baron Aleksandr Aleksandrovich Budberg** (1854–1914). Graduate of St. Petersburg University; in the Ministry of Justice, 1875–1883; Assistant Head of the Chancellery of Imperial Headquarters, 1883–1891; Assistant Secretary, then Secretary, 1891–1895; Assistant Head and Head of His Majesty's Private Chancellery to Receive Petitions, 1895–1904; member of the State Council, 1904.

Page 371, note 9. **in his memoirs.** See Witte, *op. cit.*, I, 339 (English edition, p. 227).

Page 373, note 10. **Vladimir Dmitrievich Kuzmin-Karavaev** (1859–1928). Jurist; professor; graduate of His Majesty's School of Pages and of the Military Law Academy; professor in the Military Law Academy, 1890, and in the Nicholas Academy of General Staff, 1899–1903; professor at St. Petersburg University, 1909–1913; active participant in zemstvo congresses, 1904–1905; one of the founders of the Party of Democratic Reforms; member of St. Petersburg City Duma; member of the First and Second Dumas; barrister in St. Petersburg Court of Appeals, 1913; during the civil war, a member of Yudenich's Political Conference; died in emigration.

11. **old zemstvo system of 1864.** See note 18, chapter i, p. 599.

Page 376, note 12. **Prince Sergei Nikolaevich Trubetskoi** (1862–1905). Graduate of Moscow University, lecturer (1888), and later professor of philosophy there; the first elected Rector of Moscow University; a member of the delegation of zemstvo and town men to the Emperor, June 6, 1905; made a speech on the need of liberal reforms.

13. **Fedor Aleksandrovich Golovin** (1867–   ). Member, 1898, and chairman, 1904, of Moscow Gubernia Zemstvo Board; member of the zemstvo and town delegation to the Tsar, 1905; one of the founders of the Union of Liberation; Cadet; chairman of the Second Duma; elected to the Third Duma, but resigned in October 1910; active member of the Union of Towns during the World War; Commissar of the Provisional Government, March 1917; worked in Soviet institutions since the Bolshevik Revolution.

14. **Nikolai Nikolaevich Kovalevsky** (1858–   ). Zemstvo man; member of First Duma; Cadet.

15. **Prince Dmitrii Ivanovich Shakhovskoi** (1861–   ). Active participant in zemstvo congresses, 1904–1905; one of the organizers of the Union of Liberation; in 1905 became a Left Cadet and permanent member of the Central Committee of the Cadet party; member and secretary of the

Cadet group in the First State Duma; Minister of Social Welfare, May–July 1917, in the Provisional Government; active in Soviet co-operative institutions, 1930.

Page 380, note 16. **a memorandum by Shipov.** See D. N. Shipov, *Vospominaniia i dumy o perezhitom* (Moscow, 1918), pp. 298 ff.

Page 381, note 17. **Vladimir Ivanovich Guerrier** (1837–   ). Professor; graduate in history of Moscow University; sent abroad to study, and upon his return, 1865, lectured in Moscow University; founder of a university for women in Moscow which bore his name; active in municipal affairs as member of Moscow Duma and its various commissions; author.

18. **Nikolai Aleksandrovich Khomiakov** (1850 [1857?]–1925). Son of a well-known Slavophile and poet; graduate of Moscow University; served in the Ministry of Agriculture; active in zemstvo work; elected to Second, Third, and Fourth Dumas as Octobrist; elected member of State Council, 1906–1907; chairman of Third Duma, resigned, 1910; member of Progressive Bloc in Fourth Duma; in Red Cross work with Denikin's forces; emigrated to Jugoslavia, where he died.

Page 383, note 19. **Sergei Aleksandrovich Toll** (1848– ?). Graduate of the Imperial School of Law, 1870, when he entered the Ministry of Justice and was sent to work in the Vilna Court of Appeals; in the same year was transferred to the Senate and two years later to the legislative section of the First Department of the Ministry of Justice; in 1874 promoted to be Assistant Secretary of the First Department of the Senate; 1878, Head of the Legislative Section of the Senate; Assistant State Secretary in the State Council, 1880; jurisconsult of the Ministry of Justice, 1882; member of the Consultative Board of the Ministry of Justice, 1886; became Governor of St. Petersburg, 1889, and member of the State Council, 1903.

20. **Aleksandr Dmitrievich Zinovev** (1854–1929). Gradute of St. Petersburg University in law; served in the army but retired in 1882 and lived for some years in Narva, where he was elected representative of the nobility in Peterhof Uezd and, after 1886, uezd and gubernia zemstvo member; Marshal of Nobility of Peterhof Uezd, 1897; elected Marshal of Nobility for St. Petersburg Gubernia, 1897–1903; appointed Governor of St. Petersburg, 1903; appointed member of the State Council, 1911; died in emigration.

21. **Count Aleksei Aleksandrovich Bobrinsky** (1852–1927). Attended St. Petersburg University; worked in the Chancellery of the Committee of Ministers; Marshal of Nobility of St. Petersburg Uezd, 1875–1878; of St. Petersburg Gubernia for almost twenty years beginning in 1878; at the same time presided over St. Petersburg Zemstvo assemblies; for over thirty years chairman of the Imperial Archeological Commission; became vice-chairman of the Academy of Science, 1889; Head of the Orphanages of the Empress Marie, 1893–1896; chairman of Free Economic Society, 1894; member of the Agricultural Committee in the Ministry of Agriculture; Senator, 1896; chairman of the Union of Russian Nobility, 1905; member of State Duma, 1907, and of the State Council, 1912; Assistant Minister of the Interior, 1916; Minister of Agriculture, 1916; left Russia, 1918.

Page 384, note 22. **Platon Andreevich Kulakovsky** (1848– ?). A student of Slavic languages and culture; graduate of Moscow University; taught

Russian in Belgrade and other Balkan cities, 1878; lectured in Warsaw University; editor of *Varshavskii Dnevnik,* 1886–1892; writer in Russian and other Slavic languages.

Page 386, note 23. **Union of Russian Men** (*Soiuz russkikh liudei*). This is to be distinguished from the Union of Russian People (*Soiuz russkago naroda*) a much larger organization which was founded in October 1905 and was known for its extreme conservative views, its severe criticism of the high bureaucracy, and its definitely anti-semitic tendencies. Among its most important members were Dr. A. I. Dubrovin and V. M. Purishkevich. It published its own organ, *Russkoe Znamia.*

24. **Petr Ivanovich Rachkovsky** (1853–1911). Held important position in political police investigations; in charge of police agency abroad, 1885–1902; in view of his unpopularity with Plehve, resigned in 1902 and lived in Warsaw and Paris until 1905; Vice-Director of the Police Department in the Ministry of the Interior, 1905, under Trepov; resigned, 1906, and did not return to political activity.

Page 387, note 25. **Pavel Ivanovich Astrov.** Member of Moscow District Court; lecturer at the Moscow Women's Collegiate Institute, 1912.

26. **Mikhail Yakovlevich Govorukha-Otrok** (1866–   ). Graduate of Nicholas Cavalry School, 1886; zemskii nachalnik of Belgorod Uezd (Kursk Gubernia), 1890; chairman of Belgorod Uezd, Zemstvo Board, 1901, and of Kursk Gubernia Zemstvo Board, 1908; elected member of the State Council, 1909; re-elected, 1912; member of the Council for the Affairs of Local Economy in the Ministry of the Interior, 1911.

Page 388, note 27. **Viborg Manifesto.** Drafted by P. N. Miliukov; issued as a protest after two days of deliberation (July 9 and 10, 1906) in the name of two hundred deputies of the First Duma who had gathered in Viborg after the Duma's dissolution. The Manifesto urged the population to refuse to pay taxes and supply recruits for the army. This measure of "passive resistance" was, however, to be of a temporary nature, until the convocation of the Second Duma. The Cadets, who were in the majority (120 deputies), emphasized the constitutional nature of their demand and condemned the revolt in Kronstadt and Sveaborg. On July 16, 1906, the members of the Duma who signed the Manifesto were indicted, and on December 18, 1907, were sentenced to three months' imprisonment. The prosecution undertaken by the government had the result of preventing those who signed the Manifesto from active participation in the elections to the Second Duma.

28. **zemstvo-constitutionalists.** Liberal zemstvo men, who published abroad, 1902, *Osvobozhdenie* (edited by P. B. Struve); later (1903) formed the Union of Liberation.

Page 389, note 29. **workers for this purpose.** See N. Popov, *Outline History of the Communist Party of the Soviet Union* (2 vols., Moscow, 1934), I, 135–43.

Page 390, note 30. **central committee of sailors.** It cannot be determined precisely when this committee was formed. It is known, however, that in April 1905 the Sevastopol Committee of the Social Democratic party sent representatives to organize party work among the Black Sea sailors; these representatives were active in organizing the central committee of sailors, which numbered about twenty men and which was made largely responsible for the actual preparation of the mutiny.

31. *Iskra.* The first journal of the Russian Social Democratic Labor party abroad. Published in Munich (1900–1902), in London (1902–1903), and in Geneva (1903–1905).

Page 393, note 32. **Prince Evgenii Nikolaevich Trubetskoi** (1863–1920). Professor at Kiev University, 1894; professor of the history of law, Moscow University, 1906; elected member of the State Council; leader of the Party of Peaceful Reconstruction; writer.

Page 395, note 33. *Vedomosti Peterburgskago Gradonachalnika* [*i Stolichnoi Politsii*] (*"Bulletin of the St. Petersburg Governor and of the Capital Police"*). Began publication in 1839 under the title *Vedomosti Sankt-Peterburgskoi Gorodskoi Politsii;* contained official and unofficial sections; appeared twice a week until 1843, then three times weekly; and in 1844 began to appear daily.

34. **Georgii Stepanovich Khrustalev-Nosar** (1879–1918). Lawyer; elected chairman of the St. Petersburg Soviet of Workers' Deputies, 1905; arrested and exiled to Siberia, 1906; joined the Mensheviks; fled abroad and attended London Congress as a Menshevik, 1907; lived in France; withdrew from political activities and engaged in obscure financial operations for which he was arrested in 1913; returned to Russia, 1914, arrested and imprisoned until 1917; after trying unsuccessfully to advance himself in the Petrograd Soviet, went to his native town, Pereiaslavl, where he became chairman of the Zemstvo Board; supported Skoropadsky and Petliura; with the arrival of Soviet troops was arrested and shot.

35. **"cold arms."** This is a Russian phrase meaning weapons other than firearms, i.e., bayonets, sabers, etc.

Page 397, note 36. **Semen Petrovich Yaroshenko.** Graduate of Kiev and Odessa universities with Master's degree, 1870; professor in Odessa University, 1871; Rector of same university, 1881–1890; writer.

Page 398, note 37. **Grand Duke Nikolai Nikolaevich** (the younger) (1859–1929). Grandson of Emperor Nicholas I and uncle once removed of Emperor Nicholas II; in military service from his youth; at the outbreak of the World War in 1914, was appointed Supreme Commander in Chief of the Russian forces; in 1915 when Nicholas II assumed that post, became Commander in Chief on the Caucasian Front; died in emigration in France.

CHAPTER XIX

Page 401, note 1. **Aleksandr Vasilevich Gerasimov** (1861–   ). Lieutenant General; gendarme officer; entered military service, 1883; Chief of the Department to Safeguard Public Safety and Order in St. Petersburg, 1905–1909; removed from office on account of his disagreement with Kurlov; sent abroad to watch Grand Duke Mikhail Aleksandrovich and N. S. Wulfert (later Brasova) to prevent their marriage; retired in 1914; author of *Der Kampf gegen die erste russische Revolution.*

2. **Vladimir Aleksandrovich Dediulin** (1858–1913). Graduate of His

Majesty's School of Pages and of the Nicholas Military Academy of the General Staff; entered the army, 1877; Chief of Staff and later Commander of the Gendarme Corps, 1903–1905; Governor of St. Petersburg, January–December, 1905; Adjutant General, Aide-de-Camp of the Emperor, and Palace Commandant, 1906.

Page 403, note 3. **Fedor Fedorovich Kokoshkin** (1871–1918). Professor of constitutional law in Moscow University and collaborator on the *Russkiia Vedomosti;* Cadet member of the First State Duma; State Comptroller in the Provisional Government, August–September 1917; arrested by the Bolsheviks and imprisoned with the other Cadet leaders in December 1917; murdered by sailors while ill in the hospital.

4. *Birzhevyia Vedomosti.* St. Petersburg newspaper; founded November 1, 1880, by Stanislav Maksimovich Propper, who was also the editor; published three times a week until 1885 when it was made a daily and on January 1, 1903, began to appear twice daily; a cheaper edition for the provinces began to appear in 1893; in 1905, representatives of the Cadet party, P. N. Miliukov, I. V. Hessen, and P. B. Struve, wrote for the paper, which assumed the name *Svobodnyi Narod,* but was suppressed after the second issue; beginning December 15, 1905, appeared four times as *Narodnaia Svoboda,* and was again suppressed; December 27, 1905, appeared again under the name *Birzhevyia Vedomosti,* without the participation of the Cadets; in September 1906 became the organ of the Party of Peaceful Reconstruction headed by P. A. Heyden, N. A. Stakhovich, and N. N. Lvov; finally discontinued, 1917.

Page 404, note 5. **Anatolii Federovich Koni** (1844–1927). Graduate in law of Moscow University; worked in the State Control, then in a number of District Courts; Prokuror of St. Petersburg District Court, 1871–1875, where he distinguished himself as a brilliant speaker at a number of important trials; Assistant Director of a department of the Ministry of Justice, 1875–1877; chairman of the St. Petersburg District Court, 1877–1881, and of the Civil Department of the St. Petersburg Court of Appeals, 1881–1885; lectured at the Imperial School of Law, 1875–1883; Ober-Prokuror of the Senate's Court of Cassation for Criminal Affairs, 1885–1891, 1892–1897; Senator in the same Court, 1891–1892; became member of the State Council, 1907; wrote in *Vestnik Evropy* and other journals; made honorary member of the Academy of Science, 1896; one of the founders of the Judicial and Philosophical Society; member of the Council of the Russian Literary Society; honorary member of the Military Medical Academy and of the Society of Psychiatrists.

6. **Vera Ivanovna Zasulich** (1851–1919). Russian revolutionist; began revolutionary activity in the late 'sixties, first as a Narodnik, later as a Social Democrat; in exile 1869–1875; worked for the revolution among the people in Zemlia i Volia organization and in the Workers' Union of the North, in January 1878 attempted to assassinate F. F. Trepov, Governor of St. Petersburg, for which she was tried and acquitted; emigrated, 1880; became interested in the Marxist movement, translated into Russian the Communist Manifesto and corresponded with Marx; together with Plekhanov and Akselrod founded the Emancipation of Labor Group (*Osvobo-*

zhdenie Truda) ; one of the editors of *Iskra* (published 1900–1905) and contributor to *Zaria;* joined the Mensheviks after the Social Democratic party split, 1903; in 1917 member of the Plekhanov (*Edinstvo*) Group.

7. **Fedor Fedorovich Trepov.** Father of the four Trepov brothers, F. F., Jr., D. F., V. F., and A. F.

Page 405, note 8. **Aleksandr Ivanovich Guchkov** (1862–1936). One of the founders of the Octobrist party; chairman of the Third Duma, March 1910, succeeding Khomiakov; resigned, March 1911; chairman of the Central War Industries Committee during the World War and member of the State Council; with Shulgin he received the act of abdication from Tsar Nicholas II at Pskov on March 2, 1917; first Minister of War and Navy in the Provisional Government, 1917; active in the anti-Bolshevik movements of 1917–1921; emigrated soon after the October Revolution.

9. **considerable public influence.** See Appendix 2, pp. 703–10.

10. **Pavel Nikolaevich Engalychev** (1864– ?). Lieutenant General; graduate of the Nicholas Academy of the General Staff; Palace Commandant, 1905; Chief of the Nicholas Military Academy, 1914; Governor-General of Warsaw; officer on duty to the Chief of Staff of the Supreme Commander in Chief.

Page 406, note 11. **Sergei Sergeevich Manukhin** (1856–1922). Graduate in law of St. Petersburg University; began work in St. Petersburg District Court, 1879, then in Orel District Court, and later in the First Department of the Ministry of Justice as special-duty clerk, as acting head of the legislative section in 1884, and as head in 1888; jurisconsult in the Ministry of Justice; Assistant Ober-Prokuror of the Senate's Court of Cassation for Criminal Affairs, 1890; same year returned to the Ministry of Justice as chief jurisconsult and represented the Ministry at the Congress on Criminal Anthropology in Brussels; Director of the First Department of the Ministry of Justice and Assistant Minister of Justice, 1900; Minister of Justice, 1904; member of State Council, 1906.

Page 407, note 12. **Mikhail Grigorevich Akimov** (1847–1914). Graduated from Moscow University, after which (1870) he worked in the Moscow Court of Appeals; Assistant Prokuror of the District Courts of Vladimir, Moscow, and Kiev, consecutively; Assistant Prokuror of Kiev Court of Appeals, 1881–1883; chairman of the District Court of Odessa, 1883–1887, and of Penza, 1887–1891; Prokuror of Moscow Court of Appeals, 1891–1894; chairman of Odessa Court of Appeals, 1894–1899; in the Senate's Court of Cassation for Criminal Affairs, 1899–1905; Minister of Justice, 1905–1906; member of the State Council, 1906; chairman of the State Council, 1907.

13. **Klavdii Semenovich Nemeshaev** (1849– ?). Engineer; worked on Russian railways; manager of the Southwestern Railways, 1896; appointed Minister of Ways and Communications, 1905.

Page 408, note 14. **Count Ivan Ivanovich Tolstoi** (1858– ?). Archeologist; graduate of St. Petersburg University; became member of the Imperial Archeological Commission, 1886, secretary, 1886–1890, vice-president, 1899; secretary of the Imperial Art Academy, 1889, and vice-president, 1893; chairman of the Russian Society of the Art of Printing, 1900; Minister of Education, 1905–1906; writer.

15. **Vasilii Ivanovich Timiriazev** (1849–1921). Graduate of St. Petersburg University; entered the Ministry of Finance, 1873; served as commissioner to the Paris and Philadelphia World Expositions and later took part in the organization of the all-Russian industrial exposition in Moscow; Assistant Minister of Finance and Head of the Department of Industry, Science, and Commerce, 1902; Head of the Ministry of Commerce and Industry after its establishment, 1905; resigned in 1906 and entered private business; member of State Council, 1906; again appointed Minister of Commerce and Industry, January 1909; resigned at the end of that year.

Page 409, note 16. **General Aleksandr Fedorovich Roediger** (1853–1917). Graduate of His Majesty's School of Pages and of the Nicholas Military Academy of the General Staff; served in the Russo-Turkish War, 1877–1878; in 1882 appointed Assistant Minister and later Minister of War of Bulgaria; on his return to Russia in 1883 became professor in the Nicholas Military Academy; Head of the Chancellery of the Ministry of War, 1898–1905; Minister of War, 1905–1909; appointed to the State Council, 1905.

17. **Admiral Aleksei Alekseevich Birilev** (1844– ?). Went to sea, 1859; Commander of the Russian squadron in the Mediterranean, 1900; Chief Flagman of the Baltic Fleet, 1903; Commander of the Baltic Fleet and Ports, 1904; Commander of the Fleet in the Pacific, May 1905; Minister of the Navy, 1905–1907; member of the State Council, 1907.

Page 415, note 18. **international position of Russia.** An English translation of the text of this memorandum is given in F. A. Golder, *Documents of Russian History, 1914–1917* (New York, 1927), pp. 3–23.

Page 417, note 19. *Proletarii.* Bolshevik central party organ published irregularly in Geneva, May 14—November 12, 1905; twenty-six issues in all; founded at the time of the Third Congress of the R.S.D.L. party to replace *Iskra,* which was then controlled by the Mensheviks. Responsible editor, Lenin. *Istpart* of the Central Committee of the All-Russian Communist party has republished the issues of *Proletarii.*

Page 418, note 20. **St. Petersburg example.** It is to be noted that the first Soviet of Workers' Deputies in Russia was formed May 13–15, 1905, not in St. Petersburg, but among the striking factory workers of Ivanovo-Voznesensk. They elected about one hundred delegates to represent all the strikers and demanded that all negotiations should be conducted with the whole body, thus giving unity to the strike. (See Pokrovsky, *Brief History of Russia* [2 vols., New York, 1933], II, 153–54.)

21. **General Konstantin Klavdievich Maksimovich** (1849– ?). Graduate of the Nicholas Military Academy of the General Staff; entered the army, 1867; Military Governor and Commander of troops of the Uralsk Oblast, 1893; Ataman of Uralsk Cossack Voisko, and of the Don Cossack Voisko, 1899; Governor-General of Warsaw and Commander of the troops of the Warsaw Military District in 1905; Assistant Commandant of the Imperial Household, 1915.

Page 419, note 22. **General Georgii Antonovich Skalon** (1848–1914). Graduate of the Nicholas Military Academy; Aide-de-Camp to His Imperial Majesty, Nicholas II; served in the Imperial Guards in many high posts; Governor-General of Warsaw and Commander of the troops of Warsaw

Military District, 1905–1914; an attenmpt on his life was made in Warsaw, 1906.

Page 422, note 23. **Nachalo.** Daily paper; organ of the Mensheviks; published in St. Petersburg, November 1 to December 2, 1905; close collaborators were L. Trotsky and Parvus.

24. **Novaia Zhizn.** First legal daily of the Bolsheviks, published in St. Petersburg, November 9 to December 16, 1905. In all, twenty-eight numbers appeared. Close collaborators were: V. I. Lenin, M. S. Olminsky, L. B. Krasin, M. Gorky, and others. Closed by the government; republished by *Istpart,* edited by M. S. Olminsky.

25. **Syn Otechestva.** Daily liberal newspaper; published in St. Petersburg by S. P. Yuritsyn, December 18, 1904—December 2, 1905; a supplementary cheap edition began to appear in July 1905 with G. I. Schreider as editor; among the collaborators were members of the Union of Liberation and Narodniks; beginning August 6, 1905, the paper advocated boycotting Bulygin's project of the Duma; on November 15, 1905, N. S. Rusanov, V. A. Miakotin, A. V. Peshekhanov, and V. M. Chernov became members of the editorial board and the newspaper became a Socialist-Revolutionist organ; suppressed December 2, 1905, for publishing "The Finance Manifesto" of the St. Petersburg Soviet of Workers' Deputies.

26. **Donskaia Rech.** Daily paper; editorial office transferred in 1896 from Novocherkassk to Rostov on Don; editors, M. I. Berberov and A. I. Shepkolov.

Page 423, note 27. **Aleksandr Aleksandrovich Kizevetter** (1867–1933). Graduate of Moscow University and later a member of its history faculty; professor at the Women's University in Moscow and an editor of *Russkaia Mysl,* 1904; member of the Union of Liberation; contributor to *Russkaia Vedomosti;* member of the Central Committee of the Cadet party, 1906; member of the Second State Duma; banished from Soviet Russia, 1922; professor at the Russian Emigré University and member of the philosophical faculty of Charles University, Prague; author of studies in eighteenth-century Russian social history and other works, including his memoirs, *Na rubezhe dvukh stoletii* (1929).

Page 423, note 28. **Aleksandr Apollonovich Manuilov** (1861–1929). Economist; lecturer on political economy in Moscow University, 1900; member of Moscow City Duma and Moscow Gubernia Zemstvo Assembly, 1905; Assistant Rector then Rector of Moscow University, 1905; Cadet; Minister of Education, March 15—July 17, 1917.

29. **Russkaia Mysl.** Monthly; founded in St. Petersburg, 1880, by V. M. Lavrov; reflected Slavophile ideas; S. A. Yurev became editor in 1895; later V. A. Goltsev was editor; during the 'nineties was the organ of the liberal Narodnik intelligentsia; in the Marxist-Narodnik dispute was nonpartisan; after the 1905 revolution, under the editorship of P. B. Struve, became the organ of the Right wing of the Cadets; closed 1918; resumed publication abroad, edited by Struve.

Page 425, note 30. **Vadim Andreevich Gringmut** (1851–1907). Editor of *Moskovskiia Vedomosti;* chairman of Russian Monarchist party.

Page 428, note 31. **Blaise Pascal** (1623–1662). Celebrated French religious philosopher and mathematician.

Page 431, note 32. **Nikolai Vasilevich Teslenko** (1870–   ). Graduate in law of Moscow University; barrister, 1899; studied criminology; chairman of the First All-Russian Congress of Lawyers, 1905; organizer of a circle for rendering free assistance to political offenders; vice-chairman of the Central Committee of the Cadet party; member of the First Duma.

Page 434, note 33. **Aleksei Alekseevich Suvorin** (1862–   ). Elder son of A. S. Suvorin; graduate of St. Petersburg University; at one time responsible editor of *Novoe Vremia*.

34. *"Otchizna."* Otchizna began daily publication January 24, 1906; publisher, K. F. Golovin; editor, S. K. Glinka-Yanchevsky.

35. *Vittova Pliaska.* Literally, "Witte's dance"; a play on *Pliaska Sv. Vita,* the Russian for St. Vitus' Dance.

Page 435, note 36. **Prince Dmitrii Petrovich Golitsyn-Muravlin** (1860–   ). Graduate of the Imperial Alexander Lyceum; in the Imperial Chancellery; Assistant State Secretary, 1897; member of the Council of the Minister of Education, 1903; Assistant Head, 1906, and Head, 1910, of the Fourth Section of His Majesty's Private Chancellery; member of the State Council, 1912.

Page 436, note 37. **Aleksandr Ivanovich Dubrovin** (1855–1918). Physician; one of the founders and chairman of the Union of Russian People; editor of *Russkoe Znamia;* was accused of having instigated and organized the murder of Dr. Iolloss and M. Hertzenstein, two Jewish members of the Duma, 1906; conducted a bitter campaign against Witte and later Stolypin; forced to resign his post as chairman of the Union of Russian People in 1910; owing to disagreement within this group, the influence of his paper diminished considerably; fined several times for slandering government officials and members of the Duma; shot by the Bolsheviks.

Page 438, note 38. **General Georgii Aleksandrovich Min** (1855–1906). Entered army service, 1876; appointed Commander of the Semenovsky Regiment of His Majesty's Guards, 1904; directed the suppression of the armed insurrection in Moscow, 1905, for which he was assassinated at the railway station by Zinaida Konopliannikova, a Socialist-Revolutionist, who was executed.

Page 441, note 39. **Lev Davidovich Trotsky (Bronstein)** (1879–   ). Active revolutionist since 1898; member of the *Iskra* group; vice-chairman, then chairman of the St. Petersburg Soviet, 1905; joined Bolsheviks, July 1917; chairman of Petrograd Soviet, 1917; Soviet Commissar of Foreign Affairs, 1917–1918; Commissar of War, 1918–1924; exiled to Central Asia by the Soviet Government, 1928; banished from Russia, 1929; organizer of the Fourth International.

40. *Russkaia Gazeta.* Daily Social Democratic paper, published in St. Petersburg, 1905–1906; editors, L. Trotsky and Parvus.

Page 445, note 41. **Baron Aleksandr Nikolaevich Meller-Zakomelsky** (1844–1928). General; served in the Polish campaign, 1863; studied in the Academy of the General Staff, 1866–1868; served in Russo-Turkish War,

1877–1878; held various important army positions, 1878–1906; Governor of the Baltic region, 1906–1909; member of State Council, 1909.

Page 446, note 42. **General Mikhail Dmitrievich Skobelev** (1843–1882). Took part as a volunteer in the suppression of Polish rebels, 1863; later graduated from the Nicholas Academy of the General Staff and was sent to join the troops in Turkestan; took part in the expedition to Khiva, 1873, and in the one to Kokand, 1875–1876; made general at the age of 34; placed at the disposal of the Supreme Commander in Chief of the Russian Army during Russo-Turkish War when he distinguished himself in the battle of Shipka, 1877; continued to serve in the army with the rank of Lieutenant General; in 1881, in the Transcaspian campaign, conquered the oasis of Geok-tepe, which led to the surrender of the entire region.

43. **General Mikhail Ivanovich Dragomirov** (1830–1905). Graduate of the Imperial Military Academy, 1856; professor in the Nicholas Academy of the General Staff, 1863; tutor to the Heir Presumptive, 1861–1863, and to the Grand Dukes Aleksandr and Vladimir, 1864–1866; Russian military agent in the Prussian army during Austro-Prussian War, 1866; Chief of Staff of Kiev Military District, 1869; rendered distinguished service in Russo-Turkish War, 1877–1878; Chief of the Nicholas Academy of the General Staff, 1878; continued to hold important positions in the army; Commander of the troops of Kiev Military District, 1889; member of the State Council, 1903; writer.

Page 447, note 44. **Emmanuil Ivanovich Vuich** (1849– ?). Began work in legal institutions 1871; Prokuror in the Moscow District Court, 1894; chairman of the Tula District Court, 1899; Prokuror of Odessa Court of Appeals, 1901, and of St. Petersburg Court of Appeals, 1902; Director of the Department of Police, 1905; Senator, 1906.

45. **Nil Petrovich Zuev** (1857–1918). Graduate of the Imperial School of Law; in legal institutions, 1878–1894; Assistant Secretary in the Police Department, 1894–1899, and Secretary, 1899–1903; Assistant Director, 1903–1909, and Director of the Police Department, 1909–1912; Senator, 1912.

Page 448, note 46. **Board for the Affairs of Conscription** (*Upravlenie po delam o voinskoi povinnosti*). Originally a subsection in the Peasant Section of the Ministry of the Interior; in 1900, formed into a separate department of that ministry.

47. **Vladimir Eduardovich Frisch** (1863–   ). Graduate of the Imperial School of Law; member of the Council of the Ministry of the Interior, 1905; in charge of the Food Supply of the Empire, 1909; Vice-Governor of St. Petersburg; Senator, 1915.

Page 449, note 48. **and he was right.** See V. I. Lenin, *"Left-Wing" Communism: An Infantile Disorder* (London, 1934), p. 13.

Page 450, note 49. **Rech.** Daily newspaper; published in St. Petersburg, 1906–1917; leading organ of the Cadet party; pro-Entente, and after the February Revolution favored continuation of the war and the establishment of a democratic government in Russia; opposed the Bolsheviks and their seizure of power; suppressed by the Soviet Government, but reappeared under various names—*Nasha Rech, Svobodnaia Rech, Vek, Novaia Rech, Nash Vek;* finally closed in 1918; principal editors, I. V. Hessen and P. N. Miliukov; among the contributors were I. I. Petrunkevich, V. D. Nabokov, Professor A. I. Kaminka, and others.

50. **Boris Borisovich Glinsky** (1860–   ). Writer; graduate of St. Petersburg University; after 1887 wrote mainly for *Istoricheskii Vestnik;* editor and publisher of *Severnyi Vestnik,* 1890–1891.

Page 451, note 51. **Sergei Valentinovich Ivanov** (1852–1925). Graduate of Kazan University; Head of Perm branch of the State Control, 1897; acting assistant to general comptroller of the Department of Civil Accounting, 1899; general comptroller of the same, 1902; Assistant State Comptroller, 1905; Senator, 1906; Cadet; elected member and later chairman of St. Petersburg City Duma, 1909; vice-chairman of the Extraordinary Commission of Inquiry of the Provisional Government, 1917.

Page 453, note 52. **Russia's creditors had agreed.** For Kokovtsov's own account of the negotiation of this loan, see Kokovtsov, *op. cit.,* pp. 107–22 and P. N. Miliukov, "Russkie 'liberaly' i zaem 1906 g." ("Russian 'Liberals' and the Loan of 1906"), in *Posledniia Novosti,* March 5, 1936, p. 2.

Page 455, note 53. **exile of forty-five thousand persons.** See A. A. Lopukhin, *Otryvki iz vospominanii (po povodu "Vospominanii gr. S. Y. Witte"),* ("*Fragments of Reminiscences [In Connection with 'Count S. Y. Witte's Memoirs']"*) (Moscow, 1923), p. 93.

Page 458, note 54. **Nikolai Andreevich Gredeskul** (1864–   ). Professor; jurist; political writer; member of Central Committee of Cadet party; second vice-chairman of the First Duma; professor in St. Petersburg University and elsewhere; left Cadet party, 1916, because of a disagreement, partly due to his editorship of the cheap daily, *Russkaia Volia,* founded by Protopopov.

CHAPTER XX

Page 460, note 1. **V. I. Mamontov** (1863–   ). Graduate in law of St. Petersburg University, 1887; in His Majesty's Chancellery to Receive Petitions, 1887–1895; Assistant Head and Head of the Chancellery of the Imperial Household, 1895–1900; Assistant Head of His Majesty's Chancellery to Receive Petitions, 1900–1913, and Head, 1913–1917. (See his memoirs, V. I. Mamontov, *Na gosudarstvennoi sluzhbe* [Tallin, 1926].)

Page 462, note 2. **Stepan Petrovich Beletsky** (1873–1918). Graduate of Kiev University; in the office of the Governor-General of Kiev, 1894–1899, and of the Governor-General of Kovno, Vilna, and Grodno, 1899–1907; Vice-Governor of Samara, 1907–1909; Assistant Director of the Police Department, 1909–1912, and Director, 1912–1915; Senator, 1914; Assistant Minister of the Interior, 1915–1916; executed by the Bolsheviks.

3. **Pavel Grigorevich Kurlov** (1860–1923). Graduate of Alexander Military Law Academy; attached to the Military Prokuror of the Moscow District Court, 1889; Assistant Prokuror and Prokuror of several district courts and the Moscow Court of Appeals, 1892–1903; Vice-Governor of Kursk, 1903–1905; Governor of Minsk, 1905–1906; member of the Council of the Minister of the Interior, 1906–1907; Director of the Police Depart-

ment, 1907–1909; dismissed from his post after the assassination of P. A. Stolypin in 1911 following the special investigation of his (Kurlov's) actions by Senator M. I. Trusevich and Senator N. Z. Shulgin; held responsible positions during the World War; Assistant Minister of the Interior under Protopopov, September–December 1916; died in emigration.

Page 465, note 4. **into private hands.** See Kokovtsov, *op. cit.,* pp. 374–76, 407–13, 444–45.

Page 466, note 5. **a yearly award.** Reference is here made to *arenda* (rent), a term found in Russian legislation designating a sort of reward given to outstanding state servants. Formerly this reward was given in the form of state lands in western and Baltic regions, but in 1837 this practice was discontinued in favor of a payment of so-called rent money (*arendnyia dengi*) for a certain period of time, usually twelve years.

6. **the Russian emigration.** See Kokovtsov, *op. cit., passim,* especially pp. 491–535.

7. **Ivan Grigorevich Shcheglovitov** (1861–1918). Graduate of the Imperial School of Law; held various posts in the Senate and the Ministry of Justice between 1890 and 1905; Assistant Minister of Justice, January 1906; Minister of Justice, 1906–1915; member of the State Council, 1907, and chairman, 1916; after the February 1917 Revolution, was imprisoned in the Peter and Paul Fortress; later transferred to Moscow and put to death by the Bolsheviks, August 1918.

Page 467, note 8. **Nikolai Konstantinovich Schaffhausen-Schönberg och Schaufuss** (1846–1911). Educated in the Nicholas Military Engineering Academy; military engineer; Lieutenant General; supervisor of the Moscow-Kursk railway line, later of the Nicholas railway line, and Chief of the Department of Railways in the Ministry of Finance; Minister of Ways and Communications, 1906.

Page 470, note 9. **representatives of the people.** For other accounts of this Imperial reception of the Duma members, see Kokovtsov, *op. cit.,* pp. 129–30; and Henry W. Nevinson, *More Changes More Chances* (New York, 1925), pp. 165–69.

Page 471, note 9a. **udel [lands].** Lands which provided funds for the support of members of the Imperial family except the immediate family of the Emperor. A Department of Udels was formed in the reign of Paul I and was headed by its own minister. It was subordinated to the Ministry of the Imperial Court in 1826. Between 1852 and 1856 it was again an independent department, but in the latter year it was once more placed under the Ministry of the Imperial Court, being renamed the Chief Administration of Udels in 1892.

Page 475, note 10. **Taurida Palace.** Built in 1783 by Catherine II and presented to Potemkin, "Prince of Taurida," after his conquest of the Crimea; after his death the palace was repossessed by the Crown; Emperor Paul turned it into a barracks for his guards, but his successor, Alexander I, restored it to a royal residence; used as the meeting place of the State Duma, 1906–1917; of the Provisional Government, 1917; under the Soviets has been made into a university and renamed the Uritsky Palace.

Page 477, note 11. **Trudovik [*Trudovaia gruppa*].** This group was organized in 1906 in the First Duma, chiefly by the peasant deputies headed by the intelligentsia of the Narodnik group, and included members of the Peasant Union, the Socialist-Revolutionists, radically inclined intelligentsia, and others who took a position to the Left of the Cadets and to the Right of the Social Democrats. The Trudoviks had a definite program as far as the agricultural problem was concerned. They introduced in the First Duma a bill, No. 104, demanding the alienation of privately owned land (with compensation), the establishment of a labor norm in the distribution of land, etc. After the dissolution of the Duma, Trudoviks took part in the drafting of the Viborg Manifesto, and at the same time, together with the Social Democrats, issued an appeal to the peasantry, the army, and the fleet calling them to an armed rising. The Trudoviks had one hundred four delegates in the Second Duma, where their policy was somewhat modified. In the Third and Fourth Dumas they had only fourteen and ten delegates, respectively. During the World War they took a "defensist" position. Among their most active members were: A. F. Aladin, S. V. Anikin, I. V. Zhilkin, T. I. Sedelnikov (First Duma), N. E. Berzin (vice-chairman of the Second Duma), V. I. Dziubinsky, and A. F. Kerensky (Third and Fourth Dumas).

12. **Mikhail Yakovlevich Herzenstein** (1859–1906). Economist and writer; became professor in Moscow University, 1903, and in the College of Agriculture, 1904; member of Moscow City Duma, 1905, and chairman of its finance commission; member of Zemstvo Assembly of Moscow Gubernia; Cadet; member of the First Duma; contributor to *Russkiia Vedomosti* and other papers; sharp critic of the government's agrarian policy in the Duma; assassinated in Finland soon after the dispersal of the Duma.

Page 479, note 13. **Dmitrii Dmitrievich Protopopov** (1856–   ). Member of Nikolaevsk Uezd Zemstvo Board and of Samara Gubernia Zemstvo; Cadet; member of the First State Duma.

14. **Ivan Vasilevich Zhilkin** (1874–   ). Well-known Trudovik; collaborated on *Saratovskii Vestnik;* collaborator and member of the editorial board of *Nasha Zhizn*, St. Petersburg, 1904–1908; one of the organizers and leaders of the Trudovik group in the First Duma; signed the Viborg Manifesto for which he was imprisoned for three months; abandoned political activity; collaborated on *Vestnik Evropy, Russkoe Slovo,* and other publications; after the October Revolution worked for a time in the People's Commissariat of Education.

Page 480, note 15. **Aleksei Fedorovich Aladin** (1874–   ). Studied in Kazan University, but in 1901 was brought to trial for revolutionary propaganda; escaped, and finished his education in England; returned to Russia after the Manifesto of October 17, 1905; member of the First State Duma.

Page 484, note 16. **Emperor Paul I** (1754–1801). Emperor of Russia, 1796–1801; son of Empress Catherine II (the Great); father of Emperors Alexander I and Nicholas I.

17. **Count Aleksei Andreevich Arakcheev** (1769–1834). Son of poor gentlefolk; graduate of a military school, after which he served in the army; soon advanced and made Commandant of Gatchina, where he became well known to the heir to the throne, the future Alexander I, upon whose accession he was advanced still further in the military service; accompanied the Tsar

in the battle of Austerlitz in 1805; General, 1807; Minister of War, 1808–1810; chairman of the Department for Army Affairs in the State Council, 1810; well known for his organization of military settlements, the strict discipline of which sometimes resulted in soldiers' mutinies, which were cruelly suppressed; after the Emperor's death traveled abroad, where he had a special clock made bearing the late Emperor's portrait and striking only once a day, at the hour of the Emperor's death; died in his estate on the bed which had been used by the Emperor.

18. **Vladimir Fedorovich von der Launits** (1855–1906). Graduate of His Majesty's School of Pages; entered army service, 1873; Marshal of Nobility of Kharkov Uezd, 1895; Vice-Governor of Arkhangelsk, 1901; Acting Governor of Tambov, 1902; Governor of St. Petersburg, 1905; assassinated by a Socialist-Revolutionist.

Page 485, note 19. **General Aleksandr Aleksandrovich Mosolov** (1854–   ). Married the sister of the Trepov brothers; Chief of the Chancellery of the Ministry of the Imperial Court, 1900–1917; Extraordinary Plenipotentiary to Bucharest, January 1917. (See his memoirs, *At the Court of the Last Tsar* [London, 1935].)

Page 486, note 20. **untangle the situation.** For another account of this incident, see Kokovtsov, *op. cit.*, pp. 151–56.

Page 488, note 21. **in a special edition.** See Appendix 3.

CHAPTER XXI

Page 491, note 1. **Party of Democratic Reforms** (*Partiia demokraticheskikh reform*). A moderately liberal party, to the Right of the Cadets; organized in the beginning of 1906; advocated the autonomy of certain regions, in purely local matters; approved the principle of alienation of land, but with compensation to the owners; promised to assist in the organization of trade unions and the cutting down of working hours; its organizers were: Professors M. Kovalevsky, V. Kuzmin-Karavaev, and I. Ivaniukov, and K. Arsenev, D. Stasov, M. Stasiulevich, A. Posnikov, and others.

Page 492, note 2. **confidence of those concerned.** See Appendix 4.

Page 494, note 3. **Prince Mikhail Sergeevich Putiatin** (1861–   ). Major General; graduate of the Naval School; staff officer on special duty in the Ministry of the Imperial Court, 1900–1911; Head of the Imperial Palace Administration, 1911.

4. **Count Pavel-Leopold-Johann-Stepan Konstantinovich Benckendorff** (1853–1921). Educated in Paris, then in His Majesty's School of Pages; served in Russo-Turkish War, 1877–1878; Aide-de-Camp of the Emperor, 1878; First Chamberlain of the Court, 1893; Major General of His Majesty's Suite, 1896; Adjutant General, 1905; made Grand Marshal of the Court by Nicholas II, whom he served until the end of his reign; died in January 1921 en route to emigration.

5. **her letters to the Tsar.** See *Perepiska Nikolaia i Aleksandry Romanovykh 1916–1917 gg.* (Moscow, 1926–1927), Vols. III–V (English edition, *Letters of the Tsaritsa to the Tsar, 1914–1916,* with an introduction by Sir

Bernard Pares [New York, 1924], and *The Letters of the Tsar to the Tsaritsa, 1914–1917,* translated by A. L. Hynes . . . . edited . . . . by C. E. Vulliamy with an introduction by C. T. Hagberg Wright [New York, 1929]).

Page 495, note 6. **cabinet lands.** Lands belonging to the Emperor.

Page 498, note 7. **idea of reform.** See Kokovtsov, *op. cit.,* pp. 163–65; see also Alexander Gerassimoff, *Der Kampf gegen die erste russische Revolution,* pp. 131–32.

Page 500, note 8. **Alekseevsky [Central] Committee** (*Alekseevskii glavnyi komitet*). Organized in June 1905 to provide care for children whose fathers died in the Russo-Japanese War.

Page 501, note 9. **Article 87 of the Russian civil code.** *Svod Zakonov Rossiiskoi Imperii ("Code of Laws of the Russian Empire"),* Vol. I, *Svod Osnovynkh Gosudarstvennykh Zakonov ("Fundamental State Laws"),* Part I (1906 edition), chapter x, Article 87. Provided that if measures requiring legislative sanction were urgently required when the State Duma was not in session the Council of Ministers might recommend action directly to the Emperor. Measures adopted under these circumstances might not affect the fundamental laws, the regulations of the State Council or the State Duma, or the electoral procedure of either chamber. If after the opening of a new Duma a new bill dealing with a measure thus adopted was not introduced within two months, or if the bill was eventually rejected by the State Duma or the State Council, the measure was invalidated.

10. **principle of family ownership.** The family organization among the Russian peasants was bound up with land relations. The basic trait of these relations was the communal ownership of property, and this trait characterized the great majority of peasants throughout Russia.

Page 502, note 11. **Black Hundred.** In Muscovite Russia this was the name of guilds of small tradesmen. In 1905 and later it was the name given to gangs which were inspired either by the police or by anti-Semitic, anti-revolutionary, anti-liberal, or anti-intellectual sentiments to commit violence against the persons and property of Jews, workers, students, and others. Still later the name came to be applied to reactionaries in general and to such organizations as the Union of Russian People.

Page 503, note 12. **Petr Petrovich Izvolsky** (1863–1927). Graduate of St. Petersburg University; served successively in the ministries of Foreign Affairs, Interior, and Education; Assistant Minister of Education, 1905; Ober-Prokuror of the Holy Synod, 1906–1909; member of the State Council, 1909.

Page 506, note 13. **rejection of the project.** Cf. Kokovtsov, *op. cit.,* pp. 166–68.

14. **Nikolai Nikolaevich Pokrovsky** (1865–1930). Graduate in law of Moscow and St. Petersburg universities; in the Department of Direct Taxation of the Ministry of Finance, 1889–1893; in the Chancellery of the Committee of Ministers, 1893–1899; Assistant Director of the Department of Direct Taxation in the Ministry of Finance, 1899–1903, and Director, 1904; Assistant Minister of Finance, 1906–1914; member of the State Council, 1914; State Comptroller, 1916; Minister of Foreign Affairs, 1916–1917; emigrated after the October 1917 Revolution; lecturer at the University of Kovno.

Page 513, note 15. **Nationalist party.** One faction of the Duma's Right-wing group which split in the Third Duma into a continuing Right-wing group (including Purishkevich and Markov II) and a Nationalist group which supported Stolypin. In the Third Duma these two factions had approximately fifty and ninety members, respectively, and in the Fourth Duma approximately sixty-five and ninety.

16. **Military Council** (*Voennyi Sovet*). Formed in the Ministry of War in 1838; considerably enlarged in 1865, when five committees were formed within it: (1) Committee to Supervise Military Hospitals; (2) Committee to Supervise Military Prisons; (3) Committee to Supervise Military Schools; (4) Committee of Military Codification; (5) Committee for the Organization and Formation of Troops.

Page 514, note 17. **provisions of existing laws.** Cf. Kokovtsov, *op. cit.,* pp. 218–24.

Page 515, note 18. **Minister of the Interior.** Cf. Kokovtsov, *op. cit.,* pp. 271–78.

19. **his end was at hand.** See Appendix 5.

CHAPTER XXII

Page 516, note 1. **Aleksei Nikolaevich Khvostov** (1872–1918). Graduate of the Imperial Alexander Lyceum; served in the Ministry of Justice; Governor of Vologda, 1906–1910, of Nizhnii Novgorod, 1910–1912; member of the State Duma, 1912, in which he was leader and chairman of the Right group; Minister of the Interior, 1915–1916; arrested and imprisoned by the Provisional Government; shot by the Bolsheviks in Moscow, August 1918.

Page 517, note 2. **Vladimir Aleksandrovich Sukhomlinov** (1848–1926). Graduate, Nicholas Military Academy of General Staff, 1874; served in the Turkish War on the staff of General Skobelev, 1877–1878; General, 1890; Commander of troops and later Governor-General at Kiev, 1904–1908; Chief of the General Staff, 1908; Minister of War, 1909; dismissed, June 1915, and imprisoned in Peter and Paul Fortress on the charge of treasonable negligence, but as a result of various intercessions was released and placed under house arrest; again arrested by the Provisional Government, tried, and sentenced to hard labor for life; released by the Bolsheviks, 1918, and fled to Finland; died in Germany.

3. **Assistant Minister of War.** See Kokovtsov, *op. cit.,* pp. 309–15; also V. Sukhomlinov, *Vospominaniia* (Berlin, 1924), p. 233 (German edition, W. A. Suchomlinow, *Erinnerungen* [Berlin, 1924], p. 290).

Page 518, note 4. **Lev Aristidovich Kasso** (1865–1914). Graduate of the École de Droit, Paris, and of Berlin University; later studied in Heidelberg University; lecturer in Yuriev (Dorpat) University, 1893–1895, Kharkov University, 1895–1898; professor at Moscow University, 1898–1910; Minister of Education, 1910–1914.

Page 520, note 5. **Captain Nikolai Viktorovich Treshchenkov** (1875–1915). Became gendarme officer, 1902; assistant chief of the Irkutsk Gubernia gendarme administration, 1911. As a result of the investigation instituted by Imperial order in connection with the Lena Goldfields affair, he was blamed for criminally exceeding his authority and a trial was insisted upon. Minister of the Interior Maklakov disagreed with this decision, and the matter was left unsettled until 1914 when Treshchenkov joined one of the regiments going to the front.

6. **Leonid Mikhailovich Kniazev** (1851–   ). Graduate of the Imperial School of Law; held judicial positions, 1872–1896; Governor of Tobolsk, 1896, of Vologda, 1901, of Kostroma, 1902, and of Kurland, 1905; Governor-General of Irkutsk, 1910; member of State Council, 1916.

7. **not have acted thus.** Cf. Kokovtsov, *op. cit.*, pp. 307–9.

Page 521, note 8. **Aleksandra Nikolaevna Naryshkina** (1839– ?). Close associate of the Imperial family.

9. **Commissar for Foreign Affairs.** Georgii Vasilievich Chicherin (Ornatsky) (1872–1936). Graduate of St. Petersburg University; in the Ministry of Foreign Affairs, 1896–1904; emigrated to Berlin, 1904, and joined the Social Democratic party; spent next twelve years in revolutionary activity in Switzerland, France, and, later, England; elected secretary of the Foreign Central Bureau of the Russian Social Democratic party, 1907; imprisoned in London for "enemy associations," 1917; returned to Russia, 1918; People's Commissar for Foreign Affairs, 1918–1930; headed the Russian delegations to the conferences at Genoa, 1921, and at Lausanne, 1922; retired, 1930.

Page 522, note 10. **Aleksei Nikolaevich Kharuzin** (1864–   ). Graduate of Moscow University; Governor of Bessarabia, 1904; Director of the Department for Ecclesiastical Affairs of Foreign Religions, 1908; Assistant Minister of the Interior, 1911, and Head of its Department for General Affairs; Senator, 1913.

Page 523, note 11. **Charles X** (1757–1836). King of France, 1824–1830; leader of reactionaries at court at the outbreak of the Revolution; left France in 1789; leader of the émigrés; in 1795 attempted to aid the royalist uprising of La Vendée; went to England soon after, where he lived until 1814, returning to Paris in the wake of the Allies; succeeded to the throne, 1824, at which time the Chamber was called *La Chambre retrouvée* because the elections of early 1824 had overcome a growing Leftist opposition and returned a strong royalist majority (in 1815 Louis XVIII had been so pleasantly surprised at the victory of the royalists over the Tricolor candidates in the elections of that year that he had termed the Chamber *La Chambre introuvable*) ; the reactionary policy of Charles X led ultimately to a successful revolution in July 1830 which drove him from his throne into exile in England.

12. **Extraordinary Commission of Inquiry [of the Provisional Government].** Established by a decree of the Provisional Government to the Ruling Senate, the text of which was published in *Vestnik Vremennago Pravitelstva*, No. 1, March 5, 1917. A regulation dated March 11, 1917, and published the next day stipulated that the Commission would be attached to the Ministry of Justice and that its purpose would be to investigate the illegal activities of former ministers and other high officials serving in civil, army, and navy institutions. The stenographic report of the examinations conducted by the Commission was published in seven volumes by the Soviet Government under

the title *Padenie Tsarskogo Rezhima; Stenograficheskie otchety doprosov i pokazanii. dannykh v 1917 g. v Chrezvychainoi Sledlstvennoi Komissii Vremennogo Pravitelstva* (Moscow-Leningrad, 1924–1927), edited by P. E. Shchegolev.

13. **Roman Vatslavovich Malinovsky** (1878–1918). Member, vice-chairman, and chairman of the Russian Social Democratic Labor party group in the Fourth Duma; member of the Central Committee of the Social Democratic party; at the same time served as agent-provocateur for the Police Department, as he had earlier (1905) for the Moscow secret police; dismissed from the Police Department, May 1914, by order of Assistant Minister of the Interior, General Dzhunkovsky, with a pension of 6,000 rubles a year; sent to the Bolsheviks his official resignation from the State Duma, and gave his reasons for so doing; immediately afterward left for abroad; joined the Russian volunteer army in France in 1915; was soon made prisoner by the Germans; returned to Petrograd in 1918, gave himself up to Soviet justice, and was shot, by the decision of the Supreme Tribunal.

14. **Vladimir Lyovich Burtsev** (1862–   ). As a student in the 'eighties associated with Narodnik group; arrested in 1885 and imprisoned in Peter and Paul Fortress; banished to Irkutsk whence he fled abroad; with Dragomanov and Deborii-Mokrievich published *Svobodnaia Rossiia* in Geneva, 1889; went to London in 1891, where he studied the revolutionary movement; wrote *Za Sto Let* (*"In the Course of a Hundred Years"*), 1896–1897; published *Narodovolets,* in which he advocated revolutionary terror; arrested by the English police and condemned to one and a half years of hard labor; on his release published *Byloe,* at which time he stood close to the S.R.'s; ejected from Switzerland and France, 1903–1904; returned to Russia, 1905, but went abroad again in 1907; well known for his denouncement of agent-provocateurs, such as Asef and others; renewed publication of *Byloe* in 1908; returned to Russia during the World War, and published *Obshchee Delo* in 1917; after the October Revolution left for Paris, where he again published *Obshchee Delo;* supported anti-Soviet movement; member of the National Committee in 1921 made up of Cadets and Octobrists.

15. **Petr Valerievich Kamensky** (1861–   ). Graduate of Kharkov University; member of the Third Duma; Octobrist.

Page 524, note 16. **Nikolai Georgievich von Biunting** (1861–1917). Graduate of His Majesty's School of Pages; in the Chancellery of the Senate, 1883; Vice-Governor of Kursk, 1897; Assistant Director of the Department for General Affairs of the Ministry of the Interior, 1903; Governor of Archangelsk, 1904, of Esthonia Gubernia, 1905, and of Tver, 1906.

17. **Archbishop Anthony [Karzhavin]** (1858–1914). Bishop of Tobolsk and Siberia, later Archbishop of Tver.

18. **Nikolai Petrovich Shubinsky** (1853–1920). Graduate of Moscow University; well-known Moscow barrister; member of Third and Fourth Dumas; Octobrist.

Page 525, note 19. **gubernia authorities.** Cf. Kokovtsov, *op. cit.,* pp. 336–39.

20. **Andrei Ivanovich Shingarev** (1869–1918). Zemstvo leader; physician; Cadet; member of Second, Third, and Fourth Dumas; Minister of

Agriculture of the first coalition cabinet of the Provisional Government, March 15—May 18, 1917; Minister of Finance, May 18—July 17, 1917; arrested after the October Revolution and while in a hospital was murdered by sailors.

21. **impression upon me.** Cf. Kokovtsov, *op. cit.*, pp. 291–98.

Page 526, note 22. **Vladimir Karlovich Sabler [Desiatovsky]** (1845–1923). Graduate in law of Moscow University; sent abroad by the University to study and on return lectured for a short time on the practice of criminal courts; in the Ministry of Justice, 1873; soon transferred to the Second Section of His Majesty's Chancellery; jurisconsult of the Holy Synod, 1881, and Head of its Chancellery, 1883–1885; vice-chairman of the council of the Holy Synod to superintend parochial schools, 1885; Assistant Ober-Prokuror of the Synod, 1892; Senator, 1896; member of the State Council, 1905; Ober-Prokuror of the Synod, 1911–1915; died in Moscow.

Page 527, note 23. **Ivan Konstantinovich Grigorovich** (1853–1930). Admiral; served in the Russo-Turkish War and during the Russo-Japanese War was Commandant of Port Arthur Fortress until its fall; Chief of Staff of the Black Sea Fleet, 1905; Commandant of the Port of Alexander III (Libau), 1906; Commandant of Kronstadt Port and Military Governor of the town of Kronstadt, 1908; Assistant Minister of the Navy, 1909, and Minister, 1911–1917; member of the State Council, 1913.

24. **Nikolai Evgeneevich Markov [Markov II]** (1866–   ). Engineer; until 1908 held various posts in large private railway companies; member of Third and Fourth Dumas, where he was a leader of the extreme Right group; member of the Union of Russian People.

Page 528, note 25. **with his presence.** Cf. Kokovtsov, *op. cit.*, pp. 365–67.

Page 529, note 26. **Artur Germanovich Rafalovich** (1853–1921). Russian economist; educated in France; member of the Institut de France; Director of the Russian Bank for Foreign Trade; representative in France of the Russian Ministry of Finance under Vyshnegradsky, Witte, and Kokovtsov; author of many works, including *Russia, Its Trade and Commerce, Les Coalitions de producteurs et le protectionisme,* and *Memoire sur la conférence de la paix.*

Page 530, note 27. **Mikhail Dmitrievich Chelyshev** (1866–   ). Peasant; member of Samara City Duma and of uezd zemstvo of Samara Gubernia; Octobrist; member of the Third Duma.

28. **Chief Administration of Indirect Taxation and Liquor Trade** (*Glavnoe Upravlenie neokladnykh sborov i kazennoi prodazhi pitei*). Organized in 1896 out of the Department of Indirect Taxation (*Departament neokladnykh sborov*), which had been organized in 1863 out of the Department of Taxation and Dues (*Departament podatei i sborov*).

Page 531, note 29. **limiting the use of liquor.** Cf. Kokovtsov, *op. cit.*, pp. 407–13.

30. **to be dismissed.** Cf. Kokovtsov, *op. cit.*, pp. 407–56.

31. **Petr Lvovich Bark** (1858–1937). Attended the University of St. Petersburg; entered the Ministry of Finance, 1892; Manager of the St. Petersburg branch of the State Bank, 1905; Assistant Manager of the State Bank, 1906; Managing Director of the Volga-Kama Commercial Bank,

1906–1911; Assistant Minister of Commerce and Industry, 1911–1914; Minister of Finance, 1914–(February) 1917; member of the State Council, 1915; during the February Revolution was arrested, together with other ministers; soon released, after which he emigrated; Managing Director of the Anglo-International Bank (London); knighted by King George V, 1935.

Page 532, note 32. **Fedor Alekseevich Uvarov** (1866–   ). Count; graduated from Moscow University, 1889; entered the army but retired from service, 1891, and settled on his estate, for the exemplary management of which he became famous; active zemstvo worker; member of the Special Conference to Study the Needs of Agricultural Industry, 1904; elected member of the State Council, 1909.

CHAPTER XXIII

Page 539, note 1. **Young scions . . . . such as Bakunin.** The Bakunin family of Tver enjoyed a reputation for liberalism. After the emancipation of the serfs in 1861, two Bakunin brothers, Aleksei Aleksandrovich, who was Marshal of Nobility in Novo-Torzhok Uezd, and Nikolai Aleksandrovich, who was a member of the Gubernia Special Board for Peasant Affairs, were members of a group which sent an address to the Minister of the Interior, "pointing out that the redemption dues were too heavy for the peasants, that the rule of redemption must be made obligatory for the landlords, that it was imperative for Russia to annul all classes and to grant equal rights to all good citizens and to call a *zemskii sobor.* . . . . All persons who signed this address were tried, deprived of their rights and imprisoned. . . . . Soon afterward, when they were asked to plead for pardon, all did so except the Bakunin brothers, who were released from prison but did not have all their rights restored—as did the other culprits—and for the rest of their lives were banned from taking part in any conference or holding any official position" (I. I. Petrunkevich, "Iz zapisok obshchestvennago deiatelia, vospominaniia," in *Arkhiv Russkoi Revoliutsii* [Berlin 1934], XXI, 206–7).

Page 541, note 2. **revolutionary from the outset.** See Tikhon J. Polner, *Russian Local Government during the War and the Union of Zemstvos,* in collaboration with Prince Vladimir A. Obolensky [and] Sergius P. Turin; with an introduction by Prince George E. Lvov (New Haven, 1930).

Page 543, note 3. **capture of Lvov [Lemberg].** The battle, which occurred between an Austrian army under General Auffenberg and two Russian armies under Generals Russky and Brusilov, ended in the Austrians' defeat and their withdrawal from Lvov, September 1–3, 1914, which was subsequently occupied by the Russians.

4. **General Aleksandr Vasilevich Samsonov** (1859–1914). Graduate of the Cavalry School in St. Petersburg and of the Nicholas Academy of the General Staff; served in the Russo-Turkish War, 1877–1878; appointed to the General Staff, 1884; Comandant of the Cavalry School at Elizavetgrad, 1896–1904; promoted to the rank of general, 1902; commanded the Ussuri mounted brigade and the Siberian Cossack Division in the war with Japan; Governor-General and commander of troops in Turkestan, 1909; was ap-

pointed Commander of the Second Army, concentrated on the Narev, August 1914, which was destroyed by the Germans under Hindenburg in the Battle of Soldau (Tannenberg), August 16–30, 1914; after the battle Samsonov committed suicide.

Page 545, note 5. **Chief Artillery Administration** (*Glavnoe Artilleriiskoe Upravlenie*). Formed during the reorganization of the Ministry of War, 1862–1866, from that Ministry's Artillery Department, the Artillery Section of its Military Science Committee, and the Staff of the General Feldzeug-meister.

Page 547, note 6. **Pavel Nikolaevich Krupensky** (1863– ?). Marshal of Nobility of Khotinsk Uezd, Bessarabia Gubernia, 1899; member of the Second, Third, and Fourth Dumas; chairman of the Center group in the Fourth Duma.

7. **paid him 20,000 rubles.** Stepan Petrovich Beletsky gave the following testimony before the Extraordinary Commission of the Provisional Government: "Khvostov . . . . as he had told me, had taken measures to effect a rapprochement with the nationalists and Octobrists (how successful these measures had been, I do not know) and had come to be on friendly terms with the State Duma member, P. N. Krupensky. According to the instructions of A. N. Khvostov, given in the presence of Krupensky, I paid the latter a sum of twenty thousand rubles allegedly for the organization of a co-operative store in the State Duma. When Krupensky had left, A. N. Khvostov laughingly told me that this payment was designed to influence Krupensky to reveal the mood of the State Duma" (*Padenie Tsarskogo Rezhima,* IV, 279). Khvostov confirms this statement by Beletsky in his own testimony (*ibid.,* VI, 91–92).

CHAPTER XXIV

Page 550, note 1. **Pavel Pavlovich Riabushinsky** (1871–1927). Publisher of *Utro Rossii,* a non-party, democratic daily paper published in Moscow from 1907 to 1917.

2. **Mikhail Vladimirovich Rodzianko** (1859–1924). Graduate of His Majesty's School of Pages; in the army, 1877–1882; chairman of Ekaterino-slav Gubernia Zemstvo Board, 1900; member of the Union of October 17; elected member of the State Council, 1906; member and chairman of the Third and Fourth Dumas; chairman of the Provisional Committee of the Duma after the February Revolution; participated in the anti-Soviet movement after the October Revolution, and later emigrated.

Page 551, note 3. **Sukhomlinov's trial.** See Sukhomlinov, *op. cit.,* pp. 335–60 (German edition, pp. 422–88).

4. *Razvedchik.* Began publication, 1889; at first scientific, literary, and bibliographical; later a literary and military journal.

Page 552, note 5. **Sergei Nikolaevich Miasoedov** (1867–1915). Began service in the Gendarme Corps, 1892; Commander of the Gendarmerie of Verzhbolovo, 1901; guest of Emperor William II at Romintern on several occasions; suspected of being a German agent and put on reserve list, 1907;

through his friendship with Sukhomlinov, returned to active service in 1909 as an agent in counter-espionage and intelligence work; dismissed in 1912; fought a duel with Guchkov because Guchkov accused him, from the Duma tribune, of several shady deeds (see "Iz vospominanii A. I. Guchkova" in *Posledniia Novosti,* No. 5630, August 23, 1936, and No. 5633, August 26, 1936); in 1914 returned to the Tenth Army as interpreter; again fell under suspicion and was courtmartialed and executed.

Page 554, note 5a. **General Aleksei Andreevich Polivanov** (1855–1922). Graduate of the Nicholas Military Engineering Academy and of the Nicholas Military Academy of General Staff; participated in the Russo-Turkish War, 1877–1878; edited *Voennyi Sbornik* and *Russkii Invalid,* 1899–1904; appointed Second Quartermaster General of the General Staff in 1905, and in the same year Chief of the General Staff; Assistant Minister of War, 1906–1912; member of the State Council, 1912; appointed Minister of War, 1915, and dismissed in the same year; member of a special conference attached to the Commander in Chief of the Red Armies, 1920; Soviet military expert in Soviet-Polish negotiations, 1920.

6. **"rights of the soldier."** On March 15, 1917, a commission was appointed under the Provisional Government to change all military regulations to conform with the new democratic tendencies. General Polivanov was made chairman of the commission and the army order was drafted the same day. It sought to placate the soldiers by including in the order many of the less radical innovations that had been set forth in the Soviet's Order No. 1 of March 14, which had been received with such great enthusiasm, but repudiating others, such as the election of officers by the soldiers. (See P. A. Polovtsoff, *Glory and Downfall* [London, 1935], pp. 158–60.) This order on the rights of the soldiers is not to be confused with the one promulgated by the Soviet of Soldiers' Deputies on March 22, 1917, and given in part in Golder, *op. cit.,* pp. 393–94.

7. **Aleksandr Fedorovich Kerensky** (1881–   ). Socialist-Revolutionist; first became known as defense attorney in political trials; member of the Third and Fourth Dumas; leader of the Trudovik group; vice-chairman of the Petrograd Soviet, 1917; Minister of Justice, of War, and of the Navy, and Prime Minister in the Provisional Government, 1917; in emigration; his account of the developments referred to in the text is given in his *The Catastrophe* (New York, 1927), chapters v–vi.

8. **Prince Nikolai Borisovich Shcherbatov** (1868–   ). Graduate of His Majesty's School of Pages; Poltava Marshal of Nobility, 1907; Head of the Chief Administration of State Stud Farms, 1913–1915; Acting Minister of the Interior and Chief of the Gendarme Corps; elected member of the State Council, 1915; Minister of the Interior, June–September, 1915.

Page 555, note 9. **Aleksandr Alekseevich Khvostov** (1857–   ). Graduate of the Imperial Alexander Lyceum; entered the Ministry of Justice, 1890; special-duty clerk in the Chancellery of the Minister of the Interior, 1895; Director of the Department of Economy in the Ministry of the Interior, 1900; Assistant Minister of Justice, 1905; Senator, 1906; member of the State Council, 1912; Minister of Justice, July 1915—July 1916; Minister of the Interior, July–September 1916.

Page 556, note 10. **Grigorii Aleksandrovich Krestovnikov.** Prominent Moscow manufacturer, and for many years chairman of the Moscow Chamber of Commerce.

Page 557, note 11. **General Nikolai Nikolaevich Yanushkevich** (1868–1918). Graduate of the Nicholas Academy of the General Staff; Head of the Legislative Section of the Chancellery of the Minister of War, 1905–1911; professor at the Nicholas Academy of the General Staff, 1910–1911; Assistant Manager of the Chancellery of the Minister of War, 1911–1913; professor and Head of the Nicholas Academy of the General Staff, 1913–1914; Chief of the General Staff, 1914; later the same year, Chief of Staff of the Supreme Commander in Chief; Assistant Viceroy of the Caucasus and Assistant Commander in Chief of the Caucasian Military District, 1915.

12. **General Nikolai Aleksandrovich Danilov [the Red]** (1867–   ). Graduate of the Nicholas Academy of the General Staff, 1885; Assistant Chief of the Chancellery of the Minister of War, 1905, and Chief, 1911; professor at the Nicholas Military Academy; Chief of Supplies for the Northwestern Armies, 1914–1917.

13. **General Georgii [Yurii] Nikiforovich Danilov [the Black]** (1866–1937). Graduate of the Nicholas Academy of the General Staff, 1886; Ober-Quartermaster of the Chief Administration of the General Staff, 1908, and Quartermaster General, 1909; Quartermaster General of the staff of the Commander in Chief of the Northern Armies, 1914–1917.

Page 559, note 14. **Nikolai Iudovich Ivanov** (1851–1919). Adjutant-General; held responsible posts during the Russo-Japanese War; Governor-General of Kronstadt, November 1906—April 1907; appointed Commander of troops of Kiev Military District, December 1908; Commander of the armies on the Southwestern Front against Austria during first months of the World War; on the eve of the February 1917 Revolution ordered by the Tsar to Petrograd at head of a detachment of picked troops, but was unable to reach the capital because of the revolutionary measures taken by the railway employees.

Page 560, note 15. **Article 158.** *Svod Zakonov Rossiiskoi Imperii* (*"Code of Laws of the Russian Empire"*), Vol. I, *Osnovnye Gosudarstvennye Zakony* (*"Fundamental State Laws"*), Part II, *Uchrezhdeniia Ministerstv* (*"Establishments of Ministries"*), (1906 supplement), Section II, chapter i, Article 158. This article empowered ministers to take measures in extraordinary circumstances without sovereign approval, but provided that ministers should report to the Ruling Senate concerning the measures thus taken; it provided also that ministers should report to the Senate also measures taken in extraordinary circumstances that had been given the sovereign approval.

Page 562, note 16. **General Petr Aleksandrovich Frolov** (1852–   ). Graduate of Nicholas Academy of the General Staff; Acting Chief of the General Staff, 1904; Commander of St. Petersburg Military District, 1915, and in same year Chief to superintend the supply of the armies of the Northern Front; Assistant Minister of War, 1916; member of State Council, 1917.

17. **Aleksandr Ivanovich Karpinsky** (1872–   ). Professor of neuropathology in the Psycho-Neural Institute.

18. **Sergei Dmitrievich Sazonov** (1861–1927). Educated at the Imperial Alexander Lyceum; entered diplomatic service, 1883; after serving in the Russian Embassy in London and in Rome became Minister Resident at the Vatican, 1906; in 1909 entered the Ministry of Foreign Affairs as assistant to Izvolsky, whom he succeeded as Minister in 1910; member of State Council, 1913; dismissed in 1916 and appointed Ambassador in London, but before he reached his post the February 1917 Revolution occurred; member of the Russian Political Conference in Paris and Foreign Minister of Kolchak's Government during the Russian Civil War; died in emigration.

Page 564, note 19. *sotnia.* Literally, "a hundred." A unit in the Cossack military organization.

Page 565, note 20. **Aleksandr Ivanovich Konovalov** (1875–   ). Son of rich merchant family; vice-chairman of Moscow Exchange; member of the Council of Congresses of the Representatives of Trade and Industry; member of the Fourth Duma; member of the Provisional Committee of the State Duma, February 22, 1917; Minister of Commerce and Industry in the Provisional Government, March 2, 1917; resigned May 1917 but again joined the Ministry as assistant chairman to Kerensky (September–October 1917).

21. **Aleksei Semenovich Shmakov** (? –1916). Barrister in the Moscow Court of Appeals; publicist.

Page 567, note 22. **order concerning . . . . an independent Poland.** Proclaimed August 14, 1914, by the Grand Duke Nikolai Nikolaevich, Commander in Chief of the Russian armies, in answer to the anti-Russian campaign which the Germans had been organizing in Warsaw. This proclamation was welcomed by the National Democrats, being the first stage toward the fulfillment of their aims, but the Polish followers of Pilsudski received it with no favor. An English translation of the proclamation is given in Robert Machray, *Poland, 1914–1932* (London, 1932), p. 51.

Page 568, note 23. **Vladimir Nikolaevich Voeikov** (1868–   ). General; attached to the suite of His Imperial Majesty; married to the eldest daughter of Count Frederichs; in command of the regiment of Imperial Hussars at Tsarskoe Selo, 1907; appointed Commandant of the Imperial Palace, 1913, in which capacity he accompanied the Tsar in all his movements until his abdication in March 1917; in emigration; published *S Tsarem i bez Tsaria; Vospominaniia posledniago Dvortsovago Komendanta Gosudaria Imperatora Nikolaia II ("With and Without the Tsar; Memoirs of the Last Palace Commandant of Emperor Nicholas II")*, (Helsingfors, 1936).

Page 573, note 24. **Maksim Maksimovich Kovalevsky** (1851–1916). Outstanding Russian jurist; graduate of Kharkov University; went abroad to study the history of the institutions of England and other countries; professor of constitutional law at Moscow University, 1877–1887; dismissed from this post by the Minister of Education, Delianov; went abroad, where he organized, 1901, a school for the study of social sciences; lectured in Stockholm and Oxford; returned to Russia in 1905; became member of the Party of Democratic Reforms; member of the First Duma; elected member of the State Council; member of the Academy of Science.

25. **Count Vladimir Alekseevich Bobrinsky** (1867–1927). Graduate of

Moscow University; in the army, 1890–1891; member of Bogoroditsk Uezd Zemstvo Assembly, 1892–1895; chairman of Bogoroditsk Uezd Zemstvo Board, 1895–1898; Marshal of Nobility of Bogoroditsk Uezd; member of the Second, Third, and Fourth Dumas; member and vice-chairman of the Nationalist faction in the Fourth Duma and advocate of the liberation of the Slavs of the Hapsburg Empire; cousin of Count G. A. Bobrinsky, Russian Governor-General of Galicia during the early part of the World War; left Russia in 1919.

26. **Ivan Nikolaevich Efremov** (1866–   ). Publicist; member of the progressive bloc; member of First, Third, and Fourth Dumas.

27. **Vasilii Vitalievich Shulgin** (1878–   ). Graduate of Kiev University; zemstvo member; honorary justice of the peace; collaborator and later editor of *Kievlianin;* member of the Second, Third, and Fourth Dumas; member of the Progressive Bloc, 1915; together with Guchkov requested the Tsar to abdicate in the name of the Duma; active in Denikin anti-Bolshevik movement, when he founded the newspaper *Velikaia Rossiia;* went to Soviet Russia incognito and recorded his impressions in the book entitled *Tri Stolitsy ("Three Capitals")*.

28. **Ivan Ivanovich Dmitriukov** (1872–   ). Octobrist; graduate of St. Petersburg University; lawyer in St. Petersburg, 1895; zemskii nachalnik in Kaluga Gubernia; member of Third Duma and member and secretary of Fourth Duma.

29. **Vladimir Nikolaevich Lvov** (1872–   ). Member of the Third and Fourth Dumas, where he was chairman of the Center group; after the February Revolution, member of the Provisional Government as Ober-Prokuror of the Holy Synod; after the October Revolution, emigrated; returned to Russia in 1922 and found employment in Soviet institutions.

30. **Sergei Illiodorovich Shidlovsky** (1861–1922). Graduate of the Imperial Alexander Lyceum; known for his liberal policies as a large landowner; active in zemstvo work; member of the Board of the Peasant Bank, 1899–1905; departmental director in the Ministry of Agriculture, 1905; a Left Octobrist; member and elected vice-chairman of the Third Duma, 1907; leader of the Progressive Bloc in the Fourth Duma; member of the Provisional Committee of the Duma from which the First Provisional Government was formed, 1917; member of the Pre-Parliament, 1917; emigrated, 1920. (See his memoirs, *Vospominaniia* [Berlin, 1923].)

Page 574, note 31. **David Davidovich Grimm** (1864–   ). Graduate of St. Petersburg University; Cadet; professor of Roman law at St. Petersburg University, 1901, and Rector, 1910–1911; lecturer and professor in the Imperial School of Law, 1891–1905, and in the Military Law Academy, 1896–1909; elected member of the State Council, 1907–1917; Assistant Minister of Education in the Provisional Government, 1917.

Page 579, note 32. **Anna Aleksandrovna Vyrubova [née Taneeva]** (1884–   ). Friend of the late Empress, Alexandra Fedorovna, and of Rasputin.

Page 581, note 33. **Aleksandr Nikolaevich Volzhin** (1862–   ). Graduate of Moscow University; Marshal of Nobility of Podolsk Gubernia, 1897, of Sedlets, 1904; Governor of Kholm, 1913; Director of the Department for

General Affairs of the Ministry of the Interior, 1914; Ober-Prokuror of the Holy Synod, 1915–1916; member of the State Council, 1916.

34. **Aleksandr Nikolaevich Naumov** (1868–   ). Graduate of Moscow University; zemskii nachalnik, Samara Gubernia, 1893–1897; member of the Zemstvo Assembly of Stavropol Uezd, Samara Gubernia, 1894–1897; acting chairman of the Zemstvo Board of Samara Gubernia, 1897–1902; Marshal of Nobility of Stavropol Uezd, 1902, and of Samara, 1905; publisher of *Golos Samary;* elected member of State Council, 1909, 1912, 1915; Minister of Agriculture, November 1915—July 1916; appointed member of State Council, 1916.

Page 582, note 35. **Mikhail Vasilievich Chelnokov** (1863–   ). Chairman of the Moscow Uezd Zemstvo Board, 1891–1894; member of the Moscow Gubernia Zemstvo Board and Moscow City Duma; active in zemstvo congresses; Cadet; member of the Second, Third, and Fourth Dumas; Mayor of Moscow, 1914; chairman of All-Russian Union of Towns, 1914–1917.

36. **at the Empress' treason.** The complete text of Miliukov's speech in the Duma, November 1, 1916, is given in A. S. Rezanov, *Shturmovoi signal P. N. Miliukova* (Paris, 1924?), pp. 45–61.

Page 585, note 37. **Jules Michelet** (1798–1874). Eminent French historian; chief of the historical department of the Archives of France, 1830; professor of history at the Sorbonne, 1832; occupied the chair of history and moral science in the Collège de France, and elected member of Academy of Moral and Political Sciences, 1838; distinguished himself as an adversary of the Jesuits and of Romanism; after the *coup d'état* of December 1851, as an ardent advocate of republicanism, he refused to take the oath to the Empire and as a result lost his place in the Archives and his chair in the Collège de France, to which positions he was never restored. Chief works: *Histoire de la révolution française* (7 vols., 1847–1853) and *Histoire de France* (14 vols., 1833–1862).

APPENDIX

1. SHIPOV TALKS WITH PLEHVE AND WITTE, JULY 2–3, 1902[1]

PLEHVE: I have wished for a long time to make your acquaintance, Dmitrii Nikolaevich. I have always been interested in your public activities and I have always respected them. It grieves me, therefore, that one of your latest actions has made it necessary for me to open our conversation in a manner which is not to my liking. First of all I must communicate to you our Sovereign's order. At the end of May [1902] you organized a conference of zemstvo men. This conference discussed the participation of the representatives of zemstvo boards in the Gubernia and Uezd Committees on the Needs of Agricultural Industry. When I had full information regarding the sessions of this conference and the program which it had worked out, I made a report to the Sovereign. His Majesty was quite indignant. He considers this conference an attempt to oppose the government and to deprive the uezd and gubernia committees, which are now being organized, of representatives of zemstvo boards who had been called by Sovereign order to attend these committees. The Sovereign has instructed me to express to you his disapproval and even displeasure [with your recent activities], and to warn you that if other similar conferences are organized by you, he will dismiss you from your position, in spite of the useful work you are performing, and will deprive you permanently of the right to take part in public work.

SHIPOV: Must I simply take notice of what I have been told? May I give my explanations to Your Excellency?

PLEHVE: Please tell me everything that might explain your actions.

SHIPOV: First of all I must say how deeply sorry and even grieved I am at having incurred His Majesty's displeasure. But I feel it my duty to explain that the discussions carried on by the zemstvo men in question were not of the nature later ascribed to them, as Your Excellency has just told me. The discussions which took place at the end of May in Moscow were not different from a number of similar discussions which have been taking place among zemstvo men ever since 1895. It has been a custom among zemstvo men, while attending various official congresses . . . . to gather together in order to talk over and exchange views on the most important points pertaining to everyday zemstvo work. In the course of the year such discussions have taken place at the handicraft congress in St. Petersburg and at the congress in Moscow to discuss the prevention of fires. These discussions were primarily concerned with the problem of the participation of representatives of zemstvo boards in the Gubernia and Uezd Committees on the Needs of Agricultural Industry. I will not conceal from you the fact that in the course of these discussions zemstvo men manifested a certain irritation and displeasure; and naturally so, for they could not remain indifferent to the fact that the government had ignored zemstvo institutions when attempting to solve the very important prob-

[1] D. N. Shipov, *Vospominaniia i dumy o perezhitom* (Moscow, 1918), pp. 171–197.

lems of the needs of agriculture. In this mood of irritation many zemstvo men believed that the representatives of the zemstvo boards should refuse to participate actively in the work of the committees to which they had been invited. This opinion met with objections from others, however, and no final decision on this point was made . . . . [at that time]. But in view of the seriousness of the matter at issue, the zemstvo men agreed to meet again and to invite other persons to attend their meeting. Accordingly the question was discussed at a conference in May, when the mood of the zemstvo men was calmer. This conference came to the conclusion that, since zemstvo board representatives were called by the Special Conference—which, on its part, was appointed by the Sovereign—to attend the work of the committees, refusal to participate in the work of the committees would be equivalent to a refusal to comply with a Sovereign order. The great majority of zemstvo men present decided, therefore, that the representatives of the zemstvo boards should actively participate in the work of the committees. The minority . . . . accepted the decision of the majority . . . . It should be added that all participants in the May conference agreed that the zemstvo men called to take part in the work of the committees were expected to state officially that they were expressing only their personal opinions, and not the opinions of the zemstvo assemblies, as the latter did not select them to represent these assemblies at the committees and did not give them any instructions. The participants in the May conference believed that the needs of agriculture could not be satisfied by individual measures as long as general conditions tending to retard agricultural development continued to exist . . . . These conditions, common to all gubernias, were unfavorable to the economic prosperity of the rural population, and they were as follows: (1) There exists no legal status for the peasants; (2) the education of the rural population is insufficient; (3) the position of the zemstvos, called upon to assist agricultural industry, is unsatisfactory; (4) the government's financial and economic policies are not satisfactory, consequently the rural population is overburdened with taxation.

It must be clear from what I have just said, first, that from our discussion we hoped to define how the representatives of the boards could best fulfill their duties in the committees; and, second, that we discussed general conditions unfavorable to agriculture and considered them exclusively from the point of view of the needs and well-being of the population. May I take the liberty of asking Your Excellency to communicate to His Majesty my explanations.

PLEHVE: I shall report to the Emperor all that I have heard from you, but I do not know whether or not His Majesty will alter his earlier opinion. For my part, as Minister of the Interior, I must tell you that your explanations are not entirely satisfactory. The fact that various illegal conferences have been taking place over a period of several years can in no way justify your last conference, as it cannot be considered legal. It is fortunate that in this instance the sensible majority prevailed over the minority, and that the latter submitted to the decision of the former; but it might have happened just the other way . . . . Organizations of this kind cannot be considered legal.

But let us now end the official part of our conversation. I have wished for some time to have a talk with you. So let us now talk as two private individuals. I believe that you and I have much in common, and I think that we both might belong to the same camp. I do not know that this can actually be, but I am very glad to have this opportunity of exchanging views with you. I am in favor of zemstvo institutions, and I am convinced that no state order is possible unless the public is attracted to local self-government. I do not consider it possible to govern a country with the help of an army of officials alone, and I do not consider zemstvo institutions to be incompatible with our political order. On the contrary, I believe that side by side with an autocratic rule there can exist a broadly developed local self-government. Of course, I cannot help thinking that very often zemstvo institutions are inclined to go beyond the limits of their tasks and that sometimes they pursue political aims. In the program of the May conference in Moscow you discussed the legal status of the peasant class. There is no need for me to say that this problem is not involved in the needs of agriculture, although I cannot deny that a certain connection—probably not as close as you are inclined to think—does actually exist between the two problems. But I think it necessary to say that zemstvo institutions do not even confine themselves to a discussion of problems similar to that on peasant status; very often they raise points which directly or indirectly concern the general political order of the country. You must remember very well that when zemstvo assemblies have been approached by the government on important issues—such as the matter of national food supply in the 'seventies, or of local institutions at the time of Count Loris-Melikov in the 'eighties, and so forth—some zemstvos, such as Novgorod and Chernigov, have frequently failed to confine themselves to the questions put to them, and have actually raised the point of a change in our state order. The raising of political questions by zemstvo institutions, whether it is done directly or indirectly, is contrary to the existing political order, and is therefore not only wrong but harmful in so far as actual zemstvo work is concerned. Although I am in favor of zemstvo institutions and am prepared to aid their development, as Minister of the Interior I am obliged to take into account the tendencies manifest in the higher circles, tendencies which zemstvo institutions must also take into consideration. Moreover, the raising by zemstvo people of questions of a political nature encourages tendencies which are unfavorable to any public institution, and are made use of by those who are opposed in general to the principle of local self-government. I repeat again my belief in the necessity of the broad development of local self-government, and I am prepared to establish the necessary contact between the government and public institutions; but in order that this may be possible it is necessary that zemstvo institutions in their turn do not raise any obstacles. It is my opinion that no state order can remain static and that very likely our political order will be replaced by a different one thirty, forty, or fifty years hence (I ask you, please, to see that these words are not repeated); but the raising of this question now is, to say the least, not timely. Such historical developments must take place gradually.

SHIPOV: Allow me to express to you my deep appreciation of the fact that you have considered it possible and necessary to acquaint me so frankly with your ideas on our local self-government and on its significance in our political order. If you will authorize me to acquaint my zemstvo comrades in Moscow Gubernia and other gubernias with the content of your remarks, I am sure that a considerable pacification in zemstvo circles will follow and that the zemstvo people will await more patiently the unfolding of events. Will you allow me, Your Excellency, to state my own opinion of the significance of our public institutions.

PLEHVE: I urge you to do so.

SHIPOV: I am a convinced supporter of the principle of autocracy. I believe that the autocratic form of government best suits the Russian people. In my view justice can be done and people can be more secure under autocracy than under a parliamentary regime; that is, they can be more secure when the autocrat who is the embodiment and the executor of the people's will realizes his moral responsibility before his people than when the will of the people is expressed by an accidental majority and is often the result of a struggle between various classes or a consequence of the clash of the class and material interests. I know that people have different opinions on this matter, and I consider it my duty to express to you my own point of view. But when I express my devotion to the idea of autocracy, rightly understood, I cannot identify autocracy with absolutism. I believe that an autocratic order is compatible with public freedom. What is more, I believe that under an autocracy a participation of the public in local self-government on a wide scale is essential. If an autocratic sovereign takes upon himself to execute his people's will it is absolutely necessary that he have direct communication with elected representatives of the people. Only under these circumstances will the autocratic sovereign be in a position to learn of the needs of the people and of local situations in general. The difficulties which we are now experiencing are due exactly to the fact that no contact or understanding whatever exists between the government and the public. I am far from saying that our public is blameless; in fact, I believe that the reason for the present state of affairs lies partly in the Russian public. Our public is passing through a period of [moral] sickness—its mood is one of negation; it has few ideals and no stable opinions. But if you think that public elements should participate in our state order, it seems to me you must also admit that it is essential for the government to take measures to train the public for participation in the political life of the country. Now this is possible only if the public is organized and if it is attracted to work in government institutions. Yet the gulf that separates government and public has been steadily widening, and this was particularly apparent after the circulation of the memorandum of the Minister of Finance [Witte] entitled "Autocracy and Zemstvo." In this memorandum the Minister of Finance argued that local self-government is incompatible with the idea of autocracy. It would logically follow from this premise that all those who believe in self-government, and who think it their duty to support institutions of local self-government, liberty, and independence, are politically unreliable. Can zemstvo men work in peace under such circumstances? Can it be wondered that they become excited? This memorandum was soon followed by several new legislative regulations which seemed to confirm the supposition that the government had accepted the principle outlined in the memorandum . . . . and that it intended actually and consistently to apply that principle. Lastly, the author of the memorandum was appointed chairman of the Special Conference which considers it possible to ignore zemstvo institutions while discussing such an important matter as the needs of agriculture, a matter which concerns all sides of public life. In making this point I must add that I do not think that zemstvo institutions alone, especially in their present excited frame of mind, are capable of supplying the Special Conference with the information it needs or of expressing absolutely competent opinions. But the need of ascertaining the opinions of public institutions at the present moment is not so much a question of any practical significance as one of principle.

PLEHVE: In regard to your remarks concerning the memorandum of the Minister of Finance, I must say that no one among the ministers is more convinced of the need for public independence and the development on a wide scale of public self-government than is S. Y. Witte. The main purpose of the memorandum of which you speak was to assist in the overthrow of my predecessor, I. L. Goremykin, and also to prevent the application of the statute to introduce zemstvo institutions in our borderlands [i.e., the western gubernias]; and with his stand on the latter point I am in absolute agreement. To our great shame we have not succeeded in creating a situation in our borderlands which would make it possible to introduce local self-government there. I am not an admirer of S. Y. Witte's policy (please do not pass this on either), but in all fairness I must say that he is not against public institutions. I admire his genius, thanks to which our finances are in such a good condition. I believe that future generations will be grateful to him for what is now being done for them, although I must admit that it represents too heavy a burden for our present taxpayers. I believe it exceedingly useful, therefore, to stress in the memoranda which the representatives of the zemstvo boards intend to present to the local committees the weak points of our financial and economic policies.

Now to return to what you have just said. I agree with you that at present contact between the government and the public is lacking. I admit also the necessity of bridging the gulf which exists between these two forces—the government and the public. But I cannot agree with you that under an autocratic regime contact between the government and the representatives of the people is absolutely necessary. I believe that this contact can be made through the officials of the local self-government. Well-informed men who are well acquainted with local conditions and needs can help to establish this contact. Such people would include, for example, chairmen of gubernia zemstvo boards, as they already enjoy the confidence of zemstvo assemblies and are closely associated with zemstvo work. Of course if local interests were actually to be discussed, then the elected representatives of the people would be needed to defend their particular local interests. But the Special Conference does not intend to study local interests. All that the government now needs is well-informed men. Besides, if the principle of the elective representation is adopted, the next step would be the convocation of the *zemskii sobor*.

SHIPOV: The people who are elected by the zemstvo assemblies to attend to zemstvo self-government do not always have the qualities of well-informed men. Very often the zemstvo assemblies elect to the boards people who have a talent for practical work but may not have the broad outlook or training required for the discussion of state problems. The representation of [class or group] interests has been always alien to the Russian people, and let us hope will always be so. The statute of 1890 concerning zemstvo institutions introduced class groupings in the zemstvo by differentiating between the nobility, merchants, and peasants in the zemstvo assemblies; and what were the results of this innovation? A decline in zemstvo activity as a whole and an apparent apathy in the public mood. But neither the nobility nor the merchants took advantage of the situation to represent their special class interests in zemstvo institutions. As before, these classes continued to be guided in their activities by moral principles, and continued to work together and use whatever means were necessary to satisfy the needs of the less fortunate masses. I am convinced that when zemstvo men are called by Sovereign order to participate in the work of the government they will try to represent the Russian land and Russian people as a whole and will discuss the only existing national problem, that is, the problem of Russian local people, and will not defend simply their own class interests.

PLEHVE: In any case the raising of the question of people's representation is untimely. At the present moment only the matter of establishing contact between the government and the official representatives of local government can be considered. I ask you D[mitrii] N[ikolaevich] please do not encourage discussions of this nature or of a nature similar to those of which we spoke in the beginning of our conversation. I shall try to call the chairmen of gubernia zemstvo boards to participate in the discussions in the Ministry of the Interior on various points which these institutions are competent to discuss. . . . .

I should like to hear your opinion regarding the significance of the so-called "third element" in zemstvo institutions. The contingent of persons invited by the zemstvo to work for it is growing in number and seems to be continually gaining in significance. Yet the great majority of these zemstvo workers are politically unreliable.

SHIPOV: Speaking to you quite frankly, I must say that it is my deep conviction that the future of zemstvo work rests with the "third element."

PLEHVE: You don't mean it!

SHIPOV: I have already had occasion to say that at the present moment no single group in Russia can pretend to have the leading role, and in the future this role can belong only to those public groupings which come to represent the center of the intellectual and spiritual forces of Russia; these forces, I believe, are mainly concentrated in the "third element." Of course, there are people among the "third element" who are politically unreliable—and such people can be found in zemstvo circles also—but it is hardly possible to generalize on this point and to speak of the majority of the "third element" as politically unreliable. Besides, it is very necessary to take into account that the prevailing disquiet and excitement in these circles are largely due to the indefinite position of these circles in so far as concerns their status not only in the state but also in the zemstvo. In the majority of cases these people contribute their labor to zemstvo public work quite disinterestedly.

PLEHVE: As far as their disinterestedness is concerned, I am quite convinced that these people do not serve their material interests, are satisfied with modest salaries, and work unselfishly. Nevertheless, I believe that they are concerned mainly with political aims, that is, the destruction of the present social order.

SHIPOV: I repeat that among the "third element," just as among the rest of zemstvo people, there are persons whose aims are those of which you have just spoken. But these persons are exceptions. I have worked for a long period of time among the "third element" in the zemstvo, and I must say that the majority of them are Tolstoians in the best sense of the word, that is, in the sense that they feel deeply their moral duty toward their fellowmen and wish to contribute to the general good by serving their neighbors rather than by repudiating in its entirety the principle of state order. Taking this moral ideal as their guiding principle, the "third element" is becoming a significant force, especially in zemstvo work. . . . .

The next day I visited the Minister of Finance, S. Y. Witte, in compliance with his wish as communicated to me by M. A. Stakhovich. Witte asked me to tell him in detail of my conversation with V. K. Plehve in so far as it concerned the zemstvo May conference. I gave him an account of my visit to V. K. Plehve and then narrated the opinions of the zemstvo men concerning the participation of representatives of zemstvo boards in the work of local committees on the needs of agricultural industry. After this the following conversation took place between us.

WITTE: I am very glad that you were so kindly received by the Minister of the Interior. I may have been indirectly responsible for it. I spoke to V[iacheslav] K[onstantinovich] after he had seen M. A. Stakhovich. Even earlier, when it was expected that the zemstvo men intended to organize an obstruction to local committees, I advised V[iacheslav] K[onstantinovich] to let you alone and said that it was not necessary to exaggerate the importance of this matter. Now that it is known that an absolutely correct move in this matter was taken at your conference, I find still less occasion to attach to your meetings the significance which was given them earlier.

I have your program. I may disagree with you on certain points, but that is merely a difference of opinion and convictions. I must also acknowledge that no part of your program goes beyond the points put before the committees. I find the exchange of opinions which took place in Moscow exceedingly useful for [future] work. There is no need for the Special Conference to instruct the local committees to discuss separate points of your program. What is important is to ascertain locally what are the general conditions that are retarding the development of agricultural industry. The discussion of these conditions at the conference of zemstvo men in May in Moscow has made it possible to ascertain the public opinion on this point, and consequently has made quite evident the importance of your conference. As chairman of the Special Conference, I consider it my duty to report on it to the Emperor. Tell me, how do you zemstvo people fare and how do you feel?

SHIPOV: We fare and feel very badly. The zemstvos are surrounded by an atmosphere of distrust which prevents them from working peacefully: they are continually under nervous strain. Instead of quietly attending to zemstvo problems and being concerned with the best methods of doing our work, so that the people will derive most benefit from it, we are obliged to concentrate our attention on other issues and are continually anxious not to arouse the suspicions of the administration; also to avoid various official difficulties which besiege us everywhere. It is impossible to work well when there is no contact or mutual confidence between the government and the public.

WITTE: How do you explain the fact that these conditions have recently grown considerably worse?

SHIPOV: May I speak quite frankly with you?

WITTE: I ask you to be quite frank. We talk not as a minister and a chairman of a zemstvo board but as two private individuals.

SHIPOV: In that case I shall take the liberty of saying that your widely circulated memorandum on the matter of introducing zemstvo institutions in the western regions has been the cause of much disturbance in zemstvo circles.

WITTE: Why?

SHIPOV: In this memorandum it was stated that zemstvo institutions are not compatible with an autocratic order. From this the conclusion was drawn that all persons who support the principle of local self-government and independent zemstvo institutions are politically unreliable. This argument was bound to widen the gulf between the government and the public.

WITTE: My memorandum was thoroughly misinterpreted. It does not include anything which should cause dissatisfaction on the part of zemstvo circles. I do not retract what I said in my memorandum, that is, I continue to believe that the two main points of my memorandum are absolutely correct and that their validity cannot be denied by anyone. The first point is that the drawing of the public into the work of the local government will lead to public participation in the central government. This is an axiom which has been proved by the experiences of all countries and by the theories of history. No honest-minded person will deny it. In Russia this opinion is also held by such authorities on political science as Gradovsky, Chicherin, and others. Only our dear Aleksei Dmitrievich Obolensky does not agree with me, but he is always beclouded by some theoretical fantasies and believes that the Russians are some very special people, inspired by some special ideals. Of course, I cannot agree with this point of view; I believe that all peoples are alike: English, French, German, Japanese, and Russians! What is good for one people cannot be bad for others!

SHIPOV (interrupting): Will you allow me to be true to myself and to say that I disagree with you?

WITTE: But does the position of the country grow worse when a representative form of government is adopted? Why then should we also refuse to accept it? I state in my memorandum that zemstvo institutions are a historical fact in the political life of our country and that there can be no question of their repudiation; from that I conclude that the participation of the public in local government will lead to its participation in the central government. As a minister I considered it my duty to tell the Emperor this, so that he may be aware of the direction in which the country is going.

My second point is as follows: If we have zemstvo institutions, and if they cannot be done away with, then they must be allowed to live. But actually they are not permitted to live. That is what I explained in my memorandum. Why are zemstvo institutions displeased, why are they disquieted? Because in their present organization they are left without foundation, they are hanging in the air, so to speak (making a movement with his hand). They are separated from the people by a bureaucratic wall, and they feel bureaucratic pressure from above. Zemstvo men ask to be permitted to make contacts with the lower circles of the population, but they are not permitted to do so. They ask permission to join the government machine, and are refused that also . . . . Hence they are tossing hither and thither. It is impossible to prevent the inevitable course of political development, but it is possible to retard it. To this end it is necessary to bring the zemstvo institutions closer to the people and to assign to them some important tasks. As Minister of Finance, I do not find it possible to accomplish any important economic measures directed to the improvement of the country's general position unless public forces are attracted to participation in this task. To this end, it is necessary that the zemstvos become popular institutions and that everything which separates them from the population be removed. A small zemstvo unit must be created. If under present conditions zemstvos are given numerous and urgent tasks, they will be so busy with them that they will abandon their political pursuits.

Apart from my memorandum, what else is there that is creating dissatisfaction among zemstvo people?

SHIPOV: After the issuance of your memorandum there began to appear new legislative regulations which, in our opinion, represent the application of the program outlined in your memorandum. Food supply and distribution is being taken out of the hands of zemstvo institutions.

WITTE: Here I must agree with you. Such a solution of the question of food supply and distribution was completely wrong. I had foreseen it and had warned D. S. Sipiagin, but I failed to convince him of it. First I insisted and then, I am sorry to say, I gave in. Consequently the work is being done unsatisfactorily and zemstvo institutions are naturally offended. What else?

SHIPOV: Next the regulation which set the limits of zemstvo taxation.

WITTE: Here again is a misunderstanding. There is nothing in this law that should offend zemstvo institutions. To have both local and state taxation unlimited is not considered correct or admissible anywhere. The income of the properties taxed can be taken into consideration only to a certain extent. It is at present impossible to settle permanently the limits for zemstvo taxation, that is, until the evaluation work is done; the law of June 12, 1900, is only a temporary measure. If zemstvo institutions find themselves short of funds for their own needs, as a result of setting the limits of zemstvo taxation, the requisite money will be given by the state. Why don't zemstvos use this source? In the state budget for 1901, 500,000 rubles were allocated for this purpose, but the zemstvo institutions used only 50,000. If 500,000 is not sufficient, I am prepared to raise the grant so that it will actually satisfy the requirements.

SHIPOV: If it were only a question of setting the limit of zemstvo taxation as you have just said, then, of course, such a measure would be correct and could arouse no displeasure on the part of the zemstvos. But the law of June 12, 1900, does not deal with the limit of taxation as a whole. It simply limits to a certain per cent the yearly increase of taxation and in this way interferes with zemstvo independence and the zemstvo's most essential right, namely, its right to impose zemstvo taxes. At the same time zemstvo institutions abstain from using government subsidies in the present situation from fear of losing still more of their independence.

WITTE: What else can you point out?

SHIPOV: Recently the Special Conference on the Needs of Agricultural Industry, of which you are chairman, has found it possible to ignore zemstvo institutions when attempting to solve a very important question which concerns all sides of our national life.

WITTE: I ask you to believe in my sincerity. I spoke at the Special Conference in favor of bringing the zemstvo institutions into this work, but I met with objections from D. S. Sipiagin, who was supported by A. S. Ermolov and the majority of the members of the Conference. I found it difficult even to secure the consent of the members of the Conference to the appointment of the committees in their present composition. I considered it necessary to consult zemstvo institutions on the problem which is being studied by the Special Conference, and I foresaw that failure to attract into this work zemstvo institutions would cause public displeasure. But tell me frankly, do you think that zemstvo assemblies are capable of expressing competent opinions and supplying definite suggestions on the essential points in question?

SHIPOV: Speaking frankly, I must admit that zemstvo assemblies, particularly as they are now composed, would hardly be capable of fulfilling these tasks. Nevertheless, I believe that it is absolutely essential to them to draw them into the discussions on the needs of rural economy, not so much as a matter of practicality, but as a matter of principle and of political consideration.

WITTE: I absolutely agree with you on this point. Recently I received a request from the Moscow Gubernia Committee that the zemstvo assemblies be allowed to communicate their opinions on the needs of agriculture to the Special Conference. I shall pass on this request to the Conference, but I do not know whether or not the Conference will find it possible to have it presented to His Majesty. At any rate, the first sessions of the Conference will not take place before the end of October or the beginning of November, when the sessions of uezd assemblies will be ended and when very little time will be left before the opening of gubernia sessions.

SHIPOV: Zemstvo assemblies would be willing to call special sessions in order to discuss this important matter.

Witte then proceeded to ask me about the arrest of some persons in Moscow whom the police considered politically unreliable, and whether many such arrests were made, and what impression they had had on the public. I answered that these arrests were very numerous in Moscow, and that in the majority of cases there was nothing against the persons who were arrested. I gave him several examples of this, and said that such arbitrary acts aroused the anger even of those who supported law and order. Witte listened to what I had to say, then mused: "Yet Sipiagin was a good and honest man, but unfortunately he could see no farther than this" (as he said this he closed his eyes). With this our conversation ended.

I returned to Moscow in high spirits after my interviews with the ministers. I wanted to believe that both ministers truly realized the necessity of making contact with public forces, that a language of mutual understanding could be found, and that in the near future a foundation would be laid for the establishment and consolidation of contact between the government and the public.

On the basis of what the ministers had said, I believed that both V. K. Plehve and S. Y. Witte had come to realize, perhaps against their wills, the force of public opinion and the need for making a contact with these forces which they could no longer ignore. It was a significant fact that at the time when Sovereign displeasure was being expressed to the participants in the zemstvo conference, both ministers recognized the organization which aimed at zemstvo unification, accepted it as an established fact, and spoke to me as its representative. Even if their words did not actually express their convictions, it seemed to me that they saw the inevitability of changing their policies. If bridging the gulf which separated the public from government was not the actual wish of the ministers, nevertheless they considered such a measure essential, perhaps in order to save themselves from falling over the precipice. My usual optimism was particularly strong at that time. But it did not last long.

On my return to Moscow I shared my Petersburg impressions first of all with my comrades on the board, and on July 18 I reported my conversations with the ministers to several chairmen of gubernia boards who happened to be in Moscow, and to several zemstvo men who had participated in the May Conference. I said that it was possible to conclude from what had been said, not only by the Minister of Finance but also by the Minister of the Interior, that the reactionary policy of the government was now to be abandoned and that apparently both ministers were prepared to establish contact with the public and consequently paid no attention even to the views of those who were above them. They wished that this change should take place gradually and that zemstvo institutions should raise no obstacles to the carrying out by them of certain measures. The Minister of the Interior thought that an example of such obstacles could be seen in the zemstvo's insistence on participation in the central government and in the Special Conference on the Needs of Agricultural Industry. Since I was confident of the sincere desire of the ministers to establish contact with public institutions, I suggested that we cross out for the time being Paragraph four of our May program, and in this way show our willingness to make concessions to the government for the sake of realizing our main task: the re-establishment of contact between the government and the public. My suggestion was approved by those present. We also decided to notify the members of all gubernia zemstvos of this decision, and to send them a report of my talks with the ministers. Six persons among us were given this task.

In this way the program we had worked out at the May conference, with paragraph four excluded, served as a guide for the zemstvo representatives in most gubernia and many uezd committees when they prepared their memoranda for the Committees on the Needs of Agricultural Industry. In this way, too, these committees were supplied with the public opinion on the problem under consideration, a fact which was very important. But the countermeasures and reprisals which were soon put into effect by the local, and particularly the central administration, clearly revealed that both Plehve's and Witte's statements to me of their benevolent intentions in regard to zemstvo institutions and their readiness to establish contact with the public were, to say the least, insincere.

In accordance with S. Y. Witte's wishes, I outlined in detail and sent to him in the form of a letter dated July 18 a plan by which zemstvo assemblies could, at least indirectly, express their opinions on the questions which were considered by the local Committees on the Needs of Agricultural Industry. S. Y. Witte wrote me a short letter, July 31, in which he said that he found it difficult to solve the question I had raised, without having it discussed by the Special Conference which was to start work again in November. It was apparent that this was simply an excuse . . . . I do not know even now whether or not S. Y. Witte discussed this matter with V. K. Plehve as he had promised to do. At any rate, in July the Minister of the Interior sent to all gubernia and uezd marshals of nobility [who were presiding over the local committees] a circular letter containing the statute of the Special Conference on the Needs of Agricultural Industry and stating that the "participation of the zemstvo institutions in the study of separate points of the Conference's program was not considered necessary." . . . . A little later—in September—the governors, acting in accordance with another circular from the same minister, warned the marshals of nobility of possible attempts on the part of the zemstvo assemblies to discuss the questions connected with the Sovereign's expression of displeasure with the participants of the May conference, and asked the marshals to take all measures necessary to prevent the inclusion of such questions in the agenda of the zemstvo assemblies; should such questions be included, the marshals were asked to delete them from the agenda by virtue of their special authority as chairmen of assemblies.

I shall not discuss here the repressions and prosecutions suffered by the zemstvo representatives for their memoranda to the local committees . . . . I shall limit myself to mentioning facts which concerned the activity of the Moscow gubernia committee alone . . . . [Shipov then relates how at Plehve's orders measures were taken to prevent the Moscow zemstvo institutions from expressing their opinions on the needs of agriculture.]

Such conduct on the part of the Minister of the Interior so soon after our conversation convinced me that I had been wrong to place my confidence in him. It became clear to me that when V. K. Plehve gave me such a kind reception he was endeavoring to attract me into close collaboration with him, intending to buy me off and make use of me in the ministry as a person well acquainted with zemstvo work. On the other hand, as he considered that I was held in certain esteem among zemstvo people, he thought that my collaboration might weaken the public opposition to the government. When he saw that his plans were not materializing, V. K. Plehve had soon changed his attitude toward me, and decided to take every opportunity to bring pressure to bear against me.

[On pp. 233–35 of his book, Shipov gives an account of his re-election, on February 14, 1904, to the post of chairman, for the third time, of the Moscow Zemstvo Board and of Plehve's refusal to confirm the election because of Shipov's "political unreliability."]

2. COUNT WITTE INVITES PUBLIC MEN TO JOIN HIS CABINET[2]

On October 18, 1905, I received from Count S. Y. Witte a wire . . . . asking me to come immediately to St. Petersburg. . . . . Upon my arrival, on the 19th, I, together with Count P. N. Trubetskoi, who had come on the same train with me, visited Prince Aleksei Dmitrievich Obolensky, who was at that time Witte's right-hand man. I learned from him of Count Witte's intention to ask me to join the cabinet which he was forming, and of the proposed changes in the statute on election to the State Duma. This statute had been confirmed by the Sovereign on August 6, 1905. I was at Count Witte's at 1:00 P.M., where I found Prince A. D. Obolensky.

When he greeted me Count S. Y. Witte told me that he was approaching me as a public man who enjoyed the confidence of public circles, and that he wanted to ask me to assume at that difficult time the post of State Comptroller. Count Witte made it clear that he well realized how great was the government's need of public confidence at that moment, and added that he believed that my presence in his cabinet in charge of the state control would make the public confident that state expenditures would be made in the correct manner. I answered that in principle I was willing to agree to his proposal but that I would deem it possible to accept this position only if I were confident that my presence in the government would prove useful. The government needed to inspire public confidence not on the matter of a correct expenditure of state funds but as to the replacement of the old state order by a new one in accordance with the Manifesto of October 17. In order to inspire such confidence it was necessary, I said, to attract into the government the representatives of various public circles. I belonged to the Right wing of the Zemstvo Congress of November 1904, that is, to its minority. At the present moment I was not a member of the [Bureau of] Congresses of Zemstvo and Municipal Public Men, and my inclusion in the government could be of no consequence. I pointed out the necessity of including in the government the representatives of the majority—that is, the Left wing—of these congresses and said that in order to create an atmosphere of confidence it would be necessary for the public men to be given ministerial portfolios,

[2] D. N. Shipov, op. cit., pp. 334–49. For Witte's account of the formation of his cabinet, see his memoirs, Russian edition, II, 50–66, especially 59–62 (English edition, pp. 318–26, especially pp. 325–26).

such as those of the Interior, Justice, Agriculture, Education, and Trade and Commerce. Count Witte appeared to agree with my view and said that he was not afraid of the people who professed Left-wing tendencies, but that he considered it necessary for the public men who would agree to join his cabinet to be men of strong will power, to be conscientious in their state work, and at the same time to believe in the necessity of authority in government and in the establishment of order in the country during the present transitional period. He asked me how he could get in touch with the people I had in mind. In view of the fact that on October 22 and 23 there was to assemble in Moscow the Bureau of the Congresses of Zemstvo and Municipal Public Men, I suggested to Count S. Y. Witte that he should send a wire to the chairman of the Bureau, F. A. Golovin, expressing a wish that several members of the Bureau come to St. Petersburg in order to conduct negotiations. On my part I was willing to acquaint the Bureau with the nature of the forthcoming negotiations, and expressed the opinion that the Bureau would probably elect for this purpose I. I. Petrunkevich, S. A. Muromtsev, and Prince G. E. Lvov.

Count Witte was not personally acquainted with these men and asked me to give him some information regarding them. He listened to me attentively, and then expressed the opinion that from what I had said these persons would be suitable candidates for ministerial positions. He asked my opinion as to how the portfolios should be distributed among them. I answered that S. A. Muromtsev seemed to me to be a suitable candidate for that of Justice and that Prince G. E. Lvov and I. I. Petrunkevich seemed to be most suitable for those of the Interior and Agriculture, respectively. I added that Count Witte could judge for himself, after he met them, which ministry should go to which man. Count Witte then said that he intended to offer the portfolio of Education to Prince E. N. Trubetskoi and that of Commerce and Industry to A. I. Guchkov. He asked me to draft a wire to F. A. Golovin, which he immediately dispatched. . . . . [There follows a discussion of proposed changes in the electoral law.]

With this our talk ended. As Count Witte bade me good-by, he said, "So you do not object in principle to my proposal?" I repeated that I did not object to it in principle but that I would reserve my final decision until the question of the participation of other public men in the cabinet was solved. I asked him to help me to arrange my departure from St. Petersburg that same day, and, thanks to his special orders, I was able to leave St. Petersburg by train on the night of October 20, attended by men from the army railway battalion. The train consisted of several empty third-class railway cars and one second-class car in which I was the only passenger. The cars were not heated, and no light was used until we reached the station of Kolpino. . . . .

I arrived back in Moscow on the night of October 20–21, and on the morning of October 21 I was told that on the previous day F. A. Golovin, upon receipt of Witte's wire, had called a special meeting of those members of the Bureau who were in Moscow, and that that meeting had considered it possible to discuss Count Witte's proposal immediately without awaiting the general meeting of October 22. The following persons were elected to conduct negotiations with the Chairman of the Council of Ministers: F. A. Golovin, F. F. Kokoshkin, and Prince G. E. Lvov. And these three men left for St. Petersburg on the evening of October 20.

The personnel of this delegation, with the exception of Prince G. E. Lvov, and the haste with which it left for St. Petersburg predetermined the results of the forthcoming significant negotiations, especially since the leading role in the delegation was assigned to F. F. Kokoshkin, a very young man at that time, who was carried away by the slogans recently proclaimed at the constituent meeting of the Constitutional Democratic party. On October 21 the delegation was at Count Witte's. From the start it assumed a defiant attitude, which precluded every possibility of a successful conclusion of these negotiations. Before discussion had begun the delegates stipulated that the entire conversation should be made public. Count Witte consented, and a record of the discussion was drawn up on the same day by the delegates, approved by Count Witte, and published on October 23 in *Russkiia Vedomosti*, No. 278. The basic conditions laid down by the delegation were as follows: the only possible way out of the present situation lay in the convocation of the Constituent Assembly that should work out the [new] basic laws: the Constituent Assembly should be convened on the basis of universal, equal, direct, and secret suffrage; the liberties proclaimed in the Manifesto should be immediately applied; full political amnesty should be granted. All these reforms, the delegates said, were bound to come, and it was better to grant them at once than to do so gradually and painfully through the modified State Duma. It seemed apparent from the manner in which the delegates advocated the solution of the difficulties that they were not in the least concerned with retaining and supporting the authority of the existing state power. This made it impossible for the government to conduct any further negotiations with the members of the Bureau of the Congresses of Zemstvo and Municipal Public Men, or to attract its representatives to a participation in the government.

Immediately after he had received the delegation Count Witte wired me to come immediately to St. Petersburg, and on October 22 I was there. At the same time A. I. Guchkov was also invited to come. On the morning of October 22 Count Witte informed me of his talk with the members of the Bureau of the Congresses of Zemstvo and Municipal Public Men, and that this had excluded every possibility of further negotiations. He said that he had reported to the Tsar my consent to become State Comptroller, that my appointment had been confirmed, and that on the next day, October 23, I was to present myself to His Majesty. I expressed my surprise at Count Witte's action. He knew that I had consented to join his cabinet only on certain conditions; yet he had thought it possible to report to the Tsar concerning my appointment. I said that I considered it my duty to communicate to His Majesty the considerations which I had already expressed to Witte. Count Witte and Prince Obolensky, who was also present, expressed their astonishment at my attitude. They considered it impossible for me to carry out my intention, since my appointment had already taken place. I repeated again that if His Majesty deemed it necessary to put his confidence in me, I, as a public man, considered it my duty to tell him frankly of my convictions.

At this Count Witte telephoned to Peterhof to the State Secretary—I believe it was Voevodsky—and asked him to hold up the ukase on my appointment until I had reported to the Emperor. He then asked me to call on him on my return from Peterhof.

The next day I went to Peterhof. On the boat I met K. S. Nemeshaev, who had been appointed Minister of Ways and Communications, and my second cousin, I. P. Shipov, a candidate for the post of Minister of Finance. I was received first, and it seemed to me that the Tsar had already been informed of what I was to tell him. He asked me of my recent work, recalled when he had last seen me, and stated his wish to appoint me State Comptroller. I thanked His Majesty for his gracious consideration and confidence and said that I did not possess the required administrative experience, as His Majesty was no doubt aware, but that if he still wished to choose me for this post it must be because, after laying the foundation of the new order of state administration in his Manifesto of October 17, and considering it necessary to consolidate the much-needed contact between the government and the public, the Emperor wished to attract me into the government as a public man who enjoyed the confidence of certain public circles. I was fully sympathetic with this purpose and believed it necessary to do what I could to help the realization of His Majesty's plan; nevertheless I believed that this plan could be carried out only if the government was joined by not one or another separate member of the public but by a whole group of public persons representing various shades of political opinion. Only under these conditions could the much-needed confidence between the government and the public be established and the public become confident that the rights granted to it in the Manifesto of October 17 would be fully realized. The first attempt in this direction by the Chairman of the Council of Ministers—his appeal to the representatives of the Bureau of the Congresses of Zemstvo and Municipal Public Men—had been unsuccessful. This was unfortunate; but if no agreement were possible with the representatives of a particular public organization, perhaps it would be possible to attract to the government several persons who enjoyed the confidence of various public circles. In that case my participation in the cabinet might prove of some use. But the inclusion in the government of a person like myself who belonged to the group of the public which represented a minority might very well lead to undesirable results.

His Majesty listened to me and then said: "I find your argument quite correct. Please communicate this to Sergei Yulievich." Our audience was over; and immediately upon my return from Peterhof I visited Count Witte and communicated to him His Majesty's final words.

That evening and the next day there were conferences at Count Witte's attended by Prince A. D. Obolensky, A. I. Guchkov, and myself, and M. A. Stakhovich as well. Count Witte considered it necessary to acquaint us with the circumstances which had preceded the publication of the Manifesto of October 17. On October 14 Count Witte had been called to Peterhof, and in view of the general public excitement and strikes the Tsar had asked his advice and offered him the leading position in the government. The next day Count Witte had stated to the Tsar in writing his opinion of the situation.

He had said that in his estimation there were two ways out of the difficult situation in which the country was then placed. One was to enact a number of repressive measures immediately and with the help of the military force to re-establish order. The second method was to meet the wishes of the public, to grant civil liberties to the people, and to allow them to participate in the carrying out of legislative measures. Witte had not considered that he was a suitable person to carry through the first measure, but agreed to assume heavy responsibilities if his second measure was adopted. At the same time, Witte had asked the Tsar to bear in mind the fact that the choosing of the second method would signify the abandoning of the principle of autocracy and the adoption of a regime of equity. The Tsar had chosen the second method, after which Count Witte had prepared his most humble report and the text of the Manifesto, both of which were approved by the Sovereign on October 17. Count Witte had been appointed Chairman of the Council of Ministers.

Later when he discussed with us the candidates for the ministerial positions in the new cabinet, Count Witte declared that the portfolios of Finance and Ways and Communications must be given to persons with special training, and that I. P. Shipov and K. S. Nemeshaev had already been appointed to these posts. Prince E. N. Trubetskoi, whom Witte intended to appoint Minister of Education, arrived in St. Petersburg on October 24 and took part in our conferences; but from the start he declined to accept the post.

At that time it was learned that there had become manifest among the newly formed party of "People's Freedom" and the academic union of professors a definite tendency whereby it was made obligatory for all members of these groups to decline all offers of participation in the cabinet Count Witte was forming, if such offers were made by him. Consequently the plan of drawing into the government representatives of public circles from various political groupings became practically impossible, and the only choice left to Witte was that of choosing new ministers from old administrators whose names were not odious to the public. There was great argument over the candidate for Minister of the Interior. Count Witte maintained from the start that in appointing the Minister of the Interior it was necessary to bear in mind the fact that this ministry was responsible for all secret and general police and that the person appointed Minister of the Interior in the time of revolution would have to be well acquainted with the organization of the Russian police, so that he might be responsible for the safety of the ruling house and the lives and property of the citizens. In his opinion only two persons were suitable for this position: D. F. Trepov and P. N. Durnovo.

All the public men who participated in this conference fervently opposed these candidates. They pointed out that the appointment of persons distrusted by wide circles of the Russian public and closely connected with the old regime would make it impossible for the new government to gain the confidence of the public. All members of the conference were fully agreed that it was imperative to secure the safety of the Imperial house and that it was necessary to entrust this duty to a person competent and enjoying the trust of the Emperor, and expressed their wish that D. F. Trepov should be given the position of palace commandant. But as concerned the appointment of the

Minister of the Interior they believed that . . . . the task of domestic policy could not be sacrificed to that of police and that it was domestic policy which should mainly concern the Minister of the Interior. The reasons for the objections to Durnovo's candidacy lay not only in his political views but also in his questionable moral character. A. I. Guchkov and I declared that there could be no question of our entering Witte's cabinet if P. N. Durnovo was appointed Minister of the Interior.

In the course of further discussions several candidates were suggested for the post of Minister of the Interior. Prince A. D. Obolensky mentioned the Saratov Governor P. A. Stolypin; but he was little known to us, and his candidacy did not attract the attention either of Witte or of other members of the conference. A. A. Lopukhin was also named, but Count Witte, displeased with Lopukhin's activity as Estonian governor, declined to discuss him. Count Witte wished to know our opinion of Prince S. D. Urusov. He said that he had wired to Prince S. D. Urusov to come to St. Petersburg and intended to ask him to return to active participation in the government. Prince Urusov had replied that he would come at his first opportunity, as soon as railway communication, broken by the railway general strike, had been re-established. Prince Urusov had said also that in view of the existing situation he was willing to accept whatever post should be offered him. Count Witte said that he had intended to offer Prince Urusov the post of Assistant Minister of the Interior and asked us what we thought of him for the post of Minister of the Interior. All present who knew him personally, and even those who were not acquainted with him, said that Prince Urusov enjoyed the general esteem and confidence of the public and that his appointment as Minister of the Interior appeared entirely desirable. Count Witte expressed the fear that Prince Urusov would find it difficult to direct police activity, as he was not acquainted with the complicated technique of the secret police, and again pointed out the significance of the smooth functioning of police machinery under existing conditions. He considered it necessary, therefore, that P. N. Durnovo should remain under Prince Urusov as Assistant Minister of the Interior in charge of police. This arrangement seemed acceptable to all present. Our conferences were then postponed until the arrival of S. D. Urusov, and that evening, October 24, A. I. Guchkov and I left for Moscow.

On October 25, soon after our arrival, we received from Count Witte a wire informing us that he expected Prince Urusov would arrive that day and asking us to hasten back to St. Petersburg; that evening we left for St. Petersburg. On October 26, A. I. Guchkov, Prince E. N. Trubetskoi, M. A. Stakhovich, and I went to Count Witte's. There we found Prince S. D. Urusov, who had just come. Count Witte said that he had already talked over the situation with Prince Urusov, who had agreed to accept the post of Assistant Minister of the Interior, while P. N. Durnovo would be Minister. This took us completely by surprise after all that had been said in the preceding meeting. It is most difficult to describe the indignation we felt. I asked Count Witte why, after deciding to appoint P. N. Durnovo Minister of the Interior, he had asked me to come to St. Petersburg again when he had my categorical declaration that I would not join his cabinet if this person was a member. A. I. Guchkov made a similar declaration. Prince S. D. Urusov was very much perturbed and said that he had not been aware of our opinions and that since he had agreed to be assistant minister to P. N. Durnovo, of whom the public men had such an adverse opinion, he felt most uncomfortable. Count Witte tried to explain his decision by his previous reasons. We said that we could not force him to accept our view and that he had a right to settle the matter as he saw fit, but that he had no right to invite us to participate in his cabinet and at the same time to ignore our definite declarations. In view of the situation A. I. Guchkov and I told Count Witte that we considered the question regarding our participation in his cabinet ended and our further participation in the conferences unnecessary. Count Witte asked us to delay our final decision until evening; in the meantime he and Prince Urusov would again discuss this question in his circle. We consented to this, although it seemed apparent that we would not change our decisions. Later in the day, in conversation with us, Prince Urusov tried to ameliorate our adverse attitude toward P. N. Durnovo and said that he was really better than public opinion made him out to be. As far as he personally was concerned, Urusov considered himself tied by his membership in the administration and by his two promises—the first made in his wire, and the second made during a personal interview with Witte on the day of his arrival—to accept Count Witte's offer. A. I. Guchkov and I were now determined to decline Witte's offer to us. Our considerations were as follows: Apart from Count Witte's apparent lack of sincerity and directness as well as his organic incapacity to free himself from the accepted habits and methods of the bureaucratic regime, our inclusion in his cabinet could have had significance only if the representatives of the majority of the Congresses of Zemstvo and Municipal Public Men—now joined to form the Party of People's Freedom—participated in it simultaneously with us, and if the number of public representatives included in the cabinet were sufficient to secure an influence on the state administration. But the inclusion of two of us [public men] in a cabinet composed of representatives of the bureaucracy, who were incapable of understanding just public demands, could not secure for the government the public confidence which would help the situation. At the same time the Manifesto of October 17, which called the Russian people to a new political life, made it necessary for the public elements to form political groupings, and we considered it our duty to help the unification of the persons who belonged to the minority in the zemstvo congresses in order to form a political party. We decided to explain our motives for declining Witte's proposal, and with this decision we went to see him in the evening.

As we went up the stairs in the building occupied by Witte on the Dvortsovaia and next to the Winter Palace, we saw a person in uniform whom we did not know. Count Witte, who met us in his study, apologized for being obliged to leave us for a time to receive a report from Rachkovsky. He soon returned looking somewhat perturbed, and said that it would probably be necessary to give up Durnovo's candidacy. Rachkovsky had reported that many newspaper offices had materials regarding Durnovo's past activities which exposed his moral character, and that if he were appointed minister these materials—including the well-known command of Emperor Alexander III "remove this scoundrel in twenty-four hours"[3]—would be immediately published. A. I. Guchkov expressed his astonishment that the fear of scandal was more effective than the arguments of public men. Count Witte then spoke again about the necessity of appointing P. N. Durnovo, and said that "as for the threats of the newspaper editors, due measures can be taken." I then stated that, irrespective of Durnovo's appointment, we did not think it possible at that time to enter the cabinet which he was forming, and set forth the motives which had prompted us to take this stand. Count Witte said he was sorry, and asked us to put in writing the reasons which made us decline his offer.

Before we left, Count Witte made of us the following request: In the course of our conferences the question of the forthcoming changes of the statute concerning the election to the Duma provided for in the Manifesto of October 17 had been discussed, together with the matter of the personnel of Witte's new cabinet. All public men who had participated in these conferences had spoken of the necessity of making the principle of universal suffrage the basis of the proposed changes in the statute concerning the election. Count Witte had apparently agreed with us, but he had envisaged the difficulties that would inevitably arise in the working out of these changes in the little time remaining before the election. When he said good-by, Witte asked us to prepare as soon as possible a draft of the changes in the electoral law on the basis we had expounded. We all expressed our complete readiness to do so, saying that we would try to attract to this work public men of various political tendencies. . . . .

3. THE ATTEMPT TO FORM A COALITION GOVERNMENT BEFORE THE DISSOLUTION OF THE FIRST STATE DUMA, JULY 8, 1906[4]

On the morning of June 27, 1906, Prince Orlov telephoned me to come to Peterhof on the 28th at 6:00 P.M. for an audience with His Majesty. Later in the day I received a wire confirming this invitation and informing me at which railway station a coach would be awaiting me. Still later in the day N. N. Lvov again communicated to me P. A. Stolypin's request to visit him at 11:00 P.M. In view of my forthcoming visit to Peterhof, I considered it expedient to accept Stolypin's invitation. N. N. Lvov and I left for the island, the Minister's summer home, so as to be there at 11:00 P.M. Soon after our arrival A. P. Izvolsky arrived also. Then our conversation began.

P. A. Stolypin repeated what I had already heard from N. N. Lvov and made a sweeping statement regarding the State Duma's inability to work, criticized the speeches of its members, and tried to prove the necessity of

---

[3] Another version of the Emperor's command is "Remove this pig to the Senate."

[4] Shipov, *op. cit.*, pp. 446–60.

dissolving it. He then asked me to state my opinion concerning the dissolution of the Duma. I said that according to my views and my understanding of the situation I considered the dissolution of the Duma at that moment unjust and politically criminal; I added that as far as I was concerned I could not be a party to it. . . . .

It was apparent that all I said regarding the inadvisability of dissolving the Duma was at variance with P. A. Stolypin's opinion and evidently did not please him. He soon changed the subject of our conversation and raised the matter of forming a coalition government under my chairmanship. According to his plan the cabinet would include public men invited by me. Stolypin made me understand that he wished to see A. P. Izvolsky included in the new cabinet. I expressed doubt that a cabinet so created would enjoy authority among the people's representatives and could establish the much-needed contact between the government and the State Duma. Putting aside for the time being the question whether or not it would be advisable to retain in the new cabinet the representatives of the old order and the impression which would thus be inevitably created, I said that I could not hope to obtain the consent of the representatives of the leading majority in the State Duma to participate in the new cabinet. Without such participation the new cabinet would certainly fail to receive the support of the people. I said that I was bound to admit that I enjoyed certain authority in and confidence of zemstvo circles. Recently, however, when the question was raised in the zemstvo and municipal circles regarding the needed reforms of our state order, two tendencies had become manifest. I belonged to the small minority. N. A. Khomiakov was right when he said that both he and I had become constitutionalists by Sovereign order after the Manifesto of October 17, although at the present moment, and in view of existing circumstances, I believed it absolutely imperative fully and immediately to apply to life the constitutional principles proclaimed in the Manifesto of October 17 and was prepared to assist in their application with all my power. I was certain that if I succeeded in attracting to my cabinet only my adherents, such as Count P. A. Heyden and G. E. Lvov, then my cabinet would meet with a reception similar to the one accorded that of I. L. Goremykin. At the same time such a cabinet would be averse to seeking support in the traditions of the old regime. It would inevitably become involved in conflict with the Duma, and consequently would be obliged to resign. I also pointed out that in view of the composition of the Duma, the new cabinet would have to include representatives of the Constitutional Democratic party and that the task of forming the cabinet should be given to one of the leaders of that party. A. P. Izvolsky was apparently in sympathy with what I said, and added that I might be able to persuade the representatives of the Constitutional Democratic party to join the coalition government. Then, turning to P. A. Stolypin, he said: "As to our participation in the cabinet, this decision must be left entirely to Dmitrii Nikolaevich." P. A. Stolypin wished it to appear that he was of the same opinion, but objected to some of the essential points of my argument. He said that he thought it too risky and, therefore, impossible to allow the representatives of the Cadet party to form a government, and insisted on the dissolution of the Duma. P. A. Stolypin also said that he had

invited P. N. Miliukov to come to see him, and that he had spoken to him of
the possible change in the cabinet. P. N. Miliukov had left him with the understanding, Stolypin said, that he would not decline the offer of forming the
cabinet if such an offer was made. In conclusion Stolypin said that the question of forming a new cabinet could be solved by the Emperor alone, and that
I should be able to present my considerations to His Majesty, since it had
been intended to give me an audience the next day. Apparently P. A. Stolypin
was not informed that I had already received such an invitation, and I did not
think it necessary to enlighten him, since this invitation had been sent without
his knowledge. Our talk, which had lasted till 3:00 A.M., now ended. In parting, P. A. Stolypin and A. P. Izvolsky asked me to share with them my impression of the audience I was to have with the Tsar; to this I gladly
consented.

Before my departure for Peterhof I considered it my duty to make myself
clear on the attitude of the Cadet representatives to the idea of the possible
formation of a coalition government. I asked P. A. Heyden to see P. N.
Miliukov, as I was but slightly acquainted with him, and I myself had a long
conversation with S. A. Muromtsev. Count Heyden, as it was agreed between
us, did not tell P. N. Miliukov of P. A. Stolypin's suggestion that I should
form a coalition government or of the audience which I was to have at Peterhof. Count Heyden asked P. N. Miliukov what he and his party thought of
the rumors regarding the formation of a coalition government under my
chairmanship and whether or not he [Miliukov] would agree to participate in
such a government. P. N. made a definite answer to the effect that he supported the principle of parliamentary government; consequently he considered
the proposed combination absolutely unacceptable to him; in his opinion the
new cabinet should be formed exclusively from the leading majority in the
State Duma. He made Count Heyden understand that he believed that this
question had already been decided [in his favor] and that he was prepared
to undertake the formation of such a government as soon as this task was
given him.

Since my youth I had been closely associated with S. A. Muromtsev. I
told him frankly and in detail of my conversation with the ministers and of
my forthcoming visit to Peterhof, and that the formation of a coalition government of the Cadets and those who stood to the Right of them seemed to
me the most suitable measure under existing conditions. I thought, however,
that the main, and perhaps the only obstacle would be the refusal of the
leaders of the Constitutional Democratic party to agree to such a plan. I
tried as hard as I could to make S. A. Muromtsev agree with me. . . . . .
But all my persuasion and pleading were of no avail—S. A. refused to assist
me in the formation of a coalition government. He said that he believed my
considerations were essentially correct, but he did not think it possible to
shake the already definitely accepted attitude of the Cadets on this question.
He added that P. N. Miliukov was already sure of being made premier. He
[Muromtsev] was absolutely unwilling to participate in the cabinet as premier
and Minister of Justice. In the opinion of S. A. the existing unrest among
the population at large and the general hostile attitude of the public toward
the government, an attitude for which the government alone was responsible,

made it impossible for any cabinet to expect to carry on peaceful and efficient work or to retain its position for a long time. Revolutionary unrest was inevitable and in the face of this fact any government would be bound to resort to strong repressive measures; this in turn would certainly arouse dissatisfaction in public circles and deprive the government of public support. S. A. agreed with me that existing conditions excluded the possibility of forming the government under my chairmanship, that is, he confirmed the decision of the Cadet party to refuse to participate in a coalition government; this circumstance would have made inevitable a conflict in the near future between such a newly formed government and the State Duma. These negotiations with S. A. Muromtsev and the information given me by Count P. A. Heyden regarding his conversation with P. N. Miliukov only confirmed the supposition I had elaborated upon in my previous day's conversation with P. A. Stolypin. . . . .

[In the succeeding audience at Peterhof Shipov repeated to the Tsar his earlier criticism of the recently adopted electoral system and gave the reasons for his opposition to the proposed dissolution of the State Duma.]

The Tsar then said that P. A. Stolypin had informed him that I did not find it possible to accept the offer to form a coalition government, and expressed a desire to hear my reasons. I answered that the formation of a coalition ministry made up of persons who belonged to different public groupings would, in my opinion, fully answer the needs of the moment and would establish between public elements and the government that contact which was so much needed in the transitory period of the country's political life. But unfortunately such a coalition was impossible as it met with an unfavorable response from the Constitutional Democrats, the most numerous and most influential party. I reported to His Majesty the conversations with S. A. Muromtsev and P. N. Miliukov on this point and repeated their points of view, ... [and added that] without the participation of the representative leaders of the majority [party] of the State Duma in the government I believed such a cabinet would be unwelcome to the Duma and consequently would not be able to remain at the helm for any considerable length of time. It appeared that the attitude taken on this issue by the Constitutional Democratic party had been particularly strengthened after the negotiations between P. A. Stolypin and P. N. Miliukov. At that moment, however, and under existing conditions, only the formation of the cabinet from the representatives of the majority [party] in the State Duma could prove satisfactory. The spirit of opposition which at that time was so definitely expressed by the members of the Cadet party should not cause particular apprehensions. The nature of this opposition could be explained by their lack of responsibility as members of the opposition. But if the representatives of the party were brought to participate in the government and to accept the heavy responsibility connected therewith, the existing mood of the party would undoubtedly change and its representatives, who would become members of the cabinet, would come to consider it their duty to reduce considerably the party program and would then actually meet the bills which they had signed in their pre-election campaign by paying no more than ten to twenty kopecks per ruble.

The Sovereign then wished me to explain exactly what I meant by the meeting of these bills and suggested that I speak on the five points discussed in the Duma's address: (1) the abolition of capital punishment; (2) general political amnesty; (3) the agrarian question; (4) equality for all nationalities; (5) autonomy for the Kingdom of Poland.

"The question regarding the abolition of capital punishment," I answered, "has already been studied by the State Duma; the legislative bill has already been drafted and sent to the Council, and will probably be presented to Your Majesty. As regards the second point, I believe that the Cadets will be satisfied with a political amnesty for those who have been indicted for trespassing the law in their desire to obtain liberties [i.e., constitutional and civil liberties] as soon as possible but who have not been connected with any attempts on the life and property of others." As to the agrarian question I had already expressed my supposition that the Cadets would first of all correct the mistake made in the Statute of February 19, 1861, and through recourse to the State Treasury would secure additional allotments for the peasants; they would then take extensive measures to give state assistance to the peasants to purchase privately owned lands and would resort to forceful alienation of these lands only in very exceptional cases and only if absolutely necessary. "The question of the rights of all citizens of the empire, irrespective of creed or nationality," I said, "has already been decided upon by Your Majesty in accordance with the report of Count Witte which accompanied the Manifesto of October 17. Lastly, the question of the autonomy for the Kingdom of Poland can probably be solved by the granting of extensive rights of local self-government to the population and equal rights for the development of national Polish culture."

In giving my opinion on these various points I deemed it necessary to say that all my remarks represented merely my private opinion. I added in conclusion that if the representatives of the Cadet party were called to the helm it was quite possible that in the near future they would consider it necessary to dissolve the State Duma and to have a new election for the purpose of unburdening themselves of a considerable number of Left-wing members, thereby creating a legislative chamber of the country's united progressive elements.

The Tsar appeared to be satisfied with my explanation and asked me which members of the Constitutional Democratic party enjoyed the greatest authority and were most capable of assuming leadership.

In answer to this question I expressed the following views: P. N. Miliukov should undoubtedly be considered one of the most influential members of the Cadet party, and although not a member of the Duma he was the actual leader of the Cadet group. But with due respect to his capacities, his talents, and his erudition, I thought that his conception of life was mainly that of a rationalist, a positivist; that he had little religious feeling, that is, a realization of every man's moral duty before the Supreme Being and before humanity. It was my opinion, therefore, that if P. N. Miliukov were placed at the head of the government he could hardly be expected to accept moral duty as a basis of his activity, and that his policy would not be likely to lead to that moral development of our people which was so very much needed at the present time. "At the same time Miliukov loves power and is autocratic (I used the last word thoughtlessly and I very much regret it) so that if he is placed at the head of the government it is to be feared he will oppress his comrades, and thereby interfere with their independent activities. But the presence of P. N. Miliukov in the cabinet as Minister of the Interior or of Foreign Affairs would be exceedingly useful, and even necessary, if the cabinet is to be composed of members of the Cadet party. I think that as chairman of the cabinet, S. A. Muromtsev—a man of high moral integrity—is the most suitable person."

The Emperor added: "I have been favorably impressed by my acquaintance with S. A. Muromtsev and I respect him."

I then continued: "S. A. Muromtsev enjoys particular respect as Chairman of the State Duma, and his appointment as head of the cabinet would be welcomed by broad public circles and not only by the Cadets. S. A. has a strong will; at the same time he has much tact and gentleness. If he were chairman of the cabinet, the independence of all members of the government would be secured, and under his leadership the participation of P. N. Miliukov in the cabinet would be highly useful."

To this the Emperor replied: "Yes, that is the way by which a union of spiritual and mental forces can be reached."

With these words the Emperor made it clear that the audience was over. As I rose, I asked His Majesty to forgive me if I had been too outspoken and had said anything that displeased His Majesty. I had considered it my duty, once His Majesty had deigned to listen to me, to state frankly all my opinions. The Sovereign gave me his hand and said: "I am very much pleased that you spoke frankly. I am very grateful to you for that."

Our audience had taken over an hour. I returned to St. Petersburg in high spirits; I was happy to have had the occasion to speak so frankly with the Sovereign, and was deeply moved by the confidence and attention shown me.

The next morning I visited A. P. Izvolsky and told him all that had happened at the audience. A. P. listened with great interest, approved my arguments as correct and well-founded, and said that according to rumors the Sovereign was in sympathy with my point of view and with my recommendations. A. P. Izvolsky thought it possible that S. A. Muromtsev would soon be invited to Peterhof, and advised me to warn S. A. to this effect. I answered that I was in complete agreement.

From A. P. Izvolsky I went directly to S. A. Muromtsev. I described in detail to S. A. all that I had said to the Emperor as stated above. As I proceeded with my story S. A. expressed several times his complete approval of [what I had said] . . . . but when I came to the matter of asking S. A. to make up the cabinet, he became very agitated and seemed to be quite displeased with me. He said: "Your opinion regarding the inadvisability of the dissolution of the Duma was quite correct; you were right in insisting on the formation of a cabinet made up of Cadets; but what right had you to discuss a question which can be decided only by the party?" I answered, "My right lies in my duty to tell the Tsar, as long as he wishes to listen to me, what I consider good for our country."

Muromtsev and I talked a long time, and I saw as we conversed that the prime reason why Muromtsev objected to forming a cabinet was that he considered it necessary to invite P. N. Miliukov into it. S. A. was apprehensive of the difficulties that might arise in working together [with Miliukov] and said among other things: "Two bears find it difficult to live in one den."

To this I replied, "You are already bears from one den, and I am sure that you will find it possible to live together again in a new den." In conclusion I said that no matter how great S. A.'s responsibility would be, if the Sovereign should entrust him with the formation of the ministry, he had no right to decline it but was in duty bound to accept this responsibility in order to help establish a new political regime in the country.

I visited Stolypin at 4:00 P.M. of the same day. As soon as I met him I read displeasure on his face. He opened our conversation by saying he had had some general information of what I had said to the Emperor, and that apparently I had made a good impression and my suggestions had been approved. Stolypin then asked me to relate in detail my talk with the Emperor in Peterhof, and I did so. He tried to restrain his displeasure as he listened to me, and when I had finished he said: "Now let us wait to see what will follow."

As I left P. A. Stolypin I had an impression that he would do everything possible to dissuade the Emperor from the idea of forming a cabinet of the leading elements in the State Duma. [Shipov hears from other persons reports that the Emperor had been pleased with and approved of what he, Shipov, said.] . . . .

I now considered my task accomplished and left for Moscow on the evening of June 30. I returned to St. Petersburg on July 7. In the hotel Frantsiia, where I usually stayed when in St. Petersburg, I was told that a day or so previously the Minister of Foreign Affairs had inquired when I was expected back and had requested me to visit him on my return. . . . . I soon went there. A. P. Izvolsky wished to tell me that the good impression created by what I had said to the Emperor had lasted until July 5, but after then the situation had changed sharply, and it seemed that S. A. Muromtsev would not receive an invitation to Peterhof. I asked what caused this change. A. P. answered he had no definite information, but that he supposed it was due to P. A. Stolypin's influence. After some further discussion I left. Later I saw several other persons and heard that the news of the murders of Admiral Chukhnin in Sevastopol and Major-General Kozlov of His Majesty's suite in Peterhof—and especially the effect of the Duma's plan to issue a proclamation to the people in reply to the government's communication regarding the agrarian problem—had enabled reactionary tendencies in St. Petersburg and in Peterhof to prevail and had made it easier for P. A. Stolypin to realize his intentions. As is known, the ukase concerning the dissolution of the Duma was signed on July 8, Stolypin was appointed chairman of the Council of Ministers, and the convocation of the newly elected Duma was fixed for February 1907.

4. STOLYPIN'S ATTEMPT TO INCLUDE PUBLIC MEN IN THE GOVERNMENT AFTER THE DISSOLUTION OF THE FIRST DUMA, JULY 8, 1906[5]

The dissolution of the State Duma and the appointment of P. A. Stolypin as premier made one anxious. The last hope of bringing about a union between the government and the public was gone. Nor was it to be expected that the promises of liberties proclaimed in the Manifesto of October 17 would be honestly fulfilled and the new state order peacefully established.

Owing to the fact that simultaneously with the dissolution of the Duma [July 8] the sessions of the State Council were closed, I left St. Petersburg on July 10, and did not expect to return in the near future. But on July 12 I received a wire from N. N. Lvov and M. A. Stakhovich, who insistently asked me to return. Considering all political negotiations to no purpose and unnecessary, I replied that I could not come. But on the next day I received a second telegram signed by N. N. Lvov, M. A. Stakhovich, and Count P. A. Heyden. I consulted my family and friends in Moscow, and left by express for St. Petersburg on July 14, arriving on the evening of the same day. I was told by Count P. A. Heyden, N. N. Lvov, A. I. Guchkov, and M. A. Stakhovich that P. A. Stolypin, who was forming a new cabinet, had approached the first three of these men and had also asked them to put pressure on me to take part in the government; he had said that he intended to send a similar invitation to Prince G. E. Lvov. But I did not approve the idea of my participation in the government; I said that P. A. Stolypin and I estimated quite differently the tasks of the government in general, especially at this time. I saw in Stolypin a person brought up on and permeated with the traditions of the old regime. I considered him the main culprit of the dissolution of the State Duma, who had undoubtedly used pressure in order to make it impossible to form a cabinet from the representatives of the majority [party] of the State Duma . . . . since he knew my attitude toward his policy, I was surprised that he was seeking my co-operation. N. N. Lvov, A. I. Guchkov, and M. A. Stakhovich, who had become reconciled to the dissolution of the State Duma, saw in P. A. Stolypin a man capable of co-operating with the public men and of carrying out reforms according to the Manifesto of October 17; they tried to incline me to their point of view. Count P. A. Heyden was skeptical of their opinion and was inclined to share my estimation of Stolypin's policy, but in spite of his skepticism he thought it better not to refuse to negotiate with Stolypin. He said that we should first try to become better acquainted with Stolypin's intentions and program. I held to my opinion, however, and said that for the interest of becoming better acquainted with Stolypin's program those of us who had already been negotiating with Stolypin should continue to do so, but that I personally did not find it possible to take part in these negotiations after my interview with Stolypin before the dissolution of the Duma.

On July 15 Prince G. E. Lvov, chairman of the All-Zemstvo Union, came

[5] Shipov, *op. cit.*, pp. 461–71.

to St. Petersburg to negotiate with the Minister of the Interior [Stolypin] on the matter of supplying certain localities with food. He . . . . was unaware of Stolypin's intentions concerning the formation of the cabinet, and asked for an audience. On the same day all the public men here named gathered in the hotel Frantsiia at lunch and discussed the question which interested us all. During lunch Prince G. E. Lvov was summoned to the telephone to answer a call from the chairman of the Council of Ministers [Stolypin]. When he returned to the lunch table, G. E. said that Stolypin had invited him and me, as a member of the All-Zemstvo Administration Board, to visit him in his summer house at 4:00 P.M. that day to discuss a plan to help certain districts, a plan which involved the co-operation of the All-Zemstvo Union. I had a feeling that this invitation was a trap set for us; but, as it was officially impossible to decline to make this visit, we set off to the summer house of the Minister of the Interior and were there at the appointed time. . . . .

I find it very difficult and almost impossible to give a systematic account of the conversation which followed. Both sides were excited and often interrupted each other. Disjointed opinions were expressed, and before one question was sufficiently formulated others were raised . . . . Both Prince G. E. Lvov and I saw quite clearly that P. A. Stolypin wished to attract us into his cabinet, not to secure our aid in applying the principles proclaimed in the Manifesto of October 17, but because in spite of his courage and self-assurance he feared public hostility to his measures and saw in our participation in his cabinet a means of reconciling the excited public with the government. . . . .

[To Stolypin's invitation to join his cabinet] we replied that before we could give our answer it was necessary for us to become acquainted with his political program. . . . . P. A. then announced that that was not the time for words and programs; it was the time for work. We pointed out the necessity of introducing a fundamental change in governmental policy and of convoking the new State Duma as soon as possible. P. A. said that in order to pacify all classes of the population it was necessary first of all to satisfy the primary needs of every large public group, and by so doing to attract these groups to the side of the government. People would believe actions better than words. In elaborating upon this idea, P. A. said, among other things, that it would be necessary to attract [to this work] influential Jews in order to learn with their help what concessions were necessary and possible as a means of pacifying the revolutionary mood of the Jewish people. We ardently opposed this policy and pointed out that no measure which required the sanction of a legislative chamber could be carried out without the confirmation of the legislative institutions, and said that we were at a loss to understand how, since the Manifesto of October 17, the government could decide what kind of reforms were needed without first consulting the people's representatives. P. A. Stolypin then said that as far as he was concerned he saw clearly what measures were immediately required; he was critical of the legislative capacity of the State Duma, at least in its early sessions, and again emphasized his conviction that the government would be able without any delay to grant to all classes of the population what they really needed. We called his attention to the fact that the Sovereign Power had granted the population the right to participate through their elective representatives, in the determining of the country's political life, and asked how His Majesty's government could violate this right? We admitted that legislative chambers made mistakes, as was only natural, but . . . . the population . . . . would take these mistakes into account in the next election. The mistakes made by the government, on the other hand, would only make its name more odious to the population. "How will your policy differ from that of our predecessors?" I said to Stolypin. "Did not Count Tolstoi, Sipiagin, and Plehve wish good for Russia as they understood it? Did not Count Witte say that he knew what was needed for the happiness of Russia? If their policies were harmful, they at least had the justification of being within the bounds of the old order. But how can this same road be taken now that the Manifesto of October 17 has been issued? It is my firm conviction that adherence to the old methods of government will only lead the government into the path of reaction, so that the government will not only fail to pacify the country but will even be obliged two or three months hence to resort to most severe measures of repression." At these words Stolypin grew quite excited and exclaimed: "What right have you to say that?" "You are inviting me to join your cabinet," I replied; "and I consider myself duty bound openly to express to you my convictions."

Later Prince Lvov and I tried to make clear the conditions under which we considered it possible to accept Stolypin's invitation to join his cabinet. Our conditions were as follows: that public men be included in his cabinet and their inclusion be explained in a Sovereign act as the means of establishing a contact between the government and the public; that the public men who had united on the basis of one political platform be given half of the portfolios, including the portfolio of Minister of the Interior; that the new cabinet issue a government communication defining the tasks of the cabinet; that legislative bills be prepared and introduced in the Duma immediately after its opening; that these bills deal with the most important problems of state life and be an application of the liberties proclaimed in the Manifesto of October 17; that there be no capital punishment until the legislative bodies decide in principle upon its employment.

Stolypin listened to our remarks inattentively . . . . In conclusion he said that now was not the time to talk about programs; public men must trust their Tsar and his government and, in view of the difficult conditions in which the country found itself, must accept unselfishly the invitation of the government. Prince G. E. Lvov and I saw we could not find a common language with Stolypin and that our estimation of the current situation differed fundamentally from that of Stolypin. We considered any further exchange of opinion with the Chairman of the Council of Ministers useless, said good-by, and departed.

On our return . . . . we acquainted the persons who had known of our interview with the nature and content of our conversation. Count P. A. Heyden saw in what we said a confirmation of his doubts of Stolypin's sincerity . . . . and saw no possibility of coming to an agreement which might be acceptable to the public men. The other three, N. N. Lvov, M. A. Stakhovich, and A. I. Guchkov continued to express their confidence in the desire and capacity of the Chairman of the Council of Ministers to regenerate our state order; they thought that between us two on one side and Stolypin on the other side some misunderstandings had occurred and as a result we had failed to understand each other; they were sorry that our impression of Stolypin was unfavorable . . . .

[Although Prince Lvov and Shipov had been unfavorably impressed by their interview with Stolypin, they thought it possible that, in the heat of the discussion, they had not presented clearly the conditions on which they were willing to join his cabinet. In order that there should be no misunderstanding about these conditions, which had been unacceptable to Stolypin, they wrote him a letter restating their position.]

We waited a day for some acknowledgment of our letter, and were prepared to visit Stolypin again had he expressed a wish to have further explanations from us. Considering that such an invitation might follow, we even prepared a list of members for the coalition government . . . . :

Chairman of the Council of Ministers..........P. A. Stolypin
Minister of Foreign Affairs...................A. P. Izvolsky
Minister of Finance.......................V. N. Kokovtsov
Minister of Communication.................N. K. Schaufuss
Minister of War...........................A. F. Roediger
Minister of the Navy..........................A. A. Birilev
Minister of the Imperial Court.........Baron V. B. Frederichs
Minister of the Interior....................Prince G. E. Lvov
Minister of Justice............A. F. Koni or S. A. Lopukhin
Minister of Education ....A. A. Manuilov
Minister of Commerce and Industry
　　　　　　　　　　M. M. Fedorov or V. I. Timiriazev
Minister of Agriculture.......................D. N. Shipov
Ober-Prokuror of the Holy Synod.....Prince E. N. Trubetskoi
State Comptroller.....................Count P. A. Heyden

Late on July 17 no answer had come from Stolypin; so we left for Moscow by express. On the 18th a courier delivered a letter to me in Moscow. This was a reply from Stolypin. This letter had been addressed to the hotel Frantsiia, but we had gone. P. A. had then made arrangements for it to be sent to me in Moscow by special courier. The letter was as follows:

"Dear Sir, Dmitrii Nikolaevich:

"I thank you and Prince Lvov very much for your letter. I am grieved to hear that you refuse to render your valuable and much-desired collaboration in our efforts to be useful to the country. I am also very sorry that I failed to explain to you clearly enough my point of view and left an impression of a person who fears bold reforms and is a partisan of 'petty concessions.' I believe that what we need is work and true reforms, and that we in the 200 days that are left us before the convocation of the new Duma must give ourselves entirely to the preparation and carrying out of as many measures as possible. This 'work' thus done will inspire public confidence in us better than any words we might say.

"The general outline of your program differs little from mine, and I too believe that our program should be made public. As concerns the postponement (by means of an Imperial Ukase) of the application of capital punishment and the granting of amnesty, we must not forget that the decision on these matters rests entirely with the Monarch.

"I agree that the cabinet must be of one political viewpoint, but in my opinion the crux of the matter lies, not in the number of portfolios given, but in the choice of suitable persons united by a desire to lead Russia out of the present crisis. As for the portfolio of the Minister of the Interior, so far the Sovereign has not yet relieved me of this duty. The change in the date of the convocation of the Duma, apart from other considerations, would go against our fundamental law. Please excuse this disjointed letter, caused by a rush; please excuse me, too, for taking your time. I thought when I invited you and Prince Lvov to become members of my cabinet, just as I thought earlier when I offered you the task of forming the cabinet, that Russia would gain much by your participation in the government. You have judged differently. Nevertheless, I am very grateful to you for your frank talk, your sincerity, and your apparent desire to help me in the difficult task entrusted me by the Sovereign.

"Believe me, I remain sincerely yours,

"P. STOLYPIN, July 17, 1906."

5. STOLYPIN AS A STATESMAN. HIS DEATH[6]

Stolypin made a name for himself in history not only as a victor over the revolutionary anarchy which was rending Russia in 1905–1906, and not only as Chairman of the Council of Ministers which tried gradually to transform the Russian autocratic monarchy into a constitutional one, but primarily as the initiator of the vast land reform which by transforming the peasants into small landowners gave promise of laying a firm foundation for Russia.

Stolypin was a landlord from Saratov Gubernia. He managed his estate well and knew well the peasant economy. He had learned many lessons while he was Governor of Grodno. There were no zemstvo institutions in Grodno Gubernia and the local governors were obliged to consider carefully the economy of their respective regions. An intelligent and well-educated man, Stolypin pondered for some time the hapless condition of the Russian village and came to the conclusion that the low level of rural economy and the general culture of the peasant population was due mainly to the fact that the land did not belong to the peasants and was not their individual property. He realized, too, that Russia could not become a strong power until the majority of her population—the peasants—became interested in the safeguarding of individual property and, therefore, the state order which guaranteed them this

[6] "Iz Vospominanii A. I. Guchkova," *Posledniia Novosti,* Nos. 5633 and 6537, August 26 and 30, 1936. These memoirs of A. I. Guchkov are an elaboration of stenographic notes dictated by him.

property. The Revolution of 1905 with its agrarian excesses only strengthened Stolypin's convictions on this point. It was then that he came finally to believe that the primary need of a state like Russia was the creation of a class of well-to-do peasant landowners. He realized that the interests of the landlords might suffer from such a measure because the number of day laborers would inevitably become scarce in the countryside, but to this problem he gave the answer: "Let the landlords reorganize their economy, that is their business."

Hence when he joined the government he decided to apply all his efforts toward putting into practice the agrarian reform which he had already outlined in his mind. . . . . But the drafting and elaboration of the reform was done mainly by V. I. Gurko, who, as Assistant Minister of the Interior, gave himself entirely to this work and under the guidance of Stolypin prepared the bill which became a law after the dissolution of the Second Duma. . . . . [See chapter xxi of text.]

Thanks to this law peasant private landownership made tremendous strides in Russia. Stolypin spared no money in order to consolidate and to increase the well-being of the new class created by him. He encouraged the practice of [granting the peasants] small credits; he maintained an army of land experts, land surveyors, and agronomists; he spent large sums of money on public education; lastly, he came out with a project for creating a volost zemstvo which would stand close to the peasants and raise their social level, and prepare them for self-government within the limits of their understanding. For a long time Left-wing groups in Russia had insisted on an all-class volost zemstvo. Stolypin went far toward meeting these demands by a bill which he introduced in the Third State Duma. But while he accepted the participation in the volost zemstvo of all classes of the population residing in the given volost, he based his project on the electoral law which would safeguard the wealthy minority from being overwhelmed by the huge peasant majority. His bill aroused much criticism from both Left and Right. The Left opposition did not think it sufficiently democratic; the Right opposition was generally against self-government and any further development of it. In the Duma, thanks to the efforts of our party [Octobrists], the project received the required majority vote and passed on to the next legislative chamber, the State Council. It was never discussed in the State Council, however, while Stolypin was alive, and after his death there was no longer anyone interested in it. So it remained buried and the volost zemstvo came into existence only after the Revolution of [February] 1917, and then a few months later was annulled by the Bolsheviks.

Stolypin's creative efforts in the work of the state to which he gave himself with such enthusiasm were not always within the limits of the constitutional order at which he aimed. He violated this constitution and thus undermined the state order which he tried to defend from the attacks of the reactionary elements who had established themselves firmly around the throne. A typical instance was the bill . . . . concerning the introduction of zemstvos in western gubernias. . . . . [There follows an account of this incident which is described in chapter xxi.]

By this act Stolypin aroused the entire Russian public against him. The

Left wing and the Center were indignant at such a flagrant circumvention of the constitution, while the Right wing was indignant at his treatment of its leaders in the State Council. I was Chairman of the Duma at that time, and in spite of my good relations with Stolypin I was obliged to protest against his violation of parliamentary rights. My position enabled me to make this protest by resigning from the chairmanship of the Duma. This was particularly necessary in order that no suspicion might be aroused that I and the Octobrist party, which I headed and which fully supported Stolypin's law regarding western zemstvos, were in sympathy with his clearly unconstitutional actions.

Stolypin was very much surprised at my resignation. He could not see any sense in it, as the law was issued in the form in which it had passed the Duma. I replied that: first, he had dealt a blow to our not yet firmly consolidated constitution; second, by dealing in such a way with the members of the State Council who had voted against the government he had discredited the State Council, in which all members should have an independent opinion; third, and most important, he had committed political suicide and was bound soon to lose his post.

This was quite clear to me, because I understood that having made so many enemies in various groups of society he had completely lost the support of the Tsar, who could never forgive Stolypin for bending the Tsar's will to his own.

Since I had resigned my position I took a leave of absence and on instructions from the Red Cross went to the Far East to take part in the fight against the plague epidemic which had broken out in the Russian colonies in Manchuria. I returned to Petersburg in the summer of 1911, a few days before the tragic death of Stolypin. When Stolypin heard of my return he invited me to dine with him at his summer residence on the Elagin island. He was greatly depressed. I had the impression that he realized more and more the helplessness of his struggle against irresponsible court influences. He related with bitterness how a monk—the fanatic Iliodor—supported by the Tsar, was conducting Black Hundred propaganda in Saratov Gubernia, refusing to obey the orders of the local governor, and in this way undermining the authority of the government as a whole. He pictured all this in very black colors, which seemed very different from his usual confident nature. It was apparent that he was coming to a decision to give up his position.

A few days later news was received from Kiev, where Stolypin had gone for the opening of the memorial to Emperor Alexander II, that Stolypin had been the victim of a terrorist act and was seriously wounded. I sent him an icon which he lived to receive, but when I arrived in Kiev two days later I found him dead.

The Governor-General of Kiev, F. F. Trepov, told me the details of Stolypin's assassination. All work of the Secret Police during the Kiev events had been entrusted to Assistant Minister of the Interior Kurlov and to the Chief of the Palace Guards, Colonel Spiridovich. According to Trepov, they were concerned only with the safety of the royal family, while Stolypin, in spite of the fact that the revolutionists were continually threatening his life, was left unguarded. Trepov did not mention to me any definite suspicion; but from his story I gathered that he, like myself, believed that if the persons who headed the Secret Service did not actually organize the attempt on Stolypin's life, they at least did not try to prevent it. It looked very suspicious that Stolypin's assassin, Bogrov, was the agent of the Secret Service section, and was hanged in a hurry before the arrival in Kiev of Senator Trusevich, who had come with special instructions to investigate the murder. On his return to Petersburg Trusevich told me of his impressions, which only confirmed my earlier suspicions.

Then in the Duma I put to the government a question approximately as follows: "Does the government know that some very questionable actions were allowed [in Kiev] as a result of which Stolypin was killed?" I stated definitely that we had before us a case, not of simple negligence on the part of those who were on duty, but of direct sufferance [of the murder], and I named the persons whom I accused: Kurlov, Colonel Spiridovich, Gendarme Captain Kuliabko, and a certain Verigin, who was in charge of the political Secret Police at the time of the assassination. After my speech Colonel Spiridovich reported to his chief that I had insulted him and that he wanted permission to challenge me to a duel or to defend his honor in some other way. The ruling circles wished to make light of the incident, and Spiridovich was ordered to keep quiet. But at the same time no answer was given to my question in the Duma.

I am still inclined to think that the assassination of Stolypin was at least tolerated by those in high positions. They did not know how to get rid of Stolypin and did not dare remove him without a serious reason. At one time it was intended to create for him the high post of viceroy of Siberia, but for some reason this was given up. Stolypin had many enemies among the bureaucrats and the people at the court. To add to this he ordered an inspection of the secret funds of the Department of Police. So, as the revolutionists at that time were organizing an attempt on his life, it was decided not to interfere with their plot.

When I returned from the Far East I had heard that the Finnish nationalists were preparing an attempt on Stolypin's life. Since I had concrete information on this matter, I believed it my duty, in spite of my personal dislike of Kurlov, to inform him of it and told him that the attempt might be made when Stolypin journeyed to Kiev. I wished to warn Stolypin also, but did not like to do so, as I did not want to worry him. Yet Stolypin had felt the danger that was threatening him. I heard later that he was in the habit of saying to Shulgin, a member of the Duma: "You will see! I shall be killed! And I shall be killed by members of the Secret Police."

INDEX

INDEX

A

Abaza, A. M., 263, 264, 266, 275, 278, 279, 282, 285, 648 (n. 14)

Administrative reform, Mirsky's project for, 297–98, 300–304, 315; Plehve's plans for, 112, 121–30, 227–29; Witte's attempts at, 315–23; Witte's projects for, in the First Duma, 452–53; *see also* Bureaucracy and bureaucrats; Local administration; Peasant local self-government; State Duma

Afghanistan, 259

Agents provocateurs, 117, 119, 523 n.; *see also* Zubatovshchina

Agrarian reform, *see* Peasant legislation

Agrarian uprisings, in 1902, 113–14, 122, 165, 172, 229, 234, 338; in the Revolution of 1905, 338–39, 364, 368, 380, 411, 412, 418, 449; *see also* Revolutionary movement

Agricultural committees, 62, 167, 206–7, 211, 222–25, 232, 241–42, 298, 316, 326, 334, 691–92, 695, 697, 700, 702; *see also* Peasant legislation

Agricultural Conference (1913), 197 n.

Agricultural conferences, gubernia, 166–68, 173–74, 217, 219–20, 332–33, 658 (n. 7); *see also* Peasant legislation; Special Conference on the Needs of Agricultural Industry

Agricultural Society of Poltava, 554

Agriculture, 5, 9, 57, 61, 67, 68, 71–74, 113–14, 133, 136, 159, 195–96, 197, 201–2, 203–7, 219, 221, 231, 232, 242–44, 325, 538, 691–93, 695–97, 700; *see also* Agrarian uprisings; Committee for Land Affairs; Land commune; Ministry of Agriculture; Peasant legislation; Zemstvos

Agronomic congress (Moscow, 1922), 160 n.

Aigun, Treaty of, 98, 622 (n. 11)

Akhlestyshev, N. D., 77

Akimov, M. G., 407, 410, 667 (n. 12)

Aladin, A. F., 480, 674 (n. 15)

Aleksandr Mikhailovich, Grand Duke, 260, 266, 302, 647 (n. 13)

Aleksandriia pogrom (1904), 249

Aleksandriisky estate, 294

Aleksandro-Severskaia Church, 523

Alekseev, E. I., 258, 273–74, 280, 282–84, 285–86, 287, 290, 647 (n. 10)

Alekseev, K., 254, 273 n.

Alekseev, M. V., 203, 641 (n. 3)

Alekseevsky Committee, 500, 676 (n. 8)

Aleksei, Tsarevich, 493, 520

Aleksei Aleksandrovich, Grand Duke, 255, 285, 646 (n. 4)

Alexander I, 48

Alexander II, 24, 446 n., 594 (n. 3); assassination of, 15, 108; reign of, 16–17, 108, 140

Alexander III, 5, 24, 66, 180, 182, 222, 254 n., 303, 404, 520, 530, 589 (n. 2), 599 (n. 15); illness and death of, 13–16, 18; reign of, 16–21, 131

Alexandra Fedorovna, Empress, 9, 10, 281, 289 n., 339, 451 n., 460 n., 465, 470, 493, 494, 518, 520–21, 530, 555, 566, 568 n., 578–79, 581, 582, 594 (n. 21); *Letters of the Tsaritsa to the Tsar, 1914–1916,* 675 (n. 5)

All-class volost zemstvo, *see* Small zemstvo unit

All-Russian Congress of Lawyers (March 28, 1905), 374

All-Russian Congress of the Nobility (1908), 523, 525

All-Russian Homecraft Workers' Congress (1902), 73

All-Russian Peasant Congress (July 30, 1905), 389

All-Russian Peasant Union, 441

All-Russian Union of Towns, 541, 582

All-Russian Zemstvo Union, 244, 298, 539–41, 563, 567, 583, 717–18

Altschuler, Austrian spy, 517, 552, 553

America, *see* United States of America

Amnesty for political prisoners, 395, 401, 403, 416, 417, 430, 431, 471, 575, 705, 714, 721

Amur border patrol, 527